Unlikely Warriors

D0298202

Windsor and Maidenhead

38067100545356

Unlikely Warriors

The British in the Spanish Civil War and the
Struggle Against Fascism

RICHARD BAXELL

Aurum history

First published in Great Britain
2012 by Aurum Press Ltd
7 Greenland Street
London NW1 0ND
www.aurumpress.co.uk

Copyright © Richard Baxell 2012

Richard Baxell has asserted his moral right to be identified
as the author of this work in accordance with the Copyright,
Designs and Patents Act 1988.

All rights reserved. No part of this book may be reproduced or utilised in
any form or by any means, electronic or mechanical, including
photocopying, recording or by any information storage and retrieval
system, without permission in writing from Aurum Press Ltd.

Every effort has been made to trace the copyright holders of material
quoted in this book. If application is made in writing to the publisher, any
omissions will be included in future editions.

A catalogue record for this book is available from the British Library.

ISBN 978 1 84513 697 0

1 3 5 7 9 10 8 6 4 2
2012 2014 2016 2015 2013

Typeset in Dante Mt Regular by SX Composing DTP, Rayleigh, Essex
Printed by MPG Books, Bodmin Cornwall

For Robert and María

Contents

Acknowledgements

This book has taken several years to write. Without the support of my friends and family, it simply would not have been possible and several in particular have stoically endured my divided inattention. Thanks and apologies in equal measure go to my mother, the four girls, Sophie Charles and, above all, to Heather.

I owe a huge debt to Paul Preston, Britain's foremost historian of modern Spain, who has always been as supportive as he has been inspirational. Many others – too numerous to list – have also given me the benefit of their invaluable time and advice, but special thanks must go to Michael Alpert, Jennifer Beamish, Melody Buckley, Peter Carroll, David Convery, Nigel Copsey, Ciaran Crossey, Stephen Dorril, Claudia Honefeld, Angela Jackson, Dan Kowalsky, David Leach, Alan Lloyd, Richard Lorch, Linda Palfreeman, Danny Payne, Rémi Skoutlesky, Phyll Smith, Peter Stansky, Boris Volodarsky, Don Watson, Bill Williams and Gerben Zagsma.

The committee and the membership of the International Brigade Memorial Trust were incredibly helpful and supportive, as were a number of veterans of the International Brigades and their families. I would like to extend a special thank you to the relatives of Andy Andrews, Edwin Bee, Freddie Brandler, Len Crome, Gerry Doran, Bob Doyle, Jack Edwards, Harry Fraser, Edwin Greening, Jack Jones, James Jump, Joseph Kahn, Sam Lesser, David Lomon, John Longstaff, Willy Maley, David Marshall, Max Nash, David Newman, Michael O'Riordan, Jack Shaw, Fred Thomas, Miles Tomalin, Frank West, Sam Wild and Archie Williams.

Having spent time in a number of archives during my research, I would like to express my particular thanks to John Callow at the Marx Memorial Library, Alice Locke at the Tameside Local Studies Archive and Gail Malmgreen at the Tamiment Library. Thanks also to the staff of the Imperial War Museum's film and sound archives, the Working Class

Movement Library and the People's History Museum. Dolores Long, Hilary Jones and Rickard and Carol-Jeanette Jorgensen all very kindly provided me with very much more than just a place to stay during my research trips to Manchester and New York.

And last, but definitely not least, my thanks to Sam Harrison and Steve Gove at Aurum Press and Tom Buchanan, Jim Carmody and Helen Graham, all of whom devoted a considerable amount of time and effort in helping to eliminate any mistakes. Those that remain are, as they say, mine alone.

I sing of my comrades
That once did sing
In that great choir at Albacete
Before the battle. Rank after rank
Of the young battalions
Singing the Internationale
They came from every corner of the earth
So many men from distant lands
Each with his private history
Who took to arms in the defence
Of Spain's Republic.

David Marshall, International Brigader and poet

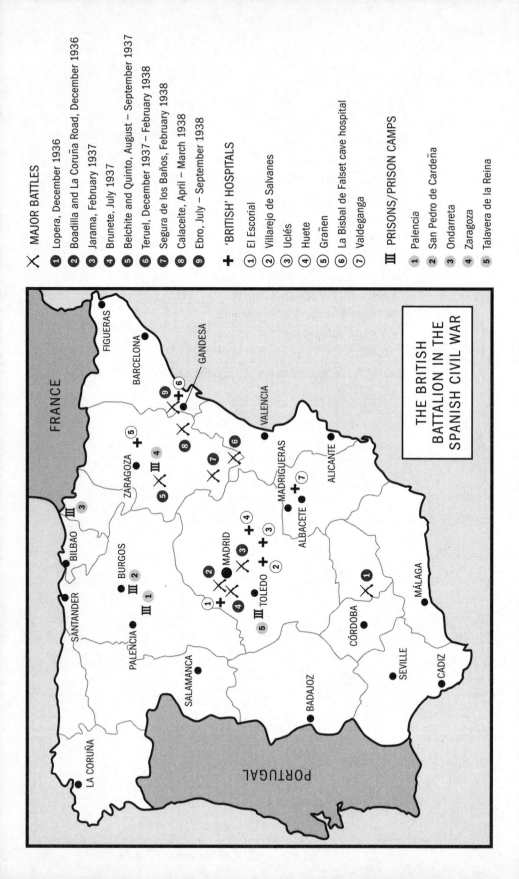

✕ MAJOR BATTLES

1. Lopera, December 1936
2. Boadilla and La Coruña Road, December 1936
3. Jarama, February 1937
4. Brunete, July 1937
5. Belchite and Quinto, August – September 1937
6. Teruel, December 1937 – February 1938
7. Segura de los Baños, February 1938
8. Calaceite, April – March 1938
9. Ebro, July – September 1938

✛ 'BRITISH' HOSPITALS

1. El Escorial
2. Villarejo de Salvanes
3. Uclés
4. Huete
5. Grañen
6. La Bisbal de Falset cave hospital
7. Valdeganga

Ⅲ PRISONS/PRISON CAMPS

1. Palencia
2. San Pedro de Cardeña
3. Ondarreta
4. Zaragoza
5. Talavera de la Reina

THE BRITISH
BATTALION IN THE
SPANISH CIVIL WAR

Introduction

On 9 June 2009, in the elegant surroundings of the Spanish Embassy in London's Belgravia, a 94-year-old Briton stood up and, leaning on a stick for support, delivered a speech imbued with the passionate idealism of a man many years his junior. He spoke clearly and eloquently, in fluent Spanish, though an occasional catch in his voice betrayed the emotional intensity of the occasion. He told of his pleasure at being invited to the reception, but acknowledged sadness that so few of his friends and comrades were still alive to witness the event, citing the words from Laurence Binyon's war poem, 'For the Fallen':

> Age shall not weary them, nor the years condemn.
> At the going down of the sun and in the morning, we will
>   remember them.

As the speech drew to an end, the man raised his right arm in a clenched-fist salute, earning thunderous applause and cheers from the smartly dressed audience of well-wishers and representatives of the British and Spanish media. The gesture also provoked the return of the salute from one of his companions, sitting in pride of place at the front of the crowd.[1]

The pensioners, six from Britain and one from Ireland, had been invited to the embassy that day to be formally presented with Spanish passports, symbols of an offer of citizenship from the country's government. As the ambassador explained, the seven (the speaker, Sam Lesser, along with Thomas Watters, Lou Kenton, Joseph Kahn, Jack Edwards, Paddy Cochrane and Penny Feiwel – nonagenarians all) were among the last survivors of the 'extraordinary men and women' from Britain and Ireland who, seventy years earlier, had left their homes to go to Spain 'to fight for democracy and freedom' as part of the International Brigades, the courageous band of volunteers from around the world who had fought on the side of the elected government in the Spanish Civil War of 1936–1939. The Brigaders' sacrifices had earned the eternal gratitude of the Spanish Republicans, eloquently expressed by Dolores Ibárruri (the legendary orator from Asturias, known as *La Pasionaria*) at a huge farewell parade held in Barcelona on 28 October 1938. 'We shall not forget you,' she had assured them, promising that, one day, they would be welcomed back to a free, democratic Spain:

> Those of you who have no country will find one, those of you deprived of friendship will find friends and all of you will find the love, affection and gratitude of the whole of the Spanish People.[2]

There was to be a long wait for the fulfilment of that promise. The dictatorship of General Franco lasted for nearly forty years, ending only with his death on 20 November 1975. But after a surprisingly peaceful transition to democracy in 1977, free elections were held in Spain for the first time since February 1936. Five years later, the newly elected socialist government of Felipe González, drawing on the memory of the defeated Second Republic of the 1930s, would decide to confer Spanish citizenship on all the surviving veterans of the International Brigades.

When the offer was first made on 26 January 1996, it came with a proviso: the veterans must renounce their own nationality. Despite the enthusiastic welcome they received on the *homenaje*, their return to Spain that year for the sixtieth anniversary of the war, few were prepared to consider this. It was not until the re-election of the Socialists, led by José Luis Zapatero, in 2007, that the Spanish parliament passed the *Ley de la Memoria Histórica*, of which Article 18 confirmed the right of the surviving veterans to Spanish citizenship without the need to renounce their current nationality. This finally allowed the government to fulfil *La Pasionaria*'s promise, leading in turn to the poignant 2009 ceremony at which the Spanish Ambassador to Britain, Carles Casajuana, graciously assured the handful of survivors that 'Your efforts were not in vain. Your ideals are part of the foundations of our democracy in Spain today.' His speech was received with gratitude and emotion by the veterans, who sat proudly clutching their new passports. 'We're a little late,' admitted Sam Lesser, 'but today I believe we can say that we have come home.'

*

The reasons that lay behind the momentous decision, all those years ago, to go to Spain had as much to do with events outside the country as within. The vast majority of the volunteers from Britain and Ireland knew very little of Spanish politics, but they had personal experience of the powerful forces engulfing Europe in the 1930s, which had encouraged many to shift politically to the left.[3] First had come the Great Depression, the catastrophic economic crisis that followed the stock market crash of 1929 and put over two million Britons out of work within a year, marches and protests against unemployment and hunger became emblematic of the period.[4] And alongside the economic turmoil came a political storm, one that had been growing since the end of the First World War and now swept across Europe, attacking and unseating liberal and democratic regimes as it went.

The birth of Mussolini's fascist Italy in 1922 was followed by the establishment of dictatorships such as António de Oliveira Salazar's Estado Novo (New State) in Portugal. Hitler's ascent to the German chancellorship – offered to him by an old guard of Prussian aristocrats in the mistaken belief that they had the power and authority to control him – followed in 1933, and the destruction of the Austrian working-class movement by Engelbert Dolfuss's 'austrofascist' regime the next year continued the unrelenting attacks on the European left.

By the mid-1930s, essentially constitutional states were themselves seemingly under threat. Both France and Spain were bitterly cleaved between left and right, while in Britain, Sir Oswald Mosley's British Union of Fascists (BUF) represented the domestic version of an ever more confident Europe-wide movement:

> It was not only from abroad that the menace came. Oswald Mosley was actively trying to build a fascist movement in Britain, and sent disciplined, uniformed groups of Blackshirts to beat up Jewish people in London's East End. British fascists also attacked unemployed workers in Merthyr Tydfil, Aberdeen and elsewhere; any hecklers or interrupters at Mosley's rallies were treated with extreme brutality. It was clear that British fascism had the same ugly face as its German counterpart.[5]

The rise of the BUF, known as the Blackshirts, induced the fear that fascism was now taking root in Britain and this led many of those targeted by Mosley's thugs to reject their long-standing pacifism, the legacy of the appalling carnage of the 1914–18 'war to end all wars'. Meanwhile, the British government's inability to prevent Mussolini's invasion of Abyssinia or Hitler's rearmament of Germany in 1935 confirmed their suspicions that appeasement of dictators was futile. With the split in the Labour Party of 1931 having stymied effective parliamentary opposition, and the leaders of the Labour movement seemingly as frightened of Communism as they were of fascism, grass-roots politics and direct action appeared to offer the only means of resistance. As one Manchester activist put it:

> Well, to me it was elementary. Here was fascism spreading all over the world, the rape of Abyssinia, the rise of fascism in Germany and the persecution of the Jews there, and the rise of the Blackshirts in Britain . . . I felt that somebody had to do something to try and stop it.[6]

Within Spain itself, the democratic Republican government had only come into existence in 1931, following seven years of military dictatorship. However, the new regime's attempts to implement what the Liverpool trade unionist and volunteer for the International Brigades, Jack Jones, referred to as 'elementary' social and educational reforms, strongly antagonised elements of the Spanish right, in particular the powerful troika of landowners, army and Catholic Church.[7] In addition, the government lacked vital support from much of the left, particularly the powerful Anarchist movement, which saw the Republic as little better than the former dictatorship. A military rising in August 1932 was a poorly kept secret and easily suppressed, but it clearly demonstrated the level of opposition facing the Republic from sections of the right. The election of a right-wing coalition in November 1933 saw the previous administration's reforms abandoned, if not overturned, and the admission of three members of the CEDA (a confederation of right-wing groups) into the cabinet in October 1934 was widely seen as the first entry of fascists into the government. A general strike was called in protest; although it failed to materialise in much of the country, in the mining areas of Asturias, in northern Spain, it escalated into an armed insurrection. The rising was put down with brutal force by Moroccan troops under the command of a man whose experience gained fighting in North Africa had made him one of the youngest generals in Europe: Francisco Franco y Bahamonde. Several thousand people were killed or wounded and up to thirty thousand were imprisoned.[8]

Elections held in February 1936 saw a victory for a coalition of Republican and leftist parties, united in a 'Popular Front'. But as political violence escalated, those parts of the Spanish right who had lost – or never had – any faith in the Republic prepared to overthrow it by force. On 13 July 1936, the murder of Calvo Sotelo, a prominent Catholic conservative politician, in reprisal for the killing of a Republican policeman, served as the perfect excuse for the leader of the military plot, General Emilio Mola. Four days later, on the evening of 17 July 1936, the military garrisons rose in Morocco, and the revolt quickly spread to the mainland. Though it was initially successful in many parts of Spain, opponents of the rising took to the streets, erected barricades and confronted the insurgents. Faced with determined opposition, the generals saw that their rebellion was in real danger of being defeated. With their best soldiers, Franco's elite Army of Africa, trapped in Morocco, the Rebel officers turned to fascist Italy and Nazi Germany for assistance. After some hesitation, both Hitler and Mussolini sent help, providing vital aircraft to ferry Franco's troops across the Strait of Gibraltar onto the peninsula, where they were able to head rapidly north, leaving a trail of slaughter and destruction in their wake. The involvement of the fascist dictatorships intimated that a Spanish military rising threatened to escalate into a European civil war.

To many foreign onlookers it was now apparent that Spain had become the latest battleground in what one British liberal newspaper, the *News Chronicle*, described as 'a world war in embryo'.[9] Fearful that yet another country was about to succumb, anti-fascists from around the globe decided to involve themselves in the Spanish Republic's struggle – in the words of one young Londoner, 'to defend democracy with deeds'.[10] Seen within the wider context of the struggle of democracy against international fascism, the volunteers believed passionately that the Spanish Republic's fight was their fight.

Meanwhile, desperate pleas for assistance from the Spanish Republican government, initially regarded with sympathy by France, met with firm opposition from Stanley Baldwin's government in Britain. Determined to avoid a wider European conflagration, and maintaining that appeasement of Germany and Italy was the best means of preventing it, the European democracies chose not to come to the Republic's aid. Instead a 'non-intervention agreement' was created, to which Britain, France, Germany Italy, Portugal and the USSR all signed up – in writing at least.

However, it quickly became apparent that the agreement strongly favoured the Rebels, who continued to receive covert assistance from Germany and Italy. Indeed, for many supporters of the Spanish government, the non-intervention pact was the real villain of the story, and they later argued that the fate of the Republic 'was settled in London, Paris, Rome, Berlin – at any rate not in Spain'. Sam Lesser never forgave His Majesty's government for the manifestly one-sided agreement imposed on the Spanish Republicans:

> We would have won if the democracies, particularly the British government, had allowed the legally elected government of Spain to purchase arms internationally, as was the right of any government to do so, but they were prevented. The French tried to send arms but the British government bullied them. Through [Neville] Chamberlain and Anthony Eden they made it clear that if the French became involved in any war as a result of supplying arms to Spain, the British government would not come to their assistance.[11]

In 1936 this had spurred Lesser, then a student of Egyptology at University College London, to become one of the first few from Britain to take the momentous decision to go to Spain; over the course of the civil war, 35,000 men and women, from over fifty countries, would do likewise. Although a number served in militia units, in the Republican navy, or as pilots and aircraft technicians, the majority fought in International Brigades, divided up into battalions based principally on the language and nationality of the volunteers.[12] The French (the largest contingent) formed a number of units, such as the André Marty and Commune de Paris Battalions; the Germans fought in the Thaelmann Battalion, Yugoslavs in the Dimitrov Battalion, Italians in the Garibaldi Battalion. Most English-speaking volunteers were placed in the 15th International Brigade, the last to be formed, which included the American Abraham Lincoln Battalion, the Canadian Mackenzie-Papineau Battalion (known, almost universally, as the 'Mac-Paps') and the British Battalion. Over the course of the war, some 2500 volunteers from Britain, Ireland and the Commonwealth fought with the British Battalion, and more than 500 were to die in Spain.

A number of these volunteers are now widely known, in particular George Orwell, though he actually fought with a militia unit rather than with the brigades themselves. In addition to the trade unionist Jack Jones, prominent Britons who joined the International Brigades included poet and writer Laurie Lee; Tom Wintringham, founder of the Home Guard and the Common Wealth Party; Winston Churchill's two nephews Esmond and Giles Romilly; (Sir) Alfred Sherman, later an ideologue and speechwriter for Margaret Thatcher; speedway motorcyclist Clem Beckett; and actor James Robertson Justice, who came to prominence in the 'Doctor in the House' films.

However, most Britons who went to Spain were neither celebrated nor famous. Rather they were ordinary men and women from modest working-class backgrounds, hailing from great smokestack cities such as London, Glasgow, Liverpool, Manchester and Newcastle.[13] Despite claims to the contrary, only a few of them were jobless when they left for Spain, with a large proportion employed in industrial occupations, including construction, ship-building and mining. Most were politically active – perhaps as many as three-quarters were members of the Communist Party – but those with an alternative political stance or who hailed from the trade union movement were also accepted. The ages of the volunteers were older than sometimes believed; the average was just under thirty, with most aged between twenty-one and thirty-five. Some even had a degree of military know-how, although it was not always particularly useful; Manchester volunteer Walter Greenhalgh, for example, had served in the Territorial Army, but had done so as a drummer and the value of his expertise was probably limited.

Despite such inexperience, the International Brigades provided some of the Republic's best troops, particularly at the beginning of the war. They were repeatedly thrown 'into the heart of the fire', on occasions demonstrating almost suicidal bravery and suffering appallingly heavy casualties; undoubtedly their sacrifice helped prolong the life of the Spanish Republic. After two years of fighting, those still alive were withdrawn by the Spanish premier, Juan Negrín, in a vain attempt to secure international help to mediate a peace with Franco. But with the military might of Germany and Italy behind him, Franco had no need – nor did he ever intend – to enter into negotiation. Bled to death, the Republic essentially collapsed and, on 1 April 1939, Franco declared victory for his triumphant forces.

Hopes of the supporters of democratic Spain from around the world were dashed. 'In Spain,' wrote French writer and philosopher Albert Camus, '[my generation] learned that one can be right and yet be beaten, that force can vanquish spirit, that there are times when courage is not its own recompense.'[14] Orwell agreed:

> Nourished for hundreds of years on a literature in which Right invariably triumphs in the last chapter, we believe half-instinctively that evil always

defeats itself in the long run . . . Don't resist evil, and it will somehow destroy itself. But why should it? What evidence is there that it does?[15]

Once back in Britain, the dispirited former International Brigaders vowed to continue the fight against Franco and his fascist and Nazi allies. With the outbreak of the Second World War many veterans chose to enlist, feeling that their war in Spain had been the first battle in a world struggle against fascism. John Londragan, a working-class Communist from Aberdeen, set out the position clearly:

I went to Spain because I was an anti-Fascist. When I went to Spain I thought I was trying to halt Hitler and Mussolini and their exploitation of Europe. We didn't succeed. Spain was defeated. So we went to war in 1939. I went through the Second World War doing exactly the same job I went to Spain to do. There was absolutely no difference at all. It was an anti-Fascist war. Both were anti-Fascist wars.[16]

During the Second World War, many veterans proved themselves to be highly motivated and experienced fighters and a number were decorated. When Hitler and Mussolini finally fell, the veterans continued their unfinished battle for Spain: campaigning for Spanish political prisoners, sending food parcels and paying for British lawyers and MPs to attend their trials. However, despite the Franco regime's imprisonment, torture and execution of political opponents, the dictator's anti-Communist stance in the Cold War climate ensured his survival right up to his death. Only then was democracy finally restored to Spain, two years after Franco's passing and forty-one years after the illegal military uprising he had come to lead.

Since the end of the war in Spain, there have been several histories of the British volunteers. Initially, they were written by the veterans themselves, or their supporters, who maintained the view established at the time: that the International Brigades were solely comprised of anti-fascists, fighting for Spanish democracy. However, George Orwell argued – and others have followed him since – that such simplistic and romantic notions of 'good versus evil' or 'democracy versus fascism' are problematic, and that the actions of Stalin and the Soviet Union during the Spanish Civil War – including the formation of the Brigades – were not quite the expression of international solidarity that some Communist accounts might suggest. A number of works, particularly those written during the Cold War, carried forward Orwell's criticisms, maintaining that the International Brigades were, first and foremost, a 'political, ideological and propaganda instrument' for Stalin, not just in Spain, but around the world.

The harsh discipline in the brigades, the desertions and executions, were all seen through the prism of the vicious purges in the Soviet Union. 'Stalin', it was argued, 'had every intention of achieving effective dictatorship in Spain, but behind an anti-fascist façade.'[17] However, just as more recent histories of the civil war itself have shown the picture to be more grey than black and white, so too have recent works on the British volunteers. Less coloured by the divisions of the Cold War, and distanced from grudges formed at the time, these have been rather more nuanced, arguing that the harsh discipline and the occasionally callous treatment of deserters are not necessarily symptoms of the 'Stalinisation' of Republican Spain, but should be seen, at least in part, as the desperate reaction of an army in a bitter struggle for its very survival. There was, after all, a war on and, as Orwell himself acknowledged, 'war is bloody'.

It is now seventy-five years since the British volunteers in the International Brigades fought in the bloody battles around Madrid. Since then, many have told their stories to interviewers, or published memoirs. However, the present study is the first to place the Spanish Civil War within the context of the volunteers' lives, rather than the other way round. It tells the story from the perspective of the participants themselves using, wherever possible, their own words. Of course, there are problems inherent in working with oral sources, particularly those recorded long after the event. Many of the interviews lack dates, locations and are frustratingly vague: 'what happened next is hazy,' admitted one volunteer candidly in his memoir.[18] Other accounts were written as 'a call to arms' or are clearly exaggerated, even fabricated.[19] As London volunteer Fred Thomas, who kept a diary in Spain, remarked sardonically:

Recent years have produced many accounts of the Civil War by fellow International Brigaders. Time after time I have read with awe the wealth of detail, the precision, the confident assertions brooking no questioning, the facts culled from memories of events and incidents of thirty, forty, or even fifty years earlier. And not one of them kept anything like even the modest personal account which I managed. Faced with such powers of observation, such capacity for total recall and seeming omniscience, my humility is complete. In excuse for my ignorance, I can say only that those same people, when my companions of those days, gave little evidence of being any more aware than was I.[20]

It is undoubtedly true that oral testimonies often fall short of providing pinpoint locations, reliable chronologies, or dispassionate and objective analysis, but this is not their strength. To really gain an understanding of a soldier's day-to-day experiences in war requires looking at the world through his (or her) eyes. As Helen Graham, one of the foremost British historians of modern Spain, has argued: 'Telling big stories through individual human lives is a very powerful way of doing history.'[21]

This work attempts to transcend the occasionally impressionistic memoirs and subjective tributes, which glorify the sacrifices of what *La Pasionaria* referred to as 'the heroic example of democracy's solidarity and universality'. Instead, it seeks to provide a more three-dimensional picture of the Brigaders and, in approaching them as living, breathing human beings, hopes to portray all the more vividly the exceptional nature of their actions. This is necessary, because only when it is understood how shocking were their experiences for the volunteers themselves can the reality of the International Brigades in the Spanish Civil War take on its proper perspective. As Orwell himself later explained:

> The picture of war set forth in books like *All Quiet on the Western Front* is substantially true. Bullets hurt, corpses stink, men under fire are often so frightened that they wet their trousers . . . a soldier anywhere near the front line is usually too hungry, or frightened, or cold, or, above all, too tired to bother about the political origins of the war. But the laws of nature are not suspended for a 'red' army any more than for a 'white' one. A louse is a louse and a bomb is a bomb, even though the cause you are fighting for happens to be just.[22]

Recruited and organised by the Communist International (though they were, of course, volunteers not conscripts) and commanded by Party appointments, many members of the International Brigades were them-selves disciplined Communists, uncompromising followers of Stalin and the Soviet Union. Others were long-standing anti-fascists who had fought and chased Mosley and his followers from the streets of cities such as London, Manchester and Aberdeen. A few were artists and poets; some were even soldiers. But many of the Britons who went to Spain were normal working-class men – and the occasional woman – who believed that the European situation of the 1930s was sufficiently serious that it demanded ordinary people to take extraordinary action. As Freddie Brandler, who served as a dispatch rider in the 15th International Brigade, declared, 'The very air was different then.'[23]

Many years after the war, Hugh Sloan, a Scottish member of the British Anti-Tank Battery, described his comrade-in-arms, musician, poet and Cambridge graduate Miles Tomalin, as 'the unlikely warrior'. Tomalin later wrote back to correct him. 'Hughie,' he replied, 'we were all unlikely warriors.'[24]

I

The Politics of Dissent

A do-gooding middle-class lady came to the Clydeside in the early
1930s and was telling a group of wives of unemployed workers how
to make a nourishing soup out of fish-heads and fish-bones. Jimmy's
mother watched with interest. 'Aye,' she said at the end, 'very
interesting. And who gets the rest of the fish?'

Judith Cook, *Apprentices of Freedom*

For a great many people in Britain, the 1930s were a time of improved life,
health and leisure, 'a period of rising living standards and new levels of
consumption'.[1] Three million new houses were built and there was a huge
increase in the number of homes supplied with electricity. Falling birth rates
meant smaller families, while improvements in medicine and diet meant
taller, larger and fitter children. The advent of hire purchase brought hitherto
unaffordable luxuries and labour-saving devices, such as the vacuum cleaner
and washing machine, within easier reach. And with the start of regular
broadcasts in 1936, the wireless radio, which had already become a
comforting presence in many sitting rooms, was joined by television,
although only a pioneering few yet owned sets with which to tune in. For
cinemas, dance halls and football grounds this was a golden age of popular
entertainment in which large numbers indulged themselves on a regular
basis. Increased car use even allowed some lucky families to take holidays at
the seaside. For those with money, for those with, above all, work, this was
no 'devil's decade' and there were no 'hungry thirties'. But these were the
lucky ones. For those without work, it was a very different existence.

The 1929 American stock market crash had sent shock waves around
the world, with tumbling prices and a serious contraction of international
trade, as sources of credit dried up. In Britain the crisis led to the most
profound economic depression of the twentieth century: factories closed

and hundreds of thousands of working people joined the growing lines of unemployed. By July 1930, there were almost two million people out of work. Incapable of finding a solution to the economic crisis, the Labour government, installed only months prior to the crash, resigned, to be replaced in August 1931 by a Conservative-dominated 'National Government'. Led by the former Labour Prime Minister Ramsay Macdonald, this coalition included a number of Labour members, causing a catastrophic split in the party. In the General Election later that year, the National Government was returned with a huge majority of nearly 500 seats, to be faced by an emasculated Labour opposition of only 52 MPs.

The economy continued to slump, while the numbers of jobless continued to climb, reaching three million by the end of 1932. The national rate was nearly twenty per cent but in parts of the manufacturing areas of the north of England, Wales and Scotland it was even higher, with as many as a third of the workforce unemployed. In response, the government implemented an austerity programme of tax rises and draconian public-sector cuts, including a reduction in unemployment benefit and the restriction of payments to no more than a six-month period. Anyone unable to find work faced an uncertain future – but certain poverty – with the forced sale of their belongings and the humiliation of having to appeal, cap in hand, for 'transitional payments' from the Labour Exchange. This required undergoing the hated household means test, overseen by the Public Assistance Committees which had replaced the Poor Law Assistance Boards, in name at least, in 1929. All belongings were included in the assessment, meaning that any household items of worth had to be sold off before money would be paid. Worse still, any income brought in by other family members was also taken into account, forcing many grown-up sons and daughters to leave home as families found themselves caught in a terrible trap: if the children were working, their income would be counted against the family's assistance payments; if not, then they were yet another mouth to feed.

Consequently, despite any overall increase in living standards, for many working-class families the 1930s were a time of poverty, misery and near-starvation. Living conditions were often overcrowded and insanitary: philanthropist Sir Ernest Simon, formerly the Lord Mayor of Manchester, described one, not untypical dwelling in a slum district of the city:

The general appearance and condition of this house inside are very miserable. It is a dark house and plaster on the passage walls, in particular, is in a bad condition. There is no sink or tap in the house; they are in the small yard, consequently in frosty weather the family is without water. In this house live a man and wife, and seven children ranging from fifteen to one, and a large, if varying number of rats.[2]

Perhaps as many as a third of the working class households in Britain in the early 1930s were 'living on incomes that were insufficient for basic human needs'.[3] First-hand experience of such appalling poverty was among the formative influences that would eventually lead many to volunteer in the Spanish Civil War: for the young Penny Phelps, later a nurse in Spain, growing up in Tottenham in north London just after the First World War meant 'being in debt, visits to the pawnshop . . . [these were] constant accompaniments of my mother's life'.[4] Many 'on the dole' worried whether they would ever find permanent employment again and were forced to search further and further afield, 'picking up work wherever you could'.[5] Mining areas such as the Rhondda in south Wales were particularly hard hit:

There were thousands unemployed. There were closed shops everywhere, dilapidated and dirty. Most houses were shabby outside. There was an atmosphere of decay everywhere. Young and old alike were forced to leave the valley for the Midlands and London regions . . . We had nothing, no job, no prospects, and no trade. We were the most under-privileged in a society of mass under-privileged.[6]

In response to the manifest injustices of the economic and political system that many working-class people endured in the 1930s, a number looked for explanations for the situation in which they and their families found themselves. 'An empty stomach makes an empty head think,' said one unemployed Scottish labourer, wryly.[7] One railwayman found himself unemployed for two periods between 1930 and 1932, in one case for nine months.

I used to go out, religiously, looking all over the show for work, you know: and it was this – continuously looking for work, and going asking for interviews, and getting snubbed, and getting treated as though I was dirt, you know, that really made me furious about things.[8]

Young Londoner James Brown grew up in King's Cross, where 'rats ran over the beds all night' and several of his siblings died as a result of the conditions in which they lived: 'We were evicted from home eleven times for non-payment of rent and the furniture thrown onto the streets,' he remembered. He later worked for a firm delivering fish to the houses of the very rich, which revealed to him the huge disparity between the lives of the poor and the wealthy. This spurred an interest in economics and he read Adam Smith and David Ricardo, among others. However, it was the writings of Jack London, particularly *The Iron Heel*, a dystopian Socialist tract, and *The People of the Abyss*, set in the slums of London's East End, that made a lasting impression on him; and on many other Britons who would later fight in Spain – George Orwell read the latter as a teenager and its influence can be seen in *Down and Out in Paris and London*. Like a character from Robert Tressell's *The Ragged-Trousered Philanthropists* – which depicted the misguided and self-defeating 'philanthropy' of workers who were, in reality, slaving for capitalist masters, and which many volunteers also cite as an important influence on their political development – Brown later laboured in the building trade, where 'you worked in the summer and starved in the winter.'[9]

For these 'working-class intellectuals', unemployed men with time on their hands, public libraries provided a haven. Many of the volunteers in Spain described a love for reading which developed during periods of unemployment: 'reading through the depression', as one Welsh miner described it.[10] Many also studied at evening classes, run by the Workers' Educational Association: 'my education didn't stop at fourteen, it was only beginning,' said Jim Brewer, a particularly well-read Welsh miner.[11] Brewer read Dickens, Thomas Hardy, T.S. Eliot's poetry and, of course, Jack London, 'all that I could get hold of', later securing himself a scholarship place at Oxford's Ruskin College. This demand for progressive literature would later be well served by the Left Book Club (LBC), founded in early 1936 by publisher and 'fellow-traveller' Victor Gollancz. The LBC was a phenomenal success, with some 40,000 members joining in the first year, and many who would later volunteer for Spain recall the political education they received from it.[12] All subscribers agreed to take the LBC's 'book of the month' for six months and the club published numerous left-leaning works, both non-fiction and fiction, in their distinctive orange covers. Among these were books by Communists or sympathisers and the LBC had a close relationship with the Communist Party; regular advertisements for the club appeared in the Communist national newspaper, the *Daily Worker*, and roughly one-sixth of subscribers were party members.[13]

Discussions about literature, religion and politics were central to the upbringing and development of many of the political radicals and 'nonconformists' of the 1930s. Labour MP Ellen Wilkinson, later the first Education Minister in Attlee's government, who was to visit Republican Spain on several occasions during the war, rejected her religious non - conformity for a political alternative.[14] However, Jim Brewer later claimed that his political outlook was formed by his religious roots in Monmouth, and by the influence of two of his uncles, both boxers, who imparted to him the code of the Marquess of Queensberry rules.[15] A sense of a tradition of political nonconformism and protest was also important to Tom Wintringham, a senior British Communist who had been arrested for sedition and inciting soldiers to mutiny in 1925 and who would take on an important role in Spain. Wintringham felt an affinity with a distant ancestor, a 'hedge preacher' who had his tongue torn out by a royal court of justice to prevent him 'carrying on subversive propaganda'. 'That hedge doctor had sent me', explained Wintringham in his memoir, *English Captain*.[16] Similarly, Lillian Urmston, who served as a nurse in Spain, was very proud of her descent from 'Jack Cade, the rebel', much to the embarrassment and disapproval of her mother.[17] This idea of a long-standing line of dissent was deliberately invoked in a booklet produced after the war to commemorate the British volunteers who had fought in Spain:

> Out of the proud traditions of Britain's past they came. Part of the long struggle for freedom, carried forward from Wat Tyler through men like Byron and movements like the Chartists, through Keir Hardie to the present day. Our modern bearers of Britain's great traditions came forward in answer to the call, ready to give their lives that freedom might live.[18]

While for some, like Oldham grammar school boy Albert Charlesworth, the Labour Party and trade unions provided a focus for their political thinking, many of these 'open-eyed' men and women found the answers and solutions offered by the traditional labour movement inadequate. The failure of the General Strike called by the TUC in 1926 (in a vain attempt to force the government to protect wages) and the split in the Labour Party in 1931 suggested, to some, that parliamentary politics and the trade unions were no longer able to defend their interests. Labour's continued inability to mount an effective opposition to the National Government's austerity programme inspired some to take matters into their own hands. Hit by disproportionate pay cuts, in September 1931 around 1000 British navy sailors mutinied at Invergordon in north-east Scotland; among their leaders was Fred Copeman, a tough young rating from New Cross in south-east London. After two days, the government backed down and agreed 'to withdraw the cuts and guarantee no victimisation'. Despite these promises, Copeman was one of those identified as a ringleader and subsequently expelled from the navy. His experience of leading men in struggles would not be forgotten:

> For me personally the mutiny was a turning point. Invergordon changed my whole outlook. I began to understand the meaning of leadership and – even more important – the meaning of politics.[19]

Fred Copeman was one of a number of British volunteers for Spain whose political consciousness was formed during a period in the armed forces. Most joined as a means of getting off the dole, rather than from any patriotic desire to serve their country. Sam Wild served with Copeman in the navy: 'I got fed up with being hungry, so I thought I'd better get some place where you can get a regular meal.' However, the disciplined life on HMS *Resolution* soon paled for Wild and he deserted from his ship in South Africa. Later recaptured, he was discharged from the navy and declared ineligible for the dole.

> I gained the reputation in the Navy of being a Bolshie. I'd taken an interest in what was going on in Russia, the struggle of the Irish people for Home Rule, and the General Strike. All these things accumulated in my mind and I began to think about things . . . It accentuated my 'anti' attitude to all things. I became anti-Queen, anti-King, anti-ruling class, anti-officer.[20]

Like Wild, Irishman George Leeson joined the navy and found it a formative experience. Based in China during the civil war between the Kuomintang nationalists and the Communist Party, he became disillusioned with the way the navy was being used:

> What we were doing was imposing ourselves on the Chinese people. What right did we have to be there? I saw the British Petroleum Company and

the Asiatic Petroleum Company and became very dissatisfied and determined to get myself out.[21]

Back home, following a period of unemployment, Leeson joined the London Underground, where he became an active member of the rank and file movement that was trying to press the conservative leadership of the National Union of Railwaymen into a more combative stance.

This disaffection with traditional labour, a feeling they were 'selling out' as one Perthshire Scot described it, led many on a search for more robust defenders of working-class interests: the radical parties of the left.[22] Some joined the Independent Labour Party (ILP), a Marxist-Socialist party established at the very end of the nineteenth century. Since disaffiliating from the Labour Party in July 1932, however, it was a party in decline, 'a regional (primarily Scottish) political force'.[23] Nan Green, who was to work as an administrator in a convalescent hospital in Spain, joined the ILP in 1929, but found her local group in Hampstead dominated by 'patronising' middle-class students. She soon became disillusioned, and joined the Communist Party after reading *The Coming Struggle for Power* by the Labour MP for Aston, John Strachey, a Communist fellow-traveller who helped Gollancz conceive the idea of the Left Book Club.[24] Green was not alone. For many on the left the only viable alternative was the Communist Party; though still relatively small, this was showing signs of growth, particularly in industrial sectors such as mining and shipbuilding hit hard by the depression.[25]

Established in 1920, the Communist Party of Great Britain (CPGB) was the British section of the Communist International, and therefore closely wedded to the line set by the Russian Party. Primarily an organisation of trusted cadres, its membership remained relatively insignificant during the first half of the 1920s. However, despite – or perhaps because of – the preemptive arrest of its leadership for sedition in 1925, the party accrued some prestige from its involvement in the 1926 General Strike. But any gains were quickly squandered by the disastrous tactic it adopted at the end of the decade, known as 'class against class', which portrayed all other leftist and social-democratic parties as 'social-fascists' and therefore to be opposed. Links with potential fellow-travellers were severed and by 1930–1 the Party's membership had dwindled to not many more than 2500. While some gains were made from Labour's collapse in 1931, gradual improvements in the economy ensured that the Party struggled to make any real inroads into parliamentary politics. As one study of the 1930s shrewdly observed, the Communist Party was 'a revolutionary party in a non-revolutionary situation'.[26] Charlotte Haldane, wife of the Communist scientist J.B.S. Haldane and herself a senior member who was widely involved in British responses to the Spanish war, explained:

> In spite of the fact that Marx and Engels had spent most of their lives in England, their doctrines had made comparatively little headway in a country where social-democracy had produced a powerful Labour Party and legal trade unions that satisfied and absorbed the socialist-minded organized workers.[27]

The Communist Party became a noisier and more serious force of resistance from 1933 onwards, once it had abandoned the suicidal policy of 'class against class'. Hitler's brutally efficient suppression of the German trade unions and the largest Communist Party in Europe provided an alarming reality check and the Party prudently moved towards support for 'people's' or 'popular fronts', seeking cooperation with other parties of the left in order to combat fascism.[28] However, leaders of the Labour Party and the trades unions, subject until very recently to attacks from Communists as 'social-fascists', remained wary of collaboration either with the Party or the various 'fronts'. Labour leaders banned members from joining the Party or any 'organisation ancillary or subsidiary' to it, and any Labour member who spoke at one of its meetings could be expelled.[29] Trade union leaders such as Walter Citrine, General Secretary of the Trades Union Congress (TUC), and Ernest Bevin, leader of the Transport & General Workers' Union (TGWU), were both extremely hostile towards the Communist Party, fully aware of the Leninist doctrine of infiltration of the union movement and furious at Communist attempts to set up rival unions.[30]

Moreover, the first rumours of the murderous nature of Stalin's regime strengthened the repugnance already felt by anti-Communists, from the left as well as the right. Trotsky's exile in 1929, the great famine of 1932 that followed the Soviet Union's policy of forced collectivisation, the purges and the show trials all confirmed – to those looking for it at least – the evil nature of Stalin's Russia. But many on the pro-Communist left, perhaps guilty of a 'siege mentality', simply did not, or could not, believe it. Even the Fabian Socialists, Sidney and Beatrice Webb, who paid a visit to the Soviet Union in 1932, failed to see the truth; probably, like so many idealists, they were victims of 'confirmation bias', better at finding evidence which coincided with their beliefs than contradicted them. Works by former fellow-travellers and supporters of the Soviets, such as French author André Gide, who returned deeply disillusioned from a visit to Russia in 1936 to write *Return to the USSR*, were dismissed as anti-Communist propaganda. Even those who had their doubts about Stalin's Russia argued that the USSR should be supported as the only friend of western anti-fascists. Leslie Preger, a young Manchester socialist who worked in Collet's political bookshop before volunteering to serve in the British Medical Unit in Spain, was appalled and disgusted by his experiences during a visit to Russia in 1934:

> I was so horrified at the workers' paradise that if I'd had any moral courage I should have come home and said that it stinks . . . It was the year after the terrible famine and there was very little food and few clothes. I stayed at a hotel called the Hotel Moscow and I had a pure wool Jaeger shirt, which cost me seven bob in those days, and when the chambermaid came in to clean the room she picked it up and was so enamoured of it she started unbuttoning her blouse. I was so horrified and so disgusted that I let her have the shirt . . . Everyone looked so fed up and so miserable.[31]

But, argued Preger, with the rise of Hitler's Nazi regime in Germany, 'it was a question of accepting the lesser of two evils . . . everyone who was against Hitler was a friend.' Winston Churchill would, of course, say much the same in 1941: 'If Hitler invaded Hell,' he remarked, 'I would at least make a favourable reference to the Devil in the House of Commons.'[32] The belief of some members of the disillusioned Labour rank and file that direct action was needed to fight injustice and inequality made the Communist Party an attractive proposition, as George Leeson explained: 'I looked around and thought the Labour Party doesn't seem to be doing very much, they are pretty tame anyway and I thought the only people who seem to be doing anything that leads to what I believe in – Socialism – were the Communists, even if they were a small group.'[33]

Manchester clothing worker Maurice Levine agreed: 'For a lot of young people . . . the Communist Party was the only political party to join.'[34] As Jessica Mitford, the only left-wing member of her infamous family, argued, 'In all the great battles for progress of the 'thirties, Communists had proved outstanding for their courage and singleness of purpose.'[35] Many others expressed similar sentments:

> The Labour Party seemed too apathetic to me . . . we had one particular Labour councillor on our branch committee . . . he should have been a Tory really . . . He went to Germany and came back praising Hitler and everything, you know, what wonderful roads they had, all this sort of thing.[36]

Denis Healey, for some Labour Party members 'the best Prime Minister we never had', was motivated to join the Communist Party, arguing that 'for the young in those days, politics was a world of simple choices . . . the Chamberlain government was for appeasement, Labour seemed torn between pacifism and a half-hearted support for collective security, and the Liberals did not count.'[37] He was one of a number of fresh-faced intellectuals to join the Party in the mid-1930s. Another was Philip Toynbee, a 'young upper middle-class Englishman' who joined while a student at Oxford in 1935 and admitted that membership gave a certain frisson of outsider excitement:

> Revolt against parental and school authority? Of course. The pleasures and inner security of belonging to a semi-secret society? Not a doubt of it. The pure romanticism of red flags and clenched fists? Who could deny it?

But it was the rise of Hitler and the Communist Party's robust response which turned his idle interest into a serious commitment:

> The Communist Party of Great Britain could easily justify its claim to be in the vanguard of the fight against a monstrous 'National' government which cared little or nothing for poverty at home and almost as little for the present reality and future international dangers of fascism in Europe.[38]

Certain regions proved especially fertile ground for Communist recruits, notably Glasgow, Tyneside, parts of London and, in particular, south Wales, where the mining communities had a well-founded reputation for militancy. One volunteer for Spain later argued that the large numbers of miners in the International Brigades, and in the Communist Party, were principally a result of the loss of respect that followed the Labour leadership's cooperation with the coal owners in the 1920s and 1930s, though feelings of solidarity with the miners of Asturias in northern Spain, whose uprising was brutally crushed by Franco and the Spanish military in October 1934, also played a part.[39] Over twenty Welsh volunteers for Spain had served prison terms for their political activities, including miners' leaders Harry Dobson and Will Paynter, both 'responsible Communists' and graduates of the Lenin School in Moscow, the finishing school for the Party's elite.[40] There were a number of Communist district and county councillors in the Welsh Rhondda area, and the South Wales Miners' Federation included a large quotient of party faithful, including the president, Arthur Horner. Having been made redundant in June 1932, Welsh miner Edmund Greening joined the Communist Party in 1934, becoming thoroughly inculcated in what he described as the 'strange way of life' of Communist politics. He attended meetings, sold copies of the *Daily Worker*, went knocking on doors to canvass for new members. Greening was in no doubt that, at that time, only the Communist Party offered a straightforward solution to the evils of unemployment: 'The Quakers, Labour and the Liberals did their best to ameliorate the bad conditions . . . but their efforts were directed to better their conditions of unemployment and not to end the unemployment.'[41]

Politics provided both an outlet and a means of gaining understanding of the causes behind their lives. One Middlesbrough volunteer described how he 'was unemployed, but in many ways actively employed politically and not concerned about being unemployed. I wasn't propping up lampposts on street corners.'[42] However, there were often other reasons for involvement in a party which could be as much a social movement as a political organisation. Discussions and meetings organised by its youth wing, the Young Communist League (YCL), provided an opportunity to meet others with a similar outlook. As one member of the Middlesbrough YCL remembered, 'we went hiking, we went camping, we had dances; it was a club as well as a centre for political activity.'[43] Another member in Mile End, east London, argued that there was a difference between joining the youth movement and its more serious and disciplined older sibling:

> To be a Communist was to be more purposeful, more militant than being a Socialist . . . There was a difference between the Communist Party and the Young Communist League. You have to go through a certain amount

of screening and dedication and education and qualification to be a member of the Communist Party, but anyone could belong to the Young Communist League, because although it did have a philosophical connection, it was mainly a social sort of thing.[44]

For another young Manchester man, it was joining the Clarion Cycling Club, named after the newspaper of nineteenth-century socialist Robert Blatchford, that introduced him to politics and instilled in him a passion for reading newspapers:

> I started reading the *New Statesman* and I gravitated from the *News Chronicle* to the *Daily Worker*. I suddenly found myself buying two morning papers – the *Manchester Guardian* and the *Daily Worker* – and then I started to read the *Class Forward*, the Glasgow Independent Labour Party paper. I became completely besotted by the whole thing; I started to think that the Soviet Union had the answer to everything from appendicitis to divorce. There was nothing that could not be cured by the dictatorship of the proletariat.[45]

During the early 1930s, Maurice Levine took part in several large demonstrations by the unemployed in Salford and Manchester, where he was finding it extremely difficult to find work. Perhaps surprisingly, Levine cited the influence of the Young Men's Christian Association on many young men growing up in Cheetham, a predominantly Jewish area in central Manchester: 'Most of them when they were about eighteen joined the YMCA for its sporting or gymnastic facilities and later took on a big part in their debating societies and came under the influence of socialist thinkers in the YMCA.'[46]

This encouraged some local young men to take evening classes in Marxism, run in the basement of a restaurant in the centre of the city, and from there to membership of the YCL or the Communist Party.[47] Levine later took part in hunger marches and in the 1932 mass trespass on Kinder Scout, an action aimed at gaining access to open spaces in what is now the Peak District National Park. At Kinder he and his fellow protestors encountered the determination of landlords to protect their property:

> I was among the first few who charged up the hill . . . we were met by a dozen or so keepers, wielding sticks and trying to intimidate the hikers . . . one fellow was struck and he struck back . . . we got on to Kinder Scout,

held a meeting with a contingent who had come from Sheffield and then
we returned . . . when we stopped, police who had been hiding in the homes
on either side of the Kinder Road arrested five men at random.[48]

A number of individuals who would later fight – and die – in Spain took
part in the action and five of the protestors received six months' hard labour
for their involvement.[49] For such as these, battles to ensure the right to roam
across the countryside were very much part of their wider struggle against
oppression. John Longstaff, from Stockton-on-Tees, was involved in
protests as part of the Ramblers' Association: 'it was a job to ensure that
our heritage and that the right of walking was free to all, and this was
probably the first political activity that I ever remember myself carrying
out.'[50]

The two features of hiking and protesting were combined for Longstaff
when he joined one of the most potent symbols of political dissent in the
1930s: the hunger marches. 'If one is to seek a major factor in the motivation
of a significant proportion of the British Battalion, one could well begin with
the hunger marches and the conditions which provoked them,' one
observer declared.[51] The marches were organised by the National
Unemployed Workers' Movement (NUWM), established in 1921 by Wal
Hannington, a London shop steward and one of the founders of the CPGB,
to publicise the plight of those without work. The NUWM became 'the
most important organisation of the unemployed during the depression'.[52]

Having grown up in a working-class community in Sunderland, near a
colliery, Frank Graham always remembered the demonstrations and parades
of the unemployed during the 1926 General Strike. As a student at King's
College in London he joined the Labour and Socialist Society before moving
to the Communist Party. However, he was forced to leave university early
when he ran out of money and returned to Tyneside where he became active
in the NUWM, taking part in another march of the unemployed to London
in 1934.[53] The same year, John Longstaff took part in another march to the
capital from 'derelict and distressed' Stockton-on-Tees, despite having 'no
idea of the distance to London and in complete ignorance of the route the
marchers were taking, or even the time it would take'.[54]

Together with the Friends of Soviet Russia and the British Anti-War
Council, the NUWM was one of a number of organisations proscribed by
the Labour Party leadership; TUC leader Walter Citrine instructed Labour
members that they should not join the marches or offer their support.

Moreover, the marchers were met with active hostility by the government, police and, seemingly, many Londoners:

> We were marching through the City of London. People from the offices around were shouting out, 'You dirty bastards, go back home, get a bloody job.'
>
> Some well-dressed men started shouting at us – 'Bloody Reds, you all want shooting.' Others were shouting, 'Go to Russia where you came from.' I could not understand why these well-dressed men, and some women, had hurled such abuse at us. I did not know what a Red was.
>
> Little did I know that I was walking by the Stock Exchange and Lloyds and the other city companies. All I knew was to see these chaps in their bowler hats and their pin-striped suits shouting words of abuse at us; they were frightened of us in those days. Unarmed, ill-clad, badly-clothed and half-starving, they were frightened of us.[55]

Many recollections by volunteers for Spain refer to their 'progression' from the hunger marches as a key stage in their political development, one of the first stepping stones on their road to war; 'a crash course in political education', as the Teeside volunteer David Goodman described it. Unsurprisingly, many hunger marchers joined the Communist Party and found that involvement in the NUWM led logically to volunteering.[56] For example, four of the leaders of a march which left south Wales for London in the autumn of 1936 later fought in Spain.[57] As Lance Rogers, one of the large number of Welsh volunteers, explained, it was 'a continuing process. Here we were in Merthyr Tydfil in a continuing struggle night and day. The Hunger March over, we left for the Spanish war. It was a fulfilment and a most natural step to take.'[58]

2

Fighting the Blackshirts

Looked at today, it may seem rather far-fetched to have imagined that England was in danger of becoming a Fascist state. But then it appeared to be well within the realms of possibility . . . Mosley was no mere illiterate house painter. He was impeccably upper class, a baronet related to many of the greatest families in the land, a product of Winchester and Sandhurst and a very handsome man of outstanding intellectual attainments and considerable wealth.

Jason Gurney, *Crusade in Spain*

While many of the men and women who went to Spain had a long history of political activism, for other volunteers it was the rise of fascism in Europe and its home-grown version in the form of Sir Oswald Mosley's Blackshirts, that principally lay behind their decision to fight.

The establishment of the British Union of Fascists in 1932 was the first serious – if only partially successful – attempt in Britain to create a mass party in the image of continental fascist regimes. Originally elected as a Conservative MP in 1918, Oswald Mosley had grown disillusioned with the Tories and infamously crossed the floor of the House of Commons to join the Labour Party in 1924, becoming Labour MP for Smethwick in 1926. Mosley developed a passion for current economic theory, and his extremely thorough knowledge of the subject led to his appointment as Chancellor of the Duchy of Lancaster in the Labour administration of 1929. Disturbed by the high levels of unemployment that resulted from the economic slump, Mosley suggested an ambitious – and expensive – plan of public works, but his suggestions were rejected by the government, from which he promptly resigned in disgust.

In Mosley's eyes, Britain possessed a weak National Government populated with unimpressive and unreliable political figures, and responsible for a political crisis that matched the economic one. Never short of self-confidence, Mosley believed he could offer a more vibrant alternative to the discredited government and, indeed, the Westminster system itself, with its 'old gang' of tired and ineffectual politicians.

Mosley gradually collected together a group of young followers, such as Labour MPs Aneurin 'Nye' Bevan (member for Ebbw Vale and later deputy leader of the Labour Party) and John Strachey, to help him press the government into taking his suggestions on board. However, in February 1930, he decided to give up his struggle to change Labour from within and, instead, broke off to form a new political party. Controlled financially and politically by Mosley, in 1931 the New Party put forward a candidate for the Ashton-under-Lyne by-election. Previously a Labour seat, the Conservatives won by just under 1500 votes, with the New Party candidate, Allen Young, polling nearly 4500. When the result was declared, Mosley and the New Party were booed by Labour Party members, who recognised that the New Party had split the vote, allowing the Tory candidate to profit.[1]

Faced with the disappointing result and the ensuing hostility of Labour supporters, Mosley's party gradually took on an increasingly fascist appearance. Nevertheless, in the General Election of October 1931 they were humiliated, gaining fewer votes than even the Communist Party. Following this disastrous showing, the New Party effectively ceased to function, and in early 1932 Mosley travelled to Italy to see Mussolini's fascism at first hand. Impressed, and firmly wedded to the belief that Britain's economic depression heralded a crisis which the political establishment lacked the will and dynamism to overcome, Mosley determined to launch a British fascist party.

Established on 1 October 1932, the British Union of Fascists (BUF) was 'slavishly imitative' of other European fascist movements. Mosley made use of all the fascist tricks: the uniforms, the grandiose stage shows, the speechifying and rolling eyes of Mussolini and, crucially, the violence. As members of the BUF later admitted, deliberately provoking violence was an essential part of the fascist programme, all part of a wider scheme to blame Communists as a justification for seizing power by force.[2]

Membership of the BUF grew quickly and at its high water mark in the summer of 1934 the party comprised 134 branches, with perhaps as many as 50,000 members. This rapid growth was partly due to members of the other, smaller British fascist parties joining, but it was also due to a genuine appeal. There is no question that Mosley possessed a remarkable talent for oratory. According to one of the foremost historians of British fascism, he was 'without peer as a public speaker in twentieth century British politics'.[3]

As the BUF's membership increased, it also gained a number of powerful backers. Foremost among these was Lord Rothermere, the owner of the *Daily Mail*, who lent his newspapers' support to the BUF's cause from January 1934. While Rothermere may have been 'more of an anti-communist than a fascist', pro-BUF reporting in the various Rothermere newspapers undoubtedly gave the movement a huge boost.[4] The infamous article 'Hurrah for the Blackshirts' appeared in the *Daily Mail* on 15 January 1934. Crucially – and despite Mosley's denials both at the time and later – the BUF also received substantial financial support from Mussolini, estimated to be in the region of £60,000 between 1933 and 1936.[5]

Mosley's belief in an impending crisis was widely shared, particularly within the Communist Party, which argued with 'all the intense, irrational fervour of street corner evangelists'[6] that the end of capitalism was nigh. Therefore, for Mosley and his followers, it was fundamental that they prevent the Communist Party from capitalising on the expected unrest. However, just as Mosley's overtly calculated fascist trappings generated huge enthusiasm among his followers, they likewise inspired suspicion, loathing and dread among his opponents. Many suspected that Mosley sought not just to benefit from a political and economic crisis, but to create it. They were determined to stop him.

Following the Communist Party's abandonment of its 'class-against-class' policy in response to the rise of fascist and authoritarian regimes across Europe, both the Communists and the Independent Labour Party appealed for a 'united front' against fascism. However, the Labour Party remained deeply suspicious of its former critics and their dramatic volte-face, and was unwilling to have anything to do with them. Thus the Communists adopted the clandestine tactic of channelling anti-fascist activity through front organisations such as 'The British Anti-war Movement', headed by John Strachey, who had left Mosley's New Party in disgust when it began to develop a fascist tone.[7]

During 1933, as support for the Blackshirts increased, so correspondingly did anti-fascist demonstrations by those perceiving themselves to be the targets of fascism: Communists, members of the Labour movement and, in particular, Jews.[8] From March 1933 onwards there were increased occurrences of confrontations between 'the radical left' and the BUF, especially in London where, on several occasions, BUF newspaper sellers were jostled, or even attacked, by Jewish activists. Other violent confrontations occurred during the year in cities such as Manchester, Stockton and Oxford. Walter Gregory, who would become a lieutenant and company commander in Spain, was involved in a number of attempts to disrupt the Nottingham branch of the BUF and was wounded in a demonstration at the city's Victoria Baths. While disrupting the meeting Gregory got into a fight with a member of the audience, before a steward hit him over the head with a chair, breaking his nose. As Gregory described, 'The Communist Party's tactics at Fascist meetings were basically simple; get as many members as possible into the meeting and then, once it was in progress, cause such disruption that the meeting could no longer continue or the disturbance would have to be quelled by Fascist stewards.'[9]

George Watters, who would fight with the British Battalion at Jarama, was involved in anti-Mosley demonstrations in Edinburgh:

> I remember gaun to a meeting in the Usher Hall, having been supplied wi' a ticket by some of the students at Edinburgh University. I landed down right in the second front seat in the Usher Hall. You'll know what sort of position I was in. My job was to get up and create a disturbance right away by challenging Sir Oswald Mosley, which I did. At that time I had a pretty loud voice. And Sir Oswald Mosley wasn't being heard. I was warned by William Joyce, better known later on as Lord Haw Haw, what would happen to me unless I kept quiet. There was a rush and in the rush I got a bit o' a knocking about and taken up to High Street. We were released wi' the Party phoning up and letting them know any bail that was being tabled. It finished up wi' us being fined £5 each. But when I was in the High Street I was accused by one o' the Fascists o' having kicked him in the eye. His eye was split right across. So I jist said at the time, 'I wish tae Christ it had been me. I'd at least have felt some satisfaction'.[10]

Another Scottish volunteer, Eddie Brown, a member of the Communist Party from 1934, was involved in anti-Mosley protests in Perth:

> Mosley came down [to the North Inch in Perth] and he had his car planked there and they were shouting the odds from that. But those of us who opposed Fascism we gave his car a push and it landed just simply in the [River] Tay . . . That finished the speechifying.[11]

In Manchester, activities centred on Cheetham, home of a large Jewish population. BUF members regularly hung out in Walter's café on Great Duncie Street, near Victoria station. From there, they would march through the area of Strangeways in order to provoke its Jewish residents.[12] Opposition was led by the Jewish-dominated YCL, 'the Challenge Club' of up to 200 members.[13] Sam Wild, active in the Manchester NUWM and Communist Party and later to command the British Battalion in Spain, 'used to take part in all the anti-Mosley demonstrations' and was involved in the 'familiar pattern of marches and anti-Mosley activity'. So effective were the counter-demonstrations, he believed, that 'Manchester effectively became a place where Mosley just could not go.'[14]

One meeting in Stockton was particularly strongly opposed and Blackshirts responded by attacking members of the crowd. The meeting was subsequently closed by the police who escorted the Blackshirts to their buses, pursued by an angry crowd of over 1000 anti-fascist demonstrators.[15] Here was incontrovertible evidence of the BUF's predilection for the deliberate use of violence against opponents, a fact which fostered a determined belief among anti-fascists that the Blackshirts had to be combated directly, on the streets, wherever they appeared. As later events would demonstrate, the main beneficiaries of the BUF's use of violence would be the Communist Party.[16]

During 1934, Mosley planned three big rallies in London.[17] The first of these, in the Albert Hall on 22 April, saw him address a crowd of 1000 people in a large and ultimately successful meeting. However, opponents were determined that Mosley's next appearance, at Olympia on 7 June, would be strongly opposed. The counter-demonstration was pre-planned in detail, and determined efforts were made to get as many opponents of Mosley as possible inside the venue. A variety of ruses were used; as one Jewish activist who would later fight in Spain explained, 'forged tickets to enter Olympia were available at every billiard hall in the East End of London.'[18] Some 600 tickets were purchased for the event, and increasingly preposterous letters were sent to the *Daily Mail* begging for tickets. One letter in particular became infamous: 'I like the Blackshirts because I want to die for my country and they seem to offer the best opportunity,' claimed the applicant.[19]

By 7.45 on the morning of the rally, 1000 people were already protesting outside Olympia and taunted anyone entering the hall: 'Hitler and Mosley, what are they for? Thuggery, buggery, hunger and war!'[20] Several hundred protestors successfully managed to get inside, although they were severely outnumbered among an audience of twelve thousand. Having already been on the receiving end of Blackshirt violence, many came determined to provoke disorder; one later described how he and a friend selected their weapons before the demonstration: 'We brought knuckle-dusters at a Drury Lane ironmonger and I well remember the exaltation of trying them on. We flexed our fingers. "A bit loose here . . . Not very comfortable on the thumb." We were expert knuckle-duster buyers.'[21]

However, the Blackshirts' brutal response entailed wholly unnecessary levels of violence. Any hecklers were violently ejected, thrown physically out of the hall. Many individuals were badly beaten.[22] These violent scenes were met with outrage by newspaper commentators and politicians, who laid the responsibility on both sides. The Labour-supporting *Daily Herald* blamed the Communists, arguing that if they hadn't been in the hall, there would have been no disturbance. Criticism also came from the conservative press such as the *Daily Telegraph* and *The Times*, who denounced the use of violent private armies and the tactics of the brutal BUF stewards.

The violence at Olympia had two significant consequences. The first was a near-collapse in BUF membership, which forced Mosley to change tactics and attempt to appeal to local populations on local issues – particularly in London's East End, where nearly half of the membership congregated. The second was that, after Olympia, the Communist Party became seen as the leading force in the fight against Mosley's Blackshirts.

Nonetheless, the Labour Party continued to reject the Communists' overtures for joint action, believing that the fascist threat was being deliberately and shrewdly overstated.[23] When the Communist Party organised a demonstration in Hyde Park on 9 September 1934, the press refused to publicise it. In response the party attempted an 'innovative' – and highly effective – guerrilla publicity campaign, led by Welsh miner and Communist Party organiser Bert Williams, who was to become a political commissar in Spain, responsible for maintaining morale – and political orthodoxy – within the Communist-dominated International Brigades. Measures included the hijacking of a BBC outside broadcast on 3 September, as a result of which the protestors were labelled 'the microphone bandits' by the *Daily Mirror*. As many as a million leaflets were thrown from London rooftops, banners were hung from buildings such as Broadcasting House and slogans were daubed across the city, including a call for 'workers to do their duty' painted on Nelson's column. The ensuing meet numbered perhaps 100,000, many times the size of the BUF contingent, who found themselves completely surrounded. This time, despite the booing and ridicule by the anti-fascists, the event remained remarkably peaceful. Faced with such organised resistance and growing official disquiet, membership of the BUF continued to decrease through 1935, with only 5000 members remaining by October.[24]

Following the explicit adoption of anti-Semitic policies, its popularity resurged. Mosley claimed to oppose the behaviour of Jews, rather than the Jews themselves, but his protestations failed to convince, particularly as his BUF foot-soldiers seemed incapable of making the same fine distinction. Unsurprisingly, British Jews were quick to see parallels between Mosley's movement and fascist European regimes and were therefore prominent among those demonstrating against the Blackshirts. Although any reading of BUF speeches, with their frequent allusions to 'alien and foreign influences', demonstrated clearly enough that anti-Semitism had been present in Mosley's movement from the outset,[25] the verbal – and physical – abuse of Jews in which many BUF members were engaging marked a change to a more offensive stance and the beginning of the BUF's move into overt anti-Semitism.

In London's East End, home of the highest concentration of Jews in Britain – some 100,000 out of a national population of 330,000 – competition for scarce accommodation, a dislike of Jewish business practices (in particular 'sweating' – manufacturing in small, often overcrowded, premises), plus naked racial prejudice, created a fertile breeding ground for the BUF.[26] Fascist branches were established in Bow, Bethnal Green, Shoreditch and Limehouse, and fights between BUF paper-sellers and Jews became increasingly common. Attacks on Jewish properties and on Jews themselves became a regular occurrence during 1935 and 1936, when the BUF campaign in the East End began in earnest 'and their campaign, at its peak, approached a siege of terror'.[27]

> In Stepney . . . the anti-Semitism was so great that you could hardly venture out of your own particular area – for instance, to go to Bethnal Green or to Shoreditch, the Elephant and Castle, Hoxton, anywhere like that, you were entering enemy territory. You could be attacked if you appeared Jewish.[28]

With signs that he was successfully tapping into popular prejudices, Mosley announced another rally at the Albert Hall for 22 March 1936. The response by Communists was rapid and widespread. According to the *Daily Worker*, in the days preceding the meeting, the East End was chalked and whitewashed every night by members of the Young Communist League and the Labour Party League of Youth. On the day of the demonstration itself, about 10,000 protestors tried to assemble outside the Albert Hall, but the area had been cordoned off, as all counter-demonstrations within half a mile were banned. Around 5000 protestors reassembled in nearby Thurloe Square, where the crowd was charged, apparently without warning, by police with batons. A report on the demonstration produced by the National Council for Civil Liberties considered the meeting to be perfectly orderly, until the police's intervention. A retired solicitor described the charge as 'unnecessary and provocative and carried out without warning and with a degree of roughness which surprised me' and several other witnesses mentioned the excessive brutality of the police. One statement, from G.C. Maclaurin, 'a bookseller from 5 All Saints Passage, Cambridge', testified to two particular features of the action:

> First, the orderly nature of the crowds. There was a certain amount of shouting but a complete absence of disorderly conduct. Secondly, the markedly provocative behaviour of the police, more particularly those on horseback . . . in many cases the horses were ridden into the crowds on the footpaths, and made to rear up in a manner calculated to alarm anyone not used to horses . . . The speeches were by no means inflammatory. Had the police had any reason to fear the proceedings would lead to trouble there was nothing to prevent them from approaching the platform and forbidding it.[29]

The Cambridge bookseller, Griffin Campbell Maclaurin, was in fact a Rhodes Scholar from New Zealand, studying at the university. He was also a Communist Party member and would be among the first contingent of volunteers to fight in Spain.

Another statement, provided by Gerald Lorimer Birch, described the treatment of an anti-fascist protestor who was arrested and beaten with a baton, solely for protesting about police brutality. According to Birch, the arresting officer repeatedly referred to the anti-fascists as 'you lot of bastards'. Birch was himself charged with 'insulting words and obstruction of police' and eventually released on his own surety at 2.50 the following morning.[30] Like Maclaurin, Birch was at Cambridge, working as a research chemist, and was a member of the Communist Party. And, like Maclaurin, Birch would leave for Spain in the late summer of 1936.

To the anti-fascist demonstrators, the success of the Blackshirt meeting had clearly been a result of the policing of the event. This was the culmination of a number of complaints against the police for their treatment of anti-fascist protestors. Max Colin, a young Jewish activist from London, had gone to the Olympia demonstration the previous October 'just for a lark, to see what's cooking'. He was stunned by his experiences:

> Well, this was an eye-opener for me. Because I'd never seen anything like it before. I'd always imagined the police as honest people who looked after other people – good blokes as it were. But the callousness of the police at that night absolutely shook me, shook me rigid . . . Both of us were walking along towards Olympia along Kensington High Street. And two policemen stopped us and: 'Where are you going?'
>
> 'Oh, we're just going up to Olympia.'
>
> 'Get back to the effing East End, you two bastards,' said the policeman. Then tried to trip my mate up.[31]

Further complaints were made about police behaviour at demonstrations in Oxford in May 1934 and at Tonypandy, in the mining areas of South Wales, the following month.[32] Six thousand Blackshirts attended the Tonypandy meeting, which was pelted with stones by 200 protestors and closed after thirty minutes. Several anti-fascists were arrested and seven received prison sentences for their part in the disturbances.[33] When a protestor complained to police about the brutal treatment being meted out by Blackshirts, he was told to 'mind his own business and run along'.[34]

Despite official denials, anti-fascists became convinced that 'the fascists were shown a remarkable indulgence by the police, both in terms of their ability to hold meetings and processions, and in their ability also to police and regulate those demonstrations themselves.'[35] Many BUF speakers felt they had little to fear from the police who, numbering many army veterans in their ranks, were regarded as natural allies.[36] While it might be argued that senior officers attempted to remain impartial, there seems little doubt that some policemen were sympathetic to Mosley and were themselves guilty of giving the fascist salute and joining in the anti-Semitic abuse.[37]

In line with the increasingly anti-Semitic nature of the movement, in April

1936 Mosley changed his organisation's name to the British Union of Fascists and National Socialists, which was shortened the following year to the British Union. The fasces symbol was replaced by a circle of unity containing a flash of lightning, smartly dubbed by opponents 'the flash in the pan'.[38] The following month, there was another massive anti-fascist demonstration in Tonypandy, where thirty-one men and five women were summonsed for incitement to riot and similar charges.[39]

During July and August, according to police reports, 600 political meetings a month were held, and Special Branch reported that 60 per cent of British Union London meetings in August were disrupted. Although the majority of anti-fascist demonstrations were organised by the Communist Party, the Young Communist League or the Communist-dominated NUWM, opposition widened over the summer, with the establishment of new organisations such as the British Union of Democrats and the Jewish People's Council against Fascism and Anti-Semitism.

Responses to the British Union differed: the Labour Party and Jewish leaders recommended 'ignoring' the Blackshirts' provocations. The Board of Deputies and the *Jewish Chronicle* consistently advised Jews not to take part in demonstrations, in order to avoid drawing attention to themselves and to prevent Mosley claiming that Jews were pro-Communist. However, the Communists continued to press for direct confrontation, fully aware that the activities of the British Union acted as a highly effective recruitment aid for the Party among Jews and others frustrated by what they saw as the passivity of the Labour Party and the Jewish leadership towards Blackshirt intimidation. Indeed, two leading anti-fascists in the London Communist Party, Lionel Jacobs and Phil Piratin, were later to admit that Communists deliberately exaggerated the violence of the fascist movement.[40]

Charlotte Haldane remembered encountering a Blackshirt rally while out on a walk with her son:

One Sunday afternoon Ronnie and I decided to go to Hampstead Heath, to see for ourselves one of the fascist meetings that were then held there by Mosley's followers. The meeting was a small one, but the envenomed anti-Semitism of the speakers was unrestrained by the indifference of most of the listeners. Ronnie did not react to the situation with any outward exhibit of emotion, but on the following Monday he joined the Young Communist League.[41]

To many working-class Jews in the East End, the Board of Deputies appeared distant and out of touch, in contrast with the Communist Party.[42] As one Jewish activist put it, 'Who do you think was defending Jews in the East End of London in the 1930s? . . . The CP were the only organisation that had the power and the organisation to oppose Mosley.'[43]

Buoyed by the gains in east London, Mosley hatched his infamous plan to march provocatively through Cable Street in the East End on 4 October 1936, to commemorate the fourth anniversary of the founding of the Blackshirt movement.

As with responses to the British Union itself, opinions on how to respond to the march differed. The initial response of the Communist Party was to recommend that Party members stay away. Not because they had decided to adopt the line of the Board of Deputies – though it is true that many in the CPGB saw Mosley as a figure of ridicule rather than a threat – but because they were organising their own demonstration in support of the Spanish Republic in Trafalgar Square, at a time when Rebel forces had just captured Toledo, only seventy kilometres from Madrid, and the Spanish capital appeared to be facing very real danger.[44]

The Jewish activist groups and the Independent Labour Party were determined to prevent the march by force, while the Board of Deputies, the Labour Party and the TUC tried to have it banned. The Jewish People's Council submitted a petition of 100,000 names complaining about the march.[45] A deputation of mayors met Sir Alexander Maxwell, deputy under-secretary at the Home Office, to try and get the march stopped or re-routed away from the East End. And former Labour leader George Lansbury wrote to the Home Secretary, Sir John Simon, asking that the march be diverted, at the same time advising Labour supporters to stay away: 'Fascist meetings are in themselves dull. The platform is dull, the speeches are dull. The "message" is dull.'[46]

By late September, the Communist Party leadership was coming under increasing pressure to cancel the aid-Spain demonstration and support the anti-fascist protest in the East End. Joe Jacobs, secretary of the Stepney branch of the Communist Party, approached Willie Cohen, secretary of the London Young Communist League, about the anti-fascist demonstration, only to discover to his horror that the party was not prepared to cancel the Trafalgar Square rally and still believed that Spain was a more important issue than Mosley.[47]

In an attempt to reach a compromise, on 30 September the *Daily Worker* instructed party members to attend the Spain rally and then to head to the East End. However, grass-roots pressure forced the Party leadership to come into line with Jacobs and, aware that many would simply go directly to the East End, on 2 October the YCL and CP finally abandoned their plans for the pro-Spain march and got behind the anti-fascist demonstration.[48] A determined and, if need be, violent response was planned. One anti-fascist later claimed that a number of dockers had guns stored on the roofs at Cable Street.[49]

Keen to show that the party was now taking the anti-Mosley demonstration seriously, Douglas Frank Springhall, usually known as Dave or 'Springie', secretary of the London district of the Communist Party and a member of the party's Political Bureau, who had twice been jailed for his activities in the General Strike and its aftermath, spoke at a meeting just before the demonstration. Springhall blamed the Home Secretary for any ensuing violence, arguing that the march should have been cancelled.[50] Anger among the mass of demonstrators, combined with a grim determination to prevent the British Union from marching, was further provoked by Blackshirts who while waiting on the Embankment chanted, 'The Yids, the Yids, we got to get rid of the Yids.'[51]

Many of those at Cable Street were experienced anti-fascist activists who had been at Earls Court and Olympia and many of them would later continue their fight in Spain. Parallels between the fight against Mosley in London and against Franco in Madrid were clear. The struggles against domestic and overseas fascism were inextricably linked for the Communist Party; the emblematic slogan, ¡No Pasarán! (they shall not pass), the use of the term 'civil war' and the quoting of the Spanish Communist La Pasionaria's dictum that 'it is better to die on your feet than live on your knees' were calculated and deliberate.[52] Barricades were built in the side streets by people who had learned what to do from photographs in the Daily Worker of the Spanish people preparing to defend Madrid.[53] 'It seemed the whole of London was turning out to stand by the Jews and the working people. All were determined that the British Union of Fascists would not get through the East End.'[54]

Alf Salisbury, a ship's fireman and acting secretary of the Stepney branch of the NUWM, was twenty-seven years old when he joined the demonstrators at Cable Street. He had been part of the East End anti-fascist protests since the rise of Hitler in Germany in 1933, and a member of the Communist Party since 1934.[55] He was in Aldgate three hours before

Mosley's march was due to take place, knocking on doors, persuading people to come out on to the streets and support the demonstration against the Blackshirts. One demonstrator recounted how 'I shared the joy of this mass of anti-fascists. The more they crowded me – and at times the pressure was so great I could hardly breathe – the more strength I drew from them.'[56] But once again the anti-fascists met with blunt official force. Alun Menai Williams, later a stretcher-bearer and first-aider in Spain, was knocked down by a charging police horse, before being dragged away to safety: '[The police] bludgeoned any unlucky protestor who had the temerity to approach, or was accidentally pushed to within touching distance of the black-shirted marchers . . . The entire police force, mounted and on foot, were engaged in a full-frontal attack on the protesting demonstrators.'[57]

Another demonstrator, Charlie Goodman, only sixteen years old, was arrested after climbing a lamp post to urge his fellow protestors to resist the police charges. Having been 'clubbed, punched and kicked all the way to Leman Street police station',[58] Goodman was sentenced to several months' hard labour. Soon after his release he travelled to Spain, joining the British Battalion on 4 February 1937.[59]

Many felt emboldened by the experience of collective action. One east London volunteer described the emotion of seeing, in among the thousands of demonstrators, banners of numerous organisations: the Communist Party, the Transport and General Workers' Union, the anti-fascist printers, and local tenancy associations:

> I must admit that I was excited. I was exhilarated by it, but I played no leading part in it. I was a very, very young man at the time, and I wasn't part of the organisation, but I was exhilarated by it. I was seeing the power of people being able to stop something that was hateful to them. It was a lesson.[60]

Alf Salisbury claimed that 300,000 people turned up to oppose Mosley, though this is almost certainly a considerable over-estimate.[61] When police were unable to force their way through the huge and determined crowd, the Metropolitan Police Commissioner, Sir Philip Game, was left with little choice but to instruct Mosley to abandon the march. 'There was a great cheer which I joined in when they marched away from Cable Street,' remembered the young Jewish activist Tony Gilbert, with great satisfaction.[62] For the anti-fascists it was a triumph, and an object lesson:

On Sunday, October 4th 1936, yet another glorious page in the history of the East London Working Class was written. East London workers irrespective of their race, or creed, irrespective of their political affiliations, Jews and Gentiles, Communists, Socialists and Labour Party supporters, demonstrated to the whole world that the best traditions of East London's militant past were safe in their hands. On that day the working class of London scored a tremendous victory against the forces of reaction.[63]

While it is true that membership of the British Union increased after Cable Street and he was still able to address Blackshirt meetings in the East End, the huge anti-fascist turnout clearly demonstrated to Mosley that the level of opposition he faced was far greater than he had imagined. It had serious consequences. Mussolini's foreign minister, Ciano, informed Mosley that the Italians viewed it as a defeat and were considering terminating their financial support.[64] The movement was soon crippled by financial difficulties, forcing Mosley to reduce dramatically the number of candidates in the 1937 London County Council elections from 143 to 30.[65]

Mosley's movement was squeezed further in the capital. First, vigorous Communist involvement in local campaigns such as housing and rent strikes and the party's opposition to evictions increased Communist support in the East End. Second, the Public Order Act, introduced in early January 1937, banned paramilitary organisations, uniforms and marches, and the Blackshirts found it increasingly difficult to hire halls for their meetings.[66] Though the act was promptly attacked by the Communist Party for giving the police robust powers to ban marches, while not making the incitement of racial hatred illegal, Home Secretary Sir John Simon later claimed that it 'worked like a charm'.[67]

Some anti-fascists, like the Nottingham volunteer Walter Gregory, played down the importance of the anti-fascist demonstrations in Mosley's failure to break the mould of British politics in the 1930s:

The attempts in which I was involved to disrupt Fascist meetings had little effect upon the fortunes of the fascist cause in Britain . . . our activities were more of a nuisance-value than of any political significance. Mosley failed because he never managed to capture the sort of support that would have given him electoral victory.[68]

His analysis may have had the benefit of hindsight. As one resident of

Hoxton remembered, 'that was not how it seemed if you happened to be living in one of the areas in which the Fascists concentrated their greatest efforts during that crucial couple of years.'[69] To many of those actively involved in confronting the Blackshirts, the danger seemed all too clear. One London volunteer later pointed out:

> I had been an observer of all this in the year preceding the Spanish Civil War. I had seen the hatred and the violence, with the resulting pattern of fear it introduced into the lives of ordinary men, and I hated the whole thing . . . we had seen what had happened in Germany. There, too, people had laughed off Hitler and the Nazi Party until they had found themselves overwhelmed by the situation and the Nazis had become the masters of the German state. Fascism was strengthening its hand in every country in Europe and those who felt strongly about it, and took no action to stop it, experienced a very real sense of guilt.[70]

While Georgi Dimitrov, the General Secretary of the Comintern, had warned the CPGB not to waste too much time and resources on 'the small fry of Mosley's BUF', the response from those under attack in Cheetham or the East End was to confront the Blackshirts directly and robustly.[71] It was a powerful and often formative experience, a key feature in the political development of those who would go on to confront fascism not just on the streets, but on the battlefield. Like young Charlie Goodman, Jack Shaw was arrested at Cable Street and sentenced to three months' hard labour in Bristol prison, far away from his home and family.[72] Upon his release he signed up on a ship bound for Spain where he arrived in April 1937. There Shaw joined the International Brigades and served as a runner in the British Battalion. Alf Salisbury's story was very similar:

> I was just one of a number of people who, as a result of what happened at Cable Street, felt that we had to do something to defeat fascism, to take up arms against it. Otherwise there would not only be many dead, but they would also throw us back a thousand years. I went to Spain.[73]

Salisbury was one of many who cited Cable Street, involvement in anti-fascist demonstrations and the spread of fascism in Europe as fundamental to their political development and the decision to volunteer for the war in Spain. The Nazi seizure of power in Germany and the Blackshirts' rise in

Britain politicised many working-class Britons, including one Manchester volunteer who 'wasn't interested in politics at all until the rise of Hitler, and then Mosley coming into the picture in England'.[74] And for the Jewish volunteers there was a more sharp-edged motivation to fight:

> Influences during that period were the rise of Hitler and the threat of fascist aggression spreading around the world in the 1930s. There was the humiliation and degradation of the Jewish communities and the confiscation of their property, so you had this feeling of kinship with the victims of Hitler in Germany. Then, over the years, there was the external aggression of the Nazi regime when Hitlerism was able to extend those same policies to other territories and new Jewish communities were the victims.[75]

The long-standing anti-fascist activist Tony Gilbert had previously had his nose broken while a member of a Jewish organisation called The Blue and White Club, which, as he put it, used to 'deal out their own medicine':

> More than a few were attracted by the Blue and White Society, which saw combat with those that would attack them as the answer. And it's one of the reasons why, in those days, a great many young Jewish people either joined or supported the Communist Party in their area, and it's one of the reasons why the East-End of London supplied so many people to enter into the struggle against fascism in Spain.[76]

A considerable number of the volunteers in Spain had been arrested fighting the Blackshirts at some stage between 1934 and 1938.[77] 'I felt we had to smash them off the streets,' declared one Scottish volunteer.[78] Londoner Harold Horne was arrested on several occasions; he later claimed that it was all made worthwhile when, during a melee at a meeting in Willesden, in north-west London, he managed to land a kick in William Joyce's testicles.[79] His fellow Londoner, Wally Togwell, a waiter from St Pancras, is typical of this type of seasoned anti-fascist campaigner: 'Wherever the fascists were, our group of the YCL was there also. I was thrown out of the Albert Hall, I took part in anti-Mosley demos at Olympia and Hyde Park, I was at Cable Street helping to erect barricades.'[80]

During the 1930s the apparent threat of the BUF pushed a coterie of experienced anti-fascists to engage in armed conflict. It is no coincidence that the areas that presented the most muscular response to Mosley's

Blackshirts – the East End of London, Manchester, Aberdeen and the Rhondda – were also home to a large number of volunteers for the International Brigades. As Maurice Levine described, 'I should say that it was the prime motive, the emergence of Fascism and Mosleyism in Britain in persuading lots of people like myself to go to Spain.'[81] Alongside nearly 2500 men and women, Levine graduated from fighting Mosley's Blackshirts on the streets of Britain, to fighting Franco's soldiers on the battlefields of Spain.

3

Aid Spain! or 'Keep out of it'?

> Over our hurried breakfast on July 19th we read the news of the 'Generals' Revolt' against the Spanish Republican government. I myself – and it is a sign of my political ignorance, even of my frivolity – was excited and pleased by the revolt, believing that it must be quickly crushed and that its suppression would be a heavy blow against reaction everywhere.
>
> Philip Toynbee, *Friends Apart*

On 18 July 1936, reports that something was awry in Spain began to appear in the British press; 'Spanish Rumours', reported *The Times*.[1] Over the next few days, hazy details began to emerge of the Generals' military rising and the desperate resistance of those loyal to the Spanish government. As elements of the Spanish left took matters – and guns – into their own hands, early reports suggested that, while the military rising might not succeed, the Republican government might not survive. Churches had been burned and terrible atrocities visited on priests and nuns, it was said, adding weight to the view that the Republican government had lost control; the situation was seen in some government circles to resemble that in Russia prior to the Bolshevik revolution.[2]

In *The Times*, a reliable barometer of British government opinion, the view was that if a democratic republic had ever existed in Spain, it had now been overtaken by its more radical supporters.[3] This presented an opportunity for some lazy stereotyping and patronising comments on the violent, cruel and, above all, 'alien' nature of Spain and its people: 'Political intolerance has taken the place of the religious intolerance of earlier ages . . . with this psychology . . . the outlook for Spain cannot but be black indeed.'[4] The devastation in Spain was contrasted with life in 'wonderful Britain'; while Spanish violence raged, 'Aren't You Glad You Live in England?' asked the *Daily Mirror*.[5]

The collapse of order in the Republican zone – seen as the beginning of a left-wing counter-revolution – suggested that the conflict had descended, in a foreign country with a wholly different political and cultural heritage, into a battle between two alien political philosophies, neither of which had any real support in Britain: 'A plague o' both your houses', as a leading article in the *The Times* put it. The Prime Minister, Stanley Baldwin, famously declared: 'We English hate fascism, but we loathe bolshevism as much. So, if there is somewhere where fascists and bolsheviks can kill each other off, so much the better.'[6] Baldwin was adamant that Britain should 'keep out of it' and so too should the other European powers. This absolute determination to keep the war within Spain's borders – 'Heaven forbid that Spain's calamity should become Europe's scourge,' as one British newsreel commentator put it – would play a crucial role in forming British governmental responses to the war.

Scarred by the horrific experiences of the First World War, much of British public opinion initially felt the same way.[7] However unfortunate the conflict might be for the poor Spaniards, it was no concern of British people, who considered it 'bad form to get hysterical about foreigners'.[8] As Winston Churchill's son, Randolph, put it brutally, 'A few excitable Catholics and ardent Socialists think this war matters, but for the general public it's just a bunch of bloody dagoes killing each other.'[9] Even the British fascist leader, Oswald Mosley, agreed. Not attracted by the ultra-reactionary Spanish Nationalist movement, he refused to campaign on the war, arguing that 'no British blood should be shed on behalf of Spain.'[10]

However, despite Randolph Churchill's obnoxious claim, there were a sizeable minority in Britain to whom the war did matter. Some had always been overtly hostile to the Spanish Republic. Among these Rebel supporters – right-wing Conservatives and elements of the military, as well as 'excitable Catholics' – the conflict was seen as a battle between the representatives of Christianity and law and order on one side (Franco was portrayed as 'a gallant Christian gentleman'), and an ungodly vicious mob on the other, who 'pitifully misguided and ignorant, had allowed themselves to be duped by the astute agents of Russia'.[11] Their views of the Republicans were coloured by stories of the worst excesses of the Republic's supporters, while their opinions of the Nationalists were reliant upon the words of the Rebel Generals' grandest supporters: 'The Spanish Revolution and Civil War seems on examination to boil down to a straight fight between the two conflicting creeds, of which the cross and the hammer and sickle are the respective emblems.'[12]

The anti-clericalism of the Republicans was contrasted with the image of the Nationalists as deeply religious people.[13] On 10 September 1936, the Rothermere-controlled Movietone News described the two factions as 'Red' and 'anti-Red' and described the entry of two Communists into the cabinet of the Socialist Prime Minister, Francisco Largo Caballero, as: 'The Hammer and Sickle are in the ascendant at Madrid.'[14] Pro-Nationalist papers such as the *Morning Post* and the *Daily Mail* printed a number of exaggerated, and often unsubstantiated, atrocity stories.[15] A gruesome report from a French tourist, which described three heads being carried around Barcelona on a platter, was not untypical. Nationalist supporters attacked the pro-Republican view of the war as a battle between democracy and fascism, or 'a struggle for liberty against tyranny', as Bertrand Russell described it.[16] Arthur F. Loveday, a Conservative MP and ex-chairman of the British Chamber of Commerce in Spain, wrote numerous letters to right-wing newspapers reiterating this point and complaining about the use of:

> Loyalists to describe Republicans who have discarded God and their King, destroyed Churches, persecuted priests, are supported by irregulars wearing the red shirt of communism and professing its doctrines and do, in theory and in fact, represent anarchy. The side described as 'rebels' represent the maintenance of law and order, the bulk of the regular army and those people who are loyal to God and the Christian Church.[17]

These Rebel supporters denied that the military rising was anti-democratic, but asserted that 'misrule and interference from Moscow had made it imperative to remove the present government from power.'[18] The Republic was perceived as little more than an offshoot of the Soviet Union, the Spanish Generals' aim being 'to save Western Europe from the menace of Russian Communism'.[19] General O'Duffy, the leader of the Irish volunteers who served with the Nationalists in the winter of 1936–7, blamed a fictional Russian 'Manual of Action' for the spate of church burnings that followed the declaration of the Republic in 1931.[20] The Asturian rising of October 1934 was also 'planned and engineered by Moscow', he argued: 'But for Russia there would be no civil war in Spain.'[21]

Franco's supporters stressed that the rising was therefore clearly the fault of the Spanish left and the responsibility of the Republican government. According to this view, church burnings, attacks on political opponents and the murder of the Spanish conservative politician Calvo Sotelo had left 'Rightists' with no choice but to attempt to reinstall order:

> At no time since the Republic has there existed anything remotely resembling democracy. The present 'Government' relying as it does on a motley crew of Anarchists, Syndicalists, Communists, Socialists, Liberals, all at discord with one another, is democratic in nothing but the name, and anyone who supposes that its victory would be a victory for democracy argues himself totally devoid of political understanding.[22]

English right-wing historian Arthur Bryant, an implacable foe of the Spanish Republic and a close friend of Stanley Baldwin, argued that:

> Red Spain is not a constitutional democracy. It is an inferno. Since July, 1936, some 350,000 non-combatants, men, women and children, living helplessly in that part of the Iberian Peninsula subject to the rule of what is euphemistically called the Valencia Government, have been butchered in cold blood, under conditions of indescribable horror.[23]

Two Catholic newspapers, the *Universe* and the *Catholic Times*, started a campaign to raise funds for Nationalist Spain and a number of aid committees were established; the largest of these was the Bishops' Committee for the Relief of Spanish Distress, presided over by Cardinal Hinsley, the Archbishop of Westminster.[24] The editor of the pro-Nationalist *English Catholic Review*, Douglas Jerrold, also set up a pro-Rebel group in Britain, called the Friends of Nationalist Spain, through which he and other like-minded Francoists such as Sir Henry Page Croft, the Conservative MP for Bournemouth, could lobby for the Nationalist cause. During the course of the war he pressed for the recognition of Franco's regime and the granting of 'belligerent rights' which would have allowed the Nationalist navy under international law to 'interfere' with British merchant shipping bound for Republican Spain.[25]

Nationalist supporters worked hard to counter what they saw as the overwhelmingly pro-Republican bias of the British press, which they believed to be 'indelibly coloured by Comintern fabrications'.[26] The claim espoused in the *News Chronicle* and the *Daily Worker* that the British government had a duty to come to the aid of the Spanish Republic evoked fury, as did the raising of £1000 in August 1936 by British supporters of the Republic; pro-Rebel voices argued that the money would have been better spent 'in the distressed areas of their own homeland than in a foreign country'.[27]

The irony of the rightist call to 'keep out of it' and the claim that the left had begun it was that Douglas Jerrold had himself played a significant role in the uprising. In early July 1936, Jerrold had been approached by an old friend, Luis Bolín, press correspondent of the Spanish monarchist newspaper *ABC*, to charter an aeroplane from Croydon to Morocco. Jerrold recruited 'a retired major' and two young women to accompany Bolín on the flight to give it an air of authenticity. The plane was paid for by Spanish millionaire Juan March, with the money channelled through Kleinwort Benson, a bank with strong links to MI6.[28] It was flown by a British pilot, Captain Cecil Bebb, who claimed not to know the details of his mission. It turned out to involve flying General Franco from his semi-exile in the Canary Islands to Morocco, so that he could join the rising and take command of the Army of Africa, the Spanish army's crack troops.[29]

Evidence of German and Italian involvement in airlifting Army of Africa soldiers across the Gibraltar Strait increased concern within Baldwin's government about the involvement of outsiders. The Foreign Office assistant under-secretary, Sir George Mounsey, considered the Spanish conflict 'one of the gravest menaces, if not the gravest, which the world has had to face since the Great War'.[30] Ignoring claims that Britain had a duty to help a democratically elected government, as *The Times* reported, the official response was to continue to do their utmost to 'keep Britain out of it' and to limit the conflict to Spain by pressing for a European-wide policy of non-intervention in the war, including an embargo on arms sales.[31] Not becoming embroiled in the war was essential if peace in Europe were to be maintained:

> Non-intervention is best for Spain: it is necessary for Europe . . . a policy of interference would defeat itself . . . it would immediately provoke counter-intervention by other powers . . . no course but abstention is open to any government which is genuinely committed to the resettlement of Europe and the reorganisation of peace.[32]

The government's attitude was expressed succinctly – and revealingly – in the advice given by Baldwin to his Foreign Secretary, Anthony Eden, very early in the conflict: 'On no account, French or other, must he bring us into the fight on the side of the Russians.'[33]

Following sustained diplomatic pressure, a 'non-intervention agreement' was signed in August 1936 by twenty-eight countries, including France, Italy, Germany and Russia. Aware that it was little more 'than a series of slightly differing accords' which had no force in law, the British government set up a committee in London to oversee the working of the agreement. However, chaired by the hopelessly ineffective Lord Plymouth, and with Spaniards not allowed to sit on or even report to it, the committee failed utterly to prevent foreign involvement.[34] As opponents of the agreement recognised, it prevented the legitimate sale of arms to the elected Spanish government while doing nothing to stop supplies to the Rebels. Clearly Hitler and Mussolini had no intention of 'keeping out of it', so the pact was utterly farcical from the outset.[35]

However, at least initially, non-intervention drew support across much of the political spectrum: even the staunchly pro-Nationalist newspaper, the *Morning Post*, argued that 'Spain must be prevented at all costs from becoming a European battleground.'[36] Likewise, the Labour and trade union movement – or at least the parts under the influence of the anti-Communists Walter Citrine and Ernest Bevin – initially, albeit reluctantly, supported non-intervention, and the Labour Party endorsed the policy at their conference at Edinburgh in October 1936.[37] As one Reading Labour councillor put it:

> It is perhaps expedient to adopt a policy of non-intervention at the present time, but there must be no suggestion of neutrality. It should be made crystal clear that we will not tolerate that our Spanish comrades are battered to submission by bludgeons of German and Italian manufacture.[38]

                                         *

For Communists and other members of the British left, such as the Independent Labour Party, there was no such equivocation. To these Republican supporters, the conflict was a fight between democracy and fascism: the Republican government was not 'red' or Communist, argued the avidly pro-Republican *News Chronicle*, but of the centre-left – and anyway, 'the violence [was] of the reactionaries' own making.'[39] The paper, believing the conflict to be of major significance to the British people, printed many 'human-interest' stories emphasising that those defending the Republic were no different from those who supported democracy in Britain. Taking a broadside at those who maintained that the civil war was no concern to Britain, pro-Republican newspapers argued that 'what is going on in Spain is extremely important for the rest of the world' for the conflict was part of the 'historical duel between the forces of reaction and progress', which had a meaning for all European democracies.[40]

The reactions of Republican supporters were dramatic and immediate: 'Arms for Spain!' In the summer of 1936, the Welsh District of the Communist Party organised a petition, calling on Stanley Baldwin to recall Parliament on the issue of the civil war.[41] 'Attendances of our [Communist Party] meetings doubled up . . . there wasn't a night of the week that we weren't campaigning somehow or other,' remembered senior Aberdeen Communist Bob Cooney.[42]

> The main activity of the Communist party from July onwards was Spain. Arms for Spain, collecting for Spain, food parcels for Spain, anything of that kind. This was almost a whole-time job of the Communist party and the [Young] Communist League from July 1936.[43]

Numerous organisations were set up across the country to raise money for the beleaguered Spanish Republic and thousands of people became involved: 'I think every democratically minded person in those days was on the side of the Republican government,' recalled one young activist from the north-west of England.[44]

This support quickly developed into tangible efforts in the form of meetings, rallies, concerts, collections of money and supplies of humanitarian aid: 'Meetings for Spain – Resolutions to end non-intervention – food for Spain – arms for Spain. It was the central point of all our Communist Party activities,' remembered one Welsh Party member.[45] 'The Spanish Aid Committee was organising meetings all over the country,' recalled a comrade from Rochdale.[46] Grass-roots members of Labour groups, trade unions and charities worked together with Communists and Socialists to raise money for medical supplies, food and clothing. Like many of his friends in Manchester, Syd Booth went to numerous meetings about Spain and was involved in collecting money, organising union resolutions and other work in support of the Republic: 'At that period in the thirties, I think, everybody must at some time or another have contributed to aid for Spain.'[47] Republican supporters came up with novel and imaginative ways to raise money, such as the selling of 'milk for Spain' tokens and a carol singing service; one group of women knitted jumpers, while sitting on full display in the window of the People's Bookshop in Battersea.[48]

Determined efforts were made to try and increase support for the Republic among the wider populace:

> [The] first task [of the British Communist Party], during the summer and autumn of 1936, was to arouse interest in the Spanish struggle among the relatively lethargic British working-class. An intensive programme of Aid-to-Spain meetings and rallies was set in motion. Following the Popular Front line, they welcomed help from any quarter where it was available. They sought to co-operate with prominent personalities and speakers of all political parties and points of view, who would address meetings and collect money. Even Conservatives were enthusiastically welcomed to the fray.[49]

Support for the Republic often transcended class lines: 'Tories, Liberals, everybody was involved in it.'[50] 'If the Spanish Republicans are crushed, it means the end of liberty, justice and culture and the merciless extermination of all suspected of caring for these things,' argued Conservative MP the Duchess of Atholl, whose enthusiastic support for the Republic would end in her losing a by-election.[51] Many intellectuals contributed to aid-Spain campaigns, including composer Benjamin Britten and poets Stephen Spender and W.H. Auden, who donated his poem *Spain* to raise money for the Republic.[52] Artists such as Henry Moore contributed by selling work, and post-Impressionist painter Augustus John auctioned a portrait for five hundred guineas in a 'Portraits for Spain' fundraiser in 1938.[53] Another artist, Felicity Ashbee, applied her talent to the battle for hearts and minds, designing a number of powerful posters for the National Joint Committee for Spanish Relief. On the literary front, Victor Gollancz and the Left Book Club published books propagandising for the Spanish government, such as *Spain in Revolt* by Harry Gannes and Theodore Repard and *The Nazi Conspiracy in Spain*, based on evidence of German intervention in the war gleaned by Arthur Koestler on a visit to Nationalist-controlled Seville.[54]

Many of the intellectuals who spoke up for the Republic, or visited it, were Communists, such as Spender, scientist J.B.S. Haldane, and writer Sylvia Townsend Warner and her girlfriend, poet Valentine Ackland.

Sympathetic 'fellow-travellers', such as *News Chronicle* reporter and writer John Langdon-Davies, and Sir Peter Chalmers-Mitchell (who wrote an account of the fall of Málaga), were used in the various front organisations, often chaired by non-Communists, but controlled by veteran Comintern propagandist Willi Münzenberg.[55] A huge network of support was organised in Britain, involving important Communist figures such as the secretary of the Relief Committee for Victims of Fascism, Isabel Brown, *Daily Worker* reporter Claud Cockburn and Ivor Montagu, the creator of the Progressive Film Institute, which used considerable amounts of Spanish footage to great effect in films such as Ernest Hemingway's *Spanish Earth*.

In January 1937 all the aid organisations were brought together under the National Joint Committee for Spanish Relief (NJCSR), born as a result of the visit to Madrid of a parliamentary delegation, arranged by former Labour MP Leah Manning, in November 1936.[56] Over the course of the war, the largest of the British Aid to Spain organisations, chaired by the Duchess of Atholl, was to raise somewhere between one and two million pounds (equivalent to more than one hundred million pounds in 2012).

In addition to the rallies, the campaigning and the fund-raising, Republican supporters continued to protest vigorously against the British government's unwillingness to come to the support of the democratically elected Republican government. Many on the left suspected that the government's enthusiasm for neutrality disguised, if not a sympathy for the Rebel Generals, then certainly animosity towards the Republicans; 'malevolent neutrality', as the Labour peer Lord Strabolgi put it. They had a point. There is no doubt that certain elements of the British government were overwhelmingly hostile to the Spanish Republic; the Foreign Office in particular appeared to be more anti-red than anti-war.[57] An official complaint to the Foreign Office was made after it appeared that a British consular representative, who had told of 'red' atrocities in Madrid, was accused by the city's British residents of never having left the Embassy.[58]

The extent of the hostility within the British government towards what was perceived as Spain's 'Kerensky government' (the provisional administration in Russia brought down in the Bolshevik revolution of October 1917) is manifest in a statement by Sir Maurice Hankey, the Cabinet Secretary, who argued that 'in the present state of Europe, with France and Spain menaced by Bolshevism, it is not inconceivable that before long it might pay us to throw in our lot with Germany and Italy.'[59] Elements in the Admiralty had also reacted with horror to the mutinies and executions of Spanish naval officers that followed the uprising. Sir Ernle Chatfield, the First Naval Lord of the Admiralty, candidly admitted that he leant 'more to the White than to the Red'.[60]

Anger among Republican supporters increased dramatically when it became clear that the government was determined to continue supporting non-intervention, despite the mounting evidence of German and Italian soldiers and arms flooding into Spain.[61] Hitler and Mussolini's representatives on the Non-Intervention Committee ran rings around Lord Plymouth; the German representative, Joachim von Ribbentrop, later joked that it would have been more accurately labelled 'the intervention committee'.[62] While *The Times* weakly noted that 'it has been realized from the first, of course, that non-intervention was a euphemism for controlled intervention . . . Controlled intervention is a great deal better than uncontrolled intervention,' a leader column in the *News Chronicle* complained bitterly that 'the game is to go on arguing, while Franco goes on advancing.'[63] As early as 1937, Admiral Sir Hugh Sinclair, the chief of the Special Intelligence Service (MI6), admitted that, as Mussolini was clearly intent on continuing his Spanish adventure, it would be 'far better to let him exhaust himself *in* Spain rather than he should "run amok" *outside* Spain'.[64]

Sir Robert Gilmour Vansittart, permanent under-secretary at the Foreign Office, later admitted that 'the whole course of our policy on non-intervention has in reality as we all know worked in an extremely one sided manner.'[65] Whether deliberately or no, Franco was certainly grateful for what he perceived to be the British government's support for the Nationalists. In June 1938 he was to write to Neville Chamberlain, Baldwin's successor as Prime Minister, 'thanking him for his friendship towards Spain and assuring him that they were both defending the same ideals and principles'. Embarrassed, Chamberlain ensured that the note was not made public.[66]

Fully aware that the Nationalists were benefiting far more from the agreement than the Republicans, the British government turned a blind eye: 'Better a leaky dam than no dam at all,' claimed Anthony Eden.[67] In support of the government's position, *The Times* argued that the major importance of non-intervention was to prevent the conflict spreading:

If the war which is tearing Spain to pieces were extended outwards across its frontiers, its cruelties and its destructiveness would also certainly be extended with it. It is therefore the first and paramount concern of every government which cares for the civilisation of Europe that the armed conflict should be confined to Spain . . . If it cannot prevent all arms traffic with Spain, it has the authority to keep it to a much lower scale than if there were no attempt at control.[68]

However, Republican supporters were outraged at the 'one-sided' nature of the agreement, which in their eyes acted as a 'cloak' for German and Italian intervention.[69] The Duchess of Atholl agreed:

The only way to avoid drifting into a position in which we become the instruments of the final strangulation of a brave people fighting against desperate odds for liberty, culture and social betterment, is to end so-called non-intervention and to restore to the Spanish Government its right under international law to buy the arms it needs and has the wherewithal to purchase. Non-intervention has not been straightforward neutrality. It has really been a concealed form of intervention. It has inflicted gross injustice on a friendly people, and to continue it any longer is to bring ourselves and France into deadly peril and make practically inevitable a European war which we should enter under the gravest handicap.[70]

Calls from those such as the Labour MP Philip Noel Baker, who argued that if non-intervention was defective, the Republic's right to purchase arms should be restored, were strongly resisted by the government.

Pressure increased from grass-roots Labour Party members and trade unionists for the leadership to abandon their support of the 'farce' of non-intervention. But senior Labour figures remained reluctant, extremely wary of Communist attempts to use the issue of Spain to entangle them in an anti-fascist Popular Front. Indeed, the *Daily Worker* had been quick to point out the significance of the events in Spain for Britain; that the success of the Spanish 'People's Front' provided an object lesson for the British working class.[71] Not until June 1937, two months after German bombers razed the Basque town of Guernica to the ground, was the policy abandoned, although that decision would have to wait until the Labour Party and TUC conferences in the autumn to be ratified.[72] By then, many trade unionists, impatient with their leadership, had reached their own conclusions about the 'treacherous non-intervention pact' and the involvement of Germany and Italy in Spain.[73] As the Liverpool Labour Party councillor and trade unionist Jack Jones declared: 'This was Fascist progression. It was real and it had to be stopped.'[74]

For Jones and the nearly 2500 other volunteers from Britain and Ireland, meetings, demonstrations, collecting food, money, medical supplies, seemed no longer the answer.[75] Spain needed arms, as one young Spaniard argued: 'We Spaniards are greatly thankful for your charity and your lint and your ointments which you send us to repair Don Quixote's wounds; but we would be much more thankful if you were to outfit him with a new lance and an up-to-date shield.'[76]

Jones' response was to volunteer for the International Brigades in order to fight for the Republican cause: 'Since the Governments of . . . Britain and France were not prepared to go to their aid . . . many of us felt that it was right to give whatever help we could in supporting them.'[77] Like other volunteers, he discovered that the aid-Spain meetings provided opportunities for those involved in campaigning for the Republic to take the next step and volunteer to fight. Speakers at the numerous meetings calling for support for Spain often quietly told potential volunteers how to find their local recruiting centre, or the one in London.[78]

John Dunlop was a young chartered accountant in Edinburgh whose increasing awareness of politics led him, in 1936, to join the Communist Party. He found his work colleagues' apathetic reactions to the military rising in Spain to be 'astounding and insupportable' and vowed to involve himself, in order to personally demonstrate to them 'the danger that this war of intervention by the Fascist Powers of Italy and Germany against the Republican Government had for this country':

Reading the *Daily Worker* and the other press of the day I was very well aware of what was happening in Spain. It seemed to me that great injustice was being perpetrated on the people there by the organisations that had revolted against the legal government of the day. I was also disgusted at the fact that the other democratic governments in Europe were not doing anything at all to help the legal government in Spain against an attack which obviously was being supported by both the Fascist Government of Italy and the Nazi Government in Germany. I felt very strongly that if they were allowed to continue their attack on the people of Spain it wouldn't be so very long before the rest of Europe was engulfed in war.[79]

For British anti-fascists, the July rising represented the latest manifestation of a phenomenon they saw sweeping across Europe. One
volunteer, part of a strong anti-fascist movement in Aberdeen, was in no
doubt that it was his 'duty to go and help the people in Spain. And the
fight, whether it be here in Aberdeen against the British Union of Fascists
or against Mussolini and Hitler in Spain, was exactly the same fight
to me.'[80]

The volunteers saw this not as a civil war within Spain, but as one more
episode in an ongoing European war against fascism:

> Nobody in the Communist Party saw the Spanish Civil War as just another
> civil war. Spain was different, Spain was about opposing the growth and
> spread of Fascism by armed force, of meeting Fascist aggression with
> aggression and ensuring the safety of democracy in the face of the Fascist
> challenge.[81]

Many of them had already participated in the fight at home, where
'attempts were being made by Mosley and company to bring about a similar
situation in Britain.'[82] This was a struggle that went beyond national
boundaries, a perspective lucidly expressed by South African-born sculptor
Jason Gurney:

> The Spanish Civil War seemed to provide the chance for a single individual
> to take a positive and effective stand on an issue which appeared to be
> absolutely clear. Either you were opposed to the growth of Fascism and
> you went out to fight it, or you acquiesced in its crimes and were guilty of
> permitting its growth . . . for myself and many others like me it was a war
> of principle, and principles do not have a national boundary.[83]

Many volunteers came from the same branch of the Communist Party,
or Young Communist League. Others were neighbours, brought up in the
same street, living the same experiences. One street in Glasgow sent five
volunteers. However, while the overwhelming majority of volunteers,
perhaps two-thirds, were members of the Communist Party, it would be a
mistake to conclude that they were all doctrinaire Stalinists, or even
Marxists.[84] The Communist Party acted as a vital conduit to Spain and it
was natural enough that some volunteers joined simply to ensure that they
would be accepted. Among them was David Lomon (originally Solomon),

a young Jewish salesman from the East End: 'I wanted to go to Spain, so I joined the Young Communist League just because, I thought, these are the people, who I could use to get over to Spain . . . I wanted to do something, I wanted to fight fascism.'[85]

The Communist Party was 'the noisiest opponent of fascism' and many anti-fascists naturally gravitated towards it, even if only as fellow-travellers:

> The reason why I joined the Communist Party is partly the reason why I went to Spain . . . My basic feelings and beliefs made me an anti-fascist, opposed to Hitler and were my reasons for joining the Communist Party and going to Spain . . . I looked around and thought the Labour Party doesn't seem to be doing very much, they are pretty tame anyway and I thought the only people who seem to be doing anything that leads to what I believe in – Socialism – were the Communists, even if they were a small group.[86]

And, of course, while the majority of the British volunteers were Communists, a sizeable minority were not:

> When I went to Spain I was a member of no party. I supported the Labour Party in its programme. I read the *News Chronicle* and had great respect for the *Manchester Guardian* and the Liberal Party because at least it was progressive.[87]

Another volunteer, the son of 'an old socialist', had been brought up 'in a free-thinking . . . progressive atmosphere at home' and remained out of the party. He was the brother-in-law of one of the political commissars in Spain, yet he saw himself solely as an anti-fascist.[88] Many senior members of the Brigades, both Communists and not, were adamant that membership of the party was not compulsory. Political commissar John Angus was quite clear about this: 'There was certainly no pressure whatever that I recall in the British Battalion to join the C.P., on the contrary, I hardly remember the topic being discussed.'[89]

Hostile newspapers, such as the *Daily Mail*, accused volunteers for the International Brigades of being mercenaries, or dupes of the Communist Party who were promised safe work behind the lines, then dragooned into active service once they arrived in Spain. The accusation was supported by

Douglas Hyde, a senior Communist and subsequent convert to Catholicism, who claimed that 'When cannon-fodder was needed, one Party organiser's job was to go around the Thames Embankment in London at night looking for able-bodied down-and-outs. He got them drunk and shipped them over the Channel.'[90] Even Manchester volunteer Alec Marcowich was convinced that 'there's three people there who I'm quite positive were recruited from the embankment, the three of them were the Scots, MacQueen, Kemp and another fellow called Henderson.'[91] The right-wing press, particularly the *Daily Mail*, obviously made much of this, despite furious denials by the British Battalion leadership in Spain and others.[92]

While most such accusations were motivated by political mischief-making, the party's need to recruit meant that on occasion 'sub-standard' volunteers did end up in Spain.[93] Will Paynter, the Welsh political commissar based at the International Brigade headquarters in Albacete in the summer of 1937, later admitted that some 'were recruited in rather rotten circumstances. One or two we had that were recruited on Trafalgar Square at about two o'clock in the morning, but they weren't much bloody good to us.'[94] George Aitken, another senior political commissar, agreed:

> There was always a core of tremendously reliable people, dedicated socialists and communists . . . But there was also, of course, quite a number of people out of work and some of them had been recruited – as far as I was informed – on the embankment.[95]

The accusation was taken seriously by André Marty, the veteran French Communist and Comintern member in charge of the International Brigades in Spain. He wrote to Harry Pollitt, General Secretary of the Communist Party of Great Britain, insisting that 'Drunkards, down and outs, criminals and others of this character are not wanted here. There should be a stop to recruiting in hostels and parks, Embankments etc.'[96]

Undoubtedly all but a few volunteers were fully aware of why they were going to Spain. However, despite the widespread coverage of the war in the press, rallies and political meetings, many knew little about the country itself, as the young writer and Communist Philip Toynbee admitted:

> Very few young English communists knew anything at all about Spain. They adored their own pipe-dream of the Soviet Union; they loved to plot

in Paris; they sang American Union songs, and they were deeply conscious of German and Italian fascism. But this easy assumption that those who were fighting the Spanish Civil War on the government side were closely akin to communist students at Oxford shows an almost ludicrous ignorance of Spanish history and the Spanish reality of 1936.[97]

Manchester anti-fascist Syd Booth admitted that the military uprising rather took him by surprise, for his knowledge of Spain was not very sophisticated: 'we discussed things in a very raw manner, you know.'[98] Walter Gregory was even more candid, confessing: 'it is astonishing how little I knew of Spain . . . The actual causes of the Civil War were barely obvious to me except in terms of the broadest generality: "The Fascists are trying to kill a democracy".'[99] One Scottish volunteer later admitted that his politics were 'more instinctive than theoretical or dogmatic'.[100]

There is no doubt that, possessing little or no knowledge of Spanish politics and history, many British anti-fascists projected their own perceptions onto the conflict and saw it simply as a battle between democracy and fascism. However, as a thorough study of the effect of the civil war on British political opinion argued: 'If, as was the case, they were in part ignorant as to what was really happening in Spain, this in no way detracted from their sincerity and self-sacrificial idealism or from its resulting influence on the opinion of millions of men and women in Britain.'[101]

As the war dragged on into 1937 and 1938, a number of volunteers, many of them wounded, were to return to Britain bringing tales of their experiences, of the Republic's lack of arms and of Nationalist bombings of civilians. Despite the risks, some who had not taken the decision to join up in the winter of 1936–7, when recruiting for the Republic was at its height, chose to volunteer. They left for Spain in defiance of non-intervention and despite the British government's implementation of the Foreign Enlistment Act in January 1937, an obscure nineteenth-century piece of legislation which made volunteering to fight in Spain illegal. One Scottish volunteer joined after listening to speeches from recently returned volunteers, despite having lost a friend and an uncle in Spain.[102]

When [Sam] Masters and [Nat] Cohen found themselves involved in it, we were a bit jealous, actually, and would have liked to have been there . . . I wanted to fight back . . . I liked the notion of having a rifle to fight with, rather than having no rifle to fight with.[103]

Over the course of the war, the worsening plight of the Republic, and the abject failures of the British government's policy of non-intervention, were to lead many who had previously been neutral to become increasingly sympathetic to the Republic's plight. 'Nationalist sins gained prominence over Republican failings,' as one later commentator summarised it.[104] By late 1938 even some, like Winston Churchill, who had initially supported the Rebel cause, had begun to have second thoughts:

> It would seem today that the British Empire would run far less risk from the victory of the Spanish Government than from that of General Franco . . . The victory of the Spanish Republicans . . . would not only be a strategic security for British Imperial communications through the Mediterranean, but gentler and reconciling forces would play a larger part . . . The Liberal and Moderate influences have waxed and the Anarchist and Communist doctrinaires and assassins are being brought monthly under the healthy restraint of military service enjoined by dire need.[105]

Opinion polls taken in Britain between March 1938 and January 1939 all showed both overwhelming support for the Republicans over the Nationalists and a shift among those who had previously been non-partisan towards support for the Republic; support for Franco stayed virtually static in all three surveys.[106] The large shift towards the Republicans was probably not a reaction to the situation in Spain alone, but also to the failure of Chamberlain's policy of appeasement towards the dictators.[107] Supporters of appeasement could point to very little that would justify the policy, except of course that, as yet, Britain and France were not embroiled in another European war.

The comment expressed by an 'anonymous working class man, aged 45', to a Mass Observation interviewer during the Munich crisis of September 1938, in which Britain and France cravenly forced the Czechs to gift the Sudetenland to Hitler, could just as easily have been about his feelings regarding Britain's role in the Spanish Civil War. 'I'm just a working-class man,' he said, 'and I'm entitled to an opinion as anyone else. We've let them down good and proper.'[108] His conclusion was later supported by an admission by Francoist minister Pedro de Sáinz Rodríguez:

Many Spaniards . . . believe that we gained our victory exclusively through German and Italian aid; I am convinced that, though this did contribute, the fundamental reason for our winning the war, was the English position opposing intervention in Spain.[109]

4

To Spain!

The most important element of Russian help was neither Russian officers nor Russian bombs but the 'international brigades', the foreign volunteer forces recruited by the communists all over the world, which have played a decisive role in the defence of Madrid. These international brigades have men of almost every country of the world, with the one exception of Russians.

Franz Borkenau, *The Spanish Cockpit*

The precise events surrounding the creation of the International Brigades were, for many years, shrouded in secrecy and much that has been written has since proved to be ill-informed. They were not, as some historians have claimed, the brainchild of Maurice Thorez, the leader of the French Communist Party.[1] Nor were they a 'spontaneous' creation by the volunteers themselves, as some Communist histories maintained; although there can be no doubt that the presence of foreign volunteers in Spain from the outbreak of the war played a vital part in their inspiration.[2] As Jason Gurney describes, the desire to fight in support of the Spanish Republic predated the creation of the Brigades:

From the very day of the rising, all sorts of individuals set out for Spain to assist the embattled Republic. It immediately appeared as the symbol of a great number of things which men held valuable but which were being destroyed all over Europe. To the Italian and German refugees, it was an opportunity to fight against the dictators who had destroyed their homeland; to the Greeks, the military who had been corroding democracy in their country; to the various Balkan peoples, it was a symbol of resistance against the variety of oppressive regimes at home; to the British and French, a chance to protest against the hopelessly corrupt and inefficient ruling cliques who were leading them into another world war or an accommodation with Hitler. The Communists had the good sense to realize the terrific force of idealism that existed and climbed on the band-wagon to exploit it.[3]

In fact, the foundation of the International Brigades, as British political commissar George Aitken observed, 'was organised by the Comintern'.[4] As the sole anti-fascist body capable of large-scale coordination across national borders, the Communist International provided the crucial mechanism that made it possible to both recruit and enrol thousands of men and women from around the world and transport them into Spain.[5] However, Soviet intervention in the war was not immediately forthcoming, nor was it inevitable.

Initially, following the military rising of July 1936, approaches had been made by the Spanish government to the USSR for aid. An agreement to provide discounted fuel supplies – which had been turned down by the British government on 22 July – was agreed by Russia on the same day.[6] But supplying arms was a different matter entirely and support for the idea was not given until the following month.

The idea of raising an International Brigade of volunteers was first mooted at an extraordinary Politburo meeting in Moscow on 26 August 1936. Soviet military intelligence (GRU) reports arriving from Spain had demonstrated the dire position facing the Republic and the fragmented state of the Republican military response to the rising was regarded by Moscow with alarm. Despite the imposition of the non-intervention agreement, German and Italian involvement was increasing and the amateurish nature of the Republican militias – some of whom were accustomed to heading off home at the end of the day – suggested that they would not be able to defeat the experienced Nationalist forces. Likewise, the pivotal role played by the army in the rising meant that officers in the Spanish military, no matter their proven record of loyalty to the Republic, came under suspicion. The inability of the Spanish Premier, Francisco Largo Caballero, to recognise the nature of the crisis facing the Republic did not help. However, Russian intelligence reports suggested that all was not yet lost.[7]

Stalin's support for the Spanish Republic was, at its most basic, a riposte to the intervention of the fascist powers in Spain. Moscow believed that the Republic should be supported – not replaced – by a People's Army, including loyal members of the military. Alarmed at the rapid progress of the Rebel forces, instructions were sent out to European Communist parties to put pressure on their governments to assist the Republic.[8] The role of the national Communist parties was crucial, for they provided the network for recruiting large numbers of anti-fascists to fight for the Spanish Republic. But their purpose was not to help turn Spain into a satellite state of the USSR, for this was not Stalin's game – at least, not in Spain and not in 1936. Stalin's main fear was German expansionism. He was keen, too, to avoid upsetting the French and British governments, with whom he was urgently attempting to establish an entente. Overt Russian involvement in Spain would obviously jeopardise this, as would the fostering of socialist or communist revolution. But covert assistance could help prevent another authoritarian right-wing regime on France's doorstep and, crucially, keep Germany embroiled in a costly war, far removed from Russian territory. Far from seeking to ensure a Republican victory, Stalin's likely aim was to prevent a Republican defeat.

On 6 September, he gave preliminary instructions to sell fifty bombers to Spain, using Mexico as a conduit. The bombers were to be supported by twenty pilots who would train Spanish pilots in how to fly the planes. Also included in the sale would be 20,000 rifles, 1000 machine guns and 20 million bullets. When the plan proved unrealistic, a more comprehensive approach was decided upon in the second half of September. Much more ambitious, this included the shipping of vital supplies, such as trucks; the clearing-out of old stock of Russian military *matériel* for Spain; the sale of new *matériel*, such as planes and tanks, and the organisation of purchasing second-hand arms in Europe; and the formation of brigades of international volunteers.

The final decision to create the International Brigades was taken by the Comintern Secretariat on 16 September. The frequent portrayal of the International Brigades as a Comintern army is however a misconception. To be sure, they were created and organised by the Comintern, com - manded by Comintern officers and their ranks were principally made up of Communists. But many of the volunteers who fought in the Brigades saw themselves as anti-fascists, not Comintern warriors.

Ten days later, Stalin decided to rapidly escalate the amount of *matériel* sent to the Republic, including modern tanks and bombers. On 12 October, Largo Caballero formally agreed to the formation of the Brigades and Albacete, a town of approximately 50,000 people, which lay on the main railway about halfway between the port of Valencia and Madrid, was chosen as their base. Following Caballero's agreement, the Communist

International began the process of recruiting volunteers. A central recruiting office was established in Paris through which volunteers from across Europe – and beyond – could be channelled. Paris was the logical choice, as France was home to many left-wing exiles from Germany, Italy and the other right-wing authoritarian governments across Europe: 'Today in Spain, tomorrow in Italy,' declared one exile from Mussolini's regime.[9] Disdainful of the officer class who had been at the centre of Spain's military coup, the Comintern selected experienced Red Army commanders, many exiled in Russia, to command the army of international volunteers. One such was the Austro-Hungarian Jew, Manfred Lazar Stern, a former captain in the Austrian army who had fought with the Bolsheviks during the Russian Revolution. Under the *nom de guerre* General Emilio Kléber, he arrived in Spain to become the first military commander of the International Brigades.

In Britain, where the government was strongly opposed to any intervention in the Spanish struggle, recruitment had to be carried out in secret, particularly following the implementation of the Foreign Enlistment Act on 9 January 1937 and the banning of volunteers under the non-intervention agreement in February. Though many families were supportive, it was not uncommon for volunteers to keep from their loved ones the decision to fight. Often the first family members would know was when a postcard arrived from Spain.[10] Albert Charlesworth from Oldham, now nineteen years old and working as a metal-polisher, deliberately didn't tell his mother, because he 'thought she might stop me'.[11] Understandably, such subterfuge sometimes created resentment, particularly if the volunteer's family were not politically committed to the Spanish Republic's cause. For example, Walter Gregory's mother was confused and distressed by her son's decision: 'She was astounded at what she considered to be my stupidity in going to fight in another nation's war. Still being able to recall vividly the horrors of the First World War she assumed that the war in Spain would simply be a repeat of its slaughter.'[12]

Clearly the decision to fight was not an easy one and, although taken in secret, was almost always a matter of conscience. London volunteer Fred Thomas was adamant that it was his decision and his alone: 'Nobody cajoled, coerced or bullied me into making the decision [to volunteer]; certainly not the Communist Party, even though, at my request, they provided the means.'[13] However, on occasions, suitable individuals were approached and asked if they would go to Spain, mostly to take political roles, such as the Communist party organiser for South Wales, Will

Paynter, and the leader of the National Unemployed Workers' Movement in Nottinghamshire and Derby, Eric Whalley, both of whom were to serve as political commissars. In October 1936, Scottish Anarchist Ethel MacDonald was invited to Spain by the Spanish Anarchist Trade Union and Anarchist Federation[14] and Nan Green, whose husband George was already serving in Spain, was asked to go to work as an administrator. Her decision was made a little easier by the generosity of Wogan Philipps, an ambulance driver in the war and the son of Baron Milford, who offered to pay for her two children to go to the famously liberal Summerhill boarding school.[15] Others, such as New Zealander Griff Maclaurin, were asked because they possessed vital military skills (he was an experienced machine-gunner), or because they had no dependents, such as Walter Gregory. He was approached by the Communist Party organiser for the Nottingham area, who told him that the Party had placed restrictions on eligibility: volunteers now needed to be at least twenty-one and unmarried, 'as there was little likelihood of a widow receiving any form of financial support from the Spanish government'. Would Gregory still be interested in volunteering? He was:

> I was wild with excitement, I was going to Spain, I was going to fight for democracy, I was going to fight against Fascism. Here was somebody really asking *me* to do something important. Not just asking me to canvass for someone else to be elected for Parliament or to a local council, but actually asking *me* to go and fight against a Fascist dictatorship! I was over the moon, I thought it was absolutely marvellous.
>
> It never occurred to me that I might be on the losing side, never occurred to me that I might get killed.[16]

Most volunteers in Britain heard about recruiting either by reading the *Daily Worker* or by attending political meetings or rallies in support of the Spanish Republic. Contacts would be made with the local Communist Party branch, which would then forward the volunteers to the party offices in King Street in London's Covent Garden; after February 1937, they were sent to a nearby office above what would later become the Dependents' Aid office at 1 Litchfield Street. Here they would be interviewed, normally by R.W. Robson, 'a tall, thin, dour' Scotsman known as 'Robbie', previously the Party's London District organiser.[17] Robson would assess their suitability in military and political terms before delivering 'a rather threatening lecture' warning of the serious risks entailed in going to Spain to fight 'in a bastard of a war [where we] would be short of food, medical services and even arms and ammunition'. 'We don't want adventurers,' he declared. 'We want people who are really anti-Fascist, who really want to play a part in the fight against Fascism in Spain.'[18]

[Robson] pointed out all the difficulties, all the hardships, 'Was I certain I knew what I was letting myself in for?' He wanted to assure himself absolutely that I quite knew what I was doing, that I was aware both politically and physically, that I was not going to Spain for a picnic or just to visit Spain to see what it was like, that my intentions were serious.[19]

The lecture was clearly effective. 'I was under no illusion as to what it meant,' remembered one Stockton volunteer.[20] Or perhaps too effective; one recruit who had travelled down from Manchester was rather taken aback by the toughness of the interview:

They put me through a right third degree; at the end I said to him: 'Don't you want me to go? What's to do with you?' . . . They were telling me how rough it was, and everything; and, you know, there's no pay, there's no this and no that and no the other and 'Why do you want to go? And now are you sure?' . . . I got the impression that they didn't want me to go! Didn't want anyone to go! I thought they were on Franco's side![21]

University student and Communist Party member David Crook, who until recently had been an MP's private secretary, was determined to fight in Spain:

Robbie was a proletarian and I, for all my reading of Marx, was not. It stood out a mile. He fired questions at me.
   'Why have you come here like this without permission from your branch? Why do you want to go to Spain? Have you had any military experience?' The Party was trying hard – and with reasonable success – to keep out adventurers, spies, saboteurs. I played my trump card: I had been in the Officers' Training Corps at Cheltenham College many of whose graduates went to Woolwich or Sandhurst. Robbie must have groaned inwardly. But I was young, keen and knew French, the lingua franca of the Brigades. He gave in. Go home for Christmas, he said, perhaps thinking that

the comforts of home and the Yorkshire climate would cool my ardour. It did not.[22]

Despite the Spanish Republic's urgent need, volunteers who Robson considered unsuitable would be rejected or, like Crook, told to go away and reconsider. Harry Fraser decided to volunteer in October 1936 and went to the office in King Street, where his party card secured him an interview with Robson:

> He said, 'Have you had any military experience?'
> I said, 'No.'
> He said, 'Do you drive a heavy lorry?'
> I said, 'No.'
> He said . . . 'Had I any medical experience?'
> 'No,' I said. 'I've got a lot of clerical experience. It might help.'
> He said, 'Oh, we've got hundreds of people that can do that . . . You're no good to us. Don't bother.'[23]

Fraser went away and joined the RAF in order to gain some military experience. He returned in September 1937 and was accepted.

Some volunteers were rejected for reasons other than political unreliability. A number of influential Communists were initially turned down, for the Party was obviously wary about being deprived of all its senior figures.[24] Despite the gains in membership during the late 1930s, the CPGB was by no means a large and powerful organisation and it was considered imprudent to risk the lives of all their political cadres on the battlefields of Spain. Initially, when the Communist George Drever lost his job (he held a PhD in chemistry and was a tutor in the National Council of Labour Colleges and to members of the Young Communist League) and tried to volunteer, he was told he was too important to lose: 'Oh no, you won't do that. You'll go back to Edinburgh and get a job.' However, by the end of 1937, the situation had changed dramatically:

> At one of the Party meetings, Fred Douglas, who was an organiser then, said: 'We've got a letter from the centre,' he said, 'that things are difficult in Spain and we want our best comrades to go.' I was single, I wasn't married at the time. So I went along . . . 'Right-oh, Fred,' I said, 'put my name down.' He says, 'Why do you want to go?' I said, 'You've just told us

that they want the best comrades to go. I consider myself to be one of the best comrades.'[25]

Labour councillor (and clandestine Communist) Tom Murray volunteered to join in 1936, but he was also vetoed: 'I was a Councillor in the city of Edinburgh, and they regarded my function as more important here, especially having a sister and a brother out in Spain.' However, by the spring of 1938, the Republic's situation was so desperate that he was asked if he was still prepared to go. He volunteered immediately.[26]

Aberdeen Communist Bob Cooney was another figure in the party considered too important to risk. But following problems in the leadership of the British Battalion during the summer of 1937, Cooney's political experience and prestige came to be seen as invaluable to the Republican cause. Even so, Harry Pollitt attempted to warn him off:

> He [Pollitt] said, 'I believe you're anxious to go to Spain?'
> I said, 'I am indeed.'
> He said, 'You realize that if you go by this time next year you may only be a name on the Roll of Honour?'
> To which I said, 'I'll be in good company if I am.'[27]

For the journey to Spain volunteers were placed under the charge of a *responsable*, usually a party member. As the majority of volunteers had never travelled abroad before – 'we didn't even know how to get to London,' laughed one Glasgow volunteer – they were ordered to purchase weekend return tickets to Paris, known as 'dirty week-enders', which got around the need for a passport. Among one group of twelve volunteers in December 1936, only one actually held a passport.[28] Volunteers were instructed to be discreet and keep a low profile: 'You may be closely questioned by the British and the French police. In answer to all their questions, just say that you are on a weekend trip and you will be alright.'[29]

> When we gathered at Victoria Station it was explained to us that, ostensibly, we were off on a day trip to Dunkirk, for which no passport was necessary. We were told to remain together at all times on the journey to Paris but to try to create the impression that we were not closely associated and had simply struck an acquaintance during our travels; this so that we would not attract the attention of the police who, because of the non-intervention

policies of the British and French governments, were keeping a sharp watch for groups of young men making their way south.[30]

One volunteer found that Victoria station was 'as thick as flies' with special agents and detectives, 'you could tell by their huge boots.'[31] The security services kept a close watch on the station and the volunteers were evidently highly conspicuous, despite all their efforts to the contrary. For example, on 23 December 1936, a party of sixteen men described as 'suspected recruits for the Spanish Government Forces' were observed by a sergeant from Special Branch, who reported that 'these men were all in possession of one-day excursion tickets London-Dunkerque. Several of them were discreetly questioned, but did not disclose their destination beyond Dunkerque.'[32] Special Branch forwarded their surveillance reports to MI5, who drew up a huge list of 4000 individuals suspected of being potential volunteers.[33] Most volunteers, however, were aware that the British authorities could do little more than take suspects' names and make threats of future problems when – and if – they returned. It 'was only intimidation. They had no legal right to do anything about it,' one volunteer recalled.[34]

Once they crossed the Channel, it was a different matter, as one young Scottish Communist discovered. Hugh Sloan, who volunteered under the name Hugh Smith, attempted to get to Spain in the spring of 1937 but quickly realised that the British and French authorities were beginning to take active steps to stem the flow of volunteers:

Before we left Dover to cross to Calais a plain clothes policeman said to me: 'We know where you're going.' I says, 'Somebody must have told you.' 'No, we know where you're going. You'll not get in.' I says, 'We'll see.'

When we landed in Calais the whole group were immediately arrested. We were taken to the police station and we were told that we would be allowed to stay until the following morning. But we were not to leave Calais or we would be arrested. They took our money from us but gave us sufficient to go to the cinema. The following morning we were deported back to England.

When I arrived back at Dover the same policeman in civvy clothes had a big laugh at me and said, 'I told you so. You wouldn't get by.' I said, 'Because you reported us.' He said, 'No, honestly I didn't.' So the authorities must have known where we were going.[35]

Another group from the Manchester Young Communist League found that there were other means of preventing them from reaching Spain. Having been accepted in London, the group set off and boarded a boat in Folkestone on the usual £3 weekend Paris ticket, but were promptly thrown off the boat by the captain. The group later worked out that two men who had volunteered with them in Manchester had been police informers or agents.

Most volunteers, however, managed to cross the Channel successfully before continuing on to Paris. Scottish volunteer John Lochore was one of a number who arrived on a weekend excursion ticket in the winter of 1936:

> With no hitches we duly arrived in the French capital and on leaving the station, by presenting our secret address to the driver, we were whizzed through a maze of streets to a wooden hut attached to a building site. The emphasis on our trip was secrecy, but I am sure the entire fleet of taxi drivers in Paris knew the address – a fact which was revealed by their casual confidence in conveying us to our 'secret destination'.[36]

In Paris the volunteers' political credentials were checked once again, as was their health and political determination:

> We were given a medical examination and we were given a final opportunity to change our minds if we wanted to, they said, 'If you want to change your minds do so now, they'll give you a ticket back and that will be the end of it.' But none of my group did.[37]

Some did turn back, or were rejected. The brother of Welsh volunteer Edwin Greening only made it as far as Paris, failing his medical examination;[38] others were rejected for a lack of political credentials. But most of the rejections were due to age; two men were turned back at Paris for being too old, despite having useful military experience gained fighting in the First World War.[39] Tom Wintringham stated that the upper limit was officially forty, but that there were many over the age of fifty: 'some of the older men had lied as cheerfully about their ages as the youngsters.'[40] In theory the minimum age was twenty-one, but just as in the Great War, many eager volunteers lied about this too; George Watkins claimed to be twenty-two, but was actually only sixteen.[41] And on occasion some of those enlisting the volunteers turned a blind eye:

Campbell, who was the organiser then, went into Ingram Street . . . [and] . . . said to Willie Gauntlett and me, 'Before I go in here,' he says, 'you better say you're 19.'

'Okay, I'll be 19 if they ask.'

They did ask. They told me, I think it was the Thursday, 'You'll be going down to London now and they'll see you in London and you better tell them ye're 20, because 19 sounds a bit young.'

'Aye, okay, I'll be 20.'

Well, when I went to London my age increased from 20 to 21: 'You better say you're 21.' And when I got to Paris that was me, 21.[42]

Benny Goodman was one of a group of YCL members who approached the Communist Party in Manchester's Fountain Street, where he told them he was twenty-one. But Martin Bobker, a leading Jewish member of the Manchester YCL, refused to accept him, realising that Goodman was too young:

We had four members, four Jewish lads, members of the Young Communist League who wanted to go to Spain. Now they were underage and I was opposed to their going because they were underage, however I was overruled . . . I fought like hell to stop them from going because they were underage and I didn't think they should go and I foresaw trouble, because all the parents of those kids blamed me for their going and I had a terrible time.[43]

Despite being under the minimum age, all the group were accepted. Goodman was only eighteen, and his true age was discovered when his parents complained to the Party:

[Battalion commander] Sam Wild gave me the biggest [bollocking] I've ever had and he said to me, 'you've got a lot of trouble from your home town, your parents are giving us hell and you've got to get back home.' So what he did, he shoved me inside the cookhouse, he did. And that more or less ended it off for me.[44]

For those running the brigades in Spain, the arrival of underage volunteers was an irritation they were keen to avoid.[45] Aware that a number of volunteers had lied about their ages, the political commissar at Albacete suggested that in future, they should provide documentary evidence of their date of birth.[46] While checks were being carried out, the volunteers waited around in Paris. Most quickly became bored, although one Liverpool volunteer who spent three days in Paris during August 1937 found the International Exhibition in full swing. The large crowds meant that it was not difficult to remain unnoticed. 'We were free to view the sights of Paris as we willed. The only condition was that we must not get into conversation with the police or any strangers.'[47]

However, Paris could hold many perils for the unwary Briton. One Lancashire volunteer was rather shocked by the behaviour of some compatriots, 'who were purely adventurers, as far as I could see. When they got to Paris, the men had heap[s of] booze and I think one actually got lost in Paris.'[48] Based in the office in Place de Combat, the city's staunch left-wing district, was the French-speaking Charlotte Haldane, now honorary secretary of the Dependents' Aid Committee, whose job it was to process the incoming volunteers and to warn them to stay away from the familiar haunts of soldiers, bars and brothels:

> The parties varied in numbers, from a mere half-dozen to twenty or thirty at a time. They were accommodated for the week-end in little, shabby, unobtrusive hotels in the quarter, whose owners' discretion and loyalty could be relied on. They all had their secret contacts, who warned them if there were any signs of undue police interest in their unregistered lodgers. In order to avert the danger that any of the volunteers should get drunk, start brawls or become involved in them, or be lured into the neighbouring brothels, the leadership had decided that, on arrival, their spare cash should be confiscated, and that each man should receive no more than ten francs daily pocket money, to provide him with a packet of French cigarettes and a couple of *bocks*. Food and lodging they received free. The 'responsable' had to carry out these instructions, and also to give the men lectures – on the routine to be followed, and on the dangers of venereal disease.[49]

Many volunteers did not take at all kindly to being lectured by a woman on subjects such as the dangers of the 'risk of us contracting an unpleasant disease' from 'casual women'. 'I never heard a woman talk like that in my life, never,' said one.[50] The no-nonsense Haldane was fully aware of their discomfort, but had no time for those who 'were apt to gape or be embarrassed when given a solemn lecture, by a woman, on the dangers of the "gay city" and of venereal disease'.[51] Her directness clearly shocked a lot of the volunteers and probably inspired her insulting nickname, 'Charlotte the harlot', though her stormy and unconventional relationship with her husband J.B.S. and the strong likelihood that she had an affair with an American *responsable* in Paris may also have had something to do with it.[52] Not that everyone heeded her warnings:

> 'We have quite a job,' [the American *responsable*] Max said . . . 'to keep the volunteers out of these dives, especially the British and Americans, who come over with more money than the others, think they must have a final fling before going on to Spain, give us the slip, get tight, spend an afternoon in one of these holes, and get a dose, so that when they reach Spain they find themselves in jail instead of in training.'[53]

With the risk of being arrested always hanging over them, most volunteers tried to keep a low profile. A number were seized in France and sent back to Britain, though for some, this only amounted to a delay. One Scottish volunteer was apprehended, charged with vagrancy and repatriated: 'They put me on the boat and put me back into London again. That was on the Wednesday. On the Friday I was back on the boat tae France again and I got right through then.'[54]

After a few days waiting around in Paris, the volunteers were sent south by train towards the Spanish border, where volunteers from a multitude of nations tried to congregate inconspicuously in the medieval and conservative market town of Perpignan. Discretion remained vital, though not all seemed to appreciate it:

> We were told to go to the Gare de Lyon and that it was all very secretive. But when I got there it seemed to be full of people going to Spain. As for being a secret, everyone was going around with a clenched fist, chanting, *Des avions pour l'Espagne* – planes for Spain.[55]

Until January 1937, volunteers were able to travel across the frontier by bus or train. However, following the ban placed on volunteering, those seeking to join the International Brigades were faced with a gruelling, hazardous climb over the Pyrenees. They were taken by *camions* to the foothills at the base of the mountains, which they knew they would have to climb in secret 'from dusk to dawn, with the French police hunting you, taking pot shots at you'.[56]

> We could dimly make out the Pyrenees, huge mountains which were being lit by long lancing pencils of light from searchlights which were placed every couple of miles apart as far as the eye could see. They were sweeping around continuously. They were the lights of the Non-Intervention Committee.[57]

Some French police and border guards were supportive of the Republican cause and turned a blind eye – 'He came past us and he never saw us but he knew we were there . . . there was no question that that French guard was sympathetic' – but others were not.[58] The groups of volunteers would creep forward, making sure to keep out of sight of gendarmes and border guards. As they progressed they were given signals by Republican supporters letting them know the way ahead was clear.[59] The volunteers would be kept off the roads and smuggled along small trails before being led over the mountains by guides, often smugglers disguised as shepherds or goat-herds:

> We seemed to wait a hell of a long time, in this blasted place, about half an hour. And then, down the road came a shadowy figure . . . And you've never seen anything like it. He was dressed in rags. And he had a stick. And a goatskin water bottle. And you've never seen such a tatterdemalion figure as this bloke. And he came around, he was barefoot.
> 'Come on, hurry up, hurry up, hurry up.'
> Everything was hurry up.[60]

Prior to beginning the climb, strict warnings were given: 'Nobody was allowed to smoke. Not drop a bit of paper. Not leave a mark anyplace to show that you'd passed over.'[61] They were also told to remove their footwear:

> We marched maybe a mile into the woods and they said 'Take your shoes off.' And they gave us these rope-soled alpargatas, they call 'em in Spain: 'Leave your shoes here and put these on.' So we got these on and then off we went marching again in the dark; no light or anything, we didn't know where we were . . . So we start climbing . . . It was murder . . . I had this overcoat on and I thought 'I can't stick this, let's . . .' so I threw the overcoat

away. About five minutes after [there was] this tap on [my shoulder] –
'Here, here's your overcoat.' They had a guide at the back making sure you
didn't throw anything away![62]

For many of the British volunteers, city-bred, malnourished and unfit,
the long, arduous and dangerous climb through 'the high, snow-filled
mountain passes in the middle of the night' was by some margin the hardest
physical task they had ever undertaken, making the hunger marches pale
into insignificance. 'Every mountain you climbed, there was another bugger
. . . you wondered when the hell you were going to get there!' complained
former sailor Fred Copeman.[63] Walter Gregory was in constant fear of
'falling into gullies and ravines, of damaging ankles, arms and legs and of
being shot at by border patrols'.[64] One London milkman, whose size
thirteen feet were too large for the Spanish rope-soled shoes, found the
climb particularly terrifying: 'I had to go on with my civvy shoes, but being
proper shoes they had leather soles and were slippery. I was hanging onto
the stones.'[65] David (Haden) Guest, a young Marxist lecturer in mathematics
at Southampton University, remembered how 'You had to feel your way
from ledge to ledge, clutching hold of the gorse; when daylight came you
were amazed that you managed to scale such precipitous heights in the
dark.'[66] Several volunteers recalled with astonishment how Ben Glaser, a
huge Jewish man from London, a member of the Unity Theatre, managed
to carry another man on his back for the last period of the climb.[67]

Not all were so fortunate and many did not make it over the mountains.
Four Americans who travelled down from Paris with one Briton
disappeared. Probably journalists or students, 'they were carrying
typewriters and things like that.' Weighed down by their belongings, they
were left behind on the trek over the Pyrenees and were never seen again.[68]

Those who did survive were rewarded by the sight of Spanish
Republican border guards 'cheering us and welcoming us' as they came
across the top of the pass.[69]

Just as dawn was breaking – the first light – we were right on top [of the
Pyrenees] and into Spain. And by God that was a vivid dawn that, because
the Mediterranean was shrouded in mist, the sun was coming up through
it and you had this enormous panorama of colour in the sky. It was just like
a Van Gogh landscape.[70]

Many volunteers' accounts of crossing the Pyrenees describe seeing
Spain bathed in a glorious morning light, 'a huge expanse of brilliant
sunshine'.[71] Clearly it was a very emotional moment:

> As we got to the top of the border, I gazed down into Spain. The sun was
> beginning to rise on the Mediterranean, lighting up Spain. I looked down
> across the lower hills and found it very difficult to believe that killing of any
> kind was going on there.[72]

Exhausted, but triumphant to have arrived at last, members of the
different nationalities began singing the songs of their respective working-
class movements; 'about the only people that weren't singing were the
British, who merely joined in with tunes that they knew.'

> But then, at last, somebody started up singing The Internationale, which of
> course we all knew, and we joined in. I find it extremely difficult to explain
> the feelings that swept through me when this singing of The Internationale
> started up. Here were we, all young men from really all the nations in
> Europe, and some from outside Europe as well, joining in this one song in
> their own language which seemed to express a yearning for the unity of
> mankind. I find it extremely difficult to explain how exhilarating this was. I
> don't think I've ever felt the same feeling at any other time in my life.[73]

5

The Army in Overalls

The canard that the Column was a force of mercenaries lured to Spain by promise of big rewards has, now, almost died the natural death due to it. The men of the Column – when they accepted pay – got no more than the ten pesetas a day (about four shillings at the present rate of exchange) which the ordinary militiaman received. But most of them received only a few pesetas when they went on leave to Madrid or their base. Nor were they 'shanghai'd' into serving in Spain. The only shanghai-ing was done by an economic and political system which so antagonised these men's every feeling that they were willing to go out and risk their lives every minute of the day to build a different order.

Geoffrey Cox, *The Defence of Madrid*

While the majority of volunteers for the British Battalion followed the usual route into Spain, some arrived by other means. A number jumped ship at Republican ports before making their way to Albacete to join up. These included Able Shipman George Forman, who disembarked at Barcelona, and William Baillie, who absconded from HMS *Lucky* at Valencia. Those arriving this way faced considerable danger; though the long trek over the Pyrenees was hazardous, Italian submarines running amok in the Mediterranean made the journey by sea even more perilous. In June 1937, the ship *City of Barcelona* was torpedoed by an Italian submarine. She sank in four minutes and at least three volunteers on their way to join the British Battalion were drowned.[1]

Later that year, Percy Ludwick, a British Communist living in Moscow, was to have a unique journey to Spain. The son of Russian-Jewish parents – his father had been killed fighting with the Red Army during the civil war of 1917–23 – in September 1937 Ludwick was visited in Moscow by Harry

Pollitt, who asked if he would volunteer to serve. Unlike almost every volunteer making their way from Britain, Ludwick travelled in style: he flew to Paris, via Stockholm, then on to Perpignan and over the Pyrenees. On arrival at the International Brigade base at Albacete he and the rest of his party had the honour of being welcomed by a brass band.[2] The young British nurse Patience Darton was another lucky enough to arrive in comfort, flown into Spain in March 1937 on an emergency mission to nurse a former commander of the British Battalion who was believed to be in danger of dying of typhoid.[3]

When Scottish volunteer John Lochore made the journey over the Pyrenees in December 1936, he was one of the last to be carried over the mountains in a bus, though he believed his journey to be just as terrifying and dangerous as the long trek endured by his comrades. In order to avoid the non-intervention patrols and border guards, the vehicle showed no lights as it climbed painfully slowly along the winding mountain roads:

> The journey lasted some hours. We rumbled on endlessly and I felt physically sick. Then the engine revved up to a terrific speed – obviously travelling downhill. There was a crash of wood. It felt like we were in a collision. Then came the quick echoes of gunfire and the crack! crack! of bullets hitting the rear of the bus. Not long afterwards the bus halted and its lights flashed. The driver alighted from his cabin, jumping excitedly. 'España! España!' he shouted. We had arrived.[4]

Once through the border, usually fortified with a cup of 'some kind of [coffee] substitute [and] a small hunk of white bread' and with the farewells of the frontier post ringing in their ears, volunteers arriving on foot would make their way slowly down the mountain pass into Spain. However, as mountaineers know, the descent is often every bit as taxing as the ascent:

> Hour after hour went by and we still seemed to be many thousands of feet from the bottom. It was debatable which was the most unpleasant, ascending or descending the mountain. At least we had the cool of the night to climb, but the heat of the day to descend.[5]

Upon reaching the road the volunteers were typically collected by lorries which drove them twenty kilometres to the garrison town of Figueras, dominated by its 'magnificent medieval fortress', which operated as the mustering point for volunteers arriving from the north.[6] During one particular journey, the lorries stopped off at a large house, where the volunteers were provided with lunch. Unfortunately, many found Spanish food to be so different from their home fare that they wouldn't touch it:

> A meal had been prepared; rice, fish, meat, beans and I don't know what else, all cooked together in the same pot. I decided that even though I was hungry I could not eat that foul-looking meal. Never again in Spain was I to refuse anything put in front of me for that meal, I understand, was a real Spanish speciality dish.[7]

Scottish volunteer Donald Renton was struck by the revolutionary (in every sense) presence of women in the militia at Figueras:

> While we had often talked about the role to be played by women in the general struggle, there for the first time we saw the militiawomen, comrades who like ourselves were either going to have or already had had first line experience in battle against the Fascist enemy . . . It brought home to me that here was a general struggle [and] that, despite the backwardness of Spain by and large, here for the first time were women beginning to play the kind of role without which the general emancipation of ordinary working people on a world scale from any form of exploitation is impossible.[8]

Billeted inside the fortress on straw palliasses, the hundreds of International volunteers were given final checks to establish their ages, political background and military experience.[9] They were also given a 'very cursory' medical examination before the political commissars at Figueras offered them a final chance to turn around and return home:

> I decided that all the English-speaking volunteers would be lined up one morning and we'd put it to them at three o'clock that afternoon there would be a show of hands of those who didn't want to go any further . . . at three o'clock there were five [who] held up their hands – sheepishly, and in fact very sadly in some respects because it was a painful experience. You see, we told them it was not a picnic they'd come to.[10]

One Scottish volunteer remembered that they were asked if, 'even at this eleventh hour . . . you want to continue going into Spain, being part of the International Brigades?' The commissar 'painted what war was all about. He painted a word picture that didn't sound very happy at all' and told them that, 'if perhaps in a fit of enthusiasm we had said we wanted to go to Spain, the offer was now being made that, "If you wish to go back nothing will be said."'[11]

At least eighty volunteers either changed their minds or were refused admission into the brigades on their arrival in Spain, whether on grounds of fitness or age, or because their behaviour on the journey (usually drunkenness) had suggested that they might be troublemakers.[12] One British volunteer 'who had been a machine-gunner in the British Army, had volunteered in London and with his record, was gladly accepted'. However, when the man arrived at Figueras, 'it was discovered that he had no fingers on his left hand. He must have kept his hand inside his pocket at appropriate moments.'[13] Another was rejected 'because he had a bad heart, in spite of all his effort to try and get through it'.[14]

Despite the demands for men of a proven political background, some 'slipped through the net', as Wallasey volunteer Jim Jump, who served as an interpreter, paymaster and clerk (among other roles) in Spain, remembered:

I met a number of people, like the Blackburn waiter, whose political awareness was nil at the time of going. I remember another man, John Smith . . . he was a Glasgow shipyard worker I think, and he told me that he went to Spain for three things: 'Loot, women and wine.' And then he added, with a touch of sadness in his voice, 'And I've never come across much of any of them.'[15]

Problems were also caused by the acceptance, at least early in the war, of a number who wished to serve in the Spanish Republican navy, or the air force. Unfortunately, most were rejected for naval service and usually ended up at Albacete, where they, not unreasonably, expressed an unwillingness to serve in the Spanish army. Here they became a problem for the political commissariat, and letters were written to Harry Pollitt asking that, in future, the party only recruit for the International Brigades. One young Englishman, intending to volunteer for the air force, was arrested at Figueras following his arrival in late 1936.[16] The report by the senior British Communist in Spain, Tom Wintringham, was suitably scathing:

> At Figueras he lost his baggage getting out of the train and failing to return in time. He then lost other trains, and sat about in this frontier town writing imaginary stories of battles with Franco's troops at Figueras (100 miles from the front) illustrated with maps. He was arrested. He carries a letter from the C.P.G.B. and a pilot's license. He left his passport and other papers in his baggage. The police here, after questioning him, asked my advice. I questioned him and felt that almost certainly he was a young fool, very completely a fool, and no use in Spain.[17]

Fortunate not to have been shot as a spy, the naïve Peter Elstob was eventually released and repatriated back to Britain with the assistance of the British consul.

Those considered to be fit, healthy and reliable were sent onwards on a slow train to Barcelona. In fact, the train moved so slowly that volunteers at the front were able to 'to jump from it as it passed an orange grove, throw oranges to comrades leaning from the carriage windows and still have time to climb aboard the last coach without having to break into a gallop'.[18]

As one group of volunteers passed through the town of Gerona, they were greeted by a band playing the Internationale and a huge, cheering crowd:

> In response to the crowd which was giving us this lavish and moving testimony of its feelings we answered with a Spanish slogan that has since gone the round of the world: 'They shall not pass!'
>
> From end to end of the train, with all the power of our lungs, we shouted it in chorus: 'No pasaran! No pasaran! No pasaran!' We liked the slogan and it was easy to remember; so we used it all throughout the journey.
>
> Every time we shouted this, the crowds that listened to us became almost hysterical. People began to laugh, and shout, and even weep. They saw in us a proof that the world had not completely forgotten them.[19]

Other volunteers spoke only of enduring a long, tedious train journey, though their boredom was swept away in an instant by the tumultuous and unforgettable welcome they received at their destination:

Our welcome to Barcelona began the moment the train pulled into the station. On the platform a band was playing and crowds both inside and outside the station buildings were cheering, singing and shouting political slogans. Against this background of noise and excitement we marched with such military precision as we could muster through the main streets of the city. It seemed as though people from miles around had left their houses, shops, offices and factories to greet us. Every building was festooned with the red flag of the Communists, the red and black of the Anarchists and the colours of the Catalan Nationalists. Every available wall was covered with posters exhorting the people to come to the defence of the Republic and to enter the fight to smash the Fascist insurrectionists.[20]

Even before the formation of the International Brigades, Barcelona had acted as an impromptu mustering point for foreign volunteers, including a number of British people caught in Spain at the outbreak of the war. Many Britons, terrified by stories of murderous 'Red' mobs running amok, fled as soon as they could, stopping only to pass on alarming stories of atrocities to receptive diplomats and journalists waiting safely just the other side of the French border. Others, however, sympathetic to the plight of what was, after all, a democratically elected government, decided to stay and do what they could for the Republic. And for some this involved taking up arms. The sculptor and artist Felicia Browne, from London University's Slade College, was painting in Barcelona when the rising began. After constant appeals that she be allowed to join those defending the Republic, Browne was eventually permitted to enlist with a militia unit in Barcelona on 3 August 1936. She was killed at the end of August in a mission to blow up a munitions train near Tardienta in Aragon.[21]

The novelist Ralph Bates, who had lived in Spain and knew it intimately, was walking in the Pyrenees with his wife Winifred when the war broke out. Both would later take up important positions in the operations surrounding the involvement of British volunteers in Spain. Initially Ralph worked for the Republican government's propaganda and information services, before becoming the first editor of *Volunteer for Liberty*, the journal of the English-speaking 15th International Brigade. Winifred, 'a devout Stalinist' even by her husband's account, worked with him as a journalist and broadcaster in the Ministry of Information before joining the British Medical Unit in June 1937.

Two Jewish clothing workers from London, Nat Cohen and Sam

Masters, were also in the Pyrenees, on a cycling holiday, when the rebellion began.[22] Both Communist Party members, they quickly made their way to Barcelona to volunteer to fight and joined up there with three other Britons.[23] The group were part of an abortive raid on Mallorca in mid-August 1936, widely expected by the Rebel forces defending the island.[24] One of them was injured in the disastrous attack and repatriated back to Britain, having only been in Spain for a month. Cohen, however, who distinguished himself in the action, was elected leader of the group when it returned to Barcelona.

The Marxist intellectual John Cornford, vice-president of the University Labour Federation, arrived in Spain with his friend and fellow Trinity College student, Richard Bennett, on 8 August 1936. Cornford wrote to his lover and fiancée Margot Heinemann, with whom he still planned to holiday in France, of his experience of Barcelona in the throes of revolution:

In Barcelona one can understand physically what the dictatorship of the proletariat means. All the Fascist press has been taken over. The real rule is in the hands of the militia committees. There is a real terror against the Fascists. But that doesn't alter the fact that the place is free – and conscious all the time of its freedom. Everywhere in the streets are armed workers and militiamen, and sitting in the cafés which used to belong to the bourgeoisie. The huge Hotel Colon overlooking the main square is occupied by the United Socialist Party of Catalonia. Further down, in a huge block opposite the Bank of Spain, is the Anarchist headquarters. The palace of a marquis in the Rambla is a C.P. Headquarters. But one does not feel the tension. The mass of the people . . . simply are enjoying their freedom. The streets are crowded all day, and there are big crowds round the radio palaces. But there is nothing at all like tension or hysteria. It's as if in London the armed workers were dominating the streets – it's obvious that they wouldn't tolerate Mosley or people selling *Action* in the streets. And that wouldn't mean that the town wasn't free in the real sense. It is genuinely a dictatorship of the majority, supported by the overwhelming majority.[25]

While Cornford set off to witness and report on Republican Spain, Bennett remained behind to work with Barcelona Radio, the voice of the Catalan Socialist Party.[26] However, while travelling around Aragon with the Austrian writer and veteran Communist Franz Borkenau, Cornford soon decided that 'a journalist without a word of Spanish was just useless' and took the decision to actively join the fight.[27] Three days later, he was on the Aragon front around Huesca and Zaragoza, serving with the militia units of the POUM, the Unified Marxist Workers' Party. From the front, he wrote an emotional letter to Heinemann:

> I love you with all my strength and all my will and my whole body. Loving you has been the most perfect experience, and in a way, the biggest achievement of my life.
>
> The Party was my only other love. Until I see you again, bless you my love, my strength. Be happy. I worked for the Party with all my strength, and loved you as much as I was capable of. If I am killed, my life won't be wasted. But I'll be back.[28]

Cornford's letters provide a revealing description of the life of a Republican militiaman in the first few months of the war. Although a devout believer in the cause, he was candid about his time on the Aragon front and the honesty of his observations compares favourably with some other accounts of the time, written in a rather more 'heroic' style. In a classic example of the type, the Communist writer and political commissar, Bill Rust, wrote that 'It was a glorious adventure to help the Spanish people crush the revolt and, whipped up by the surging enthusiasm of those days, a hundred or so virile youngsters from half a dozen different countries cheerfully fought against black reaction and military dictatorship.'[29]

Cornford's time on the Republican front line suggests not surging enthusiasm and adventure, but loneliness and homesickness. His only communication with his comrades was with one young Catalan volunteer in broken French: 'And so I am not only utterly lonely, but also feel a bit useless . . . This loneliness, and this nervous anxiety from not knowing when or how to get back, and not yet having been under fire, means that inevitably I am pretty depressed.'[30]

Remarkable self-discipline and political dedication helped Cornford to develop a more phlegmatic yet positive attitude to a life during war. Although he was, as he recognised, fighting on 'a quiet sector of a quiet front', he optimistically estimated his odds of survival to be 'a 70 per cent chance of getting back injured and 90 per cent of getting back alive'. As he also acknowledged, however:

> I came out with the intention of staying a few days, firing a few shots, and

then coming home. It sounded fine, but you just can't do things like that. You can't play at civil war, or fight with a reservation you don't mean to get killed. It didn't take long to realise that either I was here in earnest, or else I'd better clear out.[31]

Cornford provided an evocative description of the democratic nature of the militia forces with whom he was fighting:

The army is a curious mixture of amateur and professional. There is practically no shouting and saluting. When somebody is told to do something, he gets up to do it all right, but not in a hurry. Officers are elected by acclamation, and obeyed. About half the troops are more or less in uniform, in blue or brown overalls and blue shorts. The rest are more or less nondescript. I myself am wearing a pair of heavy, black, corduroy trousers (expropriated from the bourgeoisie), a blue sports shirt, and that alpaca coat, rope-soled sandals, and an infinitely battered old sombrero. Luggage, a blanket, a cartridge case (held together with string) in which there is room for a spare shirt, a knife, tooth-brush, bit of soap, and comb. Also a big tin mug stuck in my belt.[32]

In mid-September Cornford briefly returned to Britain to recuperate from an illness contracted at the front and to spend some time with his family and friends and with his lover, Margot. However, the main purpose of his trip, and its most time-consuming, was the raising of recruits for the Republic. He was determined that on his return to Spain in early October, he would not be alone.

In fact, with the International Brigades still to be formed, the drift of British volunteers to Spain had already begun. London Communist Louis 'Bobby' Hearst arrived in September 1936, spurred by the Rebels' appalling massacre of the town's defenders during their recent capture of Badajoz and the British government's apparent determination to abandon the Republic to its fate:

[When] the Rebels entered Badajoz – drowning the town in the blood of its inhabitants – and managed to join their northern and southern armies, I began to feel a compulsion, tremendously powerful, to be doing something myself.

When England took the reins of 'Non-intervention' I could hold back no longer. I put everything else aside, and decided that I could not identify myself even passively (being a Socialist both by personal conviction and by family tradition) with this political farce; I decided to go to Spain to defend democracy with deeds.[33]

Hearst later wrote his impressions of crossing the frontier from France into Spain. If a certain amount of poetic licence crept into his recollections, it is perhaps understandable:

I had a vague impression of entering 'No Man's Land'. We marched in single file. As we went I turned my head for a last look at that land of France which, perhaps, I should never see again. Just as I did so our driver comrades who had fallen into ranks as if for review, raised their clenched fists to salute us and struck up the 'International'. For a moment it was as if an electric current ran through us, paralysing us. Then we halted and returned their salute in the same way. What with the moonlight and the mountain echoes singing with us, the experience was so powerful and poignant that I cannot attempt to describe it . . . [I] was infected with the emotion around. It took hold of me. Then our leading comrades gave the word to start. 'We haven't come here to be sentimental,' they said, 'but to beat fascism. And we will beat it!'[34]

By now Barcelona was established as a meeting place for English-speaking volunteers. Nat Cohen and Sam Masters were here, having survived Majorca. Now calling themselves the Tom Mann Centuria (one of many autonomous militia units formed to confront the Rebels), they were gradually joined by other English speakers, including David Marshall, a young clerk from Middlesbrough who had been utterly miserable in his job in the local unemployment office. On seeing reports of the war in the British press he realised, 'Christ, here's a way out!' and in the summer of 1936 promptly set off for Spain, thrilled that 'if the Spanish Republican government wins the war a socialist state will be set up.' Young, bookish and a little naïve, Marshall had initially been turned back at the Spanish border, as he couldn't show membership of an acceptable trade union or political party. Fortunately, Italian volunteer Georgio Tioli, who had previously lived in London and was conveniently at hand, stepped in and persuaded the border guards that anyone so innocent was hardly likely to be a spy.[35] The two set off together to Barcelona where they joined up with Cohen and Masters. Marshall later discovered his civil service card in his wallet; much to his embarrassment it clearly stated that his union was affiliated to the TUC. He was a respectable anti-fascist after all.[36]

In August a senior British Communist arrived in Barcelona, where he introduced himself to Cohen and Masters. He was Tom Wintringham, the founding editor of *Left Review*, an urbane and cultured intellectual who had been convicted in 1926 for his part in the General Strike. Approaching forty years of age and with fifteen years of full-time political work behind him, Wintringham had some military experience, having served as a mechanic and dispatch rider in the Royal Flying Corps in the First World War; he was also the *Daily Worker*'s military correspondent, 'the leading Marxist expert on military affairs currently writing in English'.[37] Wintringham had originally been asked by Harry Pollitt to go to Spain as the Party *responsable* in Barcelona, but having arrived, and seen for himself the amateurish nature of the Spanish militias, he became convinced of the need for 'a legion of foreign volunteers'.[38] Realising the significance of Cohen's Centuria, he pointed out to Pollitt that the worth of an English-speaking unit would be considerable: 'Send ten per cent trained men if you can to act as corporals and the rest kids and enthusiasts. Most of them will come back with very valuable experience.'[39] On 12 September, Wintringham proposed to Pollitt that he would himself join, and the Tom Mann Centuria became an official British unit. Wintringham promptly deserted them to continue his Party work and spend more time with a young woman he had met in a Barcelona café, an American journalist called Kitty Bowler. This was not the first time, nor would it be the last, that Wintringham's personal and political lives would come into conflict.

While Wintringham pursued his business in Barcelona, other volunteers drifted in, including a young Glasgow member of the Young Communist League who was, as he stated proudly, 'the first to go from Scotland', having entered Spain on 19 September. Known inevitably as 'Jock', Phil Gillan proved to be a useful addition to the group, having previously been a lance-corporal in the Territorial Army, though not, he was quick to point out, through any sense of patriotism:

No way, it was the only way we could get a holiday. And you got money. You got your bounty, boot allowances and your pay when you were away at camp for a fortnight. You got two weeks' holiday and you were well fed.[40]

Two more volunteers arrived to join the Centuria together. On his arrival at the *estación Francia*, young Labour Party member Keith Scott Watson bumped into a fellow English speaker, who promptly introduced himself: 'Me name is Bill Scott and oi'm from the IRA.' The Irishman had come to Spain for the Workers' Olympiad in Barcelona, originally scheduled to be held from 19–26 July 1936 as an alternative to the Berlin Olympics, but abandoned following the uprising.

> We had little time for further confidences; two armed soldiers led us into a
> brilliantly lit waiting room. We were grouped into nationalities. Bill and I
> comprised the British section. Bill's insistence that he was *not* British caused
> a little confusion. He was pacified only by being assured that the arbitrary
> grouping was very temporary and entailed no loss of Irish independence.[41]

The Englishman, the Irishman and the Scotsman were soon united with the other English-speaking volunteers. The two working-class members of the Tom Mann Centuria, Bill Scott and 'Jock', were in a minority, for 'the earlier people tended to be more intellectual than those who came later.'[42] The presence of these young intellectuals did much to help create the myth that the Brigades were an army of poets and writers, of 'radical romantics and middle-class Marxists'[43] – a myth that later reached the level of absurdity with the claim by one British volunteer that:

> The men of the International Brigades were, for the most part, intellectuals
> and numbered many scholars amongst them; it was common for them to
> be proficient in four or five languages besides holding high degrees in
> science, the law and a multitude of other subjects.[44]

In fact, as one of the first few British volunteers to arrive in Spain admitted, they were really 'a collection of odds and sods'.[45]

Keith Scott Watson's initial enthusiasm for the war quickly waned. Not only did preparations for combat keep getting in the way of his pursuit of Rosita, a young Catalan *miliciana*, but also his idealistic notions of the glory of the Republican cause were shattered by being ordered to watch the execution of six Rebel prisoners:

> From the other side of the square a double file marched out, between them
> six men dressed only in shirt and trousers. One of them was half carried

between two soldiers, at first I thought he was ill; he was shaking with terror. They were led to the wall facing us at the end of the courtyard and left. The knees of the frightened man gave way, he slumped to the ground. His guards tied his arms to his side. All the time he was making whimpering noises, the man next to him said something in a contemptuous tone, the creature was past scorn. He was left half kneeling, half sitting. The guard withdrew, the officer gave an order, the men raised their rifles. Another officer came forward with a paper. He read aloud the names of the condemned men. I understood snatches of the charges he read out '– armed insurrection against the legally elected government of Spain . . . firing on the people . . . to be shot to death . . .'

Two of the six refused to have their eyes bandaged, they stood, their arms raised in the Fascist salute. The officer drew back. Another of the six began to sway – before he could fall, the first volley crashed out: four figures slumped to the ground. The officer gave another order, the rifle bolts clicked as another cartridge slipped into the breech. Another volley, the two remaining figures collapsed, their shirt-fronts bloody. I felt very sick.[46]

Despite this initially unpleasant experience, the English-speaking group generally found their new life not to be overly taxing or dangerous:

The days passed . . . with the peace of a disciplined routine. I learned to dismantle a machine-gun, to fire a rifle with a degree of accuracy and to drink wine from a bottle with a long spout which squirts the wine into one's mouth. This last was my most difficult feat.[47]

By the end of October, after seven weeks of training, the volunteers were becoming bored and restless. The Centuria was visited by Ralph Bates, now working for the Republican government. Despite his appearance, 'tall, stout, about forty, looking more like a master plumber than a revolutionary leader', he clearly had authority, managing to arrange the replacement of their commander and convincing the disaffected volunteers to join up with another group of English-speaking volunteers, currently training in Albacete.[48] Keen to actually get involved, they attached themselves to the German Thaelmann Battalion, in the 12th International Brigade,[49] where they were spotted by Sefton Delmer, a newspaper reporter for the *Daily Express*:

There was no missing them. They stood out from the Germans like a schoolboy team from Blues. Their cheerfulness was magnificent. But somehow, compared to those barrel-chested Germans, they looked smaller and younger and less assured – like amateur beginners put down among a group of hardy old professionals. And beginners of course, is all the British were at this time.[50]

While the Tom Mann veterans were adjusting to military life with the Germans, John Cornford was in the process of returning to Spain, now accompanied by several British fellow volunteers, including a young Communist from Hampstead, the author John Sommerfield. Passing through Paris, they encountered other international volunteers, 'mostly they were French and Poles, some of them pretty tough,' all in the process of signing up to fight for the Spanish Republic. With Paris now in the initial stages of becoming the organising centre for the International Brigades, all of Cornford's group were signed up.[51]

We advanced to the table, said our piece, were handed forms, and went through complications of translation. What was my job? Author, perhaps? The French word was *écrevisse?* Something like that. But no, it turned out to be *écrevain. Ecrevisse* was a lobster. 'Sommerfield, the celebrated English revolutionary lobster.' It was a crack to last for weeks.[52]

Cornford's group arrived in Spain by sea in October 1936, to find the town of Alicante in full revolutionary spirit. In Alicante, as Orwell would later find in Barcelona, 'the working class was in the saddle':

The streets were filling with crowds who sang with us, saluting with raised clenched fists and shouting. The traffic stopped and the whole town came out into the streets and sang and shouted. And everywhere were the Anarchist and Communist flags and banners with slogans; and on all the cars and lorries and the big buildings and the shops and cinemas and cafes were the signs and initials of the trade unions and the workers' organisations.[53]

Disembarked from their ship, the volunteers were transferred onto a train for the next stage of their journey, 140 kilometres to their north-west. As the train slowly wound its way, the group passed the time singing songs, while 'the two Johns' (Sommerfield and Cornford) puffed on their pipes, much to the bewildered amusement of the two French volunteers, who declared that only old men *'avec le barbe'* smoked pipes.[54] It was 'a long triumphant journey', with the trainload of foreign volunteers receiving tumultuous welcomes in towns and villages as they passed, just as Bobby Hearst's group had done:

> From the front of the train came faint sounds of music and cheers . . . The train hardly moved and in the stillness we could hear the strains of the *'Internationale'* . . . we all tried to see what it was, squeezing ourselves into the small window. All the windows along the whole train were crowded with men leaning out and looking forward to discover where the sounds came from.
>
> The music grew louder and we could see the lights of a station . . . The lights of the compartment flickered over heads, hands, banners and flags. Cries of *'Viva'*, deafening now as we drew into the station, drowned the music except for the boom-boom of some deep brass instrument. Over the din now rose the Republican anthem. Emerging from the darkness and stillness of a minute ago it suddenly seemed very bright, although there were only a few oil lamps burning which threw flickering lights and deep shadows. On the bright scarlet flags a few words glittered in golden letters, *'Solidaridad Obrero'*, *'Proletariat'*, *'Libertad'*, 'UGT' and 'UHP'. Big streamers carried high on two poles swaying and sagging: *'Arriba la Republica, una y indivisible'*.
>
> There were more flags, more banners being borne down the village street towards the station. There were people running, shouting, waving their hats. We wanted to get down on the platform, but it was impossible. There was not room enough to put one's foot down. The comrades behind us nearly pushed us out of the window to gain a glimpse. There were shouts of *'Viva Rusia'*, *'Viva la Republica'*, *'Abajo Franco, abajo, abajo'*, taken up by everyone, *'Abas, abas,* 'Down down', *'Vive el Proletariat Mundial'*.
>
> Spain had come to greet us.[55]

The volunteers' journey ended in Albacete, a town famous for its fine knives and daggers, dating back to medieval times when Spanish steel was the finest in the Western world.[56] Despite its history, Albacete, full of 'narrow streets, cobbles and lots of mud', was 'not old, picturesque or interesting', thought one German volunteer,[57] and was not generally remembered with fondness; one Irish volunteer described it as 'a haven for deserters, saboteurs, black marketers, spies, fifth columnists, and rumour mongers. It was', he believed, 'the most demoralising place in Spain.'[58]

> Albacete will always remain in my mind as one of Spain's most unpleasant towns. Like many large railway-junctions, it possesses no character of its own. It has two main industries, the manufacture of lethal knives and a thriving though sordid brothel quarter. Few of its roads are paved, in winter they are rivers of mud. We found one presentable café, where we would spend an evening away from the barracks.[59]

While sitting in the café, one English volunteer amused himself by identifying stereotypical national characteristics:

> The Germans delighted to sit around in a large circle singing revolutionary songs with all the precision of a steam organ . . . The French drank and played billiards, and indulged in all kinds of animated argument while wreathed in clouds of tobacco smoke. The British drank and complained.[60]

The day after their arrival all volunteers were paraded in the bullring and allocated to units, once those with useful training or skills had been identified. They were then treated to a speech by André Marty, commander of the International Brigades:

> *Camarades!* I salute you. Behind you are your homes, your families and your women. In front of you lies the task of making history, not with speeches and resolutions, but with your arms. That many among us have been pacifists will not deter you, a blow now may free civilisation for ever from the curse of Fascism.
>   Here in the battlefields of Spain are no Croix de Guerre to be won, we have no stock of Victoria Crosses for the widows of dead heroes. Be brave, my comrades, but no false heroics; we are here to kill fascists, not to commit suicide in front of them.[61]

Marty, who had been imprisoned for his part in the Black Sea mutiny in 1919, has long been a figure of loathing: 'Marty's claim to have executed five hundred Internationals in Spain earned him the reputation of "the butcher of Albacete".'[62] 'Only Stalin himself had a more suspicious nature than André Marty,' claimed Hugh Thomas in his exhaustive history of the Spanish Civil War.[63] One London volunteer certainly took against him:

> He may have been a great chap in his day, but in Spain he was both a sinister and a ludicrous figure. He was a large, fat man with a bushy moustache, and always wore a huge, black beret – looking like a caricature of an old fashioned French petty bourgeois . . . He always spoke in a hysterical roar, he suspected everyone of treason, or worse, listened to advice from nobody, ordered executions on little or no pretext – in short he was a real menace.[64]

Despite this legendary inhumanity, Marty gave the prospective volunteers not just a stark warning of what they could expect, but also a choice:

> Perhaps, he told us, there were some among us who had decided to set off for Spain in a moment of enthusiasm or in a spirit of adventure: perhaps they were not ready to face the sacrifices, big and little, that civil war demanded. If there were any of us feeling like that, they had only to hand in their name to the office before the next day, and they would be repatriated. Those who remained would have to show the most scrupulous regard for discipline: they must be prepared to defy hunger, cold, and everything else.[65]

All who changed their minds and no longer wished to volunteer, Marty promised, 'will receive a ticket back to France'.[66] How true this pledge actually was is difficult to say. Certainly the offer had been made previously, in London, Paris and Figueras, and several had already chosen to take the advice, though there is little sign of this happening after the volunteers had reached Albacete. Once enrolled in the Brigades, of course, attempting to leave Spain became much more difficult, if not hazardous. Desertion was not always looked on sympathetically.[67]

The British volunteers were also given a pep talk, 'delivered in a crisp Scottish accent' by Peter Kerrigan, a big, burly leading British Communist, who had come to Spain straight from leading the 1936 hunger marches.[68] Kerrigan, the secretary of the Scottish district of the Communist Party, had a long history of activism. He had been a member of the National Unemployed Workers' Movement in the early 1920s, having briefly served in the British Army in the last year of the First World War. A militant trade unionist, he joined the Communist Party in 1921 and was delegate to the Trades and Labour Council and vice-chairman of the Glasgow Trades Union and Labour Council, until the Labour Party banned Communists from holding office in 1925. During the General Strike he was head of the coordinating committee in Glasgow. He had also visited Russia on numerous occasions, studied at the Lenin School in Moscow and been an election agent for Communist MP Willie Gallagher in Fife. Tough, disciplined and uncompromising, Kerrigan was as 'dour and ill-tempered as only a Scot can be, utterly devoid of any trace of humour and with a total acceptance of the Party line', thought one London volunteer.[69]

However, despite his 'hard line', Kerrigan knew full well that accepting unsuitable volunteers would cause serious problems of discipline and morale. In line with the commissars at Figueras, he wrote to Harry Pollitt requesting that the situation the volunteers were likely to face should be made absolutely explicit, that 'this is war and many will be killed. They must understand this clearly and it should be put quite brutally.'[70] He stressed too that volunteers must understand that a greater discipline – self-discipline – than that experienced in 'capitalist armies' would be expected.

John Cornford's group arrived at Albacete on 13 October 1936, the day after the formation of the Brigades. Other English-speaking volunteers, many of whom were experienced soldiers, gradually joined them, bringing their number to twenty-one:

> There was [H.] Fred [Jones], twenty-nine years old from London and his inseparable friend Steve [Yates], a small cockney with a big nose and blond hair. There was Jock [Cunningham], a Scot, who had done a prison term for mutiny, he later rose to the rank of colonel. There was Joe [Hinks] an ex-fighter from the Red Army in China. There was George [Sowersby], a pale, thin young man with a red beard which made him look like Christ and Pat [Thomas Patten] a young Irishman.[71]

H. Fred Jones, an ex-Grenadier Guardsman known to all as 'Freddie', was elected leader, despite Cornford's previous experience of the war. But Cornford himself recognised the importance of military experience and confided to his friend and fellow Cambridge student, Bernard Knox, that 'I think I could handle our little lot, but I don't fancy ordering old soldiers about.'[72]

The arriving Internationals were billeted in 'a large and gloomy barracks', formerly the home of the Spanish paramilitary police force, the *Guardia Civil*, who had backed the military during the rising. They had consequently been slaughtered by the local militia, who 'could not conceal their pride when we were called upon to view the blood-spattered walls and floors of the various barrack rooms'.[73] There were now enough international volunteers in Albacete for them to be divided up by nationality and language, which meant that military training could be given in the language of the soldiers themselves, rather than in French which had previously been the official language of the volunteers. However, the multinational nature of the International Brigades still created problems: 'We saw the Spanish and the Poles, the Italians and the Germans, the French and the Hungarians, and they each had their own way of doing things,' remembered John Sommerfield.[74]

The English-speaking group were formed into a section and attached to the French Commune de Paris Battalion (also known as the Dumont Battalion, after its leader), 'a heady mixture of ex-Legionnaires, unemployed workers, kids just out of the Lycée, and the inevitable contingent, in a French unit, of semi-alcoholics'.[75] 'It was decided, as most of the officers and instructors were Frenchmen, to do it French fashion. To do otherwise, that is to let every national section execute the movements after its own national method, looked bound to produce complications sooner or later.'[76]

The training, described as farcical by one English volunteer, was supervised by their French section leader, Marcel. It caused much amusement for the locals, '[who] mimicked Marcel's "un, deux, un, deux." They had every reason to be amused. When Marcel said "a gauche" some went to the left, others to the right.'[77] A number of ex-soldiers were less amused and did not take well to having to relearn their military skills. Some began to grumble:

When they gave us orders there was nearly always muttering in the ranks. For instance, the about-turn is done to the right in the French army, and when this order was given, it was not uncommon for Italians, Poles and such-like to begin grumbling and saying it was better done to the left, as in their countries . . . The worst disciplined among us began to abuse the instructor comrades, complaining that things ought to be done in this, or that, or the other way. Their conduct made a bad example. Something serious began to develop – 'the spirit of the bourgeois barracks'. The lads

no longer did what they were asked to do, or at best they half-did it. Those
of us, the majority, whose morale remained sound, began to tear their hair.

From the ranks this state of mind made its way to the quarters and the
dining halls, where there began to be grumbling about the quality of the
food, and nagging of the comrades responsible for cooking and serving it
. . . The 'grouchers' were a tiny minority of us, but in spite of that they
managed, in the matter of a few days, to induce a demoralisation that was
almost general.[78]

However, as one *Daily Worker* reporter later acknowledged, 'all armies
grumble'. That was especially true during the long, often tedious days spent
training and hanging around in Albacete, eating unfamiliar food and, all too
frequently, suffering from dispiriting stomach complaints. Many volunteers
struggled to adjust to the Spanish diet. Sommerfield remembered that
'diarrhoea soon reached epidemic proportions', yet, at the barracks, there
were only four toilets between some 800 volunteers.[79] One Lancashire
volunteer believed that the numerous stomach complaints could be
explained very simply: 'the French shit anywhere and the Spanish shit
everywhere.'[80] Nevertheless, despite the periods of demoralisation, the
novice soldiers gradually improved:

The days of training rolled on and the brigade began to look like a military
unit at last. We marched in step now (a sight which aroused delighted
murmurs on the streets of Albacete – it was the first time they had ever seen
it), and everyone was equipped with a large black beret; the beginning of a
uniform that, for most of us, was never to materialise.[81]

The volunteers were allocated, or, rather, helped themselves to, other
items of clothing to make up what might pass for a uniform:

Some got extraordinary dark-blue short coats, some ammunition belts,
some socks, some caps, some vests, some boots, some bayonet frogs, some
scarves, some gloves. Everybody got *something* and no one got everything.
We marched off looking like a lot of scarecrows, and in filthy tempers
because of the rush and of not getting things we needed.[82]

Most of the clothing was extremely thin and wholly unsuitable to winter
in the Spanish sierra, while their own clothes were simply discarded: 'Our

civvy clothes were thrown on a gigantic heap and it was with the greatest reluctance that I parted with my best and only suit, which I had bought for thirty-five bob.'[83] '[The clothes] were just dumped,' complained one Liverpool volunteer, 'there was no checking and we realised that we would never see them again.'[84] Two thin blankets were allocated to each man, together with a groundsheet, which was supposed also to serve as a cape: '[a] depressing piece of rubberized cloth with the four corners flapping about at uneven lengths . . . No doubt it is a very useful garment, but there is no possible means of wearing it without looking like a moth-eaten bird with a broken wing.'[85] A leather belt with oversize ammunition boxes and a French First World War helmet made out of extremely thin metal completed their equipment. Rifles, bayonets and ammunition were not allocated until later.

On 29 October 1936, the English-speaking members of the Commune de Paris Battalion, poorly trained, barely clothed and still without arms, left the training base at Albacete. They were conveyed to the village of La Roda, thirty kilometres to the north-west, where they were quartered in a fifteenth-century convent. One early morning, Jan Kurzke, a German refugee from the Nazis, was on his way to wash when he was met by an arresting sight:

> On the hill stood a church pointing its square yellow tower into a cold and cloudless sky. It was an ugly church, big, plain and forbidding. I looked up and suddenly saw, high up in the belfry, what appeared to be two people hanging by their necks, their long shirts fluttering in the morning breeze. The sight of the gruesome decoration filled me with horror and fear and for some time I stood there motionless until other men noticed it too, standing round in groups looking up with incredulous eyes and speaking in whispers.
>
> I went through the gate and climbed the track towards the church, but when I came near enough I saw that the figures were not human beings, but the statues of Jesus and Mary which someone had taken from the church and hanged out of the tower. Many times I had seen these bloodstained and agonising symbols of christianity in stone, in paint, placed behind iron bars to make them look more life-like and real, but they never looked more remote, sinister and threatening than on this October morning against a radiant blue sky.[86]

While Kurzke thought the act 'stupid', he did not find it unduly upsetting or offensive. 'It doesn't matter, they are only figures,' he assured a friend. His comrade, an Irish Catholic, was less convinced, finding the symbolism deeply disturbing. For the Irishman, 'Pat', the widespread anti-clericalism in the Republic – the church-burnings, the murder of monks and nuns – was difficult to accept. Only the belief that the crimes of the Nationalists were worse, 'the massacres in Badajoz, Sevilla, Burgos', convinced him that he was 'doing the right thing'.

It was at La Roda, their all-too-brief period of training now over, that the volunteers were finally given rifles: American-made Remingtons, dating from the 1914–18 war. Though 'battered and chipped', John Sommerfield thought them to be mostly in reasonable working condition: 'Some were better than others [and] they might have been a lot better, but they were as good as any rifles to be found on this side of the war.'[87] Old though the rifles may have been, this was seen as a moment of great significance: 'we fixed the bayonet on the rifles and marched back, looking for the first time like soldiers.'[88] With the arms came their orders: the volunteers would soon be leaving for the front, 'suddenly we heard that the Fascists were almost at the gates of Madrid.'[89] Jan Kurzke remembered that the departing Internationals were given a rousing farewell by a French Communist deputy who had travelled down from Paris to meet them:

'Comrades, I am glad to have an opportunity of speaking to you before you go to the front. Most of you have handled a rifle for the first time today. Ammunition is scarce. Five rounds is all we can give you. You are untrained. You are going out to face a ruthless, well-armed and well-trained enemy. You are fighting for a great cause. The eyes of the freedom-loving people in the world are upon you. It rests with you whether democracy will survive or forever be destroyed, not only in Spain but in many other countries. I am sure you know this and you will fight well.'

We cheered and waved our rifles. He was deeply moved and continued:

'Many of you may not come back. You have come from all over Europe to lay down your lives for democracy. What you lack in weapons you will make up for in courage. I am sure you will do your best. Salud – and bonne chance!'[90]

The following morning the volunteers packed up their things and left La Roda for the grim reality of war on the western outskirts of Madrid. Here, as one small part of the International Column (as they were initially labelled), the Commune de Paris Battalion were to play an important role in the defence of the city. Despite their inexperience, their lack of training, their poor arms and equipment, these volunteer soldiers from around the world were determined that the fascists would not pass; that Madrid would be the tomb of fascism. Indeed, the advancing Nationalist forces, who had swept towards the Spanish capital opposed only by inexperienced militias, would discover its new defenders to be a very different proposition. As John Cornford wrote to Margot Heinemann, Madrid was 'a real war, not a military holiday like the Catalan affair'.[91] Unfortunately for Cornford, and for more than five hundred other volunteers from Britain and Ireland, real wars entail real casualties.

6

The Battle for Madrid

The Madrileños heard the sound of steady marching feet; at first they thought that the Fascists had broken through the city's defence, but then they heard the sound of a song that was becoming more and more familiar to their ears, as the columns marched along Gran Via towards the front. The song they heard was a song of defiance, and international solidarity and comradeship. It was the 'Internationale.' The people listened and heard it sung not in Spanish, not just in another language, but in a variety of languages. The first of the International Brigades had arrived.

Michael O'Riordan, *Connolly Column*

Once Hitler and Mussolini provided the crucial airlift of Franco's Army of Africa across the Strait of Gibraltar into southern Spain at the beginning of August 1936, the Rebel army had been able to advance swiftly northwards towards Madrid. By 10 August they had reached the old Roman town of Mérida, 175 kilometres north of Seville, linking Franco's southern zone, which comprised the south-western corner of Andalusia (including Cadiz and Córdoba), with the northern zone under General Mola, which included almost all the northern half of Spain, apart from Catalonia and a narrow strip alongside the Bay of Biscay. Pausing briefly to capture the town of Badajoz on the Portuguese border, where they shot 2000 of the townspeople, the Rebel army continued their relentless drive towards Madrid, brushing aside the poorly trained Republican militia columns as they went. However, upon reaching Maqueda, seventy kilometres south-west of the capital, Franco chose to divert his forces forty kilometres south-east to relieve the Republican siege on Toledo's famous Alcazar fortress, which housed the Spanish infantry officers' school and still overlooks the city today.

While taking the credit for lifting the siege allowed Franco to assume the mantle of leader of the Nationalist camp, it also crucially allowed the Republican forces time to prepare their defences in Madrid. But after another massacre of militiamen – Moorish soldiers killed 200 Republican wounded in the hospital in Toledo by throwing grenades into the wards – the Francoists' march towards Madrid resumed. By 1 November, the Rebels had reached the south-west of Madrid adjacent to the Casa de Campo and University City. The Madrileños, only too aware of the fate of the defenders of Badajoz and Toledo, prepared to resist the attacking Nationalist forces. On 6 November the Republican government took the 'divisive and controversial' step of evacuating itself to Valencia, leaving the defence of the Spanish capital in the hands of a military Defence Junta, commanded by General José Miaja, the so-called 'hero of Madrid'.[1] The battle for Madrid, 'the central epic of the Spanish conflict', was about to begin.[2] 'Spain was the heart of the fight against fascism,' wrote one British volunteer, paraphrasing W.H. Auden's famous poem, *Spain*, and 'Madrid was the heart of the heart.'[3]

On 7 November, with the Rebel forces poised to attack, a new force arrived in the capital to take its place alongside the Spanish defenders. Formed on 25 October 1936, the 11th International Brigade, under the command of General Kleber, consisted of some 1900 volunteers, mainly French, Germans and central Europeans.[4]

In the early hours of a grey and hopeless November morning the Madrileños heard strange and unfamiliar sounds. Waking and peering from their windows, they saw that the rhythmic and disciplined tramp of marching troops was not the arrival of the expected enemy. These men were tall, straight, not Latin at all. They marched like Prussians. Very soon the civic mood changed from pessimism to a delirious, thrilled optimism. Help had – miraculously, so it seemed – arrived. The citizens streamed into the streets to greet with typical Spanish exaltation their new comrades and fellow fighters, the Ernst Thaelmann Battalion of the International Brigade. The Communist International was coming to the rescue.[5]

International volunteers were asked by welcoming Spaniards where they were from. '"London," we shouted back, "Paris, Marseille, Warsaw." "But Russia?" they cried, "Are you not from Russia?"'[6] But, as the *News Chronicle* reporter in Madrid, Geoffrey Cox, realised, 'Madrid was not worrying who these troops were. They knew that they looked like business, that they were well armed, and that they were on their side. That was enough.'[7] The defending Spanish Republicans were jubilant:

Milicianos [militiamen] cheered each other and themselves in the bars, drunk with tiredness and wine, letting loose their pent-up fear and excitement in their drinking bouts before going back to their street corner and their improvised barricades. On that Sunday, the endless November the 8th, a formation of foreigners in uniform, equipped with modern arms, paraded through the centre of the town: the legendary International Column which had been training in Albacete had come to the help of Madrid. After the nights of the 6th and 7th, when Madrid had been utterly alone in its resistance, the arrival of those anti-Fascists from abroad was an incredible relief . . . We all hoped that now, through the defence of Madrid, the world would awaken to the meaning of our fight.[8]

The Internationals marched west along the Gran Via to the front, waving flags, carrying their guns and ammunition on their shoulders for everyone to see, while 'throngs of people' walked alongside.[9] The Brigade's destination was the red-brick buildings of Madrid's new – and still unfinished – University City. Beyond it, on the other side of the Manzanares River, lay the huge wooded area of Casa de Campo, an 'ex-royal forest, rather Sussexy to look at', thought John Cornford. 'Like an undulating Hyde Park,' wrote Geoffrey Cox.[10] Within the 11th International was the handful of British volunteers in the Commune de Paris Battalion; they were sent to occupy a ridge in the Casa de Campo, where they took up defensive positions facing Franco's elite Moroccan *Regulares*.[11]

The Englishmen had arrived in the capital a few days earlier. Their journey to Madrid had not been a pleasant one: eleven hours crammed into the back of a lorry with all their equipment, forced to lie on top of each other. And it was freezing cold.

There were forty of us and forty packs and rifles and blankets and it was an ordinary sized two-ton lorry. I was jammed against the tailboard, half squatting on the floor, rifles jabbing at my ears and eyes, people huddled all over me and breaking my ankles and dislocating my knees, while the bolts in the tail-board were boring holes in the small of my back, and then we started and the road was terrible, the roads were terrible all the way, little country lanes with bumps and curves and we went fast and it was cold, wind blew and our eyes watered, noses ran, and we were jammed together too tightly to reach for handkerchiefs or lift arms to wipe away the drops. It was the worst ride you could imagine and it went on and on all through the night for hours and hours, getting colder all the time, the discomfort becoming agony, and no relief to look forward to because no one knew where we were or to what place we were going.[12]

The sense of unhappiness with their conditions was not greatly mollified in Madrid, despite their welcome as heroic saviours. Several Britons with a military background – including their commander, the popular ex-Guardsman, 'unemployed organiser, and sincere Communist' H. Fred Jones – were fairly scathing about the Republican Army.[13] Jock Cunningham, from the Argyll and Sutherland Highlanders, and British and Chinese Red Army veteran Joe Hinks were equally unimpressed.[14] What little ammunition was available was bad and 'quite dangerous': bullets were loose in the casing, so every clip of cartridges had to be checked individually.[15] Armed with their antiquated, hideously over-complicated and, above all, unbearably heavy French St Etienne machine guns (with their tripod, they weighed over fifty kilograms), the British section of the Commune de Paris Battalion marched or, rather, struggled, slowly towards the front:

I was carrying the Etienne, and heavy as it was, the burden of its weight was rendered worse by the pressure of its ridges on my shoulder; however I shifted it some sharp piece of steel bore down upon my flesh with the strength of a hundredweight and a half of metal behind it. Added to this, I carried a pack, blanket, water-bottle, cartridges, bayonet, and wore heavy boots; someone else took my rifle for me. After twenty minutes' brisk marching all of us who were carrying the guns and the tripods (which were almost as heavy) were drenched with sweat and trembling with exhaustion. Each bearer took it in turns with the man next to him, but my relief was a little chap, and it was impossible for him to take it for more than a couple of minutes at a time. I stumbled forward rather than marched, sweat ran into my eyes, the blanket kept slipping off my shoulder; I didn't care about the war or Madrid; there was only one thought and desire in my mind – to be able to lie down – and that being beyond all possibility now, its eventual certainty so remote as to be inconceivable, I tried to contract the bounds of my imagination into the space of time that it took for each separate step, so that nothing would exist beyond the moment when I put my right foot forward until the time came to advance my left foot. It was worse than the cold in the night on the hills, it was worse than the agonies of the lorry ride, it was worse than anything I could think of.[16]

On 9 November, the 11th International Brigade launched an assault on the Rebel forces in Casa de Campo, which was promptly stymied by a counter-attacking force of vastly superior numbers. Two New Zealanders, Steve Yates (an ex-British Army corporal) and Griffith Maclaurin, the mathematician who had run a left-wing bookshop in Cambridge, accompanied by Briton Robert Symes, left the main group to set up a forward machine-gun position.[17] All three were killed.[18] 'It's always the best seem to get the worst,' mused John Cornford.[19]

Yet, the following morning, Republican forces managed to recapture the entire park, with the exception of Mount Garabitas, and Franco was forced to abandon the attack. For the English group, 'shivering with cold and weariness' in makeshift trenches overlooking the park, by 'the lonely river' Manzanares, it nevertheless remained a fearful and unpleasant time:

> It was degrading to experience. Here I lay, grovelling in a glorified ditch and gnawing a piece of earthy tinned meat between shell-bursts, listening tensely to the howling in the air for the note that would tell me that one was coming our way, flattening myself against the ground with arms folded above head, waiting for the explosion and the hail of stones and shrapnel overhead, and then taking another bite of meat. And the sun was down and the cold night coming, and there was only an angry exhausted numbness in my mind, and a despairing craving for sleep and warmth . . . At that time and place, I learned something about war that I would never forget – that its real vileness did not only lie in its physical horrors but also in what it could do to men's minds.[20]

The following day, 11 November, the volunteers were part of a 'great flanking attack on the Fascist lines at Aravaca', just to the north of the Casa de Campo. But it 'was a costly failure – the only apparent result was the loss of the University [City] to the Fascists' in the brigades' absence.[21] The attack had an extra significance for the English-speaking unit, who were involved in a freak accident. One volunteer was injured, and their group leader killed, when an ambulance broke through a roadblock formed by a steel cable. The cable snapped, scything through the unfortunate volunteers:

> I saw a wire glittering about two hundred yards ahead. It was stretched across the road about a foot from the ground. The headlights of a motor-car coming up behind us picked it out. I heard shouts of 'Alto!' from the soldiers guarding the wire. The lights rested on them for a moment and then the car, I could see it was an ambulance, passed them at terrific speed and the wire snapped and coiled through the air and it was dark again. Men were running in front of me, shouts came from everywhere . . . 'Where's Fred?' I asked. Nobody knew . . . When it was light we had some coffee, brandy and bread. I saw Alfredo [Bougère, their French commander] coming towards us looking very white, tired and distressed. He told us to step forward, while our French comrades looked on from a distance. He told us that Fred was dead. The wire had caught him around his throat and killed him.[22]

'Freddie' had been a popular leader. According to Cornford, nobody dared tell them of his death for several hours, because they were worried about the effect it would have on morale.[23] John Sommerfield in particular took Jones' death badly, thinking it 'a rotten way to die'.[24] As Jan Kurzke later remarked, miserably, '[Fred] took such good care of us and could not take care of himself.'[25] Following Jones' death, Sommerfield's group elected Joe Hinks to be their commander. The group was transferred to a front-line position in University City, close to the Philosophy and Letters building, 'a huge, ugly but inoffensive construction of red brick that stood at the edge of a miniature cliff'.[26] The building had been recently occupied by Spanish Moroccan soldiers, who had overrun the Anarchist militiamen of the Durutti Column, named after their legendary Anarchist commander, Buenaventura Durutti.[27] The English group advanced into the building itself, where they fought alongside some of Durutti's militia and a number of Asturian miners. Here London archaeology student Sam Lesser discovered that the militiamen's attitude to military discipline rather differed from his own:

> We knew that there was an Anarchist unit further on. I went over with the patrol and we found there were only two or three people there and we said,

'Well, what's happened? Where has the unit gone? They said, 'They've gone to the pictures.' We thought this was a pretty poor show.[28]

The Englishmen occupied the building for a week, sniping out of the windows at the Rebel soldiers occupying the adjacent block. 'That was mostly how you killed men in a war; there was a movement and you fired and the movement stopped,' observed John Sommerfield. 'You felt a momentary thrill of accomplishment, but it was impersonal, clay pigeon shooting; you did not think that you were making widows and orphans, robbing mothers of their children.'[29] The three writers in the group, Sommerfield, John Cornford and Bernard Knox, were reduced to 'firing from behind barricades of philosophy books at the Fascists in a village below and in the Casa Valasquez opposite'.[30] The piles of (literally) impenetrable volumes of Indian metaphysics and early nineteenth-century German philosophy gave very effective protection against Rebel small arms fire; 'they were quite bullet-proof,' Sommerfield discovered.[31] That they were confronting soldiers of the Spanish Foreign Legion, whose commander, General Millan Astray, had declared 'death to intellectuals', added a further irony. For Cornford's group, the week spent among the books was a temporary spell of contentment within an age of overwhelming discomfort and fear:

We were as happy as I think men can possibly be in the front line of a modern war. We were under cover from the deadly cold that so far had been our worst enemy. We had leisure to talk and smoke in physical comfort, and, greatest pleasure of all, it was safe to take off our boots at night. The only drawbacks to this battle paradise were the fact that we were a perfect target for artillery, and the realisation that we might be completely cut off at any moment. Here we discussed art and literature, life and death and Marxism during the long day, and as the evening drew on, we sang. Nothing delighted John more than the sort of crude community singing that is common to undergraduate parties and public bars alike . . . With John Sommerfield we formed a famous trio, and our version of 'She was Poor but She was Honest' was a thing to bring solicitous political delegations down many dark corridors to find out what was the matter.[32]

Making the most of this interlude, Sommerfield was deeply immersed in a copy of De Quincy's essays on the Lake Poets, written a hundred years earlier:

> I was with Wordsworth and Coleridge, in another place, another time . . .
> All the afternoon I read, and was on the last chapter when I heard an
> appalling crash and looked up and the room was thick with dust and smoke,
> in which figures moved confusedly . . . the call for the stretcher-bearers went
> echoing down the corridors; John's head was bleeding swiftly, Joe held his
> nose and swore.[33]

The defenders had been hit by what was later identified as a Republican anti-aircraft shell.[34] John Cornford's head injury 'was done up in a big bandage, and he looked the complete wounded hero, very romantic and all that', thought Sam Lesser.[35] Others were less fortunate; Jan Kurzke encountered a group of Polish volunteers who had been hit by shellfire:

> They all looked strangely alike; their faces pale, waxen, yellow, their eyes
> dark and still with the expression of surprise and horror of the terrible
> moment when the shell had burst upon them. Their hair was full of sand as
> if they had been buried. I fumbled for a cigarette and lit one. One of the
> wounded was talking to me in Polish and I could not understand what he
> said. He looked at my cigarette and I put it in his mouth. He sucked it
> greedily and then died, the smoke still trickling from his mouth.[36]

By 23 November, Rebel soldiers had managed to gain control of two-thirds of the area of University City, yet it had become clear that the Republican forces were now well established and that the direct frontal attack on Madrid had failed. Franco reluctantly called off the attack and the English group were moved out of University City for a short period of rest. As they marched away from the unreality of the front line, John Sommerfield encountered an incident which would remain with him for many years after he had departed Spain:

> By the open space lay two dead Fascists, one in the gutter, his head
> smashed open against the kerbstone, the brains slopping out. A big, lean
> dog with a famished look came up to the corpse, sniffed, and began to lap
> at the mess of brains. One of the guards drew his automatic and put three
> bullets into the dog. It lay coughing over the corpse, not yet dead. The

guard ran forward, his head held down, and finished the dog off with a rifle butt.

He stopped when he passed us, looked apologetic, and said in bad French, 'It has to be done. They get the taste for human flesh. It is bad . . .' His keen Spanish face, edged with a black beard, smiled deprecatingly. Sure, we said. We understand. And he looked relieved and went back to his post.

And we stood there waiting, steel helmeted, hung about with arms and ammunition, gas-masks dangling on our chests, a hundred and forty soldiers of the machine-gun company of the Marty Battalion of the International Brigade; and the rain came down, the broken water-main gushed continuously, the tall buildings gaped their wounds, and from the corpse in the gutter the blood and brains washed slowly away, mingling with those of the dead dog.

It was as good a war picture as I could think of.[37]

While the English group in the 11th International Brigade were fighting in the Philosophy and Letters Building, a second group of British volunteers had also been fighting in Madrid. Members of the 12th International Brigade, they included the original members of the Tom Mann Centuria, plus later arrivals such as Esmond Romilly, 'the fair-headed, red cheeked, seventeen-year-old nephew of Winston Churchill', with whom they had been united at Albacete.[38] Young Romilly was a popular member of the unit, described by one fellow volunteer as 'fiery . . . an attractive character . . . audacious rather than being wise'.[39] Army veteran Phil 'Jock' Gillan was rather more circumspect: '[He] was a very brave little lad who volunteered for most things, but in other ways as a soldier, you know, a big question mark . . . how he wasn't killed, really I don't know.'[40] Like other inexperienced volunteers, Romilly relied completely on the know-how of his comrades, particularly the First World War veterans Harry Addley and Arthur 'Babs' Ovenden, who had given up their successful and popular restaurant in Dover to fight for the Spanish Republic.

When the members of the Tom Mann joined the German Thaelmann Battalion at Albacete, Romilly had found them to be incredibly brave and determined fighters, often to the point of recklessness: 'With good reason, the Thaelmann Battalion had the reputation of being the finest fighting unit of the International Brigade.'[41] The reasons were not difficult to understand: as exiles from their home country, 'there could be no surrender, no return; they were fighting for their cause and they were fighting as well for a home to live in.'[42] The battalion was supposed to be given six weeks' training, but the precarious situation facing Madrid meant that the period was reduced to one day 'out in the fields'.[43] Romilly's first experience of physical training 'did not amount to much', he felt.[44]

As the Rebel armies continued their advance on the Spanish capital, the British group in the Thaelmann Battalion was involved in a number of small skirmishes. The first occurred on 12 November, when the Republican forces launched a hopelessly ineffective attack on the Cerro de los Angeles, a hill ten kilometres to the south of the city. Both the military preparations for the attack and the volunteers' proficiency were utterly inadequate: 'We hadn't even fired the rifles before we went into action,' complained David Marshall.[45] One ill-prepared volunteer mistakenly believed for some time that the operation was only a training exercise.[46] The action was 'myopic Bloomsbury Bohemian' Keith Scott Watson's first experience of being under fire and he hurriedly took shelter as bullets swept across the Republican soldiers: 'Leaves flew from the bush I sheltered behind . . . I felt a deadly cold fear inside my stomach . . . I don't want to die alone.'[47] 'Jock' Gillan was equally stunned by his first experience of the war in Spain:

> The first ten minutes of the attack were the worst. In spite of my 'terrier' [Territorial Army] training, I was just plain scared – and I'm not ashamed to admit it – the zip, zip got louder and then suddenly I knew that the air was just thick with machine-gun bullets. Did I duck? You bet I did. The funny thing was that I didn't feel afraid, but when I tried to get up off the ground, my legs wouldn't work for about three minutes.[48]

David Marshall, shot in the foot, was one of the substantial number of Republican casualties.[49] Keith Scott Watson, already stunned by the realities of military combat, witnessed the horrifying consequences of a Rebel air raid the following morning:

> Ambulances raced across the rough track, first-aid men rushed over. Twenty men had been hit, some of them were unrecognisable. The bomb splinters had torn them with a macabre humour. One boy lay on his back threshing the air with his leg, where the other should have been was a quivering bloody stump. In the fork of a tree, another was tightly wedged; he was alive and moaning, when the ambulance men touched him, he gave a high-pitched scream, a blue red tangle of intestines hung from his stomach. We

tried to lift one man on to a stretcher – he bent like an old rag doll, his spine had been severed, my arms were soaked in blood. I dared not stop and think or I should go mad. A boy, not more than sixteen, lay grinning at the blue sky as though at a remembered joke, the top of his head was taken off as one opens an egg. Those who were past aid were shot; it was the greatest mercy the ambulance men could have shown.[50]

Sickened by the slaughter and demoralised by hearing rumours on the BBC of Rebel forces entering Madrid, Scott Watson, feeling 'tired and beaten . . . was for resigning in an official way as a volunteer'.[51] He confided his plan to other members of the group, who stated that they intended to remain fighting with the Republican forces: 'You're not a Party member – you wouldn't understand. I just can't walk out,' declared Martin Messer, an Edinburgh University student and Communist.[52] David Marshall in particular was infuriated by Watson's actions and his habit of, as Romilly described it, 'rushing off to Barcelona and not taking any of the rules and regulations seriously enough'.[53] Marshall witheringly described Scott Watson as having only 'come [to Spain] for the sensation . . . certainly he was a shit and he pissed off quickly.'[54] Despite his comrades' opposition, Scott Watson 'decided that he would prefer to be a journalist rather than fight'.[55]

With little time to recover from the disaster at Cerro de los Angeles, the Thaelmann Battalion was rushed by lorry to University City, now the focus of the Nationalist assault. Both sides fought doggedly, often hand-to-hand, and Romilly and his group were involved in some of the most ferocious fighting. With the front lines separated by as little as 150 metres, buildings could be captured and then recaptured in the same day. As Phil Gillan later recounted, 'it wasn't like many of the other battles, which lasted maybe three or four days and then there was a lull after it. This was continuous, night and day, just going up the lines and back down, up the line and back down.'[56] Nobody managed to get more than a few hours' consecutive rest during nearly eight days of fighting alongside the Casa Velasquez, the School of Advanced Hispanic Studies, on the south-west outskirts of University City, and the craving for sleep became overwhelming:

The hours of sleep were precious. I can't remember any other time in my life when I have so much enjoyed the prospect of sleeping. When you felt the hand on your shoulder and heard someone saying, 'Your turn on guard now,' you would hope it was a dream and you could go on with a delicious sleep. But when you came back, chattering with cold, you were impatient with others who were like that.[57]

University City bore the brunt of the Rebel attacks and many of the Germans were killed or wounded: 'in eight days they had had over a hundred casualties – nearly all the leaders had disappeared.'[58] When the Nationalist attack eventually ran out of steam (or rather manpower), the badly depleted Thaelmanns were withdrawn to Fuencarral in the north of Madrid. Despite the terrible casualties taken by their German comrades, the English emerged unscathed from the fighting: 'Our little group almost felt guilty in having miraculously escaped with not a single casualty.'[59]

While in reserve, Romilly and three of his companions took a day's unofficial leave in Madrid. They bumped into Scott Watson, now working as a *Daily Express* correspondent, and a British delegation, who treated them to dinner and put them up in their hotel. On return to their billet Romilly was taken aside by Arnold Jeans, the Latvian leader of the English-speaking group, who had discovered that Romilly's influential connections – his 'parents and others' (perhaps even Winston Churchill himself) – had made contact with the War Office in Madrid, trying to get him out of the war. Jeans offered Romilly the chance to return home, but the offer was politely declined: 'Desperately glad though I had been to leave the Casa Velasquez, I hadn't the slightest wish to return to England then. That was all I heard of the matter.'[60]

After his vain attempt to capture University City, in December Franco changed tack and began a new offensive to the west. In response, a fortnight before Christmas, the English unit in the 12th International Brigade moved up to help stem a Rebel attack which was threatening the Republican-held village of Boadilla del Monte, fifteen kilometres west of the capital.

Within Boadilla, among the Republican forces attempting to defend the village, were the Englishmen of the 11th International Brigade. Cornford's group had set themselves up in a barn and looked on as the Republican infantry vainly tried to launch counter-attacks to stem the advancing Rebel forces, part of what Bernard Knox believed to be 'the biggest offensive the Fascists had yet launched'.[61] Hopelessly outgunned and outnumbered, the British retreated through the village, crawling on their stomachs to avoid the hail of bullets: 'One of us, I think it was David Mackenzie, was repeating slowly to himself, "Even when you have to retreat, do not run,"' Knox remembered. 'And so we walked, dragging the guns over the ploughed land that crumbled as the bullets hit it.'[62] Aware that they were in imminent danger of being outflanked and surrounded, the group abandoned the village.[63] During their retreat Knox 'suddenly uttered a fearful shriek and fell, clutching his throat'.[64] He lay, badly injured, as his comrades debated what to do:

> There was a hurried consultation and I heard David [Mackenzie], a medical student, say, 'I can't do anything with that.' John [Cornford] leaned over me. 'We can't do anything for you. Good luck, and God bless you, Bernard.' And they moved off again to fire off a couple more drums before leaving the village.[65]

Knox later described his feelings on realising that he was probably going to die:

> I have since then read many accounts by people who, like me, were sure that they were dying, but survived. Many of them speak of a feeling of heavenly peace, others of visions of angels welcoming them to Heaven. I had no such feelings or visions; I was consumed with rage – furious, violent rage. Why me? I was just 21 and had barely begun living my life. Why should I have to die? It was unjust. And, as I felt my whole being sliding into nothingness, I cursed. I cursed God and the world and everyone in it as the darkness fell.[66]

Yet, somehow, Knox managed to drag himself back to a dressing-station and survived.

Meanwhile, Romilly's group in the 12th International Brigade was involved in a melee around Boadilla, before it was captured by Rebel forces during the night of 14 December. Expecting to participate in a counter-attack the following morning, the group instead held their positions for the next three days. Surprisingly, it did not seem like such a terrible position to be in, 'there was plenty of food, wine and cognac and, apart from the digging, we had quite a pleasant time.'[67] Romilly even encountered John Cornford, whom he knew vaguely from his time at Wellington School, as Cornford's unit moved into reserve.

At Boadilla, the good fortune of the Thaelmann Battalion's British members finally ran out. A second Nationalist offensive overwhelmed the Republican defences, and Romilly's group became separated from their comrades. As they came under fire from intense machine-gunning, they tried frantically to retreat, but were caught in murderous crossfire, with bullets also coming from their own trenches.[68] Their former colleague, Keith Scott Watson, later described the volunteers' last moments as they were virtually wiped out:

> A heavy fire had broken out; bullets sang and smacked among the trees. Jeans gave his last order: 'Retreat in open formation. Birch and Jock every five hundred metres cover fire with Lewis guns. You others –' Jeans slumped down; bubbles oozed from a hole between his eyes.
>
> They ran; whining death ran with them. Romilly and Jerry were last, a cross-fire now broke out – they were surrounded. On their left they could see the turbaned Moors moving forward led by the Italian whippet tanks. Ray Cox tumbled forward, a bullet in his thigh. 'Get on, I'm done.' He sat with his back to a tree – the Moors came on, he was still firing when he was hidden from sight by the trees.
>
> Long Sid's height was his undoing – a tank machine-gunner saw him, four bullets tore into his stomach. The English rested for breath, while Sid died. Jock was the next, blood spurted from his neck; this tough little Highlander refused to die, he tied the wound in rough tourniquet and stumbled on, Jerry took his Lewis gun. Jerry didn't learn to use the Lewis gun in the army, but he knew all right. A hand of a dozen Moors tried to cut the survivors off; firing from his waist, he mowed them down like corn.
>
> Birch halted to open fire; his head snapped back, Joe saw him and turned to help. Birch was past aid; Joe gave a little cough, he crumpled, a bullet in his heart. 'Best o' luv to muvver.' Messer held him while he died. The steel whip that screamed over Messer, killed two more of the English; Harry Adley, a little ex-serviceman with a small café in Folkestone; and Bill Scott who survived the ambushes of the Black and Tans, and died in the once peaceful woods of Madrid.[69]

Six British volunteers were killed at Boadilla, which saw the end of the group's involvement in the Thaelmann Battalion. The surviving British volunteers, Phil Gillan, Esmond Romilly and Arthur Ovenden, were all repatriated to Britain.[70] News of the deaths appeared in the *Daily Worker* on

28 December, accusing German soldiers fighting for the Nationalists of having killed them.[71]

Yet, while the Republican forces – and particularly the International Brigades – suffered heavy losses at Boadilla, so too did the Rebels, forcing them to eventually abandon their attempt to break through the capital's western defences. As British volunteers such as Bernard Knox and Phil Gillan recognised, they did not 'save Madrid': 'The International Brigades played a big, big part, but it was the Spanish troops themselves that had held them.'[72] Clearly, however, the Internationals' contribution had been hugely important.

Despite the casualties, the brave last-ditch defence of Madrid inspired others to join up. By the end of 1936, Robson's efforts were beginning to pay off and volunteers were arriving from Britain in such numbers that Tom Wintringham's dream of uniting all the British (and Irish) volunteers within a battalion was becoming a realistic possibility. The first step towards the formation of a British unit came in December, with the creation of an English-speaking company as part of the 14th International Brigade. The group, 145 strong – and around a third of whom were Latin Americans, who according to one Irish member 'spoke English like Captain Flint's parrot'[73] – formed the first company of the French 14th (La Marseillaise) Battalion, commanded by a Frenchman, Lieutenant-Colonel Delasalle.[74] They were placed under the command of Captain George Nathan, a former lieutenant in the British Army with a somewhat chequered past, but who presented the very image of the British Army officer – 'an elegant, cane-swaggering, likeable type of adventurous Jew', thought the poet Stephen Spender.[75] According to a volunteer who came to know him well, Nathan possessed 'humour . . . enormous charm' and a 'magnificent air of authority and decision'. More significantly, he had 'the gift of being able to instil in others the unquestionable certainty that he knew what he was doing and it was for the best'.[76] Nathan was one of a number of Britons in Spain who would reveal a remarkable capacity for military command:

> At first sight Nathan . . . had looked to us like a man that had been humbled by poverty, wearing as he was a mixture of military and civilian clothes. In an old sweater and cheap shoes he had not impressed the leadership in Albacete; but then there were not any alternative candidates, and he was given the No. 1 Company. In Andalusia something that was similar to a

Kafkaesque transformation changed Nathan's appearance . . . [His] boots, given a spit and polish brush-up . . . glittered in the sunlight . . . His army great coat looked as though it had been tailored for him. His collar and tie were neatly set, and even his helmet had been cleaned. The chin-strap was at the correct angle, and we detected a clearer ring to his obviously acquired upper class accent, particularly when he was delivering statements that Campeau translated for the French. The affectation that he had developed all of twenty years before had arisen from the ashes.[77]

Some members of the English-speaking company had seen action before. In addition to Nathan, there were the five English survivors of the 11th International Brigade's Machine-Gun Company: Jock Cunningham, Joe Hinks, Jock Clarke, Sam Lesser and John Cornford, who was still recovering from the head wound received at University City, but refused to be left behind.[78] There were also several IRA veterans and the first of a number of Cypriot volunteers to arrive from London.[79] Magdalen scholar Ralph Fox, the author of acclaimed biographies of figures as diverse as Genghis Khan and Lenin, joined the company as political commissar a few days before it left for the front.[80] Intellectual but down to earth, Fox was a popular choice:

Ralph Fox impressed me immensely. He was a Marxist scholar and truly an egalitarian. No tabs of rank had been stitched to the sleeve of his army greatcoat . . . In truth Ralph Fox was quiet, gentle and efficient. He did not need tabs to win authority.[81]

On Christmas Eve 1936, No. 1 Company was sent to the Córdoba front in southern Spain, arriving at Andújar railway station, seventy-five kilometres east of Córdoba, early on Christmas Day. They were part of a response aimed at countering a Rebel offensive, but the action had begun badly, prompting the Republican command to release their infamous communiqué: 'During the day the advance continued without any loss of territory.'[82]

As ever, the volunteers' training was brief at best: 'We wandered over the fields and then we had a long walk and that was the training. We saw the rifles the first time we went to the front.'[83] Almost half of the recruits had not handled a weapon before their arrival at Andújar, when they were presented with turn-of-the-century Austrian Steyr rifles, part of the Republicans' hotch-potch of antiquated weaponry:[84]

They were worn out. Sometimes they jammed, they jammed so often. And the early rifles, they were so small they could explode, cause a lot of damage to the user. They weren't of much value, but they were better than nothing.[85]

The task of No. 1 Company was to capture the town of Lopera, just south of the road between Andújar and Córdoba.[86] The Company's first section, comprising mainly Irish volunteers, was commanded by Kit Conway, an experienced IRA activist, another section by John Cornford's comrade from the 11th International Brigade, Jock Cunningham, 'an ex-army sergeant . . . tough as they come', who had been in prison for leading a mutiny while in the Argyll and Sutherland Highlanders.[87] However, the attack encountered much stiffer resistance than anticipated, particularly from the air. As Manchester volunteer Jud Colman discovered, 'it was a waste of time using rifles against planes.'[88]

> After a night's rest at Andújar, the battalion marched to its positions among the olive groves outside Lopera and Villa del Rio. On Xmas day, about noon, the enemy aviation made the first attack, and sweeping low, machine-gunned our lads. The first victim of their planes was Nathan Segal of Walthamstow, who was buried a few yards from where he fell . . . Swooping down with no opposition as we had neither planes nor anti-aircraft, they made the position untenable and the Company had to withdraw.[89]

Another attempt was made to encircle the town on 28 December. However, the reinforced and well-fortified Rebel forces again resisted strongly, before counter-attacking the British positions on the 'English Crest' among the low hills, 'covered with olive-groves, planted in endless, symmetrical rows'.[90] It was here that John Cornford and company commissar Ralph Fox were both killed. Ironically, Cornford, the epitome of the heroic Byronic volunteer, died precisely as a result of his image – his white bandage acting as a perfect target for the skilled Moroccan snipers. Cornford's loss was keenly felt, not just by his comrades in Spain, but in Cambridge, where he had already established himself as a sincere, decent young man, with an enviable intellect. An obituary appeared in the *Cambridge Review*, with an afterword written by one of Cornford's professors:

I had only a brief knowledge of John Cornford, but it will never pass from
my memory . . . His belief in Communism was no youthful effervescence;
it was a still water which ran deep . . .

He had a first-rate mind; but he had also something greater – very much
greater. He was one of those who are willing to stake heart's blood upon
their convictions, turning them into a faith, and acting in the strength of
their faith.[91]

Cornford and Fox were by no means the only men lost and, faced with
a superior enemy force – aeroplanes machine-gunned the British lines 'from
8 in the morning . . . [to] 5pm at night' – the British soon had to retreat.[92]
Without the experience of the popular and calm George Nathan, who
managed to organise the withdrawal under a heavy Rebel artillery barrage,
the number of casualties would undoubtedly have been much higher.[93]

Captain Nathan's voice was heard above the din of battle: 'Retreat by
sections!' And then, a few minutes later, as some inexperienced comrades
thought to get back too quickly, Nathan's voice rang out again: 'Dress your
files! Retire in proper formation!' The running comrades halted. The
Company went back, section by section, firing as they retired. It was an
exhibition of cool leadership on the part of the commander.[94]

The battalion moved backwards and forwards over the next three days,
repeatedly re-occupying positions as the Rebels launched their own
powerful counter-offensives. However, any hope of capturing Lopera had
long passed.

Senior figures at the International Brigade base saw the operation at
Lopera, in which 300 volunteers from nineteen nations were killed and
another 600 were wounded, as a catastrophe.[95] Efforts were made to
discover why the battalion had been so disorganised and ineffective, and
André Marty and Peter Kerrigan launched an investigation. Marty accused
the French commander of the Marseillaise Battalion, Delasalle, of cowardice
and treason and claimed that he was spying for the Rebels.[96]

Many volunteers who fought with No. 1 Company at Lopera believed
that Delasalle was made a scapegoat: 'He may have been a coward, he was
certainly dandified and pretentious with an exaggerated idea of his military
capacities, but it was manifestly absurd to maintain that he was in the pay of
Franco.'[97] As one of the British admitted, 'we much preferred to believe that

there was treachery rather than incompetence.'[98] However, the diary entry of Manchester volunteer Ralph Cantor for 3 January 1937 is brief but telling: 'Trial of our Commandant De Lasalle [sic] proved to be receiving money from the Italians. Nathan chief witness . . . verdict and sentence and execution within 20 minutes.'[99]

Whether Delasalle was guilty of espionage or not, many of the British blamed him for the heavy casualties at Lopera and were not unhappy to see the back of him: 'The boys were glad he was shot, that I'll say,' said Jim Brown. George Nathan was promoted to replace Delasalle and Brown, for one, was well satisfied, for he felt that Nathan was 'a far better type of man, more reliable, more trustworthy, more honest, braver . . . a good leader he was'.[100]

The English-speaking company was transferred back to Madrid on 11 January to help contain another Rebel offensive, which had been launched at Las Rozas, ten kilometres north of Boadilla. Following the failure of his frontal assault through the Casa de Campo, Franco attempted instead to close the circle around the north of the capital. By 3 January, the offensive had captured Majadahonda and Las Rozas, cutting the main road between Madrid and La Coruña in several places.[101] Now under the command of Jock Cunningham, the companies in Nathan's battalion attempted to retake Las Rozas, but by 15 January, amid freezing weather conditions, their attempts ground to a halt and the effort was soon abandoned.

On Christmas Eve 1936 the company had been 145 strong; when they returned to Albacete the following month only 67 remained.[102] However, new volunteers flooding into Spain – 150 British and Irish in the first week of January alone – were currently beginning their training. The remaining members of No. 1 Company were sent to join up with the new arrivals. The new 'British' Battalion, of the 15th International Brigade, was beginning to take form.[103]

7

The British Battalion

The men of the battalion came from every part of the British Isles and from many other parts of the world . . . Very many had been soldiers, at one time or another: more than one had, I believe, deserted from the British Army in order to join our battalion. Some drank; some tired of training in a mud village and enlivened things by private fighting; some considered discipline unnecessary in our new sort of army. But now that there was fighting to be done, these foibles of the past were easily forgotten.

Tom Wintringham, commander of the British Battalion

Formed on 27 December 1936, the 16th Battalion of the 15th International Brigade would soon join the four other International Brigades already fighting in Spain. Initially the unit was to be named the Saklatvala Battalion, after an Indian Communist who had died from a heart attack in January 1936. Shapurji Saklatvala, MP for Battersea, was the first Communist to sit in the House of Commons. However, the name never really caught on and they were always referred to as el batallón inglés, or the British Battalion.

The new arrivals were soon united with the Britons and Irishmen in No. 1 Company of the 14th International Brigade, back from Lopera. These battle-hardened volunteers, 'whose fighting reputation made them the heroes of the battalion', received a heroes' welcome; 'a guard of honour lined the streets [and] the villagers joined in the cheering welcome':[1]

Now that was an occasion I'll never forget. These comrades had already been through the mill on the Córdoba front, at Boadilla and elsewhere in the southern regions and they carried scars of battle. Many of them had already been wounded. Some of the best known characters in the British labour movement had already been killed in the fighting in these areas.[2]

A training base was established for the battalion in the small village of Madrigueras, twenty kilometres north of the main International Brigade base at Albacete. Madrigueras in 1936 was 'a poor place with a population of 6,000, mainly families of hired labourers of absentee landlords'.[3] In December 1936, the 'very dull and depressing' winter climate of La Mancha did little to endear the village to the volunteers: 'everywhere lay under a chill and drizzling rain.'[4] One Nottingham volunteer found it particularly dispiriting:

If Albacete had been lacking in appeal, Madrigueras was little better, especially as it seemed to have an infinite capacity to attract a cold and very dampening drizzle, which enveloped the tedious uniformity of the plain of La Mancha upon which our new home stood. Like so many Spanish villages I was to see, Madrigueras was characterized by the squalor of its buildings and the almost unbelievable poverty of its peasants: a poverty which struck me forcibly even though I felt myself to be no stranger to hardship. Compared to the poor peasants of this part of Spain, the unemployed of Nottinghamshire were affluent.[5]

Sculptor Jason Gurney was also appalled by the villagers' 'really frightening' poverty.[6] He was one of many volunteers to remark pointedly on the glaring contrast between the desperate condition of the villagers and the imposing size of the church, which was 'as much a fortress as a place of worship, with a few narrow slits of windows high above the ground, a massive, iron-studded wooden door and a tall tower overlooking the village square'.[7] The church showed the signs of desecration familiar within much of the Republican zone, where the Catholic establishment, the long-standing target of a powerful anti-clerical movement, had been violently attacked for its association with the military plotters. A number of British volunteers were taken aback by the level of hostility directed at the Church, which 'had become the scapegoat for every sin of omission or commission by the ruling caste'.[8] In Madrigueras, the high altar, the pews and all signs of religious paintings had been removed and the building was now being used as a communal eating place for the villagers and troops.[9]

Explanations for the violence were soon forthcoming, with locals recounting familiar stories of the role the village priest had played in the uprising: 'We were told that the local priest had been a Franco supporter and when he . . . got wind of Franco's revolt he got up into the bell tower of the church with a machine-gun and fired on anyone who went to the local fountain for water.'[10] The priest had, they told one Scottish volunteer, been killed and hung on a hook in the butcher's front window.[11]

The volunteers were billeted around the village, mainly in locals' houses. One Glaswegian was lucky enough to end up in the squire's house, 'one of the best residencies in the village':

> The floors were in picturesquely designed terrazzo and the walls were of the best decor. There were eight rooms in addition to a very large and commodious kitchen, and in comparison to the small peasant houses it stood out like a palace.[12]

The billet was shared with a number of other volunteers, including Clem Beckett, a renowned speedway rider and 'wall of death' stunt motorcyclist, who ran a shop selling motorcycles in Oldham.[13] There was also Marxist writer of poetry and philosophy Christopher St John Sprigg, a 'quiet, thoughtful and extremely good-looking young man who would systematically dismantle, and lecture on the intricacies of the only machine gun in our possession', and who fought under his pen name, Christopher Caudwell. Other room-mates were remembered for less highbrow reasons: one 'bulky Londoner … used more swear words than anyone I ever knew', thought a strait-laced Scottish hunger-marcher.[14]

Not all the billets were so luxurious. One Londoner was put up in a hay loft belonging to a peasant family, with a number of other volunteers including 'Maro', the cartoonist for the *Daily Worker*.[15] All they had to sleep in was 'a blanket which we used for mattress and bedding combined'.[16] A number of volunteers were put in the old theatre, where staying clean was particularly difficult:

> No provision had been made for baths or laundry, nor even for the most elementary form of personal ablution. The few lavatories which existed were hopelessly inadequate for the numbers that they had to serve, with the result that the stink in the billets was really abominable.[17]

While the lack of decent sanitation caused a certain amount of grumbling, it was the volunteers' encounter with Spanish food that produced the most complaints and unhappiness. Walter Gregory's feelings on the subject were unambiguous: 'I think it could be accurately described as awful.'[18] Many volunteers found the lack of variation thoroughly disheartening: 'Beans we had, and beans and beans and beans.'[19] Chick peas or *garbanzos*, known by the volunteers as 'carbunchies', featured heavily in the diet, their flavour not improved by the British cooks' tendency to serve them stewed in water, rather than in olive oil.[20] Clearly, a number of the British cooks found preparing the alien foodstuffs utterly baffling:

> Our volunteer cooks did not realize that the French tinned meat was intended for use only for stew or soup and was almost inedible served cold, as one can serve the English 'bully' they knew. The 'tinned monkey,' as the French call it, would not make rissoles, either. Nor could we do anything with the almost uncured bacon that we got. As for 'baccalau,' which is supposed to be cod or dog-fish but is more probably dried shark, no cooks on earth can make it edible.[21]

Many volunteers suffered from stomach problems due to the dramatic change of diet: 'At first you all had queasy stomachs because of food in the oil. They fried rice. You had fried fish in the oil. Everything was in oil.'[22] English cooks based in what was dubbed the 'Harry Pollitt Field Kitchen' may have been working underneath slogans on the canteen walls such as 'An army fights and marches on its stomach' and 'Waste is an ally of fascism', but the constraints imposed on them, combined with a lack of familiarity with Spanish food, meant that their cooking was not hailed with universal acclaim.[23] 'No one seemed to know what nationality the cooks were,' said one London volunteer, 'though we were all quite clear that they had been born out of wedlock and were now fascist.'[24] One volunteer cast doubt on the origin of the meat, complaining that 'the meal we had – the time it took to prepare, and the piece of gristle, with what seemed fur – made me suspicious of the scraggy cats, and why there were so many.'[25]

Yet the villagers' obvious poverty meant that most volunteers understood that they had to 'make the best of a bad job'. One young Scottish miner summed up the spirit of acceptance and sacrifice:

> We were pretty fortunate as far as food was concerned. Despite the difficulties we seemed to get just enough to do us. We weren't looking for much. We knew that certain things had to be for the Spanish children . . . It wasn't just what we would have expected at home but we understood

the difficulties and were quite happy wi' what we got all the time we were there.[26]

There is no doubt, however, that the constant stomach complaints and sickness took their toll. Problems caused by diet were exacerbated by a lack of drinkable water, which in addition to causing serious health problems had another unfortunate consequence. Many volunteers turned to the only readily available liquid – wine, even if some found it an acquired taste: 'That red wine! I defy anybody not to pull a face when they had it, it was so dry.'[27]

Prior to Spain, most British volunteers were happy enough downing a pint of beer. Wines, had they been affordable, were considered somewhat sissyish. In Spain though, we took readily to the coarse red vino supplied liberally at meal times and usually available in the cafes. To some the question of its potency remained a constant challenge, too often unresolved until the questioner was beyond acknowledging defeat. Drunks were a damned nuisance.[28]

In his 'official' account of the war, senior British Communist Bill Rust admitted that 'Heroism is by no means synonymous with teetotalism and some of the bravest men in the field were hard drinkers at the base.' Nonetheless, 'a strict order had been issued by the Popular Front organisation in Madrigueras that during training no drink would be served to any of the Internationals.'[29] It was not long before the volunteers found a devious way to evade the ban: 'we discovered by complete accident that the way round the problem of getting drink . . . was to order what they called *cafe frio*, cold coffee, a mixture of rum and coffee.'[30] One volunteer, 'a real tough guy, a boxer', was christened 'Tom Vino' for his habit of putting wine, rather than water, in his water bottle.[31] So seriously regarded was the problem of drunkenness that Machine-Gun Company commander Harold Fry, 'the kind of man who liked a pint himself', was forced to inspect 'every water bottle, to make certain that water and not alcoholic drink was in it'.[32] The drinking culture presented serious discipline problems for the battalion leadership, who were working urgently in order to forge the volunteers into a cohesive military – and political – unit.

Within the battalion itself – and the International Brigades in general – two parallel forms of command operated. The traditional military structure was mirrored by a political command; every unit from company upwards had a political officer – a commissar – whose job was to provide political leadership. Based primarily on the model of the Soviet Red Army (though also on Cromwell's New Model Army in the English Civil War), political control was seen by the Communist leadership to be as important as military: soldiers must understand and support the war in which they were fighting. Bill Alexander, who served as both a military commander and a political commissar, was adamant that 'the character of the war, the need to create a new united army in a divided country – short of everything – gave a political complexion to all things military.'[33]

This desire for political understanding – or conformity – combined with the fact that over two-thirds of the volunteers were Communists, meant that all the senior figures in the battalion in January 1937 were Party members, seen as politically reliable by the Comintern leadership of the Brigades.[34] Inevitably, the successful operation of the system depended on efficient cooperation between the two forms of command and on the ability of the commissars to motivate and inspire the volunteers. Unfortunately, some individuals were considerably more effective than others and the system was, on occasion, placed under such extreme pressure that it virtually ceased to function at all.

The man appointed to be the first military commander of the British Battalion was Scottish journalist and First World War veteran Wilfred Francis Remington Macartney, who had 'impeccable revolutionary credentials' following his ten years in Parkhurst for spying.[35] Many were highly impressed with Wilf Macartney's military abilities; the ex-Navy man and Invergordon mutineer Fred Copeman described him as 'a highly intelligent officer, neatly dressed, who gave his orders quietly, but as if he meant them'.[36] Peter Kerrigan thought him 'very capable indeed and . . . well-respected by the men'.[37] However, by no means all the volunteers were so positive:

[Macartney was] a rich and well-educated man, a great drinker and bon viveur, and I find it difficult to believe he was ever a very dedicated Communist. In any case, it soon became evident that he had very little idea of the duties of a Battalion Commander.[38]

Others were similarly unconvinced, claiming that Macartney was 'unable to motivate those under him to give their best' and that 'his abilities as an organizer and decision-maker were rather rudimentary.'[39]

A former colleague described him as 'a fool, who became a rogue through drink'.

The man chosen as battalion political commissar was Dave Springhall, secretary of the London district of the Communist Party. Like many Party cadres, Springhall had studied at the Lenin School in Moscow.[40] Politically experienced he may have been, but Gurney, who had little time for the more rigid Communists, found him to be

> A pleasant, but hopelessly obtuse and humourless man . . . His principal function at Madrigueras seemed to be the delivery of exceedingly boring homilies at morning parades which were always prefaced with the phrase, 'Now comrades, the position is as follows.' He seemed to be a well-intentioned man who was completely out of his depth in the position in which he found himself.[41]

The battalion itself was divided up into four companies: one machine-gun group, plus three of infantry, each with their own military and political officers. No. 1 Company comprised the experienced veterans from Lopera, plus the new arrivals necessary to bring their number up to company size. It was led by Jock Cunningham, who as a veteran of the battles in University City and Lopera had proved himself to be a brave, competent and popular leader: 'He knew how to deal with men. He knew how to be severe. He knew also how to get men along with him,' said one Scottish volunteer.[42] The company's political commissar was Ralph Campeau, a 'London communist' and French-speaker, who had proved invaluable when he had served with Cunningham at Lopera.[43]

No. 2 Machine-Gun Company, which was equipped with a variety of automatic weapons, was led by Tom Wintringham, who had also now been in Spain for several months: 'Although he always said he hated war, he was fascinated by it.'[44] Wintringham also acted as second-in-command of the battalion and took on many of the responsibilities for training the volunteers in military skills and tactics. His commissar was Donald Renton, a Scottish Communist who had participated in a number of hunger marches.

The third company was commanded by Bill Briskey, London bus-driver, militant member of London Transport's 'rank-and-file' movement and experienced activist within the Transport and General Workers' Union. Another dedicated Party member, he had arrived in Spain just before Christmas and was chosen to lead the company despite his lack of military background; his political discipline was considered an acceptable substitute. Briskey's commissar was Northumberland miner Bob Elliott, a well-known open-air speaker in the National Unemployed Workers' Movement from the Blyth Valley, where he was a Communist member of the local council.[45]

The commander of No. 4 Company was Bert Overton from Stockton-on-Tees, another Communist and trade union activist who had arrived in Spain on New Year's Day, 1937.[46] A British Army veteran, having served in the Guards' Regiment, Overton was 'a mysterious, boastful character, who had all the swagger and swashbuckling antics of a typical mercenary soldier'.[47] 'He had been a brilliant Guardsman,' wrote one volunteer who had served with him, 'but that was in peacetime.'[48] Overton's commissar was Tom Devenham, a miner from Wigan, a member of the Sheffield District Committee of the Communist Party and another alumnus of the Lenin School in Moscow. He was also a First World War veteran, so possessed important military know-how, in addition to a wealth of political experience.

Military training, such as it was, was put into practice: 'it was a training which was of necessity hurried, for times were critical and men were needed.'[49] Fortunately, several volunteers had some form of military training and 'the number who had never handled a rifle before was surprisingly small.'[50] There was 'a good proportion of ex-servicemen' and many had served in the Territorial Army or other military organisation. Time spent in the Royal Navy Volunteer Reserve had given one Scottish volunteer invaluable experience of firearms and he felt that 'I was quite used to them, remarkably well used to them.' However, he added wryly, 'It was hiding from the other side's bullets. I think that was what I was deficient in.'[51]

But too many volunteers were like the Scotsman who admitted, 'I had no military experience before I went to Spain.' Attempts to rectify the novices' lack of combat skills did not impress him much: 'At Madrigueras we had a month of training – which was more or less useless.'[52] He was not alone in his dismissal of the battalion's preparations for battle. Wintringham was initially horrified by the drilling he witnessed:

The first days of training . . . were pitiable in the extreme. I did what I could to start training in tactics, but was dismayed to find that neither of the company commanders knew how to move men either on the parade-ground or the field. [One of the company commanders] . . . made his men string out and double forward at the sound of his whistle, exactly on the good old Boer War lines that I had learnt in the Officers' Training Corps at school. He loved blowing that whistle. I noted with real misery – standing ahead of the two companies and watching them move towards me in a formation intended to be that of attack – that this boy chose a nice hillock to stand on and waved his men forward with dramatic gestures. And I noted also that had I been an enemy machine-gunner I could have wiped out most of his company at ranges between six hundred and four hundred yards.[53]

When Tony Hyndman (a boyfriend of the poet Stephen Spender) arrived in Madrigueras, he was greeted by a former journalist who had been training for the past two weeks: 'Welcome to the biggest shambles in Europe.'[54] There was 'a certain amount of training and a great deal of boredom', Hyndman confessed later to Spender.[55] As Bill Rust observed, 'The desire to fight Fascism did not in itself automatically solve all the problems associated with the creation of a fighting force capable of employing scientific weapons and applying modern strategy.'[56]

Undeterred, Wintringham struggled to meld the volunteers into a cohesive, disciplined unit, under the watchful eyes of Wilf Macartney who, Wintringham claimed, with 'a quick eye and a quicker tongue . . . brought more realism into our practice manoeuvres than I have known elsewhere'.[57]

Macartney and I tried to get the ideas of cover, approach from the flanks, cross-fire and accurate fire control into the heads of our section and group leaders . . . I lectured to hoarseness on our machine-guns, on the strategy of the war in Spain, on 'communication, co-operation, obedience.'[58]

Despite Wintringham's upbeat assessment, most of the volunteers were very critical of the amount of training they received: 'We pretended to shoot at things and we pretended to be evading the enemy. We learned one or two things about camouflage. And we played at soldiers.'[59] One put it very succinctly, 'I can't even remember my training. I can remember one miserable day, only about a morning, running about a field.'[60] In addition, many criticised the training as being inappropriate for the Spanish war, and it was later suggested that the purpose was more symbolic than practical, designed mainly to keep the volunteers occupied and shore up their morale. One volunteer was utterly convinced that the training was

Not effective, not in the slightest . . . You see, it was just a case, really, of trying, what are you going to get the men to do? And so just keep them busy doing something so they don't get demoralised and keep them tough and strong as well, take them out on long route marches. About the only thing they really learned was how to take cover from aircraft. You know, they'd blow a whistle for aircraft and you scattered from the road and would lay face downwards. Even if you put your head in a load of mule manure, you did that. And the other thing was forming artillery formation, which is arrowhead formation, which it turned out wasn't a very good formation for advancing in front of the enemy anyway.[61]

Manchester volunteer Sam Wild, who was to be battalion armourer at the battle of Jarama in February 1937, confirmed that, at most, those fighting at Jarama had received six weeks' training.[62] While Tom Wintringham claimed that 'in five weeks or so they had produced some very fair infantry,'[63] in truth five weeks of basic training was 'absurdly short'.[64] The summary by Cypriot political commissar Miklos 'Mike' Economides was probably a fair one:

We didn't have a long training because they didn't have the time to train, that's how it was. The war needs you and you have to go. It wasn't really an effective training, but none the less, sufficient to kill someone.[65]

Of course, many of the problems with training were a result of the well-documented shortages of arms and ammunition:[66]

Our greatest weakness was lack of arms. The so-called Non-Intervention Pact . . . prevented the free supply of all the essentials. Gallant seamen ran the blockade with food and arms sent by the Soviet Union and Mexico. Unsung heroes like Potato Jones sailed and burst the blockades to San Sebastian time and time again. Armaments that had been bought and paid for by the Spanish Republican government were 'frozen' in France at the behest of the government there. The achievements at the front and the defence of Madrid could have been greater and more significant than they were but for the Non-Intervention Pact.[67]

Wintringham agreed: 'Guns and ammunition were scarce in the extreme' and in particular, 'the machine guns of the Second Republic's army were at this time, in February 1937, mostly a job lot of junk.'[68] Wintringham was unimpressed with the Colt machine guns, which he felt to be dangerously unreliable. He would be later proved right; all the Colts taken to the battle of Jarama were captured by the Rebel forces.[69] The French Chauchats were no better. Copeman believed they were among the most hopeless and inefficient guns he had ever handled; their susceptibility to mud, dirt, and humidity meant they jammed with monotonous and frightening regularity, earning them the reputation as the worst machine guns ever fielded in the history of warfare.[70]

> After several weeks of being weaponless we started to receive a most extraordinary variety of automatic weapons. The first of these was always known as the 'shosser', and I never discovered what its proper title was. We were provided with a dozen of them for issue to alternate sections through the three infantry companies. It proved to be the most outstandingly useless weapon that I have ever seen and the entire lot were either lost or thrown away during the first day that we were in action. There seemed to be an almost unlimited number of ways it could jam itself, which it usually succeeded in doing before it had fired more than five consecutive rounds – the shossers had apparently been made in France for the French Army, and the French must have been wholeheartedly glad to have got rid of them. Every time the gun jammed it had to be entirely dis-assembled and put together again. They were not one of the Government's best buys.[71]

If this were not bad enough, ammunition for the machine guns was particularly scarce: 'Our military training reached its zenith when for a few hours we played with and then fired two rounds apiece from a Maxim machine-gun,' noted one volunteer dryly.[72]

The Russian-made Maxim guns were at least reliable, with an extremely rapid rate of fire. The weapon's principal drawbacks were its cumbersome size and its weight for, unlike the British version which came with a tripod, the Russian Maxim was equipped with 'a miniature gun carriage which the poor No. 2 on the gun had to carry . . . It was a very heavy beast indeed . . . as you marched along over rough ground the wheels of the carriage used to bump up and down on your back.'[73] They 'also had the disadvantage of being water-cooled which, in a country like Spain, can often be a problem. There was, on more than one occasion, no water to put in them and the question arose, "Shall we put in the wine ration?" And, generally speaking, the decision was, "Yes, but let's pass it through our kidneys first".'[74]

As Jason Gurney remembered, the ordnance was no better:

> The grenades which were issued to us were ridiculous things. They consisted of a short length of mild-steel piping with half a stick of gelignite inside and a short piece of fuse sticking through the metal cap. The theory was that the grenadier lit the fuse and threw the bomb – it all sounded so magnificently simple. But it didn't work that way. The only thing we had to light the fuse with were the ordinary flint and tinder lighters which the peasants used to light their cigarettes – a flint and steel, as on a petrol lighter, with a length of yellow tinder cord impregnated with saltpetre. The system was to roll the wheel fiercely with the palm of the hand until the tinder caught a spark which was then blown up into a glow and applied to the piece of fuse sticking out from the end of the grenade, igniting it. After that you threw the bomb at the enemy. It was all perfectly simple – if you had time enough, if it was a fine day and the tinder had not got damp, if the piece of fuse had not become unravelled, and all the other ifs that made it an utterly impracticable weapon. The only advantage of it was as a morale builder, particularly with the bright yellow tinder cord braided up and worn over the shoulder like an aiglet.[75]

Other vital supplies were missing, leading Tom Wintringham to write bitterly to Harry Pollitt in mid-January, 'why on earth send us out sweets, when we are almost entirely without binoculars, compasses and good watches?'[76]

The members of the battalion did at least possess a uniform of sorts. On arrival in Spain, volunteers were issued with rough khaki clothing, which resembled battle dress, but made of corduroy. It did not greatly impress:

> Well, I suppose you could call it a uniform. We had a pair of denim trousers and a little jacket thing and a hat, but I wouldn't have called it a uniform because it was mixed types of stuff. There was no uniformity about the dress.[77]

The trainee soldiers often had to rummage through huge piles of uniforms in order to find anything with a semblance of fit, confirming the long-standing soldiers' joke that army clothing only comes in two sizes: too large and too small. The volunteers were issued with boots, but as they were made of raw leather, they often caused terrible blisters.[78] The effect was topped off with a flimsy French army tin hat. In charge of the equipment storeroom at Madrigueras was an impatient captain, James Robertson Justice, who would later become famous playing the bombastic chief surgeon Sir Lancelot Spratt in the 1954 film *Doctor in the House*. One volunteer's inability to find a pair of boots which fitted reportedly gave the captain 'a chance to indulge in a dash of what was to be, in a future career, his stock in trade – irascibility'.[79]

Brand new Russian rifles eventually arrived at the beginning of February, and came complete with a triangular bayonet that was designed to be in place when the rifle was fired. But the bayonets were extremely cumbersome and most were either lost or discarded. A number ended up being used as tent pegs. Moreover, they could be as dangerous to friend as foe; one volunteer arriving at Madrigueras in mid-January 1937 'missed the first week of the battle of Jarama having been injured with an accidental bayonet wound in the eye'. Like many of his comrades, he felt that 'the Russian habit of having a bayonet fixed was a thoroughly stupid one.' As he admitted, he learned the lesson 'the hard way'.[80] Many volunteers didn't like them, especially British Army veterans who had used the Lee Enfield, but accepted that 'you'd to make the best of what you could.'[81]

Where possible, infantrymen were given five cartridges in order to practise firing the new guns. More often, due to the critical shortage of ammunition, the instructors had to devise imaginative ways of teaching inexperienced volunteers how to sight a rifle, without ever giving them the opportunity to fire the weapon:

What they used to do was they cut a hole in the centre of a card and they looked through it, them that were training you. They were looking through to see that you were pulling the trigger and the thing wasn't moving. You were dead on the bull. That was the only way they could teach you to use a rifle, and actually you never used the rifle until you were ready for action. They didn't have ammunition to train you with at all.[82]

One volunteer remembered that, due to the 'real scarcity of ammunition', he hadn't fired more than twelve rounds on the training range before going into battle.[83] Even one normally ultra-loyal Communist who was deeply critical of 'accounts in which people claim to have been literally pulled off a train and put into the front line without any form of training whatsoever' admitted that he had only 'expended fifteen or more rounds on the improvised firing-ranges before moving up to the front'.[84]

The young Southampton Communist Ivor Hickman thought that matters were made immeasurably worse by the naïve and complacent belief that political will was enough to ensure victory: 'Is it hell!' he railed. 'You never heard of political morale turning aside a bullet.'[85] Jason Gurney's summary of the battalion in January 1937 was probably accurate: 'Many people writing on the International Brigades have described them as well-armed, highly disciplined and well-trained units. This we of the British Battalion were not.'[86]

In early January 1937, there were approximately 450 volunteers training with the new battalion.[87] There were also a number of other volunteers, either on the Brigade staff and Commissariat, such as Peter Kerrigan, or in specialist units, such as map-making, transport, engineering or trans-missions. Others were working within the crucial group of interpreters, for within the Brigades, 'the Legions of Babel', 'language sometimes presented a difficulty', as News Chronicle journalist Geoffrey Cox put it with masterly understatement.[88]

> People could just about make themselves understood in ordinary life, but in the heat of battle, over an inadequate telephone line, there was virtually no communication at all. This problem was solved by one of the most remarkable collections of human beings in history. There were altogether about fifteen interpreters of various nationalities. None of them spoke less than five languages, some of them working happily in ten.[89]

The British volunteers were utterly reliant on the interpreters, for though a few, such as Tom Wintringham and Ralph Campeau, could speak French, most only spoke English. Very few spoke any Spanish, though Sam Wild knew a few words, having spent time in South America when he was in the navy.[90] The honourable exception was Jim Ruskin, whose command of English, Russian, French, Spanish and German was reported to be 'excellent'.[91]

Training progressed and volunteers arrived, yet problems continued with both. Wintringham complained to Harry Pollitt that 'About 10 per cent of the men are drunks and funks: can't imagine why you let them send out such obviously useless material . . . Discipline is still backward, too much drinking and too much arguing . . . the lack of discipline expresses itself in erratic military performance.'[92] Furthermore, disaster struck in mid-January, when a number of Irish volunteers, already unhappy with British officers' tendency not to make any distinction between the British and the Irish, discovered that two senior Britons – George Nathan and Wilf Macartney – were believed to have played a part in British covert activities in Ireland.[93] Both were alleged to have served with the notorious Black and Tans in Ireland in the 1920s; worse still, Nathan was rumoured to have been involved in a hit squad that murdered two prominent members of Sinn Fein in May 1921. His rather chequered past also gave rise to suspicions that he could be a Franco spy.

Nathan was directed, probably by André Marty, to explain himself to his Irish colleagues. According to one, Nathan was in effect put on trial for his life. He vehemently denied that he was a spy, but admitted that he had been an intelligence officer in the Auxiliaries, the paramilitary section of the Royal Irish Constabulary, in County Limerick. However, he claimed that he was acting under orders while in Ireland and argued that, as a Jew, he was a staunch anti-fascist, and that all the volunteers in Spain were all on the same side now. According to the former High Kinder trespasser Morris Levine, Nathan's explanation was accepted by the Irish, who 'deleted all references to his past'.[94] Nathan was fortunate to have earned widespread admiration for the military skills and courage that he had demonstrated during the disastrous Lopera action.

However, resentment continued to smoulder and was reignited by a tactless report in the *Daily Worker* in early January which, in recounting the actions of No. 1 Company at Lopera, made no mention of the Irish, instead describing them all as British volunteers. A number of Irishmen were furious, and it became clear that an attempt to resolve the simmering discontent would be needed. A meeting called by battalion commissar Dave Springhall on 12 January was attended by some forty-five Irish members of the battalion. During a stormy session, a number demanded that the group leave the British-dominated battalion, while others, such as the Waterford Communist John Power who wanted to stay, vigorously argued 'that distinctions must be made between anti-fascist working-class comrades from Britain and British imperialism'.[95] Perhaps surprisingly, given their IRA past, a number of Irish republicans spoke up for remaining with the British Battalion.[96] Nevertheless, at the end of the meeting, the Irish group voted by a ratio of two to one to leave and join the American Abraham Lincoln Battalion based at nearby Villanueva de la Jara.

That a senior British political commissar should even allow a meeting in which members of the battalion could take a vote on whether to leave or remain seems to fly in the face of the International Brigades' authoritarian reputation. While the meeting may have been a political miscalculation, however, the leader of the Irish volunteers, Frank Ryan, always claimed that it was a deliberate stunt by senior British Communists, who 'wrecked' any chances of forming an Irish national unit.[97]

British reports of the split claimed that the British commanders were keen to see the back of a turbulent faction. As Londoner Charles Bloom remembered:

> The Irish were always in trouble with us, with our officers. They didn't like the British, although they joined us to fight the fascists . . . They had a long standing antipathy towards the British. I can understand that.[98]

A number of senior figures in the British Battalion were very uncomplimentary about the Irish volunteers, their view probably not helped by accounts of Irish volunteers being carried into the battalion barracks late at night by the local peasants, so drunk they could not walk.[99] According to an official account of the battalion, many British were not sad to see them go: 'The friction that existed between the English and Irish was so great that the separation was welcome[d] by both groups.'[100] Dave Springhall admitted to Harry Pollitt that 'they have now gone today to the Americans and we are frankly glad.'[101] One casualty of the split was Dubliner Terry Flanagan, acting commander of the Irish group at the time. He was held responsible by Wilf Macartney, charged with sabotage and imprisoned. Only the personal intervention of Frank Ryan, who returned from Madrid in the nick of time, secured Flanagan's release. Another was Springhall himself, who was blamed by many senior figures in the British Party for what Scottish political commissar George Aitken described as 'his grave political mistake in helping the Irish section of the British Battalion to transfer to the American Battalion'.[102]

Early February 1937 brought a further unsettling incident, when Wilf Macartney was wounded in suspicious, or at least bizarre, circumstances. As part of his parole requirements following his release from Parkhurst prison for spying, Macartney had regularly to report to the authorities in Britain and he was due to return home temporarily.[103] Prior to his departure, a farewell supper was held in his honour at Albacete on 6 February. At the end of the evening, Kerrigan was exchanging pistols with Macartney when one of them went off, wounding Macartney in the arm and ensuring that his period of leave became permanent. According to Kerrigan, Macartney had a large heavy revolver, whereas his own was a small, much lighter Belgian model. Macartney suggested an exchange and asked Kerrigan to demonstrate how it worked:

> I took the revolver in my hand and what I can't say for sure is whether or not I touched the catch or trigger, but suddenly there was a shot and he said, 'Oh, you've shot me in the arm!' We rushed him to hospital, got an anti-tetanus injection and he got patched up and went off.[104]

The event remains shrouded in mystery. Many commentators have argued that the shooting was no accident and it is certainly true that senior figures in the 15th Brigade and the British Communist Party had become disenchanted with Macartney's leadership.[105] Originally he had been seen as the only man in Spain capable of leading the British Battalion: Kerrigan wrote to Harry Pollitt on 4 January 1937 of Macartney's selection as battalion commander that 'I feel it is a very good appointment.'[106] But, by the end of January, Macartney had lost the confidence of both Kerrigan and Tom Wintringham:

> [Macartney] is far too irritable or querulous and I feel this has an effect on his ability to inspire the men with confidence in himself. I believe this querulousness is due in a measure to his anxiety to get the best possible results in a short time, but it makes him very critical of the Party . . . I do have the feeling that there are signs that there is not the complete confidence there should be.[107]

However, it seems reckless for Kerrigan to have deliberately shot Macartney, if he was about to return home anyway. Had senior Communist Party figures decided that the battalion would be better served without Macartney, there is little doubt that he could have been prevented from returning – later the same year, three senior British figures would be recalled to Britain as a result of heated infighting after the battle of

Brunete.[108] Certainly Kerrigan always portrayed the shooting to Pollitt as accidental:

> The accident was the result of a stupid mistake for which I was responsible and it was just chance that the consequences were not a great deal more serious . . . it had bad effects politically . . . Mac is a well known figure in Britain being an author etc. and it would be impossible for the accident not to be known of there.[109]

Macartney was replaced as battalion commander by Wintringham, with Harold Fry, an ex-sergeant from the British army who had served in India and China, taking command of the Machine-Gun Company.[110] It was probably a fortuitous change for, according to Gurney, Wintringham appeared to be almost universally popular, 'invariably pleasant, informal and unpretentious'.[111]

Tony Hyndman remembered that 'It took him only a few days to win the respect and loyalty of all under his command. He was cool, quick in deciding who did what, with a wry sense of humour.'[112] Though by all accounts 'a supremely modest person' and despite his lack of relevant military experience, Wintringham possessed 'enough knowledge of the elementary principles of musketry training to become the mainstay of the battalion' and was 'an absolute genius not only in his ability to inspire, but in his capacity to create weapons'.[113]

In addition to a new commander, the battalion was also appointed a new commissar, when Dave Springhall was promoted (or booted upstairs) to brigade commissar. He was replaced by George Aitken, a Scot who had served in the Black Watch during the First World War and was the full-time Communist Party organiser for the north-east of England. Aitken was 'a quiet, modest and conscientious man, who was consistently zealous for the welfare and just treatment of every man in the Battalion'.[114] The new commanders took up their posts on 6 February 1937.

Two days later, the battalion prepared to leave Madrigueras for the front, to the south-east of Madrid. In preparation for their departure, all the volunteers were confined to their quarters, though 'some old soldiers sneaked out and got drunk [and] others didn't come home.'[115] In the morning, the entire village turned out to bid the battalion farewell, 'all dressed in their Sunday best'.[116]

The children and the parents of the village assembled to wave and say farewell. The sad mothers looked on with their lined, brown faces and prematurely greying hair as their children clung to their aprons, staring in silence and wonder as the troops lined up. The men gathered, mostly old, stood in a corner respectfully touching their hats as they recognised each of their new found friends among us. There was a feeling of foreboding as they looked on, tears glistening on their cheeks. Dust rose from the square when the soldiers stood to attention. It was a brief ceremony. The commander thanked the villagers for their hospitality and promised that every man leaving for the front that day would do his proud duty.[117]

The volunteers climbed into lorries and prepared for their long, slow journey to the front line. Taking in a final view of Madrigueras and its inhabitants, they set off for the front. It was an emotional departure for one young Londoner, who could not forget the tears of a villager in whose house he had been billeted:

The whole town was out, terrifically wrought up, lined up by the lorries, shouting, saluting, laughing and crying. Maria wept bitterly, which worried and puzzled me . . . I puzzled over Maria's tears for years. Finally I concluded that for all my education and her lack of it, she knew more about life and death than I did. She foresaw what I did not: that many of us would not come back.[118]

8

Their Finest Hour?

This battle has been reported on many occasions. Suffice it to say
that it was the bloodiest of all the battles that the British Battalion
was involved in, in Spain. There was none as deadly.

Interview with Peter Kerrigan, British political commissar

What became known as the battle of Jarama began on the morning of 6
February 1937. Following the failure of previous attempts on the west of
Madrid in November and December 1936, Franco had prepared a new
offensive to the south of the capital, aiming to cut the vital road that linked
Madrid with Valencia, the seat of the Republican government since it had
evacuated itself there in November. Initially intended to be part of a
combined operation with Italian troops to the east of the city, Franco
decided to push ahead with the action even though the Italian forces,
buoyed by their recent capture of Málaga, were delayed by heavy rainfall.

Colonel Varela, the Nationalist field commander, had five brigades of
six battalions at his disposal, plus eleven reserve battalions, totalling some
25,000 men – mostly elite Moroccan *regulares* and legionnaires – backed up
by German armour.[1] The Republicans had a similar number of men
available, mustered for an impending offensive in the same sector which
had also been delayed by the weather. The Rebel offensive pressed forward
quickly and by the evening the Republican forces had been pushed back to
the Jarama River, some twenty-five kilometres south-east of the capital. The
Rebel troops were now only ten kilometres from – and within shelling
distance of – the Madrid–Valencia road. Two days later they had captured
the bridge across the Manzanares River just south of Vaciamadrid, twenty
kilometres south-east of Madrid, and threatened to cut the road. General
Miaja, in charge of the Republican defence of the capital, sent the
Communist General Lister's 11th Division from Madrid to reinforce

the defending Republican forces and a desperate Republican counter-attack on 9 February retook the bridge, allowing Republican defences to be reorganised along the heights to the east of the Jarama River.

On 11 February, a small number of Nationalist troops – having knifed the sentries, French members of the 14th International Brigade – managed to stealthily cross the railway bridge on the small dirt road which ran towards the Madrid–Valencia road. The remainder of the Rebel column crossed immediately after them, then moved forward into the Tajuña valley.[2] During the evening another Nationalist unit managed to cross the Jarama using the same strategy employed at dawn, and during the night they consolidated their position in preparation for an assault on the high ridge which overlooked them, the Pingarrón Heights.

The 15th International Brigade, including the British Battalion, was now thrown into the defence. The brigade was commanded by a naturalised Russian colonel, using the name 'Gal', who was already unpopular with the British, for his dislike of George Nathan had resulted in Nathan's transfer to the 14th International Brigade.[3] 'Gal has been given a terrible reputation as a terrible martinet and he was a bit of an arse right enough,' said George Aitken.[4] The brigade's political commissar was a Yugoslavian, Vladimir Čopić. In addition to the 600 or so in the British Battalion, the brigade included similar numbers in the Dimitrov and Franco-Belge Battalions.[5] The American Lincoln Battalion was also part of the same brigade, but at this stage was still in training at its base in Villanueva de la Jara.

Supporting the British Battalion were perhaps one hundred British and Irish volunteers who had been held back in reserve and another hundred distributed between various units, offices and hospitals in Spain.[6] Despite the loss of a large number of Irish volunteers, the battalion appeared to be in relatively good health. The commander, Tom Wintringham, was assisted by the popular George Aitken, 'the only Political Commissar who was effective without becoming sanctimonious', and had as his adjutant 'wee' William McDade, an experienced Scottish ex-army man.[7] All but one of the battalion's commanders from company level upwards had previous military experience and the only exception, Bill Briskey, had already shown himself to be a talented and innovative company commander. Briskey, as Tom Wintringham later acknowledged, 'was utter reliability combined with shrewd wiliness'.[8]

However, two of the companies were badly under strength. No. 1 was lacking many of its battle-hardened veterans of Lopera, who had been formed into the brigade guard at the rear HQ at Morata de Tajuña and did not take part in the initial action at Jarama.[9] It was also missing its widely respected commander, Jock Cunningham, who was taken ill in early February and was 'raging at being left behind with influenza'. He missed the first day of the battle, a major setback for the battalion, as the Madrid veteran was in Wintringham's opinion 'the best soldier of the lot'.[10] Cunningham's place was taken by the ex-IRA man Kit Conway, another veteran of Lopera.[11] Harold Fry's Machine-Gun Company was also badly under strength; Wintringham estimated that it only contained seventy-two men in total.[12] Though typically downbeat, Jason Gurney's assessment of the situation was probably accurate:

> By 9th February, 1937, we had built up to over 600 men. Something over fifty of them had been in action on the Cordova [sic] Front, and the remainder had received some sort of training in Madrigueras but had still not fired a shot from any of their weapons. Only one Company Commander had been in action [in Spain], and that, only as the second in command of a platoon. The Commander of the Battalion was well intentioned but totally inexperienced. The other three battalions which formed the Brigade were not very much better off. Whether Gal, the Brigadier, and his staff knew any more than the rest of us, I cannot tell. But it is quite certain that the Brigade was not the well-armed, well-trained force that various people have pretended it to have been.[13]

As one London volunteer acknowledged ruefully, 'We weren't really soldiers. We really didn't know what we were letting ourselves in for.'[14]

On the morning of 11 February the battalion was taken by train to Albacete, and then by lorry to Chinchón, about twenty-five kilometres from Madrid and fifteen kilometres south-east of the site of the Rebel advance. Here the volunteers were issued with Russian rifles and ammunition and spent a day learning how to use them. For some, this was the first time that they had ever fired a weapon in their lives.[15] The volunteers spent a tense night, knowing that, in the morning, they faced the awful reality of combat and that some would probably not survive the day.

> Around nine o'clock I decided to step out to buy some vino – a strange thing for me to do then. I was sick with fear and worry at the thought of impending action and the consequences. My idea in getting the wine was to give me Dutch courage at the vital moment. I managed to contact an

elderly peasant who introduced me to someone who supplied the vino. Back in the billet with my boots placed together as a pillow and an old blanket for a cover I lay down to try and sleep, but couldn't doze off. The rumbling of shell fire could be heard, and the drone of planes overhead. We were close to the front. I lay stiff with cold and fear, wondering what the morning would bring. Terribly lonely now for the first time since leaving Glasgow, my mind kept going back to my mother and young sister lying in their beds. I lay wondering, wondering, what would happen? I have, in circumstances of worry, been able to compare my lot with someone in a less favourable position and achieved a sense of relief by comparison, but on that night I could find nothing to equal my miserable soul.[16]

Early the following morning, the battalion moved up to the junction of the Morata–San Martín de la Vega and Chinchón–Madrid roads, arriving at 5.30 a.m.[17] Despite their understandable anxiety at the impending combat, Gurney believed that 'everybody was full of confidence, as we now had machine-guns instead of rattles, and every man had a rifle even if he did not know how to use it in any effective manner.'[18] The morning began gloriously warm and sunny:

The whole world had changed overnight. We were now away from the flat, dreary plain of Albacete into fine, hilly country; there was not a cloud in the sky, the sun was shining brilliantly and everyone looked keen and optimistic.[19]

Walter Gregory, who served as an infantryman and messenger at Jarama, remembered 'the beauty of a crisp, sunlit, early spring morning and the total absence of any artillery barrage or aerial bombardment gave no indication of the ferocity of the fighting which was now only a short time away.'[20] However, Fred Copeman, who commanded a machine-gun section, was much less impressed. He described the battalion as 'just a huge crowd. It looked like a bloody summer's outing.'[21]

At 7 a.m. the battalion reached a large farm on the road from Chinchón to San Martín de la Vega, which was operating as their cookhouse. The farm possessed a labyrinth of cellars and a *bodega* with huge wine containers. Here the volunteers were given breakfast, and a rousing speech from their political commissar, who reminded them that they were fighting 'not just for the Spanish people, but . . . for all the peoples of the world'.

Fuelled by copious amounts of coffee, the battalion set off and began to climb steeply uphill. It was tiring work, so unnecessary belongings were soon left behind. Later that day, Jason Gurney was carrying a message from Wintringham to brigade headquarters, when he came across the volunteers' discarded belongings:

I was sent back with a message to Brigade HQ and instead of following the road, I took a short cut across the open country over which the Battalion had advanced during the morning. It was sad retracing our steps. The signs of indiscipline and of a totally unrealistic optimism lay on every side. The men were not physically fit and the stiff climb, combined with the morning sunshine, had caused them to abandon more and more of their gear, so that the whole olive grove was now covered with a mass of litter like an abandoned fairground. Most of them had evidently decided that the campaign would be over in a few hours and had left their overcoats, blankets, and packs containing spare clothes and personal possessions neatly stowed as if to be collected later in the day. Others had abandoned their belongings, item by item as they climbed the hill. There was an extraordinary variety of objects among the debris – hand grenades, ammunition, machine-gun spare parts, and clothing and equipment of all kinds. But the personal items which had been jettisoned provided the strangest part of the collection. Books of all kinds – though the Marxist textbooks, which were large and heavy, lay fairly near the bottom of the hill. The rest were of an amazing variety, ranging from third-rate pornography to the sort of books which normally fill the shelves of the more serious type of undergraduate. There were copies of the works of Nietzsche, and Spinoza, Spanish language textbooks, Rhys David's *Early Buddhism* and every kind of taste in poetry.[22]

The volunteers continued climbing the hill in the direction of San Martín de la Vega, spread out in 'artillery formation'. All seemed well: 'there was still no fighting going on – at least not with us. We could hear the artillery and the like but there was no fire of any kind coming to us and we weren't firing.'[23] By 10 a.m. the battalion had reached the top of the plateau, which looked down into the Jarama valley. To the battalion's right lay the San Martín road and beyond it was the Franco-Belge Battalion. Following Colonel Gal's orders, Wintringham deployed his three infantry battalions, with No. 1 held in reserve, much to the disgust of its new commander, Kit

Conway. Wintringham watched with approval as his troops 'moved handsomely' into their allotted positions, high on the plateau. Their position was 'perfect', he thought. But the idyllic spring morning was suddenly disturbed by the sound of German bombers flying low towards them. Following the lead of the Lopera veterans, the volunteers dropped to the ground and prepared to open fire on the planes as they passed overhead. But Republican fighters quickly appeared and a dogfight ensued far above their heads, until the Nationalist bombers fled back to their lines. The spectacle of the fight 'was all rather unreal – a bit like watching a film', thought Gurney.[24]

Wintringham's satisfaction was short-lived. Minutes later George Nathan arrived and informed Wintringham that he had ordered the battalion to continue to move forward. As Wintringham now realised, 'it was clear that this offensive, of which there had been guarded talk, had become a counter-attack.'[25] The three infantry companies moved forward cautiously across the last crest of the plateau, crossing a narrow depressed track as they went:

> On the edge of the escarpment was a sunken road, whose surface was about four feet below the general ground level . . . From the military point of view, they provided ready-made entrenchments in which men could take cover and move around in comparative security. Their disadvantage was that the men, having found this haven, were understandably unwilling to leave it. And because they were as straight as circumstances permitted the original carters to make them, they were totally vulnerable to enfiladed fire.[26]

Still continuing their westward advance, the volunteers began to descend into a valley in front of them, through a narrow bottleneck between two hills: that to the right, conical and devoid of cover; that to the left, wooded and capped by a red-roofed white house. By the end of the day the British volunteers would have come up with their own name for the high ground on the left: Suicide Hill.

By 11 a.m. the three companies had reached their new positions; 'the British companies promptly straddled the two hills and the saddle between them.'[27] Conway's company was to the right, Briskey's to their left. Overton's company was in the middle, beside the conspicuous white house. At first, all seemed well, as one volunteer remembered: 'We weren't being fired on although firing seemed to be taking place – I thought so anyway.

But it wasn't until eleven o'clock in the morning that I realised that the birds that were singing were bullets whistling past and there was a fierce battle going on.'[28] Then, as they took up their new positions, Wintringham was accosted by a Russian engineers' officer, who was attempting to install a telephone link to the 15th Brigade headquarters. He ordered Wintringham to move the battalion forward beyond the two hills and attack the advancing Rebel forces, despite Wintringham's vocal objections.[29] Over the telephone link, Colonel Gal confirmed the order that the British Battalion should advance. Wintringham was assured that the British would be supported by a Spanish cavalry unit on their left and that half the Dimitrov Battalion would support the Franco-Belge Battalion to their right, who were under attack from a brigade of Moroccan infantry and, as George Nathan admitted to Wintringham, 'having quite a time'.[30]

As ordered, the British volunteers continued their descent into the Jarama valley. When they encountered advance Rebel units who had already crossed the river and began to come under heavy fire, they quickly retreated back up the hill and prepared to engage with the advancing Nationalist forces.[31]

It was by no means a perfect position.[32] London Underground clerk George Leeson was horrified to find that 'there was no cover whatsoever' among the short grass on the top of the hill.[33] Sitting exposed on the summit, the battalion was subjected to a devastating three-hour artillery and machine-gun barrage, which centred on the conspicuous *casa blanca*, before traversing along the British positions: 'Within minutes hell was let loose as shell fire began, trees disappeared, and the whizzing screaming noise shook the ground around us.'[34] The ferocity of the artillery barrage had a catastrophic impact on the volunteers:

> The first time you hear a shell explode, the first time you hear it cutting the air, let alone the explosion, it's a, well, it was for me, a tremendously frightening experience. Your stomach just turns to water. This happens to every soldier when he first hears metal tearing through the air and knows it's liable to be his finish.[35]

As Jason Gurney recognised, 'these were completely raw troops, imperfectly trained and disciplined, ordered to hold a position on an exposed hillside against heavy artillery fire. They had no entrenching equipment, nor had they received any instruction in fortification.'[36] Battalion armourer

Sam Wild agreed: 'Having no experience in actual warfare, you don't know what's going to come up. You don't anticipate artillery fire, aeroplanes, machine guns, trench mortars.'[37]

By midday, the Franco-Belge Battalion to the north had been forced back, which brought the British companies and the battalion headquarters under lethal enfilading machine-gun fire from their right: 'it seems as though a thousand bees are buzzing past my face,' described one Irish volunteer.[38] When Moroccan troops appeared on the knoll to their right, Kit Conway tried to move his men back, but was hit and mortally wounded, as was the company political commissar, Ralph Campeau, who died several days later.[39] Ironically, George Leeson later claimed that Conway had just ordered his men to stand up and show they weren't afraid of the 'fascist bastards'. One Scottish ex-army man remembered how some of the volunteers, 'more out of bravado than anything else', got to their feet when firing, instead of lying down and taking cover: 'It was just a slaughter.'[40]

> Lads still stood on the skyline . . . there was a number of shots; it wasn't like in the British Army where someone shouts for you, 'Get down on your stomachs!' You just walked on and people sort of fell down. I can even remember lads still stood on the skyline after two hours and a Scots sergeant crying his eyes out and shouting, 'Get them off the skyline!'[41]

The British held on desperately, but were cut to pieces. No. 3 Company lost their gifted but inexperienced commander, Bill Briskey, and his replacement, Scottish Communist and Lopera veteran Ken Stalker, within a short time of each other. Also lost was Christopher Caudwell.[42] 'What a waste,' wrote the creator of Biggles, W.E. Johns, who knew Caudwell well and came to be a determined advocate of the Spanish Republic's cause.[43] Caudwell, the archetypal middle-class Marxist intellectual, fought and died alongside his close friend, speedway rider Clem Beckett. During their time in Spain, the two men, from utterly different backgrounds, had become inseparable.[44]

The situation facing No. 4 Company was just as serious, for in their inexperience they were attempting to take cover behind the *casa blanca*, which provided the Nationalist artillery with a perfect target. Bert Overton watched in horror as his company was literally blown to pieces by the shelling. He was later seen by some of his men 'lying behind the ridge, weeping because so many of his men had been killed and wounded'.[45] One

London volunteer described seeing 'a lot of dead bodies which were being used as firing emplacements, or sandbags if you like'.[46]

When the barrage, at last, came to an end, the utterly stunned volunteers were attacked by no less than three battalions of experienced Moroccan infantry, who advanced skilfully and with astonishing speed over nearly two thousand metres of uphill ground. The Moroccans were highly accomplished soldiers, in their element when moving across the open terrain of the Jarama valley, and consequently most of the volunteers developed more than a grudging respect for their soldiering skills:

> To speak the truth, the Moors were brave. They knew more about fighting than we did, or I did, far more, far more. Theirs was an art, you could be lying with good cover, they couldn't hit you, but they'd pick a place to ricochet off the wall wherever you were onto you. They knew all the gags and they could hide and camouflage.[47]

Jason Gurney described the horror with which the poorly trained volunteers regarded the advance of the North African troops, effectively summarising the inequality between the two opposing factions:

> Nobody at Madrigueras had said anything about artillery fire or the genius of Moorish infantry to move across country without presenting a target for anyone but a highly-trained marksman – a category that included no one in our outfit. In the event, we were utterly unprepared for what was going to happen to us . . .
>
> [The Moroccan soldiers] were professionals, backed by a mass of artillery and heavy machine-gun fire supplied by the German Condor legion. It was a formidable opposition to be faced by a collection of city-bred young men with no experience of war, no idea how to find cover on an open hillside, and no competence as marksmen.[48]

Leeson felt that the battalion's naivety contributed greatly to the terrible slaughter, blaming 'ignorance and [a] lack of communication'.[49] Stationed behind the three infantry companies, Wintringham was desperately trying to maintain contact with his company commanders, but was reliant upon information being brought to him via a series of runners and the unreliable telephone line:

[The telephone] was to prove more of a liability than an asset. Without any maps and the use of map references, it was practically impossible to describe the situation with any degree of accuracy. Moreover, the line and telephone equipment were in such poor condition that any conversation was so mutilated as to be almost incomprehensible.[50]

Wintringham was thus deprived of the vital information he needed to command effectively:

I did not know that casualties were mounting steadily and quickly; that Kit Conway, when I lost sight of him, was not lying down to seek cover, but was dying; that the section commanders in his company were either dead or wounded; that the thin grass and weeds on the crest of the hill was being slowly mown down, as if a gigantic scythe was passing and repassing, by bullets from the machine-rifles of the Moors and machine-guns of the Germans. I did not know that the wounded I could see were only a small proportion of those limping or lifted to the rear . . . I did not know that one of my company commanders was on the edge of panic and would come running back to find me.[51]

Wintringham later recognised that 'the lack of communication between the companies on the first ridge and the Battalion headquarters was the worst blunder on the first day.' He received no messages from Kit Conway and only one from Bill Briskey, which read: 'Please send help, have bad wounded. I have a part of nos. 4, 1, 3 coys. left. Comrade com. 1 coy. wounded. We are holding out well.'[52] Though the note was written sometime between noon and two o'clock, by the time Wintringham received it, it was too late. Conway and Briskey were already dead.

Fearing that the three infantry companies were in a position that was rapidly becoming untenable, Wintringham issued the order to retire. However, an order from the 15th Brigade staff overruled his instructions, with Colonel Gal insisting that the British must 'hold on at all costs'. Ironically, Gal's brutal command may have saved many of the lives of the men on Suicide Hill; in the absence of covering fire from Harry Fry's Machine-Gun Company, any retreating soldiers would have been picked off at will.

The inability to provide covering fire was a consequence of the non-intervention agreement. When the machine guns had been hauled onto the plateau via a thirty-foot vertical scramble earlier in the day, 'it was discovered that there was no ammunition.'[53] Fry's company had been given the correct belts for the machine guns, but the belts had been filled with ammunition for German Maxim guns, rather than the Soviet versions with which the battalion had been equipped.[54] The situation was exacerbated by the actions of 'Sergeant H', in charge of the lorry sent to Morata de Tajuña to collect more ammunition. At Morata he had drunk several brandies to steady his nerves and on the return journey he crashed the lorry, killing a man. The sergeant was later discovered, 'sitting by the road-side holding his head in his hands, completely drunk'.[55]

Deprived of their machine guns, Fry's company – or the forty or so riflemen available to him – kept up a field of fire on the knoll in front and to the right of them, and on the wooded slopes beyond the road, doing what little they could to prevent the Moroccan soldiers from advancing any further.

> There we were, a whole section of machine-gunners, trained to handle machine guns, but have to use only rifles to fire on the fascists, who we could see assembled in large numbers on our left. It was terrible to see men being carried back, destroyed by the enemy, and not being able to do anything effective to help them.[56]

But by the afternoon, the Nationalists had managed to force themselves forwards and had captured the knoll and Suicide Hill, including the *casa blanca*. The perilous situation of the battalion and its mounting casualties left them with little option but to attempt to make an orderly retreat, through the olive groves and back to the battalion headquarters on the plateau, dragging their wounded comrades with them.[57] Unfortunately, as one London volunteer remembered, 'there weren't many to go back.'[58]

As they withdrew, Moroccan soldiers flooded over the top of the hill in pursuit. But here, at last, the situation began to turn in favour of the defending British. After a heart-breakingly frustrating day spent without ammunition for their machine guns, the correct calibre of shells had finally appeared, though it still needed Harold Fry and Fred Copeman to load these individually, by hand, into the belts. Just in time, Fry and Copeman brought the machine guns into operation, although Copeman was determined that the machine-gunners should hold their fire until the Moroccan soldiers were within range:

> The job was to convince our gunners that on no account must they fire until I gave the word. The Moors had a name in Spain as the most vicious troops on the peninsula; their actions had become almost legendary, and some of the younger members of the machine-gun company were already showing a fit of jitters. One young Irishman, in charge of the gun on the left, threatened to open fire and to hell with Fred Copeman. There was no time to argue the point. I sailed into him and laid him out, and shortly we needed a new No. 1 on that gun![59]

The machine guns were fired with devastating effect on the Moroccan infantrymen, who were for once caught out in the open and totally unawares; 'within sixty seconds his five guns had put over a thousand bullets among the Moors.'[60] Wintringham estimated that the Moroccan battalion 'must have lost nearly half its strength in three minutes'.[61] The Rebel soldiers quickly either dropped down out of sight and waited for the cover of darkness or, where they could, retreated out of range. This brought to an end the first day of the battle of Jarama.

The official report of the fighting on 12 February by Vladimir Ĉopić, commissar of the 15th International Brigade, made little mention of the appalling level of casualties sustained by all its battalions, mentioning instead their 'staunch heroism' which repulsed 'violent fascist attacks causing heavy losses on the enemy'.[62] However, other 'official' assessments were more revealing. In *The Book of the Fifteenth International Brigade*, published in 1938, the battalion's unquestionable achievement in holding the Rebel attack is balanced by a description of the appalling cost:

> Out of our 600 odd men there were less than 200 with us now; another 100 re-found us during the next two days. The remainder were either dead or wounded. It had been terrific slaughter and what had we achieved to compensate for it? There had been mistakes – the absence all day of our machine-guns, the bungling of the ammunition belts, the bad communications with our front-line.
>
> Yet it was our very failure to follow the laws of military text-books that was our glory that day. The stubborn, not-an-inch stand of our men, their

holding out against overwhelming fire-superiority, their courage in untenable positions, their refusal to realise when they were beaten – these were the factors that halted the Fascists for the first time in a drive that had been victorious for six successive days.[63]

Other descriptions were even more stark. Jason Gurney estimated that 'seventy per cent of those who had been holding the forward positions were either killed or wounded.'[64] Tom Wintringham reckoned that 'out of the four hundred men who had held Suicide Hill, I had only 125 left . . . less than half the battalion's strength that morning.'[65]

During the night, Wintringham and George Aitken set about regrouping the depleted remnants of the optimistic group of men that had left Madrigueras only a day earlier. An attempt was made to rescue the wounded lying out on the battlefield and a number were successfully brought in under the cover of night. But many of those wounded that first day were left behind, as Jason Gurney later discovered, when he was asked by Wintringham to reconnoitre the sunken road.

I had only gone about seven hundred yards when I came on one of the most ghastly scenes I have ever seen. In a hollow by the side of the road I found a group of wounded men who had been carried back from No. 3 Company's attack on the Casa Blanca hill. They had arrived at a non-existent field dressing station from which they should have been taken back to the hospital, and now they had been forgotten. There were about fifty stretchers all of which were occupied, but many of the men had already died and most of the others would die before morning. They were chiefly artillery casualties with appalling wounds from which they could have had little hope of recovery. They were all men whom I had known well, and some of them intimately – one little Jewish kid of about eighteen [probably Maurice Davidovitch] whose peculiar blend of Cockney and Jewish humour had given him a capacity for clowning around and getting a laugh out of everyone even during the most depressing period, now lay on his back with a wound that appeared to have entirely cut away the muscle structure of his stomach so that his bowels were exposed from his navel to genitals. His intestines lay in loops of a ghastly pinkish brown, twitching slightly as the flies searched around over them. He was perfectly conscious, unable to speak, but judging from his eyes he was not in pain or even particularly distressed. One man of whom I was particularly fond was clearly dying from about nine bullet wounds through his chest. He asked me to hold his hand and we talked for a few minutes until his hand went limp in mine and I knew he was dead. I went from one to other but was absolutely powerless to do anything other than to hold a hand or light a cigarette. Nobody cried out or screamed or made other tragic gestures. I did what I could to comfort them and promised to try and get some ambulances. Of course I failed, which left me with a feeling of guilt which I never entirely shed.[66]

The wounded were not the only men missing. During the night a number of stragglers were discovered at the cookhouse by Aitken, who attempted to cajole them back to the line; but, as he freely admits, some volunteers were pressed back to the front under the threat of his gun.[67] Another group of men was found hiding in wine vaults in the farmhouse behind the lines by Fred Copeman and André Diamant, an anglicised Egyptian now in command of No. 1 Company. Copeman and Diamant threatened to throw grenades into the vaults and almost one hundred men who had been hiding promptly revealed themselves.[68] They too were marched back to the front. Some terrified volunteers ran as far as Morata de Tajuña, though most returned to the front with Jock Cunningham the following day, despite being shattered by their experiences. John Tunnah from Edinburgh remembered that many in the battalion 'were so frightened [that] they were now all at each others' throats. They were just so edgy, so upset about the whole thing.'[69]

Coerced or not, those returning to the front would be desperately needed over the following two days. Only two hundred and seventy-five men were left, plus a Spanish company for whom Manuel Lizarraga, a Filipino sailor who had been living in Philadelphia, took over as impromptu commander.[70] Preparations began for the coming day: rifle-cleaning, setting sentries and reuniting any remaining stragglers with the companies. The Machine-Gun Company worked through the night digging in.

Stand to was at 3 a.m., with coffee served fifteen minutes later. Tom Wintringham, still stunned by the previous day's events, prepared his depleted forces as best he could, bolstered by the arrival of the unflappable George Nathan.[71] 'The Battalion still existed as a fighting unit even if there were not many of us left,' claimed Gurney, somewhat optimistically.[72] No. 4 Company, under Overton, were placed to the right, No. 1 Company well to the left – almost out of eyeshot. What remained of No. 3 Company were to the right of No. 4 Company, along the sunken road. Battalion HQ was at the rear, just behind the sunken road. Wintringham placed No. 2 Machine-Gun Company out in front, overlooking the valley and river below them. It was an unconventional move, but fully justified in Wintringham's opinion; he considered their situation to be 'magnificent', overlooking nearly a mile of the front and the only position from which they could get a field of fire.[73] As Wintringham pointedly stated, 'Well dug in, with plenty of belts and ammunition, our machine-gunners could hold that terrace – if their flanks were safe.'[74] The principal danger was the left flank, where there were no Republican troops at all, but there was also a dangerous gap to their right, between themselves and the Franco-Belge Battalion. During the previous day Nathan had specifically warned Wintringham to 'watch his right flank' and had later ordered him to send out patrols throughout the night to check on 'the hated gap'.[75]

When dawn broke, the members of Harold Fry's Machine-Gun Company were able to see a number of Rebel soldiers, '[the] best part of a Brigade', resting up in the valley. A merciless strafing from Fry's machine guns thwarted any attacks for the next few hours. However, for the Yugoslav, Franco-Belge and German battalions to the right, it was another story, with two Nationalist brigades falling upon them, as Franco's forces continued to build upon the previous day's gains.[76]

Later in the morning Dave Springhall arrived, bringing orders from brigade headquarters. Despite their losses, the battalion should prepare to make an attack, which would be accompanied by aircraft, tanks and the elite Spanish Lister Brigade, aiming to relieve the pressure on the Thaelmann and Dimitrov Battalions to their right. However, no tanks appeared and the 'air support' turned out to be three small planes, which all too quickly dropped their bombs and disappeared. This made little or no impression on the Rebel forces, who were well dug in and had set up effective machine-gun positions. In response, the Nationalists launched another artillery barrage on the British Battalion. Faced with the prospect of a suicidal 600-yard advance into enemy machine guns, Wintringham ignored the order to go forward. It was a brave decision, for Wintringham must have been aware that it could have seen him executed for dereliction of duty.

During the morning the pressure on the Dimitrov and Franco-Belge Battalions increased and Fry's machine guns began to come under heavy shellfire. Unwilling simply to sit and wait for an attack, Wintringham led a small group of men, about forty strong, in a diversionary 'fake' attack to the left of the British lines. It was a daring move and proved successful, temporarily at least, for the Nationalist artillery switched their attention from Fry's Machine-Gun Company to counter Wintringham's 'attack'.

At 3 p.m., Gal sent another order to Wintringham to launch an attack on the Nationalist forces. Again, Wintringham ignored the instruction; he believed that an assault on Fry's position was imminent, as small groups of Moroccan troops could be seen working their way forward to the right, where Bert Overton's No. 4 Company was situated. At this point the nervous Overton finally panicked, and withdrew his company right back to the sunken road, as he had been begging Aitken to allow him to do all day.[77] As shells began to fall on their positions, Overton apparently shouted out in panic, 'God Damn it! It is too bloody hot here; I am getting out of it!'[78] His withdrawal instantly removed the vital protection Wintringham had put in place for the Machine-Gun Company's flank. Without it, they were quickly surrounded. Thirty members of the company, including Fry and his adjutant, were taken prisoner.

The exact details of the seizure of Fry's company are difficult to establish, for there are a number of conflicting accounts. Confusion reigned, it appears; certainly contradictory orders were given.[79] Fred Copeman later claimed that forty Rebel soldiers 'wearing the uniforms of our own dead, came up from the valley singing the "Internationale"', and that this ruse enabled the capture of Fry's company.[80] His account is supported by Jimmy Rutherford, one of those captured. Rutherford explained how the members of the Machine-Gun Company had been ordered to expect a Spanish battalion to take up positions to their left, which contributed to the deception's success:

> We heard, during a lull in the firing, the singing of the International, and saw a body of men advancing towards our position, giving the anti-fascist salute and shouting 'Vivan las Brigadas Internacionales!' At that distance and because of the similarity of dress, we mistook them for the Spanish Battalion. When they were about 30 metres from our positions, our Commander recognised them as fascists by their Mauser rifles and the dress of their officers. So he immediately gave the order to load and fire.[81]

Perhaps more likely, however, is that the troops that infiltrated the Machine-Gun Company were members of the Spanish Foreign Legion, replacements for the North African troops who had suffered such heavy losses the previous day.

George Leeson, a section commander in the Machine-Gun Company also captured that day, believed that Harold Fry mistook the advancing Nationalist soldiers for deserters and stood up and told his company to cease fire.[82] Whatever the truth of the story, when it was realised that their comrades had been seized, Bert Overton tried to make amends by leading a charge in a desperate attempt to retake the trenches. The Nationalist soldiers simply mowed them down with their own machine guns: 'Out of the forty of us who started out, only six returned.'[83]

Wintringham was hit by a bullet in the knee as he ran towards the Machine-Gun Company's positions to establish what had happened. He departed for hospital, leaving the battalion under the command of Overton, who pleaded for permission to withdraw. Wintringham refused. Following Wintringham's departure, George Aitken 'became very dissatisfied and disturbed at Overton's conduct [for] he did not appear . . . to be exercising any real control over operations'.[84] Overton begged Aitken to ask the brigade for permission to withdraw but, just as Wintringham had earlier, Aitken refused. Soon afterwards, 'in a very nervous state', Overton was panicked by a fascist flare fired over the battalion's position and fled, taking a third of the battalion with him. He was not seen again until the following day, claiming he had been stunned by a grenade. With the battalion down to two hundred men and effectively without a commander, the return in the evening of the experienced Jock Cunningham, still sick with fever but accompanied by about sixty stragglers, came not a moment too soon.

The third day of action saw the depleted ranks of the British Battalion still clinging, somehow, onto their positions on the plateau: 'When morning dawned, we were still holding the sunken road. There was no food. A meal had been brought up the previous night, but most comrades had been unable to contact the food wagon. For many it was the third day without food.'[85]

As the battalion came under increasingly severe crossfire, Cunningham was forced to withdraw from the sunken road, whereupon a number of Nationalist tanks appeared. Without any specialised equipment to face such an enemy, the battalion was forced to retreat further:

> About 1 p.m. I heard the tanks on our left . . . At that moment, a tank shell
> burst a few yards away. Across to the left a big tank, bigger than any of ours,

loomed up. Behind it swarmed Moors. Their main fire was on the Spanish Company on our left. Simultaneously, the din on the right became terrific. Nothing could live in the face of such fire . . . In those days we had no anti-tank guns, no grenades, no anti-tank material. The left flank broke, and the rout spread to the whole line. The slaughter was terrible. One would see five men running abreast, and four of them suddenly crumple up . . . Here and there, little groups rallied to stem the Fascist advance. Five or six times, a little bunch of Number 1 Company under André Diamint [sic] held up the Moors. Finally, they too, had to give up the unequal fight.[86]

It appeared that the battalion's tenacious attempts to hold their position were finally over.

The despondent survivors made their way back to the battalion cookhouse:

Dispirited by heavy casualties, by defeat, by lack of food, worn out by three days of gruelling fighting, our men appeared to have reached the end of their resistance.

Some were still straggling down the slopes from what had been, up to an hour ago, the front line. And now, there was no line, nothing between the Madrid road and the Fascists but disorganised groups of weary, war-wrecked men. After three days of terrific struggle, the superior numbers, the superior armaments of the Fascists had routed them. All, as they came back, had similar stories to tell: of comrades dead, of conditions that were more than flesh and blood could stand, of weariness they found hard to resist.[87]

Some 180 men were gathered at the cookhouse, where Frank Ryan and Colonel Gal attempted to hearten the shattered volunteers. Gal explained that their retreat had left a gap, which there were no other troops available to fill. Despite their exhaustion, despite all that they had suffered over the previous three days, the volunteers agreed to return to the front. They began marching west along the main Morata–San Martín road:

The crowd behind us was marching silently. The thoughts in their minds could not be inspiring ones. I remembered a trick of the old days when we were holding banned demonstrations. I jerked my head back: 'Sing up, ye sons o' guns!'

Quaveringly at first, then more lustily, then in one resounding chant the song rose from the ranks. Bent backs straightened; tired legs thumped sturdily; what had been a routed rabble marched to battle again as proudly as they had done three days before. And the valley resounded to their singing:

> 'Then comrades, come rally,
> And the last fight let us face;
> The Internationale
> Unites the human race.'

On we marched, back up the road, nearer and nearer to the front. Stragglers still in retreat down the slopes stopped in amazement, changed direction and ran to join us; men lying exhausted on the roadside jumped up, cheered, and joined the ranks. I looked back. Beneath the forest of upraised fists, what a strange band! Unshaven, unkempt; bloodstained, grimy. But, full of fight again, and marching on the road back.[88]

★

Sounding suspiciously like a Comintern propaganda creation, the story of what became known as 'the great rally' is actually corroborated by many witnesses and has become a powerful image of the British Battalion's involvement in Spain. Londoner John 'Bosco' Jones related the story in disbelief – and he was there:

I think maybe there was seventy-five of us . . . I'll never forget it. And as we walked up this main road, there are things I can't believe but . . . Someone burst out and started singing the Internationale. We were stone mad when I think about it. And as we moved up, troops from all around, Spaniards and all others, rallied. And we found ourselves in a small army! Going forward, with Cunningham in front . . . And the fascists fell back.[89]

Marching along the road, the volunteers fought their way to within 100 yards of the sunken road. The Rebel forces were caught unawares; finding enemy soldiers on their flanks, they assumed that fresh reinforcements had been brought up and retreated to Suicide Hill and the knoll. It was a lucky break for the battalion, but as Tom Wintringham later stated triumphantly:

A battalion that does not know how to be defeated deserves an occasional stroke of luck . . . The biggest and best organized drive that Franco had so far made had been stopped – within a few miles of its starting place. Arganda Bridge was ours. The Madrid-Valencia Road was ours. Madrid lived.[90]

As some in the battalion realised, it had been very close: 'The thing I remember most about the battle of the Jarama was looking down that road to Valencia and realizing that there was only me and two or three other fellows holding those fascists back . . . they could have *walked* into Madrid or Valencia just like that if they'd known, it was crazy!'[91] But the volunteers' courage, and the deception that enabled them to fool the Rebel forces into thinking they were faced by more than a handful of men, had held the line at a critical moment for the Republic.

During the night of 14–15 February, Spanish units were brought up, and the gap in the line was finally plugged. Both sides dug defensive fortifications and a stalemate ensued, which neither side was able to overcome. The positions remained virtually static for the rest of the war.

The three days of fighting from 12–14 February had seen the inexperienced British volunteers almost annihilated. During the first day alone the battalion had lost 225 out of its original 600 men.[92] Over the course of the battle, the Republic lost fifteen square kilometres of territory and at least 10,000 men, while the Nationalists lost more than 6000.[93] Contemporary accounts, written for audiences in Britain, portrayed the losses as a worthwhile sacrifice, for the Republican forces had achieved their principal objective in preventing the Rebel advance from cutting the vital road between Madrid and Valencia. The report of the battle in the *Daily Worker* understandably placed a strong emphasis on both the valour of the volunteers and the relevance of their sacrifice to those in Britain:

You have never read and you never will read a story greater than this.

When you have read it, you will know why there are no words in the English language capable of doing justice to this 'epic of valour unequalled in all history' – the epic of the Anglo-Irish Battalion of the International brigade at Arganda Bridge: The epic of British and Irish men who 'endured so that they might possibly prevent such things happening in our native land.' When you have read how the Anglo-Irish Battalion saved Arganda bridge – and saving it helped to save Madrid, and Britain and all Europe from war and death, you will understand why the young general in

command said that in all his career he had 'never seen such tenaciousness
and bravery'.

Nothing that we can do will ever fully repay our debt to these men who
fought for us and died for us.[94]

It was, as Hugh Thomas acknowledged, a 'brave performance'.[95] It may
even have been 'the greatest single contribution to the victory of Jarama,
and thus to the survival of Madrid', as one historian has claimed.[96] However,
the battle provided a brutal wake-up call for those who had naïvely believed
that the rightness of their cause would ensure victory. Accounts by those
that fought as foot-soldiers at Jarama often stress the blunders and the
carnage, rather than the valour:

Whenever I have met survivors of that battle, in hospitals or camps, Spain
or England, everyone with whom I have spoken has voiced, in one way or
another, the feeling that the ridge was untenable; that the three companies
should not have been left there, or that a mistake was made somewhere on
that first day which they, lying close to the earth among the bullets, could
not be sure about but suspect. The feeling of all my friends who survived
that fighting can be summarized in the name that they have given to their
position . . . They call it Suicide Hill.[97]

Scottish volunteer and Territorial Army veteran Frank McCusker put it
simply: 'It wisnae a battle at a', it wis a bloody slaughter as far as we were
concerned. They had everything and we had nothing . . . The International
Brigade got a real beatin' up there.'[98]

9

'The old men waiting patiently'

> On this now quiet Front each of us adjusted in his own way towards
> an acceptance of the filth and discomfort, lack of sleep and hard
> toil. One and all, we closed our minds to what we knew was sure
> to come sooner or later, probably sooner. Unable to wash, except
> rarely, we dug dirt from our eyes, nose and mouth, accepted –
> albeit reluctantly – the myriad flies which swarmed everywhere,
> especially in the discarded trench we used as a latrine, and
> compared dugouts as, not so long ago, we might have contrasted
> the relative merits of different beds.
>
> Fred Thomas, *To Tilt at Windmills*

The three days of fighting from 12–14 February 1937 had dealt the British
Battalion a near-mortal blow. Of the 630 men who had gone into action on
12 February, only 80 were left unscathed when the battle ended three days
later.[1] None of their commanding officers, from company level upwards,
were still in the line. Tom Wintringham, the battalion commander, was in
hospital with a leg wound. Kit Conway and Bill Briskey had been killed and
Harry Fry had been captured, his fate uncertain. Bert Overton, who had
deserted his post, was in hospital, awaiting an imminent investigation into
his actions. The political commissars had fared little better: battalion
commissar George Aitken and No. 3 Company commissar Bob Elliott were
both still on the front line, but Ralph Campeau had been killed, Donald
Renton had been captured and Thomas Degnan had been hospitalised with
a lung injury.

The dismal task of sending letters of condolence was begun. Many were
written personally by Harry Pollitt; the letter received by the family of Allan
Craig, a volunteer from Glasgow who died in hospital from his wounds on
22 February, is typical:

Comrade Craig, together with so many others of the finest and bravest section of the British people, has played a magnificent part in preventing the fascist hordes from gaining ground and cutting the Valencia road to Madrid.

It can truly be said that it is the British section of the International Brigade which has been most instrumental in saving Madrid in the critical battle, and the courage and heroism of the brave fighters for liberty is beyond all words, fighting as they were against the almost overwhelming forces of German and Moorish troops.

Our Comrade Craig's name will live for ever in the annals of history as one who saw his duty to the peace loving forces of the world, and who gave his all to save the peoples of Spain and the world from brutal fascist oppression.[2]

However, confusion and mistakes regarding the disappearance or death of brigade members were by no means unknown and delays were inevitable, adding to relatives' heartache. Confirmation of the deaths of a number of brigaders at Jarama did not arrive in Britain until July 1937, while announcements of the deaths of volunteers such as David Mackenzie, reported in the *Daily Worker* as having been killed in Madrid on 5 December 1936, later turned out to be mistaken.[3] As one volunteer complained, 'obituaries have been written and much misery caused – only to find they had the initials wrong or that the man was on long leave and the company records were destroyed and he was written down as "missing".'[4]

To help replenish the battalion's numbers, some eighty new volunteers from Madrigueras were rushed to the front, even though most of them were yet to receive training. Taxi driver Harry Stratton, who had only arrived at the start of February, had not even handled a rifle. He did not consider this to be much of a handicap, as 'Jock McCrae had taught me rifle drill with a walking stick on the train going up.'[5]

Fortunately, on 16 February, the British sector on the Jarama front was strengthened by the arrival of a new battalion of volunteers who had come to join the 15th International Brigade: 'the American battalion, the Lincolns, had reached the Brigade.'[6] Dressed in their First World War uniforms, the Americans made an arresting sight:

They came marching along the road, only about three hundred yards from the Fascist lines, concealed by a shoulder of the hillside and a bend in the

road, and presented a startling appearance as many of them were wearing
the 'dough-boy' uniforms of the 1914–18 war. There were about five or six
hundred men dressed in what seemed to me an utterly bizarre costume
belonging to the days of silent films. And here they came, striding along
with the apparent intention of proceeding straight on into the fascist lines,
just around the corner of the road. The explanation, as it turned out, was
comparatively simple. The organization in the USA knew that there was a
shortage of uniforms in Spain, so they had followed the simple expedient
of outfitting the men from US Army surplus stores.[7]

The Americans did not have to wait long for their first taste of action.
As they dug protective trenches, Italian bombers passed overhead dropping
small objects. 'Lookee, boss,' cried black American volunteer Oliver Law
to his commander, Robert Hale Merriman, a graduate student at the
University of California, 'they're dropping propaganda leaflets.' Almost
immediately, a series of huge explosions rocked their positions. As silence
gradually returned, Law exclaimed, 'Boss Merriman, them sure was
powerful leaflets.'[8]

On 27 February, General Gal, newly promoted to the rank of divisional
commander, ordered an attack by the 15th Brigade on the strongly held
front between San Martín de la Vega and the hills of Pingarrón. In what
was later described as a 'well planned, but poorly executed' attack, the
battalions were faced by such well-directed Nationalist machine-gun fire
that many volunteers simply refused to advance. Those who tried were
shot to pieces.

We were all in trenches, we were told on the morning that there would be
air cover, there would be a bombardment. There was neither. We were just
rushed over the top to face crossfire and machine-guns. It was a slaughter.
We didn't stand a cat in hell's chance! I saw lads, my comrades that I'd learnt
to love, die and some of these boys never fired a bloody shot.[9]

Merriman himself had originally refused to give the order to advance,
believing it to be 'a pointless exercise in suicide'.[10] However, he was
overruled by Vladimir Čopić (now brigade commander), who ordered Dave
Springhall and Lieutenant George Wattis, a highly experienced British Army
veteran, to ensure that Merriman either obeyed the order or was replaced.
Merriman managed to persuade both Springhall and Wattis of the futility

of the action, but they were unable to countermand Ĉopić. Instead, they nobly remained with the Americans and joined them as they went 'over the top'. Merriman and Springhall were both wounded almost immediately, though Wattis, showing impressive coolness under fire, continued to urge the reluctant troops forward.[11] The Americans suffered particularly heavily in the attack, losing more than 120 killed and 175 wounded. Twelve British were killed instantly, with another twenty falling during the day.[12] The advance was a disaster, 'because there's no way you can send men against machine-guns without losing some. It was just physically impossible.'[13]

With the deadlock unbroken, both sides dug into increasingly well-protected trenches. However, the loss of life continued, with snipers taking a steady toll: one unfortunate volunteer 'was killed standing near the battalion headquarters by a bullet which entered the right hip, fractured the pelvis and came out through the testicles'.[14] Some volunteers were lost taking foolish risks, even if from the best intentions: Bernard Bolger, known as 'The Admiral', was killed in no man's land while searching for letters or papers he could recover and send back to the relatives of the fallen.[15] The Hackney bookmaker had been promoted to battalion adjutant in February, but as an official note admitted, 'this comrade did not appear to be at all suited to his position.'[16]

More significant in its impact on the battalion was the injury in March 1937 of the highly popular and recently promoted Captain Jock Cunningham, who was hit in the side by a machine gun in an attempt to clear a Nationalist-occupied trench.[17] Cunningham was replaced as battalion commander by the 'quick-tempered' and relatively inexperienced Fred Copeman, which caused great concern among the company commanders.[18] A 'natural rebel', he was a divisive figure, described by Gurney as 'one of the strangest characters I knew at Madrigueras . . . an exceedingly large and brutish man . . . everyone was frightened of him as he charged around the place threatening to beat everyone's brains out, and looking as though he was quite capable of doing it.'[19] One stretcher-bearer at Jarama was similarly unimpressed: 'I think Copeman was a bit of a nut.'[20] Yet, despite a tendency to use his fists to instil discipline that ensured that he was never universally popular, many volunteers held Copeman in respect. The Scot John Tunnah, no admirer of Copeman as a soldier, nevertheless believed that he 'held it all together' at Jarama.[21]

While new arrivals had gone some way to restoring the battalion's numbers, repairing the damage inflicted on morale by the appalling level of casualties was a different matter.[22] A handwritten note by Aitken acknowledged both the loss of morale and its obvious causes:

> Many comrades are beginning to show signs of exhaustion and nervous strain. The signs of nervous strain on the part of many is no doubt partly due to the fact that the vast majority of the leading forces in the battalion have been killed or wounded since the beginning of the present action.[23]

'After what they had seen on the Jarama,' many volunteers developed a disenchantment with the war.[24] 'Morale was very bad' and the surviving brigaders were feeling 'very depressed . . . we'd had a right hiding . . . so many lads had been lost . . . a lot of the officers and sergeants and people had been killed.'[25] As one Mancunian recognised, 'the symptoms of this lack of discipline after Jarama were disinterest and no enthusiasm to fight. They never refused an order but they didn't fight with enthusiasm like they did in the early days, there was a sort of apathy.'[26] So bad was morale that one volunteer believed that almost half of the volunteers had 'had enough, [and that] it was on the cards that we might have retreated out of it'. Faced with the very real prospect of being killed, a number of volunteers took the decision to leave the front without permission. As Frank Ryan admitted: 'Some grumbled and groused. Some begged for leave; some took it without asking.'[27]

Copeman noted worriedly that the desertions spread right through the battalion: 'groups of men, led by some of the finest members of the battalion, were leaving the line without permission.'[28] Many of the desertions were short-lived – to the nearby towns of Morata, Chinchón and Aranjuez, or to Madrid itself – but not all:

> For many an unauthorized weekend in Madrid was not enough; they were determined to get out of the country altogether. Some of the deserters got as far as Barcelona, where they threw themselves on the mercy of the British Consulate, and at least one man that I know of made his way from Jarama all the way back to Figueras, over the Pyrenees into France, and eventually back to England.[29]

The volunteers' reasons for leaving the line were understood: 'the effect of heavy casualties, lack of sleep, bad food, living continuously in the front line, was in my opinion quite natural,' said Copeman.[30] However, military discipline dictated that desertion could not be condoned, whether the men had volunteered or not. 'The question of leave is not merely a question of "humanity", it is a military and political question,' declared the Welsh political commissar Will Paynter, who had been sent out by the Party to help restore morale and address the problems facing the battalion.[31] Just as in any other army deserters, if caught, were brought back to the battalion. As one Manchester trade unionist explained, 'Some got away and some didn't. Some were snaffled and put in prison for a time. But it was like any other army, if you deserted and got caught you were punished.'[32]

Opinion on how to respond to the spate of desertions differed between the Brigade leadership, with whom the battalion had developed a 'bad name', and the British leaders of the battalion itself. Copeman complained that 'a man did not become a traitor to the Republic simply because he found it impossible to overcome a desire to get to Madrid.' His claim that 'at Brigade headquarters the political side were demanding ruthless action'[33] was corroborated by George Aitken, who was approached at Jarama by higher officers and a civilian on the idea of trying, and possibly shooting, some of the deserters:

> I said, 'You'll do nothing so long as I'm here. You'll certainly do nothing of the kind.' It would have been absolutely disastrous. I said, 'All these men are volunteers from Britain. If ever it got back from here that you were shooting volunteers, it would be absolutely catastrophic, we're trying to recruit people'.[34]

Aitken maintained categorically that he remained 'totally opposed' to the shooting of volunteers, and he adds weight to Copeman's claim that there were bitter fights behind the scenes to resist this ruthless response.[35] John Tunnah recalled 'demands that a death penalty should be introduced for deserters or cowardice' but insisted that these calls were resisted by the battalion's leadership, who recognised that they were dealing with 'men, some young, some old, who weren't soldiers, who didn't know what they were getting into and seemed to be a bit surprised when they found that the fascists were firing real bullets at them.' Tunnah claimed that 'neither Copeman, nor Sam Wild would have any part of this and they argued very, very early on, they both argued, very violently . . . against any death penalty for any reason.'[36]

The response of the Communist Party leadership in Britain to the deserters was less draconian than that suggested by some of the Brigade commanders. Believing that the British and Irish volunteers were, in the main, good anti-fascists who had been placed under intolerable conditions, the Party sent out 'the cream of its leadership' to try and lift the troops' spirits.[37] On one of these visits in March, several volunteers were taken out of the line for a rousing pep talk by Harry Pollitt himself, who reminded them how vitally important their contribution was in the war against fascism. In general, the volunteers spoke very positively about Pollitt's appearance, for 'it gives you a lot of confidence when these people come and visit you.'[38] Many were impressed with Pollitt's oratorical skills:

> I remember Harry Pollitt came out and, man, were we naïve, but he moved us. What we really needed was guns, but he spoke to us, and what a speaker! The best I've bloody heard in my life. He'd bring tears to a glass eye.[39]

However, not all were so affected. Manchester volunteer Walter Greenhalgh felt the effect of Pollitt's pep-talk was actually rather limited and believed that 'the euphoria only lasted a very short time.'[40] Greenhalgh's description of Pollitt's visit is very similar to that of author and poet Laurie Lee, which suggested that Pollitt was able almost to bewitch the volunteers with rhetoric, until the end of the speech when 'the spell and magic' broke. He describes the brigaders:

> Plucking at his sleeves and pouring out their grievances, asking to be sent back home. 'It ain't good enough, you know. I bin out 'ere over nine months. Applied for leave and didn't get no answer. When they going to do something comrade? . . . eh?'[41]

While Lee's memoir is partly fictional, it is undeniable that during the long period on the Jarama front 'one of the biggest political problems facing the British concerned leave and repatriation.' The problem was compounded by a number of the British military and political leaders who had given unauthorised promises of leave following a fixed period of service in Spain.[42] Considerable disillusionment developed from the realisation that these promises were unlikely to be fulfilled:

> It was only now that people began to realize that nothing had been said in King Street about coming home, or even being given local leave, and no

one had had time to think of it before. Now that the Battalion had been reduced to the level of a mere holding force on an inactive front we began to feel that the granting of leave was possible and that we deserved it. Approximately 800 men had passed through the Battalion between 15th February and 15th March, and now less than 200 men were left in the line. None of us had enjoyed a night's sleep out of uniform or a decent hot meal for several months. There was no relief from the continual fear produced by snipers and occasional mortar shells. We . . . began to feel that we were in a trap from which there was no escape.[43]

As one Scottish volunteer realised, 'while you could volunteer in, you couldn't volunteer out.'[44] Bernard Knox, who had been badly wounded at Boadilla, put it rather more bluntly: 'The soldier is in it for the duration; the only way he can get out is on a stretcher, or in a box.'[45]

As the time spent in the trenches lengthened, many volunteers found that the shift from intense action to 'humdrum trench warfare', in which 'the all-out offensive and defensive warfare of the early days had been replaced by a far more static form of confrontation', offered no improvement in their conditions and did nothing to lift their spirits.[46] Even the 'official' history of the 15th International Brigade recognised the disheartening impact that the long period at Jarama had on the volunteers:

Trench warfare . . . tested morale almost as severely as did the big battles of February. Monotony can often be as trying as heavy fighting. As the long vigil by the Jarama – the longest on record of any unit – dragged on, wall newspapers recorded less the enthusiasms of young recruits and more the cynicisms of 'old soldiers'.[47]

Clearly the political commissars had a tough job on their hands to maintain morale. However, it was to the military leaders, Fred Copeman and Jock Cunningham, that the practicalities of rebuilding the battalion fell.[48] Their first task was to make sure that the trenches were deep and sophisticated enough to offer protection from Nationalist machine guns and artillery shells – no easy task in the crumbing Jarama soil, which 'collapsed at the first artillery bombardment'.[49] Despite their efforts, as time in the trenches wore on, enthusiasm for digging decidedly waned. Copeman admitted, '[It's] no small matter to get men to dig when they've been in the line some thirty days without a break.'[50]

Life in the trenches was made immeasurably worse by the appalling weather during March and April 1937. It rained relentlessly for long periods, making it virtually impossible to ever get warm and dry: 'We just sat in the trench and the rain poured in . . . you sat there and let the puddle form . . . it was cold, it was damp,' said former 'ragged-trousered philanthropist' James Brown.[51] *Daily Worker* journalist Claud Cockburn (whose writings from Spain were published under his *nom de plume*, Frank Pitcairn) was left in no doubt that this greatly added to the volunteers' misery, though his response suggests a certain lack of sympathy:

> It rained and it rained and it rained. They had all got the impression that they were going to sunny Spain. They'd all seen the posters. And the main source of discontent and grumbling and so on – all armies grumble – but the grumblings of these people were the feeling that somehow they had been swindled by the weather.[52]

The rain and freezing wind made it very difficult for the volunteers to keep the trenches – and themselves – clean. Orders were issued from battalion headquarters warning that 'The attention of all comrades is drawn to the regulations concerning the use of latrines. Only the latrines provided must be used. The co-operation of all comrades in this connection will do much to preserve the health of the battalion.'[53]

However, a battalion report admitted that 'there were times when, in spite of urgent need, there was a reluctance to let the pants down in the face of the icy wind, and one would try to wait for at least a momentary let-up in the rain'.[54] Shortages of paper added to the discomfort, with one volunteer recalling 'one visit to the latrine when all I had was one cigarette paper'.[55]

The lack of clean clothes and washing facilities meant that the familiar scourge of trench warfare – body-lice – quickly infested everyone. One ex-sailor had experienced rats and fleas, 'but never had I had before the dreaded experience of lice on my body . . . [it] was the most lowering form of human existence.'[56] Another wrote a sardonic letter to a friend back home:

> I am not wounded. I am but lousy . . . I have, luckily, escaped anything serious up to now. But lice, no. They have at last overcome me. What frightful company to have thrust upon you! And there is no way of getting rid of them, until we move right out of the front line. And so each morning begins with a delousing exercise. Doesn't this appeal to you?[57]

At first, there was general embarrassment and an understandable unwillingness to admit to carrying the parasites: '[you] wanted the confirmation that other people had them before you'd admit that you had them [yourself] and everybody was lying about it.'[58] But as the outbreak quickly spread, the desire for even momentary relief from the terrible itching of the bites soon overcame pride or squeamishness:

> By this time everyone up in the line was infested with lice: translucent, yellow brutes which looked like sugar ants. They lived principally in the seams of any garment where they remained comparatively quiescent during the day, becoming violently active at night. Their bite produced large, raised weals that itched like hell. Up to now I had been able to avoid this particular form of misery. Down at Brigade HQ it was easy to keep clean and wash clothes regularly. But up in line it was a very different situation. Most of the men up there had not moved out of the trenches for more than sixty days. Their bodies and their clothes were filthy. Water was scarce as it had to be carried up over the hills and Gal had ordered that no fit man was to be allowed out of the trenches, even for an hour, owing to the shortage of man-power. There was no insecticide and the only effective method of dealing with the lice was to run all the seams of your clothing through a candle flame at regular intervals. The lice popped and hissed in a most disgusting way as they and their eggs hit the flame, but the treatment was partially effective. It was a most depressing business to see civilized men squatting around hunting through their clothes and persons in pursuit of vermin like a bunch of apes.[59]

The insanitary conditions of the trenches meant that, inevitably, there were outbreaks of disease, such as a major spate of scabies in May.[60] Of greater concern were typhoid and dysentery, which had the potential to substantially weaken the battalion's fighting ability. Battalion orders of 15 May complained that:

> Waste food is still being deposited indiscriminately in and around the lines and already a plague of flies are [sic] infecting the sector. These flies are a deadly menace to health being Typhoid and dysentery germ carriers.
>
> In the interests of the health of the battalion, company commanders and other responsible comrades will take immediate steps to stop this criminal

behaviour. The offenders will be brought before the battalion commander and disciplinary action taken against them.[61]

The issue cropped up regularly in orders. Moreover, there appeared to be a great unwillingness among volunteers to be inoculated and 'many had to be detained in the disciplinary Battalion before they finally agreed to the injections.'[62]

The poor quality of the food, which had caused so much grumbling while the volunteers were training at Madrigueras, became an issue once again:

> Food was beginning to get worse. Mule flesh seemed to be the only meat available. This had a tendency to turn into small lumps of rubber when cooked. I never succeeded in swallowing it, though I often used it as chewing gum.[63]

While Copeman's claim that 'it was now usual to receive soup literally packed with maggots' is probably an exaggeration, at least one volunteer described throwing away food that contained larvae.[64] One Greek Cypriot, utterly fed up, lost his temper and threw his ration over the top of the trench, before launching into a furious tirade about the terrible food and cooks. His company commander responded by sending him to the Brigade base at Morata for punishment. However, his superiors at the base, probably having some sympathy with his complaints, responded leniently and he was sentenced only to two days' 'chores'.[65]

Problems with drunkenness also reappeared:

> Another way of surviving the boredom was by drinking. There was frequently a lack of food on Jarama, but never any shortage of liquor. There was a ration issue of red wine, and in addition supplies of prohibited brandy and anis were always available.[66]

During June, Bill Meredith, the commander of No. 2 Company, reported that five of his men had been drunk, complaining that 'fighting has been going on in the trench and some drastic action should be taken as an example to the rest of the Battalion.' The men received ten days in a labour battalion and had five days' pay stopped.[67] But while the spate of drunkenness was not condoned, it was widely understood.

Sometimes comrades became the worse for drink. To deny that would be denying human nature . . . Somehow or other one could not be too hard on the few comrades who drank a glass too much at times. One never knew what the next day would bring.[68]

What the discontented volunteers really wanted was to get out of the line for a few days, an opportunity to take off their lice-infested uniforms and clean themselves up. The Brigade leadership were fully aware of this, but with manpower critically short, it was no easy task. However, on 5 March, the battalion was, at last, relieved from front-line duties and sent to Morata de Tajuña for rest and recuperation and a clean-up. 'It was great to get a good wash, but shaving was a painful process. I was the fourteenth to use the same razor-blade, and I had a three week growth of beard,' remembered one London volunteer.[69] And the period of leave was painfully short. Only four days later the men were returned to the front.

Discipline remained a problem as the period spent in the front line continued to lengthen. Will Paynter tried to arrange periods of leave for those stuck in the line for week after week, but found that this could only be achieved in the unlikely event that there were men available to replace them. Finally, though, during April, welcome news arrived that the volunteers were to be withdrawn from the front once and for all:

In the midst of so much demoralization and boredom, a rumour began to grow that our Brigade was due to be relieved for rest and reconstruction. We knew that there was a build-up of new recruits around Albacete. There were all sorts of stories about the new Officers' School said to have been started under Merriman, Wintringham and others who had recovered from wounds received at Jarama. And there seemed to be a lot of activity around Brigade HQ which could indicate some sort of re-organization. Finally, orders came through one morning that we were to be relieved that night by the *Quatorzième*, which threw the whole Battalion into a fever of excitement.[70]

On 28 April 1937, after seventy-five days at the front, the battalions of the 15th International Brigade prepared to be taken out of the line.[71] Before leaving, an 'impressive memorial service' was conducted by George Aitken and Fred Copeman for the members of the battalion killed at Jarama and a stone memorial, in the shape of a five-pointed star, was erected.[72] Aitken gave an eulogy to the fallen:

> They were our friends. We had come to know them intimately. They shared our joys and our sorrows in the days of training. They fought side by side with us in fierce battles. They lived with us day and night in the trenches, shared the same dug-outs, stood on guard by our side, shivered with us in the cold nights and huddled close to us when on many a night the rain poured down in torrents.
>
> How could we help growing fond of them and sorrowing at their passing. They lie here now sleeping their long last sleep.
>
> But let us not think they have laid down their lives in vain. Their sacrifice prevented the fascists gaining Madrid and has made it almost impossible for them to do so now. Through their magnificent courage and steadfastness they, in a period of great difficulty, paved the way for the new victories now being recorded and for the final defeat and driving out of Spain of the beasts of fascism.[73]

Following a moment's silence, 'while still the bullets whistled overhead and cracked around . . . the two companies of British and two of Spanish troops came to attention' and the service was concluded. The men were then withdrawn to Alcalá de Henares, where a decent meal was the main priority of most, though a number took the opportunity to get 'blind, paralytic drunk'.[74]

This precious time away from the front was however dominated by a battalion meeting, held during the evenings of 27 and 28 April, to discuss the actions of Bert Overton, who 'had been taken to the Brigade to face some pretty serious charges, first in connection with the early battles, second, on his rank and, third, on his conduct while in hospital'.[75]

The meeting was chaired by Bert Williams, previously Communist Party organiser for the Midlands, who had replaced George Aitken as battalion commissar the previous month when Aitken was promoted to brigade commissar. Aitken himself outlined how the terrified Overton had 'lost his head' while at the front and how his actions, many in the battalion felt, had directly led to the capture of Harold Fry's Machine-Gun Company.[76] Though it is unlikely that his presence would have made any difference to the verdict, Overton was not at the meeting, and therefore had no opportunity to defend himself.

During a predictably hostile meeting it was alleged by members of his own company that, in addition to his demonstration of cowardice in the face of the enemy, Overton had thrown a Mills bomb into the company's ammunition dump in order to justify the retreat.[77] Overton's actions after the battle did not help his case: there was general outrage when it emerged that while in hospital convalescing, he had promoted himself from sergeant to captain and had since been claiming the appropriate pay.[78] The battalion decided overwhelmingly that Overton's actions warranted a court-martial. This was duly held at Brigade headquarters, in front of Kerrigan and Aitken, and Overton was convicted of desertion in the face of the enemy, stripped of his officer's rank and sentenced to a period of service in a labour battalion.[79] A week later he was sent with a punishment battalion to the front, where he was 'killed by a shell while carrying munitions to a forward position'.[80]

It has been alleged that Overton was either murdered, or deliberately put in a position where he was certain to be killed.[81] While there is no evidence to support the first accusation, the second probably has some truth to it. Although the odds facing any member of the battalion in the front line were probably not much better, working in no man's land, repairing barbed wire defences and digging trenches, is obviously extremely dangerous. After the terrible blood-letting at Jarama, it seems unlikely that many volunteers would have grieved for Overton.

The British brigaders' relief at their time out of the line was, again, to be short-lived. On 4 May the battalion's leave was cancelled and it was returned to its former positions.[82] This bitter blow caused much resentment, prompting Alec McDade to pen the lyrics to a satirical song, sung to the tune of 'Red River Valley':[83]

> There's a valley in Spain called Jarama,
> That's a place that we all know so well,
> For 'tis there that we wasted our manhood,
> And most of our old age as well.
>
> From this valley they tell us we're leaving,
> But don't hasten to bid us adieu,
> For e'en though we make our departure,
> We'll be back in an hour or two.

Oh we're proud of our British Battalion
And the marathon record it's made,
Please do us this little favour,
And take this last word to Brigade:

'You will never be happy with strangers,
They would not understand you as we,
So remember the Jarama valley,
And the old men that wait patiently.'

The battalion remained in the line until 17 June 1937 when, finally, they bade farewell to the Jarama valley for good, and were taken by lorry to their new base at Mondéjar, fifty kilometres east of Madrid. Mondéjar was 'a small dusty village on the plateau above the [Tajuña] river, with cafes around the square and the inevitable dominating church' which had been virtually levelled by local Anarchists.[84] Walter Gregory was one of many who didn't take to Mondéjar, finding it 'filthy . . . hardly a scenic delight'.[85]

Following their relief from front-line service, the problems of poor food, boredom and, above all, lack of leave, could however be overcome, temporarily at least. That a certain level of disillusionment had set in during the long period in the line is hardly surprising. The horrific levels of casualties in the battle itself, and the conditions in the trenches in which they festered for nearly four months, would have sorely tested any army. 'We have had difficulties but these are due principally to the long period in the line,' argued George Aitken.[86] And while many in the battalion were clearly at an extremely low ebb, some volunteers accepted the difficulties phlegmatically. John 'Bosco' Jones later argued that much of the Jarama period had not been as intolerable as they had believed at the time:

We'd made it quite snug and food was bearable. Enough food. For wartime conditions of soldiers it wasn't too bad. We had a shower bath that used to come round during the day. You know we needed it about once a week. We had a barber that used to come down once a week. We had a dentist. We got all that treatment. You know, it was quite liveable.

However, Jones continued pointedly, 'no one wanted to stay in trenches for two months. With no leave.'[87]

Finally, at Mondéjar, a number were at last able to take a few days' rest in nearby Madrid. Comfortable billets in beautiful countryside soon helped to improve morale. Training resumed in earnest and the battalion remained at Mondéjar until the end of June 1937. The battle for Brunete, held in the full glare of the Spanish summer sun, awaited.

While conditions facing the battalion during their long vigil on the Jarama front had been cold, wet, monotonous and often dangerous, they were considerably better than those facing their comrades in the Machine-Gun Company. Most had been killed outright: 'Out of the original 120 finally some twenty-nine of us were herded together.'[88] The survivors were surrounded by Spanish troops and asked if they were Russians.[89]

> Somebody spoke and I heard a voice say, 'Don't shoot,' they thought we were Russians with the uniforms at first. Somebody shouted, 'Ingles?' If it hadn't been for that, Fry would have been shot and we would have been shot one at a time . . . They were going to shoot us. We were all lined up.[90]

Having steeled themselves for their certain fate, the reprieved prisoners were able to breathe a temporary sigh of relief. Moroccan soldiers on horseback arrived to take charge of them and after a thorough search and the removal of their money, valuables, ammunition and rifles, the prisoners had their hands bound and were quickly led away from the front. At first, 'whips were employed very readily on those who lagged behind,' though when it was discovered that the prisoners were English, not Russian, the beatings and abuse stopped.[91] Nevertheless, several did not survive the forced march:

> When we were taken prisoner we were compelled to march through this valley in such a manner that we were under fire from our own line. There was a lot of dead ground in this area and the Fascists who were escorting us, while able to keep a certain amount of cover themselves, compelled us to appear in the sight of our own comrades who were manning the sunken road. A number of our comrades were killed in the course of this march through Death Valley.[92]

At least one of the prisoners was killed by a stray bullet from the Republican lines, while others were cold-bloodedly executed by their captors.[93] One prisoner was given permission to smoke, but 'as he reached in his tunic-pocket for a cigarette, the guard who had given permission riddled his stomach with bullets from a sub-machine gun. The hand shot out of the tunic-pocket, holding a cigarette.'[94] Another volunteer was killed by the same burst of machine-gun fire.[95] When Edward Dickenson, company lieutenant and second-in-command, protested over the shooting, he was taken aside and shot through the head:

> Being taken with his own papers still on him Ted was singled out by the Fascists and told he would have to fight for Fascism or die. That man chose death. He marched up to a tree like a soldier on parade, did a military about-turn, and said: 'Salud, comrades!' the second he died. I felt like fainting.[96]

Company commander Harold Fry was lucky not to suffer the same fate. He was initially identified as an officer due to his uniform, but all the prisoners denied this, claiming that Fry was wearing the uniform of the company secretary. Fry probably owed his life to the quick thinking of Dickenson, who had deliberately ripped the insignia from his comrade's uniform when they were captured.[97] The outraged and horror-struck survivors were then marched to a temporary holding area for prisoners in a barracks at San Martín de la Vega, where they spent what most expected to be their last night. Their fears appeared to be confirmed by the visit of a priest, who informed them that they would all be shot in the morning.

Whether the priest lied deliberately or not, he was mistaken. Having been held in the barracks for two days, the prisoners were moved to a jail in Navalcarnero, thirty kilometres south-west of Madrid, where they were interrogated, fingerprinted and their heads were shaved. Here the sixteen British prisoners were paraded standing on the back of a truck, guarded by proud members of the *Guardia Civil* and filmed by Movietone News. A still image from the newsreel appeared in the *Daily Mail*, accompanied by a typically hostile caption:

> These are the first pictures – exclusive to 'The Daily Mail' – of some of the misguided and hapless British prisoners who were captured by General Franco's forces on the Jarama front. They were sent out to Spain by Communists with promises of work at £6 a week, but the first most of them knew of their real fate was when they were given arms and drafted to the Reds' front line.[98]

The prisoners were held at Navalcarnero for four days, nine to a cell, before being transferred to a concentration camp in an old dilapidated factory in the town of Talavera de la Reina, some eighty kilometres further south-east into the Nationalist-held zone. Here they were worked hard for ten hours a day, with little food and the most basic living and sanitary facilities. Several were still carrying wounds sustained at Jarama: Donald Renton had been wounded in the legs, Harold Fry had a broken arm and both Jimmy Rutherford and George Watters had been beaten virtually unconscious.[99] Abuses continued and many of those who had initially been in reasonable health soon fell ill from stomach and lung diseases. Due to the overcrowding and filth, soon 'everyone was dirty and covered in lice.'[100]

> Our conditions were almost unendurable. We were starved. Our only food was two helpings of beans per day, served in the crudest fashion possible. In our cells we slept on the ground without straw or covering. Some of us who had overcoats when we were captured had been relieved of them by the Moors, and our suffering during the cold nights was almost unendurable. We huddled together for warmth. The sanitary arrangements were primitive and during the whole term of our imprisonment we had no facilities for a decent wash.[101]

The weekend following their arrival at Talavera, the prisoners were visited by press reporters sympathetic to the Nationalists, and lurid accounts of the volunteers and their reasons for fighting in Spain appeared in the world's newspapers. Notable among the ludicrous claims were that the company's North American former boxer, Yank Levy, had been recruited in a brothel and that Jimmy Rutherford had been 'ruthlessly kidnapped from his parents at the tender age of nineteen'. Rutherford later dryly remarked how the reporters were 'filming us doing all sorts of things, but neglecting to film our prisons'. Nevertheless, the publicity led to somewhat improved conditions.[102] The prisoners' situation was helped further by a visit from the international correspondent of the *Daily Telegraph*, Philip Pembroke Stephens, who had heard that there were British and Irish prisoners in the camp. One grateful inmate remembered how Stephens did what he could to help the British, though he 'made no secret of the fact that he himself supported Franco'.[103]

The prisoners were taken individually to be interrogated by Don Pablo Merry del Val, the son of the former Spanish ambassador in London, who was a lawyer and 'a senior official in the Nationalist Ministry of Press and Propaganda'.[104] Del Val spoke impeccable English in an upper-class accent, having been educated at Stonyhurst, the same Jesuit-run English public school as a number of Rebel officers, including the head of the Nationalist press office, Luis Bolín.[105] A report from one of the prisoners describes how del Val told them 'that they had one chance to save themselves from being shot dead, and this was to fight on the fascist side against the Reds'.[106]

The interrogations were detailed and thorough, covering the volunteers' initial decision to fight, the journey to Spain and life in the brigades, including training and the role of particular individuals. Prisoners soon discovered that del Val was extremely well-informed: he knew for instance that the first commander of the battalion had been Wilf Macartney, whom he also correctly identified as the author of *Walls Have Mouths*. Wisely, the prisoners played down their roles in the battalion. Archie Williams pretended he had come to Spain looking for work, rather than to join the Republican Army, and claimed to be happy to have been captured by the Nationalists. But he was very careful not to answer many of the specific or incriminating questions put to him.[107]

Subjected to frequent death threats from the guards – '*Esta noche todos muerto*' – the prisoners could do nothing but watch as Spanish Republican prisoners were taken out of the prison every night in a van – which became known as the 'Agony Wagon' – and not brought back again.[108]

A covered Chevrolet truck drew up at the prison gate, guards came out. They called the name of the victim, handcuffed him, packed him into a lorry which drew off followed by a sedan, containing an officer and priest. Five minutes later a squad of Legionaries marched up the cemetery road to a bullet-riddled stone wall. A ragged volley of shots cracked out; a blood stained stretcher is put to us again and a quiet body is dumped into the pit.[109]

Understandably, the constant executions had a severely depressing effect on the prisoners. Not only did they realise it could soon be their fate, but also many of the executed Spaniards and Internationals had become their friends. Yet, despite the terrible conditions, some prisoners appear to have maintained a remarkable *sang-froid* and brave efforts were made to keep up morale. Under the influence of 'Yank' Levy, a baseball game was held on 19 May, between teams formed from inmates (Stanley) Giles' Gorillas and (James) Pugh's Panthers, 'two well known giants of the baseball world' as

Archie Williams recounted in his diary: 'The gates were opened early and by ten o'clock the crowd was immense at least 7 Spaniards and 14 hens were in a fever of expectation. The two cockroaches were also in a fever of expectation but of a different kind.'[110]

Somewhat rough and ready, 'a pick-shaft was the bat and two rolled up shirts were the ball. Running the bases one had to wind his way round the plentiful lumps of cow-dung.' Williams' notebook relates that Giles' team won, by fifteen to nine. Unfortunately the Nationalist authorities felt that the energy that had been expended on the game could be better used in the dismal task of digging graves for those executed in the camp.

After three bleak months at Talavera, the prisoners were transferred to Salamanca jail to be tried collectively by a military court for 'aiding a military rebellion'. 'In other words,' pointed out Donald Renton, 'the Fascist characters who had risen in military rebellion against the legally elected Spanish Republican Government were the same characters charging us with military rebellion.'[111] The brigaders were 'represented' by a lieutenant in the Spanish Foreign Legion, who remained silent throughout the proceedings. The trial was conducted entirely in Spanish, and as the translator provided spoke almost no English, the defendants understood virtually nothing of the proceedings. None of the prisoners were given an opportunity to speak, even if they had possessed enough Spanish to be able to do so.[112] In line with Franco's proclamation of 9 March declaring that any foreigners captured under arms would be shot, five prisoners received death sentences. The remainder were given twenty years' imprisonment, with two sentenced to serve their entire term in solitary confinement.[113]

Following the trial, the prisoners were transferred under Italian guard to the Model prison in Salamanca, where they were told the sentences were to be carried out. Their faint hopes were not improved by the shooting of thirty-seven Spanish Republicans on the day of their arrival. However, unbeknown to the prisoners, negotiations were under way between the Republicans and Nationalists, via the League of Nations, over a possible prisoner exchange. While discussions continued, the men remained in the prison, five still under sentence of death, until May 1937, when they were finally informed that Franco had magnanimously decided to pardon them and that they were to be exchanged for a similar number of Italians held by the Republicans.

The captured volunteers left Salamanca on 27 May by truck, arriving at Fuenterrabia, near the border with France, at 10 a.m. the following day, where they were paraded in front of a huge crowd and the world's media.[114] The Franco regime was determined to make the most of the propaganda opportunity: 'The fascist officers roared *"Viva Espana, arriba Franco!"* Comrade Stuldreher [actually George Stuhldreer, from Tottenham in London] was stood in front of a camera and forced to shout the same words.'[115] The transcript of 'a short address read to the men on behalf of the Generalissimo', a typical example of Francoist propaganda, was printed later in *The Times*:

You have been induced by false propaganda to take arms against our cause. You have been told that you were serving the cause of humanity and justice against tyranny and oppression. Your experience has enabled you to judge for yourselves [the] attacks on unarmed populations, the violation of women, the looting of sacred treasures in the churches and museums. Many of you were present at the execrable scenes which demonstrated that you were not fighting for a just cause, but for foreign Muscovite barbarism. The human feeling that you have encountered in the National camp, the respect for life and conscience, have shown you that civilisation is on this side, that generosity and chivalry, traditional among the Spanish people, are honoured today more than ever by the Spain of Franco. We could have kept you as hostages, or at least have attempted to exchange you for our prisoners. But Franco is not accustomed to commercialising his generosity.[116]

Just prior to their release, the prisoners were forced to sign two documents: first, an agreement not to return to Spain and second, a letter addressed to Franco personally, stating they had not been badly treated. The wording used by some prisoners was suitably ambiguous: 'We are overjoyed at what we have seen in Spain. We thank you for our freedom.'[117] Once again, the prisoners were photographed and had their fingerprints taken. For one of them, this would have dramatic consequences.[118]

The first group, twenty-three in all, was exchanged at the end of May.[119] They marched across the frontier through a crowd with their arms raised in the Fascist salute. A small number of volunteers remained in prison, including George Leeson, Maurice Goldberg and Liverpudlian Robert Silcock. Leeson was released in September after a campaign in the UK, and Goldberg and Silcock – the latter of whom was in hospital faking illness, hoping it might save him from being shot – were finally released in November 1937.[120] Why they were held back is unclear; in his history of the

British in Spain, Bill Alexander suggested that it was motivated by anti-Semitism.[121] It could also have been, as Carl Geiser, the American brigader and POW, suggested, because the Nationalists hoped to discourage the released prisoners from saying anything unfavourable when they returned home to Britain.[122]

IO

'The May Days'

And what is a Trotskyist? This terrible word – in Spain at this
moment you can be thrown into jail and kept there indefinitely,
without trial, on the mere rumour that you are a Trotskyist – is
only beginning to be bandied to and fro in England. We shall be
hearing more of it later.

George Orwell, 'Spilling the Spanish Beans'

To many in Britain who take an interest in the Spanish Civil War, the May
Day uprising in Barcelona, and the brutal suppression of the POUM that
followed, is seen as the conflict's central story. This 'civil war within the
civil war' has been a useful weapon for those looking to take pot-shots at
the Spanish Republic, and has seemingly provided them with ample
ammunition. As one historian, sympathetic to the Republic, recently
confessed:

If I were asked to name the single non-military event which had done most
harm to the wartime Republic, both within Spain and internationally, I
would name the kidnapping, followed by torture and assassination,
followed by incredibly bogus, self-righteous efforts to deny or cover-up the
'disappearance' of the leader of a small anti-Stalinist Marxist party, the
POUM.[1]

However, as one of the best-known British volunteers in Spain declared,
'so much political capital has been made out of the Barcelona fighting that
it is important to try and get a balanced view of it.'[2] That volunteer's own
account of the May events, *Homage to Catalonia*, published in 1938 under
the author's pen name of George Orwell, has become the most widely read
memoir by any of the Britons in Spain, if not the most widely read book on

the civil war in English. However, it is by no means the only British volunteer's account of the Barcelona 'May Days' and, like any memoir, it is best read alongside other accounts and situated within the wider context of the war itself.

Orwell, under his real name of Eric Blair, served in Spain alongside a number of British volunteers in a Republican militia as part of a unit organised by the Independent Labour Party. Following the rising in July 1936, the ILP offered support to their sister organisation the POUM, *Partido Obrero de Unificación Marxista*, a small Marxist – though anti-Stalinist – party based primarily in Catalonia.

Leading ILP figure John McNair, a businessman and good linguist, was sent out to Spain on a fact-finding mission, and was asked by the POUM leadership if the ILP could help by providing medical supplies. The ILP held meetings and raised money; they bought medical aid and an ambulance, which was sent to Spain at the end of September. On their arrival, one of the two drivers, who had military experience, promptly joined the POUM militia. The other, convinced that an armed response to the uprising was justified, returned home to persuade the ILP to send a military contingent to fight in Catalonia.[3]

This put the ILP leadership in a difficult position. Like many others on the left in Britain, their horror at the appalling slaughter of the First World War, and their determination that it should not be repeated, had hardened into a resolute pacifism. But younger members of the party, not bearing the scars of the Western Front, saw things differently. No less appalled by the rise of European fascism than their countrymen (and women) who volunteered for the International Brigades, they saw the conflict in Spain as part of a revolutionary struggle against fascism and were determined to fight alongside their brothers in the POUM. The go-ahead for volunteering was given at the end of 1936, and requests for volunteers appeared in the ILP paper, the *New Leader*, in December 1936 and January 1937.

The first group of twenty-five volunteers left Britain on 8 January 1937, led by Bob Edwards, a former hunger-marcher and member of the ILP National Committee who had been the party's candidate for Chorley in the 1935 General Election. Although a political veteran, Edwards, the second of those two ambulance drivers in September 1936, possessed no military understanding. One of the ILP group later described him witheringly as 'knowing nothing about military affairs. He might make a good Salvation Army officer,' adding that the ILP group in Spain were happy when

Edwards returned to Britain and happier still when he stayed there.[4]

As in the International Brigades, ideological commitment was paramount: the group elected a political commissar and established a five-man political committee. However, volunteers from other political parties were generally accepted.[5] For example, Stafford Cottman, a member of the Young Communist League and veteran of battles with Blackshirts in east London and Bristol, heard that the ILP and the Communist Party were appealing for volunteers. He applied to both, intending to take whichever offer came up first. The ILP were the quicker to respond, so he happily joined their group.[6]

At the ILP's St Bride Street office in London, Cottman met Edwards, McNair and their colleague, Fenner Brockway (the ILP's candidate for Norwich in a by-election in 1935), who were interviewing potential recruits. They apparently had no problem with his YCL membership, but asked about his military experience; most likely more in hope than expectation, as very few of the ILP volunteers had any military training.[7] Also, as R.W. Robson was doing at the Communist Party office in King Street, some warnings of the risks involved were given. Thereafter, despite some ineffective efforts on the part of the police to prevent them getting to Spain, including an anonymous – and bogus – tip-off that the border between France and Spain was closed, the contingent set off, travelling via Paris and Perpignan and arriving in Barcelona at the end of January 1937.[8]

Like Cottman, George Orwell had contacted the Communist Party about joining the International Brigades but Harry Pollitt, irritated by the writer's upper middle-class background and suspicious of his politics, flatly turned him down. Orwell turned to the ILP; keen to help, they gave him a letter of introduction to John McNair, who had returned to Barcelona in October as the Party's representative and to establish an office there.[9] Orwell arrived in Spain in late December 1936, before the main ILP group. He found Barcelona in the throes of revolution, and was spurred to write his famous description of the city:

> When one came straight from England the aspect of Barcelona was something startling and overwhelming. It was the first time that I had ever been in a town where the working class was in the saddle. Practically every building of any size had been seized by the workers and was draped with red flags or with the red and black flag of the Anarchists; every wall was scrawled with the hammer and sickle and with the initials of the

revolutionary parties; almost every church had been gutted and its images
burnt . . . Every shop and cafe had an inscription saying that it had been
collectivised; even the bootblacks had been collectivised and their boxes
painted red and black. Waiters and shop-walkers looked you in the face and
treated you as an equal. Servile and even ceremonial forms of speech had
temporarily disappeared. Tipping was forbidden by law; almost my first
experience was receiving a lecture from an hotel manager for trying to tip
a lift-boy. There were no private motor cars, they had all been com-
mandeered, and all the trams and taxis and much of the other transport
were painted red and black. The revolutionary posters were everywhere,
flaming from the walls in clean reds and blues that made the few remaining
advertisements look like daubs of mud. Down the Ramblas, the wide central
artery of the town where crowds of people streamed constantly to and fro,
the loudspeakers were bellowing revolutionary songs all day and far into
the night . . . In outward appearance it was a town in which the wealthy
classes had practically ceased to exist. Except for a small number of women
and foreigners there were no 'well-dressed' people at all. Practically
everyone wore rough working-class clothes, or blue overalls, or some
variant of the militia uniform. All this was queer and moving. There was
much in it which I did not understand, in some ways I did not even like it,
but I recognised it immediately as a state of affairs worth fighting for.[10]

Orwell immediately abandoned any plans of reporting on the war and
arranged to meet McNair in order to volunteer, though – at least initially –
McNair was no more taken with him than Harry Pollitt had been. However,
the letter of introduction and McNair's realisation that he was talking to the
author of *Burmese Days* and *Down and Out in Paris and London* changed his
attitude dramatically and he escorted Orwell to the POUM militia base at
Barcelona's Lenin barracks. The famous author's place in the ranks of the
militia was quickly recognised as a major coup and the POUM's English
newspaper, *The Spanish Revolution*, appealed for others to join him.[11]

At the barracks, the ILP volunteers were given basic military training.
Orwell's military experience ensured that, very soon, he was in charge of
training the young, green recruits in marching and other aspects of military
discipline. Orwell admitted that 'the so-called instruction was simply parade-
ground drill of the most antiquated, stupid kind; right turn, left turn,
marching at attention in columns of threes and all the rest of that useless
nonsense.' As there were no actual weapons in the barracks, two weeks'

marching and an introduction in the use of rifles and machine guns was, for many, the limit of their training. Orwell knew full well that a number of important skills weren't being taught: 'If you only have a few days in which to train a soldier, you must teach him the things he will most need; how to take cover, how to advance across open ground, how to mount guards and build a parapet – above all, how to use his weapons.'[12]

On 2 February 1937 the group were sent to the front at Monte Trazo in the hills near Zaragoza in Aragon, 250 kilometres west of Barcelona. The group formed one section of a Centuria; they were led by portly 45-year-old Russian-born Belgian Georges Kopp, whose involvement in the war had begun, so he claimed, by the smuggling of arms into Spain.[13] The unit was organised on democratic militia lines, so there were no signs of rank, no titles, no badges, no saluting; and military orders were agreed by discussion among all ranks. As Orwell admitted, 'discipline was difficult to impose and officers had to rely on the enthusiasm of the men as they had little hope of enforcing an unpopular order.'[14]

Initially placed with a Spanish unit, Orwell and a Welsh volunteer, Robert Williams, soon joined the rest of their British colleagues, where Orwell was disappointed to discover that he had been sent to what John Cornford had earlier described as 'a quiet sector of a quiet front'.[15] The enemy lines were over 700 metres away on an adjacent hillside, too far to shoot at accurately. It was probably just as well: the unit had too little ammunition to participate in any meaningful action, so 'the thing to do was to hold the line.'[16] While Orwell believed the group to be 'an exceptionally good crowd, both physically and mentally', another member felt that many were rather more 'booksy and political' than military in bearing.[17] The major weakness of the unit, however, was that soldiers were extremely poorly equipped for the trenches:

No hats, no bayonets, hardly any revolvers or pistols . . . no maps or charts . . . no range-finders, no telescopes, no field-glasses . . . no flares, or Very lights, no wire-cutters, no armourers' tools, hardly even any cleaning materials . . . there was not even any gun oil.[18]

Most had no idea about weaponry and the first five injuries that Orwell witnessed were the result of accidents, rather than enemy shooting. One volunteer felt that the unit was very slap-happy and unprofessional in their handling of armaments, ammunition and equipment. Volunteers were known to drop their weapons, setting them off, and accidental self-inflicted wounds – many of them from back-firing rifles – were common. Orwell found the young militiamen to be incredibly brave, but also incredibly reckless, often standing up in full view of the enemy. Initially Spanish soldiers laughed at the English habit of taking cover and lying prone to shoot – although, following high casualty rates, a propaganda campaign was eventually launched to encourage Spanish militiamen to follow the example of the *extranjeros* (foreigners).[19] Fortunately, the enemies' shooting was usually no better than theirs. Their most effective weapon was probably the megaphone, which the Spanish soldiers used to harangue their counterparts in the Nationalist trenches, explaining that they were fighting men of their own class and urging them to desert.

While the stalemate meant that the risk of death from snipers or shellfire was small, conditions were undoubtedly tough, with poor food, freezing cold weather and the irritations of rats and lice. Like the International Brigades on the Jarama front, the ILP group at Huesca, sixty kilometres north-east of Zaragoza, suffered from dreadful infestations of lice, which multiplied much more quickly than they could be killed:

> All of us were lousy by this time; though still cold it was warm enough for that. I have had a big experience of body vermin of various kinds, and for sheer beastliness the louse beats everything I have encountered . . . The human louse somewhat resembles a tiny lobster, and he lives chiefly in your trousers. Short of burning all your clothes there is no known way of getting rid of him. Down the seams of your trousers he lays his glittering white eggs, like tiny grains of rice, which hatch out and breed families of their own at horrible speed. I think the pacifists might find it helpful to illustrate their pamphlets with enlarged photographs of lice.[20]

The only reliable meal was breakfast and many, Orwell included, badly felt the cold. Consequently much of the time was spent building fires and foraging for food. 'In trench warfare five things are important: firewood, food, tobacco, candles and the enemy. In winter on the Zaragoza front they were important in that order, with the enemy a bad last,' Orwell believed.[21]

> When we were not eating, sleeping, on guard or on fatigue duty we were in the valley behind the position, scrounging for fuel. All my memories of

that time are memories of scrambling up and down the almost perpendicular slopes, over the jagged limestone that knocked one's boots to pieces, pouncing eagerly on tiny twigs of wood.[22]

Much time was also spent engaged in political arguments, where 'the conflicting party "lines" were debated over and over'. Orwell did not endear himself to his comrades by laughing at what he felt to be their political naivety.[23] Like Pollitt and McNair before them, many volunteers were acutely aware of Orwell's 'cut-glass Eton accent' and east Londoner Frank Frankford said he disliked the 'supercilious bastard' on sight:

> He really didn't like the workers . . . It was his attitude in discussions that I didn't like, his attitude towards the working class. Two or three of us said that he was on the wrong side, he should be on the other side . . . I rather think he fancied himself as another Bernard Shaw . . . There was no depth to his socialism at all.[24]

April saw the arrival of copies of *The Road to Wigan Pier*, in which Orwell made the infamous claim that the middle classes were taught that the working class smelled. Neither this, nor his habit of setting aside time every day to write, helped to ingratiate Orwell with his working-class comrades.[25] Bob Edwards, who also took a personal dislike to Orwell, later unfairly described him as 'a journalist observer [and] bloody scribbler'.[26]

By April 1937, the lack of action was beginning to frustrate some of the group. Feeling that they had come to Spain to fight fascists, not to be shot while foraging for firewood on the freezing mountainsides, Orwell and Stafford Cottman discussed the prospect of leaving for the International Brigades. Many of their comrades, including Bob Edwards, tried to talk them out of it, but the pair recognised that the real battle against Franco's forces was being fought at Madrid:

> Here we were on the Aragon front with very little happening, you saw the enemy miles over there as a little moving dot on the landscape. You didn't really feel as though you were making a useful contribution to the Spanish Civil War.[27]

When the ILP group were pulled out of the line on 25 April and sent on leave to Barcelona, Orwell and Cottman decided to use the opportunity to try and join the Brigades:

> When we went on leave I had been a hundred and fifteen days in the line, and at the time this period seemed to me to have been one of the most futile of my whole life. I had joined the militia in order to fight against Fascism, and yet I had scarcely fought at all, had merely existed as a sort of passive object, doing nothing in return for my rations except to suffer from cold and lack of sleep.[28]

Orwell approached 'a Communist friend, attached to the Spanish Medical Aid' in Barcelona to enquire about joining. Asked to see if other members of the column could be persuaded to come with him, Orwell returned to talk to his comrades. John McNair was obviously keen to hold on to the prestigious author, so a meeting was held on 28 April, allowing any ILP members who were considering enlisting in the International Brigades to air their grievances. Two days later Orwell spoke to a senior British Communist in Barcelona, Walter Tapsell, previously the circulation manager for the *Daily Worker*, who had been instructed by the Communist Party to mingle with the ILP members. Orwell discussed the question of joining and a confidential report was sent to Harry Pollitt describing his disaffection:

> The leading personality and most respected man in the contingent at present is Eric Blair. This man is a Novelist and has written some books on proletarian life in England. He has little political understanding and 'He is not interested in party politics, and came to Spain as an Anti-Fascist to fight Fascism.' As a result of his experiences however, he has grown to dislike the POUM and is now awaiting his discharge from the POUM militia.[29]

However, events were to overtake Orwell's desire to join the International Brigades. On their arrival in Barcelona, the British ILP section had found the city to be in a state of high tension and much changed from the Barcelona that Orwell had so vividly described the previous January: 'The militia uniform and the blue overalls had almost disappeared; everyone seemed to be wearing the smart summer suits in which Spanish tailors specialize. Fat prosperous men, elegant women, and sleek cars were everywhere.'[30]

Propaganda for the new Republican Popular Army had replaced that for the militias. Government attempts to restore in the Republican zone the kind of centralised authority which had virtually collapsed following the military rising the year before were receiving strong support from the Communist Party, who had their own reasons for wanting to limit the power of the Anarchists and their militias. Moves had already been made against the POUM, which had earned the enmity of Stalin by their condemnation of the Moscow show trials in August 1936 and the expression of solidarity with Trotsky made by their leader, Andreu Nin. Stalin was determined that Spain should not become a fertile breeding ground for Trotskyists and other 'deviationists' critical of the Soviet Union; if he had any agenda in Spain beyond keeping Hitler embroiled in a war for as long as possible, it was to eradicate all forms of perceived Trotskyism.[31]

During April, many of the POUM's newspapers had been closed down, and a number of members had been expelled from factory committees. With tensions rising, the May Day parades in Barcelona had been cancelled to prevent disorder.

The simmering violence was brought to the boil on 3 May by the government's attempt to take over the Telefónica (the Barcelona telephone exchange) held by members of the CNT, an Anarchist trade union. Having infuriated government officials by eavesdropping on official phone calls, the occupiers had refused to admit three lorry loads of Guardia Civil sent by the local police chief to remove them. Shots were exchanged and Anarchists across Barcelona, supported by members of the POUM who believed that the government was attempting to roll back their revolutionary gains, erected barricades and prepared to defend themselves. Meanwhile the Communists seized their opportunity by accusing the POUM of being 'Trotskyists' and agents of Franco. The false association of the POUM with Trotskyism was crucial in identifying them as enemies within, as one International Brigader admitted:

We heard the word 'Trotskyist' many times. It was synonymous with 'defeatist' or 'fascist'. A Trotskyist was one who claimed to be anti-fascist but, because he did not accept the current political 'line' of the Republican government, was in fact said to be helping Franco by destroying the unity of the Republicans.[32]

Caught up in the fighting, the ILP group helped defend a number of the

POUM's buildings. After collecting weapons from the Hotel Falcon, Georges Kopp and a small number of POUM militiamen, accompanied by Orwell's wife, Eileen O'Shaughnessy, took refuge in the POUM executive building on Las Ramblas, the wide thoroughfare linking Plaza Catalunya with the seafront. During the six days of street fighting that followed, the group watched as hundreds lost their lives and many more were arrested.[33] The fighting ended only on 6 May, when six thousand Republican Assault Guards arrived in the city and the barricades began to be dismantled. Orwell's view of the events was crystallised by an encounter in the Hotel Continental with a supposed Russian agent, who was explaining to foreign refugees that the whole thing was an Anarchist plot. Orwell watched him with disdainful fascination, for – journalists aside – 'it was the first time that I had seen a person whose profession was telling lies'.[34]

Meanwhile, other British volunteers witnessed the fighting from the other side of the barricades. Peter Harrisson, a Communist Party member and journalist from Portsmouth, had travelled to Spain in late April, driving a lorry full of Vermicine, an insecticide for killing lice. As he waited in Barcelona for papers permitting him to continue to Albacete, he saw a large crowd gather outside the telephone exchange where, he was told, there had just been some shooting, following 'a revolt by the Anarchist FAI and the Trotskyist POUM against the Catalan Government and the Communists'.[35] Safe inside a flat in Calle Balmes used by the British Medical Unit, Harrisson watched on as:

> An Anarchist armoured car appeared at the top of Balmes coming our way firing indiscriminately to keep up its spirits. From our fourth floor balcony we would watch it slowly approach the barricade and drive slowly past raking it with machine gun fire while the police and other government supporters would reply with all the weapons they possessed and try to roll hand grenades beneath the armoured car. To add to the sound of battle, snipers on the roofs around would join in.[36]

Once the street fighting had died down, Walter Tapsell talked to John McNair and Stafford Cottman about the ILP's role in the uprising. According to Cottman, both were wary of the dedicated Communist, but Tapsell assured them that he accepted their version of events, apparently admitting that he believed the 'POUM was being used as a blind' and that members of the Spanish Communist Party 'were not without knowledge or responsibility'.[37] Tapsell's report on the ILP group certainly states that they denied involvement in the shooting and were furious that the *Daily Worker* had accused them of 'rising and stabbing the Government in the back'.[38]

Tapsell may have continued to believe that some ILP volunteers might yet be persuaded to join the International Brigades. However, incensed by Communist portrayals of the POUM as fascist agents, Orwell and the other volunteers unsurprisingly rejected his attempts. Correctly surmising that they would be seen as politically unreliable within the Communist-dominated International Brigades, they returned to the Huesca front on 10 May, with the POUM group now part of the 29th Division of the Republican Army.

One of the ILP group, David Wickes, a member of the Luton Socialist League, did in fact request permission to join the International Brigades. Aware of the propaganda value, Tapsell strongly recommended he be accepted and Wickes was permitted to join.[39] But despite gaining promotion to assistant battalion paymaster and being wounded in action, Wickes remained under suspicion 'because of [his] ILP associations'.[40] A superior's assessment was that Wickes' 'activity appears good, but has a tendency to take up Trotskyist positions and should be watched for that reason'.[41] No doubt their suspicions of Wickes' lack of political will were later confirmed by his refusal to participate in a firing squad.

Ten days after returning to the front, Orwell – having previously been rather disparaging about Spanish marksmanship – was hit in the throat and almost killed. Mocking him for his earlier criticisms of the unsoldierly nature of the ILP unit, Frank Frankford claimed that, had he kept his head down, as any good soldier would have done, Orwell would not have been hit. Orwell described vividly the experience of being shot:

> It was the sensation of being *at the centre* of an explosion. There seemed to be a loud bang and a blinding flash of light all round me, and I felt a tremendous shock – no pain, only a violent shock, such as you get from an electric terminal; with it a sense of utter weakness, a feeling of being stricken and shrivelled up to nothing . . . The next moment my knees crumpled up and I was falling, my head hitting the ground with a violent bang which, to my relief, did not hurt. I had a numb, dazed feeling, a consciousness of being very badly hurt, but no pain in the ordinary sense . . . I thought, too, of the

man who had shot me – wondered what he was like, whether he was a
Spaniard or a foreigner, whether he knew he had got me, and so forth. I
could not feel any resentment against him. I reflected that as he was a Fascist
I would have killed him if I could, but that if he had been taken prisoner
and brought before me at this moment I would merely have congratulated
him on his good shooting.[42]

The bullet narrowly missed Orwell's carotid artery and he suffered
considerable blood loss, along with nerve damage which paralysed his vocal
cords and his right arm. Serious though it was, the wound was not as bad
as it initially appeared and Orwell was walking around within a few days,
even if he lost the ability to speak properly for a time. By 10 June, however,
a depressed Orwell had accepted that he was no longer fit for military
service and now determined to leave Spain. He left the POUM hospital and
returned to Barcelona to rejoin his wife, who was working as a secretary in
the ILP office.

Back in Barcelona Orwell experienced first-hand the vicious and
slanderous campaign now being waged against the POUM. In a particularly
nasty slur, a cartoon was circulated in which the POUM's hammer and
sickle mask had slipped revealing a swastika underneath. ¡Fuera la careta!
'Tear off the mask!' the posters proclaimed. On 16 June, following
Communist demands, the Republican government banned the POUM. All
rank and file members were disarmed and its leaders were arrested. After
interrogation and brutal torture at a house in Alcalá de Henares to the east
of Madrid, used by the Spanish Communist head of the Republican air force,
Ignacio Hidalgo de Cisneros, Andreu Nin was murdered by his interrogators
and buried in a nearby field in an unmarked grave. There seems little doubt
that this was a Russian operation: the group responsible included the senior
NKVD operative in Spain, Alexander Orlov, and the operation was led by
NKVD assassin Iosif Grigulevich, a close associate of senior members of the
Spanish Communist Party.[43]

As associates of the POUM, the British ILP members were also
persecuted. A young Scottish member, Bob Smillie, was arrested trying to
cross the border into France, ostensibly for carrying illegal arms – though
this was probably a pretext, for the 'arms' consisted of two ancient hand
grenades from which the charges and fuses had been removed. Smillie was
thrown into prison and died there of appendicitis, probably exacerbated by
the poor treatment he received.[44] Two days later, when John McNair

returned from a visit to London carrying ILP mail and money, as well as documents for the members' repatriation to Britain, he was arrested as a suspected POUM courier, although he managed to talk his way out of jail.[45] Following Eileen Blair's discovery that her room had been searched, she, Orwell and McNair, realising that they were at imminent risk of arrest, prudently decided to leave Spain as quickly and quietly as possible. Though a handful stayed to fight on with other units, most of the remaining ILP volunteers elected to do likewise.

Trapped in the trenches on the Jarama front, the men in the British Battalion were informed by their political commissars of events in Barcelona:

> News of the fighting was greeted with incredulity, consternation and then extreme anger by the International Brigaders . . . The anger in the Brigade against those who had fought the Republic in the rear was sharpened by reports of weapons, even tanks, being kept from the front and hidden for treacherous purposes.[46]

According to battalion commander Fred Copeman, the brigaders were outraged: 'Why, men asked, was it possible that these people could obtain arms and even tanks, so far in the rear, when the front line was starved of ammunition?'[47]

It is not surprising that many in the British Battalion reacted with such hostility, overwhelmingly reliant as they were on Communist propaganda: 'how were we to know anything different?' asked one British volunteer.[48] It was near impossible for those on the front line to obtain objective news; their post was censored and the only newspapers available were those which put across the Communist Party line:

> We were not too well informed, newspapers, Spanish or British, came to us in a hit or miss way, often none at all for several days. Spanish papers were either the Communist *Mundo Obrero* or the Socialist *El Socialista*, neither noted for objective reporting. Anyway, printed in Spanish they were, regrettably, unintelligible to three quarters of the British. Irregularly we saw the British *Daily Worker*, unavoidably several days old, and sometimes *Reynolds News*, a now defunct Co-operative Party publication which, as a Sunday paper, was likely to be even more behind events.[49]

Besides, as several volunteers openly admitted, very few knew much about the complexities of Spanish, let alone Catalan, politics: 'of . . . the wide range of passionately held beliefs of so many parties from Liberals to Communists, not forgetting Anarchists and Trotskyists, Left Republicans and Separatists, we knew little or nothing.'[50] Even a senior figure such as Len Crome, who rose to become chief medical officer for the entire 35th Republican Division, knew little personally of what was happening in Barcelona and therefore took on trust the information he was given:

> I was very badly informed about it all. I wasn't taking too much interest either, you know. At the front, in the army, we didn't know what was happening . . . The International Brigades were run by Communists and I believed what I was told.[51]

However, not every member of the battalion swallowed the Party line whole. Jason Gurney was certainly not convinced by the propaganda and the attacks on the POUM and the Anarchists:

> It was impossible then to discover the truth about these events, but they served to heighten the feeling that the Communists were in control of the situation and that they would exploit it to suit their own advantage without any sort of consideration for anyone but themselves. The official Party now produced a mass of palpably absurd propaganda, claiming that the POUM were in alliance with Franco who, for all his faults, certainly would not have allied himself with a small party of dissident Marxists . . . There were the wildest rumours, spread officially and unofficially – the POUM had linked up with Franco supporters in Barcelona to raise a revolt in our rear but had been wiped out by the loyal forces of Party stalwarts defending peace and democracy.[52]

John Angus, meanwhile, summarised the feelings of some less rigid members of the battalion when he acknowledged that 'the POUM was perhaps not as black as it has sometimes been portrayed', admitting frankly that 'undoubtedly Nin was the victim of a frame-up.' Nevertheless he still believed that the attitude of the Anarchists and the POUM 'was not at all helpful to winning the war'. Though not actually fifth columnists, they were, he believed, 'politically innocent, naive people' who were 'very remote from reality'.[53] This rather patronising view prevailed widely within the battalion: 'Experience had shown that any argument with Anarchists would pass through all the debating levels to a national conference, and then no results would be achieved. It was always better to do the job yourself and leave them to it.'[54]

However they might have felt about the POUM and Anarchists, the volunteers in the trenches at Jarama could legitimately argue that they played no part in the suppression. Other Britons, however, were certainly involved. David Crook, a casualty at Jarama, had been sent to the Officer Training School at Pozorrubio, 130 kilometres north-west of Albacete, after recovering from his wounds.[55] While convalescing, Crook was approached by George Soria, a Soviet agent working for the Communist newspaper *Imprecor*, who recruited him for the Republican Military Intelligence.[56] After being trained in intelligence work by Ramón Mercader, later to become infamous as Trotsky's murderer, Crook was charged with befriending and reporting on members of the POUM such as the Austrian Communist Kurt Landau, who Crook identified for his 'bosses' and described as having been 'kidnapped, put in a wooden crate and loaded on to one of the Soviet ships bringing food or arms to the Republic'. Landau disappeared mysteriously in 1937; if Crook is to be believed, this explanation solves the mystery of his fate.[57]

Crook inveigled himself into the ILP's Barcelona offices, where he copied documents and passed them on to the Russian embassy and to his handler, Hugh O'Donnell, who had originally been connected with the British Medical Unit, but was also working in a clandestine capacity for the PSUC, the Communist-dominated Socialist Party of Catalonia.[58] Crook spied on members of the ILP contingent such as commander Georges Kopp, John McNair and the Orwells and passed on his findings to O'Donnell:

I was to become friendly with these people – especially the 'Trotskyists' – get to know their views, activities and contacts, and write reports on them, which were to be handed to 'Sean.' The hand-over method was to place the report in a folded newspaper and pass it inconspicuously to Sean in a café or sometimes in the hotel lavatory. Sean would give me instructions as to new targets of observation and our next time and place of meeting.[59]

Other British volunteers were prepared to play their part. En route to Spain at the end of May 1937, one Scottish volunteer was part of a group approached in France by a Spanish emissary to discuss the May Days. The Scot was quite clear about the POUM, believing that it was 'causing obstructions to the unification process needed to fight the war . . . [it was] a Trotskyite-type party that was open to any kind of provocateur to enter.' The volunteers were asked a simple question: 'If the situation in Barcelona worsened, would we go to the support of the Government to help put an end to that situation in Barcelona?' Their answer was clear: 'Without exception the whole group agreed that we were prepared to do this.'[60]

Senior members of the British Communist Party were also involved. As early as 6 May, stories in the *Daily Worker* accused Anarchists of precipitating the street fighting by their seizure – rather than their defence – of the telephone exchange. *Daily Worker* reporter Claud Cockburn accused the Anarchists and POUMistas of being armed with weapons 'which they had been stealing for months past', including 'tanks, which they stole from the barrack just at the beginning of the rising'.[61] The calumny was repeated by Ralph Bates when he visited the battalion at Jarama on 14 May and lectured the volunteers on the 'Disorders in Catalonia'. One Manchester volunteer remarked that Bates' speech made it absolutely clear to all 'that P.O.U.M., Trotskyists and spies engineered it'.[62]

In Britain, the May events were played out in the pages of newspapers sympathetic to the ILP and Communist Party. Pro-Republican newspapers such as the *News Chronicle* followed the Party line, with John Langdon-Davies describing the event as 'a frustrated POUM putsch'.[63] Claud Cockburn's reporting in the *Daily Worker* was particularly virulent. In an article published on 11 May 1937, entitled 'Pitcairn Lifts Barcelona Veil' (probably a deliberate reference to the anti-POUM poster in Barcelona), Cockburn claimed that German and Italian agents, 'in cooperation with the local Trotskyists', were preparing 'a situation of disorder and bloodshed'. He went on to claim that:

> The POUM, acting in cooperation with well known criminal elements . . . planned, organised and led the attacks in the rearguard, accurately timed to coincide with the attack on the front at Bilbao . . . In the plainest terms the POUM declares it is the enemy of the People's Govt.[64]

To further damn the POUM, the *Daily Worker* published an interview with ILP volunteer Frank Frankford, given to Sam Lesser, the former International Brigader now working as a radio broadcaster in Barcelona.

Deliberately edited to suggest that Frankford was accusing members of the POUM of fraternisation, the piece included the utterly unfounded claims that the POUM battalion commander was a fascist agent and that arms for the May uprising had been supplied by the Nationalists.[65] As one former member of the battalion who went on to support the ILP claimed: 'International Brigade comrades normally perfectly honest and sincere will swear that they actually witnessed material evidence of the P.O.U.M.'s complicity with the Fascists – evidence that solely existed within their incessantly propagandized minds.'[66]

Other pro-Communist papers stepped into line and joined the attacks. Incensed by an article in the *New Statesman* on 22 May which accused the POUM of having stolen guns and tanks from the government arsenals, Orwell wrote a typically acerbic response:

In reality, by far the worst offenders in this matter of keeping weapons from the front, were the Government themselves. The infantry on the Aragon front were far worse-armed than an English public school O.T.C.; but the rear-line troops, the Civil Guards, Assault Guards and Carabineros, who were not intended for the front, but were used to 'preserve order' (i.e. overawe the workers) in the rear, were armed to the teeth. The troops on the Aragon front had worn-out Mauser rifles, which usually jammed after five shots, approximately one machine-gun to fifty men, and one pistol or revolver to about thirty men. These weapons, so necessary in trench warfare, were not issued by the Government and could only be bought illegally and with the greatest difficulty. The Assault Guards were armed with brand-new Russian rifles; in addition, every man was issued with an automatic pistol, and there was one submachine-gun between ten or a dozen men. These facts speak for themselves. A Government which sends boys of fifteen to the front with rifles forty years old, and keeps its biggest men and newest weapons in the rear, is manifestly more afraid of the revolution than of the Fascists.[67]

Stafford Cottman was later expelled from the Young Communist League for his pro-ILP writings on Spain, in particular his accounts of the Barcelona uprising published in the *Socialist Leader* and the *News Chronicle*. He also sent an account to the *Daily Worker*, but it was never published.[68]

The arguments between supporters and opponents of the POUM were (and still are) set within a wider dispute over whether the war or the revolution needed to be given priority in Spain. In Orwell's words, this argument became 'the donkey on which everyone pinned their tail'. The Communists' claim that if the war was lost, there could be no revolution, was not unreasonable, as were their demands for greater centralisation and a traditional army structure. As Orwell stated, 'it was a little better, though only a little, to lose the revolution than to lose the war'; clearly if the war was lost, there could be no revolution.[69]

Frank Frankford certainly accepted this argument and its logical consequence: '[the] taking away [of] the rights of the democratic militias and handing them over to a popular army.' Yet despite his reluctant acceptance that 'from a military point of view that was the thing to do', he still believed that 'it altered the whole spirit of the revolution.'[70] As Orwell noted, 'On paper the Communist case was a good one; the trouble was that their actual behaviour made it difficult to believe that they were advancing in good faith.'[71] The problem was, of course, that the Communist line was self-serving, the screen behind which they sought to justify the eradication of the POUM.

The suppression of the POUM continued to resonate in Britain long after the end of the war. But for many Communists, including a number of those who had served in the International Brigades, the issue remained a distraction. The former political commissar (and later assistant general secretary of the CPGB) Bill Alexander always maintained that the political repression instigated by the Republic was completely justified: 'The Republic had to safeguard itself against internal enemies. Injustices and mistakes were inevitable, but the Government erred, if anything, on the side of complacency and lack of vigilance.'[72]

Others went further. In 1976, Bob Cooney denied that Orwell had even fought in Spain, that all he had done was to 'hover around the cafés'. 'George Orwell did get a bullet, but it was in the back of the neck,' he claimed, 'and it was a Republican bullet, when he was escaping over the Pyrenees.'[73] Ten years later Frank Frankford was still claiming that he had heard carts at night travelling between the POUM and Nationalist lines.[74] Other former members of the battalion, such as Frank Graham, remained absolutely convinced that the POUM had been an enemy of the Spanish Republic:

When on May 4th reports reached us that the POUM (a so-called 'left-wing' socialist party) had revolted and was trying to overthrow the government in Barcelona we were outraged although not surprised. For months it was known that the leadership had been working secretly with Franco and many of its members were former falangistes (fascists) who had been unable to escape to the south when Franco invaded Spain.[75]

Graham's is now very much a minority view. Many see the May Days and the attacks on the POUM and ILP which followed very differently. Within Britain, the most widely read account of these events and of the war itself is still that of Orwell, who was understandably scarred by his six months in Catalonia. Drawing from their reading of Orwell, many develop the belief that Stalin, the Communist Party and bitter sectarianism were responsible for the Republic's defeat. This view of the 'Stalinist terror' in Spain was reinforced by Ken Loach's film *Land and Freedom*, in which Jim Allen's screenplay falsely portrays American International Brigaders shooting Republican militia. Furthermore, over the years it has been frequently and, quite wrongly, alleged that thousands of members of the POUM and other left-wing organisations were, like Nin, brutally tortured and murdered in Communist prisons in Spain.[76] In fact, as Orwell himself acknowledged: '[Spanish Premier Juan] Negrín and the others have kept their heads and refused to stage a wholesale massacre of "Trotskyists". Considering the pressure that has been put upon them, it is greatly to their credit that they have done so.'[77]

This is not to argue that Stalin was the great advocate and defender of Spanish democracy. As historian A.J.P. Taylor convincingly argued, it is highly unlikely that the USSR aided Spain on principle. Stalin would have welcomed peaceful relations with Nazi Germany if at all possible: 'Conflict in Spain was more welcome to the Russians than conflict near their own border.' Stalin had two aims in Spain: first, to keep the war going as long as possible to tie down Germany, and second, to eradicate the 'Trotskyist' left, wherever it cropped up.[78] On 23 July 1936, Georgi Dimitrov, General Secretary of the Comintern, had warned that any policy that might lead to a dictatorship of the proletariat in Spain must be avoided, and as early as the following year Franz Borkenau recognised that '[the Communist Party] have ceased to be a revolutionary party and become one of the mainstays of the anti-revolutionary force.'[79]

Such fratricidal purges may have contributed to the demoralisation of government supporters and undoubtedly damaged the Republic's reputation abroad. They were not, however, the primary cause of its woes: the greater military experience and efficiency of the Nationalists was more significant. It should therefore be remembered that Stalin's Russia was the only major power to assist the Republic. Ultimately, the most dangerous obstacle facing Republican Spain was not Stalin's terror, but the colossal level of intervention in support of Franco by Italy and Germany, which was allowed to continue wholesale by Britain and France's determination to maintain the 'farcical' non-intervention pact.

II

¡Sanidad!

Those of us who have the good fortune to be spared the experience of participation in armed conflict are probably unable to appreciate fully the sheer chaos that pervades the battlefield.

Nicholas Coni, *Medicine and Warfare*

The burning need to act, to *do something*, created among a small but dedicated number in Britain by Spain's descent into civil war, took a number of forms. While some donated money, attended political meetings, or even chose to join the fighting, others turned their efforts towards trying to help alleviate the suffering of those caught in the turmoil. Not content with merely collecting money for medical supplies, a number of men and women from Britain and Ireland went to Spain. However, no doctors and only one nurse, the daughter of the eighth Lord Howard de Walden, Priscilla Scott-Ellis, volunteered to serve with the Nationalist forces;[1] the rest went to join the Republican medical services.

Three separate medical missions were established in Britain, and each sent staff and equipment to Republican Spain. The first, and smallest, was organised by the Independent Labour Party, which though in a pretty moribund state in 1936 – the party only had about 5000 members and was deeply in debt – nevertheless made impressive fundraising efforts. Having managed to collect over £1000, in September 1936 they bought an ambulance which was driven to Spain and handed over to the POUM.[2]

The second was the Scottish Ambulance Unit (SAU). This had been established by Sir Daniel Stevenson, the wealthy 85-year-old former coal exporter, Lord Provost of Glasgow and Chancellor of Glasgow University, following an appeal for money north of the border:[3]

There was a tremendous amount of money being poured into the

expedition by the people of Scotland. It was a quite extraordinary and
exhilarating manifestation of the spirit of the Scottish people that in spite of
their – I would almost say – abject poverty at that time, with enormous
unemployment and industrial depression, they were still eager to give
towards the support of Republican Spain what little they could from the
little they got.[4]

Led by Fernanda Jacobsen, 'their middle-aged Scots commandant [who]
was as indefatigable and bossy as Florence Nightingale herself',[5] the Scottish
Ambulance Unit set out from Glasgow on 17 September 1936.
Unfortunately, the unit was dogged with controversy right from the outset.
Jacobsen was suspected to have close links with the British government;
one volunteer with the unit noticed that on her arrival in Valencia, she was
warmly greeted by Captain Lance, the British military attaché – later
dubbed the 'Spanish Pimpernel' when he was discovered to be involved in
evacuating Nationalist sympathisers from Republican Spain.[6] In fact,
Jacobsen believed that the unit's role should be to help both sides and used
the ambulance unit to ferry Rebel sympathisers from embassies in Madrid
to Valencia. As one brigader observed, 'They had come out to give medical
aid, but did not seem to sympathise with the People's Army.'[7]

To make matters worse, there were rumours of the unit's involvement
in helping British deserters escape from Spain. Some members took a
relaxed attitude to the unit's clandestine activities:

> Regarding smuggling people [deserters] out of the embassies, it was minor
> really. It saved a lot of bloodshed and it saved a great deal of unfriendly
> propaganda abroad, which would have done the Spanish Republican cause
> no good. Therefore it was a satisfactory solution to the problem of these
> people who were hiding in the various embassies and in various friends'
> houses in Madrid. They were taken out of the embassies by the Scottish
> Ambulance Unit down to Valencia to be shipped across to Gibraltar.[8]

However, many members of the unit were firmly opposed: three later
left to join the International Brigades, while another returned home.[9]

There were further damaging allegations. In October 1936, one member
approached Hugh Slater, then working as a British journalist in Madrid,
claiming that the entire unit had been arrested and imprisoned in Aranjuez,
south of the Spanish capital. He blithely admitted that 'most of the members

of the Unit' had been involved in looting and revealed a number of gold
and silver items of contraband. Slater immediately reported this to the
Communist Party, noting significantly in his statement that 'the usual
practice in Spain is to shoot looters.'[10] Seven members were sent home and
with their departure, the unit was essentially unable to function. The
remaining members, including Fernanda Jacobsen, returned to Britain on
30 July 1937.[11]

The third medical mission to Spain – and by far the largest – began as a
result of a request for medical aid in late July 1936 from *Socorro Rojo
Internacional* (International Red Aid) to Isabel Brown, the Communist
Secretary of the Relief Committee for Victims of Fascism.[12] In response, the
Spanish Medical Aid Committee (SMAC) was formed the following month
under the leadership of Dr Hyacinth Morgan, the Catholic medical advisor
to the TUC, with Peter Spencer (Viscount Churchill) and Viscountess
Hastings as joint treasurers. Described as having 'a People's front character
. . . composed mainly of London doctors, or British doctors and Labour
MPs',[13] the SMAC was drawn from a broad cross-section of the left.

The committee's first meeting was held on 1 August and an advertisement placed in the press appealing for doctors, students and nurses. Pleas
for donations were answered quickly and generously – within three days
of its formation SMAC had collected £1550 (equivalent to about £300,000
in 2012). Kenneth Sinclair-Loutit, a young London medical student and
Communist, suggested buying an ambulance with the money and the first
left for Spain two weeks later, accompanied by a group of medical
volunteers.[14] Many more would follow: over the course of the war, SMAC
managed to organise around 150 men and women and eighty-two British
ambulances.[15]

The first British Medical Unit (BMU) comprised four doctors and four
medical students, together with a number of nurses, assistants,
administrators and drivers. Sinclair-Loutit was appointed as the unit's
coordinator, but his first impressions were not encouraging. The Communist
administrator, Hugh O'Donnell, was 'without medical qualifications', the
quartermaster was actually 'a driver and nothing more', one nurse was
'devoid of any experience and training' and the driver himself, who had been
'thrust upon the unit by the party, on the grounds that he was a driver and
could speak Spanish, turned out to be unable to drive a car, and to have
forgotten the few words of Spanish he had learnt several years before'.[16]

Unlike the British Battalion, where there was a strong sense of class and political uniformity, the BMU (like SMAC itself) was a diverse group, with members 'divided by age, sex, class, intelligence, political allegiance, and mental stability'.[17] Most of the doctors were young, middle class, political and often ambitious, for the civil war provided the opportunity to learn quickly under the demands and pressures of warfare.[18] 'We were all novices,' admitted Dr Len Crome. 'I don't know anyone who had any experience of military medicine before.'[19] Nurses were also mainly young and Spain offered them the opportunity to take on roles and experience beyond those offered in the UK. Some were apolitical, driven more by 'humanitarian considerations' than by politics:

> Most of the nurses who came out that I met were politically conscious and knew why they were coming out. But there were a few who just went out to be nurses for a humanitarian reason and had no idea which side they were on even when they went out there.[20]

Apart from doctors and nurses, the unit included ambulance drivers, stretcher-bearers and administrators, whose backgrounds were also diverse. The unit offered the chance for volunteers to participate in the struggle without fighting on the battlefield, though the work was certainly not without risk; several members of the BMU were killed in Spain.

Viscount Pater Churchill established an office for the unit in Barcelona and selected a small farm in Grañen, near Huesca on the Aragon front, as the site for the first hospital, arguing that it 'was the only place that drained the whole front *and* gave two ways back if we had to move'.[21] Following an intensive operation to clean the farm, the hospital was opened with twenty-five beds and two operating theatres.[22] Casualties from the Aragon front, mainly Germans, soon started to pour in; one particularly exhausting three-day period saw the arrival of nearly two hundred patients. The work was nevertheless spasmodic in nature, adding to the stress: periods of frantic, intense activity alternated with long periods of interminable boredom, and several of the British staff soon discovered that they were unable to cope. Some resorted to drink, others elected to return to Britain.

Fortunately new recruits arrived at the end of September, including Reading doctor and Communist Reg Saxton, and a number of nurses, such as Annie Murray from Edinburgh:

During the first attack [in Aragon] I was on night duty and, because of this, the war made a deep impression on my mind; for sick people are usually more ill at night, and our senses being more acute at night to the grue-someness, the awful suffering of the men, especially those with abdominal wounds and haemorrhage for which one can do little, became burnt on my mind. In those days many of the soldiers were under twenty years of age, and I shall never forget those young men with their bodies torn and their limbs smashed.[23]

Problems soon developed in both the hospital at Grañen and the Barcelona office. A report described 'intermittent contact between members' and a general lack of organisation. Worse still, the report complained, 'the atmosphere among the English in Barcelona is the atmosphere of the English in India.'[24] A number of doctors quickly gained a reputation for being imperious and aloof, and Sinclair-Loutit in particular was seen as prickly and difficult. Particular criticism was levelled at the administrator in Barcelona, Hugh O'Donnell. According to Winifred Bates, the political *responsable* for the nurses, O'Donnell 'installed himself as Secretary to the Unit and a kind of link between London and the hospital at Grañen.'[25] A power struggle developed between Barcelona and Grañen, with the Barcelona office frequently making decisions over the head of the Grañen hospital. These difficulties were exacerbated by the TUC's threat on 25 November to withdraw financial support for SMAC, unless Communists were excluded from the unit.

At the end of January 1937 Viscount Churchill was replaced by Rose Davson (known in Spain as Rosita), who was regarded with great suspicion by senior British Communists, as she had previously worked for the British Embassy and Diplomatic Corps.[26] Her political 'unreliability' does not appear to have been ameliorated by her personality; cold and unfriendly, she seems to have been widely disliked in Spain. Winifred Bates stated pointedly: 'I pointed out the undesirability in my opinion of appointing Rosita in any position where she had to deal with human beings.' Her conclusion was biting: 'As a human being I sometimes want to offer her pity; as a revolutionary I have no more use for her than I have for a fascist.'[27] Later that spring, Davson was held responsible for the death of an Irish nurse, Ruth Ormsby, in a fire in the BMU flat in Barcelona: 'Two girls flung themselves from the window because they could not get out of the door. Both were badly burnt. There was no handle on the door because Rosita took it off,' wrote Bates. Yet, despite this and constant attacks on her from both Bates and Bill Rust, Davson earned the respect of, among others, SMAC secretary Leah Manning, and was still in place at the end of the war.

Problems were also evident in the hospital itself. Some were the result of political machinations – the influence of a clandestine Communist Party cell within the unit was widely resented – but many were personal and based on petty jealousies. Two recently arrived nurses, one of whom 'became involved in a passionate Lesbian love-affair' and the other 'whose sexual promiscuity seemed to shock the Spaniards', had to be sent back to England in mid-October.[28] By November, Sinclair-Loutit was becoming increasingly unpopular, partly due to his clumsy party manoeuvrings, but also to his rivalry with another young London doctor, Archie Cochrane, and his public relationship with one of the British nurses.[29] However, Sinclair-Loutit was one of a number to believe that the hospital's principal problem was not the squabbles within the unit or with Spanish medics, but that it was based on a quiet sector of the front. On the days 'when no wounded arrive . . . people quarrel for lack of occupation, and because they dislike the shape of each other's ears', grumbled Australian nurse Aileen Palmer, in a letter to her family.[30] By the end of the year, despite opposition from those who wanted the SMAC to remain in control of the unit, Sinclair-Loutit had persuaded the committee that they should move to the main Madrid front, where they could be more use to the Republic.

Dr Alexander Tudor-Hart, an experienced surgeon and a long-standing Communist, arrived in December 1936 and was quickly put in charge of the unit. The decision was taken to incorporate the medical unit within the International Brigades themselves and it was transferred to the 14th International Brigade, under the control of the Spanish Republican Army. Reg Saxton remembered that 'upon arriving at Albacete . . . we signed some document saying that we would put ourselves under military discipline.'[31] A number of medical staff were extremely – and not unreasonably – unhappy about losing their independent status, signifying that the medical volunteers were now in breach of the non-intervention agreement, just like the volunteers in the British Battalion. The changes also meant that new arrivals would no longer be placed in a single 'British hospital' but would be scattered among a number of hospitals in Republican Spain.

In early 1937, the main English group was transferred to Madrid. They worked first at a new hospital in Torrelodones, north of Las Rozas, before moving in February to the small village of Villarejo de Salvanes, sixteen kilometres from Morata de Tajuña on the Jarama front. During the ensuing battle, the unit's Herculean efforts were unable to prevent huge numbers of casualties dying at the front while waiting for ambulances, or in aerial bombardments. Seven hundred casualties poured in during the four heaviest days' fighting, and 'even the most gravely wounded had to be left lying in the open air until they could be attended to.'[32] More than sixty surgical operations were carried out each night, with the medical staff like 'cogs in a machine, working in a frenzy, and dropping down to sleep whenever there was a chance'.[33] The conditions were utterly gruelling:

> One became almost an automaton, you know, you were just going on, keeping on and keeping on ... the patients would come in and the wounded would come in, we were doing what we could for them. Many were dying and a few were surviving and were sent on and some wanted to go back and did go back. It seemed to go on for weeks and weeks, one got the impression it would never end ... We slept when we could, mattresses on the floor in some of the odd rooms that were not being used. We grabbed food when we could get it, we had short breaks when we could to get a little fresh air when the rush wasn't too wild ... But generally it was a hard slog all the time.[34]

It quickly became clear that establishing a rapid chain of evacuation from the battlefield would be vital if lives were to be saved:[35]

> When the British Battalion went into action for the first time we had a battalion doctor, an ambulance which belonged to the battalion and which ferried our own wounded to the dressing-station and operated a shuttle service between the front line and the dressing-station, and four or five stretcher-bearers assigned to the battalion. Two problems immediately became obvious. First, the distance from the front line to the dressing station was about four or five kilometres – a long way for even a superficially wounded man to travel under his own steam. Secondly, four or five stretcher-bearers, not per company, but for a battalion of 600 men engaged in heavy fighting, were far too few. Although this appears to be a fearful picture, and although men most certainly died outside the dressing-station while awaiting attention, wounded men at the front would still have had to be dragged to safety by their fellow soldiers, no matter how many

stretcher-bearers were available. The expectation of being carried from the front, under fire, and on a stretcher, is totally unrealistic. At Jarama, battalion headquarters served as an assembly-point for the wounded and they waited there for the ambulance to collect them and transport them to the dressing-station.[36]

After Jarama, the BMU officially became part of the *Sanidad Militar*, within the 35th Division of the Republican Army. However, the lack of a specific British medical unit to serve the British Battalion was proving problematic. British casualties would often end up in hospitals where nobody spoke English – not only was this distressing for individuals, it also made accurate diagnosis more difficult. An exasperated Walter Tapsell raised a number of other problems:

> There are often outstanding cases of quite innocent medical mismanagement. Wounds go undressed, men discharged without examination . . . Another big complaint is the fact that 27 Ambulances have been sent out here, but our Battalion is terribly badly served in this respect. Only the other day it took 7 & ¾ hours to get a wounded man to hospital on a quiet day . . . Why the hell [Alex Tudor] Hart and the other people peacefully stand around and allow this state of affairs to continue beats me.[37]

Keeping track of casualties was also extremely difficult. Three months after the end of the Jarama battle, letters were still arriving from London complaining that relatives had received no news of members of the battalion believed to have been killed or captured.[38] The response blamed the problems on the hard-pressed hospitals:

> We are not told by anybody when our men are sent to Hospitals, or when they are killed. Nor are we supposed to divulge the information. Nobody knows . . . The Hospitals issue no lists of incoming patients and outgoing patients, or nationalities . . . Everybody is working like mad and the main thing is not lists but care of the wounded.[39]

Establishing whether or not a volunteer had been killed was unbearably time-consuming and complicated:

> This is often impossible. We don't know it and there is no way of knowing

it. We find out in the lines, but the chaps here (and I myself) have no conception of dates, day of the week and etc. Only approximate dates can be set in many cases.[40]

One possible solution to the numerous problems was the establishment of a specific English hospital situated between the Madrid and Teruel fronts. This would complete a chain of hospitals able to efficiently evacuate wounded soldiers from the front. The hospital was set up in Huete, 'a little village north-east of Barcelona', where it occupied 'a large sixteenth century religious building around a spacious courtyard'.[41] Unfortunately, as a report complained, it received 'almost no support from Britain':

> We realise that one of the main weaknesses [of the unit at Huete] was the poor relationship between ourselves and the people of Britain . . . we feel that if the necessary help is forthcoming from Britain, we will build in Spain a hospital that will be a permanent monument to the solidarity of the British people.[42]

In any event, Huete was over one hundred kilometres away from the site of the next battle involving the British, at Brunete, west of Madrid. Consequently, in preparation for the forthcoming offensive, the Republican 35th Division (of which the International Brigades were part) set up a hospital in El Escorial, twenty kilometres from Brunete, in early July. When the Republican offensive was launched, ambulance driver Wogan Philipps was glad that the period of rest was over, as 'it was much harder to keep one's morale up when doing nothing.'[43]

Brunete soon put huge demands on the Republican medical services: during the course of the battle, there were in the region of 25,000 Republican casualties, there was virtually no water and the casualty rate of stretcher-bearers exceeded that of the infantry.[44] Welsh first-aider Alun Williams described the situation for the wounded as 'diabolical': the medical unit ran out of morphia within the first hour, with more than half of the seriously wounded dying within an hour.[45] This was despite the hard-pressed surgical teams working sixteen-hour shifts and achieving an astonishing work rate, with around a thousand operations carried out by Republican medical services operating just behind the front line. As English nurse Penny Phelps, who was based at El Escorial, recalled: 'By noon ambulances could no longer enter the yard . . . it was full of the wounded on stretchers. Although our organisation was better than on the Jarama, some casualties were already dead before we could do anything for them.'[46] One British volunteer, wounded during the Brunete fighting, remembered the hospital completely overwhelmed with casualties: 'it was really desperate with everybody stretched to the limit, stretcher cases right along the corridor in the hospital right through the lobby and right out into the open, waiting for attention.'[47]

Julian Bell, Virginia Woolf's nephew, who had been determined to go to Spain despite his family's opposition, was one of those killed at Brunete. Bell had volunteered as an ambulance driver despite the tough conditions – much of the driving was done at night, without lights, and on one occasion Bell and his partner drove their ambulance over 500 miles in two days. The popular Bell considered his time in Spain to be 'a better life than most I've led'.[48] His life was further cheered when he discovered that his old friend from King's College in London, Archie Cochrane, was working at the hospital to which he had been assigned. During the battle, Bell set off to help fill in shell-holes on the roads to speed up the evacuation of the wounded. Caught unawares by a Rebel counter-offensive, he was sheltering underneath his ambulance from bombardment near the village of Villanueva de la Cañada, when he was hit by a horizontally flying piece of shrapnel. When Bell arrived in hospital, Cochrane discovered that the shell fragment had penetrated deep into his friend's chest and that there was nothing that he could do, except to make his last moments as comfortable as possible.[49] Bell's last words were, 'Well, I always wanted a mistress and a chance to go to war, and now I've had both.'[50]

Peter Harrisson, who had previously been working as the administrator at Huete with Alex Tudor-Hart, never forgot Brunete and 'having to hold a wounded man down onto the blood-soaked operating table, while the surgeon cut away his arm without enough anaesthetic to kill the pain'.[51] Another doctor recalled:

We had counted up to ten thousand people who went through our hospital, wounded, lightly wounded, severely wounded or dead. We had a big marquee where we put the people lying on the grass on primitive stretchers, those who were alive but nothing could be done for them, waiting to die, covered in flies and dust and not even cleaned up properly. Some French doctors attached to the hospital used to go out at night and give lethal injections to those who were absolutely beyond salvation. I could not bring myself to do it, but I did not disapprove of it when you saw bodies lying in the dust beside you still breathing.[52]

However, in the stress and confusion that were endemic in the hospitals during battle, mistakes could all too easily be made, with potentially catastrophic consequences:

> One night, in the middle of the night I walked into the tent and found this male nurse, ex-veteran of Indo-China, French, leaning over a good-looking, blond athletic looking person with a syringe in his hand. When I asked him why he was doing this, he said, 'Look, his brain is hanging out.' When I put my hand on the man's hair what dropped out was about a fistful of congealed blood; the brain was not at all affected. He was an Englishman. I never found out who he was, but he was saved.[53]

At the end of the Brunete battle the British medical unit was withdrawn to the Aragon front. In September 1937 the medical units were fully integrated into the Republican Army, and now reported to the Spanish government, rather than the SMAC in London. Some doctors, such as Reg Saxton, returned home temporarily on leave, while others went permanently. The latter included Archie Cochrane and Kenneth Sinclair-Loutit, who took the nurse Thora Silverthorne, now his wife, with him.[54] On 11 October, the constant dangers facing the medical volunteers were amply demonstrated when the original British hospital at Grañen was destroyed by Nationalist bombers.

During the autumn of 1937, as the British Battalion were fighting in Aragon, a report complained vociferously about the 'hair-raising' conditions at the British-supported and Spanish-run hospital in Uclés, near Tarancón (seventy-five kilometres south-east of Madrid), which had received no supplies of soap for months, no clean sheets and 'impossible food'.[55] Hospital administrator Nan Green's account of the appalling standards of hygiene made disturbing reading:

> They used to throw amputated limbs out of the window and into the moat . . . and so the moat was full of rats. All the patients got lice and so did our nurses, who used to come home in tears. Our nurses used to stand the beds in tins of disinfectant because the rats used to get into the beds of paraplegic patients who didn't know if they were being chewed or not.[56]

Not surprisingly, it was recommended that no more British casualties should be sent there.[57]

The following spring saw an urgent reorganisation of the medical provisioning, forced upon the Republic by the huge Nationalist offensive which drove through Aragon to the Mediterranean, catastrophically splitting the Republic into two. The medical units, like the fighting units of the International Brigades, were severely debilitated by a lack of supplies and equipment. As the English nurse Margaret Powell remembered:

We fairly frequently had to do amputations, for instance, without anaesthetics. But sometimes, I had one man, I can remember very well . . . who was brought in and said 'You can take it off, if it has to come off, without an anaesthetic, I can bear it.' And, he did. And he didn't complain and nobody had to hold him down. The thing that seemed to grieve him most was that he wouldn't be able to fight anymore.[58]

The shortage of supplies meant that performing operations without anaesthetic was far from uncommon. One Scottish volunteer underwent surgery after being hit in the head by a bullet:

This doctor came in and looked at the X-ray and started, 'Right.' So here he started cutting in to my head, but there was nae anaesthetic. I don't know if it was pliers he was using but he couldn't get hold of the bullet and you could hear the ding . . . They left me alone for a couple of days then a little dapper chap came in. He was a dentist. He said, 'Have you got a bullet in your head?' 'Aye.' He says, 'Aw, well, I'll see to that.' So they brought me in. It was like one of these Hollywood things, they had everybody in, even the cleaners were in to see what was happening. He pulled the bullet out right enough. He had the pliers. He asked me if I wanted the bullet. I said, 'No, you can keep it.'[59]

Liverpool volunteer Bob Clark, wounded in the right arm and the side of his head, was told that he needed an operation, but that 'owing to the ghastly shortage of anaesthetic . . . all operations, except amputations or internal, had to be done with the local emergency injection.'[60] And it was not just medical supplies that were lacking: 'The facilities were very poor really, compared to the needs which we had. We were always short of people, always short of supplies, always short of transport.'[61] Mundane items, such as blankets, often ran short during major battles. Nurse Patience Darton had to overcome her own misgivings and insist categorically that blankets must not be buried with the dead:

> I had terrible arguments there with the stretcher bearers who wanted to take my blankets to wrap the people in to bury them, and I said no, I must have the blankets to keep people alive with – [I] had to pull the blankets off them.[62]

In the summer of 1938, following the urgent rebuilding of Republican forces, the Republic was to strike back at the Nationalists by launching a big attack across the Ebro River in Catalonia, 130 kilometres south-west of Barcelona. During the offensive, a small hospital was established behind the advancing soldiers, but as everything had to be carried across pontoon bridges by lorry, or ferried across in boats during the night, the facilities were necessarily limited. Serious casualties had to be taken back across the river to an improvised hospital set up by Len Crome, now commander of the medical service for the Republican 35th Division, in a large cave near the small Catalan village of La Bisbal de Falset. Leah Manning visited the hospital in the summer of 1938, and bravely sat with a young Welsh brigader she knew from home who had been mortally wounded in the stomach. She followed to the letter the instruction given to a young Spanish trainee by an experienced English colleague: 'never leave a boy to die alone – go and hold his hand and talk to him.'[63]

> At about four o'clock, the boy opened his eyes. He stared at me. In a voice of astonished wonder he said 'Leah Manning!' Then smiling – quietly, 'You see, I made it comrade.'[64]

The battles in the Sierra Pandols and Caballs, at the southern end of the mountain range running through Catalonia, were among the worst experienced by medical staff in Spain, for the task of getting the injured off the mountains under fire was extremely challenging. 'The pronouncements by the Generals that "War is Hell" are mere words,' said Alun Williams. 'Hell is a product of the imagination and without substance. War is real and unimaginable.'[65] Often the nearest ambulance was more than a kilometre from the front line, making the stretcher-bearers' work virtually impossible.

Where possible, they worked at night, hoping that the wounded could wait that long.[66]

The mythology of the Spanish Civil War includes heroic stories of wounded brigaders 'deserting to the front' from hospitals. Despite the ring of Comintern propaganda, some of these tales do have an element of truth to them. Walter Gregory was wounded in July 1938 and managed to make his own way back across the Ebro, where he was ferried to a hospital at Mataró:

> I had only been at Mataro for a few days when Sam Wild appeared along with two or three other comrades from the Battalion. They had come to the hospital with a sackful of mail for the wounded and Sam asked how I was feeling. Having seen the plight of so many of my fellow fighters I felt it honest to reply that I was well on the way to recovery.
>
> 'You don't look right yet,' said Sam, 'but we're off to the "Pimple" [the British nickname for a hill overlooking the battlefield]. We couldn't take it and now we're in a reserve position. There's a lot to be done and we can use you. How about coming back with us? There's a lorry outside and you can travel in the back. We'll just have to make sure that no one sees you trying to leave 'cos if they do you'll be back in that bed in no time.'
>
> How could I turn down such an offer? Sam grabbed my freshly laundered uniform, threw an arm round me to lend me some support, and had me out of the hospital and into the back of the waiting lorry in a matter of minutes. He threw a few old sacks over me and said that he would help me to get dressed later when there was time. The journey back to the Battalion was not one I would care to repeat.[67]

London surgeon Harry Bury remembered other men attempting to leave hospital and return to their units before they were fully recovered:

> A Cockney taxi-driver . . . came in with some nasty flesh wounds in his legs. After a few days he found he could walk again. But when we would not discharge him prematurely, he escaped and tried to get back to his unit. He was arrested by the military police, however, and was brought back to the hospital, where we decided to keep him locked in a stable until he was fit. Another, character named [Noel] Carritt (related to the poet), had received a leg injury. He was also keen to leave as soon as he could, and tried to persuade us that he was fit by lying on his back and waving his legs in the air.[68]

While some of the wounded chose to escape from hospital to return to the fight, others found different ways of overcoming the tedium of convalescence. Among these was Scottish volunteer John Tunnah:

I was in the hospital lying flaked out in bed. As I grew better (the big windows were open because it was very hot) I managed to hop and hobble over to the window just to see what was going on in the street. There was a flat roof opposite and all these darling girls were waving to me and smiling and shouting to me in Spanish and by signs and everything, always hanging out washing on the line on the flat roof. So each day this happened in the morning and I steadily improved. And nobody said anything to me. I just shouted over, 'When better I come see you'. 'Oh great!' So the day came when I was on crutches, I went out of the hospital just across the road, the girls saw me and welcomed me in. And I thought they were introducing me to their mother, anyway I was there half an hour before the penny dropped. And it was a brothel! 'You're not!' 'Si, si.' They were ever so pleased to tell me. So I said, 'Well, I've always liked you when I see you from there.' They said, 'Oh no, you're not well, you're wounded.' 'I'm well now!' And I wasn't a bad looking little fellow and I went on so much that this girl said to me, 'Alright'. So I went upstairs and of course I was weak and I was wounded and I tried and I tried and tried and it was hot and the sweat was rolling off me. Eventually she said, 'Enough, enough! Stay there.' She went over to the hospital. Two blokes came running over, upstairs, rolled me off the bed on to a stretcher, carried me out of the brothel on this stretcher and back to the hospital where they all knew by this time. And they were leaning out of the windows and gave me a great cheer, somebody shouting, 'A good advertisement for that place!'[69]

Many volunteers for the Republican medical services experienced gruelling and often terrible conditions. However, there is no doubt that important lessons were learned; and not just by the volunteers themselves. During the war, a number of hugely significant advances were made in the treatment and management of casualties, many of which, such as the improvements in organisation, the treatment of fractures and the use of blood transfusions, were to prove of great value in the Second World War.[70] Conventionally, Franco's army included, the role of medicine in war was to get as many men back on the front line and fighting as quickly as possible. However, as New Zealand doctor Douglas Jolly explained, the Republican medical services instead aimed to save as many lives as possible, for 'in our army a wounded comrade is not thought of only as a potential military asset.'[71] Crucial to saving lives was the implementation of an efficient chain of evacuation, the provision of decisive early treatment and the rapid expedition of casualties from the battlefield to hospital.[72]

The first link in the chain were the stretcher-bearers, who rescued casualties from the battlefield, often under intense enemy fire. As the stretcher-bearers were frequently working in no man's land, with no protective trenches or covering fire, a great number were killed or badly wounded and their casualty rate could exceed that of infantrymen.[73] Australian nurse Agnes Hodgson estimated that seventy per cent of stretcher-bearers were killed bringing in wounded.[74] The job required bravery to the point of recklessness: 'It took guts to walk into a front line where you made an attack and were beat back and you went crawling out at night, in the grey dark to pick up the wounded. It took guts. Very few of us had guts like that.'[75] As one Scottish volunteer remembered, 'they were getting gunners, riflemen, and suchlike, but then they said, "What about stretcher bearers?" Nobody was volunteering for stretcher bearers.'[76]

The small number who did volunteer ferried casualties to the first aid post, where medics dressed wounds, splinted fractures, applied pressure dressings or tourniquets, administered morphine for pain relief, and gave anti-gas gangrene and anti-tetanus injections. Situated at the front, this was an extremely hazardous position: 'Front line doctors were a rarity and their casualty rate was very high.'[77]

From the first aid post, the wounded were taken by ambulance or mule to a classification post in the rear; also not an easy task, for there were never enough ambulances and the few that were available were 'invariably subjected to Fascist artillery fire'.[78] Keith Scott Watson was convinced that this was a deliberate and calculated strategy by the Nationalists:

> I had long lost the illusion that the red cross meant anything in modern war. A hospital was an easy target. 'What was the use of wounding the Marxist swine if one allowed them to recover?' – that was not Fascist logic.[79]

Any wounded who survived the journey would be assessed for treatment according to the newly implemented system of triage, which essentially categorised patients as lightly wounded, needing urgent attention, or, all too often, beyond help. The system had been initiated by

Archie Cochrane, who ran it with the assistance of nurses such as Margaret Powell. Sometimes heart-breaking choices were involved:

> Men poured in as fast as the few ambulances and trucks that we had, to bring them in. I was then in ward and the only nurse in the ward. And I had to decide who should be treated. And many died then because I couldn't divide myself into six. And this was, I think, the most terrible thing that happened to me in all my life.[80]

Once assessed and categorised, casualties would be forwarded to the next stage of treatment; either an evacuation hospital away from the front, or, if they were in need of urgent intervention, to one of the mobile field hospitals.[81] Here they would be operated on by a 'remarkable' team of doctors who, working 'under the most difficult and heart-breaking conditions, performed wonderful feats of surgery'. Alun Williams was convinced that 'a severely wounded soldier's potential for survival was increased 100%' by the doctors, whose 'dedication and work . . . was bordering on the miraculous'.[82] Later, in the lead-up to the Second World War, Len Crome's experience of such improvements in medical organisation and the evacuation and treatment of casualties saw him given an important advisory role to the Royal Army Medical Corps. And the 1942 manual written by Douglas Jolly, *Field Surgery in Total War*, which drew heavily upon his experiences in Spain, became a primary text for British army doctors.[83]

Many of the medical advances in the Spanish Civil War were a direct result of the perilous lack of resources and the sheer numbers of wounded, which forced the doctors to seek imaginative and novel solutions. Dr Alex Tudor-Hart pressed for first-aiders to be made aware of the latest thinking on medical treatment, particularly relating to fractures which required careful splinting and padding to minimise shock.[84] Dr Harry Bury developed a keen interest in the treatment of complicated fractures by the 'closed method', picked up from the work of pioneering Catalan surgeon Dr Josep Trueta:

> My special interests were the casualties treated by the Dr. Trueta method of enclosing the whole of a shattered limb in plaster. The flesh wounds received no dressing, and so a lot of pus was generated inside the plaster cast (we had no anti-biotics then). When we opened the plasters after the

bone had had time to knit, it was full of maggots. The smell was terrible, but the wound was clean and healthy. Dr Tudor working at a hospital in Mataro, on the other hand, preferred to cut out a small window in the plaster in order to drain the pus. I decided not to do this as I was convinced that the maggots contributed to the healing process.[85]

However, it was the improvements in the transfusion of blood developed by another pioneering doctor, the Canadian Norman Bethune – assisted by Reg Saxton – which were probably most revolutionary and significant:[86]

The need was apparent for blood transfusion. So he [Bethune] collected together equipment, skilled people . . . and started the Madrid Blood Transfusion Service . . . he started this institute, recruited blood donors and got blood which could be stored in refrigerators.[87]

Blood transfusions were reserved for the most urgent and blood was stored by using the novel procedure of keeping it on ice. With limited time for matching blood groups effectively, the hospitals mainly relied upon supplies of blood group O, the universal donor.[88] Inevitably, volunteers were called on to donate the urgently needed blood, as Nan Green remembered:

Being fortunate to be the Universal Donor, and a sedentary worker, I was recruited to give some of my blood by direct transfusion, an unforgettable experience. Lying down beside a seriously wounded man, on the point of death, I watched as the colour came back to his lips, his breathing improved and he turned back towards life. Nowadays the transfer of blood is a far more scientific business and the simple grouping used at that time has become immensely more complex (I wasn't even given a Schick Test [for susceptibility to diphtheria], there wasn't time). During those early days of the Ebro campaign I actually gave 200cc of my blood, three times in little over two weeks. I felt no ill-effects, except that my legs seemed rather heavy for a day or two afterwards.[89]

Likewise, the process of giving the transfusion, as Reg Saxton described, was somewhat primitive:

I had a long rubber tube and a funnel so I delivered the blood into the patient
by pouring it into a funnel and it came down a tube and it went through a
cannula into a patient's vein. It worked very well, but of course it was a bit
tedious and troublesome and the sterilising wasn't too easy. We just had to
wash it out and boil it up and do it again.[90]

Saxton also investigated the use of cadaver blood for transfusions: 'There
are lots of dead people around who have no further use for their blood, it
might be as well, if it were feasible and safe to make use of some of that.'[91]
However, a lack of time, materials and the opportunity prevented him from
actually attempting the procedure.

These innovations undoubtedly saved numerous lives, not just in Spain,
but in the war that followed. Many volunteers recognised that they owed
their lives to the work of the British medical unit, led from the front by the
dedicated Dr Len Crome, whose work earned almost universal respect.
Douglas Jolly later argued that 'in Spain I saw the Army Medical Corps grow
from a rudimentary ill-equipped, inadequate organisation to a disciplined,
efficient body of which no modern army need be ashamed.'[92] As one
admiring English International Brigader later remarked, 'War is a bloody
business, and Len [Crome] saw more bloodiness than most. But all who
were treated by Len Crome and his team knew that everything that could
be done for them, would be.'[93]

12

'The good looking students'

The battle of Brunete saw the finish of the 'heroic' phase of my diary keeping. It remained to the very last word, naive, coy and very proper; but the realities of war, especially contrasted with the relative picnic of our own particular experience of the post-battle Jarama front, brought home to me the inadequacy of some of my pious platitudes of earlier days.

Fred Thomas, *To Tilt at Windmills*

Finally released from the Jarama front, the British Battalion had been returned for some sorely needed rest and relaxation to Mondéjar. The facilities were typically basic; volunteers were forced to sleep where they could, although there was food and wine available. The morning after they arrived, the process of restoring themselves to something resembling an army began; 'weapons were cleaned, clothes washed and new clothes were issued.'[1] They would have barely three weeks.

On 6 July 1937, the Republic launched an ambitious offensive twenty-five kilometres west of Madrid, not far from the site of the battles around the La Coruña road the previous December. While General Miaja, 'the saviour of Madrid', was officially in charge, the Brunete offensive, as it became known, was the brainchild of gifted Republican military tactician Vicente Rojo. His plan was to release the Rebel stranglehold on Madrid with a double-pronged attack designed to break through the Nationalist lines at two separate points: one at Brunete heading south-east, the other to the south of Madrid heading east, and designed to meet up with the first at Alcorcón. It was by some way the largest Republican action so far; 'if we cannot succeed with such forces, we will not be able to manage it anywhere,' declared the Republican President, Manuel Azaña.[2]

The soldiers in the International Brigades were supplied with new

THE GOOD LOOKING STUDENTS'

equipment and, for the first time, officers were issued with revolvers and proper uniforms. While Fred Copeman's claim that 'the 15th International Brigade was well known to the military commanders as the finest fighting unit on the peninsula' was typical of his bravado, the British commander had good cause to believe that morale had been restored and that the battalion was back in good order after the bloodbath and long vigil in the trenches at Jarama.

> Brunete was an action where we had everything. We had the arms. The battalion was 660 [strong]. Every man was trained and the commanders knew their job . . . We had tanks in numbers and types never before seen. They rumbled by with guns bigger than any visualised in Spain. Arms seemed to be plentiful and the air force knew its stuff. No longer the single fighter against a dozen Franco planes; whole squadrons, capably manoeuvred, flew over during the day ensuring that no enemy spotter planes came within a hundred miles of our sector.[3]

In fact, the whole 15th Brigade was at peak numbers. It now comprised six battalions, divided into two regiments. In the first, commanded by Jock Cunningham, were the British, and the two American battalions, the Lincolns and the Washingtons; in the second were the 24th Spanish, the mainly Yugoslavian Dimitrovs and the Franco-Belge Battalion.[4] The experienced George Nathan was chief of operations for the brigade, and the British Battalion itself was under the command of Copeman, who had taken over from Jock Cunningham in March, when he was wounded.[5] 'What a contrast to Jarama,' remarked one volunteer, though wiser heads wondered if their position was quite as strong as some might believe:[6]

> When we went into action at Brunete we had one automatic rifle, similar to a Bren gun. And we had six Maxim machine guns for a Battalion. Now that in itself was ridiculous. That was all that we had. The remainder were simply rifles, you know, the ordinary rifle.[7]

While the battalion itself was lacking in heavy weaponry, the 15th International Brigade had been joined at Brunete by a new artillery unit, the British Anti-Tank Battery, usually known as the 'anti-tanks', which was formed in May 1937 from forty men training at Madrigueras. They represented something of an elite; Fred Copeman claimed that he deliberately chose intellectuals to be members, 'good-looking students . . . as a kind of apartheid' to keep them apart from the 'roughnecks' in the overwhelmingly working-class infantry companies.[8] Copeman also insinuated that some of the men were homosexual and that this was another reason for separating them: 'they were too good looking for me. If you get a good-looking lad among twenty big husky men, well,' he claimed, 'he's going to turn that way whether he likes it or not.'[9]

Whether or not some of the men in the anti-tanks were homosexual, Copeman's version of the selection process is not supported by members of the battery. Bill Alexander, the unit's political commissar, stated categorically that Copeman had 'nothing' to do with choosing the British members of the anti-tanks.[10] And as Fred Thomas, who served with the unit from May until the end of the war, recounted: 'Somebody chose the forty or so of us and omitted the known drunks and general nuisances, but not Fred Copeman.'[11] The members were actually selected by Malcolm Dunbar, their commander, and his assistant, former journalist Hugh (actually Humphrey) Slater:

> On June 6 the order came through to the first Battalion of Instruction that an English company of 35 men, including an officer and sergeants, should be sent at once to the base to form an English-speaking Anti-Tank Battery. Hugh Slater, political commissar of the English company and I made out a list of names, and next morning we left taking with us Jack Black as second in command. Apart from Black and myself, the men were new recruits from England who had never been to the front.[12]

Ronald Malcolm Loraine Dunbar, the first commander of the anti-tanks, was a French and Spanish-speaking journalist who had arrived in Spain on 9 January 1937.[13] The son of Lady Dunbar, he was public-school educated and had read Economics and History at Christ's College, Cambridge.[14] Described as a 'very, very delicate sensitive person', the highbrow and enigmatic Dunbar seemingly 'never got intimate with anyone'; even Hugh Sloan, who was Dunbar's *enlace* (runner) and spent a great deal of time with him, never really came to know him on a personal level.[15] However, his respect for Dunbar remained undiminished:

> Captain Dunbar, for all the time I knew him, was a very remote, private, uncommunicative person, who always maintained an aloofness and

remoteness from the people he associated with. He always remained an
enigma to me. I never ever once had any kind of personal talk with him,
only through the orders and military requirements he had to give. He kept
everybody at their distance . . . But he was a very, very courageous and
dependable soldier, in my opinion probably one of the best of the volunteers
that ever went to Spain.[16]

Like George Nathan, Dunbar was to reveal previously hidden qualities
in Spain, eventually becoming the leading military figure among the British
volunteers.[17] But he was no 'true believer', only joining the Communist
Party in November 1937.[18] Even as late as July 1938, when he was Chief of
Staff for the 15th International Brigade, Dunbar's political work was
described as weak.[19] Instead responsibility for ensuring political orthodoxy
in the battery lay with Scottish political commissar George Murray, who
was also a clandestine agent for the Republican military security, the *Servicio
Investigación de Militar* (SIM).[20]

Well-led and well-staffed, the Anti-Tank Battery was also well-
equipped, with three brand new, state-of-the-art Soviet semi-automatic
45mm guns; as one volunteer stated proudly, 'the gun was at that time in
advance of anything in use in any other army'.[21] When the US military
attaché visited the battery in late 1937, he spent some time carefully
examining the guns.[22] Fitted with optical sights which, combined with the
flat trajectory, made them extremely accurate, they were capable of firing
both armour-piercing and high explosive shells, had a range of up to 16km
and were effective against even heavy tanks at distances of up to three
kilometres.[23] The battery was taught how to use the new guns by Russian
instructors, assisted by an Italian linguist who spoke Russian and could
translate the names of their various parts.[24] The volunteers were left in
no doubt of the weapons' importance: 'When we were first created, we
had a reception at divisional headquarters, and told the guns were of more
value than our lives.'[25]

Many volunteers enjoyed being part of an elite unit and were hugely
relieved that they would not have to do any more marching:

Each gun-crew was a small team, and at rest – and even sometimes close to
action – had certain advantages over the infantryman. For example, because
each gun was towed by a lorry, members of the battery were able to stow
more material among the ammunition boxes than a 'foot-slogger' could

carry – a few books, writing paper, the simplest things which made life more tolerable.[26]

Designed to be operated by a team of nine, all of whom were expected to be able to function in each and every role,[27] the guns were transported by teams of two or, preferably, four men, though for longer journeys their pneumatic tyres meant that they could be towed behind a truck. However, the initial excitement rather waned when it was realised just how much physical effort was required to fire the guns and, above all, to manhandle them into place.

> This was great fun. We were playing at soldiers in the pleasantest way possible, with no enemy to answer back. So we vied with each other in our martial posturing and felt very warlike. I think, if truth be told, there was a slight decline in this exuberance when Dunbar, our C.O., called us to order. For then we found how big and heavy these guns were! Of course, trucks would transport them and us on journeys of any length (though we frequently found later that trucks were by no means always available) but basically they had to be manhandled. In the firing position the long and solid legs were splayed wide; on the order 'Prepare to move,' these were lifted by two men apiece, run together and clamped fast with an alarming clash of metal. Then with all eight of the gun crew at different positions, 'Lift!' and the bods at the tail end heaved up; 'Move!' and as they pulled the rest pushed until, with much heaving and staggering and losing balance, the thing was moving. On a good, smooth, macadamed road it was relatively easy. On rough fields with hillocks and deep ruts everywhere, it was decidedly not.[28]

The unit quickly developed a reputation for being highly effective; Welshman Jim Brewer felt that the Anti-Tank Battery was 'the best unit we ever served in'.[29] Even Fred Copeman admitted that the 'anti-tank company were bloody good . . . and they had plenty of courage'.[30]

The anti-tanks were initially attached to a Spanish Republican unit at Jarama where, too late to be involved in any of the front's major actions, they had to be satisfied with taking the occasional pot-shot at the Rebel lines.[31] Dunbar devised ramps leading to a number of firing positions, so that the guns could fire a few rounds to destroy a machine-gun post, then be quickly moved back out of sight.[32] But on 3 July, the battery rejoined their compatriots in the 15th International Brigade, in preparation for the forthcoming action.

At the same time, the resting volunteers had been informed that they were about to return to combat. For some, the thought of having to undergo once more the hell of Jarama was too much to contemplate and a number promptly deserted, just as the battalion was leaving for the front.[33] The remainder, some six hundred strong, left Mondéjar on 2 July, after being presented with a banner made by the grateful women of the village.[34] Their gruelling journey, which required skirting Madrid, took most of the night and ended finally in the foothills of the Guadarrama, near San Lorenzo de Escorial, forty kilometres north-west of Madrid. Once unloaded, they spent the night hidden among the woods near the village of Torrelodones, before moving down to the bottom of the foothills in the morning. Here they prepared for the forthcoming attack on the village of Brunete, which lay on the plain in front of them, baking in the full heat of the Spanish summer sun.[35]

Initially held in reserve, the 15th International Brigade was soon thrown into the battle to assist a Spanish unit which had been unable to capture the resolutely defended village of Villanueva de la Cañada, en route to Brunete.[36] Perhaps considered too important to lose, the Anti-Tank Battery was held back during the attack, much to their astonishment. Scottish volunteer John Dunlop was particularly critical of the decision not to use their guns to knock out the strongpoints in the village. It was 'sheer bloody incompetence', he railed.[37]

While the Washington Battalion advanced on the northern end of Villanueva, the British and Dimitrov Battalions launched an assault on the south, in an attempt to cut off the defending force. However, a number of attackers were hit by machine-gun fire and by snipers strategically placed in the high church tower, 'a converted Islamic minaret . . . sticking out like a sore thumb', which forced them to dive for cover.[38] Walter Gregory and a Welsh comrade were among those who came under fire. Later that day, Gregory returned to look for his friend:

When I had dived for the safety of the roadside ditch he had been right beside me and now, safe from the fire of the machine-guns, I turned to look for him.

'Are you alright Taff?'

There was no reply.

I worked my way back along the ditch and saw him lying on his face. I rolled him on to his side. He was dead. A bullet had gone through his forehead. His mouth hung open and was full of flies. His tongue, which had swollen from thirst, was protruding. His eyes were still open and covered with those blasted flies, which were also working their way into his ears. It is a picture which has stayed with me for forty-five years and one which I am certain will never leave my consciousness.[39]

In temperatures of over forty degrees centigrade, the Republican attackers remained 'pinned down . . . [behind] a ridge . . . four to six hundred yards away from the village' until nightfall.[40] The terrain was extremely unpleasant; 'dry sandy soil cut into ravines and deep gulleys, with no cover . . . the fields were covered with dry grass and stubble easily set alight by bombs and shells.'[41] Their discomfort was accentuated by an acute shortage of water, for the volunteers' water bottles had been taken away to be refilled when the battalion had moved off. Some of the men made matters worse by drinking wine and several members of the battalion were urgently dispatched to find supplies for their parched comrades, who 'were dying of thirst'.[42]

Albert Charlesworth was among those sent on the search for water. Crawling along under cover, he found himself trapped by rifle fire from the village and prudently took shelter until nightfall. As darkness approached, he cautiously resumed his search, keeping a wary eye on the church tower. Suddenly:

A terrible hullabaloo went out. Firing burst out in all directions, there was shouting, there was screaming. After a few minutes I could hear the voice of Fred Copeman crying, 'Stop firing! Stop firing!' And very shortly the firing did stop and everything went deadly quiet.[43]

Walter Gregory later recounted what had happened:

At dusk there was a commotion in the village and all of those around me started to peer over the top of the ditch to see what was happening. A party of women and children were slowly leaving the village and making their way down the road toward our position. They were closely packed together and casting fearful and anxious glances to left and right as they moved forward. We started yelling at them to get a move on, to get away from the village as fast as possible, to get off the road where they were so visible, to get behind our lines where they would have some protection. As they drew nearer we saw that they were being used as a human shield by a group of Fascist troops who were crouching behind them and forcing them forward, in tight formation, at bayonet-point. These heroes then started firing at us from behind their living armour and we had no alternative but to return their fire. With great regret I have to state that quite a few of those poor women and their children were killed and wounded by both Fascist and Republican bullets which missed their intended targets. It was a side of war that I had never seen before and, thank God, I was never to see again.[44]

As other accounts describe, the 'crowd of women, children and old men, and about forty young men' called out '¡Camaradas!' before the soldiers hiding behind them opened fire.[45] The Republicans were left with little choice but to shoot back, knowing full well that this would cause civilian casualties.[46] Fred Copeman later admitted that he ordered two machine-gunners to return fire:

I hissed to them, 'Get ready to fire all you've got, and don't be sentimental.' At the top of my voice I yelled to our men, in the semi-darkness, 'Listen carefully. When I blow the whistle lay down and don't move.' With the next breath I blew the whistle, and Ginger and Bill let everything rip along the flat surface of the road . . . Not a nice sight. One old lady was dead in front. Happily she didn't know what had hit her. A few more of the women were wounded . . . Only three of the men remained alive.[47]

Already enraged by the defenders' ruse, their blood was raised further when Bill Meredith, the popular commander of No. 2 Company, was shot while going to the aid of a wounded man lying in the road. 'People were very, very angry about this . . . we took no prisoners,' admitted one London volunteer, candidly.[48] As many as half a dozen Nationalists were executed, including the mayor of the village.[49] Fred Copeman later confessed to personally executing a Rebel officer who was attempting to surrender, partly in response to the shooting of Meredith:

A few minutes afterwards someone appeared in front of me with a Spanish civilian. It was the enemy commander of artillery coming to give himself up. All I saw was the Colt revolver he was waving around aimlessly. I was taking no chances. He dropped like a brick.[50]

Following the Rebels' failed escape attempt, Villanueva de la Cañada was captured by the combined units of the 15th International Brigade at midnight. Little of the village remained:

> It was a vision of what would be only too familiar in the future. A village reduced to rubble, seen in those pictures of villages on the Somme from the First World War. It had been defended by small fortified positions on an old front line protected by barbed wire. Huge bomb craters everywhere and overall the stink of the decaying enemy dead buried beneath the rubble, and flies, flies and more flies.[51]

The battalion had also taken heavy casualties; during the attack, fifty men had been killed or wounded.[52] However, the night offered the opportunity to resupply, and the parched and sun-struck volunteers gratefully restocked themselves with food and, crucially, water. They spent the night sleeping rough in the deserted, ruined village.

The following day, the British followed the American battalion as they advanced east towards the heights in the distance, which lay across the River Guadarrama and only three kilometres from Boadilla, the scene of the massacre of Esmond Romilly's group a few months earlier. The key highpoint – their target – would later be named 'Mosquito Hill' after the noise of the countless bullets buzzing overhead. As the troops moved out of the village and into the open, several aeroplanes appeared in the sky, heading towards them.

> Some aircraft – three Junkers 52s – came over. We got down, the Americans got down. The 'planes passed overhead and immediately the Americans got up. We stayed down. The Americans got up and started to advance, the 'planes circled back – had seen them – circled back and dropped bombs on them . . . We found that quite a large number of Americans had been killed by these bombs.[53]

'When we moved forward again to take up our position, we had to pass where the bomb had landed, a massive bomb-hole with the dead still lying around,' remembered one Manchester volunteer.[54]

As the British advanced towards Mosquito Hill, the Anti-Tank Battery was moved up to the bank of the River Guadarrama, where they were spotted by Nationalist aircraft; by this stage, these were coming over 'one after the other . . . picking you off at their leisure'.[55] 'It's just the world's worst bloody sensation,' remembered Fred Thomas, 'flattening out with your face in the dirt, shrapnel and muck falling all around and on top of you.'[56] Veteran Communist and hunger-marcher Sid Quinn watched as four bulls, which had been 'grazing quietly and peacefully away', were slaughtered by a barrage of machine-gun and shellfire. 'I thought it was tragic,' said Quinn, 'but that was war.'[57] The Anti-Tank Battery suffered their first mortality when they were spotted by Nationalist artillery. Fraser Crombie, a veteran Scottish campaigner against the means test, was hit in the shoulder by a shell and killed instantly. 'We were caught with our pants down,' Hugh Sloan admitted.[58] It was both a shock and a warning of what lay ahead.

As brigade commander Vladimir Ĉopić realised, the strong Rebel defence, combined with their air superiority, was decisively slowing the Republican advance.[59] Brigade runner Frank Graham discovered that Ĉopić was right to be worried. Moving ahead of the main British contingent (on a white horse, according to Bill Alexander), Graham had seen that their target, the crucial Romalillos Heights, appeared to be neither defended nor occupied. However, by the time the battalion approached the heights, Nationalist soldiers were moving into position and were able to begin firing on the Republican forces advancing towards them:

Now if we'd reached the top of that hill, we might have won the battle, because below was the road. But we had no mobile, we had no trucks, we were on foot carrying all our packs and that, and the heat. It took them all the time to reach the fortifications . . . As they came to the fortifications I saw two or three people [Nationalist soldiers] on the top of the hill and I knew it was over.[60]

A two-hour barrage from Rebel artillery allowed even more reinforcements to be brought up. The British managed to move slowly forward and captured a number of secondary ridges, but they remained pinned down and, with existence 'almost unbearable under the boiling heat and the flies',[61] the number of casualties began to mount alarmingly. They included Charlie Goodfellow, battalion second-in-command and a good personal friend of Fred Copeman. A legend later developed that Goodfellow died because he was wearing a pair of jinxed leather boots, which had originally been issued to Copeman:

> Some time previously, when the officers were issued with uniform, mine included a pair of cavalry boots. I was wearing them one day when the Commander of the Army came to inspect the sector. Having got into the trench with the boots on, I found I could not climb out without taking them off, and I made up my mind that they were no good to me. Young McIlroy immediately grabbed them and was killed while wearing them. A few days later Bill Meredith took them over and had them on when he lost his life at Villa Nueva [sic] . . . There was an extra sharp crack from an exploding antitank shell, and I looked round to find Charlie's brains spread over my shoulder. His head was blown off less than three feet away from me. I hadn't a scratch. Charlie had waited so long to get home, and now it was too late. I gave an instruction that the boots were to be buried with him.[62]

The secondary ridges were as near as the British ever got to capturing the Romalillos Heights. They held on, stranded in an extremely exposed and dangerous position where communication with other Republican troops was almost impossible. As Fred Thomas discovered, his regimental commander was struggling to stay in contact with the officers under his command:

> [Jock Cunningham] was there, issuing orders, sending messages right and left, endeavouring to cope with what was obviously a critical situation. Then as the telephone operator at his side failed repeatedly to contact some required unit, Cunningham saw us.
>
> 'You two, get this fucking message to them quick, and there's only one fucking way, over the top!'
>
> Even now the memory is still vivid. A fierce fascist attack was raging and, as George [Baker] and I edged ourselves cautiously over the parapet of sandbags, bullets whistled and cracked past us. For perhaps fifteen minutes we crawled about, never daring to lift our heads an inch from the dirt, shrinking into petrified hulks when a shell or mortar burst nearby. Then we gave up. I clearly remember that getting back was even worse; it is much more frightening when it's all coming from behind you! Falling

ignominiously into the trench we confessed our failure to deliver the message.

'What message?' asked Jock.[63]

Just as they had done the previous day, supplies of ammunition, food and water ran short. The River Guadarrama, which they had crossed earlier, was dry and the soldiers dug holes in the sandy riverbed allowing a small trickle of water to percolate through. However, 'these were soon abandoned when it was discovered that a little way upstream were some bloated corpses of mules laying in the river bed.'[64] A number of men were sent to refill the water bottles, which one Scottish member of the anti-tanks realised 'was a risky thing to do, you know, because crawling around you could have been picked off'.[65] As night fell, they were withdrawn to the Nationalist-built trenches overrun during the initial advance.

Over the next two days increasingly desperate attempts were made to capture the heights, but bombarded by air and artillery, facing a well dug in and determined defending force which was growing in strength every day, Copeman came to realise 'that without support we would not gain the top of Mosquito Hill'.[66] David Anderson, a Scottish officer then serving with the Lincolns, agreed:

> Mosquito Hill was a position that we absolutely couldn't capture with the means that we had. It was absolutely impossible. I mean, they had domination, and as a matter of fact as we lay in that position down below Mosquito Hill, we could see right behind, the lights of the supplies going up to the Fascists' positions. It wasn't long before we realised that the position that we held was absolutely impossible. And then of course we had to withdraw. It was the end of the offensive as far as the Republican Government was concerned.[67]

On 11 July, depleted and exhausted, the British and American battalions were moved temporarily into reserve positions. Two days later, as the extent of the casualties became evident, Harry Pollitt wrote to Will Paynter at Albacete, asking for details 'of all comrades who have been killed and wounded and especially in regard to death certificates'.[68] In reply, Paynter admitted that 'the action is still on and it is not possible to send a complete list of the dead. We do not wish to make the mistake of reporting people dead who are not.' However, it was already abundantly clear that the Brunete offensive had taken a devastating toll on the entire 15th Brigade: both the American and Canadian battalions had lost half their strength[69] and significant British losses included a number of key figures:

> When we do send the complete list you will realise how heavy our losses have been, not so much in numbers but in quality.
>
> Two company commanders have been lost, one killed and the other seriously wounded. [Charlie] Goodfellow, second in command, has been killed. G[eorge]. Brown [company political commissar and a leading Manchester Communist] and [hunger march organiser Robert] Elliott have been killed and represent a big weakening of our political forces.[70]

Matters took a serious turn for the worse when, on 18 July, Franco launched a huge counter-attack, supported by at least 300 aeroplanes and a similar number of artillery pieces. Meanwhile, Ĉopić estimated that the British Battalion now numbered only 208 men.[71] The remnants were divided into two groups, the first led by Joe Hinks, the Madrid veteran who had demonstrated 'great ability and technical skill' and who had replaced the overwrought and exhausted Copeman as commander of the battalion.[72] The other group was led by Daily Worker correspondent Walter Tapsell, who had transferred to the battalion as a political commissar, infuriated with his Party work in Barcelona:

> I have lived here for over a month now, at my own expense. There is no pay for the job I am supposed to do. Thank you kindly for the appointment, the next time you want an office boy, advertise in the Daily Worker will you?
>
> Let me say quite frankly I am tired of being fucked about. I came out here to fight. I did not come out here for more political jobs, nor do I want one.[73]

Showing dangerous 'rank-and-filist tendencies', Tapsell had strongly resisted being sent to Albacete to carry on the political work he had been attempting to do in Barcelona, arguing that 'it will be a good thing for the Party in the eyes of the men if one of the communists is NOT a Political Commissar or Military Officer, and just mucks in with them.'[74] But despite his enthusiasm for the fight, both his and Hinks' groups, hopelessly outnumbered and overwhelmed, were soon forced to withdraw when

General Enrique Lister's elite Communist Fifth Regiment was pushed out of Brunete itself. The battalion retreated back across the Guadarrama, where the two groups were reunited. When the Republican forces established a new line on the other side of the river, only forty-two men remained in the battalion.[75] But the Nationalist counter-attack had at last spent itself and on 25 July the British were pulled out of the line.

During the three-week battle, the Republic had gained over forty square miles of territory, but the losses had been extensive: over 25,000 casualties, and a correspondingly disastrous cost in armour and aircraft.[76] The British lost a number of key figures: along with George Brown, Bob Elliott and Charlie Goodfellow, they included Bill Meredith and the anti-tanks' popular second-in-command, Jack Black. The loss of Black was a major blow: 'he was the best-liked lad in the whole outfit, a wonderful fellow, always full of fun. When things got rough he could keep geeing you up.' The same volunteer remembered Black's capacity 'to produce a packet of Lucky Strike when things were at their worst',[77] although another member of the battery remembered this ability rather less fondly: 'Every time we went into action, we'd get Lucky Strike cigarettes and Jack coined a phrase, "When in trouble boys, smoke a Lucky." Every time we got Lucky Strike cigarettes, we knew we were in trouble.'[78]

Matters were not helped by anxieties that even the notoriously resilient Fred Copeman had begun to crack up under the strain. But most significant was the loss, in mid-July, of the experienced and popular Major George Nathan. It was also, by some accounts, a death that could have been avoided. One Welsh volunteer who was near Nathan when he was killed admitted that he was 'a superb commander' but considered him to be 'excessively brave . . . [he would] never bend to enemy fire, which was incredibly foolish.' Caught in an enemy bombardment and having allegedly refused to lie prone, Nathan had been hit by a shell or bomb fragment.[79] Nurse Penny Phelps treated the mortally wounded and virtually unrecognisable Nathan in hospital; his situation, she quickly realised, 'was quite hopeless'.

> A casualty was carried into the operating-theatre. A weak voice said, 'Penny, don't you know me?' I had a fearful shock. It was George Nathan, now a major commanding a regiment. He was in great pain. I gave him an injection, put the anaesthetic mask on his face and we began to operate. A piece of shrapnel had pierced the liver, diaphragm and lungs and had lodged

in the spine. It was quite hopeless. After the operation we took Nathan
upstairs. I stayed with him having given an intramuscular saline infusion
and repacked his wounds. Our best officer was dying.[80]

During the evening, avoiding any danger of an air attack, Nathan was
given the special military funeral befitting his prominence among the British
volunteers. Most of the leading figures of the brigade attended. George
Aitken gave the funeral oration; as he spoke he 'could hear both Gal and
Cunningham sobbing, sobbing away; probably feeling that they once hadn't
been on too good terms with the great soldier'.[81]

On 28 July, a request was made for volunteers to go back in the line,
although the battalion was clearly in no position to do so, with survivors
'lying almost dead to the world with fatigue, with the heat, the thirst and
the lack of food . . . they were half dead with exhaustion.'[82] The order
sparked what was essentially a mutiny: 'perhaps as many as 60 or 70', as
John Angus put it carefully, 'expressed . . . a reluctance to return to the
front.'[83] It was wisely countermanded, and the battalion and anti-tank units
were temporarily moved into reserve before returning to the villages from
which they had departed, so optimistically, only three weeks earlier.[84] The
Anti-Tank Battery was billeted in the picturesque mill town of Ambite, 'a
setting straight from the Sussex Downs', while the battalion returned to
nearby Mondéjar.[85]

> Our return to Mondéjar was in sharp contrast to the noisy enthusiasm the
> villagers had shown at our departure. Then, they had seen a strong,
> optimistic battalion setting out to do battle with the Fascists, and they must
> have thought that a Republican victory was as good as guaranteed. Now
> they witnessed a small band of weary and despondent men gathering back
> at base. It must have been unnerving for them to see such a transformation
> in so short a time.[86]

The volunteers' refusal to return to the front had been defended by both
Walter Tapsell and George Aitken, who felt that the battalion was in no
physical or mental condition to continue the fight. Aitken protested to his
Corps commander[87] about what he called a 'bloody terrible' decision:

> I marched up with my interpreter, saluted and told my story about the

conditions of the troops and that this was an impossible order; the people were in no condition, they were half dead with exhaustion. And I remember he just looked across the table at me and said very quietly, 'We may all be dead before morning.' That clicked me back on my heels, so I said to him, 'Well, in that case, there's nothing more to be said,' and I just saluted and came out.[88]

Provoked, no doubt, by the horrendous number of casualties, Tapsell went even further, openly criticising the Republican battle strategy and rashly accusing Gal of gross incompetence: 'only stupidity or a deliberate disregard for life would keep men in such an exposed position [on Mosquito Hill]. Gal isn't fit to command a troop of Brownies, let alone a People's Army.'[89] A report by 'Gallo' (Italian Communist Luigi Longo, a senior member of the Comintern who had been involved in the creation of the International Brigades) estimated that less than half of the 15th International Brigade remained by the end of the battle.[90] According to Tapsell five out of every six British volunteers had been either killed or wounded.[91]

Having initially seemed to augur so well, the failure of the offensive was particularly devastating. Even a visit by the legendary orator Dolores Ibárruri, *La Pasionaria*, could not restore the morale of the shattered British volunteers:

Pasionaria came to see us and addressed us. Well, it wasn't very effective because we knew that we had suffered a defeat and she was speaking in Spanish anyway, which we didn't understand and the interpreter wasn't very effective. So it was rather a damp squib . . . [She was] a real firebrand, she was a commanding personality, she did stand out and I've no doubt that to someone who understood Spanish, her form of address and so on was very effective. But it was the wrong place for a woman to be and the wrong place to make speeches, because a hell of a lot of our chaps had been killed . . . everybody was exhausted.[92]

Back in Mondéjar, arguments raged over the strategy and tactics of the battle and the actions of the British Battalion leadership. Walter Tapsell repeated Copeman's criticism that capturing Villanueva de la Cañada had merely allowed Franco's forces enough time to bring up reinforcements, and other senior British figures agreed.[93] Gal wanted Tapsell shot for his earlier insubordination, but was persuaded to back down by Fred Copeman

– who went, backed up by Joe Hinks' Machine-Gun Company, to brigade headquarters to remonstrate with Gal. But Tapsell's criticisms did not end with Gal – he also accused Jock Cunningham of being out of his depth as regimental commander. Nathan and Aitken thought much the same; when they told 'the highly strung' Cunningham that he had placed two battalions in the wrong place, he had responded furiously by going on strike and refusing to take any further orders.[94]

While many of the arguments were over military tactics, the disagreements had their roots in personal feuds. Will Paynter held Aitken partially responsible for the acrimonious rows that developed, accusing him of having shown 'a disturbing complacence'.[95] Dave Springhall claimed that there was a total disintegration of the battalion leadership after Brunete, and though Aitken denied that the situation was so serious, he did admit that certain 'leading comrades' had collapsed under the incredible strain. Bert Williams, a political commissar then working with the Americans, was, apparently, 'at the end of his tether', Copeman 'was in a very bad state' and Tapsell was 'in a state of distress', 'absolutely demoralised, and not quite normal'.

Both Tapsell and Copeman essentially had nervous breakdowns during the Brunete battles. Indeed Tapsell was physically detained for some days after his outburst, Aitken believing that 'he was not at the time fully responsible for his actions . . . The circumstances were abnormal and above all Tapsel[l] was abnormal and his conduct abnormal.'[96] It was important to recognise, Aitken continued, 'what three weeks battle such as we went through at Brunete can do to some men'. Paynter accused Tapsell of unwittingly encouraging anti-brigade feeling and general disaffection:

This showed itself in the statements he [Tapsell] was making to all and sundry and very loudly about the whole offensive and about the new Spanish Army. For him the whole offensive had been a ghastly failure and a severe defeat while the new Spanish forces were worse than useless – a menace. It is no exaggeration to say that he was talking as one panic-stricken. He was also loudly criticising in front of all the men the whole conduct of the operation – shouting about our lack of artillery and aviation, creating the impression that the British Battalion had had a specifically raw deal, had been deliberately placed in all the tough spots, a suggestion which was absolutely false and which, in the frightfully difficult circumstances then prevailing, was criminal and dangerous.[97]

In a letter to the Party Secretariat on 9 August 1937, defending himself against Aitken's accusations that he was 'whipping up discontent against the Spanish troops', Tapsell argued that:

> In plain fact, and it is hard to state this, on every occasion we were with Spanish troops in this engagement they let us down. Their behaviour on every occasion either resulted in serious casualties, or the immediate loss of positions won by us at heavy cost. This is a fact.[98]

Raging against 'pious prattle' that avoided any criticism of the Spanish forces by refusing to face up to this fundamentally important issue, Tapsell – who clearly loathed Aitken – rebutted the brigade commissar's allegation that he was 'a bad influence in the British Battalion' and reminded the Secretariat that, only six weeks earlier, Jock Cunningham had himself been 'demanding that Aitken be sent home as utterly useless'. He argued that 'Aitken's temperament has made him distrusted and disliked by the vast majority of the British Battalion who regard him as being personally ambitious and unmindful of the Battalion and the men.'[99]

Nor did other senior figures escape Tapsell's wrath. He railed against Paynter and Bert Williams and alleged that Cunningham 'fluctuates violently between hysterical bursts of passion and is openly accused by Aitken of lazing about the brigade headquarters doing nothing'.[100] Feeling that Fred Copeman had been badly treated – 'but, quite frankly, I am not Copeman and am not going to be shoved out of the way in this fashion'[101] – Tapsell was also very unhappy about discussions surrounding what he believed to be 'the annihilation of the British Battalion', a plan to incorporate it into the American battalion.

The five leading figures were called back to Britain in late August 1937 to try and resolve the disputes. After an exchange of bitter accusations and counter-accusations, Harry Pollitt ordered Cunningham, Williams and Aitken to stay in Britain, while Copeman and Tapsell were to return to Spain.[102] Cunningham took the decision personally, as did Aitken, who wrote a furious letter protesting 'against the decision to send Comrade Tapsel[l] back to Spain. This decision, in my opinion, is monstrous and dangerous and the decision that Comrade Copeman should also return to Spain is a grave mistake.'[103]

★

Ironically, while Aitken, Cunningham and Williams raged at not being allowed to return to Spain, many of the men still there, disheartened and demoralised, had decided that they had had enough of fighting for Spanish democracy. A list drawn up on 26 July included the names of thirty-six deserters, 'some of them with first class records';[104] an official report admitted that 'the English battalion has fallen victim to a wave of collective desertions, which has begun to effect [sic] the American battalions. The officers are not excluded from this process of demoralization.'[105] Will Paynter had already explained the likely repercussions in a letter to Harry Pollitt:

> I am anticipating quite a deal of trouble when it is all over. First, from the position of divisions that exist among the leading people, since this action seems to [have] aggravated the position. Second, from the men, who will raise with new energy the demand for repatriation or leave to England. This has already been raised with me by many of the men who are now in the hospitals.
>
> Then there is the whole question of the Battalion. When things have cleared we shall be able to see the position better and be able to judge what our forces are. But it is clear even now, that we shall not be able to put a Battalion in the field unless we get reinforcements. Even when those who have been lightly wounded have recovered, I estimate that our strength will be less than 150.
>
> Our casualties have not been only killed and wounded. There have been, as could be expected, a number of desertions. To my knowledge at the moment we have ten such in Madrid and seven in Albacete, whom I have to interview today. They absolutely refuse to go back to the front in all cases. They constitute a hell of a problem for me, but I shall do the best I can, and endeavour to keep them in Spain. To send them home would be to acquiesce in desertion and leave a bad effect upon those who stood loyal and solid.[106]

The difficulties experienced at the base after Brunete, wrote Paynter, were the worst he had encountered in Spain: 'the toll of desertion has been heavy. We have over twenty in Albacete, and are informed that there are more in Madrid and Valencia.' Nevertheless, he argued that a draconian response would be a mistake:

While we must condemn this form of conduct, we must also understand it. The men who have come to us have all been in Spain for more than six months. Almost without exception they have served at Jarama since the 12th Feb. Many have been once wounded. All are exhausted and in bad nervous condition. Many of them have previous excellent records. Their past records prove that they are not just cowards.[107]

Paynter felt that the deserters should be isolated from the battalion, though not treated as prisoners. Those that would accept work building railways and roads should be encouraged to do so, although 'for the worse types, the isolation will have to be continued.'

The dire situation facing the Republic meant that the battalion leadership was in no position to allow large numbers to return home. Many were treated leniently and, once rounded up from Madrid and Barcelona, were ordered to dig trenches, or jailed for a few days at Albacete. However, for confirmed recidivists and, worse still, 'Trotskyists', the punishment meted out could be much more unpleasant.

13

¡Disciplina Camaradas!

One afternoon, at the time of the siesta, we were digesting our *garbanzos* when a sleek Spanish captain, in a Sam Browne and polished boots, summoned us to an *hora political*. Nobody was interested, and after an argument he forced us downstairs at the point of his gun. We sat sullenly in the shade of some olive trees while a Spanish commissar read an article from *Frente Rojo*, a badly printed paper that was always pretending that the Republic was winning on all fronts, even when retreating. After the interpreter had made translations in four or five languages, questions were invited. The British gave one concerted roar: '*When are we going home?*'

Interview with British volunteer John H. Bassett

The problems experienced during training at Madrigueras, the mass of desertions at Jarama and Brunete and the widespread disenchantment with the war that followed, presented the leadership of the battalion – and the International Brigades themselves – with serious problems. So far, attempts to overcome the difficulties had not been particularly successful. The withdrawal of the battalion to Alcalá for rest and recuperation at the end of April had been marred by (perhaps understandable) drunkenness; further-more the period of leave had been cut short, compounding the battalion's unhappiness.[1]

Two months later, just as the battalion was leaving for the Brunete front, several returning deserters promptly deserted again. Clearly, the situation could not continue, but the battalion leadership was in a tricky position. As George Aitken had argued at Jarama, the view of the battalion as volunteers ensured that any idea of shooting deserters was completely unacceptable, not to speak of its 'absolutely catastrophic' effect on potential volunteers back home.[2] Balanced against this, of course, was the reality of warfare: for men to leave the line, especially while under fire, simply could not be condoned.

The brigades' predominantly Communist leadership reacted according to the Party's line that the conflict in Spain was not a civil war, but an anti-fascist war. Volunteers were therefore required to be trustworthy, dedicated and reliable anti-fascists: 'Political indoctrination was more important than military indoctrination,' claimed Jim Brewer.[3] Political discipline was held to be every bit as important as military; indiscipline – whether drunkenness, insubordination or even desertion – was seen as primarily a consequence of lack of political development. Serial offenders were seen as sabotaging the anti-fascist cause in Spain and as traitors to their class. These 'political unreliables' must be removed from the battalion and deposited where they could not spread their cynicism and defeatism. Occasional transgressors, however, were treated with some understanding; as Will Paynter argued, 'the whole aim is to try and reclaim them.'[4]

Discipline was maintained and imposed by the system of political commissars. All units, from brigade down to company level, were allocated commissars who were, theoretically at least, expected to represent the Popular Front composition of the Brigades, where soldiers in uniform were not allowed to wear political emblems and all political meetings were forbidden without the express permission of the Ministry of War.[5] It was a laudable policy, if somewhat undermined by the fact that every political commissar in the battalion was a Communist, and many were experienced Party cadres, educated at the Lenin School in Moscow.[6] Peter Kerrigan made it explicit when he wrote to Harry Pollitt in early 1937: 'please note that this is a Popular Front War therefore no hammer & sickle on the Battalion Banner and no Party Slogans.'[7]

> The Political Commissar's work is in the spirit of the People's Front and not of any one Party. The right of Party organisation exists but is a matter separate from the commissar. No commissar must hold any party function nor act in a way which associates him exclusively [with] any particular party.[8]

The commissariat's command structure mirrored the military ranks. Commissars were theoretically subordinate to military commanders.

During a conference of British political commissars in November 1937, the differences in role between the military and political leadership were clearly laid out:

> Between the Political Commissar and the military commander there should be a harmony [sic] relation in which the tasks of both are discharged efficiently. The Military Commander give[s] the orders, the Political Commissar prepares, advises, sees to it that the morale is such that the orders are understood and executed promptly.[9]

However, as Jason Gurney pointed out, 'the confusion between political and military functions or responsibilities was never entirely resolved throughout the history of the International Brigades.'[10] Commissars' willingness to accept a subordinate role could depend on the particular personalities involved. Certainly Fred Copeman claimed that he had to resist attempts by commissars to exert military as well as political authority:

> Ever since my taking over the battalion there had been some friction, based on my refusal to accept the right of Political Commissars to influence military organisation and discipline. The Brunetti [sic] action had brought a spate of demands for harsher punishment of those who had left the line. My attitude was for punishment, yes, but within reason and commensurate with the crime – if such existed – bearing in mind that most of our men had already been wounded at least once.[11]

Some political commissars believed themselves qualified to be involved in making military judgements, despite orders confirming that this was specifically not part of their role:

> The Commissars' mission is political and moral education and vigilance, not technical leadership or military command.
> Commissars [are] to maintain [a] close and constant relationship of mutual information and co-operation with command. They will participate in decisions taken by commanders in an advisory capacity. They will sign jointly with the commanders the orders and reports issued by the commanders.[12]

That a number of commissars, such as Vladimir Ĉopić, Hugh Slater and

Bill Alexander, later became military commanders, added to the blurring of lines between the two chains of command.

Officially, however, the role of the commissar was to look after – or watch over – the men (and women) in his charge; 'to inspire officers and soldiers with [the] highest spirit of discipline'. The commissars were responsible for maintaining morale and political orthodoxy. Frequent speeches, meetings, and cultural and sports activities were all part of a process of fostering a sense of political unity. The commissars' slogan, '¡*El primero en avanzar, el ultimo en retroceder!*' (the first to advance, the last to retreat!), was not entirely rhetorical: three British Battalion commissars and several company commissars were killed in Spain.[13]

Many volunteers accepted the commissars' work as important, even necessary. Ambulance driver Wogan Philipps's description is typical of those more favourably disposed towards the role:

> They were political rather than military people, but they were certainly soldiers too, and took on all the duties of soldiers. They were more educated, more politically minded than the ordinary soldier could hope to be . . . They were there to explain things; what the war was about; what defeat would mean. They were to educate, keep the morale up and to see that through ignorance the troops didn't get fed up and depressed. For it was their war; they were fighting for their interests, unlike soldiers in large imperialist wars. Again, the commissars were there to hear even the smallest complaint, discuss it, and try to put it right. Everything was to be explained. There were no orders which could not be discussed. It was a democratic army, and the commissars were the links between officers and men. Their job was to be the friends of every single soldier, and always accessible.[14]

Commissars therefore 'acted as links between the men and the command . . . they received complaints and criticisms.'[15] As one Liverpool volunteer put it, 'I mean, if you're convinced, you're a much better person, much better soldier. And if you know what you're doing, and why it's being done, it stops all the grumbling.'[16] The commissariat served as a means of allowing volunteers to vent their unhappiness, even if little could actually be done: 'The political commissar is a comrade whose job is to promise everything you ask for and to blame it on Albacete when he doesn't get it for you,' complained one battalion member.[17] Jason Gurney admirably summed up what was expected:

The function of a Political Commissar at its best is very similar to that of a Chaplain in the British Army. His first job is welfare. He serves as a buffer between officers and soldiers, and functions as the source of moral authority. He endeavours to fulfil these tasks without possessing any kind of power. He cannot give orders but must operate entirely by virtue of persuasion.

However, as Gurney added, 'that is the theory: in practice he may be something approaching a Secret Police spy, of whom everyone is terrified.'[18] Just as important as any 'pastoral' role was the commissars' responsibility for keeping watch for, or on, malcontents, political dissidents, spies and traitors: 'Commissars must pay special attention to fight espionage and provocation in the ranks of the Army, cooperate with the command to maintain among combatants careful antifascist vigilance and train in the observance of military secrecy.'[19]

Gurney was never convinced that the International Brigades were a likely target of Franco's spies and believed the Communists were being paranoid:

One of the inherent defects of the Communist Party is a passion for conspiratorial activity and its corollary of suspicion. Throughout the War the leadership was convinced that among the International Brigades there were a number of people who were Fascists who had joined with the purpose of spying and sabotage. Personally I consider this proposition to be ludicrously improbable. Practically none of them spoke Spanish without which it would have been absolutely impossible to pass back and forth through the enemy lines, and since Franco had complete mastery of the air, there was very little about our troop movements of which he was not aware . . . There is no doubt that Franco had spies in plenty, but they were Spaniards, and they were employing themselves much more efficiently than they would by sitting around in the trenches of Jarama. The same thing was true of sabotage. The amount of sabotage which an individual soldier in the line can commit is strictly limited by the circumstances of his being confined to a small area. If a man wants to commit sabotage he does not join an infantry regiment where he has less privacy than he would enjoy in prison. He can only operate if allowed freedom of movement – as in the case of the partisan fighter. I certainly know of no single instance of planned sabotage during the time that I was in the Brigades.[20]

Members of the National Unemployed Workers' Movement on a hunger march in October 1934. *Press Association Images*

Oswald Mosley inspects his British Union of Fascists storm troops prior to their abortive attempt to march through the East End of London on 4 October 1936. *Getty Images*

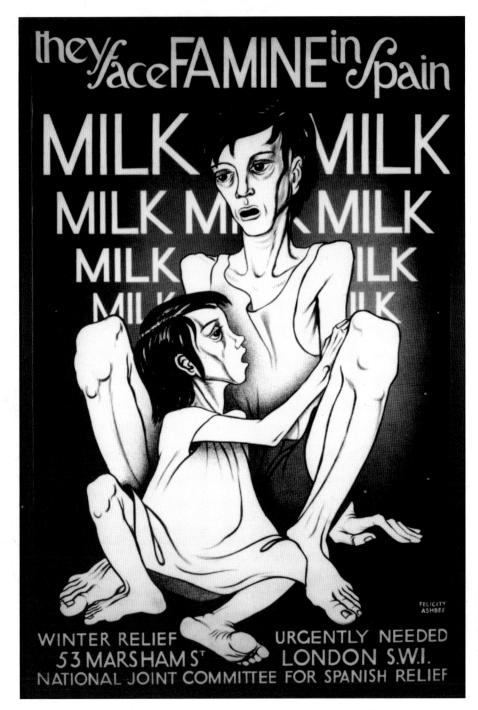

One of a series of posters designed by the artist Felicity Ashbee for the
National Joint Committee for Spanish Relief. *Felicity Ashbee*

The Tom Mann Centuria in Barcelona in September 1936. Left to right: Sid Avner, Nat Cohen and his Spanish girlfriend Ramona, Tom Wintringham, Italian Georgio Tioli, Australian Jack Barry and David Marshall.
Marx Memorial Library

Three early arrivals from Britain who would take on senior roles amongst the British volunteers. Left to right: 'Jock' Cunningham, George Nathan and Ralph Campeau.
Imperial War Museum

The 'Marxist intellectual' John Cornford, who was killed whilst fighting with the British Number One Company at Lopera on 28 December 1936.
Marx Memorial Library

Surviving members of the Thaelmann Centuria, Arthur 'Babs' Ovenden and Esmond Romilly, on their return to London in December 1936.
Marx Memorial Library

'Old men waiting patiently': British Battalion members at Jarama in May 1937. Battalion commander Fred Copeman is in the centre (wearing beret and Sam Browne belt). To his right (with pipe) is company commander Bill Meredith, who was killed at Villanueva de la Cañada in July 1937. To Copeman's left is battalion commissar Bert Williams and next to him is Copeman's friend, Charlie Goodfellow, who was killed at Brunete. Alec Cummings, who disappeared in mysterious circumstances in the Sierra Caballs in September 1938, is standing second from right (with bandaged hand). *Marx Memorial Library*

Members of the Machine Gun Company captured at Jarama on 15 February 1937. Company commander Harold Fry is seventh from right and Jimmy Rutherford, who was later executed by the Nationalists having been recaptured following his return to Spain, is third from right (partly obscured). *Marx Memorial Library*

The British Anti-Tank Battery. Commander, Hugh Slater, is standing in the very middle of the second row (with cap and jacket). To his left (in cap and leather jacket) is battery second-in-command Jeffries Mildwater. *International Brigade Collection, Moscow*

Members of the British Anti-Tank Battery. Otto Estensen far left, one of a number to command the battery and gun commander, Chris Smith, far right. *Marx Memorial Library*

Members of the Anti-Tank Battery relax at their base in Ambite in late 1937. Cultural officer Miles Tomalin is playing the recorder and Otto Estensen is on mandolin.
Marx Memorial Library

above: Members of the POUM militia training in Barcelona (December 1936 to January 1937). To the rear of the column, a head taller than his comrades, is British volunteer Eric Blair, better known as George Orwell.
UCL Library Services, Special Collections

Daily Worker reporter Claud Cockburn (left) and battalion commander Fred Copeman photographed in 1937. *Magnum/Gerda Taro © ICP*

Popular battalion commissar Walter 'Wally' Tapsell, who was killed at Calaceite on 31 March or 1 April 1938. *Marx Memorial Library*

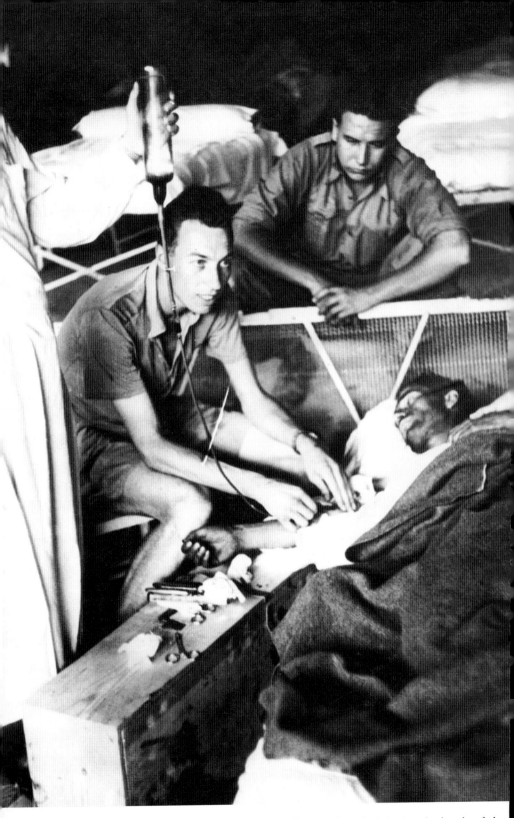

Doctor Reggie Saxton giving a blood transfusion in the cave hospital during the battle of the Ebro in the summer of 1938. *Imperial War Museum*

entist J.B.S Haldane (left) and his Canadian assistant Hazen Size demonstrate procedures
counter gas attacks in December 1936. *Imperial War Museum*

nadian Doctor Norman Bethune and companion in front of the mobile blood transfusion
in 1937. *Imperial War Museum*

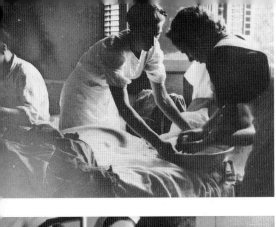

left: British nurse Patience Darton (in white) training a Spanish nurse.
Angela Jackson/Patience Darton

above: An advanced dressing station at Brunete in July 1937. The man on the far left (in shorts) is usually identified as Anthony Carritt, but is more likely to be older brother, Noel, who served with the medical services. Anthony was wounded at Villanueva de la Cañada and died of h wounds in hospital. *Marx Memorial Library*

above: Doctor Alex Tudor-Hart and nurse Thora Silverthorne in a field operating theatre.
Marx Memorial Library

below: Drawing by unknown British volunteer of the ambush by Italian Nationalist forces at Calaceite, 31 March 1938. *Marx Memorial Library*

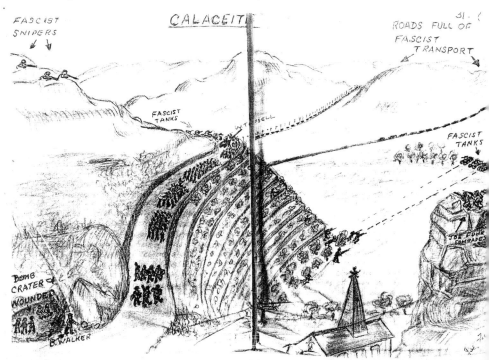

above: Republican offensive at Brunete, July 1937.
Marx Memorial Library

left: Two 'tough' commanders of the British Battalion: Bill Alexander (left) and Sam Wild.
Marx Memorial Library

left: Irish Republican leader, Frank Ryan, who died as a prisoner of war in June 1944.
Marx Memorial Library

right: The 'English Captain', Tom Wintringham, in July 1937.
Imperial War Museum

The British Battalion's field kitchen. *Marx Memorial Library*

Communist Party General Secretary, Harry Pollitt, addresses the battalion, during one of his several visits to Spain. *Marx Memorial Library*

British Battalion officers prior to their departure from Spain. Left to right: battalion quartermaster Lieutenant 'Hooky' Walker, political commissar Alan Gilchrist, battalion commissar Bob Cooney, former battalion commander George Fletcher, unknown, battalion commander Sam Wild, unknown, Irish Number One Company commander Johnny Power and Scottish Company commander Bobby Walker. *Marx Memorial Library*

British Officers of the 15th International Brigade on Hill 481 near Gandesa, in July-August 1938. Back row, left to right: brigade political commissar Peter Kerrigan, Sam Wild, battalion secretary Ted Edwards. Front row, left to right: Bob Cooney, anti-tanks political commissar Alan Gilchrist, unknown and (in peaked cap) George Fletcher. *Courtesy of Stefany Tomalin*

Surviving members of the British Battalion at Marsa on 23 September 1938. Standing in the centre of the second row (in leather jacket and cap) is Sam Wild, with Bob Cooney squatting in front of him. Third from left is Peter Kerrigan with Bobby Walker (smoking a cigarette) five to his left. 'Hooky' Walker is standing third from right (in cap). *Marx Memorial Library*

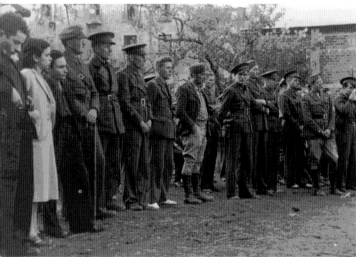

below: Margaret Thatcher's ideologue, Sir Alfred Sherman, as sketched by Clive Branson at San Pedro de Cardeña. *Marx Memorial Library*

above: 15th International Brigade officers at the Barcelona farewell in October 1938. Seventh from left is Bob Cooney, Malcolm Dunbar is visible fourth from right. *Marx Memorial Library*

The British veterans
are welcomed home,
December 1938.
Imperial War Museum

left: Former International Brigader David Lomon, photographed at the Marx Memorial Library in 2012, with his portrait by Clive Branson. *IBMT/Marx Memorial Library*

right: The British Battalion banner, presented to the veterans by the grateful population of Barcelona. *Marx Memorial Library*

British and Irish veterans of the International Brigades are presented with passports at the Spanish Embassy on 9 June 2009. Left to right: Thomas Watters, Lou Kenton, Joseph Kahn, Sam Lesser, Penny Feiwel, Jack Edwards and Paddy Cochrane. *Getty Images*

Yet the commissars were not the only ones keeping tabs on volunteers; three special brigades, comprised mainly of German Communists, were charged with the identification and elimination of fifth-columnists and 'Trotskyists'.[21] A system of informers and spies also existed within the ranks, including covert members of the SIM, the Republican Army's intelligence services. These probably included Welsh company commissar Brazell Thomas, who was killed in the summer of 1938, and machine-gunner and military censor Joe Garber, who was sent to Russia for training while in Spain.[22] As one disgruntled volunteer complained, 'The Communist Party had its members watching all the time, nobody being trusted, except those with membership cards of the Communist Party.'[23]

And while some volunteers might have appreciated the work of the commissars, many volunteers felt them to be an unnecessary annoyance and resented their often patronising lectures, 'making them the most disliked men in the Brigade . . . Political Commissars persist in treating us as children or political ignorants,' complained one Manchester volunteer.[24] One Scot was infuriated by commissars 'telling us all what we should do and what we shouldn't do . . . He was saying that you should join the Communist Party, you should fight for Russia, they are the saviour of mankind – a lot of absolute rubbish.'[25] Jim Brewer believed that the majority of his colleagues in the Anti-Tank Battery were highly educated autodidacts from the working-class movement who understood full well why they were fighting for the Republic. In his view, all that the political commissars' speechifying achieved 'was to get our backs up'.[26]

Of course, some commissars were better received than others. George Aitken, Walter Tapsell and Bob Cooney were generally well thought of, while their more po-faced comrades, who as Fred Thomas complained, 'indulged themselves and us in platitudes', were dismissed disparagingly as 'comic stars'.[27] Tom Murray, himself a political commissar, recognised that the job required sensitivity. When the experienced and respected Cooney was taken sick, a junior commissar attempted to address the battalion in his place. As Murray admitted, he 'made such a hell of a mess of it' that Murray felt compelled to step in to counter the junior's 'rather heavy, lugubrious type of speech'.[28] And, as Scottish volunteer John Dunlop recounted, some members of the battalion hated the whole system of political commissars on principle, seeing it only as more 'party bullshit'.

Barney Shields was in the Machine Gun Company along with me and of course [having served as a regular soldier in the British army for some time] was first rate in his weaponry. But we had to stand guard one night on Battalion headquarters, which were in a house in the square in Mondéjar. Barney Shields came on duty and he was as drunk as a lord. Anyway he was put on the middle watch of the night. He was stationed in the hall of the house, just on to the hall one of the doors led into Wally Tapsell's bedroom. Now Wally Tapsell was the Battalion commissar. One thing about Barney was that he had a dislike for commissars. He was there to fight, he didn't need any commissars to tell him why he needed to fight. A pet aversion of Barney were the high boots that the commissars all wore. Commissars were probably about the most highly paid people in the Battalion. Once they became a commissar they all seemed to go and get themselves these high laced boots which nobody else seemed to wear. Of course as soon as you saw somebody with high laced boots you figured he was a commissar.

Well, Wally Tapsell unguardedly left his boots outside his door, hoping that somebody would come and polish them up for the morning. Now in the middle reaches of the night Barney was feeling that he needed to go to the lavatory. He also knew that he was supposed to stay on duty. However, he saw those boots, and he thought, 'Well, this is an ideal opportunity', first of all to relieve himself and also to indicate what he thought of commissars. So he promptly filled up the boots. And of course next morning when Wally Tapsell came to put his feet into the boots he got a very unpleasant surprise. I wasn't there unfortunately to hear what he said but I am sure they were not the kind of things that a commissar ought to say in public.[29]

Resentment was not aimed solely at the commissars. The traditional hierarchy that existed within the Brigades was also a cause of dissatisfaction:

The contrast between the conditions of the men and the officers was one of the first things to disturb me. This did not seem to me a workers' army, with its differences between the privates and the officers. It was an army which maintained class differences.[30]

To some extent, of course, this was true, for a traditional military structure certainly prevailed in the Brigades; they were no revolutionary army. During the period of leave at Alcalá in the spring of 1937, the distinctions made between officers and lower ranks caused much unhappiness, as this entry from the diary of Manchester volunteer Ralph Cantor reveals:

> Disturbing feature of this war is the distinctions which are too acute for justification. A sergeant receives more than double a volunteer. An officer more than 4 times as much and higher officers more. Also acute distinctions in food and accommodation. Grumbling over separate doors for officers and men in one case.[31]

Later in the war, at the new British base in Tarazona de la Mancha (which had replaced Madrigueras by the end of July 1937), what one volunteer described dryly as 'limited cooking facilities' meant that a political commissar issued a notice stating that only officers, instructors and a limited number of staff members were permitted to eat at the headquarters mess.[32] A note to Harry Pollitt from an anonymous volunteer pointed out that many volunteers 'feel downhearted at times' and that certain issues 'have caused hell among us'. Among these, it was being asked, 'Why do officers eat separate and sleep on beds while we sleep on the ground?' And rather more pointedly, 'Why do some guys go to Albacete all the time and we don't get leave?'[33]

The issue of leave, which had first arisen at Jarama, was without doubt the major problem facing the British.[34] Perhaps as many as ten per cent of the battalion deserted at some time during the war.[35] After the long period in the line at Jarama, it is hardly surprising that volunteers were desperate for leave. As Will Paynter complained to Harry Pollitt, a number of volunteers, 'some of our most courageous men in the big battles', were threatening that if leave was not granted, they would take it anyway.[36]

Rather more serious than the issue of leave was that of repatriation. A number of volunteers who received letters from Britain telling of family disasters, illnesses or bereavements unsurprisingly pestered the political commissars for permission to return home. And to some extent the problems and arguments over repatriation were of the Party's own making. Commissars frequently wrote to London furiously complaining that volunteers had been given promises of repatriation following a fixed period of service, which the leadership of the battalion in Spain was simply not in a position to grant. As one commissar admitted, 'Many of them claimed, I think honestly, that they had been told when they joined up in England that they were signing-on for only a limited period of some months and would then be able to return home.'[37]

In a letter to London in the spring of 1937, Walter Tapsell sought assurances from Harry Pollitt that he had received 'my note to stop the D[aily]W[orker] publishing nonsense about volunteers coming out here and being free to volunteer home. You would pity me if you knew the trouble the hours and days of combating such stuff which this throws on me.'[38] Three months later, following the battle of Brunete, Will Paynter wrote to Pollitt explaining why, in his opinion, there was still 'widespread' and 'serious' unhappiness among many of the volunteers: 'it is said, that from volunteers we have become conscripts . . . we have come to Spain and we are to be kept here until we are wounded or killed.' Paynter suggested that the policy on repatriation should be reconsidered, and that all volunteers who had been in Spain for six months or more should be eligible for leave to Britain, especially if they had been wounded on more than one occasion:[39]

> There should be a clause to the effect that the comrade understands the conditions and obligations attached to his enrolment. He should sign this, and this would liquidate all possibility of am[b]iguity. We still get people who say that they have not been informed that they are here for the duration of hostilities at least. They say that they were told that they would get a leave home at the end of six months. One man who came in November and is now in the venereal disease hospital, actually tells us that he was promised he could be home by January or February. Of course, we don't believe all these tales, but we would like to remove all possible doubt on this matter. We feel that because of the difficulty in getting recruits some comrades in England like to skip over these things which might stop some volunteers coming out.[40]

In fact, George Aitken negotiated an agreement with the Party that 'all of the men of the original No 1 Company, who had been in Spain from 8 to 9 months, should be given the opportunity of going home' and that 'the original battalion people had also to be allowed to return home gradually after 8 months service and according to length of service.'[41] Yet the problem still didn't go away; in September 1937 around twenty members of the battalion refused to obey orders and demanded to be sent home, claiming that both Aitken and Jock Cunningham had promised they would be sent home after two months' service.[42] There was widespread bitterness within the battalion that senior Party figures were getting preferential treatment and were being repatriated, while the ordinary soldiers weren't.

> There was a very strong rumour about this time [just after Brunete] and it seemed official that the remnants of the British Battalion were to be given home leave, it must have been strong since I wrote home to that effect. When it came to the crunch, it was just the officers and party members that went. I began to feel more alone than ever since I seemed to know no one from those early days.[43]

As Ralph Cantor complained in his diary: 'Political Commissariat makes grave error, or shows favouritism, in sending comrades to England and other decisions. Much grumbling.'[44] Political commissar John Angus confirmed the level of bad feeling: 'What made the situation infinitely worse, and added to the general atmosphere of cynicism and demoralisation, was that the entire British leadership from the battalion right down to company or even lower level, had, in fact, been allowed to go home either on leave or permanently.'[45]

Walter Tapsell pointed to the fact that a number of volunteers had been repatriated after Jarama and vehemently denied that there was a policy of protecting Party cadres, but few took the denials seriously.[46] Matters were not helped by insensitive actions such as George Aitken's proposal that Liverpool commissar George Coyle, another Lenin School alumnus who had been in Spain for six months, should 'not go back into the line, but that we should try to protect such comrades as much as possible since we had already lost so many of our best Party comrades'.[47] This was despite Coyle's earlier actions: he had proved to be a 'disappointment in Spain' when he 'deserted from the front at Jarama and took a few days leave in Madrid without permission for which he was placed in a labour battalion'.[48]

To some volunteers at least, this rather contrasted with the way other members of the battalion were treated. London volunteer Alexander J. Anderson, when asking to be repatriated, was informed that 'all leave outside Spain, repatriation on other than grounds of complete physical incompetence for any form of military service, is completely forbidden to Party members.' In support of the Party's position, Tapsell maintained that repatriation had been denied to senior Party figures, just as it was to soldiers in the line:

Cunningham with 4 severe wounds, one bullet in his lung and his left arm stiff, leaves today to rejoin the battalion. McDade with more or less permanent paralysis of his left arm ditto. Tommy Wintringham is down to about flyweight with typhoid, has doctors orders to return to England, but must stay here to make his recovery and rejoin the battalion directly he can stand.[49]

The issue of repatriation was probably irreconcilable, for there was a clear contradiction between volunteer status and membership of the Republican Army. With many believing that they were volunteering for a limited period and that, as volunteers, at the end of this period they would be allowed to return home, conflict was inevitable, especially once the International Brigades had been incorporated into the Republican Army and the volunteers were informed that they must remain in the Brigades until the end of the war.[50] As one volunteer admitted, 'I should think that if they were honest, almost every member of the British Battalion wanted to go home at some time or other, because it was a war of unusual hardships, of unusually high casualties.'[51] But the problem was undoubtedly exacerbated by the promise of limited periods of service in Spain, though it seems unlikely that this was a deliberate attempt to trick potential recruits; instead R.W. Robson, and others, were guilty of making promises that they were not in a position to keep.

Of those who did desert, a number of men were caught roaming around Spanish ports trying to board a ship, while others were found in the bars and fleshpots of Barcelona. Few volunteers' accounts mention time spent in Barcelona's red light area, but there is no doubt that some did visit brothels:

> It was said that in Barcelona if you wanted to know where the English group was, that you'd only got to go in the brothel area . . . We used to go in groups into the brothel area. Why not? Don't forget we were all seeking life at that time. There was a war on.[52]

The idea seems neither to have surprised nor offended the local villagers. Liverpool brigader Jack Edwards later remembered how the girls in the village used to tease him about visiting his *tía* (aunt) while on leave in Valencia. Confused, he asked his sergeant, who explained to him 'Well, when they say aunt, they mean prostitute.'[53] The issue was also widely accepted within the battalion; prophylactics were supplied to men who were going on leave and medical treatment made available for those returning to the front.

A short leave was granted for three days; those that had been at the front the longest were entitled to go. A notice to this effect was posted up. After the return of the lucky men from Barcelona, another notice was posted informing all men that if they thought they had caught a dose to report to the *medico*. Nobody of course reported. Another notice followed stating that all leave men were required to have injections against typhoid. Naturally all leave men turned up. Although when on leave the temptations of the flesh were very great, the rate of venereal disease was unbelievably low; the notice board method never failed.[54]

Many volunteers were young, inexperienced and feared, with some reason, that they might not survive their time in Spain. As one young Australian ambulance driver later recounted:

At this period of my life, I was 23, I was not very good at either love or sex, or shall we say love and sex. There were half a dozen young women I met in the course of my service who attracted me, Angela H[aden] G[uest], Patience Darton, and a few Spanish 'nurses' etc. I never got as far as to make a romantic suggestion, they all seemed out of reach (I was immature, or something). When in Barcelona I visited a sort of red light district, and was rather appalled at a professional exhibiting herself outside a sort of booth which I suppose was a crude brothel.

I found a not unattractive 'sensible looking' woman of about 35 and suggested spending the night with her. She said she was otherwise engaged but took me to a room where we had what can only be described as 'surgical sex', after which in a very business-like way she completed the 'surgery' by washing my parts with a solution of permanganate of potash.[55]

Likewise, the urbane John Peet was soon persuaded to overcome his reluctance:

I was slightly shocked by the idea, as a knight in shining armour fighting for the Spanish Republic, we should do anything as sordid as to go to pick up a couple of girls off the street. But taking into consideration the fact that most of us did not seriously expect to return alive from Spain, I managed to overcome these feelings and joined in.[56]

However, many volunteers did not succumb to temptation; in a letter to his wife, Ivor Hickman claimed that 'most of the men have remained celibate ever since they arrived in Spain'.[57] Liverpool brigader Bob Clark, wounded at Gandesa in July 1938, was convalescing in Barcelona following an operation. While wandering around the city, he stopped for a cup of 'ersatz coffee' in a café:

After sitting at the table for a matter of five minutes, I was approached by a young girl who was sitting at the next table. I was able to enquire why she was doing this. Her age she told me, was seventeen, but she looked even younger. Asking her why she did not work in a Government factory, her reply was that the money was not so bad, but she was not worrying about money, when it was almost impossible to buy anything with it. Food, tins of corned beef, sardines, canned milk or cigarettes, these were the real money. A tin of milk was worth almost half a week's wages. I was later to learn that some sailors [who] were landing at Barcelona, their ships mostly carrying cargoes of coal to supply the Electric Power Station, as the main water-driven electric power at the town of Lérida had been captured by the Fascists, were able to live for weeks in these women's homes by just supplying the household groceries. It was not any use arguing with this young prostitute, but feeling very sorry for her as she seemed a nice kid, I gave her a handful of tobacco which I had bummed off some English seaman earlier on.[58]

While some deserters were picked up in Barcelona's brothels and bars or hanging around the ports waiting for a ship, a few succeeded in returning home to Britain. One such, the brother of political commissar George Brown, had disappeared from the battalion crying, 'This isn't war, this is bloody madness, I've had enough!'[59] Getting out of Spain was not easy, though, for deserters attempting to return home couldn't always depend on help from British consular officials.[60] In the spring of 1937, John Lochore's attempts to gain the assistance of the staff at the British Embassy in Barcelona were singularly unsuccessful:

Our first interview was with an object who possessed the most revolting projecting teeth and hair parted down the middle of his head. He swanked an old Etonian tie and spoke as if he had swallowed an overgrown plum. He insulted us and said we had no right to take part in a war that was none of our business: we had broken the law and no help of any description could be given to us to re-enter the United Kingdom, since we had taken part in a war that our government had banned! His only advice was 'to try and get into Britain and take the consequences.' It was significant that he took all our names and descriptions before he told us to be on our way.[61]

Those caught attempting to desert were arrested and usually returned to the battalion for punishment. Welsh volunteer Taffy Foulkes, who had been 'absent' for some time, was spotted by Jack Jones trying to board a ship in Barcelona and persuaded to return, where his commander Sam Wild 'simply told him not to be a bloody fool again'.[62] Despite the reputation for iron discipline in the Brigades, Will Paynter stressed to Harry Pollitt that 'on the whole, deserters are treated with extreme leniency.'[63] Those who had simply taken off for a few days were usually put in the guardhouse, or required to dig trenches or latrines. Battalion orders of 9 December 1937 detailed three volunteers who were punished for overstaying leave; their only punishment was the loss of pay for those days.[64]

More serious misdemeanours could result in a court-martial in front of a panel of officers, including the base commander and adjutant.[65] But in general, the battalion leadership preferred corrective discipline which they felt would not be detrimental to the war effort. As Copeman recounted, a labour section was created within the battalion, keeping many punishments in-house:

Our punishment for defaulters would be three days in the labour section. That meant a midnight job in No Man's Land, digging sapping trenches, building listening posts, or erecting barbed-wire entanglements.[66]

The work was extremely hazardous, with a very real risk of injury or death, and some volunteers suspected it was a convenient means to get rid of problem volunteers. But as Bob Cooney later pointed out, 'the same thing happened in the British Army.'[67] The purpose of the disciplinary battalions and 're-education camps' was to help the Republican Army achieve victory, rather than provide forced labour.[68] While sending a volunteer into a situation in which he was highly likely to be killed seems akin to murder, it is unlikely that many volunteers would have seen it that way. As the casualty rates show, they regularly faced odds that were not much better – one-fifth of British volunteers were killed and very few survived the war without being wounded at least once.

Serious offenders not sent to labour battalions could be thrown into one of the Republic's very unpleasant jails. Will Paynter interviewed about twenty-five deserters from the battalion who had ended up in jail:

> Among them are some good types who have collapsed. They constitute a very big problem for us, since in the main they refuse to return to the Battalion, in some cases refuse to do anything but reiterate the demand to go home. Obviously, to repatriate them means to give encouragement to desertion, and in the present circumstances, there is a danger of this, without any encouragement.[69]

Paynter recognised that he was in a difficult position, for to offer the imprisoned volunteers 'soft' jobs behind the lines would create considerable resentment with those still fighting in the line, 'and rightly so,' he wrote. 'It is a snowball that is already getting bigger each day that passes.'[70]

One such prisoner was ex-Guardsman Tony Hyndman, the lover of Stephen Spender. Suffering from a stomach ulcer after fighting at the battle of Jarama, Hyndman was promised by George Nathan that he and a friend would soon be repatriated and, in the meantime, would be given safe jobs at the Brigade base. However, the pair were later informed that the military situation was now so desperate that every man was needed at the front and they would be drafted. Both promptly deserted. Picked up in Valencia, they were thrown into jail.[71] Walter Tapsell wrote of Hyndman:

> This chap will be freed in a few days. They want to send him to work on a farm, but in view of your letter I am recommending – public disgrace, dismissal with ignominy for cowardice and desertion. They will offer the alternative of return to the line, but this chap is an arrant coward.[72]

Jason Gurney, not usually one to defend the Party's actions, was similarly unimpressed with Hyndman, describing him as 'a member of Stephen Spender's set who came to Spain and hated it, deserted, was captured and held in prison until rescued by his protector'.[73]

Spender had indeed attempted to use his influence in the Party to secure Hyndman's safety, managing to persuade Peter Kerrigan that Hyndman was unsuitable for front-line service and recommending him as a private secretary. Kerrigan promised Spender that he wouldn't have to fight, but later broke his promise. Feeling guilty and responsible for Hyndman's decision to go to Spain, Spender spent several months trying to help him, though he doubted anything could be done and worried whether anything should be:

> The dead call for more dead, and if the brave have spent themselves how can one justify hoarding the weak? Yet I could not give up on a life which might be saved, and which was of no value in this war, in order to satisfy a state of mind with which I sympathised.[74]

In a letter to Harry Pollitt, he made reference to Hyndman's health problems and to promises that he would be repatriated home:

> I would like, in the most serious manner possible, to draw your attention to the fact that if Comrade Hyndman has a perforation of his ulcer, which would necessitate a serious operation, he would almost certainly die . . . Supposing Comrade Hyndman dies, his death will fall into a very different category from that of other members of the Brigade, because it will have been totally unnecessary and served no useful purpose.[75]

The Communist Party authorities were outraged and a report was made against Spender by the notorious American political commissar and SIM agent Tony de Maio, 'for recommending a deserter for such a confidential job'.[76] Nevertheless, Hyndman was at least repatriated in 1938. Others were not so fortunate: when the Internationals were withdrawn from Spain at the end of the year, several British and Irish brigaders were still imprisoned at the prison at Castelldefels, just outside Barcelona.[77] One of them, a Scottish electrician called James Fisher, who had been convicted in Britain for razor slashing and deserted in Spain, had been in jail for over six months.[78] He was eventually released in May 1939.

Deserters were not the only 'undesirables' to receive brutal treatment. Volunteers suspected of 'deviant' political views which could undermine political unity within the Brigades were particularly singled out. Following the tumultuous events in Barcelona in May 1937, any sign of political nonconformism, usually labelled 'Trotskyism', was seen as dangerous, even treacherous. A number of volunteers found themselves marked as political dissidents, but one who appears to have been particularly victimised was Manchester volunteer Alec Marcowich.[79]

Despite having a history of antagonism with Peter Kerrigan, whom he had opposed at a Communist party meeting in 1932–3 and described as 'a bully, an arrogant bloody big man', Marcowich arrived in Spain, as part of a group led by Bob Cooney, in the autumn of 1937. He was initially given a glowing report, but quickly made himself unpopular with the battalion leadership when his 'rank and file' attitudes led him to accuse them of purloining chocolate and cigarettes: 'Stuff was being taken from us and was not going to the sources that it was meant to . . . and I made the bloody mistake of projecting their grievances and taking the can for it.'[80]

But what nailed his reputation as a troublemaker was his raising of the contentious issue of repatriation at a battalion meeting in front of Sam Wild and Bob Cooney. The matter was deemed so serious that Marcowich was sent to Brigade headquarters under close arrest, though, like Joseph K, in Kafka's *The Trial*, he was not informed of the charges levelled against him. His punishment was to be posted to a corrective battalion containing some thirty men, all of whom were political, rather than criminal, transgressors: 'there wasn't a deserter amongst us,' claimed Marcowich. The unit was given tasks such as building defences, but it also took part in a number of highly dangerous actions: '[We were sent] Behind the fascist line, to get positive military information, but in the process of doing so, the law of averages was that certain problems were going to be solved, namely the elimination of people who were politically contentious.'[81]

Having been declared by the commissariat to be 'a provocateur, a Trotskyist, and a generally pessimistic element',[82] Marcowich was to spend the remainder of the war mainly in jail or in correction battalions. Bob Cooney later remarked:

> One character we had to get rid of was Alec Marcovitch, a man from Glasgow who had been expelled from the Party. He was a Trotskyist but professed repentance and came out in the same party as myself. When we got to Tarazona he got very drunk and I dressed him down for defeatist talk . . . Bill Rust said the sooner we get rid of him the better, but we failed. We were stuck with him.[83]

Marcowich only escaped at the end of the war when the guards disappeared, allowing the inmates to break out. He eventually made it home in mid-February 1939, after spending time in an internment camp just over the French border from which he was rescued by the British vice-consul. To this day his name remains inscribed upon the wall in a church in Castelldefels prison.

Clearly Marcowich was badly treated by the battalion political and military leadership. It seems likely that his 'Trotskyism' and long-standing feud with Peter Kerrigan counted against him. As Cooney's remarks show, they were keen to be rid of someone they saw as a troublemaker and, as a volunteer, he should rightfully have been sent home. But it is unlikely that Kerrigan, or his political superiors, would have seen it that way. The Commissariat constantly turned down requests for repatriation from volunteers, many of whom had months of front-line service and had been wounded at least once. To have refused to repatriate a 'good comrade', while sending home a 'Trotskyist' troublemaker, would have set an unpalatable precedent. Hence the imprisonment of Marcowich, Hyndman and a number of other trouble-making political dissidents, some of them for long periods. Others 'who did not conform', as Cyril Sexton put it, were sent to the 're-education centre' of Camp Lukacs.[84]

According to Will Paynter, the camp (named after the Hungarian General Paul Lukács, who was killed in 1937 at Huesca) had been established in order to offer deserters an opportunity for rehabilitation, as an alternative to more draconian forms of discipline, for 'the penalty for desertion is harsh in any army, especially in wartime.' However, as volunteers, the inmates unsurprisingly felt less than grateful for being locked up in a prison camp and Paynter was not exactly greeted with open arms when he visited: 'I had to talk myself out of a really difficult position and explain the problems of repatriation, the reasons for the camp and the alternatives they could have had to face had I not pressed for this camp, before their anger and bitterness subsided.'[85]

As the British commissar at the camp, John Angus, confessed, it 'was, in fact, a prison camp'. Angus, 'a very inexperienced, young, 23 year old', was placed in charge of the British volunteers in the camp, where 'the staff consisted of one young Italian who was more or less human, and a considerable number of Germans from the Soviet Union, who were really a pretty grim lot!'[86] However, Angus discovered that while the Germans treated the prisoners of their own nationality 'with great severity', they were quite prepared to leave the British prisoners to him. Angus believed that there were actually very few 'bad elements' among them and eventually Paynter managed to get the majority of the men released and back to the battalion in the spring of 1938.

As John Angus had discovered at Camp Lukacs, other nationalities appeared to have a harsher approach to indiscipline. For example, Fred Copeman was told by the commander of the Franco-Belge Battalion that 'he had improved the discipline of the battalion since three of its members had been shot.'[87] In contrast, while at least two members of the British Battalion were indeed executed in Spain, neither of them were shot for desertion or for political offences.

The first, who fought under the name 'Allan Kemp', had been caught with another volunteer attempting to desert to the enemy lines during fighting in the freezing conditions at Teruel in December 1938. When searched, Kemp was found to be carrying a map of the British machine-gun positions and 'was shot by firing squad . . . because in order to carry out his desertion he was prepared to betray the lives of his comrades by giving information to the fascists'.[88]

A statement appeared in the International Brigade journal, *Our Fight*, justifying this ruthless punishment:

> The death sentences imposed on the two deserters from the British Battalion received the complete approval of a Battalion meeting yesterday . . . We are at war – not play. All our energies are bent on winning the war. Anything that stands in the way must be crushed. If the safety of a Battalion – if the safety of the Republic demands that the lives of a few deserters be forfeit; we will act in the necessary manner.[89]

In fact only Kemp, the elder of the two deserters, who was believed to be the real instigator of the plan, was actually executed. His companion was treated more leniently and sent to a labour battalion.[90] Not that he fared much better; he was killed by enemy shellfire while digging fortifications shortly afterwards.

The second volunteer to be executed was Maurice Ryan from Tipperary, an Irish corporal in the Machine-Gun Company. During the fighting in the summer of 1938, Ryan played a central role in one of the less savoury episodes involving British and Irish volunteers in Spain. John Dunlop recalled:

I was just at the edge of a small hill. Right above my head, just inches above my head, there was a long burst of machine gun fire but it was coming in the wrong direction. It wasn't coming from in front of me, it was coming from behind me and it was just hitting the top of this ridge, just above my head. I looked back and I could see this gun, one of our own machine-guns, actually firing. It appeared to be firing on us, so that more or less ended our attack.[91]

Dunlop reported this to his battalion commander, Sam Wild. After investigating, they established that they had been fired on by Ryan, who 'was flaying drunk . . . [and] was overpowered and arrested'.[92] There was already much suspicion surrounding Ryan, 'a very mysterious fellow', according to Jim Brewer.[93] Ryan had made a number of wild claims, including that he had been in both the Irish Free State Army and the IRA, that he had previously worked as a gigolo in France and that his brother was a colonel in the Nationalist army.[94] 'A huge man, a bull of a fellow' and 'a tremendous drinker', he had had a number of run-ins with the volatile Fred Copeman, one of which had left Ryan in jail nursing a bruised jaw.[95] The Machine-Gun Company's political commissar, Tom Murray, had also complained that Ryan had refused to obey orders and had threatened him with a hand grenade.[96] 'Bourgeois extraction . . . Family fascists . . . Had fascist leanings once. Jailed for disruption . . . Should be very closely watched,' read the assessment by Ryan's superiors.[97] His friend Eugene Downing recalled:

He was a bit of a problem in the battalion. He was a larger than life character. He was from Limerick and according to himself had been to university in England. He was a tall, burly person, a complete extrovert and fearless. He was also an excellent machine gunner. On the occasion of Pandit Nehru's visit to the battalion at Marsa, he demonstrated his skill with that weapon knocking chunks out of a tree across the valley. He could be [a] very amiable and amusing character. Unfortunately, he was always kicking against the pricks, in a manner of speaking.

On one occasion when I was on sentry duty at battalion headquarters he was placed in my care until the following morning on a charge of being drunk and abusive. He just lay on the ground and went asleep. The following morning he used his charm and powers of persuasion to induce me, when I was going off duty, to fetch his mess tin when I returned to the camp and bring it back to him. To me this was above and beyond the call of duty, but he succeeded in getting me to do it.[98]

Ryan was charged with firing on his own comrades, and Divisional headquarters gave orders for him to be executed by members of the British Battalion. On 5 August 1938, he was taken for a walk by battalion commander Sam Wild and his adjutant George Fletcher, who informed him of the decision. Ryan responded calmly; 'You wouldn't do that Sam would you?' '[Sam] Wild told him to go ahead of them and then they shot him in the back of the head . . . George Fletcher was in tears over that,' admitted John Dunlop.[99] While some volunteers continued to believe that Ryan had been a fascist saboteur or a spy, the truth was probably rather more prosaic, as Eugene Downing acknowledged sadly: 'Vino was his downfall.'

Several volunteers have alluded to other executions carried out without due process. According to Welsh volunteer Billy Griffiths, company adjutant Tommy McGuire was complaining to Sam Wild about one of the men:

> Sam said, 'Why don't you shoot him?'
> 'I haven't a pistol,' said McGuire.
> Sam called for his batman, Bush, and asked him about a pistol he had asked him to clean. Bush handed the pistol in its holster to Sam, and Sam, in turn gave it to McGuire with the parting words,
> 'No more complaints about X!'[100]

Griffiths doesn't mention the name of the victim, so the report is impossible to verify. However, more than one brigader did disappear in mysterious circumstances. Michael Browne, known in Spain as 'Poona' Browne and a volunteer with two years' experience in the Colonial Police, was the brother of Felicia Browne, the first British volunteer to be killed in Spain.[101] Browne was later alleged to have been executed by his company commander 'Taffy' Evans after deserting.[102] The battalion leadership were undeniably suspicious of Browne: 'Owing to the fact that he has been in the police force and having such an <u>adventurous</u> past, he should be watched.'[103] However, as he appears to have acquitted himself well in Spain, displaying 'intelligence and a capacity for leadership' according to the report by his political *responsable*, his summary execution cannot be confirmed.[104]

Other uncorroborated rumours abound, such as those surrounding Welsh company commander and political commissar Alec Cummings. Wounded at Villanueva de la Cañada, Cummings was commended for his bravery and promoted to the cadres service. Yet, after having what seems to have been a breakdown, he had become, according to his superiors' assessment, 'increasingly disillusioned and resentful and was now threatening to desert . . . if he returns to England he should be watched'.[105] Cummings refused to return to the front, complaining bitterly of having been passed over for promotion. Political commissars Harry Dobson and Bob Cooney, battalion second-in-command George Fletcher, and the new Party secretary, Billy Griffiths, held a meeting to decide his fate:

> The man was well known. It was too dangerous to allow him to continue in command even if he were prepared to do so. If we showed undue leniency, it could affect moral adversely. Dobson was for a Court Martial organized by the Brigade with our recommendation that he be shot! I supported Dobson.[106]

Despite the recommendation of Dobson and Griffiths, Cummings wasn't shot; both Cooney and Fletcher opposed the idea. Nonetheless, Cummings failed to survive the war, disappearing in the Sierra Caballs in September 1938 having apparently become 'demoralised and unsteady'.[107] As with the cases of 'X' and Poona Browne, the evidence regarding his fate remains inconclusive.

The Communist Party's determination to protect the reputation of the International Brigades meant that some inglorious deaths were hushed up, and this has helped to fuel the conspiracy theories. For example, Dewsbury Labour councillor Clem Broadbent 'was accidentally shot . . . with a bullet in his head', probably by a member of the Spanish Lister Battalion.[108] On 9 September 1938, Broadbent died in hospital of a fever induced by his wound and was buried in a communal grave in the hospital cemetery. Clearly concerned that 'Trotskyist' elements in the Labour Party and ILP back in Britain might use the shooting to attack the Spanish Republic, it was recommended by Alonzo 'Lon' Elliott, a senior British Communist who worked at the political commissars' headquarters in Madrid, that 'it would be more convenient to give notice in England that comrade Broadbent had fallen in combat.'[109]

★

Many critics of the Brigades, both at the time and since, have tended to focus on their political, rather than their military agenda.[110] For detractors, the Comintern's involvement in the foundation and organisation of the International Brigades has ensured that they have always been seen as a Comintern army, an agent of Stalin's expansionism and the subversion of the Spanish Republic for his own ends.[111] The harsh discipline and rigid political orthodoxy within the Brigades, maintained by the threat of prison camps – and worse – have been seen as an extension of the show trials and purges occurring in the Soviet Union. Numerous allegations have been made of the routine execution of International Brigaders, 'pour encourager les autres'; that André Marty, 'the butcher of Albacete', supposedly admitted to personally ordering, if not actually overseeing, the execution of more than five hundred international volunteers.[112] This accusation by Daily Express reporter Sefton Delmer is typical:

> The Stalinist execution commandos – not so different from the 'Vehme' murder squads in Germany – even went so far as to use the clash and clamour of the battle to shoot down from behind the men whom they had on their deathlists. I remember hearing from both German and British Internationals that after the battle of Morata [on the Jarama front] none of them quite knew which of their comrades had been killed by Franco and which by Stalin. And it was the same story in battle upon battle after that. The stone cairns put up as memorials to the 'Heroic fighters for Freedom,' however, carried the names of all the fallen without differentiation as to who had killed them.[113]

Within the British Battalion, however, the leadership's determination not to execute deserters was maintained throughout the war. And despite the awkwardness it could cause, some volunteers were repatriated, even if they had committed misdemeanours during their time in Spain. One such was actor James Robertson Justice, who had been working in the Quartermaster's stores and the hospital in Madrigueras until he was accused of having a morphine addiction. Described as 'at best, an opportunist and careerist', he was believed to be 'thoroughly disruptive in causing [a] great deal of Anti-French feeling which culminated in several fights'. Rather than ending up in prison, Justice was expelled from Spain in late spring 1937.[114]

It would also be a mistake to think that there was no tolerance of political unreliability. Though 'true believers' were considered the ideal, many whose political development was seen as unsatisfactory were nevertheless accepted. Senior British figures in Spain criticised for being politically 'weak' and 'undisciplined' included Sam Wild, Jock Cunningham, Fred Copeman and Malcolm Dunbar, all of whom rose to senior ranks.[115] Furthermore, the case of Eugene McParland, from Birkenhead, demonstrated that the power of the SIM in the Brigades did not always go unchallenged. McParland had arrived in Spain in the summer of 1937 and was accepted into the Brigades despite suspicions of a criminal background in the UK.[116] Having arrived with papers stating that he had a medical condition and was only suitable for auxiliary services, he was sent to the auto-park and was working as a driver when he was, apparently, 'arrested in mistake for some-one else'. The error was admitted to McParland on the day he was arrested, yet he was still held in prison for three days and when released, was sent to the front line, despite his medical papers. Bob Cooney's letter to American brigade commissar John Gates was highly critical of the high-handed workings of the SIM's agents:

> I think that something should be done about the slovenly methods of the S.I.M. My impression is, that when they found out that they had made a mistake in the case of McParland, they hung on in the hope of finding a charge to justify his arrest. This impression is strengthened by a conversation with Comrade Ivan, whose attitude is a distinctly bureaucratic one . . . Comrade Ivan tries to justify himself by saying that 'MacParland deserves to be arrested anyhow'. This is irresponsible talk and such an attitude puts weapons in the hands of bad elements. In the interests of the good working of this Battalion, I hope that you will get this matter cleared up.[117]

McParland was repatriated in August 1938. That the commissar of the British Battalion, a senior ranking British Communist, should be able to criticise the workings of the SIM in this way, suggests that the authority of 'Stalin's goons' within the International Brigades was not as absolute as some might have believed.

This being war, of course mistakes were made. East Ender Jack Shaw was one of many volunteers to complain about the unfair and random nature of the punishments handed out:

> Colonel Gal was quick tempered. We had just marched to the rear when

suddenly Gal drew up in his staff car, got out and pounced on Frank Butler and myself. Holding his pistol to my head he shouted and cursed at us for being deserters and cowards, and had us both thrown into gaol. Imagine our feelings. We were dirty, unwashed and starving and thus we were greeted coming out of battle.

However, hasty decisions made in the heat of battle might be reconsidered once the situation and the individuals concerned had calmed down:

Next morning, Gal sent for us in his dug-out. There he stood before us an abject figure, tears in his eyes and asking our forgiveness. He told us he was ashamed of his actions and promptly made up for them by providing us with what we considered at the time to be the finest thing in the world – food, hot and appetising and plentiful. The question can be posed, in what other army would a high ranking officer bow his head and apologise to two ordinary soldiers?

'This,' argued Shaw, 'is why the International Brigade was different.'[118]

14

The 'turn of the tide'

The battle started as a Republican offensive, but ended as a rout.
Interview with Welsh volunteer Alun Menai Williams

Following investigations into the failures of the Republican forces during the Brunete offensive, the 15th International Brigade was incorporated into the 35th Division, under the command of General 'Walter' (the *nom de guerre* of Karol-Waclaw Swierczewski), the Polish Red Army colonel who had commanded the 14th International Brigade at Lopera the previous winter.[1] It was also reorganised, with the Canadian Mackenzie-Papineau Battalion (the Mac-Paps) replacing the crack Dimitrov Battalion, which was transferred to the 129th Brigade.[2] In recognition of his outstanding military talents, Malcolm Dunbar, commander of the British Anti-Tank Battery, was promoted to the brigade staff as chief of operations, and was replaced in turn by his second-in-command, the 'very much upper middle class' but rather less well regarded Hugh Slater.[3] Tom Wintringham, now recovered from his wounds at Jarama, and following a spell at the officer school at Pozorrubio, joined Dunbar on the brigade staff. By August 1937, the battalion was just over 400 strong, of whom just under half were British. From now on, the British members of the battalion would always be outnumbered by Spaniards.[4]

With Fred Copeman still recovering from his breakdown at Brunete, the battalion's acting commander, Joe Hinks, rejoined his Machine-Gun Company on 12 August. He was replaced by Peter Daly, a former IRA man 'from a long line of Irish revolutionary stock'.[5] Daly had previously served as a section leader and company commander in the 20th Anglo-American Battalion of the 86th Brigade, a unit formed hurriedly from new arrivals and recovering casualties in March 1937 to help stem a Rebel push in the south of Spain near Córdoba.[6] Following the return of the British to their battalion in June, Daly had risen quickly through the ranks, becoming a captain after Brunete.[7] While 'a popular appointment', some wondered if he might have been promoted rather too quickly: 'I would suspect that his knowledge of military strategy and tactics was no greater than that of our previous commanders, but he had that easy-going nature and lack of reserve which seems to be a feature of many Irishmen.'[8]

On 18 August 1937, the 35th Division was transferred to the Aragon front to join a new offensive aimed at capturing the town of Zaragoza. The operation was intended to divert Franco's attention away from his northern campaign, which had seen the Nationalist forces advancing ominously towards Santander. For the battalion, it meant another long and tiring journey:

> In the heat of a Spanish mid-summer this long, dusty journey by lorry proved both wearisome and wearing . . . the terrain there was the very worst: bleak, exposed, unproductive, treeless hillsides which offered no protection from the elements and scant cover from enemy fire. It was a dreadful and dreary landscape which seemed to gnaw into one and erode the spirit.[9]

The British rested briefly in the small village of Azaila, before beginning an attack on the town of Quinto, a strongpoint near Zaragoza, on 24 August. They found Quinto defended in similar fashion to Villanueva de la Cañada the previous month: 'the church with its dominating tower, had been converted into a fortress, with machine-guns bristling from the windows and emplacements.'[10] The attack was led by the American Lincoln Battalion with the British in reserve, but the British Anti-Tank Battery was used to blast the numerous strongholds with their high-velocity Soviet guns, which were 'accurate enough to shoot explosive shells through windows'.[11] Nevertheless, 'the tenacity of the Nationalist garrisons astounded the attackers.' During the street fighting, which eventually secured Quinto the following day, Tom Wintringham was again wounded, this time more seriously:

> I walked down the side of the street, scouting. I wanted to find a house we could set on fire so that it would set fire to the church. I was just having a good look round, nipping round corners and doors very quickly so they couldn't shoot me, when WHACK – a bullet hit me on top of the shoulder.[12]

The injury would eventually lead to the 'English Captain' being invalided home from Spain in November 1937.[13]

While the other battalions of the 15th Brigade fought to capture Quinto, the British Battalion was ordered to attack Purburrel Hill, a small high point – and a natural stronghold – overlooking the town. 'We were told that this hill was only lightly held and that we, the British Battalion, should be able to take it,' remembered Cyril Sexton, from Croydon.[14] Expecting little resistance, the battalion began its ascent:

A gentle slope led up towards the top of Purburrel and here we started to advance and again we came under heavy fire . . . Then the sound of aircraft. I thought that this is it. Caught out in the open with no trench nor fox hole to dive into: the enemy bombers came over and we waited.[15]

However, the Nationalist pilots mistook the defending force for Republicans and 'instead of bombing us they went over and bombed their own troops at the top of the hill. White flags began to appear, but there was some shooting from their lines and the flags soon disappeared.'[16]

The attackers soon discovered that the defenders' positions had been expertly fortified.[17] When the British tried to rush the top of the hill they were met with 'murderous' machine-gun fire, which forced them to scrabble for shelter:

We sought what natural cover there was, every undulation in the rocky ground, no matter how insignificant it appeared at a first, casual glance, housed one or more men trying to bury themselves in the unyielding earth to avoid the bullets which flew ceaselessly overhead. Rifles and hand-grenades were useless against the armaments massed on the higher ground above us . . . Those of us fortunate enough to have survived the first onslaught sought what protection we could, as throughout a long, hot and bloody day we waited for the sun to go down and the arrival of darkness to shield our retreat from those bullet-swept slopes.[18]

Repeated attacks were met with fierce and determined resistance, and Peter Daly prudently withdrew the battalion to await artillery support, despite the orders of Ĉopić, the 15th Brigade commander. During the night a Rebel patrol was captured, having left the hill in a desperate search for water, confirmation both of the strength of the defences and the inadequacy of the water supply. Had the battalion time to wait, the defenders would have been forced by their thirst to surrender – but the hill's strategic importance meant there was no time for patience.

On 26 August the battalion made a new attempt to capture the hill, but this time the defences were first bombarded by the Anti-Tank Battery. Thanks to the accuracy of the guns – and the thirst-induced weakness of the defenders – there was little resistance to the ensuing frontal assault and the hill finally fell to the British. After the disappointment of the Brunete campaign, the capture of the hill was a major and morale-boosting achievement.

> We were extremely proud of our capture of Purburrell [sic] Hill. It had not been the simple and straightforward exercise that we had initially been led to believe, and had proved, instead, to be one of the most heavily fortified positions that fell to the British throughout the war.[19]

Nonetheless, the position had taken two days to capture and several volunteers had been lost, including commander Peter Daly, who was mortally wounded on Purburrel Hill on 25 August and died of his wounds in hospital ten days later. He was replaced by his adjutant Paddy O'Daire, another long-standing political activist, who had been fighting in Spain since Lopera. O'Daire was also popular and respected, 'a hell of a nice chap', and had a phlegmatic and undogmatic – not to say prescient – view of the war: 'All war's a muddle. And the side that's in the worst muddle is the one that's going to lose.'[20]

The eventual capture of Quinto itself was to lead to one of the 15th International Brigade's less glorious episodes. Of more than five hundred prisoners taken, at least a dozen were executed by volunteers enraged at the loss of so many of their comrades in the street fighting: 'we just grabbed those guys, lined them up and shot them right there,' admitted one American volunteer.[21] Several officers were shot by General Walter personally, in retaliation for the loss of his close personal friend, the Polish chief of the 35th Division medical services, Mieczyslaw Domanski, known in Spain as Doctor 'Dubois'.[22] One badly wounded prisoner was the subject of a fierce argument. American volunteers wanted to call a political commissar to decide whether he should live, but an ex-mobster nicknamed 'Crazy O'Leary' ended the argument by shooting the Spaniard through the head.[23]

★

On 27 August, the brigade advanced twenty kilometres south-west, passing through the small village of Codo, recently abandoned by the Nationalists. Their target was Belchite, 'a fortress-like feudal town in the Spanish manner, compact, enclosed and ancient', which lay five kilometres further along the road.[24] However, the action at Purburrel Hill had seen the British Battalion's numbers sink to just over 100 men and the unhappiness displayed at Mosquito Hill had returned.[25] When the battalion was ordered to advance on the town of Mediana de Aragón, ten kilometres north of Belchite, to confront approaching Nationalist reinforcements, several men refused. Only when Paddy O'Daire appealed to the battalion's Communist Party members were the recalcitrant and unhappy men persuaded to obey the order. Reluctantly, the battalion marched on Mediana and made a 'short and sharp' attack. The Nationalists were forced back into the town, the battalion taking up positions on the adjacent hillside.[26]

Meanwhile, the Anti-Tank Battery and the other battalions of the 15th Brigade were engaged in a desperate assault on Belchite itself. The three guns in the anti-tanks fired 2700 shells in two days; one gun was fired at such a rate that its barrel burst and it had to be withdrawn from action.[27] The Americans finally captured Belchite on 6 September, following some of the most desperate hand-to-hand fighting seen in Spain, as members of the 15th International Brigade advanced house by house. The town was reduced virtually to dust: 'The slaughter was quite immense,' remembered Scottish first-aider Roddy MacFarquhar, who attended some of the wounded at Belchite and Quinto. 'I had to organise the evacuation of the wounded and the dead. It wasn't a very nice thing, a lot of them had been lying [there] for days.'[28]

This brought the Aragon offensive to an end. Quinto, Belchite and nine hundred square kilometres of territory had been captured. Many volunteers were jubilant that, at last, the Republican forces were winning battles and gaining ground: 'the list of our victories was beginning to lengthen: Purburrel Hill, Quinto, Mediana, Belchite. Never before had we advanced so successfully,' claimed Walter Gregory, triumphantly.[29] Nevertheless, the offensive had failed to achieve its principal objective, the capture of Zaragoza, and neither had it relieved any of the pressure on the northern front. By the end of the month Santander was in Nationalist hands; two months later, so was the entire northern Republican zone.

★

Following the assault on Belchite, the British were pulled out of the line for ten days in urgent need of rest.[30] On 4 September 1937, Will Paynter wrote to Harry Pollitt, advising him that yet again the battalion was in a perilous state, with only sixty active volunteers, and complaining that 'for the past three months there has only been a trickle of volunteers coming in.'[31] While the volunteers were in reserve, the official decree incorporating the International Brigades into the Republican Army was published on 23 September 1937. This confirmed that all Internationals fighting in Spain would be required to remain in the Republican Army until the end of the war. It also ruled that there must be a quota of Spanish soldiers in the International Brigades; that there must be a Spanish battalion in every international brigade, a Spanish company in every battalion and a Spanish section in every company. From now on all orders were to be given in Spanish and men were no longer to be trained, in British Army style, lining up in columns of four, but in the Spanish style of threes.[32] At the International Brigade bases, cadres 'began to do all the files and correspondence in Spanish . . . [changing] from French to Spanish'.[33]

The decree also formalised the hierarchical nature of the Republican Army. The intention was to differentiate it from the more egalitarian militia units that had sprung up after the uprising, which many Communists argued were militarily unsuited to the war against Franco's forces and were, of course, bastions of Anarchism and Trotskyism. Orders stated that 'all officers will be saluted by men in uniform':[34]

> The Republican forces were moving out of the era of guerrilla militia and becoming an army and we were to become part of the Fifth Army. This was a big political issue in Spain and in order to be an army all the free and easy atmosphere where we called [Major] George Nathan 'George' all had to go. There was to be insignia of rank.[35]

Senior figures in the battalion and the Party argued that the changes were militarily necessary. Bill Rust was absolutely clear on the importance of discipline and the saluting of officers, for 'difficult operations against the highly-trained Italian and German troops demanded a military skill which could not be achieved without stern military discipline, and required officers accustomed to command and to act without hesitation.'[36] A relieved Fred Copeman began to feel that 'the Battalion again began to look something like an efficient military unit.'

I was determined that in future an advance would be under the strict discipline of capable officers. An officers' mess was organised, with its own cookhouse and other amenities. All men, from section leader upwards, had meals with the battalion commander. Men were expected to salute all officers. This at first was a knotty problem. I decided the best way to overcome it was to start by saluting every man myself, irrespective of rank, whom I met in the village. It was surprising how quickly the lads took this up and, with few exceptions, came to make a point of getting their salute in first.[37]

A number of volunteers, referred to disparagingly by one London volunteer as 'anarcho-socialists', continued to argue 'that all men should eat together' and that 'officers should not have separate tables,' despite the officers' contention that they needed to talk things over privately and their growing belief in the military necessity of separation.[38] But while Bill Alexander, who was to take command of the battalion at the end of the year, admitted that 'the emphasis on the role of officers, which included saluting, caused some discussion', he claimed that 'among the British it did not cause great concern.'[39]

On 11 October 1937, the 15th International Brigade was briefed for an operation against the Aragon town of Fuentes de Ebro, twenty-five kilometres south-east of Zaragoza, which had held out during the previous month's offensive. The battalion was still at a dramatically low ebb when they arrived at Fuentes, numbering around 150 in all: 'That was the British Battalion at that time at Fuentes, because all the rest were "hors de combat", they were in hospital,' remembered one London member of the Machine-Gun Company.[40] According to the hopelessly ambitious plan, a Spanish battalion was to be carried forward on tanks, while the other three battalions, including the British, were to launch an assault on the Rebel lines before advancing on Zaragoza. However, just as at Brunete, though 'military-wise they sounded lovely' the 'venture had a high degree of audacity', which required 'a high degree of preparatory training and discipline'.[41] Sadly, this was not forthcoming.

Hugh Sloan, Bill Alexander's runner, saw the disaster unfold. When the operation was launched in the early morning of 13 October, he counted forty-seven Republican tanks and watched as they sped forward at full tilt, throwing off the troops who were trying to cling on and leaving them far behind to be shot to pieces.[42] The tanks themselves fared little better, for 'the Fascists were ready for them – they'd got bottles of petrol and a number of the Russian tanks were set alight.' Timing was vital, but 'the Fascists were alerted, the planes bombed too early, the artillery bombed too early and the tanks were late.'[43] Insufficient Republican artillery and air support made matters immeasurably worse. It was, thought Sloan, '[a] ridiculous charge like the charge of the Light Brigade – a gallant effort but a stupid effort.'[44] One Canadian volunteer was especially scathing:

> I think the High Command had seen too many documentary movies of the Russian Red Army exercises. There was a very famous one which I saw myself in Spain called *Red Army Exercises* in 1936 . . . the army advancing with the whole battalion put on the back of tanks. Some guy in the High Command had seen this thing and thought it was appropriate for Fuentes de Ebro. Whereas it might have been quite okay on the flat plains of the Ukraine, it was completely unsuitable for the terrain we were attacking over.[45]

As the disaster unfolded, panicked brigade staff ordered the Anti-Tank Battery to advance on the Rebel forces. But none of the guns were able to open fire and second-in-command Jeff Mildwater was injured before the battery was wisely withdrawn.[46] The British Battalion also lost another commander: Harold Fry, the commander of the Machine-Gun Company at Jarama, who had returned to Spain in the summer. Standing in for Paddy O'Daire, who was away at the officers' training school at Pozorrubio, Fry was killed on 13 October, along with several others:[47]

> [Fry] was telling me that they will always run when the tanks come . . . he must have believed it . . . he had a walking stick and the other chap that was with him . . . his commissar [probably Eric Whalley from Mansfield], the two of them stepped over the trench and walked, how they do it in the films, walking ahead and without batting an eyelid as the bullets went flying by, until they just got shot down.[48]

The Nationalist soldiers were able to keep firing for hours while the Internationals had to sit it out. They simply didn't have enough ammunition: 'We just didn't fire back. We were only reserving everything we'd got, in case we were attacked.'[49]

With the humiliating failure of the attack, the British remained in the line for ten days before being withdrawn and placed in reserve. There was a numerical reorganisation of the 15th International Brigade in the autumn, with the 16th British Battalion renumbered as the 57th Republican Army Battalion. The British were now well represented on the brigade staff, with Malcolm Dunbar continuing as Chief of Operations. The outstanding linguist, Jim Ruskin, fluent in eight languages, was appointed Chief of Transmissions, while Lieutenant Edwin Bee commanded mapping. Captain Clifford Wattis, previously with the American Lincolns, had been made responsible for Brigade supplies and Ernest Mahoney, the manager of a left-wing bookshop in London, put in charge of the Brigade postal service.[50]

Fred Copeman and Walter Tapsell returned to Spain at the end of October, and the following month they took up the roles of battalion commander and commissar respectively, Copeman replacing Paddy O'Daire who had now been accepted into the senior officers' training school (for military units of battalion size and over).[51] Bill Alexander was moved from the Anti-Tank Battery to become Copeman's adjutant; the company commanders included the tough, long-standing Manchester volunteer Sam Wild, and George Fletcher, an army veteran with fifteen years' service (and who had taken temporary command of the battalion for three weeks after the death of Harold Fry in October). Fletcher was 'very much a military man. I don't think he had a political idea in his head,' said Jack Jones.[52] The third company commander, partly in keeping with the new Republican decree for Spanish representation, but also based on his obvious competence, was Spaniard Lieutenant Cipriano (sometimes spelt Cypriano), 'a twenty-six year old illiterate peasant from Aragon, [who had] emerged as a natural leader, showing . . . courage and initiative'.[53] At the same time, three volunteers were nominated for the Republican Navalperal medal for their 'exceptional bravery and devotion to duty' in Spain: Chief of Staff Malcolm Dunbar, Irish leader Frank Ryan, and Lancashire volunteer George Buck, 'a thick-set tough guy' who had been the first to reach the top of Purburrel Hill and had torn down the Rebel standard.[54]

As ever, training continued, both military and political, while the volunteers' welfare was also taken care of in other ways:

In the Battalion there was regular training of all kinds, with a young Soviet Red Army instructor attached for a time. Special emphasis was laid on digging in, mobility, and use of ground and cover. Physical health and morale were improved by the provision of regular meals, washing facilities and sufficient sleep, together with concerts, sports and short leaves to Madrid.[55]

The frequent political meetings were seen as an important part of maintaining morale and honing the debating skills of the politically dedicated. Those who had come to Spain as 'simple anti-fascists' looked on with amazement, if not necessarily with interest:

I just listened. We were all sat there, some in the shade, some in the sun, and I just listened to the arguments and it was there I realised what an ignoramus I was, in terms of politics. They were all getting up; somebody over here would quote from Lenin and somebody would quote Marx, and so on. They were quoting by the yard! I thought, 'God help us, how do they know all that?'[56]

At the beginning of October, the brigade held a 'sports gala', for 'discipline,' the commissars argued, 'socialist competition and comradeship is the road to victory.' 'Sport,' claimed one, 'is truly international and can make a more lasting impression than any other activity.'[57] In addition to a football match between the different companies, there were field and track events.

Meanwhile, within the educated and intellectual milieu of the British Anti-Tank Battery, a cultural life thrived. The cultural *responsable* and principal driving force was popular poet, musician and Cambridge graduate Miles Tomalin, who was well-known among the British for his beautiful playing on the recorder.[58]

At night, everything quiet, I'd hear a recorder. This was Miles doing his guard duty on the frontline trench. He'd be playing some old French tune from the seventeenth century or often, Santa Maria. I'm quite sure he entertained the enemy as well as us. You're walking through the night and feeling a wee bit on your own and the trenches aren't that deep, hearing Miles playing, 'Da da da da'.[59]

Helped by Jim Brewer, Tomalin edited a 'wall newspaper' called 'Assault and Battery News', often not much more than a notice-board pinned to a tree. 'We used to put this paper up with various articles from the lads and they used to come from far and near to have a look at this,' remembered Brewer. He was not bragging; the wall newspaper was genuinely popular:[60]

> The wall newspaper is also worth seeing. We have a unique character who runs it and most of our other 'cultural' activities. In addition to playing a particular type of whistle with great skill he writes and produces sketches and 'songs', edits the paper and sets off competitions on everything from military strategy to those which determine whose girl is better looking.[61]

Such was its, and Tomalin's, success, that he was later promoted to take responsibility for the cultural education of the entire 15th International Brigade.

By mid-November the battalion numbered 105 British and Irish volunteers, with another 49 in training and 11 in officer school. Despite the return of volunteers who had recovered from wounds suffered during the Aragon campaign, there were still too few British members of the battalion to make up a standard company in the British army. It was hoped that new arrivals would bring the numbers up to 200 by the end of the year, but with the battalion aiming to increase to the standard Spanish army strength of 700, it was clear that any aspiration for the unit to comprise equal numbers of English-speakers and Spaniards was wholly unrealistic.[62]

The senior Party *responsable*, Bill Rust, who returned to Spain as the *Daily Worker* correspondent, wrote a confidential report on the current state of the battalion. Rust believed that morale and discipline were generally good, and that even the few 'undisciplined types' were more amenable than they had been in the past. However, he also discovered what he felt to be a general 'anti-brigade feeling' among officers. In particular, he argued that many of the battalion's problems stemmed from its commander, Fred Copeman, who 'refers almost without exception to the Brigade in a disparaging fashion . . . he, on occasions, goes out of his way to oppose the Brigade.'[63]

Rust claimed that these sentiments were widespread among senior figures in the battalion: '[Copeman] has also been successful in infecting C[omra]de [Bill] Alexander his adjutant with the same attitude and S[am] Wild has a long established anti-brigade tradition. Also [Ted] Edwards – battalion sec[retar]y is just a weakling who swims with the tide – in this case against the brigade.' According to the report, only Walter Tapsell, the battalion commissar, spoke up for the brigade staff; he was thus 'treated by Copeman and Wild with contempt'.[64] Rust reported that Tapsell was furious over his treatment by Copeman, and was threatening to approach Harry Pollitt and raise the threat of expulsion from the Party. He also claimed that Copeman was launching attacks on Communist Party officials in Britain, accusing 'everyone who didn't come out to Spain or volunteer to do so as running away from the struggle', and the 'fucken party members' of a lack of discipline. The 'egotistical' Copeman was, argued Rust, showing a lack of respect for the Party. In a statement rather revealing of his priorities, Rust complained that, on one occasion, Copeman had 'kicked the Mondéjar CP out of their rooms in order to provide the Battalion with a cantine [sic] for 24 hours'.[65]

Ever the political orchestrator, Rust argued that 'what is wanted of course is not to dispose of Copeman but to control him'. He acknowledged that Copeman possessed many 'sterling qualities as a battalion commander' and admitted he did not know 'of anyone who could replace Copeman from the standpoint of the good qualities he possesses'.[66] Rust suggested that the matter be raised with Pollitt, though as he felt that the threat of expulsion from the Party would not mean 'a terrible lot to Copeman', he recommended the Brigade leadership should advise him 'that unless he ceases his present slanderous attacks that he will be degraded and if need be sent to prison.'[67]

As the end of 1937 approached, attempts were made to entertain the members of the battalion and restore their morale. At the beginning of December Walter Tapsell organised a sports fiesta, including a boxing competition held in the bullring in Mondéjar, in which Salford Communist and hunger marcher Joe Norman, a former runner-up in the lightweight division in the British Navy's boxing championship, acquitted himself well:

There was a Canadian Golden Glove Champion who hadn't got a fight – he was fourteen stone. I was ten at the most. They said, 'Will you go and box him?' I said, What, him?' 'Oh, go on, give the lads a . . .' I knocked him out. It was one of the finest days out I've had. All the Spaniards for miles around packed into this bullring and all the troops who were near. It was a great day.[68]

While Norman did well in the boxing, football teams formed from members of the battalion and the anti-tanks did not; both were soundly beaten by Spanish teams.[69] However, it did little to spoil what for many volunteers was a particularly memorable day, 'the first time that the local inhabitants had ever heard British music played on mouth organs, combs, etc.'

> This was the first time we had seen so many pretty girls at once. Every Spanish soldier present began to pay his respects and soon the English lads were practising their meagre Spanish, so very little interest was taken in the efforts of the artists. What with the giggling of the girls, the noise of the innumerable children and the 'Olés' shouted by the large numbers of peasants who seemed to have flocked from miles around and were brimming over with excitement and exuberance of spirits, it was the nearest approach to Bedlam that one could imagine.[70]

A few days later, the fiestas and the sports days, the training and the discussions came to an end. After two months out of the line, the battalion was to be called upon once again, to try and ensure that the Republic's attempts to build upon the advances made in Aragon during the autumn would not be dashed.

On 10 December 1937, the 15th International Brigade departed Mondéjar and Ambite for the final time, the whole population of Mondéjar turning out to bid them farewell. Transported by train to the town of Alcañiz, twenty kilometres south of Caspe, they were then informed that they would have to march a further sixty kilometres to the front. Their initial dismay was mollified when the volunteers were informed that all the Republican lorries would be needed to transport Nationalist prisoners captured in a surprise Republican attack about to be made on the isolated city of Teruel, high in the mountains in southern Aragon.[71]

The attack began on 15 December, with the Republicans aiming to pre-empt a forthcoming Nationalist offensive at Guadalajara, the plans for which had been discovered by Republican spies.[72] At first, all went well. The elite Communist Fifth Regiment surrounded Teruel by the evening, and Republican soldiers were fighting in the city itself by 21 December. Republican supporters all over the world believed the victory signalled a turning point in the war and a demonstration of the might of the new Republican Army; the headline in Britain's News Chronicle hailed Teruel as 'the turn of the tide'.[73]

On Christmas Eve, despite the vicious hand-to-hand fighting which was still going on in the city, Republican leaders proclaimed a dramatic victory. Quartered in the village of Mas de las Matas, sheltered in a pleasant valley twenty kilometres to the south of Alcañiz, the British volunteers held an ecstatic celebration:

> A very boisterous night ensued during which it was announced that the whole Battalion would take part in a victory and homage parade the following morning. There was no doubt about it, the Battalion paraded in a style that even a British sergeant major would appreciate. The small village square was a blaze of glorious colour with the flags of the Spanish Republic, the almost American-looking flag of Catalonia with its crimson stripes, the black and red flag of the anarchists, the red flag of Soviet Russia and numerous pieces of bunting. After a number of speeches by the Commander and representatives of the Popular Front, the rest of the day was declared a general holiday. The day concluded with a grand dance in the village hall. It was more of a rugby scrum than a dance but was declared by the villagers to have been the most hilarious and entertaining in the memory of the oldest inhabitants.[74]

A Christmas feast of pork, wine and nuts was organised by the battalion's resourceful quartermaster, Lieutenant 'Hooky' Walker. The arrival of Harry Pollitt bearing letters from home was a surprise and popular gift for the volunteers – 'God bless him,' wrote one grateful soldier in a letter home.[75] All the British members of the battalion were no doubt honoured to receive in addition a signed photo of Pollitt; more welcome perhaps were the food parcels from Britain, containing a Christmas pudding, cigarettes and chocolate, which were generously shared with those in the battalion of other nationalities. During the celebrations Pollitt made a short speech, whipping up enthusiasm, and the following morning he presented the battalion with a banner, paid for by contributions made in Britain.

However, not all the volunteers were ecstatic about the celebrations. The separation of ranks continued to cause discontent, even among the Party faithful. Commissar Frank West complained: 'I was pretty browned off with the old Christmas business, having an officers' dinner and a squaddies' dinner. When the shit was being served up, we were all together weren't we?[76] Other members of the battalion were equally riled; Manchester volunteer Charles Morgan was disgusted with what he saw of the inequalities between the Brigade headquarters and those in the line. 'Brigade headquarters made me vomit,' he raged.

> When I saw conditions there after what I'd come out of, the very poor food, bad organisation, it was like the Ritz Hotel with meat, coffee with milk, cigarettes, four course dinners with champagne, the lot. That made me very bitter. If they could get it for them, they could get something better for the boys.[77]

Two days after Christmas, Fred Copeman was rushed into hospital for an operation to remove his appendix. He was later invalided home after complications set in. However, Bill Alexander, his widely respected adjutant and a 'fearless disciplinarian', replaced Copeman as commander of the battalion and the equally tough and fearless Sam Wild was promoted to become Alexander's adjutant.[78] As snow began to fall, the battalion began making their preparations for returning to the front.

The International Brigades had initially been held back from the action at Teruel to give them time to recover from the losses sustained in Aragon. There had also been doubts over their physical and mental readiness to return to the fight. As late as December 1937, General Walter, commander of the 35th Division, was complaining about the standard of training in the English-speaking battalions:

> A month ago I was with the English and Canadian battalions of the 15th Brigade. It is difficult to convey in words the state of weapons and how dirty, especially the rifles. The bores of their barrels were not much different from a seventeenth-century musket barrel found at Belchite. No fewer than 95 per cent of the rifles had no bayonet or cleaning rod, all lost since time immemorial. There was only a handful of cleaning rags in the brigade.[79]

Other problems were making themselves apparent. Tensions between the various national groups within the Brigades and with the Spaniards themselves were endemic and deeply troublesome: 'I found that national pride was one of the chief features in the life of the International Brigade,' remarked one volunteer.[80] Now, arguments between the English and Spanish-speaking members of the battalion flared up when Bill Alexander wanted to demote a Spanish officer and two Spanish corporals for disobeying an order to occupy a forward position. Alexander was overruled by Ĉopić but, as Will Paynter noted, the International harmony was not helped by the fact that 'none of our Battalion officers know more than a few words of Spanish.'[81]

Moreover, there were tensions within the 15th Brigade itself, and these were exacerbated by the overwhelmingly American leadership of the Brigade, who 'by August [1937] . . . were playing a big role'. Copeman believed that 'the Americans were struggling for military control as an indirect road to political power. In the end they gained both.'[82] From September 1937 onwards, both the base and the training school at Tarazona de la Mancha had been commanded by an American, Major Allan Johnson, who had been a regular officer in the United States Army.[83] According to a report by an (American) political commissar, 'the Americans demonstrated a feeling of superiority . . . towards the Canadian, Latin American, Spanish and Negro comrades'.[84] Both the American and British leadership believed the Canadians to be undisciplined and rather too 'rough around the edges', and the feelings went both ways. The Canadians clearly resented the American influence, with one Canadian volunteer complaining that the 15th Brigade was run by 'a clique of American Jews'. Many other disparaging remarks were made about the Americans, whom the Canadians in particular felt to be rather less hardy than themselves. As one observed acidly, 'I think most of them would starve to death in a grocery store.'[85]

Some volunteers sympathised with the Americans and their ambitions. One Scottish volunteer was convinced that the two American battalions comprised more politically experienced men than the other battalions in the brigade and that the American political commissars, Jonny Gates and Steve Nelson, only wanted influence within the brigade that was 'commensurate with their contribution'.[86] However, another Scottish volunteer, David Anderson, who served with the British, the Mac-Paps and the Americans, felt that there was a clear difference between the different national units:

> The Americans were good organisers, exceptionally good organisers. But at the same time they were childish in their outlooks. If you were good at anything, to them you were exceptional. The British, down to earth, just accepted things and that was that; but the Americans were different entirely, they organised things for their own comfort . . . I think too that the British were better fighters. They could accept hardships and the hardships were

really bad. The Americans couldn't, didn't, accept hardships to the same extent. I think the British were exceptional, you know, as far as fighting was concerned.[87]

All the problems, worries and disagreements were set aside, however, when the appalling conditions in which the Republican Army were fighting necessitated urgent reinforcements. Consequently, the 15th International Brigade was called up and on New Year's Eve, the British Battalion left Mas de las Matas for the Teruel front.[88] Soon after, on 8 January 1938, came news that despite the freezing conditions, Republican forces had managed to capture Teruel. Yet, within days, a Nationalist counter-offensive threatened to win back the Republicans' hard-fought gains. In response, on 14 January the 15th International Brigade was moved to the tip of the Republican position. There they were to bear the full brunt of a Nationalist attack comprising some 80,000 men, backed up with a mass of artillery and the largest air force so far seen in the war.

> We were ordered to take up positions on a sector of the front which gave a magnificent view of Teruel . . . Pushing my way along one sector I brushed against a pair of feet which were protruding through one side of the trench, evidently belonging to some poor devil who had been buried probably by shellfire and left where he fell. Although this was my first taste and actual sight of death on the battlefield, I felt rather casual about it. But I was glad that the two protruding feet were in a semi-mummified condition and covered by a pair of socks.[89]

Conditions were way beyond anything the volunteers had so far experienced in Spain. In temperatures that sank to twenty below zero at night, more men died at Teruel from the cold than were killed in battle, and the men 'concentrated on the desperate necessity not so much of getting warm, as of preventing freezing'.[90] Dressed in their threadbare uniforms, the conditions were unbearable. The cold and nearly a metre of snow made fighting virtually impossible, and soldiers struggled desperately to prevent themselves and their equipment from freezing:

> A useful device for protection of the body was to cut a slit in a blanket which could then be slipped over the head to act as a poncho. It broke the snow-filled winds, but allowed freedom of movement. Machine-gun locks had to

be taken out, wrapped in cloth, and carried near the body to prevent them from freezing up. Rifle-bolts often had to be warmed in the hands or the trouser-pockets before they could be moved. There was one benefit from the extreme cold. Everyone was lousy, for washing was impossible, but even the lice were too cold to crawl and bite.[91]

As one Scottish volunteer remembered, 'it was the coldest winter they'd had in thirty years . . . it snowed in Valencia and that is very improbable, even in January.'[92] In the Arctic conditions, the oranges left over from the celebration at Mas de las Matas froze solid.[93]

> It is impossible to describe just how cold we were. Sleep was just a bad joke. All we could do was jump out of the lorry and run up and down across the fields until we were absolutely exhausted and then flop down huddled together as best we could with our blankets and try and sleep for half an hour until, with every part of you freezing again, you pushed each other out of the truck to repeat the running up and down process.[94]

The battalion was deployed on the precipitous hill of Santa Bárbara, which overlooked the Alfambra River and dominated the northern approach to Teruel. The Machine-Gun Company took up position in old Rebel emplacements on the cliff edge and the Anti-Tank Battery was sited where they could support the battalion. The guns were well-placed and camouflaged, including one on the cliffs of Santa Bárbara itself, and were employed in 'knocking out machine-guns, or persuading fascist platoons, invariably advancing in a group, to retreat rapidly to safety'.[95]

But after holding on desperately for three days, a huge Nationalist artillery barrage on 18 January forced the defending German International Brigaders and Spanish marines to retreat off El Muletón, a mountain just north of the British positions. The three British rifle companies were ordered to leave the safety of the heights and to move down into the valley and across the Alfambra River. They took up a dangerously exposed position alongside the Canadian battalion, who were close to breaking under the devastating enemy artillery barrage.[96] Hurried attempts were made to dig-in, in preparation for the huge Rebel offensive everyone knew was coming.

On 19 January came a huge bombardment of the British positions. Garry McCartney, a Scottish volunteer in the Machine-Gun Company who observed the barrage from the hillside overlooking the valley, described how the Nationalists 'saturated' the British position with shell and machine-gun fire before sending their aircraft to bomb it.[97] Another member of a British gun crew perched on the cliff watched on helplessly:

> Over our heads was a squadron of Italian bombers painted black. How evil they looked . . . In a few moments the horrible shrieks of falling bombs split the afternoon air. Hour after hour that squadron of bombers dived and machine-gunned the trenches of the infantry, the only opposition being one battery of three light anti-aircraft guns and they were a long way off. It made one sick to realise that over there the bombs were falling on our own mates. What a hell on earth it must have been.[98]

The battalion held on doggedly, though all the volunteers could do was to cower in the trenches, hoping for the barrage to end: 'You could hear the screaming of the bombs and always the screaming seemed to be coming towards the back of your neck.'[99] Some Nationalist planes flew very low, picking out their targets: 'You could see them as they dived down at us. You could see the pilot looking out and looking at us as he's firing at us.'[100]

> It was harrowing in the extreme to experience a dive-bomber strafing. I'd never even thought about such a thing before. For those who've never experienced it I hope they never will. It's a frightening thing to be trying to get as close to the earth as possible with bullets besplattering all over the place.[101]

Gradually, the overwhelming superiority of the Nationalist forces began to push back the defenders. However, a determined last-ditch defence held the position – if only just – and forced Franco's forces to give up their direct assault on Teruel. For their astonishing tenacity in the face of an overwhelmingly superior force, the members of the British Battalion were personally commended by Lieutenant-Colonel Modesto, the commander of the Republican 5th Army Corps. Walter Tapsell was singled out for praise for his work as political commissar and Bill Alexander was promoted to captain.[102]

Twenty-one members of the battalion were killed at Teruel, thirteen of them from No. 1 Company alone.[103] In all, the battalion lost one-third of its strength.[104] As Sam Wild put it, typically dryly, 'the battle of Teruel was a major victory for the Republican forces, which later became a major defeat for the Republican forces.'[105] A brief memorial service was held at the rear of the British positions and Bill Alexander planted a memorial to the dead.[106] On 3 February the depleted British force was withdrawn, but as Franco's counter-attack gained momentum, their period of rest and recuperation was to be short-lived.

With little time to recover, the British and the three other battalions of the 15th International Brigade were transferred to the small village of Segura de los Baños, seventy kilometres north of Teruel. The British were to be part of a diversionary attack, designed to take the pressure off the Republicans still defending Teruel. Following initial successes by the Americans and Canadians, achieved mainly due to surprise, the British joined the position in preparation for an assault on the village of Vivel de Río Martín, eight kilometres south of Segura de los Baños, the main objective of the attack. But the ultimate outcome was a familiar one. Well-protected by German-built fortifications and with superior numbers and armaments, particularly Italian airpower, the Nationalist forces were able to gradually force the Republicans back. As Bill Alexander admitted:

> The operation had been carried out with drive and competence, and the Brigade and the British Battalion were again singled out for commendation by the 5th Army Command. However, it had not succeeded in its aim of drawing pressure away from Teruel.[107]

The eventual failure of the Republicans' winter offensive was confirmed when, on 21 February 1938, the Republican Army were forced to retreat from Teruel, giving up the city and the territory which they had fought over so doggedly. The British Battalion were withdrawn from Segura de los Baños and sent into reserve at La Puebla de Valverde, a beautiful village surrounded by mountains twenty kilometres south-east of Teruel. After a fortnight, they were moved to the village of Lecera, ten kilometres south of Belchite, where they remained during January and February, living 'in stone barns, huddled together against the bitter cold'.[108] Here attempts were made to make good a little of the devastation inflicted on the battalion by the freezing temperatures.

> After Teruel there were numerous complaints that nobody had been able to bath for weeks, so Brigade decided to create one. Heated by a wood fire,

about eight men could shower at the same time – which was three o'clock in the morning, in January! Most men only got a pint of water each, though![109]

Training recommenced. General Walter later observed that the 15th Brigade improved dramatically after Teruel, noting approvingly 'that the 15th sometimes seems completely different from what it was a short time ago.'[110]

With the battalion desperately short of manpower, two British volunteers who would become key figures in Spain took on new roles. Bob Cooney, described by one volunteer as 'a boyish-looking chap with very bushy eyebrows and hair that grew straight up', was an experienced activist from Scotland who had studied at the Lenin School in Moscow, yet he joined the battalion as a soldier.[111] In addition, Bill Alexander had been wounded, leading to him being invalided home. Consequently, 'Sam Wild became Battalion Commander. A Lancashire lad, Sam proved in subsequent battles to be the greatest commander the Battalion had yet possessed.'[112]

15

Bearing Witness

We, the journalists in Madrid, were not in the front line, but we were near enough to get something of its atmosphere. It was stimulating as well as tiring. We did not share in the feeling to the same degree as these people fighting for their lives, but we tasted it, and I, for one, found it good.

Geoffrey Cox, *Defence of Madrid*

During the course of the civil war, the British security services recorded the details of over four thousand men and women they believed to be making their way to Spain.[1] While the majority of these were volunteers for the International Brigades, the list also included a large number who went either as supporters or witnesses, or to report on the conflict. The Spanish war was a major news story in Britain, and in addition to the 'fact-finding' tours and delegations sent out by organisations eager to express solidarity and offer their support, many British newspapers and newsreels posted correspondents to Spain.

Among those travelling to Spain as reporters and observers were some whose motives were rather more covert. Foremost of these was Harold 'Kim' Philby, who worked as a foreign correspondent for *The Times*, receiving a decoration from a grateful Franco in March 1938. However, Philby was also working for Russian intelligence, having been recruited as a Russian spy by an experienced KGB agent, Edith Suschitsky, the wife of British doctor Alex Tudor-Hart, who was serving with the British medical services in Spain.[2]

Another was Hungarian-born writer Arthur Koestler. Described as 'the only significant writer to stare death in the face in Spain and return to write about it', Koestler approached Comintern propagandist Willi Münzenberg soon after the rising and was persuaded to go to Seville to find evidence of

German and Italian intervention in the war; 'he was, in effect, a Communist spy.'³ Koestler's findings later appeared on the front page of the *News Chronicle* and were passed by Münzenberg to the Non-Intervention Committee in London. Koestler returned to Spain in January the following year, unwisely choosing to remain in Málaga when it fell to Nationalist forces, a decision he later recognised to be 'downright crazy'.⁴ He took shelter in the house of the British acting consul, Sir Peter Chalmers-Mitchell; both Koestler and his host were sufficiently apprehensive of the Rebel occupation for Chalmers-Mitchell to prepare syringes and morphine tablets in order to commit suicide.

On 9 February Koestler and Chalmers-Mitchell were arrested at the house by three Nationalist officers, including Rebel press officer Luis Bolín. Chalmers-Mitchell was soon released, but for Koestler it was the beginning of three months' imprisonment and his 'dialogue with death'. Every night he heard the pitiful sounds of groups of prisoners being led away for execution and fully expected his fate to be the same. However, he was fortunate in having a number of influential friends and Franco commuted his death sentence. Following considerable international pressure, Koestler was released on 14 May, after signing a declaration not to further involve himself in the affairs of Spain. But he never forgot that hundreds of those sharing his imprisonment had been given a very different type of release. Koestler drew heavily on his experiences in the Spanish jail for *Darkness at Noon* and he dedicated *Dialogue with Death*, the second part of his Spanish testament, to a young militiaman called Nicolás, whom he met briefly in prison before the Spaniard was taken away to be executed.

While covert work such as that undertaken by Philby and Koestler entailed obvious dangers, the job of foreign correspondent in Spain was itself not without risk. It also required numerous logistical and political obstacles to be overcome. Both the Nationalists and Republicans attempted to exercise control over the press, albeit via differing means and with correspondingly varied levels of success. The Nationalist Press Office, led by the arrogant and widely loathed Luis Bolín – later responsible for the frantic denials of the bombing of Guernica – employed less than subtle means to ensure that only the Nationalist perspective was reported. As the American *Chicago Daily Tribune* correspondent, Jay Allen, observed, 'the Rebels do not like newspapermen who see both sides.'⁵ Peter Kemp, one of a small number of Britons to volunteer for the Rebel forces, admitted that 'The Nationalists . ... confident like all good Spaniards that only fools or scoundrels would deny the justice of their cause,' made little attempt to cultivate the foreign press, seeing journalists as 'at best a nuisance and at worst potential spies'.[6]

Transgressors were swiftly kicked out of the Nationalist zone, with over thirty reporters expelled over the course of the war. The *Times* correspondent George Steer fell out with the Nationalists late in 1936, as Kemp witnessed:

It seems that the Nationalist authorities eventually decided to grant the journalists' pleas for a visit to the Madrid front. They laid on a specially conducted tour, starting from Toledo. There were not only English and American journalists, but French, Italian, German and some South American as well. There were some senior Staff Officers from the Army, to explain the situation as it should be presented. A senior official of the Ministry of Press and Propaganda was in charge. A fleet of cars was assembled, ready to leave from the hotel at 8.30 in the morning. Soon after nine o'clock the party was ready to start, but there was no sign of Steer. After waiting a while in a fury of impatience, they were about to start without him when he appeared on the steps of the hotel with a set, exasperated expression on his face. In clear tones he addressed the assembled party:

'You pull – and pull – and pull – and nothing happens. You pull again . . . and the shit slowly rises. That's Spain for you,' he roared, 'in a nutshell.'[7]

Even those sympathetic to the Nationalist cause could find themselves ejected from the Rebel zone. *Daily Express* correspondent Sefton Delmer was expelled allegedly for writing accounts of mass executions or, as he was informed by the Nationalist authorities, '[for] publishing intelligence likely to be of use to the enemy, and secondly of writing a report calculated to make the Spanish armed forces look ridiculous.' Delmer later discovered the real reason for his expulsion: 'the Germans were coming', and witnesses, particularly from the foreign press, were explicitly not welcome.[8]

The Republicans' approach to foreign visitors was rather more sophisticated and open, recognising that the press were an important weapon in the war and needed to be handled carefully if they were to be wielded effectively. The smooth and able Constancia de la Mora, the English-educated grand-niece of the Republic's former Minister for the Interior, Miguel Maura, personified the Republicans' approach to the media. She was, according to Republican censor Arturo Barea, 'an efficient organiser, very much a woman of the world, who had joined the Left of her free choice'; certainly she was popular among the foreign correspondents.[9] Nevertheless, the Republic still frustrated reporters on occasion, for the censors, such as Barea and his Austrian girlfriend Ilsa Kulscar, worked hard to ensure that reporters and visitors saw and reported only what the Republican authorities wanted them to.[10] According to News Chronicle reporter Geoffrey Cox, 'Fräulein Else [sic] . . . used to criticize our stories from the angle of a journalist as well as an official, even chided us for not having enough "human interest" in our first air-raid stories.'[11]

Some reporters felt that the situation demanded the setting aside of traditional journalistic impartiality, for the two sides were not equal; this was, after all, a military rising against a legitimate, democratic government. American journalist Martha Gellhorn, who had arrived in Spain with Ernest Hemingway in the spring of 1937 to report on the war for the American magazine Collier's Weekly, lambasted the writing of dispassionate, neutral reports that tried to remain above the fray, famously condemning them as 'all that objectivity shit'.[12] However, the use of 'reportage', which was both partial and subjective, and designed to appeal to the prejudices of a particular readership, was the cause of much criticism.[13] Many stories that appeared in British newspapers were little more than propaganda. The News Chronicle reporter John Langdon-Davies, no Communist but an unwavering supporter of the Republic, found the coverage of the war in much of the British press to be so partisan that it was impossible to believe that those writing the stories, let alone the readers, could actually think they were true.[14]

Arthur Koestler later admitted how Willi Münzenberg had encouraged him to deliberately contrive atrocity stories as part of the Republican propaganda campaign.[15] Even Peter Kemp reluctantly acknowledged the Comintern's efforts on behalf of the Republic:

The Republican press campaign, ably directed by the Comintern – as Arthur Koestler has shown – was brilliant, unscrupulous and effective. I learnt to my surprise that the Nationalist armies and air force were manned almost exclusively by German and Italian mercenaries, and that the cause for which I had risked and nearly lost my life was fascism. There was hardly any mention of the vital Russian help to the Republicans.[16]

Poet Stephen Spender was taken aback to find himself attacked after writing an article for the *New Statesman*, in which he had stated that the International Brigades were Communist controlled. According to Spender, 'the correspondent agreed that the facts in my article were true, but he said that nonetheless I should not have written them'; Spender was informed that he 'should consider not the facts, but the result which might follow from writing them.' 'Apparently, truth,' Spender concluded, 'like freedom, lay in the recognition of necessity.'[17]

Famously, George Orwell wrote stinging criticism of the coverage of the war in British pro-Republican newspapers, such as the Communist *Daily Worker* and the liberal *News Chronicle*:

No event is ever correctly reported in a newspaper, but in Spain, for the first time, I saw newspaper reports which did not bear any relation to the facts, not even the relationship which is implied in an ordinary lie. I saw great battles reported where there had been no fighting, and complete silence where hundreds of men had been killed. I saw troops who had fought bravely denounced as cowards and traitors, and others who had never fired a shot hailed as the heroes of imaginary victories; and I saw newspapers in London retailing those lies and eager intellectuals building emotional superstructures over events that had never happened. I saw, in fact, history being written not in terms of what actually happened but of what ought to have happened according to various 'party lines.'[18]

Despite originally intending to report on the war himself, Orwell was contemptuous of the foreign correspondents: 'It is the same in all wars; the soldiers do the fighting, the journalists do the shouting,' he wrote, scathingly.[19] Orwell is perhaps being unfair, for a number of foreign reporters were killed while reporting the war, including the news photographer (and girlfriend of Robert Capa) Gerda Taro, killed at Brunete in July 1937, and the three correspondents accompanying Kim Philby, whose car was hit by a Republican artillery shell at Teruel on New Year's Eve 1937.[20] It was dangerous and often unpleasant work, as *Daily Express* journalist Keith Scott Watson discovered when searching out his former comrades in Madrid. Directed into the Faculty of Medicine, which had just been recaptured by the Thaelmann Battalion, and shown into the basement by a medical orderly, he encountered a horrifying sight:

What I saw sent a chill down my spine ... There could not have been more than fifty Moors, but in that eerie light, there seemed five hundred at least. All were dead; some sat in chairs, others sprawled across tables or lay in twisted heaps on the floor.

'Those boys won't do no more looting. They killed the bloody rabbits, hens and sheep and ate 'em. What they didn't know was that they had been injected full of germs by the professors. They didn't have time to kill the animals before they beat it, the Moors found 'em and ate 'em germs and all. There's enough bacilli in here to lay out Madrid.'

I fled up into the sunlight. I felt I should never be clean, what foul disease was on my clothes or in my lungs? I sweated with worry as I remembered a text-book with disgustingly vivid plates showing the ravages of obscure diseases. A hot bath and carbolic soap seemed my only hope of salvation.[21]

The battles for Madrid in the winter of 1936–7 were 'the central epic' which captured the imagination of journalists in Spain and their readers around the world. Being thrown into Madrid and experiencing the defence of the city alongside its inhabitants had a profound effect on many correspondents. 'This first week of the attack on Madrid presented an almost unique journalistic spectacle,' remarked Geoffrey Cox, for whom Madrid was to offer the opportunity of a lifetime.[22] Twenty-six-year-old Cox had been rushed into Spain to replace his predecessor, who had been arrested by the Nationalists. No searching out the battlefield was necessary; it could all be reported simply by looking out of the window:

We could get much of our news simply by standing at the windows of the Telephone Building. Spread out beneath us, as if on a football field, was the greatest battle waged in Europe since the fight for Warsaw in 1920. This city and countryside, which looked, at first glance, no different from the 'Madrid and its environs' at which parties of tourists were taken to gaze in the summer, was the setting for a struggle on which the eyes of the world were fixed. It seemed unreal in the extreme that those figures moving apparently innocently below us were engaged in the business of putting each other to death as rapidly as possible. It was like watching some fantastic puppet game – indeed, the American staff of the Telephone Company, anxious to avoid words like 'the enemy' which would appear to commit them to support one side or the other, talked habitually of the 'home side and the visitors.'[23]

As Rebel forces advanced ominously on the capital, foreign corre-spondents placed bets on how long Madrid would hold out; not many expected it to be more than a few weeks. On 6 November, rumours of Moroccan soldiers crossing the Toledo Bridge swept the capital and 'the Seville radio station was putting out messages that the rebels were almost in the Puerta del Sol . . . in newspaper offices all over the world sub-editors were preparing headlines: "Franco Enters Madrid!"'[24] But only a few days later, it was not Nationalists, but Internationalists, that Geoffrey Cox and the other reporters witnessed marching along the streets.

I was drinking coffee in the bar of the Gran Via when I heard shouting and clapping outside. I walked out to the pavement edge. The barman and his assistant followed me. There were few enough customers to be attended to that grey morning.

Up the street from the direction of the Ministry of War came a long column of marching men. They wore a kind of khaki corduroy uniform, and loose brown Glengarry caps like those of the British tank corps.

They were marching in excellent formation. The tramp, tramp of their boots sounded in perfect unison. Over their shoulders were slung rifles of obviously modern design. Many had scar-red tin helmets hanging from their belts. Some were young; others carried themselves like trained, experienced soldiers.

Each section had its officers, some carrying swords and revolvers. Behind rolled a small convoy of lorries, stacked high with machine guns and equipment. At the rear trotted a squadron of about fifty cavalry.

The few people who were about lined the roadway, shouting almost hysterically, 'Salud! Salud!', holding up their fists clenched in salute, or clapping vigorously. An old woman with tears streaming down her face, returning from a long wait in a queue, held up a baby girl, who, too, saluted with her tiny fist. One of the charwomen from the hotel stood with tears pouring down her face. The cars racing along the street stopped and blared their horns.

The troops in reply held up their fists and copied the call of 'Salud!' We did not know who they were. The crowd took them for Russians. The barman turned to me saying, 'The *Rusos* have come. The *Rusos* have come.'

But when I heard a clipped Prussian voice shout an order in German, followed by other shouts in French and Italian, I knew they were not Russians.

The International Column of Anti-Fascists had arrived in Madrid. We were watching the First Brigade of what was to develop into the most truly international army the world has seen since the Crusades.[25]

The arrival of the International Brigades made a powerful impression on the normally hard-bitten war correspondents. Herbert Matthews of *The New York Times*, who had remarked when reporting the war in Abyssinia that 'the right or the wrong of it did not interest me greatly,' came to see the volunteers as 'the finest group of men I ever knew or hope to know in my life'.[26] Other reporters, including the normally conservative Sefton Delmer, also came to develop sympathy with the city's Republican defenders:

Despite all I had seen of the brutality and contempt for justice of the Reds, despite my own antipathy to Marxism as a demagogic fraud, despite all this and much more, I nevertheless found I was being swept along in the exhilaration of Madrid's refusal to abandon the fight. I found myself sharing the thrill of the reverses which the Reds were inflicting on the side I would certainly have chosen had I been a Spaniard and forced to decide between the ugly alternatives of Franco and Caballero.[27]

Likewise, Noel Monks' experiences reporting for the *Daily Express* in the Basque areas with the Nationalists and in Bilbao and Madrid with the Republicans utterly transformed his view of the conflict. George Steer, expelled by the Nationalists, famously became a staunch supporter of the Basque cause and his account of the infamous destruction of the Basque town of Guernica in April 1937 by German and Italian bombers, an event immortalised by Picasso's painting, was one of the most influential reports to come out of the war. With Monks, Christopher Holme of Reuters and Mathieu Corman of *Le Soir*, Steer was one of the first reporters to arrive in Guernica to witness the devastation. His report, which appeared in *The Times* on 28 April 1937, left no doubt where the responsibility for the bombing lay; it was what Steer called 'the most elaborate attack upon the civilian population staged in Europe since the Great War'.[28]

Guernica, the most ancient town of the Basques and the centre of their cultural tradition, was completely destroyed yesterday afternoon by insurgent air raiders. The bombardment of this open town far behind the lines occupied precisely three hours and a quarter, during which a powerful fleet of aeroplanes consisting of three German types, Junkers and Heinkel bombers, did not cease unloading on the town bombs weighing from 1,000lbs. downwards and, it is calculated, more than 3,000 two-pounder aluminium incendiary projectiles.

Steer described in graphic detail how the town was deliberately targeted on market day and 'systematically pounded to pieces' in order to inflict the maximum of death, destruction, terror and panic:

The tactics of the bombers, which may be of interest to students of the new military science, were as follows: First, small parties of airplanes threw heavy bombs and hand grenades all over the town, choosing area after area in orderly fashion. Next came fighting machines which swooped low to machine-gun those who ran in panic from dugouts, some of which had already been penetrated by 1000lb. bombs, which make a hole 25ft. deep. Many of these people were killed as they ran. A large herd of sheep being brought in to the market was also wiped out. The object of this move was apparently to drive the population underground again, for next as many as 12 bombers appeared at a time dropping heavy and incendiary bombs upon the ruins. The rhythm of this bombing of an open town was, therefore, a logical one: first, hand grenades and heavy bombs to stampede the population, then machine-gunning to drive them below, next heavy and incendiary bombs to wreck the houses and burn them on top of their victims.

The only counter-measures the Basques could employ, for they do not possess sufficient airplanes to face the insurgent fleet, were those provided by the heroism of the Basque clergy. These blessed and prayed for the kneeling crowds – Socialists, Anarchists, and Communists, as well as the declared faithful – in the crumbling dugouts. When I entered Guernica after midnight houses were crashing on either side, and it was utterly impossible even for firemen to enter the centre of the town. The hospitals of Josefinas and Convento de Santa Clara were glowing heaps of embers, all the churches except that of Santa Maria were destroyed, and the few houses which still stood were doomed.[29]

Steer's devastating article provoked outrage and fury, as well as panic in Nationalist circles, and 'did more to engender anti-Nationalist hatred internationally than any other incident in the war'.[30] Franco's followers in Britain recognised that the incident was a major propaganda victory: 'nothing illustrates better the superiority of Republican propaganda over Nationalist than the Republican story of Guernica', argued Peter Kemp.[31] Nevertheless, he and a number of other Nationalist supporters continued to deny, despite all the evidence to the contrary, that the town had been bombed by German planes:

> [Guernica] was the Communists' most single propaganda *coup* of the war, and it created a myth which, fostered by the skill of Agitprop and immortalized by the genius of Picasso, has passed into history. According to this myth Guernica was razed by German Stukas and an experiment in dive bombing. The truth is that the town, an important communications centre and a divisional H.Q., was bombed by the Nationalist air force – not the German – who hit the railway station and an arms factory; later it was dynamited and set on fire by the retreating *milicianos* – mostly squads of Asturian miners.[32]

Reports of the bombing led to a widespread feeling of sympathy in Britain for the Basques and, following the efforts of the Basque Children's Committee, established in May 1937, nearly 4000 Basque children were evacuated from besieged Bilbao to Britain, with protection from the British navy.[33] Unsurprisingly, as Steer later recounted, many of the children were deeply traumatised by their experiences of the war and being separated from their parents.

> Distinguished persons were to notice that these war-terrified children sometimes stole apples, broke windows with stones, teased little girls, and on one occasion used knives upon a cook who had inadvertently first cut one of their number. The anti-Red herring fleet came out to drag again.[34]

In the main, though, the children were welcomed and many people donated time, money and more to their welfare. Following the fall of Bilbao and demands by Franco, the British government made 'increasingly desperate' efforts to repatriate the refugees and most were later sent back to Spain. However, amid concerns about their fate – and that of their parents – under the Nationalists, over one thousand still remained in Britain at the start of the Second World War.[35]

Steer himself left Spain, reluctantly, in August 1937, just prior to the fall of Santander. His account of his time in Spain and the Basque regions, *Tree of Gernika*, was written with astounding speed and published the following year. While Steer's romantic attachment to the 'industrious' Basques and his disdain for the 'idle' Spanish earned him a number of criticisms, not least from Orwell, his work was nevertheless seen as sufficiently damaging to the Nationalist cause that he was informed they would shoot him if he were ever to return.[36]

Many Britons travelling to the Republican and Rebel zones did so on 'fact-finding tours', intent on seeing the conflict for themselves and offering their support. There were only a small number of visitors to Nationalist Spain, mainly due to the Nationalist command's loathing of anything foreign, combined with the genuine unpopularity of Franco's regime in western democracies. Visitors included retired army officers, right-wing Tory MPs, businessmen such as Arthur F. Loveday, sympathetic journalists such as Arnold Lunn and Douglas Jerrold, and writers such as Hilaire Belloc. Most were Nationalist supporters rather than neutral observers and the British pro-Franco organisation, the Friends of Nationalist Spain, sponsored at least half of them.

The majority of visitors were invited by the Republicans, who received over one hundred British 'war tourists', from a wide variety of social and political backgrounds, over the course of the war. Fully aware of the importance of foreign support for their cause, the Republican Spanish Embassy funded delegations to visit Spain, often paying for them to stay in plush, expensive hotels and dining them in sophisticated restaurants.[37] However, visitors were carefully chaperoned and most saw little of Republican Spain – heavily bombed areas and unscathed churches aside – returning to Britain exhausted by a whirl of official receptions, and bearing reports that reliably put across the Spanish Republic's perspective.[38] One group of clergy who visited Madrid, Valencia and Barcelona came home denying the existence of an atheist movement in Republican Spain: 'One way or another, travellers became vehicles for Spanish Government propaganda in their own country.'[39] In response, the British government eventually restricted such trips, requiring all participants to sign a declaration not to express political opinions or take sides.[40]

Some visitors were encouraged to visit by British Republican supporters already in Spain. They included novelist Sylvia Townsend Warner and her partner, the poet Valentine Ackland, who were invited in mid-October 1936 by Tom Wintringham. The couple were later lampooned by Stephen Spender as left-wing day-trippers:

> A communist lady writer, and her friend, a lady poet. The Communist lady writer looked like, and behaved like, a vicar's wife presiding over a tea party given on a vicarage lawn as large as the whole of Republican Spain.[41]

Spender visited Spain himself, having initially declined Harry Pollitt's suggestion that he join the International Brigades – Pollitt had allegedly advised Spender that the best contribution he could make to the Party would be 'to go out and get killed, comrade, we need a Byron in the movement'.[42] Instead, Spender accepted a request from the *Daily Worker* that he attempt to discover the fate of a Soviet supply ship, the *Komsomol*, which had disappeared in the Mediterranean in December 1936. Spender accompanied Republican volunteers Wogan Philipps and George Green, who were driving an ambulance to the International Brigade base at Albacete. In Barcelona, he was astonished to hear the voice of English surrealist poet David Gascoyne booming out of a loudspeaker attached to a lamp post on a street corner.[43] Gascoyne had been working for the Republican Propaganda Ministry since October 1936, translating news bulletins into English during the day and broadcasting them each evening at 6 p.m.[44]

While searching for his ex-boyfriend, Tony Hyndman, Spender had an infamous encounter in the trenches of Jarama with an English International Brigader, who he doesn't name but was probably Michael Livesay, a young volunteer from Southsea who had dropped out of his studies in architecture.[45] Livesay, a fluent French and German speaker, was working as George Nathan's interpreter at Jarama.[46]

> We walked back to headquarters for luncheon. As we did so, M——, aged eighteen, born of a Liberal family, told me how he had run away from school because he identified the Spanish Republic with the cause of Liberalism. But now he found that the Brigade was run by Communists, for whom he had no sympathy. I pointed out that, although this was true, the Republic remained a Liberal cause. 'But I don't know about that. All I see are the Communist bosses of the Brigade,' he protested. I said: 'You are under age. Shall I try to get you out of here?' 'No,' he answered. 'My life is

to walk up to the ridge here every day until I am killed.' He was killed, though on a different front, six weeks later.[47]

While Spender had been preparing to go to Spain, a cross-party delegation of six British MPs, led by the Labour member for Broxtowe in Nottinghamshire, Seymour Cocks, had arrived in Madrid, where they were welcomed by prominent Republicans including the Socialist deputy, Margarita Nelken, and the Foreign Minister, Julio Álvarez del Vayo.[48] Two British volunteers, Esmond Romilly and Lorrimer Birch, met the delegation late one evening in a hotel in Madrid's Grand Via and when it became too late to return to their unit, one of the MPs kindly offered to let the two young English fighters share his room.[49] The offer was not entirely without self-interest, for during the night, he made a pass at them and 'far from enjoying a restful night, they had to defend themselves continuously against his incorrigible assaults.'[50] Never one to overlook an opportunity, Romilly threatened to publicly denounce the MP unless, on his return to England, he publicly declared his support for the Republic. Both Romilly and the MP kept to their bargain; both were killed in the Second World War.

The same month, Romilly's close friend, the young Oxford Communist Philip Toynbee, came to Republican Spain as part of an international student delegation: 'A French anarchist militiaman asked us which front we were going to, and it was bloody hard to have to say, to Valencia and Madrid, just to look around.'[51] After meeting Keith Scott Watson, then working with Sefton Delmer in Valencia, Toynbee's delegation moved on to the capital.[52] Embarrassed by his unheroic role in the civil war, Toynbee jumped at the chance to participate – as much as anything to be able to brag to his friends back in England, he confessed later. He was taken to the front at Casa de Campo: 'I took one shot, through sandbags, at the flitting figure of a Moor between the ruins. [I] felt mildly afraid, but also exhilarated.'[53]

The poet W.H. Auden spent six weeks in Spain, arriving in mid-January 1937. On return his poem *Spain!* appeared as a pamphlet, with all the proceeds going to support the Spanish Republic. He paid a visit to Valencia, finding it to be a city where revolution was in full swing, just as Orwell and John Langdon-Davies had found Barcelona:[54]

We stared at the tops of the tramcars passing below. There were many arms around waists, a sight common enough in Hyde Park or on Hampstead Heath but charged with revolutionary significance in the Plaza de

Catalunya. Jaume enjoyed what he saw. 'Revolution is a great aphrodisiac,' he said.[55]

In the spring of 1937 Dr Hewlett Johnson, the 'red' Dean of Canterbury, arrived in Madrid as part of a large delegation. They were encountered in the Hotel Florida by Sefton Delmer and a group of British International Brigaders who had realised that Delmer was a reliable source of drinks and cigarettes:

> Into this robust and boisterous hostelry one morning at the end of March 1937, there marched a bevy of sedate and dignified British VIPs of forbiddingly progressive aspect. All of them shone with gleaming benevolence. The women had their hair done up in those telephone ringlets over their ears which in Englishwomen indicate a special state of highmindedness. They wore chintz frocks and rope sole shoes, apparently under the impression that Madrid was in the tropics and warm all the year round. The men, more sensibly, were in tweeds and flannels.
>
> One of them with a white mane of hair framing a beaming pink dome seemed familiar. Could it be? Could it possibly be? I walked over to the desk to inspect the registrations. Yes it was: Dr. Hewlett Johnson, Dean of Canterbury.

The Dean's party had been sent to the hotel from Valencia, where the hotel was probably believed to be rather more salubrious than it was. As Delmer was fully aware, two Moroccan sisters had previously resided in the Dean's room, from which the pair had been busily plying their trade to certain British volunteers on leave in Madrid:

> The Dean had hardly settled into his rooms when there was a knock on the door. He opened it. Outside in the corridor stood a small group of Britons who had come from the front to visit the Moorish girls. This, of course, the Dean was not to know. He assumed that these young fellows whom he had heard talking English were a delegation of Freedom Fighters wishing to honour their eminent comrade, the Red Dean. So he talked to them very kindly, praised their readiness for service and sacrifice, and gave them a little impromptu homily on the Christian virtues of the cause for which they were fighting. Then he blessed them and withdrew once more into his room.

'You could have knocked me down wiv a fevver,' was little Tich's true-to-type but not very original comment on the scene, when he told me about it.

The abashed serenaders stole down the corridor and promptly called around at my room to find out if I knew the new location of Farida and Fatima. All of them, that is, except a rough redheaded fellow whom I knew as Jock. He had been drinking downstairs and had reeled up to the Dean's door only just in time to see the party break up and the Dean disappear inside what Jock thought was Fatima's room. Jock completely mis-understood the situation. Instead of coming to my room with the rest, he hung around and waited on in the corridor. He waited and he waited, and he waited. At last his patience was exhausted. In a fury of righteous indignation he went up to the Dean's door and hammered on it with his fists. 'Come oot, yer old bustard!' he roared. 'Ye've been mair nae twenty minutes in there! Yer time's oop. Come oot!'

Fortunately we heard him, and Jock's comrades were just in time to prevent him from smashing the door down and to take him away. And even more fortunately the Dean did not open up, and so was spared from discovering what his soldier visitors were really after, and the true meaning of the touching little scene in the corridor.[56]

★

It is little surprise that paying a visit to the International Brigaders was the aim of many visitors to Republican Spain, eager to demonstrate support for the 'British volunteers for liberty'. In particular, Harry Pollitt clearly felt a responsibility towards the British Battalion and visited it five times between February 1937 and August 1938.[57] His first visit, travelling covertly under a Spanish passport, was made in the last days of February 1937, following the bloodletting at Jarama. He attended the International Brigade base at Albacete before meeting British volunteers at Morata and taking the time to see British casualties recovering in Republican hospitals. Returning at the end of June 1937, he again visited a number of hospitals, and was escorted round Madrid by political commissar George Brown and Party functionary Ralph Bates. His third visit that year was over Christmas 1937 at Teruel, when he brought over five hundred letters for the British volunteers. Pollitt visited twice the following year; on 14 April 1938, during the retreats; his visit was remembered not for his political rhetoric but precisely for the lack of it. Pollitt told the volunteers:

I'm not going to tell you what a good job you're doing. I'm not going to tell you that you're heroes and that you're history, because enough people have told you that already. What I propose to you is to give you a resumé of the end of the football season and the beginning of the cricket season.[58]

This, claimed the volunteer who described it, was rather better received than if he had given them a political harangue.

Pollitt's last visit to Spain was in August–September 1938 when 'the comrades had just come out of the front line, after one of their most terrible nights, having been under fire from trench mortars the whole time'.[59] He spoke in detail on the current political situation in Britain and Europe and before returning home, made another visit to the wounded convalescing in Republican hospitals.[60]

Another popular visitor to the battalion was the renowned scientist Professor J.B.S. Haldane. Described by one volunteer as 'a huge man [who] almost filled the door', Haldane arrived in Spain in Christmas 1936 on a three-month visit. He gave lectures on the dangers of gas attacks 'only to find the Spaniards were already doing it very well without my help'.[61] 'Many hundreds of Englishmen have come out to Spain to help the cause of democracy since July 1936,' Haldane wrote. 'Many have given their lives, others have shed their blood. Few or none can have been as useless as myself.'[62] On this point, Fred Copeman agreed with him:

Old Haldane was there. More bloody nuisance than it was worth . . . He insisted on being on the front line . . . and he had a little tiny revolver . . . he would hop on the step and hold this bloody thing and I would go up and every time I would say, 'What bloody good do you think you are? First of all you're taking two blokes' room, two blokes could sit where your fat arse is, so get down . . .' I'm being told politically that J.B.S. Haldane must not get killed, he's too valuable. Keep him out of the line. He was all the time in the bloody line. After about three months of it, I had a long talk with him. I said, 'Look, you've done enough bloody talking old fat man.' I said, 'You've got to go home. You've got to go home.'[63]

Haldane took Copeman's advice but returned to visit the British at Mas de las Matas on the Teruel front with Pollitt in December 1937.[64] On that occasion, Manchester boxer Joe Norman treated the visitors to a rendition of a Russian folk song, despite the opposition of his fellow brigaders:

'Nobody wanted to hear it, but Harry Pollitt insisted I had a democratic right to sing.'[65] The purpose of Haldane's final visit to Republican Spain was to inspect the Republican *refugios* (bomb-shelters) 'with a view to humbly (or not so humbly) suggesting that London might have as good ones as Valencia'.[66]

The same month, Labour Party leader Clement Attlee arrived in Spain with two members of the party's executive committee, Ellen Wilkinson and Philip Noel-Baker.[67] The highlight of their trip was a visit to the battalion at Mondéjar, late in the evening of 6 December, where, as Attlee himself recorded, the volunteers were paraded in the village square to greet them.[68]

> This was an impressive scene in a Spanish village by torchlight. The Brigade had saved the Republican cause in Spain. Serving in its ranks were men of diverse views, but animated with courage, self-sacrifice and devotion, united in the fight for freedom.[69]

To loud cheers, No. 1 Company was renamed the Major Attlee Company in the Labour leader's honour.[70] Accompanied by 35th Republican division commander General Walter, the visitors were greeted by a volley of shots 'in welcome and in memory of the fallen' and introduced to the members of the battalion by Fred Copeman. Ellen Wilkinson promised to return to Britain and 'fight with all her energy against the blockade which posed under the name of non-intervention'.[71] Perhaps carried away with the emotion of the event, Attlee gave a clenched fist salute and referred to the 'farce' of non-intervention, planting a hope in the minds of the parading soldiers that he would return home and overturn the policy.[72]

> We had hoped that this deputation of the Labour Party might have some effect on the British Government. We had hoped that it might have helped to induce the British Government to change their attitude towards the rightful legal Republican Government of Spain. But . . . we couldn't see any results apart from an increased measure of support generally from people in Britain . . . unfortunately it didn't persuade the British Conservative government of the day that it should alter its attitude to the Spanish Republican Government.[73]

Back in Britain, Harry Pollitt opened a newspaper to see a photograph of Attlee 'paddling in the sea with his daughter somewhere in North Wales. It was a happy picture.' In contrast, Pollitt noted bitterly, 'the No.1 Company of the British Battalion, to which Major Attlee gave his name . . . have waded through blood.'[74]

While in training in the spring of 1938 the battalion received a number of visitors, including Sefton Delmer, and Bill Forrest of the *News Chronicle*. Pandit Nehru, the future Prime Minister of India, arrived on 17 May 'with a team of men from India, and the Machine-Gunners put on an impressive show, using the Maxim guns to shoot at targets some distance away'.[75] The following month, just before the Ebro offensive, Carmel Haden-Guest, the wife of Labour MP Leslie Haden-Guest and mother of volunteer David Guest, visited the battalion at the Fontaubella Valley (known by the British as 'Chavola Valley'). She took a number of items for her son, including an invaluable pair of binoculars, together with much-appreciated cigarettes, always in short supply.[76] The battalion was also visited by a deputation of students, including a young Edward Heath, then the Chairman of the Federation of University Conservative Associations.[77] The future Prime Minister admitted to Jack Jones that he was highly impressed by the volunteers:

> They were tough hardened soldiers, burned by the Spanish sun to a dark tan. Their morale was high and they still genuinely believed that they were going to throw back General Franco's troops.
>
> As we drove back into Barcelona one could not but admire these men, civilians at heart, who had had to learn everything of a military nature as they went along. They would go on fighting as long as they could, that was clear.[78]

However, the visitor probably remembered most fondly by the volunteers was the black American singer Paul Robeson, who visited in October–November 1937, accompanied by Charlotte Haldane. Robeson's performance for the battalion, accompanied by his wife on the piano, made a strong impression on those lucky enough to see him. 'Of course we're all shouting, everybody's shouting, "Sing Ol' Man River!" And he sang for quite a long time. He was one of the greatest people I have met.'[79] 'When the end of his repertoire came he was overwhelmed with enthusiastic cheering and clapping,' Cyril Sexton remembered.[80]

★

Not all visitors were as welcome as Robeson, Pollitt and the Haldanes – or as Errol Flynn, who encountered a group of British volunteers training at Madrigueras, jumped on top of a bar and raised a toast to them.[81] As Jason Gurney recounts, many in the battalion rather resented some of the 'war tourists':

> Every aspiring writer to the left of centre in politics endeavoured to get himself a trip to witness the agonies of the Republic. We were told to be on our best behaviour and avoid any kind of 'negative' remark, but the visitors were always so well surrounded by Political Commissars that there was little danger. Most annoying of the visitors were the type that said, 'God, I wish I was able to stay out here with you fellows' – the implication presumably being that their activities were so important that their presence could not be afforded, while us lucky chaps had the leisure to enjoy the real fun.[82]

Even the great American writer Ernest Hemingway, a 'black-haired, bushy-moustached, hairy-handed giant' who visited the battalion in December 1937, was not welcomed with open arms.[83] At least, not by Fred Copeman, who after demanding of Hemingway 'Who the hell are you?' brusquely told him to 'piss off'.[84] Hemingway also visited the British Anti-Tank Battery, but seems to have made no better impression there:

> On one occasion when the anti-tank battery were situated in the hills for a week or so somewhere in the Aragon, time and place not remembered, but before Franco's offensive began, I had an experience involving two inquisitive Americans. As I had been up a good part of the night I was snatching some sleep under an olive tree when I was awakened by Jimmy Arthur, a dour imperturbable Scot from Edinburgh. He was on guard and had his rifle slung over his shoulder. In his typically direct way Jimmy growled, 'There's a couple o' bastards up on the trucks examining the guns.' 'Did you give them permission?' I asked. You just don't allow strangers under any circumstances to mess about with your guns. 'No, ah didnae,' said Jimmy, 'the bastards just went up on their own.' When I looked at the two men on the trucks I immediately recognised Ernest Hemingway, the author, as one of them. I knew him from his photographs. The other man was an American 'lootenant' who was attached to Brigade headquarters

and who flaunted his officer's uniform ostentatiously. Being a bit crabbit on being awakened out of my sleep and feeling my proletarian resentment at too much ostentatiousness, I had already formed an antipathy to the lieutenant. I growled back at Jimmy, 'Well, order them off and if they don't get off, shoot them!' It was purely an expression of mood, born out of my coal pit expressions, and not an order. But the two men must have heard me for they got down off the truck at once, got into their car and drove off without a word. I remember thinking to myself at the time that a novelist's job was to write about people not things, and here were two dour Scots characters Hemingway might have got some copy from. Many years later Hemingway took his own life. I always had the feeling that Jimmy Arthur was the kind of morose character who might have saved him the bother.[85]

16

The Great Retreat

> We may take it as an incontrovertible fact that men cannot be
> changed overnight from conquered into conquerors. Anybody who
> speaks of an army falling back in order to go on fighting is simply
> employing verbal subterfuge. The troops that fall back, and those
> that give battle, are not the same men.
>
> Antoine Saint-Exupéry, *Flight to Arras*

Despite the freezing weather that gripped Spain during the winter of 1937–
8, volunteers still flocked to the Republic's cause. During January
reinforcements 'were arriving at the Albacete base at the rate of nearly thirty
a week'.[1] However, the terrible casualty rate experienced during 1937 had
made an impact: 'within the Party there was growing opposition to what
was known as inner-party conscription. Recruiting was not easy. There was
a reluctance among leading comrades to volunteer.'[2] As Bill Rust brutally
summarised the situation: 'The 1938 and late 1937 recruits had no illusions;
they knew they had come to face death.'[3]

The time-consuming process of training new recruits into soldiers
continued. IRA man Bob Doyle, a platoon commander at Tarazona de la
Mancha, demonstrated to his unit of thirty volunteers how to dig foxholes
and defend oneself against air attacks. Despite having to train his men with
wooden rifles, the severe lack of equipment and the mauling the battalion
had received at Teruel, Doyle was impatient to get to the front and play a
more active role in the fight:

Around February 1938 news came of a draft being sent to the front on four
lorries. I had received no instructions to be part of it, but I wanted to go, so
I jumped up on the last lorry – and the others on it thought I was supposed
to be there. Halfway to Belchite I was discovered and brought in front of

three International Brigades officers. They asked me why I had disobeyed orders and told me that my duty was to stay in the training base and to train other volunteers who would be coming over from England. I told them I wanted to be a machine-gunner, and that I needed practical experience. They then suggested that I had come here to get experience at the expense of the Spanish people – which I hotly disputed. After being given a severe ticking off, I was allowed to stay.[4]

Doyle would get his chance soon enough. On 7 March 1938, Franco launched a colossal offensive against the Republican forces in Aragon. Thirteen divisions, plus a huge number of tanks, artillery and anti-tank guns, backed up with over 900 aircraft, were massed for the push through to the Mediterranean. The Nationalist forces outnumbered the defending Republicans by almost five to one.[5] As Peter Kemp triumphantly reported, what began as a series of breakthroughs swiftly turned into a rout, as the Republican lines virtually collapsed:[6]

General Franco gave the Republicans no time to recover from their disaster at Teruel. Within a fortnight of the recapture of the town he had regrouped General Davila's Army of the North in seven Army Corps along a line running from the Pyrenees to Teruel, poised for the greatest offensive of the war. This time the campaign was to be conducted along the blitzkrieg lines advocated by the Germans. Concentrating an overwhelming superiority of aircraft, artillery, tanks and troops, the Nationalists shattered the Republican defences and in less than six weeks swept across Aragon to the borders of Catalonia and the Mediterranean coast; cutting Republican Spain in two, this offensive virtually settled the outcome of the war.[7]

As the Republic struggled to hold the huge Nationalist onslaught, the 15th International Brigade was rushed up to Belchite, the town captured by the American Battalion the previous autumn. Late on 9 March, the recently promoted commander of the battalion, Sam Wild, received orders from the American Chief of Staff, Bob Merriman, to establish a new defensive position on the high ground nearby.[8] Close by were the Americans of the Lincoln-Washington Battalion and a group of fifty men from the Spanish 135th Brigade, who told Wild that they had been in retreat throughout the previous day and night.

The battalion's position was quickly overwhelmed as the Nationalists swept forward, supported by a huge machine-gun, artillery and air barrage. Motorised units punched holes in the Republican lines, again in a forerunner of the *Blitzkrieg* tactics which would be used with devastating effect during the Second World War. 'In the defence of these positions the Adjutant, No. 1 Company Commander and about thirty men were killed and wounded,' reported Wild.[9] Forced to abandon the position, the battalion retreated towards Belchite to avoid being surrounded.

However, Belchite offered no sanctuary. Bombarded with anti-tank and anti-aircraft shells, the British Battalion and the members of the Anti-Tank Battery had to retreat swiftly out of the town, as they were again in danger of being cut off.[10] In the process, the anti-tanks were forced to destroy one of their guns that couldn't be moved and low-flying Nationalist aircraft destroyed another. With the battery effectively destroyed, most of its men were incorporated into the British Battalion. 'The defence of Belchite', wrote the unit's former commissar, Bill Alexander, 'was the last battle of the British Anti-Tank Battery'.[11]

Outnumbered and outgunned, the survivors fought on in loosely connected groups, all reeling under the huge Nationalist offensive.

> We made our last stand from behind a low wall at the end of the main street. We were on the point of withdrawing when we saw what we took to be a group of our own struggling towards us. Sam Wild ordered us to give covering fire. The little group . . . disappeared from our view. We never saw them again.[12]

The attempt to defend Belchite delayed the Rebels' capture of the town, but only for a day. It fell to Nationalist soldiers from Navarre on 10 March.[13]

Having abandoned Belchite, Wild was 'requested' by Jim Bourne, the American Brigade political commissar, to 'put the Battalion on a hill in a castle'. Wild flatly refused, believing that the castle was an obvious target for enemy artillery, but Bourne personally instructed three machine-gun units to take up the position. As Wild noted tersely in his report, the machine-gunners 'were blown up with their guns'.[14]

Such was the speed of the Nationalist advance that many Republican soldiers had little option but to turn tail and run for their lives. There was panic, terror and chaos as the survivors marched past the evidence of what looked to be a complete collapse of the Republican lines: 'As we moved over the plains we found a lot of people had abandoned stuff; we found other Brigades' equipment that had been left.'[15] Bob Clark became separated from the battalion, only finding them again on the road to Lecera, ten kilometres to the south:

> The evidence of an army in retreat was everywhere. Here a large lorry loaded with hundreds of picks and spades lay with its back axle in a ditch, the driver's heavy leather coat lying discarded on the roadside. Farther along, another lorry had run into a clump of trees, hundreds of rifles neatly stacked constituting its load. A dead Spaniard lying with a bullet hole neatly drilled through his head and a number of bullet holes in the lorry's mudguard, testified to enemy aircraft strafing. Everywhere lay empty and full ammunition boxes, odd rifles, bayonets, gas-mask containers, discarded greatcoats. A donkey with a raw, bleeding wound hobbled pitifully alongside the road. A sheep bleeding from a ghastly wound on its back excited our pity and young [Walter] Sproston [from Manchester] who had a kind heart decided that we should put the animals out of their misery, which was soon done with a couple of shots.[16]

After three days of an exhausting fighting retreat, targeted incessantly by Nationalist artillery and aircraft, the battalion arrived at Lecera, only to discover that it had already fallen into Rebel hands.[17] Warily circuiting the town, they continued eastwards, aiming for Hijar, a further twenty kilometres down the road.

On the morning of 12 March, having marched all night, the main surviving group of the battalion rested in an olive grove adjacent to the road, but 'early in the morning soldiers occupying the hills dominating the road began jumping down the hills in panic. They stampeded along the road, jumping camions and shouting that the Fascists were on us.'[18] The battalion wearily accepted that they had no choice but to press on and march through the following night if they were to get to Hijar before the enemy:

> Once again we had an all-night march – this time across difficult country. None of us [had] slept since the morning of the ninth – nearly seventy-two hours. We had been through an intense mental and physical strain. Little wonder that some of our lads collapsed on that gruelling trek over the hills. Sam Wild gave me his flask filled with cognac and I dropped behind trying to revive men who had walked to the limit of their endurance and had finally collapsed from exhaustion.

None of us who took part in that dreadful march will ever forget it . . .
The heat was well-nigh unbearable. We were exhausted, foot-sore and our
throats were parched. My boots were in tatters, my feet torn and bleeding.
Many of the others were in similar shape. It was difficult to keep our column
intact. We were in the middle of a rout. Thousands of men from other
Brigades were also on the march and mixed with them went the fleeing
civilian population.

The scene beggared description. As the long black column climbed
wearily up the steep rocky hillsides, enemy planes came swooping and
machine-gunning their helpless victims. Franco had eight hundred planes
on the Aragon front against the Republican's sixty. I did not see a single
Republican plane the whole of that dreadful week.[19]

Now aware that they were in the middle of the largest Nationalist
offensive of the war, Brigade staff officer George Wattis warned Sam Wild
to be wary as they approached Hijar, fearful that it too was already in Rebel
hands.[20] Wattis was right to be concerned; despite their exhausting forced
march, they had once again been overtaken by the Nationalists. 'They were
already in there, the Fascists were already in there,' lamented Bobby
Walker, an ex-Scots Guardsman from Edinburgh.[21]

As the shattered and now utterly dispirited members of the battalion
trudged away from Hijar, Bob Clark was one of a small group ordered to
destroy a vehicle dump to prevent it falling into the enemy's hands. Thanks
to the delay, Clark was separated once again from the remnant of the
battalion. Terrified of being left behind, he hurried to try and catch up:

I had just reached the turn of the road when suddenly loud cries of 'Rojo'
split the air. I gasped as I saw about thirty or forty Fascist troops with a light
machine-gun scrambling down the hillside towards me. Hesitating for the
fraction of a minute, my heart stopped beating. But the prospect of being a
prisoner of Franco frightened me into immediate activity. With one record
breaking leap, I jumped off the road down the slope into the valley, landing
with a tremendous crash into the middle of a vegetable garden where the
soft soil broke my fall. A rapid burst of machine-gun fire, the whine of bullets
specially intended for me, what should I do? Lie there and chance them not
seeing me? But once again the horror of being captured overwhelmed me.
The longer I lay there the less chance there was of getting away to the
temporary safety of the hills. As I lay recovering my wind and nerve, I took

stock of my surroundings. Much further down the valley gushed a narrow river, the sides of the banks being densely covered with long rushes offering excellent cover. If that river could be reached I would be half way to safety. I remembered my earlier training at Tarazona where it was instilled in our minds that to beat a machine-gun one had to anticipate the mind of the gunner and do something different. Taking a deep breath, praying that this particular machine-gunner had not got a bead on me and counting three, I suddenly jumped up and in a few moments had run a distance of about thirty yards and down I flopped. My luck was in, the bullets whined harmlessly over my head. After a short rest and rolling a little to the left, once again I sprang to my feet and in a last desperate, staggering, zig-zag run I reached the friendly rushes. It was a close shave. The bullets missing by inches cut a swathe through the tops of the rushes. I lay there for about five minutes, with sudden bursts of fire to remind me that he, the gunner, was still waiting.[22]

Clark eventually managed to escape his tormentors by wading an ice-cold river and scrambling desperately up the opposite bank, all the time trying to present as small a target as possible. While he lay recovering, the main group of British continued their march along the road. Stopping to take up an overnight position on a hilltop between Hijar and their objective, Alcañiz, they awoke to discover that Nationalist forces had again managed to infiltrate the Republican lines. When a patrol ordered by Brigade staff to investigate the town did not return, it was clear that Alcañiz had already fallen to Franco's troops.[23] Wearily the disheartened volunteers turned off the road and headed north over the rough, mountainous country towards Caspe, which lay twenty kilometres and twenty-four hours away. It was, remembered Frank Graham, 'a terrible journey . . . [with] no food, no water'.[24]

On 15 March, six days after the battalion had begun their defence of Belchite, the 150-strong remnant of the British Battalion finally arrived at Caspe. But even here there was to be no respite. Instead the exhausted soldiers were forced to fight a desperate rearguard action, in what Sam Wild complained to the new Brigade Chief of Staff, Malcolm Dunbar, was an impossible position.[25] Despite Wild and Dunbar's efforts to organise a defence, by the end of 15 March, Caspe too had to be abandoned. Moreover, attempts to make an organised fighting retreat from the town were rendered virtually impossible by 'a sustained Fascist infantry attack'. As the action descended into frantic bouts of hand-to-hand fighting, 'events grew very confused . . . I abandoned any attempts to give orders to what remained of my company: it was simply a case of each man for himself . . . no longer were we organized in battalions, now we were simply the remnants of the XVth International Brigade,' recalled Walter Gregory.[26] While Bill Alexander later praised the 'prodigies of valour' of the Brigade's defending units, Sam Wild's assessment was rather more sober: 'one Company Commander killed and one company Commander was wounded and the acting battalion commissar was also wounded and Observation officer and over 30 men.'[27]

The British were the last Republican troops to leave Caspe. During the withdrawal, Bobby Walker suddenly noticed that Wild had disappeared:

He'd sent out a patrol . . . [who] were taking a long time and he'd got impatient and walked up to see what they are doing . . . so I walk along up this road in the dark, the banks on one side and I see the group and I walk up and there's Sam with his hands up and the Fascists were there . . . So I came up and there's a gun put in my way . . . and I look at Sam and he gives me a nod . . . I looked at the chap in front of me with a rifle . . . seemingly instinctively I hit him and I ran across the road . . . What happened to the others I wasn't aware of . . . I found out afterwards that when they turned round Sam hit one . . . [and] they got back to the battalion.[28]

By 16 March all that was left of the battalion was a group of twenty men, the sorry remnant of the six hundred who had gone into battle at Teruel.[29] The following day they managed to reunite with what was left of the 15th International Brigade at Batea, a further thirty kilometres to the south-east, where they were at last able to take stock and, more importantly, to take some rest.

During those ten unhappy March days, the three brigades of the 35th Division (the Eleventh, Thirteenth and Fifteenth) resisted the enemy in the Aragon as best we could in rear-guard fighting, endlessly digging in wherever possible and impossible, keeping the enemy at bay for several hours or even days with little flanking support, and having to fight our way out of encirclement time and again. But the odds were too great. We were no match for the huge steel juggernaut that rolled on relentlessly crushing underfoot everything in its path.[30]

On 19 March, two days later, as the volunteers were regrouping on the eastern side of the Matarraña River, Republican forces bolstered with reinforcements managed – temporarily – to halt the Nationalist advance.[31] The same day, the International Brigade base at Albacete was closed down and transferred to Badalona, a suburb of Barcelona, which lay safely within Republican Catalonia.[32]

Understandably, the diabolical experiences of the previous ten days had left many volunteers' morale in tatters:

Dirty, in torn uniforms, unshaven, stunned, sullen, hungry and dispirited, they were sitting or lying on the ground, many without rifles, wearing soled 'alpargatas' on their feet. Our brigade had lost about one thousand men killed, wounded or missing. The men spoke little. They swore a lot. They demanded to know who was responsible for the ignominious retreat, for the death of so many of their comrades, comrades who they had come to know and love, with whom close friendships had been forged and tested, not in the conventional atmosphere of offices, workshops or homes, but in the crucible of the many battles of the brigade.[33]

Men blamed the battalion leadership, the brigade leadership, the army leadership and the Spanish government itself. One Welsh veteran accused Sam Wild and the rest of the members of battalion headquarters of having 'buggered off and left everybody to find their own way to safety. Wild and the HQ should have been bloody shot.'[34] Wild responded in a written report, 'I complained to brigade after the Caspe action . . . stating at the time that the lack of written orders was responsible for a lot of the confusion.'[35] In truth, there was not much he could have done.

Prodigious efforts were made to return the handful of survivors to some sort of meaningful fighting force. Men separated from the main group gradually drifted into Batea in ones and twos. Irish leader Frank Ryan arrived from Madrid, where he had been editing *The Book of the Fifteenth International Brigade*.[36] A number returned who had recovered, or were still recovering, from their wounds and the arrival of a group of prisoners from Camp Lukacs, led by their political commissar, John Angus, showed the seriousness of the situation the battalion, and the Spanish Republic itself, was facing.[37] Numbers rose at one stage to 650, the highest number ever, but the battalion was now overwhelmingly made up of Spaniards. There were barely enough British left to form a company, let alone a battalion.

On 26 March, ten days after their arrival at Batea, the battalion left for the small town of Corbera. The following day, Sam Wild, having been promoted to captain, was sent to Barcelona for rest and medical treatment. His place was taken by the experienced military man, George Fletcher, while political commissar Walter Tapsell returned from sick leave.

Four days later, on 30 March 1938, south of the Ebro River and 100 kilometres south-east of Zaragoza, Franco resumed the Aragon offensive. All four battalions of the 15th International Brigade were sent to the front alongside the Spanish Listers and as they marched along the road from Gandesa to Alcañiz, they were bombarded by Nationalist aircraft. However, the 'bombs' failed to detonate, for they were filled not with explosives, but with leaflets advising the Republican soldiers to surrender and promising that they would be treated 'with justice'. There was one significant caveat: 'This does not apply to war criminals, who will be dealt with severely for the crimes they have perpetrated against the Spanish people.' The British were in no doubt that the threat applied to them.[38]

The volunteers advanced cautiously towards the small village of Calaceite, dominated by its church on the summit of the hill, which lay on the main road from Gandesa to Alcañiz. The battalion spent the night camped outside Calaceite and, having woken before dawn on 31 March, made their way forward through the village.[39]

Having been given orders to take up positions one kilometre beyond Calaceite, but unable to find the exact location referred to, George Fletcher sought help from members of the Spanish 100th Brigade, but only received 'very vague' information in response. An enquiry concerning the exact location of the enemy forces was met with 'a wave of the hand in the direction in which my Battalion was travelling'.[40] Not satisfied, Fletcher sent the head of the 15th Brigade cartography department, Lieutenant Bee, to Brigade headquarters; Bee returned with a Spanish lieutenant to guide them to their correct position. As daybreak approached, Fletcher ordered the British No. 1 Company to accompany the Spanish lieutenant to their allotted position, acting as an advance guard for the remainder of the battalion. The main force followed 500 metres behind, marching 'in artillery formation, one file on each side of the road, with scouts ahead of us and on both flanks' and with the Machine-Gun Company bringing up the rear.[41] Moving forward, they were confronted by a group of six tanks that approached them out of the trees alongside the road.[42] As Bob Cooney admitted, 'we took it for granted . . . that they were our own tanks.'[43] 'We were soon disillusioned,' he was to recall. 'With terrifying suddenness the tanks opened fire on us. Another group of tanks emerged from the wood on the right, and simultaneously hordes of Italian infantry appeared yelling their heads off. It was a shambles!'[44]

Scouts had been sent ahead, but having to move across rough country, they were either left behind or ran into the Nationalists and were unable to warn the battalion of the huge Italian force approaching them.[45] As the Italian tanks and infantry 'poured fire into the leading companies of the Battalion', some cool-headed and fearless individuals made a vain attempt to fight back:

> The tragedy of the position was revealed when George Ives threw an empty tin can at the tanks to try and bluff the enemy that we had bombs. Had we a supply of hand grenades that morning, there would be a far different story to tell.[46]

After recovering from their initial shock, a number of British machine-gunners eventually managed to open fire and force the tanks to withdraw, but not before George Fletcher was wounded in the shoulder by a burst of machine-gun fire from one of the tanks.[47] He gave the order to scatter and make for the hills, telling Lieutenant Bobby Walker on the way up the hill to take command – though, as Walker quickly recognised, 'there wasn't a lot to take over.'[48] Using a similar ruse to that employed by George Ives, Walker did his best to get everyone away from the road as quickly as possible:

> I climb[ed] up to the top of the hill and there's two groups of fascist formations coming up, about twenty in each formation . . . I wasn't carrying a weapon and as I looked over they shouted, '¡Arriba España!' . . . I picked up a stone, pretended it was a hand grenade, pulled the pin, lobbed it and they all went down and that gave me a bit of a breather.[49]

In the confused melee the battalion lost some of its senior and experienced members. Among those killed was Walter Tapsell, who 'was wearing the cap which denoted that he was a commissar . . . this was just curtains for poor Wally.'[50]

Wally Tapsell was at the side of the road. He shouted to the Fascist officer

standing up in the tank turret, 'You bloody fool! Do you want to kill your
own men?' Wally thought they were our own tanks. We all expected that
the Lister division were ahead of us and hadn't realised that the front had
broken. The Fascist officer in the tank turret opened fire with a revolver
and shot him dead. It all happened so quickly.[51]

Manchester volunteer Syd Booth hadn't been in the country longer than
a month and was taken utterly by surprise by the Nationalist soldiers. 'I was
just a stretcher-bearer,' said Booth, 'I was petrified . . . there's all the bullets
and everything going flying about, I couldn't even think, my mind stopped
thinking.[52] Booth was very lucky to be saved by his sergeant, who screamed
at him to take cover before dragging him to safety, but at least fifty members
of the Major Attlee Company were hit by Italian gunfire and more than one
hundred – including Frank Ryan, who had only just rejoined the battalion
– were surrounded and forced to surrender.[53]

The survivors scattered, most with little option but to run for their lives.
John Angus was part of a small group marching at night to escape the
attention of Nationalists. However, in the darkness, Angus's men ran into
a group of Nationalist Italian soldiers:

> After marching across country for some hours, we found ourselves in the
> middle of the night, quite suddenly, on a road on which Italian troops
> were resting. It seemed that it would attract more attention to try and run
> away than to stay put, so we simply sat down in a group and rested on
> the roadside in a gap between the two companies and when they moved
> on we rose and moved on with them. This was a pretty hair-raising
> experience and after a few minutes an Italian officer came along and
> said, 'Who are you?' In our small party of about half a dozen there was
> a young American, Johnny, a physicist from the middle west, who
> was carrying a field telephone and he answered smartly, in Italian,
> 'Telecommunications'. The Italian officer was apparently satisfied with
> this answer and marched on ahead. I must say that this was a very
> uncomfortable moment indeed.[54]

Syd Booth was one of a small number following the huge figure of Lewis
Clive, a rowing gold medallist in the 1932 Los Angeles Olympics. Lost
behind the Nationalist lines for nearly ten days, they marched at night,
sleeping during the day; eventually, Booth became convinced that the group

was going in the wrong direction and broke off on his own. He quickly ran into trouble:

> Somebody started shooting at me. So I waited; counted out the rounds and then up and I ran right into a crowd of Spaniards. So I fired at 'em . . . and I ran into some more. And I'd got my rifle like that and the clip was still open . . . I'd fired all the shots. So they just looked at me and took it off me . . . I thought, 'Ah, this is it now.' This is the end . . . They turned out to be Loyalists, Spanish soldiers, you know, ours.[55]

Others were not so fortunate. One Scottish volunteer, when he became separated from the main force, hid in a ditch as Italian tanks passed alongside. After three days of vainly trying to find his way back to the battalion, he was taken prisoner by a Spanish cavalry unit.[56]

The main bulk of the battalion, comprised of those who had either been on patrol or were in the Machine-Gun Company, retreated eastwards, trying to make contact with the front line, which was being pushed steadily east by the Nationalists.[57] They were gradually joined by others trying to do the same, including one group led by Walter Gregory, temporarily promoted to lieutenant and company commander. Having reached Calaceite, only to find it occupied by Nationalist troops, Gregory cautiously skirted the village and headed east for Gandesa. After marching for about fifteen kilometres, the group made contact with sixty more survivors from the battalion who, led by Malcolm Dunbar, were making a defensive stand on the junction of the main road and the road heading north to Batea and Caspe.[58] They were joined there by another group accompanying Bob Cooney, now standing in for Tapsell as battalion commissar. Cooney had initially been captured at Calaceite but, showing great presence of mind, had escaped the attention of his guards by surreptitiously sitting down, before taking his chances and making a run for it.

By 2 April, Dunbar's group had swelled to about 200, as troops from a number of Republican units – and a small tank – joined them. He ordered Cooney's men to make for Gandesa, but on approaching the town, Cooney found that this too had fallen. Dunbar elected to make a stand a short way south-east of Gandesa, wisely choosing a position in a steep cutting, where it was almost impossible to be outflanked. As dark began to fall, the main force were retreating east, heading towards Cherta when they were greatly cheered to meet Sam Wild, back from Barcelona, and Lieutenant 'Hooky'

Walker, who had come looking for them in a lorry laden with food.[59] Walter Gregory bravely remained behind with his group and held up the Nationalist advance by firing madly and throwing grenades to dupe the Nationalist soldiers into thinking they faced a larger force than actually existed. Having managed to repulse a cavalry attack and survive a sporadic artillery barrage, Gregory prudently withdrew his small band at midnight and hurried to rejoin the main force. They eventually caught up with them at Cherta, and waited until the morning of 3 April for a boat to ferry them across the River Ebro.[60]

Other stragglers crossed the bridge between Mora de Ebro and Mora la Nueva. However, the route was closed when British engineer Percy Ludwick and a team of *zapatores* rigged the bridge with explosives. A huge series of explosions ensured that 'the bridge was wrecked . . . [and] . . . the road to Catalonia at Mora de Ebro was blocked.'[61] Finding no other way across the river, former rower and strong swimmer Lewis Clive managed to swim across, despite the strong current. Others, less confident in the water, were carried away and drowned.

As the survivors of the Calaceite disaster gradually found their way back to safety, east of the River Ebro, Will Paynter wrote to Harry Pollitt in London, breaking the terrible news of the previous month's events, including the admission that 350 members of the battalion were yet to be accounted for.[62] Confiding to Pollitt his belief that the catastrophic defeat at Calaceite – where more than three hundred had been killed, wounded or captured – 'could have been avoided if the leadership was better',[63] he argued that the Brigade should never have allowed a situation to develop in which men were sent walking into tanks, that there should have been better scouts, and that the battalion commander, George Fletcher, should have got his men away quicker when they were attacked. He also argued that, had hand grenades been carried, it might have been possible to attack the tanks.[64] That a large number of the men at Calaceite 'had never seen action before and had never had training' had also contributed to the catastrophe. However, admitting that 'Time after time our troops have been cut off or tricked because of the inexperience of our commanders', Paynter recognised that the fundamental cause of the retreats was the Nationalists' overwhelming superiority, not just in men and arms, but also their 'knowledge of military tactics and supply of trained officers'.

In fact, the Republican Army had been virtually annihilated by Franco's colossal advantage in soldiers, arms and *matériel*. Percy Ludwick estimated that as many as 1500 International Brigaders, including political commissars and officers, had been killed, wounded, or taken prisoner.[65] As the Republican forces collapsed under the Nationalist onslaught, many senior figures in the battalion believed they were witnessing the final defeat of the Republic:

It is with great sorrow that I have to report that we have lost many of our best comrades and that the Battalion has suffered a severe reverse . . . as you can guess, the strain has been terrific and our boys are not in very good shape . . . [Clifford] Wattis wanted to pull out immediately for Barcelona and said he had camions already fixed, [Sam] Wild was for refusing to go into the line again and Bob [Cooney] was wobbly.[66]

It was clear to Paynter that Wattis, 'a brave man and excellently trained officer', was one of many who had reached the end of their tether and now only wanted to return home. '[Wattis] has had enough and cannot be strongly trusted,' he felt. Many figures in the Brigade were similarly disheartened and, understandably, a feeling of defeatism was widespread. When Billy Griffiths escaped over the bridge at Mora, he encountered a Republican artillery battery hidden in the woods and asked them for directions to Brigade headquarters. The American in charge informed him shortly that 'There is no Brigade – no Division – no army. It is all over. The best you can do is get out of this country as fast as you can.'[67]

With Franco's capture of the Mediterranean town of Viñaroz on 3 April, and another sixty kilometres of coastland shortly afterwards, by mid-April 1938 the Republic had been split in two.[68] It was the most serious crisis the Spanish government had faced: 'On it hangs the fate of democracy in Spain and, it may be, of Europe,' warned the *News Chronicle*. The call to the International Brigades was clear: 'If they should fail, not they alone, but all of us would be the losers.'[69] Nationalist supporters in Britain crowed in triumph:

The war in Spain is over. The Red chiefs, who have never at any time showed the slightest capacity for disciplined manoeuvre, but merely gangster-like for shooting from cover until they are outflanked, have been pushed into an impossible position where their forces are already cut in two and they are threatened imminently with the loss of Barcelona.[70]

However, the Republic was to be granted a reprieve – and from a most unlikely quarter. Had Franco advanced north, as his German advisors were urging him to do, there was little to prevent him reaching Barcelona, which might well have forced the Republic to surrender. This, however, he chose not to do. Franco's aim, it appears, was not just military victory, but a *limpieza* – a purge intended to 'clean up' all the opponents of Nationalist Spain.

Once it was clear that there was no imminent danger of the Rebels continuing their advance, the physically and psychologically shattered remnants of the battalion were withdrawn for further rest, recuperation and rebuilding. The process was helped considerably by the temporary opening of Spain's border with France between March and May, which allowed new supplies of arms and ammunition to reach the Republic. Under the command of Sam Wild and their new commissar, Bob Cooney, the battalion's numbers were boosted by new arrivals and Spanish conscripts.[71]

> Wild and Cooney set about the task of restoring morale with a vengeance, for they fully realized that their men were far too preoccupied with the recent lengthy retreat. They appreciated that every one of us was aware of the immense Fascist superiority in men and weaponry, and also of the advantage which they held over us in terms of their organization and communications . . . Sam, perhaps more than anyone else I met in Spain, appreciated that men who were occupied, no matter how depressing the circumstances in which they found themselves, were far less likely to think of defeat than if they were left to their own devices.[72]

Efforts were made to restore political discipline which had been lost during the retreats. Foremost among these was the creation of the 'activist movement', formed from 'a small group of young Communists who pledged themselves to master their weapons, to study the art of modern war, to set an example in discipline and fighting morale, to develop personal initiative and set the pace in all Battalion activities'.[73] Bob Cooney claimed, probably in an excess of enthusiasm, that 'they performed wonders in speed and efficiency – then challenged the cynics, "Beat that!" Thus the cynics were subtly drawn into competition with the activists, and before long our

Battalion was virtually 100 per cent activist.'[74] In fact, as Bill Alexander admitted, the movement was ignored, if not actually mocked, by the more world-weary members of the battalion, who never took the initiative seriously.[75]

For many of the battalion, after the terrible hardships endured during the retreats, the break from fighting during the late spring and early summer of 1938 was nevertheless a great relief. The volunteers were kept busy with 'training, marching or rifle practice' and 'the procedures for crossing rivers', while at night Lewis Clive swam clandestinely across the Ebro to reconnoitre the Nationalist positions.[76] Benefiting from regular food and sleep, and safe from the daily risk of death, some came to see this as one of their most pleasant periods in Spain: 'In this happy existence, which was really enjoyable, we were out in the fresh air and we were sleeping under the open sky. The weather was fairly good and we were getting plenty of exercise and plenty of food.'[77]

Under their new 15th Brigade Commander, Major José Valledor, a veteran of the Asturias uprising of October 1934, from 1 June the British were based near the Catalonian village of Marsa, in 'a pretty valley, with rugged hills and mountains around'. The volunteers would christen it 'Chabola Valley' after the small rough shelters they constructed under the hazelnut bushes that proliferated in the *barrancos*.[78] They spent their longest period of rest and training of the entire war here, and 'the more ingenious and talented members of the Battalion constructed a number of brush huts in an amazing variety of architectural styles.'[79]

In a few days excellent dugouts had been built and the construction of a wooden building to house a library was commenced. Most of us stripped to the waist as the weather was quite hot and it was soon difficult to say which were Spanish and which were English. The Valley in a few days presented a strange appearance with many hundreds of almost naked men busily building comfortable quarters and generally preparing themselves for a long stay.[80]

As had been the case during training at Madrigueras and Mondéjar, desire for English food took on increased importance; 'whenever there was a lull in conversation about anything important food cropped up.'[81] As Nan Green observed, 'one might have thought that this dwelling on food . . . would have made people gloomy, but it didn't. It cheered them up.'[82] Jim

Jump later recalled with great amusement a conversation about food with his friend, recorder player Miles Tomalin:

> When we had nothing to do, we started discussing what was the most typically British item of food. We rejected things like sausage and mash and fish and chips, eggs and bacon and even things like Haggis and Yorkshire pudding and we decided in the end that the most typically British food, because it couldn't have been invented by anyone else, was a baked jam roll – quite illogical and stupid. And then I remember Miles [Tomalin] said to me, 'When we get back, let's form a society "For the defence of the British pudding"' and I said, 'Let's call it "The Pudding Club"' and he threw a book at me![83]

Cyril Sexton was another brigader to remember with great fondness the interlude at Marsa, where he enjoyed the luxury of 'hot baths and a change of uniforms'. Indeed, on 8 July the battalion was visited by a travelling van fitted out with hot showers.[84] Many volunteers also took the opportunity to lose themselves in a book. Their ranks included a number of voracious readers and they had amassed a huge library of English books; these were stored at a nearby *hacienda*, where they managed to rig up electric lighting and could read long into the night. 'It was a strange, argumentative army of thinkers,' remembered one.[85]

Part of the process of boosting morale was the holding of cultural and sporting events, such as the big fiesta that took place on 18 July. Unfortunately, the event did not turn out as planned: following too much drinking and general excitement, there was a terrible accident. The event began badly when Lieutenant 'Hooky' Walker, who was in charge of dinner arrangements, got 'rolling drunk' and was placed under arrest by a furious Sam Wild.[86] But much worse was to come. One of the central events of the fiesta was a competition between two of the best machine-gunners in the battalion, Irishman Maurice Ryan (who was an excellent shot when sober), and one of the Bennett brothers from Birmingham:

> On a piece of level ground near the village we sat and listened to the speakers, then milled around trying to get through the crowd and so nearer the pretty young girls among the guests. Then came ghastly tragedy.
> During the afternoon they held a machine-gun competition, to see which team could get into and out of action quickest, firing off a couple of

rounds in the process. At the finish of one heat bad control allowed someone – God knows who – to fiddle about, with the result that one poor bastard got a bullet at point-blank range right through his guts and another one through an arm and a leg. The first will be dead by now. Even with doctors on the spot he'd lost far too much blood before they took him away. What a lousy way to go. Somebody was at fault and in my opinion it was the first and second in command of the Battalion and the chap in charge of the gun for the careless way they allowed loaded machine guns to be handled. But I suppose it's easy to judge. Anyway, that finished the Fiesta.[87]

The following day the 15th International Brigade was reviewed; the battalion had been restored to over five hundred men divided among five companies, though Spaniards outnumbered Internationals. At a battalion meeting called just under a week later, on 24 July 1938, the American 15th International Brigade political commissar, Johnny Gates, confirmed to the volunteers what many had guessed; that they were to cross the Ebro in a major new offensive back through Aragon.[88] The battalion was given its orders: once across the river they were to advance through Corbera and Gandesa in a bid to cut the road linking Aragon and the Nationalist front line.

For the survivors of the retreats the previous spring, it was a moment of great satisfaction. As morale had grown, so had a desire to return to the fight to seek redress for the defeats of the past. Now, if all went to plan, they were to be the ones advancing and it would be the Nationalists who were forced to retreat. 'What exhilaration!' exclaimed Walter Gregory. 'We were on the move again, we were taking the initiative and we were on top of the world!'[89]

17

The Last Throw of the Dice

In the spring our forces had been thrown back across the Ebro as a major fascist offensive drove a wedge through the Republic to the Mediterranean. The right-wing press in Britain was jubilant and prophesied the imminent fall of Barcelona. Valencia was threatened and indeed the end seemed near for democracy in Spain.

Then three months later the world suddenly gasped. Despite the constant attention of the Italian airforce, our army advanced on a one hundred and fifty kilometre front to a depth of thirty kilometres. Over five thousand prisoners were taken together with large quantities of military equipment. The fascists were well and truly on the run.

George Wheeler, *To Make the People Smile Again*

During the nights of 23 and 24 July 1938, advance units of the 80,000 strong Republican Army of the Ebro under the command of the Spanish Communist General Juan Modesto moved stealthily up to the banks of the River Ebro. The British Battalion was driven by truck to the muster point for the 15th Brigade, concealed within a well-wooded area, and then marched the remaining thirty kilometres to their crossing point near Ascó. While experienced and dedicated soldiers like Walter Gregory and George Wheeler, a London wood-machinist, were triumphant at returning to the fray, former member of the British Anti-Tank Battery Fred Thomas was less happy. Accustomed to being transported around by lorry, Thomas found life as a 'foot-slogger' an unpleasant shock:

My boots, issued to me in Murcia, somewhat tight from the beginning and only worn rarely since, soon began to hurt, a nail in one foot, a blister on the other. Second-hand (or more) when I got them, this was hardly surprising. My blanket choked me, my packstrap cut into my shoulder, the night was stifling hot – in short, I never felt less like a revolutionary in my life.[1]

The following night, Republican forces began to cross the river at sixteen separate points along an eighty-kilometre front. The Hungarian Internationals were supposed to lead the way, but a heated argument developed between their commander and the prickly Hugh Slater, now on the 15th International Brigade's staff. Slater was demanding divisional approval before allowing the impatient Hungarians to cross and the argument was only settled by the actions of Percy Ludwick, the brigade fortifications expert and engineer, who fired his pistol, the agreed signal for the start of the crossing.

The British followed the Canadian Mac-Paps over the fast-flowing Ebro, half the battalion crossing a temporary pontoon bridge which Bobby Walker described as so unstable that 'one or two fell off and had to grab the barrels and climb back on.'[2] More bridges further upstream allowed tanks and other vehicles to cross.[3] Some brigaders came by boat: Walter Gregory, accompanied by five other volunteers, was rowed across by two Spanish locals; Bob Clark crossed in a lifeboat built for sixty people, though it was carrying many more than that.[4]

As several volunteers remembered, 'the crossing of the Ebro at night was a remarkable performance', 'it was a very, very dramatic moment in time for everybody.'[5] Returning to the fight in which they had suffered so terribly the previous spring gave many a feeling of grim determination, though tinged with the familiar and understandable anxiety that preceded going into combat:

We got into rowing boats; everyone was silent and thinking about the fighting to come. The Spanish and International Brigaders had muffled even the oars. I had a lot of equipment, rifle, about 100 rounds of ammunition and my blanket tied round my body. Inside the blanket I carried my few odd personal items, including an empty mess tin and a filled water bottle.[6]

Just like the capture of Teruel six months earlier, the crossing of the Ebro was hailed by Republican supporters around the world as a moment of huge significance. The *Daily Worker* proclaimed the offensive to be a huge boost for Republican morale, particularly after the traumatic experiences suffered during the retreats of the previous spring:

> The atmosphere of enthusiasm and determination, as revealed by their talk, has to be seen to be believed. They fully realise all this battle means to Spain and to democracy throughout the world. Many of these men . . . were in the Aragon retreat.[7]

Initially, the offensive caught the Nationalist forces on the western bank of the river woefully unprepared. However, the British advance received an early setback when a vehicle became stuck on one of the pontoons. Then – within two hours of the first troops crossing – Nationalist aeroplanes began attacking the temporary bridges, to the horror of Scottish volunteer Hugh Sloan:

> The Franco aeroplanes were coming down the river, bombing and attacking us continually before we got across. Our anti-aircraft guns were blazing at them and there was tremendous buzzing of splinters from the shells buzzing through the air as if we had been invaded by an extraordinary mass of bum[ble]bees.[8]

As the morning progressed, the Nationalist air attacks became ever more intense. Bob Clark quickly realised that, struggling to cross the river, the Republican forces were sitting ducks:

> The sky was overcast by scores of black enemy bombers all heading for the river. A deadly sickly feeling was in the pit of my stomach as I watched those black hordes with hardly any opposition, except for a dozen or so AA guns on the opposite bank of the river, droning their way towards that fateful stream. The low, dull rumbling of many bombs hitting the ground made even the hill on which we sat tremble with the concussion. Over four hundred tons of bombs were dropped in one afternoon.[9]

The crossing was further hampered when the Nationalists opened a lock upstream, raising the water level and dramatically increasing the flow of the river.[10] The now battle-hardened and experienced soldiers were fully aware of the dangers of being caught out in the open, on the bridge or in a boat.[11] However, the thoughts of Percy Ludwick, surrounded by the constant threat of death, were not for himself. Believing that he and his comrades 'had a good chance of survival by rushing or rowing to a comparatively safe place', he instead displayed a stereotypically English concern for the fate of the animals ferrying supplies across the Ebro:

> But what of the poor mules swimming across the river, or crossing by the footbridge, carrying weapons for our troops? Their chances of survival when caught out in the open were far less. We were so much pre-occupied in saving our own skins, that sometimes we did not have the time to save our mules. The dumb animals were terrified at the hideous whistling of the falling bombs. They panicked, reared, brayed piteously and many were slaughtered, if not by the bombs, then by the merciless strafing. But, on the other hand, several of our men gave their lives in saving, or trying to save, the dumb animals.[12]

Once across, however, the soldiers were able to advance rapidly. By the afternoon of 25 July they had covered over fifteen kilometres and were within two kilometres of Corbera, a village that lay between them and their principal target, the small town of Gandesa, seen as the key to the Ebro offensive. Here the advancing International Brigades and other Republican troops were greeted by astonished and jubilant supporters:

> As we turned a bend in the road we were surprised to find quite a large number of peasants, men and women, lining by the side who loudly cheered us on. One old chap seemed overcome with emotion at the sight of the Catalan flag being carried at the head of the Battalion . . . Rushing forward towards the standard he clutched it passionately and smothered it with kisses.[13]

But the battalion was soon held up by a pitched battle with Rebel soldiers hidden in the hills alongside the roads. Gradually the battalion's superior numbers began to count and when the Nationalist position was eventually destroyed with the help of grenades, their attackers were discovered to be two young Moroccan soldiers, probably no more than sixteen years of age. Anxious to secure Corbera, the battalion pressed on as quickly as possible, but they came under renewed heavy firing from an adjacent ridge and one volunteer was hit. Only when their Republican flag was spotted did the firing stop; it then became apparent that the shots were coming from their comrades in the Spanish Lister Brigade.[14]

By the evening the road to Corbera was clear, allowing the Spanish 13th Brigade to take advantage and capture the village. However, lack of supplies, especially food and water, were becoming problematic as the battalion's supply line became dangerously over-extended. Only mules, notoriously awkward beasts at the best of times, were available to bring up supplies; according to Bob Cooney, 'one particular animal was dubbed "Chamberlain" by the muleteer because it constantly made off in the direction of the fascists lines.'[15] 'We had no backing,' one Scottish volunteer realised. 'We were just a front line capable of this operation, but with no reserves. And no equipment to make up for losses.'[16] Casualties faced a dreadful journey to safety and hospital treatment:

> During the first three days any wounded had to be carried some 6 to 10 kilometres by our stretcher-bearers. No ambulances had been able to cross the pontoons, which were now under constant bombing by Franco's air force. Thus, for about 3 days it was our stretcher-bearers who had the task of getting our wounded over the Ebro, if a wounded man died a shallow grave would be the final resting place.[17]

One volunteer, a chemist from Aberdeen, never forgot seeing a young comrade hit by machine-gun fire:

> I remember one lad, he came from Lancashire. He was very, very slightly made. He weighed, I would reckon, about seven stone seven pounds, eight stones at the very most. But I had seen this little lad pulling a Maxim machine gun for miles. And he had run past the cave where the Moors were and threw in a grenade. There was a machine gun burst of fire and his arm went swinging round his side, and he said, 'Gee whiz, I thought my arm was off.' Well, he didn't realise that his arm was only hanging by a tendon.[18]

When the badly damaged remnant of his arm had to be amputated, the young volunteer was utterly distraught, crying, 'What am I going to do now when I go back into civilian life?' Believing that his whole future had vanished, he seemed simply to give up hope. He died the following day.[19]

In increasingly difficult conditions, the battalion pressed on towards Gandesa.[20] But by now the element of surprise was no longer with them.

Coldly determined to regain any lost ground and seeing an opportunity to annihilate the Republican Army, Franco rushed up reinforcements, and the Republican forces, crucially short of motorised equipment, were met by fierce resistance from Nationalist forces, particularly aircraft and artillery fire.[21] With the constant bombing and shelling limiting the opportunity to bring up supplies from across the river, the Republican troops were now close to starving. Fortunately, one Scottish volunteer made a lucky find:

> Three days after we had crossed the Ebro I was sent to headquarters with a message. On returning across the river, perhaps about a kilometre on the south side, I came to a village that had been evacuated. Now our units were perhaps another kilometre or two further on. When I reached this evacuated village in the hills I was surprised to find dumped at the gable end of the very first building into the village a stack of loaves of bread and wooden boxes which on examination turned out to be tins of sardines. I had learned to contend with hunger so I was delighted to find this. I gathered as many loaves of bread and sardine tins as I could carry . . . the boys appreciated them very, very much. This had been perhaps their third day without eating anything, other than any rations they had about their person. I call this a minor miracle, the minor miracle of the loaves and fishes.[22]

Just three months after their unsuccessful attempts to prevent Gandesa from falling into Nationalist hands, the British Battalion approached the town determined to erase the terrible memories of the retreat and return it to the Spanish Republic. As Republican forces battered the town itself, the battalion was ordered to capture a hill, just over a kilometre to the east, nicknamed 'The Pimple' by the British. 'Hill 481' overlooked Gandesa, and though not the highest hill in the vicinity, its capture was vital if the attack on the town was to stand any chance of success.

The British Major Attlee Company launched an assault on Hill 481 early the following day. However, as at Purburrel Hill the previous August, its Nationalist defenders refused to submit easily, for they were fully aware of its strategic importance and it had been expertly fortified. To make matters worse, the hill's natural defences were almost as impregnable as those constructed by the Rebels; 'it was practically a sheer rise in front of us,' one veteran of No. 1 Company later recalled.[23] Billy Griffiths was hugely intimidated by the task facing the battalion:

It was only a small hill, hardly enough room for a dozen or so men on the top. Yet the flanks were protected by covering fire from Gandesa. A frontal attack left little room for the deployment of many men and was well protected by [a] 4ft barbed wire fence and booby traps. When this position was reached one was met with showers of hand grenades. With artillery, or a supply of mortars, or concentrated attack from low flying aircraft, they could have been blown out. These we did not have. We had to depend on small arms.[24]

The first attacks were made during daylight, but with virtually no support either from tanks and aircraft or, crucially, from artillery, it was a suicidal mission; the volunteers faced 'a withering, murderous reply of shells, rifle and machine gun fire' from the hill's resolute defenders.[25] Bob Clark watched as his comrades threw themselves forward against the Nationalist defences, only to be viciously driven back:

Suddenly the cry 'Adelante' (Forward!) was given and Britishers and Spaniards, among whom were youths of seventeen years, with loud yells clambered over rocks past trees from which the leaves were dropping like a day in a park in autumn cut by thousands of bullets. The whole crest of the hill was a death trap. The whining of bullets was amazingly consistent. A number of heavy mortar bombs sent up cascades of earth and stones. There was the cry of wounded and the plaintive cry of a Spanish youth who kept calling for Sanidad . . . the fire was overwhelming.[26]

It was an almost impossible position to attack, for as Walter Gregory quickly realised, the battalion were also being hit from Nationalist positions placed on the surrounding heights and from machine-guns on the top of high buildings within the town itself: 'It seemed at times that every hand was set against us, especially when enemy artillery, which had been rushed to the front in great number, joined in pouring an almost continuous fire into our positions.'[27] Jack Jones, badly wounded in the shoulder, was one of many casualties of the first day's fighting:

Once more I had clambered up the hill with my comrades, taking cover where we could and firing at the enemy wherever he appeared. The bullets of the snipers whizzed over, grenades and shells were striking the ground, throwing up earth and dust and showering us with shrapnel. Suddenly my shoulder and right arm went numb. Blood gushed from my shoulder and I couldn't lift my rifle. I could do nothing but lie where I was. Near me a comrade had been killed and I could hear the cries of others, complaining of their wounds. While I was lying there, to make things worse, a spray of shrapnel hit my right arm. The stretcher bearers were doing their best but could hardly keep up with the number of casualties. As night fell I made my own way, crawling to the bottom of the hill. I was taken with other wounded men down the line to an emergency field hospital at Mora del Ebro where I was given an anti-tetanus injection. The place was like an abbatoir; there was blood and the smell of blood everywhere.[28]

On 30 July, No. 2 Company joined the attack on Hill 481, but they had advanced only a few metres when they were spotted and cut to pieces in a hail of bullets. Such was the rate of fire from the Nationalist defences that the attackers were trapped; able neither to advance nor retreat without presenting 'an inviting target', they could only take shelter and await the cover of darkness. As Walter Gregory exclaimed:

What a prospect! Twelve hours of lying on rocky soil, every fragment of which seemed intent on burying itself in our bodies, of being continually shot at, of having nothing to eat or drink, of being driven half-mad by the ceaseless attention of the most malevolent flies in the whole of Spain, and of hoping that by staying still the attention of a Fascist marksman would be distracted by movement elsewhere.[29]

It was not long before Gregory joined the growing list of casualties. No. 2 Company suffered particularly heavily, as Bob Cooney recounted:

When the company made its first assault, Lieutenant John Angus was in command. He fell, seriously wounded in the chest. His successor, Lieutenant Walter Gregory, got a bullet in the neck. Sergeant Bill Harrington took over, till he too was seriously wounded and Corporal Joe Harkins . . . assumed command. Joe Harkins fell, mortally wounded, just before Lieutenant Lewis Clive, the original company commander – returned from hospital.[30]

With all the military commanders killed or wounded, the political commissar, Jonny Powers, was forced to take emergency command.[31] A desperate charge by No. 3 Company the following day saw them come within fifteen metres of the crest of the hill, before being thrown back by a sustained and intense barrage of Nationalist fire. During the night, another attempt, supported by the Spanish Listers and the 13th Brigade, was similarly repulsed.

As July moved into August, the attempt to capture the hill became increasingly desperate, and casualties mounted alarmingly; Bob Cooney reported that the battalion 'was reduced to company strength'.[32] Even for men now hardened to the brutal realities of warfare, the number of casualties sustained at Hill 481 was deeply shocking. Many of them were popular, long-standing members of the battalion, such as No. 4 Company commissar Mike Economides, who had fought alongside John Cornford and Ralph Fox at Lopera in December 1936 and had been in Spain ever since. Another was the former political commissar of the anti-tanks, Alan Gilchrist, now promoted to deputy battalion commissar, struck down by two bullets in his right lung. Olympic rower Lewis Clive was killed, as was the outstanding mathematician David Guest, hit while using the binoculars his mother had given him when she visited the battalion the previous June.[33]

> David was probably the only man that I knew at that time who had a pair of binoculars and a compass that his mother had brought out for him . . . I got to Johnny [Connors] and shouted to him [from] no more than about three or four yards away, 'Come down David, you've got to come off that hill, they can see you.'
>
> I dared not go up any higher because there was a point where I would be observed. 'Just a minute,' he said, or some words like that and the next thing I knew he was falling backwards and he was dead. He was shot clean through the head . . . Johnny Connors and me we pulled him down, we couldn't even bury him because we had no spades or equipment. We just had to cover him up with a little blanket he had and buried him that night.[34]

Both Guest and Clive were sufficiently well-known to be commemorated in the *Illustrated London News* in mid-August.[35] Such was the impression created by Clive's death that it moved one of his old school-friends to write to the school newspaper, *The Eton College Chronicle*:

> So Lewis Clive has died fighting for his ideals. That would be appropriate if it wasn't so tragic. Spain has dealt with my generation . . . in quantity and

quality. I'm terribly sorry Lewis is dead. He really was one of the comparatively few people who put into practice what they preach – and he preached very high from the start, which is a pretty difficult thing to do at the age of 12 at Eton. He was incorrigibly idealistic, and I have often laid siege to his castle, at lunch in the City, but never with the slightest success. He did me a lot of good, and a lot of other people too.[36]

Many less well-known volunteers also lost their lives on the hill. George Wheeler remembered the moment when his friend and comrade Lawrence Pryme was hit:

We were making a night attack from another position on Hill 481. All of a sudden the clouds spread a bit and there was a burst of moonlight and I heard Lawrence cry, 'Oh I've been hit.' And then it was silent for a minute and I crept up behind him and I said, 'How are you Lawrence?' He said, 'Oh I'm done for. Don't bother, leave me.' And I looked at him and his legs were completely useless, they were turning around as if they were on a bit of string, the blood was pouring out so I couldn't leave him. I said, 'Hold on Lawrence, hang on to my hand.' And I tried to pull him and as I did so his heavy leather ammunition box was scraping on the ground. Another burst of firing came, I carefully undid his buckle and discarded his ammunition box. I knew it was going to be terrible to get him off that hill. By that time another comrade, [Douglas] Sutton, came to help. I lay down and eased Lawrence Pryme onto my body and Sutton pulled me by my shoulders, using me as a stretcher. He pulled me and pulled me until we got to cover and they took him away. He died on the way to hospital. I was smothered in his blood, my trousers were absolutely saturated and they stayed like that for ages.[37]

The battalion's last, futile attempt to capture 'The Pimple' was made on 3 August 1938. Trapped on the hill, they sustained terrifying numbers of casualties in the sweltering summer temperatures as the hopes and enthusiasms generated by their triumphant return across the River Ebro bled slowly away. With the battalion unable to capture the vital hill, the Republican offensive effectively foundered. As George Wheeler acknowledged, 'the offensive so brilliantly planned and executed by Colonel Modesto and the Spaniards under Lister was brought to a halt in our sector at Hill 481.'[38]

The bitter disappointment of the failure of the Ebro offensive, the loss of many well-known and popular comrades, and the diabolical experiences on that hill came as a shock to even some of the more battle-hardened volunteers. Scot John Dunlop was utterly disheartened: 'It really was a hellish place to be. I think that was just about the time when I really felt the lowest in all my life. I can't remember a time when I really felt so low.'[39]

Peter Kerrigan later wrote a report on the Hill 481 action, revealing 'facts that I cannot write about in the Daily [Worker]', particularly the pitiful conditions of the volunteers:

> From the 25th to the morning of the 30th they had nothing to drink but a little water, sometimes going for a day without this . . . They are fighting and marching over mountains, the rocks of which have cut their Spanish shoes to pieces. Many are literally barefoot as well as being in rags because of wear of clothes. Nobody has had a wash since the start of the offensive.[40]

Kerrigan was raising a familiar complaint. Jack Jones also pointed out that 'sometimes we went for a day without water, which we badly needed to moisten burning lips and parched throats.'[41] Moreover, the 'rags' in which members of the battalion were fighting offered little or no protection from the burning sun above and the sharp rocks beneath them. One volunteer described having to wear two pairs of trousers at once, 'one of which has no flies, the other no backside'.[42] In the eyes of Croydon volunteer John Peet:

> The state of our uniforms at this time was medium to catastrophic. We were all at that time haunted by lice. We had in most cases no change of clothing which meant that you were sleeping in your clothes and encouraging the lice. Shoes were an extreme problem. The *alpargatos* were war economy *alpargatos* . . . [which had] a very poor composition rubber sole which inevitably split after a few days' use.[43]

On 6 August, after thirteen days of continuous action, the British Battalion – or what remained of it – was moved into reserve. Only 150 of the 558 who had crossed the Ebro on 25 July still remained. The failure led senior Communist Party figures to begin taking a more realistic view of the likely outcome of the war and to discuss 'for the first time, the possibility of saving some of the key men who would be of better value at home'. As

Billy Griffiths admitted, this was 'the first indication that we could lose the war, and a readiness to face the complete extermination of the International Brigade'.[44]

A monument to the Internationals killed on the Ebro was constructed by Percy Ludwick's Republican engineers. Undiscovered throughout the Franco years, it still lies in the Sierra Pandols. Among the names on the monument are those of Lewis Clive, David Guest and Welsh commissar Harry Dobson, all killed on Hill 481, and another British political commissar, Morris Miller from Hull, who was killed nearby. It also bears the name of Walter Tapsell, killed at Calaceite the previous March.[45]

After their withdrawal from the front line for a brief rest, a rumour reached the battalion on 9 August that some British volunteers were to be given foreign leave. Two days later, the rumour was confirmed; all those who had been in Spain for longer than fourteen months would be eligible to apply for home leave. But initial hopes were dashed when it was revealed that only a maximum of thirty at a time, from the entire 15th Brigade, would be allowed to go, and then only for six days.[46] And all thoughts of repatriation were put to one side when two days later, on 11 August, the Nationalists launched a counter-attack in the mountains to the south of the Sierra Pandols. The 15th International Brigade was recalled to defend the almost 1000 metre high Hill 666, which had been occupied previously by the 11th Republican Division. With no transport available, the volunteers had to march across country from Gandesa, arriving at Hill 666 on 15 August, where they would face 'another eleven days of hell on the sheer precipices of the limestone mountains of the lower River Ebro'.[47]

On 24 August the British Battalion took over the exhausted Lincoln's positions, sheltering behind stone parapets on the main height of the Sierra Pandols.[48] The climb to their position, situated precariously on top of the mountain, was so exhausting that one of the mules bringing up food collapsed and died when it reached the top. 'Hell of a position that was,' said Syd Booth.[49] Former Stockton hunger-marcher John Longstaff, now a tough, experienced veteran of the Spanish war, remembered the hill without fondness:

The higher I walked the more I could smell the dead. It was getting darker and only a few Republican soldiers could be seen. The entire position was

bad. The few bits of brushwood growing showed signs of having been
burnt. I then realised what the smell was; burnt bodies, for the dead could
not be buried in the rock. I went from one defensive position to another
until finally reaching the main defence position. This was of rock walls, no
more than about one metre high. The walls had been built completely of
rock, as Hill 666 was nothing other than rock. It was evident that both the
Republican Army and Franco's forces had suffered heavy casualties for,
despite the height and strong winds blowing, everywhere was the stench
of those burnt bodies.[50]

The top of the hill was made up of 'nothing but blackened twigs of this
heathery plant and just cracked stones', remembered John Dunlop, who
was aghast to discover that 'there was no possibility of building trenches.'[51]
High in the Sierra, the position offered no cover from artillery and aircraft,
just hard, bare rock, baking in the August sun. The Nationalists rained
artillery fire on the British positions, the explosions creating rock splinters
every bit as lethal as the shells themselves. The British scrabbled to find
some sort of cover, as they were subjected to a massive bombardment 'the
like of which none of us had ever experienced', followed by an attack by
'two fascist infantry battalions'.[52]

> Aerial bombs, artillery, mortars, machine gun fire raged all day from dawn
> and pinned us in our stony crevices in a continuous state of high anxiety
> with frequent bouts of terror as all kinds of missiles fell around us; dust and
> falling stones were everywhere . . . In the blazing heat of that stony hell one
> could smell the revolting odour of excreta, urine and the ominous smell of
> putrefying corpses insufficiently buried in the crevices of the Sierra Pandols.
> There was hardly a patch of soil on these mountains; everywhere were
> pieces of shrapnel, dud bombs and shells.[53]

Perched on top of the hill, they could see in the distance Hill 481, the
scene of their earlier frustration and disappointment. Meanwhile 'fascist
bombers came over 60-100 at a time from dawn to dusk; all day the artillery
rolled, the deadly mortar fire never ceased.'[54] All the British had to respond
with was rifle and machine-gun fire. For first-aider Alun Menai Williams,

> [It] was the worst time in the war. Not for terror, I'd got over that . . . The
> agony of the Pandols was that I couldn't do much for the wounded. Day

and night we were being bombarded by aircraft, mortars, shelling and there was no cover. The casualties were horrendous; it was a big, open-air abattoir.[55]

The following day, the shattered survivors of the battalion were relieved by a Spanish unit and they returned, briefly, into reserve. The battalion was commended for their bravery on Hill 666 but, as too often, the cost had been substantial. In addition to the loss of assistant battalion commissar Morris Miller, Sam Wild was injured in the hand by a shell splinter and was replaced by George Fletcher.[56] A number of battalion officers were sent home, including secretary Ted Edwards and former commander, the popular Irishman Paddy O'Daire. At Hill 481 O'Daire had greatly impressed Jack Jones by insisting on carefully reading a French military manual, even under heavy fire: 'An outstanding example of sang-froid!' Jones remarked admiringly.[57] Jones himself, now recovering from his wounds, was also repatriated home, as was Tom Murray, another Labour councillor. Alongside Jones and Murray, André Marty had ordered that two further members of the battalion, 'Yorkie' Clem Broadbent and company commissar Lewis Clive, should be sent back by the end of September 1938; all four were standing as councillors in the November municipal elections.[58] In the event, with Clive having been killed on Hill 481, only Jones and Murray survived to return; Broadbent, accidentally shot by a member of the Lister Battalion a month later, died in hospital from his injuries.[59]

At the end of August, the last remaining gun of the British Anti-Tank Battery was transferred to the 13th (German) International Brigade. The half-dozen British in the unit were, perhaps a little reluctantly, united with their fellow-countrymen in the Machine-Gun Company:

We had been spared much of the foot-slogging, the rifle-humping, the exhausting route marches and other trials of strenuous training undertaken as a matter of course in the Battalions – and had paid for this when necessity arose. Not for us the 'fatigues' and 'general duties' – supplying guards for this and that. Nor had we been plagued by an overdose of authority from zealous NCOs or politicals. But over and above this, we had been spared the worst any man can face in war – to be called upon time after time to go 'over the top' under intense and deadly enemy fire.[60]

Once again, their respite was short-lived as Franco, now with absolute air superiority, began to make his superior forces tell. Fleets of aeroplanes, sometimes two hundred at the same time, circled over the Republican lines dropping in excess of 5000 kg of bombs every day. They met with scant resistance from the Republic's pitifully inadequate anti-aircraft defences and hopelessly outnumbered fighter planes.[61] A mass of artillery added to the deluge of shells raining down on the Republican defenders, until parts of the line were unable to hold and Franco pressed home his advantage.

On 7 September the British were rushed to one of the gaps in the front near Ascó, in the nearby range of Sierra Caballs.[62] Faced with overwhelming numbers of Nationalist soldiers and unrelenting artillery and aircraft bombardments, the British Battalion somehow managed in a feat of almost suicidal bravery to capture Hill 356, where they cowered as Nationalist aircraft and artillery units furiously attempted to blast them off the mountainside:

We all saw an enemy squadron curving round in the sky to our left . . . As the planes straightened to begin their approach to our positions we could see the dark shapes of bombs falling from beneath them. We had no trenches, no protection, we just lay flat on the ground with our arms covering our heads. The bombs burst all about us. The impact was terrific. The ground trembled and heaved, and clouds of swirling dust reduced visibility to a few inches. Some perhaps prayed for the safe deliverance from the holocaust which engulfed us; I cursed the fascists and the Non-Intervention Committee, and those back home who were too blind to see what was happening in Spain . . . If the bombing was horrendous, the constant barrages of artillery fire which we attracted right from the outset of our offensive were little better . . . How we came to hate planes and cannon and how different would have been our sentiments if they had been ours and not those of the fascists; but they never were.[63]

According to Bobby Walker, most of the aircraft were German, comprising Dorniers, Messerschmitts and Stukas in their hundreds: 'the whole front, everyone who was watching must have been saying, you know, we don't stand a chance here.' With thousands of shells dropping on them every day, the battalion clung on to the top of Hill 356 for a week until, with the front somehow stabilised, it was withdrawn and put in reserve.[64] Of the 150 men in Walter Gregory's company who had crossed the Ebro on 24 July, only two dozen now remained.[65] While the arrival of new equipment, including Czech light machine guns, was welcome, it was the renewed rumours of repatriation that provided the main talking point among the volunteers.[66] Some were willing to fight for as long as necessary, but others, such as London volunteer John Bassett were exhausted by the 'long period of almost continuous action' and 'had seen numbers dwindling as death, wounds and illness took their toll'.[67] Bassett had come to see the Republic's defeat as inevitable and now longed only to go home.

> As the apprentice, I had been allotted the end of the line, adjoining a narrow macadam road along which I expected to see enemy vehicles at any minute. All day, men would crawl over me and relieve themselves at the end of the trench. I ceased to bother to brush the flies off my face. I dreamed of tea in my mother's house in suburbia, of pints of mild and bitter in oak-beamed pubs, and I could not help wishing I had never come.[68]

But Bassett and his comrades could not return home just yet. The Spanish Republic, reeling under a series of near-mortal body blows, would call upon them one last time. After nearly two years of bitter fighting in often appalling conditions, the last battle of the British Battalion, the 57th Battalion of the Spanish Republican Army, would provide a suitably appropriate and sombre final moment.

18

Defeat and Withdrawal

When the International Brigade was withdrawn from Spain I took part in the big final march in Barcelona. Oh, I couldnae explain it. I was wantin' tae cry. We went marchin' doon and the reception we got from the people – women and everything, a' kissin' and huggin' us and all the rest o' it. It's a thing I'll never forget, never.

Interview with Scottish volunteer Bill Cranston

On 21 September 1938, Spanish Premier Juan Negrín – hoping to shame the western democracies into pressing Franco for a similar action – announced to the League of Nations the Republic's intention to repatriate all foreign volunteers from Spain. Following General Rojo's advice, Negrín had come to accept that the withdrawal of the exhausted Internationals, whose military contribution was now marginal, would not unduly affect the Republican Army. Negrín believed that, after nearly two years of combat, often at the forefront of battle, 'their military efficiency had fallen off' and that the influx of new volunteers was 'negligible'.[1] Some members of the battalion also felt that the volunteers' contribution was waning, that 'the Spanish loyalists were in the happy position of being able to do without the Internationals . . . [that they were] getting stronger and stronger . . . Or this is what we were told, anyway,' added Syd Booth.[2]

The following day Bob Cooney was informed by the 15th Brigade staff of the plans to withdraw the International Brigades. But the British could not return home quite yet, for they were needed for one last action which would allow the Spanish troops who were to replace them enough time to move into position. Cooney assured the battalion's commissars that they would only be at the front for a short time before they were relieved 'for a long rest'.[3] Nevertheless, he instructed the commissars not to inform the men. Many of them, even some officers, were thus unaware that this would be the British Battalion's final action in Spain:

> While some members of the British Battalion and some members of the XVth Brigade may have known of Negrín's intentions, I most certainly did not. Nor for that matter do I know of one man in my Company who knew what was afoot. As far as No. 2 Company was concerned we were simply going into action again: we had no inkling that we were about to embark on our final fight with the Fascists.[4]

Despite the secrecy, many discovered the truth, or were at least able to guess. And some in the battalion viewed the prospect of one last action with severe misgivings:

> We were going in for our last fight on Spanish soil. Our thoughts inevitably turned to our homes in Britain and the loved ones who waited for our return. We could not help but speculate on our chances of coming out alive. It was a cruel test.[5]

Bobby Walker remembered thinking, 'Well, I've lasted so long, so if I can survive twenty-four hours it will be good.'[6]

Therefore on 21 September, late at night, the 15th International Brigade was recalled to the front to replace the 13th (Dombrowski) Brigade, which had suffered heavy losses at Sierra de Lavall de la Torre, just south of the main road halfway between Gandesa and Ascó. Initially held back, on 23 September the battalion, still under the command of George Fletcher, moved up to the front for their final action on Spanish soil.

> While we were marching up to the front, I saw lying on the footpath close to where we were going a small book and since anything to read is better than nothing, I bent down and found to my great delight it was a copy of the old Temple Press edition of *As You Like It* by William Shakespeare. So the whole day of September 23 when we were crouching behind a wall and waiting to be called up from the reserve into the front line two to three hundred yards ahead, I managed to not just read but learn by heart considerable stretches of the play, which I must say is a very effective way of taking your mind off the fact that shells are exploding left and right of you at frequent intervals.[7]

Their position was neither safe nor easy; in fact it was dangerously exposed, dominated by higher ground from which Franco's forces sprayed the battalion's positions with machine-gun and rifle fire:

Unfortunately we had been put up overnight on to a hill which had defences already prepared for us by the engineers. But the defences were prepared on the wrong side of the hill. They were prepared on the forward slope of the hill, in full view of the enemy. They should have been prepared on the reverse side of the hill, so that the enemy would have had to come at us over the crest, and where also we would have been immune from machine gun and tank fire. That in fact was the downfall of the Company, because on the very last day that we were in, not long after daylight I was in position on the right flank of the Company and we were strung round this hill in trenches, some of which were only two or three feet deep. They had not been dug nearly deep enough.[8]

Sheltering from the withering Nationalist fire as best they could, the exhausted troops attempted to dig defensive positions in between the Canadians to their left and the Americans on their right. However, many were so tired that they fell asleep and one group, located out in front of the main position, awoke on the morning of 23 September to find themselves surrounded by Nationalist soldiers pointing machine guns at them. They were taken prisoner and quickly led away.[9]

The day's action began with a five-hour artillery barrage, and only intensified as 'Franco's army attacked and attacked, again and again with his artillery, tanks, aircraft and his infantry.' Completely overwhelmed, the Americans were forced to retire, bringing the British under attack from the positions previously occupied by the Lincolns: 'we seemed to get into position just as they prepared to attack and the shells and tanks came over.'[10] Major Attlee Company bore the brunt, remaining stubbornly in their positions until their trenches were overrun.[11] 'They were just coming down on top of them from the rear. There was nothing we could do about it,' remembered John Dunlop.[12] Many were killed or captured in the brutal hand-to-hand fighting, including a number who had been in Spain ever since the battles of Madrid during the winter of 1936.

We had a warm time almost from the start. Never before had I experienced such a pounding as the enemy guns inflicted on us. The ground trembled beneath us. Almost before one shell exploded we felt the crash of the next. Our brains reeled from the concussion. The trenches we occupied had suffered from the previous day's bombardment. Today's affair threatened to destroy them entirely. At some points the parapet was blown away and we could only move along the trench by clambering over mounds of earth and rock, thus exposing us to infantry fire.

Towards midday, our position became untenable. The hill on our right flank was occupied by the enemy with the result that we came under enfilading fire from the right, gradually creeping round to our rear. The artillery bombardment intensified and under cover of the barrage the Moors came over – a savage yelling horde. There was a hand to hand fight for the trench, but the result was obvious from the start.[13]

With enemy fire seemingly coming from all sides, communication quickly broke down and it became virtually impossible for the battalion to do anything more than take shelter from the hail of bullets. Then the order was given to retreat. In the mayhem, two machine-gun teams were left behind and temporarily forgotten:

When I went outside, there's nobody there. So I got out of the trench and had a look round the hill and the bloody hill's deserted! So I went back, I said, 'There's nobody here, only me and you!' 'Oh,' he said, 'Let's break the gun down and get away then! They must have retreated.'. . . Just as we were doing that, Jack Nulty [actually Nalty] . . . the machine-gun commander came up. He said, 'Come on you two . . . I've had to come back for you. I forgot you two were here!' . . . Down the hill we went, to the bottom . . . and Johnny Logan [Lobban] and one or two more were there taking a rest. We only had a few more yards to go and we would've been with the battalion . . . [but] they'd got to the top by then, set their machine guns up and sprayed us . . . And Jack Nulty got shot through the head, he got killed; Johnny Logan was killed; Cliff Lacey, Bill Feely got wounded . . . And that was on the day after we should've been withdrawn.[14]

At 1 a.m. the order finally arrived withdrawing the 15th International Brigade from the line. In its final forty-eight hours' fighting, some two hundred members of the battalion were killed, wounded or missing.[15] A great many men who had been talking, only twenty-four hours earlier, of their return home, never made it back: 'We lost a great deal of men in these two days, men who would have come home,' remembered one heartbroken Scottish volunteer.[16] While Bobby Walker managed to get through the day, one of his friends did not. Walker did what little he could for his companion in his last few moments of life:

> Little Johnny Logan was on a stretcher and he asked me for a cigarette. I said to him [that] I could hear him breathing through a hole in his chest, over his lung. I said, 'No Johnny, you don't want a cigarette' . . . Finally I realised he'd probably be dead before we got to the ambulance, so he had his cigarette.[17]

Their last action had been just 'as bloody as any other battles the Battalion had fought'.[18] The battalion observer, Ivor Hickman from Southampton, 'was killed by almost the last bullet of the day whilst reconnoitring the enemy positions'.[19] George Green from Stockport, who had originally driven to Spain for Spanish Medical Aid in an ambulance with Stephen Spender, had later transferred to fight with the International Brigades. While serving with the battalion at Hill 481, he had received a minor head wound and his wife, Nan, who was working at Valdeganga hospital, had helped patch him up:

> Learning of the coming withdrawal [of the International Brigades] George had insisted on returning to the Battalion to take part in the final action with his British fellow-soldiers. He came through our HQ with a note stating that he had been discharged from hospital at his own request. We spent an hour together eagerly discussing which of us would reach England first, and how it would come about; who would see the children first – and we agreed that George should not shave off his beard until they had seen it, because Grandpa Green [who was looking after their two children while they were in Spain] had told us that they were fascinated by the idea of a bearded daddy. The 22 September had been fixed for the withdrawal of the British Battalion, our little group in the Divisional HQ (mostly drivers, mechanics, American and Canadian) was to engage in training their Spanish successors and we had no date fixed for our departure . . . The 22 September came and went. Though I was still at the front, I sighed with relief that George was not on the casualty lists I had studied daily with dread.
> On the night of the 23rd, two chaps came and wakened me.
> 'George is missing,' they said.[20]

Green had gone to Spain because he strongly believed that fascism 'which is threatening everybody's home and everybody's safety . . . can be decisively beaten in Spain and if it is beaten in Spain then it is beaten forever as a world force'.[21] But – in a personal tragedy for Nan and their two children – George, 'who . . . came out of hospital still with his old wounds bandaged up, was to die in the last hour of the 23rd September 1938.'[22]

Several days later, Peter Kerrigan wrote to Harry Pollitt, expressing in a letter which he described as 'the most difficult I have ever written in my life' his shock at the terrible outcome of the last British action:

> The irony of it is that this last action took place on September 23rd, the day <u>after</u> Dr. Negrin's speech at Geneva, which announced the repatriation of the volunteers . . . I could give dozens of individual acts of heroism but what is the use. The list of citations which I enclose, tells in brief official terms of the acts of deathless glory which were played out against a background of the cutting to pieces of our very bravest. I was at the beginning of the British Battalion. I saw what No. 1 Coy. came through at Córdoba and I will never forget when I was told what our casualties were in those first 3 days at Jarama. But nothing can compare with the end of our battalion.[23]

Former battalion commander Fred Copeman, now back home in Britain, was devastated that 'the war in Spain had ended in defeat' and severely depressed to think of 'so many fine lads [who] had died, had given their all'.[24] It was a tragic and heart-breaking end to their time in Spain, though, in many ways, a fitting final act. Despite their unquestionable bravery, the men in the British Battalion were simply outnumbered and outgunned. Raw courage and a belief in the essential 'rightness' of their cause 'could not overcome inexperience, poor coordination and superior military force'.[25]

The battalion was finally withdrawn in the evening of 24 September and its few remaining British members made their way back across the Ebro to the safety of Republican Catalonia. Fred Thomas managed to hitch a lift with a friend in a lorry: they sat 'sombrely, sadness and joyous relief making a hash of our emotions . . . if either of us wondered what had been achieved since we went over that pontoon bridge on the 26th July, the thought remained unspoken.'[26] Two days later the battalion was posted to the small village of Guiamets, near Marsa, 'where', Bob Cooney remembered, 'we entered billets for the first time since December 1937.'[27] There, during the evening of 30 September 1938, the British were brought up to date on the current political situation beyond Spain:

> We heard news of the sell-out by Britain and France of Czechoslovakia. And in the darkened church of Guiamets where we were billeted, we listened to Bob Cooney telling us about the Munich settlement and we knew it wasn't bringing us peace, it was bringing us war.[28]

At the end of 'a long, tragic, but exciting meeting', the surviving members of the battalion stood up and repeated a pledge made by Cooney: 'We will never rest until the Chamberlain government is destroyed and Czechoslovakia is restored to its proper frontiers of 1938.'[29] John Peet wrote a bitter letter home to his parents, railing against Chamberlain's signing of the Munich agreement which had cravenly given in to Hitler's demands for the absorption of the Sudetenland, the areas of Czechoslovakia lying alongside the German border, into his Greater Germany:

> At first, people here simply could not credit the betrayal of Czechoslovakia by Chamberlain. Although the British Government only followed the same road of concession to fascism which they have been following for years, people had a hope that somebody would wake up before it was too late. War has been postponed, but nobody can possibly believe that Hitler will rest content with the Sudeten German areas, when apparently he can have anything for the threatening – as long as it isn't our 'Empire'.[30]

The surviving volunteers drew two conclusions from their fight in Spain and the Munich settlement: first 'that the Spanish Republican Government was going to be defeated' and second 'that the Second World War was now inevitable'. 'They were,' acknowledged Hugh Sloan, 'both depressing conclusions.'[31] While anger at what they saw as British duplicity ran high, it was tinged with sadness and regret.

These feelings came to a head on 5 October, when the British members of the battalion bid a painful farewell to their Spanish comrades, who were returning to the front to continue the fight. In a brief ceremony, Sam Wild presented the battalion and Spanish banners to the Spanish commander, Lieutenant – now Captain – Cipriano. Two hundred Spaniards formed a line of threes and broke out in the Republican national anthem, *El Himno de Riego*, as the Spanish Battalion of the 15th International Brigade set off back to the front. Welsh volunteer Edwin Greening was one of many to watch through floods of tears.[32]

> Finally, the now completely Spanish 35th Division, headed by 25 year old Pedro Maten Merino, formed ranks and marched off to the West – back to the Ebro holocaust on the right bank of the river, while we foreign volunteers marched in the opposite direction – towards the East.[33]

The volunteers were sent north to await repatriation. On their way, however, they took part in the first of two events which had been planned to formally mark the withdrawal of the International Brigaders from Spain. On 17 October all the foreign volunteers in the 35th Division were reviewed at a big rally, just outside the town of Vimbodi, thirty-five kilometres north of Tarragona, in front of André Marty and Luigi Longo, the commanders of the International Brigades.[34] Several British and Irish volunteers received promotions and commendations: both Malcolm Dunbar and Sam Wild were promoted to major, and John Power, the Irish political commissar who had tried vainly to persuade the Irish contingent to remain with the British Battalion at Madrigueras in early 1937, was promoted to captain.[35]

The volunteers were then driven by truck to Ripoll in northern Catalonia, twenty-five kilometres south of the border with France, where they arrived on 18 October. The 350 British were housed in a freezing cold theatre where they slept as best they could, wrapped up in all their belongings. In his history of the British in Spain, Bill Alexander later casually remarked how they 'were comfortably housed' at Ripoll, but the volunteers who were there saw it very differently: 'There was no heating and it was bitterly cold. We slept, fully clothed, overcoats as well,' insisted Welsh veteran Edwin Greening.[36] Meanwhile, preparations for the return to civilian life continued:

> This was no longer an army. The organisation was there; from Brigade to Company to Squad. There were officers and there were ranks. They ate and slept in different places and maintained the facade of a military hierarchy, but there was a difference. It was transitional and everybody knew it. Tomorrow, or the next day, we would become just Tom, Dick, or Jack – with no distinction.[37]

They remained at Ripoll until the evening of 28 October, when they were driven to Barcelona in preparation for a final, farewell parade in front of a huge, cheering crowd, held underneath the protection of Republican planes flying overhead. After the terrible experiences suffered by the volunteers, the Spanish population's emotional expressions of gratitude towards the men and women from around the world who had risked – and all too often given – their lives could not help but remain with them for many years. As one Welsh brigader proudly remembered, it was his fellow-countryman, Jim Brewer of Rhymney, who carried the flag at the head of the British Battalion 'as we marched and sang the songs of the British and international working class'.[38] For Brewer, the flag-bearer, it was a sombre reminder of the losses the battalion had suffered: 'It was a very poignant moment because you were thinking about the chaps who wouldn't be coming back and all the battles that you'd been in and then there was the bloody shame of leaving the Spanish people in that situation.'[39]

The remnants of the International Brigades, a few thousand in all, set off nine abreast, led by military bands, from the bull ring at the end of Diagonal, one of the city's main thoroughfares. The 15th International Brigade, the last to be established, brought up the rear and as the parade set off, John Peet quickly discovered that 'keeping in step proved difficult, because bands all along the route played different marching tunes.'[40] The crowds did not make marching with military precision any easier, for 'all the girls of Barcelona apparently wanted to kiss and embrace "the heroes" . . . at one point I was actually forced to my knees as the girls embraced me.'[41] Suffering from malaria, Bob Cooney joined his fellow convalescent Sam Wild on a balcony overlooking Diagonal, from which they watched the volunteers march past.

> As the Battalion marched, hundreds of thousands of flowers were thrown by the vast multitude of people. I shall never forget the tears the Internationals shed, and the tears the young and old men and women of Spain and Catalonia showed on their faces as we marched by them. I felt proud and very sorrowful.[42]

At the end of the parade, a huge rally was held at which important Republican figures, including President Manuel Azaña and Prime Minister Juan Negrín, expressed their thanks to the Internationals. For many the final parade was the highlight of a poignant day: 'It was really emotional,' said one volunteer, 'I think I saw more tears from people in the streets than I've seen all my life.'[43] The description of the parade by former anti-tank volunteer Fred Thomas captured the full emotion of the occasion:

> For an hour and a half we made our slow way through some of the principal streets in one long glut of emotional excess. I was not the only Brigader sometimes reduced to tears: we, who were leaving the fight, were yet receiving the heartfelt homage of the Spanish people.
>
> In the street of the 14th April the March ended, and then came the speeches. From a platform full of important people from many countries as well as of the Republic, Dr. Negrín, Prime Minister, addressed us and the vast crowds. Then came President Azaña followed by the chief of the Army of the Ebro. Finally we recognised the spare figure of the indomitable 'La Pasionaria' who quickly had the crowd roaring their approval of her every word . . . one sentence stands out – 'Come back, as honoured sons of Spain.'[44]

The famous speech of gratitude delivered to the Internationals by Dolores Ibárruri, the Communist deputy from Asturias forever known as *La Pasionaria*, was characteristically eloquent, even if British nurse Patience Darton could not see Pasionaria for her tears.[45]

> It is very difficult to say a few words in farewell to the heroes of the International Brigades, both because of what they are and what they represent. A feeling of sorrow, an infinite grief catches our throat – sorrow for those who are going away, for the soldiers of the highest ideal of human redemption, exiles from their countries, persecuted by the tyrants of all peoples – grief for those who will stay here forever mingled with the Spanish soil, in the very depth of our heart, hallowed by our feeling of eternal gratitude.
>
> From all peoples, from all races, you came to us like brothers, like sons of immortal Spain; and in the hardest days of the war, when the capital of the Spanish Republic was threatened, it was you, gallant comrades of the International Brigades, who helped save the city with your fighting enthusiasm, your heroism and your spirit of sacrifice.
>
> And Jarama and Guadalajara, Brunete and Belchite, Levante and the Ebro, in immortal verses sing of the courage, the sacrifice, the daring, the discipline of the men of the International Brigades.

For the first time in the history of the peoples' struggles, there was the spectacle, breath-taking in its grandeur, of the formation of International Brigades to help save a threatened country's freedom and independence – the freedom and independence of our Spanish land.

Communists, Socialists, Anarchists, Republicans – men of different colours, differing ideology, antagonistic religions – yet all profoundly loving liberty and justice, they came and offered themselves to us unconditionally.

They gave us everything – their youth or their maturity; their science or their experience; their blood and their lives; their hopes and aspirations – and they asked us for nothing. But yes, it must be said, they did want a post in battle, they aspired to the honour of dying for us.

Banners of Spain! Salute these many heroes! Be lowered to honour so many martyrs!

Mothers! Women! When the years pass by and the wounds of war are stanched; when the memory of the sad and bloody days dissipates in a present of liberty, of peace and of wellbeing; when the rancours have died out and pride in a free country is felt equally by all Spaniards, speak to your children. Tell them of these men of the International Brigades.

Recount for them how, coming over seas and mountains, crossing frontiers bristling with bayonets, sought by raving dogs thirsting to tear their flesh, these men reached our country as crusaders for freedom, to fight and die for Spain's liberty and independence threatened by German and Italian fascism. They gave up everything – their loves, their countries, home and fortune, fathers, mothers, wives, brothers, sisters and children – and they came and said to us: 'We are here. Your cause, Spain's cause, is ours. It is the cause of all advanced and progressive mankind.'

Today many are departing. Thousands remain, shrouded in Spanish earth, profoundly remembered by all Spaniards. Comrades of the International Brigades: Political reasons, reasons of state, the welfare of that very cause for which you offered your blood with boundless generosity, are sending you back, some to your own countries and others to forced exile. You can go proudly. You are history. You are legend. You are the heroic example of democracy's solidarity and universality in the face of the vile and accommodating spirit of those who interpret democratic principles with their eyes on hoards of wealth or corporate shares which they want to safeguard from all risk.

We shall not forget you; and, when the olive tree of peace is in flower, entwined with the victory laurels of the Republic of Spain – come back!

Return to our side for here you will find a homeland – those who have no country or friends, who must live deprived of friendship – all, all will have the affection and gratitude of the Spanish people who today and tomorrow will shout with enthusiasm – Long live the heroes of the International Brigades![46]

'And that,' said Jim Brewer, 'was the end of our effective service.'[47]

The former brigaders returned to Ripoll to await their repatriation. Meanwhile, determined efforts were made to track down the other Britons still in Spain in their numerous capacities and locations. This was no easy task: John Peet remembered it as 'almost the busiest [time] I have had in Spain. First I was on a delegation going round the hospitals, visiting the wounded comrades, making lists, taking particulars, and so on.'[48] Overall, the attempt resulted in a list of 145 volunteers still with the battalion and another 44 at Ripoll. Other Britons were scattered around the Republican zone: a number at Valencia and Barcelona, some in the Spanish 129th Artillery Division and others in various hospitals whether as patients, or as doctors, nurses and administrators. While the British Communist Party was undoubtedly doing what it could to ensure that no one was forgotten, a letter from the British Secretariat in London to the Spanish Secretariat in Barcelona on 17 November makes it clear that they were also mindful of the potential propaganda value for critics of the Republic of British volunteers rotting in Republican jails.[49] Ten brigaders were released from the brigade jail, though the unfortunate Alec Marcowich was not one of them.[50]

All returning volunteers were required to complete a questionnaire on the nature of their political and military experiences to date and, crucially, their political reliability and potential contribution to the cause in the future. Billy Griffiths assisted the senior American political commissar, Jim Bourne, on a committee convened to decide which members of the battalion were to have the honour of being admitted into the Spanish Communist Party.[51] The questionnaires, and the volunteers' records, were assessed by leading political figures in the Brigades and divided into five categories: cadres, good, fair, weak and bad. André Marty made the definition of 'bad' absolutely clear:

Have shown themselves to be largely useless or harmful to the antifascist cause in Spain. Not all should be regarded as political enemies, but without exception their defects are serious ones, such as constant drunkenness, cowardice coupled with indiscipline, disruptive tendencies, trotskyist tendencies etc.[52]

Even widely respected and senior figures in the battalion were not above harsh criticism. Major Sam Wild, though described as 'disciplined, steady [and] brave' and having performed 'exceedingly well', was nevertheless criticised for having a 'not very good attitude towards Spanish comrades' and for drinking too much.[53] However, it was generally accepted that the Internationals had been essentially used as 'shock troops', and that there was a danger of judging them too harshly:

> The standard set has been a high one. One must bear in mind the fact that the comrades have been tested in exceptionally severe circumstances during many months of fighting, and this has made a very big demand on their political morale and physical resources. Our estimates inevitably reflect to a considerable extent the judgement of the leading Party comrades in the fighting units – a judgement which has generally been severe and has often unconsciously had as the perspective the continuance of the comrades in shock fighting units.[54]

Other assessments were also required before repatriation could begin. On 12 November, each veteran was interviewed by the Evacuation Control Commission and given a visa to return home to Britain. Unfortunately, bureaucracy delayed matters, and as the period of waiting lengthened, tempers began to fray. 'It was a fairly miserable time,' remembered John Peet. 'We were just waiting to go home. There was bad news from the front. The food was miserable, we were high up in the mountains and it was cold as hell and raining.'[55] As Fred Thomas admitted, 'the simple truth was we were all thoroughly sick of this seemingly endless and increasingly unpleasant day-to-day existence'.[56] Telegrams were sent to London trying to establish the cause of the delay and a call was made in the *News Chronicle* for the Internationals' speedy return. Finally, at the beginning of December 1938, following pressure from sympathetic MPs in Britain and a delegation of volunteers lobbying the British consul in Barcelona, 305 British volunteers prepared themselves to leave.[57]

The realisation that they were, finally, about to depart Spain for good brought mixed feelings. Though of course they were anxious to get home, it is clear that many felt that 'they were leaving unfinished the task they had undertaken.'[58] Welsh brigader Edwin Greening was 'glad that the unequal struggle was over, but sad that the people of Spain were being left to fight it out against the combined might of Franco-Italian-German-Portuguese Fascist forces'.[59] Volunteers were warned by the censors not to try and take out journals or diaries, though Fred Thomas fortunately ignored their instructions. Anyway, he found that 'my diaries were passed easily enough by virtue of my having been appointed as Censor!'[60]

On the evening of 5 December, last-minute preparations were made for departure. 'We were issued with civilian suits and I got a very thin suit in a very nasty sort of Levantine mauve,' recalled an unimpressed John Peet.[61] Just after midnight on Tuesday 6 December 1938, the 320 men of the British Battalion lined up and marched smartly through the deserted streets of Ripoll to the railway station. Following speeches from the mayor of Ripoll and André Marty, Bob Cooney replied, 'thanking Ripol[l] for its hospitality and Spain for the privilege of bearing arms against Fascism'.[62] At dawn, the departing volunteers boarded their train, and to the sound of a military band playing the *Internationale*, the train drew slowly out of the town. Thousands of the local population were present to bid the International Brigaders farewell:

> No one could have hoped for a more appreciative, more generous farewell than we. Most of the populace turned out with flags and banners, showing their feelings openly with tears as well as cheers. As our train pulled out of the station, we saw as a last reminder of Spanish friendship, elderly José of our favourite café waving his Left Republican flag and calling out 'Long live our British comrades. Long live the International Brigades!' With almost unbelievable generosity we were each issued with a tin of bully for the short journey to France; gladly I recall that nearly all was handed back at the border.[63]

The final entry in John Peet's Spanish army pay book stated: 'Authorised to leave for France with 200 French francs [about £2].' 'So much for the mercenaries of the International Brigades,' he wrote. As the train approached the French border, Percy Ludwick took his final look at the Republic he had fought to save:

The last person we saw on Spanish soil was an old peasant woman, dressed in black, with a black headdress on, standing on the railway embankment. She raised her right hand as the carriage passed her and gave us the clenched fist Popular Front salute. We returned the salute and shouted, 'Viva la Republica Española!' We were glad, very glad to have remained alive, to be on our way home to be reunited with our dear ones. But we also felt sorry, very sorry, for leaving Spain.[64]

With the battalion's departure, only a few British and Irish still remained in Spain, such as Sam Lesser who was working as a broadcaster in Barcelona, and Lon Elliott, based at the headquarters of the political commissars in Madrid. One of their final tasks was to box up the records of the British Battalion, which were later sent to Moscow for safekeeping.[65] Several medical workers also remained behind to continue their work in the Republican medical services. English nurse Lillian Urmston accompanied the pitiful retreat of Republican refugees into France:

I don't know how many babies I delivered, I don't remember how many sick animals I looked after, but quite often mules were wounded that could still be used and it's a horrible thing to give first aid to a wounded mule and then watch it be loaded and made to pull its load up steep hills towards the base of the Pyrenees.[66]

Urmston was able to cross the border without too much difficulty, as she still had her passport, which she had shrewdly hidden in her underwear when she arrived in Spain. However, alongside other refugees, she was then imprisoned in an internment camp in Elne, just south of Perpignan. The French authorities demanded that the refugees be separated by nationality but, determined that they should remain together, 'we refused, so they put more barbed wire around us and said until we obeyed orders there was no water.' They were eventually transferred to a concentration camp at Argelés-sur-Mer, on the Mediterranean coast five kilometres south-east of Elne, which over time received up to 100,000 refugees. In the camp there was effectively no food or water: 'I'll never forget the sight of gaunt, emaciated men, women and children giving the clenched fist salute and saying "we'll meet again in Spain when it's free."'

After two weeks Urmston was released from the camp by the British consul, though she initially refused to leave her Spanish friends and comrades. Like the former International Brigaders who had already departed, Urmston left with a heavy heart, feeling that she was deserting her friends and comrades: 'at the station the horror of what I was doing leaving the Spanish people [struck me] and I broke down and cried.' The departure of Scottish nurse Annie Murray was similarly tinged with sadness, though her final experience of Barcelona also left her with a memory she found difficult to forget:

> As we were coming out of Spain – the Fascists were getting to Barcelona as we were getting out – I was with the Spanish surgeon and some of the others as we came through Barcelona. We found a whole lot of children, oh, dozens of them, with their hands off, completely off. The Italians had dropped anti-personnel bombs marked 'Chocolate', 'Chocolatti'. The children were picking up these things – they hadn't had chocolate for years – and they just blew their hands off. This Spanish surgeon that I worked with, he was in tears. We all were.[67]

But by far the largest number of British still in Spain were those taken prisoner during the retreats in the spring and the battalion's final battles in August and September 1938. By the time Franco triumphantly declared the end of the civil war on 1 April 1939, most former volunteers had been repatriated. Some, however, such as the popular Irish Republican leader Frank Ryan, would never return.

19

'You'll all be shot!'

There's a prison in Spain called Palencia
'Tis a place we know all too well
It was there that we gave of our manhood
And spent months of misery and hell.

Surrounded one day by Italians
Who with guns bought by Chamberlain's gold
Blown to hell by artillery and avion
That's how our brave comrades were sold.

Alternative version of Jarama song, by British
prisoners of war in Spain[1]

Many International Brigaders taken prisoner by the Nationalists were never heard from again. No doubt they had been summarily executed and buried in unmarked graves – most, especially if they were officers, machine gunners or, in particular, political commissars, were killed on sight, following Franco's proclamation of 9 March 1937 that any foreigners captured under arms would be shot.[2]

The order was officially rescinded in April 1938 in response to pressure from Mussolini, who wanted to barter the volunteers for Italian soldiers captured by the Republicans, and a warning from the British government, who wrote to Franco promising 'the strongest possible reaction on the part of H.M. Government if the clauses relating to the Geneva Convention were not rigorously adhered to'. But even after this date prisoners continued to be executed. A secret report compiled by a member of the British consular staff at the end of the war admitted: 'I am informed confidentially that any International Brigader taken in the Ebro offensive was asked one question, "When did you come to Spain?" If he replied after the 19th July 1936 he was shot *sin formacion de causa*.'[3]

Aware of the Nationalists' attitude towards foreign *Rojos*, Italian soldiers at Calaceite, scene of the disastrous ambush on 31 March, went through the pockets of their prisoners charitably 'destroying incriminating literature, removing signs of rank from officers' uniforms, assuring the captured Internationals that they'd be better treated if they appeared to be only ordinary soldiers'.[4] The grateful British volunteers, realising that this might save their lives, readily agreed; not surprisingly, Communist Party members wisely kept a low profile.[5] Nevertheless, one group of prisoners was marched to the main square in Calaceite by members of the *Guardia Civil* and lined up against a wall in front of machine guns. The volunteers had little doubt as to what was about to happen: 'We thought, "this is it."'[6] However, the group was very fortunate; they were spotted by an American journalist accompanying several Italian army officers who, aware of the Internationals' value in a prisoner exchange, managed to persuade the *Guardia Civil* not to shoot them. Stunned, though now thoroughly relieved, the prisoners were led away and locked up.

Salford Communist Joe Norman was one of a group taken off to be incarcerated in Gandesa, which had recently fallen to the Nationalists:

We heard the tide of battle rolling further away. We felt very lonely. We passed back down the road, with hands on heads, back to Gandesa. We had had nothing to eat for 2 days, we were tired, hungry, miserable and forlorn. We did not feel any better after we had been sneered at by a *Daily Express* reporter.

We sat on the ground in the town square when he came up and started asking questions, to which he did not care for the answers. He stood jeering and sneering at us for some time and then he left with the remark, 'You'll all be shot.'

Nobody bothered to bid him farewell.[7]

Over the next two or three days, other prisoners were gradually brought together in a disused church in the Italian-controlled town of Alcañiz. Conditions offered a nasty foretaste of the treatment the prisoners could expect in the Nationalist zone. The sanitary facilities were appalling, with 'excrement being piled a yard thick . . . The stench from this filth and from empty sardine and meat tins was terrible.'[8] When the prisoners were transported the 100 kilometres by train to the military academy in Zaragoza, they were crammed into cattle trucks, 'packed in so close we had to stand for the whole 36 hours of the journey. We could scarcely move and we had nothing to eat.'[9]

Over one hundred British and Irish prisoners of war were eventually brought together in Zaragoza, where the guards had orders to shoot at anyone showing themselves at the windows. The captured International Brigaders were instructed that they would now be required to salute in the fascist style, though the demand was bravely and ingeniously subverted:

> We came to this decision: we'd make a compromise. On the command to give the Fascist salute we would raise our hand and give the British salute, raise our hand slightly and then back again to the forehead and down. This was the compromise. Now you've never seen such a shambles. When the order was given it was like seeing a hundred tick-tack men at a racecourse, all waving their arms about in different directions . . . So the question of a salute fell by the wayside.[10]

The prison authorities reluctantly abandoned their demands for the fascist salute, which was celebrated by the prisoners as a welcome and badly-needed 'morale-boosting victory'.[11] The salute was soon revealed to have been conceived in preparation for a forthcoming visit by representatives of the foreign press sympathetic to Franco, and, on 3 April, the American *New York Times* reporter William Carney and the British correspondent for *The Times* Kim Philby arrived at Zaragoza. To demonstrate Nationalist generosity, the prisoners were given a meal, including an apple, just prior to the reporters' arrival. However, in a more honest demonstration of their captors' attitude, the apples were promptly taken back once the reporters had departed.

Carney sent back glowing reports of the Rebels' treatment of prisoners, describing how 'foreigners were treated exactly like Spanish prisoners.'[12] His reports were later lampooned in a cartoon called 'As Mr Carney Saw Us' by Jimmy Moon, a laboratory technician from London, which portrayed the prisoners relaxing in comfortable surroundings.[13] While Carney was no supporter of the International Brigades, his reportage of the camp in the *New York Times* nevertheless served to bring international attention to bear on the prisoners' plight. As Irish POW Bob Doyle realised, this 'triggered the start of moves by the US State Department for our release, and to increase pressure on the regime in Spain to improve conditions'.[14]

The visiting foreign reporters were accompanied by Don Pablo Merry del Val, the son of the Ambassador to London. The prisoners were informed that del Val, who spoke perfect English, would be interviewing them and that all would have their fingerprints taken.

As some prisoners quickly realised, this placed young Scottish volunteer Jimmy Rutherford in mortal danger. Rutherford had been a member of the Machine-Gun Company captured at Jarama the previous year and, as a condition of his release, had signed a pledge not to return to Spain. During his second spell in Spain Rutherford had wisely adopted the *nom de guerre* of Jimmy Smalls to disguise his identity. Aware that Rutherford's real identity was in danger of being uncovered, Joe Norman tried to help: 'We knew Jimmy was in trouble. We had a quick discussion . . . and it was decided that I should take Jimmy's place in the finger print line up. We all kept our fingers crossed.'[15] Norman's fellow Party member and hunger marcher, Garry McCartney, was standing next in line to Rutherford; when 'Merry del Val, passing up the ranks, had passed Jimmy [by] two or three steps,' he thought that the ruse had worked. But their hopes were dashed when del Val turned around, walked back to take a closer look at Rutherford and said to him, 'I've seen you before.'[16] The unfortunate Rutherford was promptly led away, and on 24 May 1938 he was shot for contravening the agreement he had signed the previous May.[17]

Three days after the fateful parade, the other British and Irish prisoners were taken out of the camp and marched to the railway station. On the way, the humming of 'revolutionary marching tunes' by some caused a certain amount of conflict between the prisoners, with several complaining that this would lead to further punishment. Four men were particularly unhappy and 'offered to throw in their lot with the Fascists'. They were not the only ones feeling disheartened and demoralised; numerous prisoners were deeply apprehensive of the fate awaiting them:[18]

Particularly at the beginning there were many who had bad reactions to the general conditions. Nerves were on edge, and emotions subject to violent vacillations. Even some of the Party members were subject to despondency and the next moment to the highest optimism. From their own subjective reactions, comrades' opinions were expressed to the following effect – the war will soon be over; there was sabotage and traitors in the Battalion; the C.P. was to blame for our position – we will soon be tried; sentence may be death or long imprisonment; we will be taken from the concentration camp to prisons or put to work; our people at home do not know anything about us; we may never get out of here etc. – and then to the hopeful opinions that we would be released soon, that it would be good propaganda for Franco to let us go.[19]

The anxious prisoners were transferred by train from Zaragoza to Burgos, in the heart of Nationalist Spain. During the two-day journey the prisoners were hardly fed and were allowed even less exercise. Late in the evening of 8 April, they finally arrived at their destination: the 'sinister and forbidding' prison camp established in the old decaying monastery of San Pedro de Cardeña, fourteen kilometres south-east of Burgos. The convent, built in 1711 on the site of the first Benedictine monastery in Spain, was, so they were told, 'the last resting place of El Cid', but by the time the British prisoners arrived it was in a state of decay: 'only the scale of its architecture gave any inkling as to its earlier grandeur.'[20] As they were marched through the massive wooden gates, one prisoner, looking up, noticed that 'ironically, the monumental work over the main doorway was that of a horseman, lance in hand, on a fiery charger, trampling down Moors.'[21]

As Joe Norman quickly discovered, the conditions in what was, essentially, a concentration camp were brutal, overcrowded and insanitary:

More than 600 I[international] B[rigad]ers from 20 different countries were all crammed into one long room that looked like a dungeon. [The] walls were 6 feet thick and the floors were made of stone. Even [in] the middle of the day the light was so bad [that] you could hardly see to the other end of the room.[22]

The Internationals were packed together in the 'very unpleasant' living quarters, which were shared with the 'mice and rats on the floor',[23] there were not enough blankets and there was 'little light and awful ventilation'.[24] 'San Pedro,' summarised Walter Gregory succinctly, 'was a terrible place.'[25]

For the first few weeks, keeping clean was impossible, as there was only one tap for the entire group of 600 men.[26] Conditions improved marginally when the Internationals were divided between the second and third floors and had three taps between them. However, as a number of the prisoners later reported, this still only allowed 'five minutes per person per day to wash our plates three times, wash ourselves and our clothes. Obviously,' the report continued, 'with such restrictions and little clothing, we were bound to be filthy.'[27]

For many prisoners, 'worst of all was the lavatory convenience, which was outside in the square.'[28] There were so many prisoners and so few toilets that inmates often had to queue for hours. There was 'no water, so the faeces were piling up and sometimes that was about two feet high'.[29] As numerous British prisoners were suffering from stomach-related illnesses such as dysentery, they were not always able to restrain themselves while waiting in the long toilet queues, which added considerably to everyone's misery.[30]

Not surprisingly, such filthy and insanitary conditions proved a fertile breeding ground for fleas and lice: 'Up in the front lines on the Republican side we all had lice,' admitted Garry McCartney. 'But that was nothing to the millions of lice and fleas that were part and parcel of every hour that we were in that prison camp.'[31] As former battalion runner Tony Gilbert remembered, 'they became a part of us. There was no way of getting rid of them.'[32]

Any prisoner still carrying combat wounds, or who fell ill while in the camp, could expect little help. Diseases such as scurvy, malaria and enteric fever were widespread, for medical facilities were extremely limited, with only five doctors divided between the International prisoners. As always, difficulties were caused by language problems and on occasions medical workers misunderstood descriptions of symptoms. One volunteer from Liverpool suffering from constipation was treated for diarrhoea for several days before the mistake was recognised.[33] The situation was certainly not improved by the hospital; described by one volunteer as little more than a 'shed where the men were lying in the corner', it was run by priests, who were not generally sympathetic to the International prisoners. It is hardly surprising that during their imprisonment in San Pedro de Cardeña 'several died . . . they just pined away'.[34] In fact many volunteers were absolutely convinced that this was no accident, but that 'they were letting people die off. That's what it amounted to,' believed Bruce Allender.[35]

The inhospitable conditions were exacerbated by the dire lack of decent food. As the prisoners quickly realised, 'the food wasn't enough to keep us going,' and most were virtually starving.[36] The principal diet consisted of a thin soup of warm water flavoured with olive oil, garlic and breadcrumbs, accompanied by one small bread roll per day.[37] At lunchtime and in the evening the prisoners were also fed a spoonful of white beans which, very occasionally, contained a small piece of pork fat. The issue of food stretched prisoners' self-discipline to the limit and was the cause of numerous arguments, particularly on the rare occasions when the meagre rations were augmented with sardines. These were served in large frying pans, around which the ravenous prisoners would crowd, hoping to grab the opportunity to scoop some of the nutritious oil onto their meagre portions of bread. The occasional chance of a second helping caused a further frantic scramble: 'When all were served, some prisoners would dive towards the pot when the sergeants weren't looking.'[38]

Many prisoners soon accepted that it was vital to prevent the degrading spectacle of men scrabbling for food, which the Nationalist guards seized upon both as confirmation of their prejudices towards the prisoners and as an excuse to beat the desperate, starving men. Alarmed at the widespread feelings of demoralisation and anger directed at the Party and Brigade leadership, a number of Party members had already surreptitiously made themselves known to each other. Despite the dangers associated with political activity, they formed a Communist Party committee to try and help restore discipline and, with it, morale.[39] Only four days after their capture at Calaceite, Danny Gibbons, a Communist Party branch secretary and member of the General and Municipal Workers' Union in London, had convened a meeting of Party cadres and established a committee – known by the other prisoners as 'the secret six'.[40] Determined attempts were made by members of the committee and other senior figures to persuade prisoners to exercise greater self-discipline, to behave 'as members of the International Brigade and not as defeated and demoralised prisoners', despite the provocation and their starving conditions.[41]

> When we were taken down for food there were two huge bins of soup or something akin to soup, and we were told: 'Help yourself.' No queues. And hungry men, not knowing how to speak to each other, going forward, putting in a cup or a plate and pulling it out, with the Fascist guards standing by with their riding crops and sticks beating us in order that we did not linger over taking what was within the bins. This was the kind of treatment. Now we couldn't continue in a situation like that. And we, the British, through the committee, organised a queue. We decided that we should get away from the camp as mentally and physically fit as possible. So we suggested through the committee to the various Internationals they should follow the lead of the British.
>
> And we went out first on the following day or so and we lined up in file in order to move forward to get the food. The rest of the prisoners followed

behind the two files that we had made, thereby denying the opportunities of the Fascists to say, 'This was only a rabble, we'll have to beat them to get some sense into them.' And this was a good tactic that we started off. The queue became part and parcel of our routine. It didn't matter who was first or whatever. But we followed in a queue, rather than going up in a charging mob to grab the food that the Fascists would have loved to see us continue to do, so they would have the opportunity of beating us indiscriminately.

I am in no doubt that the Fascists did this as a means of deliberately humiliating the prisoners. No question about it. It wasn't just a question of inefficiency on their part. They did this quite deliberately.[42]

Numerous former inmates of San Pedro recount the widespread brutality of the regime and the violence meted out to the prisoners. 'We never dreamt that guards could be so brutal to other human beings,' said Garry McCartney, also a member of the Party Committee.[43] Prisoners were warned that any unwillingness to obey regulations would result in the offenders being 'shot like dogs'; while no prisoners were actually executed at San Pedro, they 'were treated with the utmost cruelty by the guards, being belaboured with heavy bamboo staves and even rifle butts on the flimsiest pretext, or none at all'.[44] Many were convinced that the violence of the jailors was a deliberate attempt to provoke and intimidate them.[45] Certainly, as Dublin IRA veteran Bob Doyle remembered, any sign of resistance was met with an immediate and violent response from the guards:

> We were continually beaten. We were beaten with sticks and rifle butts, we were beaten if we broke ranks and to make us break ranks; before we woke in the morning; when we went to get our food.[46]

The main culprits for the violence were three sergeants, nicknamed 'Froggy', 'Tanky' and 'Sticky', who apparently harboured a general loathing of the brigaders. Froggy, named after his 'bulbous blue eyes', appeared to dislike the British in particular – and the feeling was undoubtedly mutual; one prisoner described him as 'the most disgusting specimen of humanity you will ever see'.[47] 'Tanky' had been wounded in an Italian tank when fighting against the British Battalion at Calaceite on 31 March 1938. He was, thought one prisoner from London, 'a dapper little dandy, a pretty boy with dark, curly hair and a well-trimmed moustache . . . the most evil man that

I ever knew . . . Tanky was the enemy, he hated us like mad.'[48] Beatings were often doled out by 'Sticky', named for his willingness to use a large heavy stick to beat the prisoners: 'with the least provocation and without any . . . [he] would lash out with a heavy stick at all and sundry.'[49] Bob Doyle was sent to the 'sala de tortura' by 'Sticky' for having the temerity to sit down while eating, rather than standing in line as the prisoners had been commanded:

> As I entered I was surrounded by sergeants, including Sticky. 'So you refused to fall in!' they screamed. Before I could answer, four of them closed in and began raining blows on my back, shouting, '¡Rojo! ¡Rojo!' ('Red! Red!') and in their frenzy they sometimes missed their target and hit each other instead. I was wearing only a light khaki shirt. I managed not to scream, doubling up as I protected my face and head with my hands. Two had heavy sticks, another had a heavy strap and Sticky had his favourite 'bull's penis' . . . The beating lasted ten minutes. Sweating and panting, the four called for a soldier to take me back to the others, where I had to stand at attention facing the wall until everyone had been beaten.[50]

Every day a handful of men would be selected for vicious night-time beatings:

> The men would be taken one by one into a small room where there were ten or a dozen Fascists. When the victim entered he immediately received a terrific blow in the face, and he was punched from one man to another right around the room. Then sticks and whips were used. If he fell to the floor he was kicked again to his feet, until finally he could rise no more.[51]

On top of the beatings, prisoners were subjected to interrogation, sometimes by members of the German Gestapo, who were effectively given free rein in the camp. In general the questions concerned the prisoners' political background, why and how they had come to Spain, their rank, who were the officers in their unit and whether they had been bearing arms when captured. As part of the interrogations, Cuban, American and British prisoners were singled out for subjection to psychological tests, which contained two hundred detailed questions relating to their family relations, politics and trade union background. Questions attempted to ascertain whether the prisoners would return to Spain if released, and 'what they thought of the destruction of churches in Red Spain and the murders and assassinations'. Others asked: 'What do you understand by Socialism, Communism, Democracy? To which countries do you give your social sympathies? What do you think of Red Spain, Franco Spain, Soviet Russia, your own country?'[52]

The tests were conducted under the supervision of Antonio Vallejo Nágera, previously a teacher of psychiatry in the Spanish Military Sanitary Academy, assisted by two German scientists and Gestapo agents. Vallejo, who had been appointed chief of the Psychiatric Services of Franco's army, was, if not actually a follower of Nazi race theory, certainly an advocate of 'a personal notion of eugenics' which divided people into groups along the lines of castes.[53] The purpose of his tests was essentially threefold: to confirm fascist notions of racial superiority; to find substantiation for Franco's propaganda; and to discover who were the leading elements in the camp. Or, as Vallejo outlined in a paper published in 1938 on the San Pedro tests, he was attempting 'to establish the high incidence of Marxist fanaticism in the mentally inferior and the presence of antisocial psychopaths in the Marxist masses', and, crucially, whether 'Marxist fanatics' could be transformed through re-education: 'We initiated serial research in Marxist individuals, in order to find the potential relationships that might exist between a subject's biopsychic qualities and political-democratic-communist fanaticism.'[54]

As part of the study, measurements of all parts for the body were taken, especially the head, in line with Nazi anthropometrical theories which attempted to draw links between psychological, physical and racial characteristics: 'One of them measured me, while the other jotted down the readings . . . then I was photographed naked.'[54] Many not surprisingly found this a humiliating experience: 'The indignity was dreadful because we were photographed in the nude, not all of us, but most of us, and I had my privates callipered and why should this be? I don't think I was built extraordinarily different to anyone else.'[56]

The prisoners were unimpressed by the pseudo-scientific nature of the examination and understandably dismissive of its objective, which Bob Doyle believed was a deliberate strategy 'to demoralise us and make out that we were subhuman, and could not be normal to have come and fought in the International Brigades'.[57] As one of Doyle's fellow prisoners succinctly put it, the tests were designed 'to show to the world what a lot of morons we were'.[58] If so, they must have been a great disappointment to Vallejo, who was forced to accept that 'most of the fighters came to help democracy, and many of them proudly confessed their democratic and anti-fascist ideas and were enthusiastic in defending the Republic'.[59] Garry McCartney was certain that some of the answers were not what the interrogators expected, or wanted, to hear:

[We] were given an intelligence test. I was asked two questions: Which eye did Nelson lose in the French wars? And name one of the longest rivers in the United States of America. I mentioned the Mississippi as one of the longer rivers. I didn't know which eye Nelson lost, though I did know he had lost one . . . But there was one lad, he was an English comrade, he was asked a question about the planets. This was his pet subject. Not only did he answer the question that was put to him but he made a further technical observation that must have mesmerised his questioners.[60]

The keen astronomer was actually George Wheeler, the London wood-machinist. Asked to name the planets, Wheeler was confidently able to list them, in the correct order, from Mercury through to Pluto. '"Pluto?" queried an officer. "Pluto" replied Wheeler. "Discovered in 1930 by the American astronomer Clyde Tombaugh."' Realising that his interrogators' information was out of date, Wheeler knew that he had 'scored one over them'. 'There were no more questions,' he remembered with great satisfaction.[61]

Guards thought up other ways to humiliate the prisoners, such as throwing half-smoked cigarettes to them, so they could watch and laugh at the prisoners' nicotine-starved scrabble; when the prisoners got wise to the trick and refused to rise to the bait, they were offered cigarettes to which cordite had been added.[62] A number of prisoners were subjected to the astonishingly sadistic and terrifying experience of being dragged out of their quarters at three o'clock in the morning, 'taken down to the courtyard [and] made to face the wall' as though they were about to be shot.[63]

[A] favourite amusement of the guards was to take a prisoner into the courtyard, stand him against a wall and fire bursts from a machine-gun close to his head and watch the effect. Then, having thoroughly enjoyed their 'joke,' the guards would march him back to the cells again.[64]

Not satisfied with the beatings and other intimidations and humiliations, the camp authorities were determined to break down resistance by forcibly imposing Nationalist values on the prisoners: 'From the first day at San Pedro, we were subjected to Fascist culture . . . [and] the priests, who were political commissars, organized public reading of Fascist literature,' protested the official report.[65] Essentially this required all prisoners to display respect for the Francoist regime and the Catholic Church. Prisoners were forced to attend mass and listen to propaganda speeches given in Spanish (which many of the British and Irish didn't speak); these included a lecture from the Bishop of Burgos, who charmingly addressed them as *'el escombro de la tierra'* (the scum of the earth). Prisoners of all nationalities were instructed to read out Francoist propaganda in their respective language, but the British volunteers' ability to dupe some of the less worldly guards by ingeniously claiming that they were not English, but Scottish, Welsh or even Canadian, made a mockery of the exercise and helped bring it to an end.[66]

At the daily parades all prisoners were ordered to chant Francoist slogans, but here too, as Garry McCartney remembered with great satisfaction, there were opportunities for surreptitious victories:

> We were taken down every night to salute the flag. And the officer of the day or whoever it was that was conducting that ceremony would give the Fascist calls. He would say, *'Espana!'* And all the voices in the courtyard would say: *'Uno!' 'Espana!'* – *'Grande!'* and *'Espana!'* – *'Libre!'* Now we kept quiet with the first two, 'One Spain', a 'Grand Spain'. But when it came to the third one suddenly the 400 voices of the Internationals would shout out *'Libre!'* meaning, 'A free Spain!' It was like a Hampden roar![67]

Prisoners were also instructed that, when saluting, they were to bellow *'¡Fran-co!'*, to be chanted in two distinct syllables. However, many joined in with George Wheeler, who amended the shout to a more satisfying alternative:

> With volume and enthusiasm we English-speaking prisoners shouted 'Fuck You!'
> The guards would come in among us swishing their sticks and yelling *'¡mas fuerte!'* – much louder. And with even greater gusto we would respond with, 'FUCK YOU! . . . FUCK YOU!'[68]

These small victories were important morale-boosters to many of the prisoners and helped to counteract the 'harsh and monotonous environment of San Pedro'. Apart from keeping out of the way of the guards, there was little to occupy the prisoners' time or minds, so a number of activities were devised to distract them. Unofficial lectures were given on suitable subjects, including a history of the International Brigade, Marxian philosophy and, later in the year, 'a good discussion on the Czechoslovakian position'.[69] However, a course of lectures on English working-class history started by Lionel Jacobs, a member of the Communist Party committee, had to be abandoned following pressure from the camp authorities.[70] And although a handwritten newspaper, The San Pedro Jaily News, was published for three months, it was prudently discontinued when copies started falling into the hands of the guards.[71]

Perhaps surprisingly, the prisoners were permitted a May Day celebration, which involved the singing of 'The Valley of Jarama' and 'The Red Flag'. As in the battalion itself, singing was an important and popular activity and in the camp it became a form of protest, lyrics being changed to more apposite versions: 'Hold the Fort' became 'Hold Madrid' and 'Union Men Be Strong' became 'I.B. Men Be Strong'.[72] The success of the May Day event led the Party Committee, or 'House Committee' as it was now known, to organise an international choir in which men from thirty-six different nationalities sang together.

However, 'the most popular way to isolate ourselves from the daily horror of life in the filth of San Pedro' was playing chess, with pieces carved from bread or soap.[73] One German prisoner was so proficient that he could 'play twelve games simultaneously and usually win ten of them', or play blindfolded games and still beat most opponents.[74] Another prisoner, an American who had played chess competitively in the US, gave a series of lectures on the game and recounted famous contests from the past: 'To hear him talking – in our squalid surroundings – with such knowledge about a game once played [by] Napoleon on the island of St. Helena, was an uplifting and inspiring experience,' remembered an eternally grateful George Wheeler.[75]

On 11 June the camp received an official visit from Colonel C.C. Martin, the British military attaché in Burgos. The visit clearly offered the opportunity to raise grievances about the regime at San Pedro, but the Party Committee, worried that some prisoners would be concerned only with their own personal complaints, 'organised responsible comrades to do the talking'.

They were partially successful and managed to raise a number of significant issues, including overcrowding, the presence and role of Gestapo agents and the threat to the German and Italian prisoners, the endemic beatings and the lack of basic medical provision.[76] However, one prisoner who tried to complain personally to Colonel Martin came away from the encounter convinced that 'he was only interested in knowing who in England was responsible for our recruitment.'[77] When a letter from R.W. Robson to the British Foreign Office later in the year referred to the 'alarming and disgusting reports' of the treatment and conditions at San Pedro, the official reply made light of his claims, arguing that 'a member of the staff of our agency at Burgos has paid periodical visits to the camp at San Pedro de Cardena [sic], and I find that his reports do not lend support to the allegations of ill-treatment and bad conditions in the camp.'[78] Accounts of Martin's visit by those in the camp told a different story: that the prisoners' refusal to perform the fascist salute in front of the British attaché, despite the order being given twice, had led to renewed beatings.[79]

The principal and most welcome purpose of Martin's visit was to bring the news that 100 British and Irish prisoners were to be exchanged and moved to Palencia. However, existing suspicions and dislike of British government representatives were not allayed by his instruction that all those exchanged should contribute £4 towards the cost of their repatriation. All the prisoners refused; one suggested that Colonel Martin should perhaps try and collect it from Robson at Litchfield Street. Nevertheless, Martin's information was proved correct when, the following day, 100 prisoners left San Pedro and were taken to the Italian-run camp at Palencia, ninety kilometres away. Unfortunately, here they stayed for four more months, waiting for the Nationalist authorities to receive notice that a similar number of Italian soldiers had been released by the Republicans. Eventually, on Saturday 22 October 1938, confirmation was received and the British were transferred to Ondarreta prison in San Sebastián.[80] Two days later, an initial group of forty British International Brigaders was released and allowed to march over the French border to Irun; they were led by Clive Branson, a talented artist from Battersea, who had made a number of highly accomplished sketches of San Pedro and inmates, such as David Lomon and Alfred Sherman.[81] The group finally arrived back in Britain at Victoria station on the evening of 25 October 1938. The remainder were released over the next few days.

Meanwhile, in San Pedro, there was a slight improvement in conditions during August, probably inspired by the Nationalists' successes on the Ebro battlefield. The prisoners were finally permitted to send and receive post and a small number were lucky enough to receive money. A house fund was organised, to which recipients donated ten per cent. It paid for medicine, writing paper and tobacco and chocolate for prisoners held in solitary confinement.

On 8 September San Pedro was visited by Lady Austen Chamberlain, wife of the half-brother of Prime Minister Neville Chamberlain and a supporter of Franco and Mussolini. In preparation, the camp authorities cynically issued the inmates with clean uniforms and shoes, although the impression they were attempting to create was ruined by marching the prisoners in the rain for an hour before the visitors' arrival. Lady Chamberlain inspected the parading prisoners, asking them as she went along the line why they had gone to Spain. Their unfailing response, 'To prevent fascism', was not well received; nor was their refusal to offer her the fascist salute. She swept out of the camp, affronted.[82]

The temporary improvement in conditions was not to last long. When several British volunteers captured in the Sierra Pandols arrived in September 1938, two new sergeants were put in charge of International Brigade prisoners. The use of violence was correspondingly stepped up, with prisoners regularly being taken out at night to receive beatings for alleged infringements of discipline.

> Their riding crops, loaded, were continually in use. Many comrades were taken out to be beaten. During the day for alleged crimes, they would take the names of prisoners, and last thing at night, take the comrades out, either to stand at attention in the cold, or to be beaten, or more often both.[83]

Matters worsened considerably when, during the night of 13–14 November, six German prisoners managed to escape from the camp, understandably terrified of being sent back to their homeland: 'The Gestapo used to go round the camp telling the Spanish fascists that they would shoot the German I.B.ers when they got back to Germany if the Spanish Fascists didn't.'[84] When the escape was discovered, the guards concluded that other prisoners must have assisted the Germans and the remaining inmates endured what George Wheeler remembered as 'a reign of terror'.[85]

> The captain in charge of the camp, the commandant being absent on leave, paraded us outside and made a speech. He called us cowards, that if we believed in our ideals, we would never have been taken prisoner alive. He would like to invite every foreign Consul to be present to see the lot of us being shot. Such a speech was the prelude to the terrific beatings we underwent for the next few days. Hardly any of the 650 Internationals escaped a blow or beating. The six prisoners who had been on night duty, during the time of the escapes, were horribly beaten. Kennedy, an English prisoner, was one so beaten . . . that he was in hospital for a fortnight.[86]

The German escapees were recaptured only three kilometres from the French border. Brought back to the camp, they were 'savagely beaten'. Their ultimate punishment remains unrecorded, but is not difficult to guess at: 'We never saw or heard from them again,' said George Wheeler.[87]

The Party Committee came under considerable pressure to organise some form of resistance to the upsurge in violence, but they were held back by the belief that the prison authorities were deliberately trying to provoke the prisoners to react. Therefore the committee refused to sanction any form of protest, arguing that many other nationals besides the English would suffer as a result of unilateral resistance. Instead, they proposed writing a letter detailing the brutal excesses exacted within the camp and giving it to Colonel Martin on his next scheduled visit on 20 November. However, Martin never showed up, so a complaint was made to the American consul instead. This precipitated an inspection by the *Guardia Civil*, after which 'matters eased a little,' the official report admitted, although 'blows, beatings and isolation cells continued to the end of our stay.'[88]

As Christmas approached, the prisoners were permitted to organise a concert. The event was seized upon as an opportunity to demonstrate to the camp authorities that, despite the death of a number of comrades, attempts to demoralise them had failed. It was also hoped that a demonstration of culture might foster a less antagonistic climate in the camp and reduce the beatings. This was, in fact, what happened. The authorities' initial refusal to allow rehearsals was lifted following an agreement that no revolutionary songs would be performed and, as Christmas approached, the level of repression did diminish slightly. Beatings became less frequent and the prisoners 'were even taken to a river and given a bar of soap to bathe'.[89]

The Christmas concert was performed in the prisoners' quarters, in front of a 'tantalising back-cloth depicting giant Christmas trees laden with appetising sandwiches, bottles of wine, pairs of fine boots and all the other good things which, to the prisoners, were above price'. It was painted by a talented Swiss scenic artist, and the prisoners apparently 'enjoyed the cynicism'.[90] Performed in front of the guards and their commanding officers, the concert included songs sung by prisoners from a number of different nations:

> The show began with eight German prisoners, who astounded our jailers with their rendition of 'Stille Nacht' and 'O Tannenbaum', after which the audience burst into a round of applause and 'Olé! Olé!', which could be heard all over San Pedro. In the grimness of our surroundings it was impossible to forget that these same Germans had suffered more than anyone from the wrath of the Fascists and the Gestapo and faced a bleak future, even death.[91]

Particularly well-received by the prisoners themselves was a performance of an abridged version of The Barber of Seville, with Cuban Internationals playing the female roles, much to the hilarity of the guards. However, the opera was less well received by some of the senior officers present, who recognised it as a satire of camp life.[92] The show's climax was a performance by an eighty-strong choir comprising Internationals from America and every European country represented in the camp, earning cheers of approval from prisoners and guards alike. For the prisoners, there was an extra, surreptitious pleasure: 'To the inner amusement of all prisoners, at each performance, some of the fleas in our straw sacks left us and established new residence with our guests.'[93]

As 1938 became 1939, the seventy-five British and Irish prisoners remaining at San Pedro continued to hold on to the hope that another prisoner exchange would be arranged. Eventually, on 23 January, most of them left the camp for San Sebastián's grim and overcrowded Ondarreta jail; there they awaited finalisation of the handover arrangements, though with 'no books, no chess, and no opportunity to exercise'.[94] At the end of the following month, sixty-seven were released; but as there were insufficient

Italian prisoners, ten Britons remained in San Sebastián for a further three months, eventually being released, just after the end of the war, on 5 April 1939.[95]

While extremely relieved at their own release, the prisoners were aware that an unfortunate handful of British and Irish still remained in Nationalist hands. These included Tom Jones, a miner from Wrexham, who was only released on 20 March 1940. Prisoners of other nationalities also remained imprisoned in Franco's Spain, and faced an uncertain future:

> We always knew or felt by virtue of the fact that we had the British Government's representative Colonel Martin seeing us on a few occasions, that the British people would be making agitation and calling for our repatriation. We always felt that we at some time would be repatriated. But the comrades from Central Europe, particularly the German comrades, they had no chance, because they had escaped from Nazi Germany to go into Spain to fight Fascism. And one could only conjure up what happened to these comrades after we left the camp. Despite the fact that all of us had the sticks over our backs at some time or other, we were a restraining influence, I think, on the Gestapo and on the Fascist guards from really going to town on prisoners. But when we left who else was there to speak? There were no visitors coming on behalf of the prisoners that remained from any of the Fascist countries, Hungary, Poland, Yugoslavia, Italy, Germany – there was nobody coming to speak on their behalf or to do what they could for prisoners. And we can only imagine what happened to them after they were sent back to their various countries that Hitler was in complete control of.[96]

Relief at returning home was further tempered by the knowledge that not all their fellow prisoners had survived incarceration in Nationalist concentration camps.[97] A number had died in San Pedro and were buried in the grounds of the former monastery:

> There were three or four comrades [who] died during that period while I was a prisoner. The same coffin was used for all of them. The body was put into a box, taken down and up-ended into a hole that had been dug by the Spaniards. The box was then taken away again, with the priest giving the last rites, whether the dead person had wanted them or not.[98]

Several other British and Irish failed to survive imprisonment in

Nationalist Spain. Welsh ex-boxer Tom Picton suffered a similar fate to Jimmy Rutherford, being shot in Bilbao prison in April 1938. Lionel Large, a journalist from London captured during the retreats, succumbed to exposure the same month. And at least one British ex-prisoner died after his release as a direct result of the brutal and callous treatment received in San Pedro de Cardeña. On 10 November 1938, Walter Legge, from Grimsby, lost his battle with the enteric fever he had contracted in the camp.[99] And Legge's death was not to be the last.

On 12 June 1938, Irish Republican leader Frank Ryan had left San Pedro with the large group of prisoners on their way to Palencia. However, Ryan was not bound for freedom. Instead he was led away in handcuffs and taken to Burgos.[100] At his trial three days later, having been accused – probably mistakenly – of overseeing the execution of Nationalist prisoners captured during the Brunete offensive, Ryan was sentenced to death.[101] Despite a big campaign in Britain and Ireland to secure his release, he never returned home. Instead he was transferred to Germany; suffering from ill-health, Frank Ryan died in Dresden in June 1944 in circumstances that remain controversial.[102]

20

The English Rebels and the Irish Bandera

It was only in July, 1936, when all seemed lost, and the red flag seemed to have triumphed over the Cross, that God raised up, in the person of General Franco, a patriotic and God-fearing man to deliver Spain out of the hands of Satan and his Communist legionaries.

General Eoin O'Duffy, *Crusade in Spain*

While almost two and a half thousand men and women from Britain and Ireland volunteered to join the Republican forces, less than a quarter of that number elected to join Franco's 'crusade'.[1] And if the volunteers from Ireland are excluded, the numbers are even more imbalanced: over two thousand volunteered for the Republic from Great Britain, yet only a handful joined the Nationalists. The disparity cannot simply be explained by the greater support for the Republicans that existed in Britain; while opinion polls estimated that over six times as many Britons supported the Republicans as the Nationalists, volunteers for the Republic exceeded those for Franco by a magnitude of a hundred. In the main, it seems that the rebellion's British supporters were simply not prepared to turn their sympathy into active participation. There was a general consensus among conservatives that non-intervention was probably best for Spain, and certainly best for Britain and Europe. This view was shared by Mosley's British Union of Fascists, which supported the policy of His Majesty's Government on the war and attacked the Labour Party for 'putting Spain above England'.[2] While some grassroots members of the BUF no doubt sympathised with the Nationalists, Mosley believed that 'no British blood should be shed on behalf of Spain.'[3]

Franco's supporters may well have felt, too, that Nationalist Spain simply did not need their help. Once the Army of Africa, safely transported across

the Gibraltar Strait, had linked up Franco's southern zone with the northern
zone of General Mola, the war seemed to be going Franco's way. And, of
course, Franco had the support of Nazi Germany and fascist Italy, who over
the course of the conflict sent respectively 19,000 and 80,000 men –
accompanied by a huge amount of military *matériel* – to fight in Spain.
Franco could also count, at least initially, on a steady supply of mercenaries
from Spanish north Africa; as many as 75,000 Moroccan soldiers fought for
the Nationalists during the civil war.

No equivalent organisation to the Comintern existed because it did not
need to. While the arrival of the International Brigades in November 1936
and several Republican offensives initially gave Franco, or at least his
German and Italian allies, pause for thought, the Nationalist war effort was
unlikely to be affected one way or the other, even in propaganda terms, by
the arrival of a handful of English-speaking volunteers. There were no
international brigades within the Nationalist ranks; with one significant
exception, groups of English-speaking volunteers did not serve together in
Franco's army, but in Spanish units, where they were expected to speak
Spanish rather than their native tongue. This was Nationalist, not
Internationalist, Spain.

Probably the first Briton to volunteer for the Rebels was the Old Etonian,
'blunt, hard-drinking playboy' and 'bold amateur pilot' Rupert Bellville.[4] 'A
tall, broad-shouldered, fair-complexioned man of about thirty-five,' Bellville
had spent his later teenage years in Andalusia, where he had developed 'a
bullfighting obsession and a love of the privileged, comfortable lives of the
Spanish rich'. Bellville personally attended the funeral of José Calvo Sotelo,
the leader of the conservative *Renovación Española*, who was killed by
policemen of the Republican Assault Guard on 13 July 1936 in retaliation
for the murder of their colleague, Lieutenant José Castillo. When the army
rose up four days later, Bellville – together with his friend, Edward Arthur
Donald St George Hamilton Chichester, the Marquess of Donegall –
promptly volunteered to fight with the Nationalists.[5] After a brief stint as a
journalist, writing pro-Nationalist pieces for right-wing newspapers in
Britain, Bellville fought alongside Spanish friends in the the Spanish fascist
movement, the *Falange*, for three weeks, before their murderous tendencies
became too much for him:

Horrified and disgusted by the frequent spectacles of atrocities committed
by some of the anarchists and communists in the villages and countryside

of that backward region, he was little less shocked when required himself to take part in firing squads to execute the criminals; eventually he left his unit. What had especially sickened him, apart from a natural revulsion at the shooting of prisoners, was that the victims went on twitching and writhing for some minutes after death and he never could believe that they were really dead.[6]

Not much was heard of Bellville until the following September, when his reckless character brought him brief renown. Somewhat the worse for wear after a good lunch, Bellville had unwisely decided to fly to Santander with a Spanish friend, bearing gifts for the conquering Nationalist forces:

> The Nationalists had launched their final assault on Santander, whose fall was expected hourly. Bellville had his aeroplane in San Sebastian when a report came through that the town had surrendered. Resolved to be the first to welcome the victorious army, he and a Spanish friend of similar temperament, Ricardo Gonzalez, of the famous sherry family, loaded his aircraft with crates of sherry and brandy, took off from San Sebastian and soon afterwards landed on the airfield at Santander. A swarm of blue-clad soldiers surrounded the aircraft and Bellville and Gonzalez climbed out with glad shouts of 'Viva Franco!' and 'Arriba Espana!' when they realized with astonishment and dismay that these were Republican militiamen and that Santander was still in enemy hands.[7]

Both were imprisoned by the Republican Basque militia for more than ten hours, in constant danger of being shot. Only the entry of the Nationalist forces into Santander saved their lives when they were released in exchange for Nationalist prisoners.[8]

Two other compatriots of Bellville who joined up early in the war were Noel Fitzpatrick and Gilbert Nangle, a pair of professional soldiers and adventurers.[9] A Sandhurst graduate and an experienced and competent soldier, Nangle had previously served with the British Army and the French Foreign Legion, but his propensity to drink himself senseless and open fire on his comrades (due apparently to 'legionnaire's blues', a legacy of his years of fighting in the desert) made him somewhat of a loose cannon.[10] Nangle's friend Fitzpatrick (whose real name was Noel Skeffington-Smyth) had also served with the British Army, though his career had been somewhat less distinguished, as he cheerfully admitted:

I decided that the career of a regular officer was not for me – an opinion which I believe my new CO also shared. In his confidential report on me, which I had to sign, he stated, 'No troops would ever follow this officer, except out of idle curiosity.'[11]

Having joined the Spanish Foreign Legion, the *Tercio*, in September 1936 – they were among the first to enter the Alcazar in Toledo after Franco's forces broke the Republican siege of the fortress – Nangle and Fitzpatrick were transferred as liaison officers to the Irish Bandera of General O'Duffy.[12] Their brief experience of life with the Irish volunteers – who were no happier taking orders from English officers than were their compatriots fighting for the Republicans – prompted them swiftly to seek a return to Spanish regiments: 'I've just done a stint with that shit O'Duffy and now I'm here trying to arrange a posting back to my old *bandera*,' Fitzpatrick declared in the spring of 1937. When O'Duffy's band returned to Ireland, Nangle and Fitzpatrick got their wish and were transferred back to the 15th Bandera of the Foreign Legion. Both survived the war: Fitzpatrick left Spain in the summer of 1937, following an injudicious admission during the heat of an argument that he was a Freemason, for 'in the eyes of almost all Nationalist supporters, freemasons the world over were in league with the communists.' Nangle left, for family reasons, in December.[13]

Of the other Britons to serve with Franco's forces, there are a number of whom very little is known. Patrick Campbell fought in the Spanish Foreign Legion before being withdrawn from service in October 1938.[14] 'Stewart' and 'Little' (both *noms de guerre*), two deserters from the Royal Marines, and another deserter from the Royal Navy, Reginald Victor Kellet from Wakefield, fought on the Lerida front with the 16th Bandera.[15] Canadian 'Tug' Wilson and an English sailor listed only as 'Yarlett' deserted from HMS *Barham* at Gibraltar in October 1936 to join the Nationalists, but quickly came to regret their decision when they were falsely accused of poisoning a well.[16] As another Nationalist volunteer realised, 'it is much easier to get into a war than out':[17] they were sent to the front line with the 7th Bandera, where Yarlett was killed and Wilson was badly wounded in the leg. Wilson slipped out of Spain with O'Duffy's Irishmen when they were repatriated in the summer of 1937.[18] Michael Larringa, the son of a Liverpool ship owner, who had retained his Spanish nationality, enrolled in the Nationalist artillery and Cecil Owen, from a half-Spanish family, served in the Carlist militia, the *Requetés*, before joining the 13th Bandera of the Legion. Owen was killed during the battle of the Ebro in August 1938.[19]

Rather more is known of two other British volunteers, for they both wrote memoirs of their Spanish experiences. They arrived in the late autumn of 1936, just prior to the battles for Madrid. The first was the Welshman Frank Thomas, 'the black sheep of a prosperous family . . . right-wing, restless and immature'.[20] In October 1936, bored, in search of adventure and 'unable to suit himself to everyday life', Thomas decided to volunteer to fight with the Rebel forces. He candidly admitted that it was not the Nationalist cause that drew him to Spain; rather, 'conscience compels me to say that it seemed to me the opportunity to enquire into a professional soldier's life.'[21] However, a dislike of Communism also played a part, echoing the response of many on the right who saw the civil war as a struggle between order and religion on one hand and anarchy and godless Communism on the other. In Thomas's opinion, the foreign volunteers could be divided into four clear groups: religious crusaders, criminals, fascists, and adventurers such as himself.[22]

Thomas sailed from Liverpool to Lisbon where he contacted the insurgents' office, and on 12 October 1936 he obtained a visa to enter Spain at Badajoz, scene of the brutal massacre two months earlier.[23] Like many Britons who fought in Spain, Thomas spoke no Spanish; unlike those fighting on the other side, he had no organisation, or group of comrades, to rely upon:

> I alighted on the platform of remote Badajoz, where my ignorance of the local tongue was brought cruelly home. However, with the aid of a midget dictionary purchased at home in one of the famous threepenny and sixpenny stores, I managed to convey the idea that I was neither an anarchist nor a spy.[24]

Thomas's fellow-countryman, 21-year-old Peter Kemp, hailed from a rather different background.[25] While a craving for adventure played a part in Kemp's decision to volunteer, he was more politically driven than Thomas:

> I had been active in politics in Cambridge, where my traditionalist, Tory

opinions caused me to view both communism and fascism with equal loathing. But of the two, I believed that communism presented the greater danger to Europe. In 1936 the threat from Germany and Italy was not clear, at least to me, as it became later, and at the beginning of the Civil War the Nationalists were not receiving very obvious or extensive help from either country.[26]

After making contact with a Nationalist agent in Britain, who gave him an introduction to officers based at the Rebel headquarters at Burgos, Kemp departed Britain for Spain in November 1936, armed with press accreditation from the pro-Nationalist *Sunday Dispatch* in order to evade the non-intervention officers. Kemp's distaste for fascism led him to reject the *Falange* and join instead the Carlist *Requetés*, the militia of the fanatically Catholic (anti-Bourbon) monarchists, based in Navarre, adjacent to the Basque Country in north-eastern Spain. As Kemp discovered, 'this was a civil war not only between Spaniards, but also between Basques.'[27]

Having endured a long, slow train journey to Burgos, Frank Thomas instead decided to join the Spanish Foreign Legion and was sent to Valladolid, in the heart of Nationalist Spain. For risking his life for the Rebels, Thomas was paid just under four pesetas a day, less than half the sum volunteers for the Republic received. Though admitted 'for the duration of the campaign', he was offered a final opportunity to change his mind, for his lieutenant was clearly doubtful over Thomas's ability to cope with the brutal life of a *legionario*:

> The Spanish Legion must be one of the few military forces where men are drilled by the use of whips. Drastic and medieval, like so much of Spain, but often necessary with some of the brutal animals which are attracted to their peacetime ranks . . . during training, the whip is applied to all parts of the body – some of its exponents being particularly adept at picking out their spot – by anybody from the rank of corporal upwards, even for the most trivial offences.[28]

Fortunately for Thomas, foreigners were exempt from being whipped, though an exception had been made for the unfortunate deserters from HMS *Barham*, Wilson and Yarlett, whom Thomas encountered while training in the Foreign Legion's headquarters at Talavera de la Reina on the River Tagus 100 kilometres south-west of Madrid. When Thomas met the two, they were sincerely regretting their decision to join the Legion and looking for an opportunity to get out as quickly as possible.

As Peter Kemp also discovered, punishment in the Nationalist army could be astonishingly brutal:

> There was a grimmer side to the discipline, which reminded me how far I was from the O.T.C. The day after my arrival two troopers reported for duty incapably drunk; apparently they were old offenders. The following evening [their Catalan officer] Llancia formed the whole Squadron in a hollow square in the main barrack-room. Calling out the two defaulters in front of us, he shouted, 'There has been enough drunkenness in this Squadron. I will have no more of it, as you are going to see.' Thereupon he drove his fist into the face of one of them, knocking out most of his front teeth and sending him spinning across the room to crash through two ranks of men and collapse on the floor. Turning on the other he beat him across the face with a riding crop until the man dropped half senseless to the ground. He returned to his first victim, yanked him to his feet and laid open his face with the crop, disregarding his screams, until he fell inert beside his companion. Then he turned to us: 'You have seen, I will not tolerate a single drunkard in this Squadron.' The two culprits were hauled, sobbing, to their feet to have a half-pint of castor oil forced down their throats. They were on duty next day, but I never saw either of them drunk again.[29]

After only two days of basic training, Thomas and his fellow legionaries were sent to the front. His first action was on 21 October on the outskirts of Navalcarnero, thirty kilometres south-west of Madrid, on the road from Talavera de la Reina:

> The enemy, seeing our troops advancing down the opposite slope with fixed bayonets, remembered previous appointments in Madrid and were out of the trench and away . . . Eighteen kilometres of ground, a large village of strategic value, a plentiful supply of arms and munitions, and a few prisoners – who, according to an old Spanish custom, were immediately shot – had been gained at little cost.[30]

The legion continued to move towards Madrid, finally coming to a halt at the furthest edge of Casa de Campo, overlooking the Manzanares River. Thomas was among the Nationalist soldiers who crossed the river and occupied the Hygiene Institute within University City. Here Thomas fought against the International Brigades, who were putting up a formidable resistance to the Rebels' advance on the capital. During their action at University City, over three-quarters of Thomas's Bandera were killed or wounded.[31]

Initially, the well-connected Kemp joined a cavalry unit, though he soon found it insufficiently exciting and adventurous for his taste. Not that his time was entirely without incident:

> We received orders to mount. We closed in to join the troop in the cover of some olives on a small hill. I noticed my companions pointing and talking excitedly; following their gaze I saw, some distance away to the right, a mass of dark specks moving across a wide gully. What could this be but our enemy? We drew our sabres, formed line and cantered down the hill and up the opposite slope. As we came over the crest San Merano gave the order, 'Charge!' Spurring our horses, we swept downhill in a cheering line, leaning forward on our horses' necks, our sabres pointed. In a moment of mad exhilaration I fancied myself one of Subatai's Tartars or Tamerlaine's bahadurs. Whoever, I exulted, said the days of cavalry were past? Preoccupied with these thoughts and with my efforts to keep station I never thought of looking ahead at our target; nor, it seemed, did anyone else. For the next thing I knew was that we were in the middle of a bleating, panic-stricken, herd of goats, in the charge of three terrified herdsmen. A sharp crack on the elbow from the butt of my carbine shattered my dreams; so ended my first and only cavalry charge.[32]

Impatient for action, at the end of December 1936 Kemp transferred to an infantry unit based on the south-western outskirts of Madrid, at Carabanchel Bajo. It was a dramatic contrast, 'as sudden as it was uncomfortable: if the inactivity of the cavalry had bored me, the street fighting scared me stiff.'[33] The position occupied by Kemp's platoon was a salient pushing right into Republican-held territory, surrounded on three sides. With enemy soldiers sometimes no more than ten metres away, all conversations had to be carried out in a whisper. The only means of reaching the horribly exposed position was by crawling silently through a tunnel; 'even the dead had to be sent out through the tunnel, for there was nowhere we could bury them.'[34]

Our only line of communication with Company Headquarters and the rear was the tunnel of sandbags. Through this had to come all our food, water, ammunition and supplies; through this we must evacuate our wounded. It could only be done at night, which meant that a wounded man might die before he could receive proper attention, for we had no doctor. Water was so scarce that there was no question of washing, or even of cleaning our teeth. In a few days we were all infested with lice. Our food, which consisted chiefly of mule steak and dried codfish, was cooked at Company Headquarters.[35]

While the futility of daytime attacks had been learned during the fighting in the latter months of 1936, sniping and occasional night-time raids still took their toll. Kemp was not sorry to depart the position when his group were withdrawn to Getafe, south of Madrid. A fortnight later the position at Carabanchel was blown up by a mine, killing a whole company of men in the process.

By the beginning of February 1937, Frank Thomas's three and a half months of service and dedication had earned him promotion to *legionario de primeraclase* (lance-corporal). Having also taken on the role of captain's batman, he was not personally involved in the attacks over the Jarama valley, which proved so costly to both sides. However, many of his comrades and friends were killed, one of whom he claimed had 'been wounded on the sixteenth [of February] by an explosive bullet in the right groin – indubitably fired by a member of the British Battalion'.[36] Like many on the Nationalist side, and many of their supporters, Thomas had believed that he was fighting Russian troops in the International Brigades; at Jarama he came face-to-face with a number of captured brigaders from the British Battalion:

In San Martin one day I was requested to act as interpreter to seven English prisoners before they were sent back beyond the battle area. I found that five of them were Scotsmen, one a Londoner, and the seventh a Canadian. One claimed to be the son of an Edinburgh clergyman, but the others were ordinary workmen, much the same as those who can be seen at the local Saturday afternoon football match. They claimed to have come out to Spain to get the soft jobs they had been told they could have as ambulance drivers, or some other non-combatant work. Given weekend tickets to France and a sum of money, they had arrived in Spain via Perpignan (the International

Brigade centre in France). They found themselves without option but to join the Brigade, and had been sent to Albacete for training – which I knew to be true from a 'daily order' I had found up the line. They said this was the first time they themselves had been in the line. They admitted that Brigade losses had been heavy, a fact we also knew from the constant stream of deserters, mainly French, who came over, and that, of the Anglo-American Battalion's commencing strength of 650 men, only 200 remained, a statement partly confirmed later by the British Communist Party in a bulletin giving their dead as 100 and 300 wounded. One thing worth noting were the new Russian rifles with which they were armed, while their thick khaki uniforms showed us up; their fine khaki greatcoats were especially sought after.[37]

Unlike Thomas, Peter Kemp was directly involved in the Jarama fighting. After a short visit home to visit his dying father at the start of 1937 – sadly he arrived in England twenty-four hours after his father's funeral – Kemp returned to his unit on 9 February, three days after the start of the Jarama offensive. At Jarama, Kemp observed the almost suicidal disdain of Nationalist soldiers towards the digging of trenches:

> In my experience Spanish troops, even the crack Foreign Legion, could never be induced to construct proper trenches; they seemed to think – especially the *Requetés* – that it was a sign of cowardice to dig in securely . . . men exposed themselves quite recklessly to enemy fire, even clambering onto the parapet in their eagerness to get a clearer shot – often to slump forward riddled with bullets.[38]

Posted to the south of Madrid, overlooking the valley of the Manzanares River, Kemp and his fellow *Requetés* were on the receiving end of a huge Republican counter-offensive, aimed at encircling them.[39] Kemp's outfit lost one hundred men – a third of their strength – killed in the two-day battle, which he describes vividly:

> My throat was dry, my face hot and my hands shaking as I feverishly loaded and fired my rifle. With a great effort I pulled myself together and began to fire more slowly, checking my sights, resting my elbows on the parapet and taking careful, aimed shots. This had a steadying effect on me and I began to feel much better. I began, too, to feel a kind of pity for my enemies,

exposed in the open to this murderous fire; so that, as I aligned my sights on one of them and pressed the trigger with a slow steady pressure as I had been taught, I found myself praying that my bullet might put him out of action, but not maim him grievously for life . . . Many fell; some lay down where they were and fired back at us, others turned and ran in all directions, looking for cover, not realizing that this was the most certain way of being killed . . . The bombardment intensified as a new wave of attackers surged forward, in much greater strength than the first . . . Our ears were throbbing with the explosions, our eyes almost blinded with dust; not so blinded, however, that we could not see that the enemy was getting closer, finding his way surely round to our left flank. Bullets from his light machine-guns were slapping against the parapets and whistling by our heads. Sometimes a Requeté, carried away by excitement, would clamber up on the parapet, half out of the trench, to get a better shot; in a moment he would slump back, torn with bullets, or fall forward over the parapet to roll a few yards down the slope in front.[40]

During the fighting at Jarama a new unit of English-speaking volunteers joined the Nationalist forces: a group of Irish volunteers led by General Eoin O'Duffy, an IRA member during the Irish War of Independence and commander of the Irish police force, the Garda Síochána, from 1922 to 1933. By the early 1930s, O'Duffy had become an admirer of Mussolini and in 1932 he founded the fascist Irish 'Blueshirt' movement, which numbered almost 50,000 members in its heyday. Following an acrimonious split in 1934, O'Duffy decided to establish a new National Corporate Party, known as 'The Greenshirts', but it never gained as much support. By 1936, with the movement in crisis and his political star clearly on the wane, the Spanish Civil War offered O'Duffy a chance to regain personal prestige by the formation of an Irish Catholic Brigade to fight in Spain.

After the outbreak of the war, reports in the Irish press told of burning churches, executions of clergy and the exhumation of nuns' bodies, all claimed to be 'part of a well-organised movement for the destruction of the Church and religion and civilisation throughout the world'.[41] Many Irish priests added their voices to call for men to go to Spain to protect the Church and O'Duffy capitalised upon popular perceptions of the Spanish Republic's anti-clericalism, telling how 'boys and girls dressed as priests and nuns may be seen on the streets carrying buckets of dirty water in mockery of holy water.'[42] O'Duffy cited the experiences of a Captain C.J. McGuinness who, he claimed, had fought with the International Brigades in Spain and had witnessed 'a rare orgy of blasphemy' as troops donned sacred vestments and mimicked mass, while 'a depraved looking Slav was breaking the cover of the Mass book, laughing like an idiot'.[43] McGuinness apparently concluded that 'The Madrid Government is one hundred per cent Red and violently opposed to the Catholic Church. Any Irishman fighting for or defending this regime is defending the enemy of his Faith.'[44] O'Duffy agreed: 'General Franco was holding the trenches, not only for Spain, but for Christianity.'

Overwhelmingly, the Irish volunteers' Catholic faith, combined with anti-communism, was the main driving force behind their decision to go to Spain.[45] Dublin volunteer William Geraghty believed that 'Europe was in danger of being overrun . . . by atheistic communists'; 'Ireland Declares war on Communism!' announced the *Irish Independent* triumphantly.[46] Shocked and appalled by the attacks on the Church and clergy, over five thousand men initially declared an interest in joining O'Duffy's volunteers, though only 670 had actually arrived in Spain by the end of 1936.[47]

Once in Spain, the Irish group headed south by train for Cácares in Extremadura, stopping off in Salamanca en route for lunch. There they encountered the disdainful Peter Kemp, who was no more impressed with the 'portly' General O'Duffy and his Irish 'Brigade' than Nangle and Fitzpatrick were:[48]

> The 'Brigade' was in fact equal in strength to a battalion, but O'Duffy was granted the honorary rank of General in the Spanish Army. Few generals can have had so little responsibility in proportion to their rank, or so little sense of it. Whatever the ostensible purpose of the Irish Brigade, O'Duffy never lost sight of its real object, which was to strengthen his own political position. He therefore gave the most responsible appointments to his own political supporters, regardless of their military experience; one of the most important he gave to an ex-liftman from Jury's Hotel in Dublin, a man who knew nothing of soldiering and was prepared to learn nothing. In favour of such men as this he declined the services of experienced ex-officers who did not happen to belong to his party . . . To his men he was known as 'General O'Scruffy' or 'Old John Bollocks'.[49]

Rather unwisely, lunch at Salamanca was served with wine, which few of the Irish group had ever tried before. But, according to Kemp, gamely making up for lost time, many of the group drank so much that they had to be physically assisted back onto the train:

> I knew it was going to be sheer bloody murder with the boys drinking all that wine on empty stomachs . . . when the time came to get back onto the train the boys were so drunk it was all we could do to push them back into it . . . When we'd got them all back in, and the train was ready to start, the band struck up the Spanish National Anthem, and all the officers and generals came to attention and stood at the salute. And all the time the band was playing, there was one of our lads – as drunk as a coot he was – leaning out of the carriage and being sick all down the neck of an old general.[50]

In another parallel with their compatriots fighting with the Republicans, the majority of the Irish had never fired a rifle before arriving in Spain, though perhaps twenty per cent of them had some form of military experience, either in the First World War or fighting with the IRA. Therefore all began a tough regime to bring them up to a standard acceptable to the Spanish officers who had been assigned to their Bandera, awaking early and training for six hours a day, six days a week.[51] The full brutality of the Spanish war was revealed to them at Cáceres, when several Bandera witnessed the shooting of fifteen Republican prisoners by members of the *Guardia Civil*:

> I was the only one, nobody seen me and I climbed up the tree. And the tree was so close to the wall I was able to lean on the wall with my arms folded and there I witnessed [it]. The soldiers were all there lined up in a square, in one, two, three squares. And I said to myself, 'What's going on here?' Next I seen at least seven or eight taken out and they were lined up. And the first man was handcuffed and the next man wasn't handcuffed but they'd put a binding rope around him, same as the next man, same as the next man. And their hands were together with their elbows at their sides. And not a sound was heard. I remember I wanted to cough, I nearly choked myself, to prevent myself from coughing. What is going on, I said? Next a little officer came over and what he says I don't know. Then he took out a black handkerchief and went up to them. Some of them did take it. I couldn't see any guns or anything like that but eventually I did. I heard the commands in Spanish, to come to attention. Next up comes the rifles. Next they aim . . . Then all of a sudden, I seen them fall into the ground dead. I

presumed they all were dead. But to make sure they all were dead the officer came along, took out an automatic and shot them in the head. And he didn't actually put his hand down to pull them on their side. He just booted them to put them in the position that he wanted before he shot them.[52]

As the bleak realities of military life took over, the lack of mail from home, the terrible weather and difficulties adjusting to the Spanish diet all combined to lower the band's original high spirits. 'It is not possible to get a meal in any hotel in Spain without the meat, fish, fowl, vegetables, in fact everything, swimming in olive oil,' complained O'Duffy.[53] Many in the Bandera succumbed to boredom and homesickness and a number to drinking and gambling, despite almost half their pay going towards the cost of their German uniforms. While William Geraghty claimed that 'we were never paid money to enable us to go out and get drunk,' there seems little doubt that drunkenness was endemic among the members of the Irish Bandera.[54]

Finally, on 17 February 1937, following a surprise visit and inspection by Franco, the Irishmen left by train for Valdemoro, west of the Nationalist offensive at Jarama. Two days later they advanced eastwards, in battle formation in case of artillery or air attack, towards the Jarama valley.[55] Spying a group of 600 soldiers moving towards them, a small number of the Bandera's commanding officers approached, and identified themselves as the *Bandera Irlanda de Tercio*:

> Instantly, the captain to whom he spoke stepped back one pace, drew his revolver, and fired point blank at Lieutenant Bove, but missed him. Captain O'Sullivan and Lieutenant Bove quickly returned their fire from their revolvers. 'The enemy,' shouted Lieutenant Bove, and then turned to double back with the others to his company – under a heavy fusillade. Lieutenant Bove and Sergeant Calvo were killed before they had retreated more than ten yards. Captain O'Sullivan, Sergeant [George] Timlin and Legionary McMahon got back safely. Their escape was not short of miraculous.[56]

The ensuing fire-fight lasted for almost an hour, both parties suffering a number of casualties. These included Lieutenant Tom Hyde from Cork, the first of O'Duffy's volunteers to be killed. As casualties mounted, the enemy bid a retreat, leaving a number of dead on the battlefield. The 'enemy' force was later revealed to be a band of Falangists from the Canary Islands. In an inquiry into the disastrous misunderstanding, the Irish were absolved from all blame and the Falangist unit was disbanded. However, suspicions of the military qualities of the Irish remained among many Spaniards.[57]

The Bandera was sent to Ciempozuelos, thirty kilometres south of Madrid and just west of the Jarama valley. The place had only been captured a few days earlier; when the Irish arrived they found it still looking like 'a town of the dead' with 'not a living person to be seen in streets or houses', and littered with the bodies of over a thousand Republican soldiers, 'many still unburied or only half-buried with a few inches of clay'.[58] The Bandera took up positions in trenches in the high ground overlooking the town, 'one of the most vulnerable on the Jarama river', where they were heavily shelled every day, 'sometimes for hours at a stretch'. Tom Murphy, from Newbliss in County Monaghan, remembered being taunted by Irish volunteers among the Republican forces:

> Our trenches were maybe a few hundred yards [away]. Frank Ryan used to speak on the speaker, he says, 'Irishmen go home! Your fathers would turn in their graves if they knew that you'd come to fight for imperialism. This is the real Republican Army. The real, real men of Ireland.'[59]

Under incessant, torrential rain, the position quickly became as sodden as those occupied by their compatriots in the Republican trenches.[60] Their welcome release came on 12 March, when the Irish volunteers were charged with assaulting the village of Titulcia, set on the heights opposite them. The attack was part of a diversionary attack designed to take pressure off the Guadalajara sector, which had seen the Italian soldiers of the *Corpo Truppe Volontarie* comprehensively routed by their compatriots in the Garibaldi Battalion of the International Brigades.

It was by no means an easy assignment. Titulcia was well defended by the Communist 11th Regiment, who had fortified the village and set up well-protected machine-gun emplacements. The Bandera were expected to advance across the sodden valley floor of the Jarama, negotiate their way over a canal, and then attack, uphill, against a virtually impregnable target. Although pounded by heavy and accurate shellfire, they managed to struggle through the sodden ground until darkness arrived – when, faced with little other option, the Bandera's new commander, now Major

O'Sullivan, ordered the retreat. Several men were killed and more wounded in the action, though the soft marshy land saved many lives, absorbing much of the impact of the exploding shells.

The following day, the Bandera was ordered to retry the attack, but with no air, artillery or flanking support, General O'Duffy overruled the order and eventually managed to obtain permission to call off the action. This effectively marked the end of the Irish Bandera. On 24 March, the commander of the Spanish Foreign Legion, General Yagüe, recommended its dissolution and his proposal was soon echoed by a disillusioned O'Duffy.[61] Despite the claim by Harold Cardozo, the Daily Mail's 'special correspondent with the Nationalist forces', that 'the Irish Brigade, though small in numbers, was also one of the foreign units which could be relied upon,' Yagüe had never been convinced of the worth of the Irish unit, or its leadership.[62] As the Bandera descended into infighting, they were withdrawn, first to Talavera then, on 10 May, to their initial training base of Cácares.

Here they were joined by Frank Thomas, who had been wounded in an action near Toledo in May. After an agonising crawl to safety, he was given emergency first aid before being taken to a hospital in an improvised ambulance.[63] Transferred to another hospital in Cácares, Thomas encountered the members of O'Duffy's Irish Bandera who were awaiting their repatriation to Ireland. Having become disillusioned with life in the Legion, which he described as 'intense periods of engagement with the enemy . . . followed by long periods of idleness, drilling, drinking and playing endless games of cards', Thomas decided that his eight months' service would suffice.[64] He had also come to believe that the raw Spanish soldiers increasingly being drafted into the ranks of the Legion were not prepared to match the sacrifices of the extranjeros fighting alongside them:

> Now that the Legionarios were beginning to run, how long would it be before we suffered a real defeat – and if there was one thing I hated, it was the thought of being taken prisoner by the Reds, as a foreign veterano and corporal to boot! If Spaniards could not stand their ground – and Fascists and hundreds of others in civilian jobs were hanging about risking nothing – why should I, a mercenary adventurer, do so?[65]

Like others on the right in Britain who had been initially sympathetic to the Rebel cause, including Winston Churchill, Thomas was coming to recognise that a Nationalist Spain allied with fascist Italy and Nazi Germany could present a major threat to British interests. When the Irish Bandera left for Portugal by train on 17 June 1937, O'Duffy smuggled Thomas out of Spain disguised as a member of his Blueshirts. The Spanish debacle marked the end of O'Duffy's attempts to revive his political career, although he later declared that he had no regrets: 'We have been criticised, sneered at, slandered, but truth, charity, and justice shall prevail, and time will justify our motives. We seek no praise. We did our duty. We went to Spain.'[66]

In a review of O'Duffy's somewhat vainglorious memoir, *Crusade in Spain*, George Orwell portrayed the Spanish episode rather differently: 'General O'Duffy's adventures in Spain do seem in one way to have resembled a crusade,' he wrote, 'in that they were a frightful muddle and led to nothing in particular.'[67]

While the Welshman and the Irishmen had departed, the Englishman still remained. Having survived the Jarama bloodbath following the fall of Santander in the autumn of 1937, Peter Kemp drew upon his influential social contacts and persuaded his friend Merry del Val to talk to General Millán Astray, the founder of the Foreign Legion, about a transfer to the unit. Kemp might have been a snob, but he was no coward, for the Legion 'were deployed, like the International Brigades on the other side, as "shock troops" in situations of the most critical importance or the greatest danger'.[68] Consequently, at the end of October 1937, Kemp joined the 14th Bandera of the Spanish Foreign Legion, at Getafe, south of Madrid, though he was taken aback and affronted to find that the other officers did not welcome foreigners, and treated him with 'distrust and resentment'. 'I shit on Englishmen,' Kemp's company commander informed him coldly.[69]

Posted to the Teruel front in the winter of 1937, Kemp found the Legion's officers and rankings to be rigidly segregated: 'Officers travelled in first-class carriages, five to a compartment, sergeants in second-class carriages and the men, singing lustily all the way, in cattle trucks.'[70] At Teruel in December, in one of the worst Spanish winters for many years, Kemp found himself pitted in the abominable conditions against American and Canadian volunteers in the International Brigades:

Our casualties were [to] frost-bite more than the enemy and we had to lie down to sleep, we had to lie down in the snow and we didn't have any greatcoats because they never arrived. No fires were allowed. There used to be five or six people every night who, when we woke up in the morning, they were as stiff as boards. I'd have to comb the frost out of my hair and get the icicles out of my nose. I spent most of the night walking around. The people who were stupid and didn't wake up were the people who took half a bottle of brandy – and that was the killer.[71]

With the Republicans driven out of Teruel, Kemp joined the huge Nationalist offensive of March 1938. At Caspe, conceivably fighting against his own countrymen in the British Battalion, 'often at hand to hand – my company suffered seventy-five per cent casualties, and I myself was wounded three times.'[72] During an attack on Republican defences at a monastery overlooking nearby Belchite, Nationalists pummelled the enemy virtually without reply, enabling Kemp's unit to capture the defences almost without firing a shot. Among the items found in the Republican trenches was a sack of mail for the American and Canadian International Brigaders:

> Some of the letters I had to examine were tragically moving; letters from sweethearts, wives and even, in one or two cases, children. It was horrible to feel that many of these men, who spoke my own language and who had come even further from home to fight for a cause in which they believed as deeply as I believed in ours, would never return to enjoy the love that glowed so warmly from the pages I was reading.[73]

Ensuing attacks made on trenches around the town were strongly resisted, earning a vicious response from the victorious Legionaries, who were 'shooting the wounded as they gasped for water'. Disgusted, Kemp resolved to speak to his company commander: 'I had not come to Spain for this,' he declared.[74] But when Kemp asked where the order for the execution of prisoners had originated, he was taken aback by his company commander's heated response:

> 'As far as we're concerned, from Colonel Peñaredonda [sic]. But we all think the same way ourselves. Look here, Peter,' he went on with sudden vehemence, 'it's all very well for you to talk about International Law and the rights of prisoners! You're not a Spaniard. You haven't seen your country devastated, your family and friends murdered in a civil war that would have ended eighteen months ago but for the intervention of these foreigners. I know we have help now from Germans and Italians. But you

know as well as I do that this war would have been over by the end of 1936, when we were at the gates of Madrid, but for the International Brigades. At that time we had no foreign help. What is it to us if they do have their ideals? Whether they know it or not, they are simply the tools of the Communists and they have come to Spain to destroy our country! What do they care about the ruin they have made here? Why then should we bother about their lives when we catch them? It will take years to put right the harm they've done to Spain!'

He paused for breath, then went on: 'Another thing; I mean no offence to you personally, Peter, but I believe that all Spaniards – even those fighting against us – wish that this war could have been settled one way or another by Spaniards alone. We never wanted our country to become a battleground for foreign powers. What do you think would happen to you if you were taken prisoner by the Reds? You would be lucky if they only shot you!'[75]

However, as Kemp knew, it was not just foreigners who were shot out of hand. The previous day, he had personally witnessed a surrendering Spanish lieutenant of the *Caribineros* shot through the head.[76] Two days later, on 14 March 1938, the attitude of many senior Nationalist officers towards their enemies was made explicitly clear to Kemp in a shocking encounter with Colonel Peñarredonda:

At noon next day we were still resting on our cliff-top when I was ordered to report to Cancela [Kemp's company commander]. I found him talking with some legionaries who had brought in a deserter from the International Brigades – an Irishman from Belfast; he had given himself up to one of our patrols down by the river. Cancela wanted me to interrogate him. The man explained that he had been a seaman on a British ship trading to Valencia, where he had got very drunk one night, missed his ship and been picked up by the police. The next thing he knew, he was in Albacete, impressed into the International Brigades . . .

I was not absolutely sure that he was telling the truth; but I knew that if I seemed to doubt his story he would be shot, and I was resolved to do everything in my power to save his life.

Kemp spoke to his immediate superior who agreed to spare him, subject to his superior de Mora's consent. De Mora's reaction was the same;

sympathetic, but he was not prepared to make a decision and passed Kemp further up the chain of command.

I found Colonel Peñaredonda sitting cross-legged with a plate of fried eggs on his knee. He greeted me amiably enough as I stepped forward and saluted; I had taken care to leave the prisoner well out of earshot. I repeated his story, adding my own plea at the end, as I had with Cancela and de Mora. 'I have the fellow here, sir,' I concluded, 'in case you wish to ask him any questions.' The Colonel did not look up from his plate: 'No, Peter,' he said casually, his mouth full of egg, 'I don't want to ask him anything. Just take him away and shoot him.'

I was so astonished that my mouth dropped open; my heart seemed to stop beating. Peñaredonda looked up, his eyes full of hatred:

'Get out!' he snarled. 'You heard what I said.' As I withdrew he shouted after me: 'I warn you, I intend to see that this order is carried out.'

A stunned Kemp led the prisoner away. He briefly considered advising him to make a run for it, but observed that his Colonel had ordered two legionaries to follow them to make sure that his orders were obeyed. Realising that he had been left with no choice, Kemp prepared himself to break the news to the doomed British International Brigader:

It was almost more than I could bear to face the prisoner, where he stood between my two runners. As I approached they dropped back a few paces, leaving us alone; they were good men and understood what I was feeling. I forced myself to look at him. I am sure he knew what I was going to say. 'I've got to shoot you.' A barely audible 'Oh my God!' escaped him.

Briefly I told him how I had tried to save him. I asked him if he wanted a priest, or a few minutes by himself, and if there were any messages he wanted me to deliver.

'Nothing,' he whispered, 'please make it quick.'

'That I can promise you. Turn round and start walking straight ahead.'

He held out his hand and looked me in the eyes, saying only: 'Thank you.'

'God bless you!' I murmured.

As he turned his back and walked away I said to my two runners: 'I beg you to aim true. He must not feel anything.' They nodded, and raised their rifles. I looked away. The two shots exploded simultaneously.[77]

A few days later, in a desperate fight for a strategic position on a hill overlooking Caspe, Kemp was wounded in the throat by a bullet and in the arm by grenade fragments. Ironically, the injuries probably saved his life. Although, the following day, Caspe fell to overwhelming Nationalist forces: 'The International Brigades, particularly the 14th (British), had fought a gallant and determined action, inflicting terrible casualties on the 16th Bandera and ourselves; our own company had barely twenty men left, out of the hundred and ten with which we had started the battle.'[78]

While convalescing in hospital in Zaragoza, Kemp met the English nurse Priscilla 'Pip' Scott-Ellis, who had been serving with the Nationalist armies since the previous autumn.[79] Kemp was quite taken with Priscilla, finding her to be 'a cheerful girl with a great sense of humour' and a 'sympathetic drinking and dining companion'.[80] Scott-Ellis had volunteered to serve in Spain principally due to her affections for the son of Prince Alfonso de Orléans and Princess Beatrice Saxe-Coburg-Gotha, Queen Victoria's granddaughter.[81] Despite the Nationalists' access to better supplies, particularly food, her work as a nurse seems to have been no less exhausting or shocking than that endured by the medical staff on the Republican side. During March 1938, Scott-Ellis was working 42-hour shifts, with only six-hour breaks. However, her time out of the line was rather more civilised, allowing her to socialise with her numerous aristocratic connections. She apparently enjoyed her dinner with Kemp, finding him 'good-looking' and pleasant company.[82]

Once recovered, in May 1938 Kemp returned to the Bandera until he was seriously wounded during the Republican Ebro offensive on 23 July 1938, this time by an enemy artillery shell:

I barely heard the explosion: I was conscious of it only as a roaring in my ears, a hammer blow on the left side of my face and a sickening dizziness as I fell to the floor. My mouth seemed to fill with a sea of pebbles; as it fell open the sea resolved itself into a deluge of blood and the pebbles into fragments of my back teeth; twice more the flood welled up into my mouth to pour in a widening pool across the floor. I watched with a detached bewilderment, changing to near-panic. 'Oh God!' I prayed, 'don't let me die now, like this, in terror!' I took a grip on myself, remembering how someone had once said to me, 'You're never dead till you think you are'.[83]

Initially, doctors did not expect Kemp to survive, but he was extremely lucky to be operated on by one of the finest surgeons in Nationalist Spain, Captain Tomás Zerolo, who had studied in London and chatted happily away to Kemp in English about London life. Kemp was doubly lucky perhaps, because the wound ensured that he took no further part in the fighting. After a spell in hospital he returned home to convalesce. By the time he had recovered, foreign volunteers to Franco's 'crusade' were no longer required – for the Spanish Civil War was over.

21

From Spanish War to World War

In two and a half years of bitter and bloody fighting we British volunteers left some hundreds of our comrades on the battlefields, their graves desecrated and unmarked by the fascist victors. History will tell we lost many battles. We know that the cause for which we fought and so many died, lived on. Less than one year later the battle was at last joined between much of the free world and the evil of Hitler fascism. Too late for a whole generation of Spaniards, just in time for so many others.

Fred Thomas, *To Tilt at Windmills*

Slowly, the veterans of the British Battalion made their way home. Travelling north through France by rail, they were instructed not to fly flags or banners and their train was diverted around Paris to avoid any pro-Republican demonstrations of support.[1] After a long, tedious journey, they finally arrived at Dieppe where the train ran directly onto the ferry bound for Britain. Having endured a very rough crossing, the three hundred veterans arrived at Newhaven on 7 December 1938 to find that little had changed since their departure, for some as long as two years earlier: they were met with an interrogation by customs and Foreign Office officials, who checked off their names, because they had left the country without passports, as representatives of the British security services looked on. 'The Foreign Office officials looked very stern – "Your train's up there." But we didn't bother with that. We just laughed at them, sung our songs and up onto the train and away we went to London.'[2]

Their arrival at Victoria station was a very different experience. The exhausted soldiers, many of them heavily bandaged and a number on crutches, disembarked to find that a vast crowd had assembled to welcome them home: 'In darkness, thousands packed the surrounding streets to greet us, and to recognise relative or friend among the dishevelled and unshaven men, markedly unburdened with luggage after our long absence.'[3] While no members of the British government were on show to offer thanks and bestow honours, the mass of family members, friends and supporters greeting the returning volunteers were accompanied by Labour dignitaries Clement Attlee, Stafford Cripps and Will Lawther, President of the National Miners' Federation, as well as the Communist Party leaders Willie Gallagher and Harry Pollitt.[4] Among the waving Union Jacks were flags bearing the names of British trade unions and left-wing political organisations. Others bore one simple phrase: '¡No pasarán!' Edwin Greening was one of many to find it 'a very moving scene'.[5] Years later, George Aitken, the former political commissar, who had also turned up to welcome the returning volunteers, still recalled the tremendous welcome with excitement:

> It had only been announced the day before that they were arriving. There was such a crowd, unbelievable. The square in front of Victoria was absolutely chock-a-block, right down the road and up Victoria Street. And in the station. But you know who was there? Ted Heath! Ted Heath was there![6]

Sam Wild and Bob Cooney responded to the welcoming speeches from the assembled dignitaries before the brigaders moved off, the cheers of their supporters ringing in their ears:

> At Sam's word of command we formed up behind the flags of all the nations whose sons had made Spain's cause their own. Led by drums and bugles we passed through the barrier. I will never forget the scene that followed. Drums and bugles were drowned out by the cheers of the welcoming crowd. It seemed as if all London was there to welcome us. The line of police, arms interlocked, sweated and strained in a vain effort to hold the crowd back. In the end they gave up the struggle and some of them added their cheers to those of the multitude. Our hands were seized, our backs were thumped. Warm friendly words were shouted to us. And so, brimming with happiness that brought us near to tears we marched into London. We were HOME.[7]

The veterans paraded through the centre of London, stopping to lay a wreath on the Cenotaph for their fallen comrades, before marching to 10 Downing Street to deliver a petition calling for the end of the British government's policy of non-intervention in Spain. Initial plans by the police to prevent the volunteers from reaching their intended destination melted away when they were faced with a rank of disciplined soldiers in step behind Sam Wild, who 'marched through bearing our standard and told the inspector in charge that he was going to deliver our petition come hell or high water'.[8]

> Arriving at the entrance to Whitehall near Trafalgar Square, we noted that dozens and dozens of foot police had cordoned off all of Whitehall from the marching demonstrators and that the mounted police were waiting at the rear of those ranks.
>
> Sam Wild stopped the International Brigaders with Spanish words of command. All International Brigaders halted, lowered the flags and stood at ease; the drill movement was worthy of the Battalion's veterans.
>
> The police were amazed at the sight of around fifty men, at words of command in a foreign tongue, halting and standing at ease. The next moment we wrapped the flags around the poles, each pole now acting like a pike. The crowds in the rear were impatient and wanted to press forward, but the International Brigaders who had not carried the flags now kept the crowds back. I was one of the flag bearers at the front. Sam Wild marched smartly to a police officer and words were exchanged. Not more than two or three minutes elapsed, then Sam returned, and again gave commands in Spanish that the flags were to be unfurled and to stand to attention, then in Spanish, 'Adelante'. As we did so the ranks of the police opened to let us through.[9]

As Scottish veteran Tommy Bloomfield realised, 'the police didn't care to have the stigma of batoning wounded veterans of Spain, so common sense prevailed and we were allowed to deliver our petition.'[10]

Similar welcomes awaited returning volunteers around much of the country.[11] In Ireland, seven volunteers making up the final detachment of the 'Connolly Column' were met by a welcoming party at Dublin's Westland Row station. They marched to the traditional site of left-wing public meetings, the corner of Middle Abbey Street and O'Connell Street, where Father Michael O'Flanagan, a radical priest and prominent Republican who had been barred from clerical duties, saluted them.[12]

The following month, on 8 January 1939, 9000 people attended a memorial rally for the former International Brigaders and the Spanish Republic at Empress Hall in Earls Court, London, with at least 2000 more waiting outside.[13] Chaired by Fred Copeman, 411 survivors of the battalion were presented to the audience, who joined in singing 'The Valley of Jarama', the *Internationale* and *El Himno de Riego*, the anthem of the Spanish Republic. Welsh brigader Jim Brewer 'had the privilege of carrying the battalion banner and led all the banners of all the nations down into the arena'.[14] Harry Pollitt declared to prolonged cheering that:

> We shall not cease to fight for the principle for which these men have laid down their lives. We shall stand by the struggle of the Spanish people until their victory is won and until the cause of peace and democracy has triumphed.[15]

Messages of solidarity were received from prominent supporters of the Spanish Republic, including the Duchess of Atholl, Clement Attlee and Liberal MP Wilfrid Roberts. An appeal for donations by the veteran Republican supporter Isabel Brown raised £3000 for the dependents of International Brigaders killed in Spain.

However, despite the speeches and the rallies, many volunteers were left with mixed feelings. While thankful and relieved to be safely home and alive, many felt a tinge of regret for having left the Spanish Republic to fight on without them:

> Probably a majority of the surviving British members of the International Brigades had guilty consciences. We were back home safely, but we had been ordered to leave Spain in its hour of greatest need. If a call had gone out for us to return to Spain a large proportion would, I think, have gone.[16]

In Hemingway's famous novel of the Spanish Civil War, *For Whom the Bell Tolls*, a frantic young Maria is forced to abandon Robert Jordan, the mortally wounded foreign volunteer. In reality, of course, the converse was true; the often distraught foreign volunteers were forced to abandon the dying Republic, *la niña bonita* as it was known in Spain. For Hugh Sloan the homecoming was so painful that he 'couldn't bear to talk about Spain and the sense of loss that I felt'.[17] Others experienced similar feelings of grief and anger: Chris Thornycroft, who had served with Esmond Romilly's group in Madrid in the winter of 1936, 'returned to England a rather embittered young man . . . I felt Spain and the Spanish people had been abandoned . . . [it was] a betrayal of a whole people.' Thornycroft railed against the western democracies' non-intervention policy, which he felt had been 'short-sighted and unfair'.[18] Bernard Knox, another veteran of the early battles for Madrid, felt Britain too was being betrayed:

> I watched in utter despondency as the British government persisted in its policy of appeasement and the prospect of victory in Spain receded fast as Hitler and Mussolini gave Franco a steadily increasing preponderance in weapons and troops. The sellout in Munich in 1938 plunged me into despair; it seemed to me that Chamberlain and his sinister Foreign Secretary Halifax were intent on making England a junior partner of Hitler's Drittes Reich.[19]

'I was so confident that the cause of righteousness would prevail, that I never thought we could lose,' said Sam Wild, ruefully.[20] The bitter disappointment spurred a determination not to desert the Spanish Republic and not to abandon the fight against fascism. The veterans of the Spanish war, 'at home, but not to rest', as Bill Alexander described it, made a pledge:

> We are returning to our respective countries not for celebrations in our honour, not to rest, but to continue the fight we helped to wage in Spain. We are merely changing the fronts and the weapons.[21]

Some veterans turned these words into tangible actions. In early 1939, Lou Kenton, who had served as a dispatch rider and driver in the medical services between July 1937 and February 1939, drove a lorry of food across the Spanish border and the food was distributed among the fleeing refugees.[22] Efforts were made on behalf of former International Brigaders from other nationalities, many of whom faced severe hardship. Thousands were held in the Republican internment camps in southern France and those from nations hostile to the Republic faced an uncertain future. George Leeson, himself a former prisoner of war, worked in Paris from September 1938 for Spanish Aid. He helped supply the refugees and former brigaders in the camps with food and other supplies; he also helped smuggle several dozen people out of the camps.[23] Former ambulance driver Wogan Philipps chartered a ship, paid for by donations, which transported 5000 Spanish Republicans from France to Mexico. Medical administrator Nan Green also travelled on the boat, while senior Communist Party functionary Winifred Bates remained in France to provide aid in the camps.[24] When Max Laufer, a German doctor held with his young pregnant Spanish wife in the French concentration camp at Argelès-sur-Mer, wrote to Harry Bury, the former British Battalion medical officer, Bury guaranteed full responsibility for their keep and arranged their passage to England, where the couple lived with Bury and his wife for the next year.[25]

There was also a pressing need to provide for British veterans who had been badly wounded in Spain, or faced difficult circumstances on their return. Not all the homecomings were easy, or even happy. Rose Kerrigan found her husband much altered on his return:

> There was a terrible change in him, he was quite morose and he seemed very within himself. He was really going grey and this was because he'd seen all the people who had died in Spain, having to take their effects home and see some of the people['s relatives].[26]

After arriving home, Walter Gregory was asked to talk to the family of one of his friends in Spain. He found the process of informing them of the death of their loved ones deeply harrowing:

> A friend of mine got killed out there and they asked me to go and see the relatives. His mother gave me a terrible, terrible time: 'Did you see him in the coffin?' Well, of course, a soldier doesn't get a coffin. And, 'Did you have a few flowers?' He was killed at Teruel in mid-winter, you don't get flowers at Teruel, and 'Did his friends go?' Well, of course, his friends were in the front line, which were a few yards away. One of the worst experiences in my life, that was.[27]

Many volunteers faced difficulties returning to their previous home lives, for while some relatives had been supportive of the decision to volunteer, others had not.[28] The cautious advice given by recruiters to 'say nothing and leave in the middle of the night' had proved devastating to some families; they had suffered serious financial hardship and harboured deep feelings of resentment at being abandoned.[29] Harry Stratton's pregnant wife, Winnie, had been bitterly angry when he chose to leave her without a word and disappear to Spain; he returned home to find she had later miscarried. Not surprisingly, repairing their relationship was a very 'slow and painful' process.[30] Other veterans encountered hostility in the workplace. When Scottish medical volunteer Roderick MacFarquhar arrived home, he was astonished to find that he 'was regarded with some degree of horror by some of the more sedate members of my union, the Railway Clerks' Association'.[31] George Leeson found much the same when he tried to resume his job with the London Underground; he was informed by a representative of the personnel department that 'We have here an instruction from head office that you are not to be re-employed on London Transport in any capacity whatsoever.'[32]

Cyril Sexton, formerly a member of the Royal Navy Volunteer Reserve, was repatriated from Spain after being hit through the cheek by a machine-gun bullet at Gandesa. He tried hard to find work back in Britain, to no avail: 'No one was interested in an individual that had been fighting fascism for two years.'[33] Aware that many returning brigaders faced genuine hardship, which did not reflect well on the Communist Party, a campaign was launched to raise money for the families and dependents of those killed or badly wounded and fund-raising meetings were held around the country. Sexton joined other veterans travelling around Britain and spoke at innumerable meetings on behalf of the Spanish Republic.[34] Charlotte Haldane and other members of the International Brigade Dependents' and Wounded Aid Committee (IBD&WAC), of which she was honorary secretary, visited the homes of those in need, assisting them with claims.[35] The committee supported numerous struggling veterans: Liverpool volunteer Frank Deegan later recalled that he and two others 'received small sums of £1.25 each for four weeks till we had settled down'[36] and when young hunger-marcher John Longstaff returned from Spain to two months of unemployment, he was granted 'fourteen shillings a week'.[37] However, money was always short and the issue of finding work became a pressing concern:

> In view of the fact that a good many members of the Battalion have now returned home and that the wounded are gradually being discharged from hospital or medical treatment as fit, I have been considering the question of how best they could be found employment . . . It is quite clear that the Dependents' Aid Committee cannot continue to support them indefinitely. But I consider that when we are compelled to discontinue their allowances, we should not simply abandon them to U.A.B. [Unemployment Assistance Board] or to their own efforts to find jobs.[38]

Nonetheless, some veterans felt that the Party should have given more support to those who had been wounded in Spain. Manchester volunteer Walter Greenhalgh took the view that the Party had made good political capital out 'of the lads coming home' but had failed to care for them sufficiently in the aftermath, being more concerned with the forthcoming war in Europe: 'They ignored them: "there's another battle to fight, so that's it".'[39] Certainly, the IBD&WAC's financial position was precarious; a situation not helped by the actions of a 'small core' of veterans who attempted to swindle money from it. One man was accused by a furious Charlotte Haldane of having 'made a profession' in writing begging letters.[40]

In March 1939, three months after the main party of volunteers returned and as the Spanish Republic was drawing its final agonised breath, the veterans established an organisation dedicated to continuing the struggle against Franco. The aims of the International Brigade Association (IBA), as laid out in its constitution, were:

> To carry on in Britain the spirit and tradition of the International Brigade as front-line fighters for the defence and advance of democracy against Fascism; for the rapid development of common action and purpose among all anti-fascist people; to spread the truth about the struggle of the people, Army and Government of Republican Spain and to win all necessary support for the Spanish Republic. By this and other activities, to honour the immortal memory of those who fell in Spain.[41]

With its own publication, the *Volunteer for Liberty*, the IBA was open to all who had fought in the war, not just Party members. Indeed, membership was extended even to renegades such as Tom Wintringham, who had been forced to resign from the Party in 1938 over his affair with the American journalist Kitty Bowler, falsely accused by André Marty of being a 'Trotskyite spy'.[42]

As in the battalion itself, Communists took on the leading role and ensured that the IBA maintained a close relationship with the Party, even if there were often disagreements between the leaderships of the two organisations over strategy and tactics.[43] The security services thus saw the IBA not as 'an Old Comrades Association for Members of the British Battalion of the International Brigade' but as a 'Communist controlled organ of party propaganda', and the association was closely monitored by

Special Branch.[44] But with over five hundred British dead left in Spain, the IBA could count on wide support from many in the Labour movement, and beyond, who continued to campaign for the Republican cause. On 25 January thirteen London engineering workshops imposed an overtime ban and joined with men from eight building sites to stop work early and march on the Prime Minister's office in support of Spain. A week later, over a thousand engineering workers were addressed by Communist MP Willie Gallagher before they too marched on Downing Street.[45]

Not all veterans of the Spanish war rushed to join the IBA, and not all continued to follow the Party line as they had generally been prepared to do while in Spain.[46] Some former volunteers had become deeply disillusioned with the Communist Party; they included Fred Copeman, whose departure was officially announced by the IBA in the *Volunteer for Liberty*:

> In reply to many enquiries we wish to state that Fred Copeman is no longer a member of the association. He was removed from his position of chairman for conduct prejudicial to the good name of the International Brigade. His writings and statements in no way reflect the policy of the International Brigade Association.[47]

In fact, the cause of the split was rather different: Copeman quit the Party in a row over a potentially fraudulent expense claim by a former political commissar.[48]

Many veterans, nursing personal or political criticisms of the Party and no longer held in its iron grip, did however now feel free to voice complaints that had been suppressed in Spain. One row saw accusations and counter-accusations fly back and forth over suspected desertions during the brigaders' retreat through Aragon in the spring of 1938. According to Edwin Greening, the argument had begun in Spain when two other Welsh volunteers, Lance Rogers and Jim Brewer, had attempted to interrogate him about his precise whereabouts during the retreats. Greening responded furiously, demanding that every member of the battalion should be made to reveal how he had survived. As Greening was aware, there were many occasions when headlong flight – essentially every man for himself – was the only available option. While this hardly counted as desertion, it was nevertheless not an event the battalion and Communist Party leadership were keen to broadcast.[49]

Scottish volunteer Robert Armstrong, wounded in the leg at Lopera in December 1936, was another who now felt free to raise criticisms. Armstrong had been repatriated back to Britain after a long convalescence and his experiences in Spain – he believed that the battalion leadership had failed to honour an earlier promise to repatriate him – led him to leave the Communist Party and, in his words, 'become a Trotskyist'. Unsurprisingly, this led to a major falling out with his comrades and a bitter war of words. In an article penned for *Workers Fight* (the journal of the Revolutionary Socialist League, a short-lived Marxist organisation affiliated to the Fourth International), Armstrong listed various hysterical allegations that had been thrown at him since his defection – that his wound had been self-inflicted, that he had deserted and that he suffered from 'a dangerous mental disease' – before responding with a well-aimed counter-attack:

> It is important to remember that 99 per cent of the Brigaders were voicing precisely the same sort of criticism. Sick men, useless for further service, were kept hanging behind the lines for twelve, fifteen, and even eighteen months before they were sent home. The existence of the officer caste, the police controlled training bases, and the insane policy of no repatriation created widespread hostility and engendered swift demoralisation. Most of the Brigaders were demoralised. I know that this is a very delicate point to touch upon, and one which will be passionately denied by many who were themselves demoralised. The personal prestige these comrades derive from having been in Spain is seriously undermined, they think, by such an assertion. Why should it be? These men were not demoralised because they were afraid of soldiering, but because they were treated like foreign pawns in the international political manoeuvres of the Spanish Government.[50]

Like George Orwell, Armstrong was scathing of the apparent willingness of many veterans to swallow the Party line on the Moscow show trials and the suppression of the POUM:

> Just as the rank and file members of the Communist Party believe implicitly and in defiance of all reason, the grotesque confessions extracted after months of fiendish torture from the lips of the Moscow trials prisoners, or believed the insane libel published in the 'Daily Worker' recently that Franco had taken the members of the P.O.U.M. under his protection, so will they believe, even without the slightest knowledge of us [Trotskyists]

in many cases, that we are drunkards, ruffians, neurotics, Jew baiters, pilferers and careerists willing to sell ourselves to the Gestapo for a regular wage rather than a lump sum of thirty pieces of silver.[51]

Others joined the attacks. Londoner Edwin Hall, who according to Jason Gurney had been a former member of the British Union of Fascists, and another disgruntled veteran, John Murch, described to the *Sunday Dispatch* how they believed they had been duped by the Communist Party into going to Spain and now regretted their action.[52] A further damaging attack came from Captain George Wattis, who had returned in April 1938. In front of a Commons committee chaired by the staunchly pro-Franco Sir Henry Page Croft, Wattis accused the Brigades of having been thoroughly infiltrated by Soviet intelligence, and alleged the widespread use of executions to maintain discipline.[53] This was certainly not the case, within the English-speaking volunteers at least, but Wattis was one of many who formed an abiding resentment of the 'political manipulation' within the Brigades.[54]

At a meeting on 17 March 1939 in Northampton town hall, Scottish veteran D. Davidson joined Hall and Peter Kemp, the former volunteer for Franco, on a platform where all three agreed that 'Franco was right in Spain.' One of the veterans recounted the trial of the two British deserters at Teruel, though omitting the crucial detail that the men had been carrying maps of the Republican machine-gun positions when caught. He also brought up the execution of a drunken British machine-gunner, though he did not mention Maurice Ryan by name. Davidson and Hall were extremely critical of the dominant role of the Communist Party in the International Brigades and its involvement in the suppression of political dissent. As Hall complained, 'All our leaders were people in official positions, like school-teachers. They were all Communists. I did not go there to fight for Communism. I went there to fight for democracy.'[55]

The ex-International Brigade Anti-Communist League, of which Davidson and Hall were both members, claimed that a third of the 300 men who had recently returned to Britain had joined their organisation. By doing so, it somewhat overplayed its hand, undermining its credibility in the eyes of many supporters of the Brigades: Bill Alexander later dismissed the League as comprising only ten members, the majority of them deserters who had 'promoted themselves in fanciful accounts of their battle experiences'.[56] Nevertheless, the complaints of disenchanted former volunteers were seized upon by Nationalist supporters, who had long maintained that the International Brigades contained thousands of Soviet troops and that the Spanish Republic was little more than a Russian puppet state; 'Red Spain is Communist!' read one placard at a demonstration outside Parliament.[57] This testimony, allied with that from victims of the suppression that followed the May Days, would provide the foundation for persistent claims that the volunteers were, if not actually 'dupes', as the *Daily Mail* called them, then 'heroic victims' of Comintern propaganda. While the attacks were clearly an irritant, however, Alexander and his comrades in the IBA were much more concerned with the situation in Spain.

At the beginning of 1939, Franco launched a huge offensive in Catalonia; by 26 January, Barcelona had fallen to a determined Nationalist advance. One month later, on 27 February, with the end of the war seemingly imminent, Britain and France formally recognised his government, an act decried by the *News Chronicle* as 'the shameful culmination of one of the blackest chapters in this country's history'.[58] The subsequent feeble response to Germany's annexation of Bohemia and Moravia in March only added to veterans' sense of disgust at the democracies' craven attitude to Hitler's expansionism. Of course, they were hardly alone in their criticisms of appeasement; on Chamberlain's return from Munich the previous September, Winston Churchill had warned the Prime Minister that 'You were given the choice between war and dishonour. You chose dishonour and you will have war.'[59]

With the Republic abandoned by Britain and France, many in Spain felt that defeat was now inevitable: 'it means the end of us,' Sam Lesser's Spanish secretary cried despairingly.[60] Aware that Franco would refuse to negotiate even if the Republicans laid down their arms, Spanish Prime Minister Juan Negrín determined to continue fighting the war, in the desperate hope that the international situation would change. But, in the end, it was events within Spain that sealed the Republic's fate. In March 1939, a revolt was launched against Negrín's government by Socialists, Republicans and elements of the military who believed, despite all evidence to the contrary, that a negotiated, peaceful surrender could still be secured. As the Republic collapsed, Nationalist forces were able to march into Madrid virtually unopposed.[61] Finally, on 1 April 1939, came the catastrophe that many of the former brigaders had both predicted and feared, when a triumphant Franco proclaimed victory for the Nationalists and the end of the civil war.

Those who had been part of the struggle to save the Spanish government were distraught: 'When Madrid finally capitulated . . . I was like a kid. I cried. I sobbed my heart out,' admitted former ambulance driver Max Colin.[62] 'It was a terrible, terrible thing when the whole struggle collapsed,' remembered Scottish nurse Annie Murray.[63] For Lou Kenton, who had only recently driven aid from Britain to Republican Spain, the news, however much he had expected it, was still an awful blow: 'The depression set in for me,' he confessed, 'the realisation that we had lost.'[64]

The manner of the Republic's final defeat, following the uprising launched by previously loyal Spanish army officers, provoked particular anguish and bitterness:

The Republican Government was defeated, not so much by the Fascist troops in the field, as through the treachery of some of the leaders of the Madrid command. The people's army in Catalonia had fought an heroic rearguard action all the way to the French border, finishing up in France. The only troops in modern history to be forced out of their own country.[65]

Nevertheless, many veterans' determination to continue the fight was undimmed by the end of the war. John Longstaff made this explicitly clear to Winston Churchill, in a chance encounter with him in Parliament in 1939:

I was asked to visit the House of Commons to see Sir Stafford Cripps regarding the suspension of some Labour Party members and the disbandment of the Labour Party League of Youth. Cripps happened to see Churchill in a corridor and introduced me to him as a young Socialist who had fought in the Spanish War. Churchill asked if those Britons who fought in Spain would fight for Britain. I pointed out that our fight in Spain had been for Britain and indeed we would fight if the Nazi or Fascist armies took on the British people.

Briefly I explained to him why Franco now controlled, but not conquered Spain. I pointed out that had Non-intervention not been applied, the Spanish people would have defeated Franco during 1936. It was apparent to me, even though I was confronted by one of the most virulent campaigners against Socialism and even though he had originally supported Franco, that he would fight the Nazi and Fascist powers.[66]

While campaigning and fund-raising for the now exiled Spanish Republic continued, many veterans' minds turned to the impending European war against fascism. Over the summer, Harry Bury and his Spanish girlfriend prepared themselves for the forthcoming conflict with Germany by renting 'a nice little house on the cliffs at Gorleston [just south of Great Yarmouth] for a very small rent. Many people were leaving the exposed east coast for safer (so they thought) places, and there were a lot of empty houses.'[67]

Others, however, were restless to participate and gave accounts of their experiences and the lessons they had learned during their time in Spain. Medical workers in particular had developed skills which they believed could make an important contribution. Dr Alex Tudor-Hart gave a lecture to the British Postgraduate Medical School in April 1939 on the 'Böhler' closed method technique for the treatment of fractures, which had been refined in Spain.[68] And Fred Copeman began giving talks on aerial bombardment, based on his own experiences in the civil war.[69] Interestingly, Copeman complained that his lectures were often heckled by Communists, who were calling for the installation of deep air-raid shelters in Britain's conurbations. Copeman's response showed how far he had travelled from the Party: 'Little did they know', he claimed, 'that the Government was well aware of the need, and that action was already being taken.'[70]

With war looking inevitable, many veterans prepared to enlist in the British armed forces. However, in late summer 1939 they were suddenly forced to question the very notion of a continuing war against fascism and the Communist Party's place in the vanguard of that struggle. On 23 August Vyacheslav Molotov and Joachim von Ribbentrop, the foreign ministers of the Soviet Union and Nazi Germany, signed the infamous non-aggression pact between their two countries, forcing Communist Parties around the world to discard anti-fascism in favour of 'anti-imperialism'. Clear notions of continuity with the struggle in which the Spanish veterans had participated were shattered overnight. Difficult enough for any Communist to accept, the signing of the pact left many former volunteers utterly dumbstruck and brought simmering disagreements among the veterans to a head.[71] Though many Party members argued that Stalin had been forced into the agreement by the intransigence of Britain and France, Tony McLean, who served as a research clerk and military censor in Spain, admitted that 'the Hitler-Stalin pact put all of us in a terribly false position.'[72] Others found it similarly hard to swallow:

Like so many other Communists or near-Communists at the time I was dazed by Stalin's volte-face. For years the international Communist movement had made 'Hitler means war' one of its rallying cries, and called for an anti-fascist alliance against him; now Stalin had signed a pact with the devil incarnate. Lots of people explained his motives at length, and some of the explanations made quite good sense, but it was hard to take.[73]

George Aitken was one of numerous veterans to leave the Party following the Nazi-Soviet pact, later becoming a leading figure in the Labour Party.[74] London volunteer David Lomon had done the same upon his return from Spain, believing that the Labour Party 'had a bigger voice than anyone else'. The events of August 1939 confirmed to him that he had made the right decision: 'I was pleased I didn't join the Communist Party because, being Jewish, well, that Stalin should link up with [Hitler], was unbelievable.'[75] Sailor Albert Cole, who served in the Spanish Republican Navy on a torpedo boat before joining the British Battalion, was in no doubt that 'Quite a few I knew in Liverpool fell away gradually from the Party [over the pact].'[76]

However, by no means all the veterans felt this way, many suspecting that Britain and France were trying to encourage Hitler to expand east, rather than west.[77] Manchester volunteer Josh Davidson believed that 'it was quite obvious to anyone who was interested in the political situation, at that stage, that the efforts . . . [of] the British and the French were [aimed at pushing] Germany into war against the Soviet Union.'[78] Davidson and others who remained loyal to the Party maintained that the pact was a perfectly legitimate, if tactical, means for the USSR to curtail German aggression and expansionism and that Stalin had little option. East Ender Joe Garber was absolutely clear: 'I wasn't really shocked. Truthfully. I thought to myself, it's two wily sods, they're playing for time. It was like a game.'[79]

There was little time to adjust to the new Party line. Only one week later Hitler invaded Poland and Britain's consequent declaration of war on Germany followed two days thereafter. Harry Pollitt, who had a significant personal investment in the Spanish struggle and the British volunteers, immediately proclaimed it an anti-fascist war, just as the volunteers had been fighting in Spain. In a pamphlet released on 12 September entitled *How To Win This War*, he also accepted that the British rulers were simultaneously engaged in an imperialist war, arguing that Communists should therefore see both Hitler and Chamberlain as enemies.[80]

Many veterans agreed with him and moved to continue their fight against fascism by volunteering for the British armed forces. As Charlotte Haldane put it, 'all those who had fought in Spain, or taken part in the anti-Nazi struggle in any way, responded with enthusiasm to Pollitt's declaration.'[81] Manchester YCL member Bernard McKenna, a former POW at San Pedro, regarded it very much as a continuation of the battle he had fought in Spain and once more volunteered to take up arms against fascism.[82] Bill Alexander was instructed to join up by the Party, who informed him that 'we need Communists in the forces.'[83]

Such a sense of continuity was not to last long. On 24 September, news brought from Moscow by Dave Springhall would instil a crisis within the Communist Party, split its leadership, and lose it virtually all the goodwill it had earned in its staunch support for the brave British volunteers who had fought for the Republic in the Spanish Civil War.

During a Communist Party Central Committee meeting held in London on 24 September 1939, a huge argument erupted over the line to be taken on the war in Europe. Party ideologue R. Palme Dutt maintained that it was an imperialist war which would bring no benefits to the working class, and that the CPGB should oppose it. A contrary view was argued strongly by Harry Pollitt, who could not accept that this was an imperialist war in the same way that the 1914–18 conflict had been. However, the decision was taken out of their hands when Springhall, who had been acting as British representative at Comintern headquarters, returned from Moscow during the evening. He brought clear instructions from Moscow that Dutt's interpretation was the correct one: this was an imperialist war and it was to be opposed. Consequently, an official announcement accepting Moscow's position was made at the beginning of October:

> This war is not a war for democracy against Fascism . . . It is not a war for the liberties of small nations. It is not a war for the defence of peace against aggression . . . The British and French ruling class are seeking to use the anti-fascist sentiments of the people for their own imperialistic aims.[84]

Two members of the central committee who opposed the motion, Pollitt and John Campbell, editor of the *Daily Worker*, were replaced by Palme Dutt and Bill Rust.[85] While sound arguments had been put forward for supporting the war, Stalin had spoken. The choice was simple: either accept the diktat, or leave the Party.[86]

The Party's abandonment of its long-standing war against fascism was mocked as 'the greatest U-turn in twentieth century British history' by opponents, many of whom already took a scathing view of its stance on the Moscow purges, the activities of the NKVD and the Comintern in Spain, and the Nazi-Soviet pact.[87] At the same time, many powerful and influential figures who had previously backed the Party over its defence of the Spanish Republic found the new line utterly incomprehensible; they included Aneurin Bevan, who wrote that the Communist Party 'shame their own dead in Spain'.[88] Even die-hard Party loyalist Claud Cockburn found the change of policy difficult to stomach, later describing the manoeuvre as 'totally futile'.[89] Any remaining goodwill towards the Party was dashed by Stalin's invasion of Poland on 17 September, the announcement of the agreement dividing up the country with Germany five days later and, above all, the Soviet invasion of Finland on 30 November.[90] The IBA's criticism of Labour leader Clement Attlee, who had spoken out against the invasion of Finland, did little to counter accusations that the association was no more than 'a tool of the Communist Party'.[91] Many loyal and influential supporters of the Spanish Republic were outraged, including journalists George Steer, John Langdon-Davies and William Forrest, who saw the Soviets' action in Finland as a parallel to the fascist powers' intervention in Spain.[92] Paradoxically, Fred Copeman, who had just left the Party, felt his decision was vindicated by their political somersaults: 'The news of the Party's reversal of policy in regard to the war was, in a way, a pleasant surprise to me – maybe, I thought, I was not completely wrong.'[93]

The new line put the former International Brigaders, who had gone to Spain, as they had described it, 'to defeat Hitler', in a very uncomfortable position.[94] Nevertheless, some veterans did manage to accept the Party's opposition to the war, including the former Communist Party branch secretary in Manchester, Patrick Curry. 'One imperialist power was as bad as another,' he argued, believing that any move that supported the Soviet Union should be backed, for 'we were defending the base of socialism.'[95] Others took much the same view and were happy to 'keep out of it':

This was a Capitalist war and I had no real desire to fight for the rich who would be trying to prevent their counter-parts in Germany from grabbing some of their properties. I wasn't a pacifist. If I was called upon I would join up, but my energies would be directed in trying to end the battle as soon as possible. Workers get no benefits from that type of war.[96]

In mid-November, their voices were rejoined by that of Harry Pollitt, who stated that his earlier position had been a false one. He explained his temporary mistake by citing 'the strong personal feelings which had been aroused by what I had witnessed in Spain, and the responsibility I felt I had in regard to the sacrifice made by the British Battalion of the International Brigades'.[97]

However, the British volunteers' sacrifice in Spain meant that many veterans, and Communists too, were determined to continue their fight against the Nazis, despite the Party's opposition: '*The Daily Worker* told me it had turned from an anti-fascist war into an imperialist war overnight. Neither I nor any of my comrades took any notice,' declared the future Labour Chancellor of the Exchequer, Denis Healey, who had joined the Communist Party in 1937 but left in the autumn of 1939.[98] Many veterans of the International Brigades felt the same way, believing, as anti-fascists, that joining the British armed forces at the outbreak of the Second World War was their duty. Tom Wintringham argued strongly that 'any war against Nazi Germany was a step in the right direction.'[99]

Liverpudlian Jack Edwards 'stopped and thought' before deciding that the Communist line was wrong and that, despite any loyalty he felt to the Party, fighting fascism should take precedence:

I came home in February 1939 and within a year I decided I was going to join up again, this time in the RAF. I joined because it's the same bloody fight. There was a big argument politically: whether the fight against Hitler was the same fight as we had in Spain – and I argued it was. A lot in the Communist Party said we should be anti-war, but I never agreed with that. I said it's the same bloody war, actually, that was going on when Hitler started in September, it was the same war as was going on in Spain.[100]

As senior *Daily Worker* functionary Douglas Hyde later admitted, 'those who had fought in Spain or had been in direct conflict with fascism in Britain tended to welcome the chance to "have a go at the Nazis" under any banner, even that of Chamberlain.'[101] More veterans determined to join up. Cyril Sexton joined the ill-fated British Expeditionary Force in 1939 and was in France by Christmas. Later evacuated via St Malo, he was fortunate;

many of his unit were drowned in the disastrous sinking of RMS *Lancastria* in June 1940.[102] Sexton went on to serve in West Africa, India, Burma and the Dutch East Indies.[103] Another former brigader, Albert Charlesworth, volunteered for the RAF in 1939 and 'flew as a pilot for the rest of the war – out in India, supply dropping in Burma'. Within the air force, where his exploits in Spain were widely known, Charlesworth was nicknamed, of course, 'the Red Baron'.[104]

The German invasion of France in May 1940, and the subsequent collapse of the French government, swiftly brought to an end what had been seen as the 'phoney war' and forced the Communist Party to re-evaluate its position.[105] In consequence, the official Party line shifted, moving from opposing an 'imperialist war' to backing a 'people's war'. Drawing on the lessons learned in Spain, the Party argued that the civil war had demonstrated that fascism was not invincible and that resistance was not futile, but could only be effective if conducted by a truly democratic government. This heralded the beginnings of some sense of continuity for the veterans. As Sam Wild put it: 'Only the working class can do the things the Spanish people did and form a People's Army capable of producing men like Modesto, Lister and Campesino, who stand in such striking contrast to Ironside, Pétain and Gort.'[106]

At an IBA rally in July 1940, slogans included 'The People Defended Spain!' and 'Only the People can Defend Britain!' It was now claimed that the International Brigades in Spain had been fighting for British, as well as Spanish, democracy.[107]

For 32 months of the struggle we denounced the assassins of the Spanish people with demands that 'Chamberlain Must Go'. In the present grave situation we repeat the demand. Chamberlain Must GO! And with him all the friends of Franco and supporters of Fascism in Britain.[108]

The Party argued that the 'guilty men', to use Michael Foot's infamous phrase, were too cordial with the fascist dictatorships and could not be trusted to oppose them, citing the fraud of non-intervention in Spain. Clearly, while the Communist Party and IBA leadership saw Hitler as a threat, they could not see the British establishment, or Winston Churchill, as saviours.

But, one year later, in June 1941, dramatic events in eastern Europe would force the CPGB to launch a complete volte-face. On this occasion, the decision was not so much a product of Stalin, as of his erstwhile ally, Hitler. Nazi Germany's treacherous invasion of the Soviet Union, in the early hours of Sunday 22 June 1941, brought the Molotov–Ribbentrop pact to a swift and dramatic end. The British government now had the dubious honour of the full and enthusiastic support of the Communist Party in the war against the Nazis. For loyal followers of the Party line, the difficult period of the 'imperialist war' could finally be laid to rest: the conflict was now an anti-fascist war, just as it had been in Spain.

22

Return of the Anti-Fascist War

> I had parachuted, in uniform, behind the Allied lines in Brittany to
> arm and organize French Resistance forces and hold them ready
> for action at the moment most useful for the Allied advance . . . I
> was one of the few people in the US Army who could speak fluent,
> idiomatic, and (if necessary) pungently coarse French. When [my
> Professor] asked me where I had learned it, I told him that I had
> fought in 1936 on the northwest sector of the Madrid front in the
> French Battalion of the XIth International Brigade. 'Oh,' he said,
> 'You were a premature anti-Fascist.'
>
> I was taken aback by the expression. How, I wondered, could
> *anyone* be a *premature* anti-Fascist?
>
> Bernard Knox, *Premature Anti-Fascist*

The abrupt 'about-turn' performed by the CPGB following Germany's
invasion of Russia on 22 June 1941 finally allowed Communists 'to escape
free from the embarrassing situation into which their "revolutionary
defeatism" had landed them'.[1] For many Spanish veterans, it was a great
relief to be able to abandon a line they had never really believed in. They
could take up the anti-fascist struggle once again and 'the lessons of Spain
could now be applied to the war in Europe.'[2] Many, like Max Colin, promptly
did so: 'When the Germans attacked Russia and the line changed, I changed
too. With that end, I decided to volunteer for the forces.'[3] Others, such as
David Crook, who had been in China at the outbreak of the war, did likewise:

> This, for me and other Communists, changed the nature of World War II
> from an imperialist to an anti-fascist war. In this, I felt I had a stake, as I had
> had in the anti-fascist war in Spain. And I decided to return to England and
> join the armed forces.[4]

However, not everyone was convinced by the Communist Party's sudden conversion to enthusiastic warmongering, even if Orwell had shrewdly predicted it three years earlier: '[if] Great Britain enters into an alliance or military understanding with the U.S.S.R.,' he had written, 'the English Communist, like the French Communist, will have no choice but to become a good patriot and imperialist.'[5] Tom Wintringham, who had supported the war from its outset, was particularly scathing about the Party's most recent about-face:

> Communists who have been saying that this is a simple imperialist war, a continuation of 1914–18 . . . will now doubtless change their line. But who will believe in their sincerity, or find it possible to act with them as allies or associates, unless at the same time as they change their line they admit freely and frankly that the line they have been taking in the past was wrong, non-marxist, contrary to the interests of the working class and of the revolution?[6]

Not surprisingly, many in the government were just as sceptical.[7] As Conservative politician Lord Swinton, the chairman of the Home Defence (Security) Executive committee (established by the Prime Minister in May 1940 to tackle all matters relating to the defence of Britain against a fifth column), elegantly put it: 'It is clear that the Communist game is still the same; but it is being played on a much better wicket.'[8] In Whitehall, the copying in early 1940 of Dave Springhall's secret lecture notes, in which he had stated that the Communist Party was urging comrades in the armed forces to initiate all effective action against the war, would not easily be forgotten.[9] Despite the Communist Party's shift to enthusiastic support for the war, former International Brigaders who attempted to enlist found themselves prevented from joining up.

Volunteers had found it difficult to enlist in the armed forces since the very beginning of the war. When John Longstaff had resigned from his job as an engineer – a reserved occupation – in order to join up, he had been informed by the colonel in charge of recruitment that 'we are under instruction not to recruit any person who fought with the International Brigade.'[10] Likewise, James Maley, who had served in the Territorial Army before going to Spain, tried to enlist in 1940 and was put down for the RAF after taking his medical. However, he was later informed that he was exempt from serving in the forces 'because of his time in Spain'.[11] When he responded to an RAF advertisement for short-service commissions for pilot officers, John Peet had discovered much the same:

> Almost by return of post I was summoned to appear before a board. Three or four affable officers questioned me on my qualifications, nodding agreeably when they heard I was fluent in German and had considerable first-hand knowledge of central Europe. My favourite sport? Skiing seemed appropriate, as a thoroughly upper-class pursuit, and it had the additional advantage that the chances of being asked immediately to show my prowess were fairly low.
>
> In giving biographical details it seemed wisest to omit the Spanish episode. So, without stretching the truth unduly, I gave the impression that I had continued teaching in Prague until rudely interrupted by Hitler in March 1939. It was a short and friendly interview, and the senior officer concluded by saying that, of course he could not give a final answer right off the bat, but it might not be a bad idea if I started considering how to wind up my private civilian affairs at short notice.
>
> A week or two later an official letter arrived: we have to inform you that you are unsuitable for a short-service commission. I showed the letter to a senior man in our organization, the International Brigade Association.
>
> 'So you are another of the rejects,' he said. 'It seems that all applications for commissions in the armed forces are being screened by the Special Branch at Scotland Yard, to keep out anybody who has actually been through a modern war.'[12]

In fact, a policy restricting the admission of former International Brigaders into the armed forces had been put in place in January 1939, shortly after the British Battalion's return from Spain.[13] As Roger Hollis, MI5's representative on the HDSE committee admitted, names were checked against a blacklist supplied by the security services.[14] MI5 and the War Office were extremely concerned that many former volunteers had been indoctrinated by senior British Communists, such as Bill Rust and Dave Springhall, particularly during the period when they were awaiting repatriation at the end of 1938:

> It was known that throughout the civil war in Spain, lectures were given on Communist doctrines to all units of the Brigade by political commissars, detailed for the purpose, and it was noticed further that among those

political commissars attached to the British Battalions were certain notorious Communists, well-known to the Security Service as having, in the past, been active members of the underground section of the C.P.G.B. concerned in spreading revolutionary doctrines amongst members of H.M. Forces.

After the British Battalion had been withdrawn from the line it was noticed that a body of about 300 of them had been kept embodied in a small village near the Franco-Spanish frontier and were undergoing training in revolutionary propaganda. This fact was openly referred to in the 'Daily Worker', which stated plainly that the intention was to make use of these men for propaganda purposes after they returned to this country.[15]

A 'secret and personal' memorandum stated that 'the presence of such men in the Army would obviously be highly undesirable from the point of morale and discipline.' Furthermore, it was stated that no veteran should be aware of the policy's existence: 'These instructions should be regarded as secret and care should be taken that no man reported should become aware that he is viewed with suspicion.' Attempts to enquire into the exact nature of the ban, or to elicit evidence that it even existed, were met with official silence. In a debate in the House of Commons on 23 May 1939, the Home Secretary, Leslie Hore-Belisha, resolutely refused to disclose to Labour MP Ellen Wilkinson the contents of the secret memorandum regarding the policy towards former members of the International Brigades. And an article in *The People* newspaper the same month, alleging that a ban existed forbidding civil war veterans from admission into the armed forces and the Territorial Army, met with a curt denial:

> The General Staff have of course issued no such order, and for your own information I may add that all that is done, is to make enquiries into the bona-fides of any would-be recruits, or men already serving in the forces, who are known to have served in the International brigade in Spain. Quite a number of men merely did so from a spirit of adventure and are now serving happily in H.M. Forces.[16]

Of course, this was true, for the memorandum clearly stated that the intention was not to prevent all International Brigaders – or Communists for that matter – from serving in the forces:

It may be added that the purpose of the circular referred to above, and the instructions issued to recruiting Officers, was not necessarily to prevent any man who had served in the International Brigade from serving in the British Army, but to ensure, as far as possible, that no man should be allowed to serve, whether Communist or not, who had become imbued with revolutionary ideas which would render his presence in the ranks undesirable.[17]

However, much was clearly open to interpretation and despite the apparent intention of the policy and the denials of its existence, a large number of men were denied admission into the armed forces precisely because they were former International Brigaders.[18] While the instigators of the policy may have intended that distinctions should be made between 'good anti-fascists' and dangerous 'revolutionaries', this high-minded aim did not always play out in practice.[19] When, on his second attempt, John Longstaff successfully managed to enlist, his commanding officer accused him of having fought for the 'Reds' in the Spanish war, despite Longstaff's categorical denials:

'No sir. I fought for the Spanish Republican government, sir.'
'They were the Reds.'
'No sir, I fought for the Spanish Republican government, sir. I fought in the International Brigade. I fought in the British Battalion. We were not Reds, sir, we were volunteers helping to fight fascism.'[20]

Despite the top secret nature of the memorandum, talk of a restriction on former International Brigaders persisted. Senior figures in the IBA and Communist Party had actually become aware of the policy as early as the spring of 1939, partly due to a tip-off from David Marshall, once a member of the Tom Mann Centuria. He had been warned by colleagues in the labour exchange of the existence of a blacklist containing the names of locals who shouldn't be called up: 'leading lads of the YCL, the odd drunk . . . perhaps the odd petty criminal . . . and ex-brigaders'.[21] More solid evidence came when a copy of the memorandum itself was passed on to the Communist Party. Former British Battalion secretary Ted Edwards had been working as a clerk in the Territorial Army, having served in a similar position in the Royal Artillery before his time in Spain.[22] But his job didn't last long; on 14 April 1939, with no explanation, he was dismissed with a week's notice. Though Edwards wasn't told, his commanding officer had been shown a letter from the deputy Assistant Adjutant General of Northern Command, stating that Edwards was associating with active Communists and 'was not a suitable man to be engaged in a military office'.[23]

Several days afterwards, Edwards contacted Chris Smith, formerly of the British Anti-Tank Battery, and showed him the War Office memorandum which, as Smith described it, stated that 'on no account must people who have been in Spain be accepted either into the Territorial Army or the Regular Army.'[24] Edwards was arrested by Special Branch and questioned on suspicion of copying and passing on documents, an accusation confirmed by a search of his lodgings on 22 April 1939.[25] Smith was picked up at his workplace the following morning and questioned as to where he had seen the letter, and who else might have seen it.[26]

Special Branch were anxious to discover first why, despite the restrictions placed on Spanish veterans, Edwards had encountered no problems gaining a position in the Territorial Army and, second, how he had managed to obtain a copy of the secret instructions. The former was explained simply enough when Edwards' commanding officer admitted that because Edwards had previously been employed as a clerk in the Royal Artillery, he had not bothered to check his background. Lax security had also enabled Edwards to obtain the memo. Although secret documents were kept locked in a desk in the commanding officer's office, the report noted pointedly 'Key kept in lock permanently.'[27] Edwards was tried in camera under the Official Secrets Act and was given eighteen months' hard labour in Wakefield prison, with the recommendation that he should not be accepted into any of the armed forces on release.[28]

With their route into the military blocked, some veterans looked for alternative ways to carry on the fight against the Nazis. Renowned scientist and Communist J.B.S. Haldane approached several Spanish veterans known to him from his visits to the battalion in Spain.[29] Haldane was involved in top-secret work for the navy, following a disastrous submarine accident in June 1939 in which ninety-nine men aboard HMS *Thetis* lost their lives. Among the Spanish veterans and exiles who assisted him were Juan Negrín, the former premier of the Spanish Republic, German Communist Hans Kahle, former British Battalion commander, and political commissar Bill Alexander, and three other former volunteers: Patrick Duff, George Ives (who had trained as a radio operator in Moscow in January 1936) and former political commissar Donald Renton.[30] Alexander's acceptance for such secretive work is particularly surprising, given that the security services were fully aware of his role in Spain and knew that he was a serious, disciplined and long-standing Party member.[31] Yet, while some of his former comrades were being rejected by the armed forces, he and the others were able to work on vitally important and top secret work for the navy.[32]

Haldane's experiments aimed to discover the most successful method of escaping from sunken submarines, examining individuals' reactions to pressure and the effects of carbon dioxide. The volunteers were sealed into a chamber containing high levels of the gas, which were then increased still further. Within an hour all were panting severely, particularly Duff, who was still convalescing from a wound received in Spain.[33] It was extremely unpleasant and dangerous work, as tests were frequently pressed forward until the human guinea pigs lost consciousness: 'One of our subjects has burst a lung, but is recovering,' reported Haldane; 'six have been unconscious on one or more occasions; one has had convulsions.'[34] Haldane himself suffered seizures from hypoxia on a number of occasions and one of his teeth exploded when he compressed too quickly.[35] All the participants undoubtedly risked their lives; as Haldane explained, 'I chose these men as colleagues because I had no doubt of their courage and devotion.'[36]

Unfortunately, Haldane's membership of the Communist Party meant that many in the Admiralty and security services were unhappy at his participation in secret work and his use of civil war veterans.[37] Despite letters of support arguing that his research was invaluable to the war effort, it was eventually decided that 'the personality of Professor Haldane and the presence of his assistants . . . compromises the smooth working of the Admiralty Experimental Diving Unit.' The volunteers were summarily dismissed and Haldane's work was curtailed.[38]

Attempts by another prominent figure from Spain to provide veterans with the opportunity to continue the fight also met with official resistance. In May 1940, Tom Wintringham wrote a famous article for the *Daily Mirror* calling for a 'citizens' army', earning himself the popular nickname of the 'red revolutionary'. While in Spain Wintringham had seen for himself the contradictions between military discipline and democracy, and had come to believe passionately that soldiers must feel free and understand and support the war they were fighting, even – or perhaps especially – if they had been conscripted.[39] To Wintringham, the war in Spain had demon-strated the power of the democratic character of an army: better morale, the ability to organise resistance behind enemy lines, and the advantage of small semi-autonomous units, often commanded by NCOs.[40] Thus he argued, from both a political and military perspective, for more power and importance to be given to the lower ranks; in many respects, applying the line of the Catalan POUM to the Second World War.[41]

'We are hampered by capitalism,' argued Wintringham in his bestselling 1940 publication, *New Ways of War*, '[when] what we need is socialism.'[42] In this Wintringham's view was very similar to that of George Orwell, who maintained that 'we cannot win the war without introducing Socialism, nor establish Socialism without winning the war.'[43] Wintringham's proposals for the network of local defence volunteers established in May 1940 – later the Home Guard – clearly set out his democratic vision:

> The future of the Home Guard is to be recognised as democracy's answer, and an effective answer, to the Nazi technique of aggression. If we choose only to copy totalitarian methods we shall never catch up or surpass the Nazis. But if we set free and mobilise the initiative of our people in a democratic way, in a way similar to that in which this defensive army of volunteers was raised and trained, I believe we shall find and develop ways of taking the offensive also, new methods of war, which the Nazis are doomed by their ideas and their organisation never to be able to understand or copy.[44]

Wintringham argued that, by providing defence in depth, the Home Guard could ensure that Britain was not reliant on one single line of defence and that this would prevent invading Germans from repeating the *Blitzkrieg* tactics practised to such devastating effect elsewhere:

> A battalion that I commanded helped to hold the last road into Madrid. It consisted of men and boys no different from you who read these lines. Many of them had received only ten days' training. None of them had more than six weeks. They had a few machine-guns, all of them over twenty years old. But these 500 men held up 2,000 of Franco's infantry, commanded by Reichswehr officers and backed by German guns and German planes. Our battalion was scattered by German tanks. It reformed when the tanks had gone and took back the ground. That also is the spirit of the People's War.[45]

Having seen for himself the German tactic of infiltration whereby small mobile units were used to punch holes in enemy lines, Wintringham tried to use his connections to impress on the British military command lessons learnt in Spain, but with little success.[46] While his writings on warfare, such as his 1940 pamphlet *How to Reform the Army*, were widely popular, his attacks on the 'Colonel Blimps', the army's incompetent and reactionary traditionalists, made him few friends in the War Office. Frustrated, he decided to take the initiative: on 10 July 1940, backed by money from Edward Hulton, the owner of *Picture Post*, Wintringham established his own guerrilla warfare training school at the house of Lord Jersey, a friend of Hulton, in Osterley, west of London, and staffed it with Spanish veterans.[47]

Wintringham took command, with his American girlfriend, Kitty Bowler, acting as administrator. Hugh Slater, the former Chief of Operations and commander of the British anti-tanks in Spain, took the role of Wintringham's adjutant. Slater later wrote a manual called *Home Guard for Victory*, which instructed readers how to defend villages, towns, suburbs, factories and public buildings, oppose glider landings and hunt tanks. It included a chapter on street warfare, which drew substantially on lessons gained from the defence of Madrid in the winter of 1936–7 and Belchite in the autumn of 1937.[48] Instructors at Osterley included the Canadian Bert 'Yank' Levy, who taught knife-fighting 'and other unorthodox fighting skills'; he later collected these into a manual of guerrilla warfare techniques featuring graphic accounts of hand-to-hand combat and how to destroy enemy vehicles.[49] Three refugee Spanish miners taught impromptu anti-tank strategies.[50]

Traditionalists in the army were understandably horrified at the prospect of Wintringham and his 'Marxist hooligans' training armed bands of revolutionary vigilantes in the black arts of guerrilla warfare. 'They're teaching them street-fighting – just planning to murder us in our beds!' protested one appalled ex-Tory Cabinet minister.[51] The government responded by prohibiting known Communists from joining the Home Guard and instructing that any current members should be reported to the police and expelled.[52] The War Office ordered the training school's immediate closure, but Wintringham defied the order and many left-wing MPs helped him overturn it. Osterley's reputation grew quickly during the summer of 1940. Over 250 Home Guard volunteers attended each week and some regular units were even sent there for training.[53] No doubt the reputation of the classes in camouflage, held by surrealist artist Roland Penrose, was not harmed by his beautiful wife, Lee Miller, posing naked underneath a camouflage net to demonstrate its effectiveness.[54] However, in September 1940, Churchill ordered that the Home Guard were now to be seen as regular soldiers and Osterley was prudently taken over by the War Office. Slater was quietly transferred to an anti-aircraft regiment and Wintringham, who had been refused an officer's commission, eventually resigned from the training school in June 1941.[55] By the summer, he and all his staff had gone. 'The Blimps were back in control.'[56]

Some veterans engaged in rather more covert activities to continue their anti-fascist war. Indeed, a number came to the attention of the security services for their involvement in espionage, either directly against Germany or in support of the Soviet Union. As the *Daily Worker*'s foreign correspondent after the end of the Spanish Civil War, Sam Lesser, admitted, 'the Soviet intelligence services did use the International Brigades for recruiting agents of their own.'[57] In addition, the Brigades provided Russian intelligence with vital resources, particularly passports, a number of which were later used by Soviet agents. Trotsky's assassin, Ramón Mercader, allegedly travelled to Mexico using the passport of a Canadian International Brigader.[58]

Perhaps the most significant spy among the British veterans was Alex Foote. During his time in Spain, Foote had served as a driver for both Jock Cunningham and Fred Copeman and as a courier between London and Spain, officially transporting Red Cross supplies though in reality carrying documents between King Street and the battalion's Communist Party command.[59] Foote had been recruited by Red Army intelligence at the end of the war, having been suggested as a possible foreign operative by Dave Springhall.[60] In October 1938 he was given a passport and made contact with his handler in Geneva, known only as 'Sonia'.[61] In December 1940, 'Sonia' departed for the UK, leaving Foote with ciphers and orders to continue transmissions and maintain contact with Alexander Rado, a Hungarian-born Soviet intelligence agent.

Between the fall of France in 1940 and the beginning of 1943, Foote was charged with learning German and building up a ring of reliable informants. However, by April 1943 he had become nervous that German intelligence had penetrated his cell. His suspicions were correct. Having identified Foote as 'Jim', the technical expert in a Russian intelligence network called 'Red Three' which was supplying the Soviets with reports of military information from German-occupied areas,[62] German agents tipped off the Swiss authorities and Foote was arrested by the Swiss police at the end of November 1943 for using a clandestine wireless transmission set.[63]

Foote was released on 8 September 1944. With Russian intelligence, cautious as ever, keen to be sure he wasn't a British agent, he was flown to Moscow for interrogation and then posted back to Berlin with the aim of 'gaining German background before going to Argentina to work against the United States'.[64] However, while in Berlin, Foote approached British Intelligence staff, claiming that he no longer worked for the Russians and wanted to work for the British instead. The British officer interviewing him didn't believe a word of it, seeing in Foote only 'a very sick man, tired of playing for the Russians, wanting to go home to England – to write an interesting book'.[65]

Nonetheless, MI6 interviewed him, hoping to use him as a double agent and sensing he might be persuaded to identify other British ex-International Brigaders who were working for the Soviets. Although, when shown photographs of suspected agents, Foote was able to identify only Rado, he otherwise proved to be a very useful source, providing information on Russian radio ciphers and operational procedures. MI6 were particularly interested in his knowledge of the Soviets' use of fake passports.[66] The American security services were less happy with Foote's information: Foote later wrote of his exploits in a book, *Handbook for Spies*, in which he claimed that in Moscow he had been told he would have 100 contacts in the US. Whether true or not, his claim caused panic in America.[67]

Other former members of the British Battalion also worked as Soviet agents, having been approached and recruited in Spain. One of the first to be uncovered was Birmingham volunteer (Charles) Oliver Green. Before serving in the Spanish Civil War, Green had been an active Party member in Birmingham, responsible for the Midlands Agit-Prop Department.[68] Arriving in Spain just before the battle of Jarama, he worked in the Republican propaganda services, based in Madrid, and, as one of the Party's trusted elite, was invited to join the Spanish Communist Party. He was also recruited by Soviet intelligence; upon his return to Britain, he was reactivated by the GRU (Russian military intelligence), setting up a spy ring for which he recruited a number of former International Brigaders, including Lon Elliott (now a member of the editorial board of *Volunteer for Liberty*) and Joe Garber.[69]

In May 1942, Green was arrested for forging petrol coupons and upon searching his home Special Branch discovered a number of classified War

Office documents. Interviewed on 11 August at Brixton prison, Green admitted that he had been recruited as a Soviet agent while in Spain and that he was part of a spy ring. Refusing to name any of his fellow agents, his discretion was rather undermined by discussing the agents with R.W. Robson at King Street following his release from prison. MI5, who were listening in to their conversation, gratefully wrote down the names.[70]

While the relatively low-level espionage of Green's circle was not seen as a significant threat by the security services, the case of the Communist Party's National Organiser, Dave Springhall, was taken far more seriously.[71] As a senior figure in the British Party since the 1920s, one who had moreover been jailed for his involvement in the General Strike, Springhall had been monitored by the security services for some time. Moreover, Springhall was believed to be responsible for the Party's underground work among members of the armed forces and suspected of building up contacts in order to conduct espionage.[72] Unsurprisingly, MI5 were determined to keep him out of the military at all costs:

> I think that you will agree that this man's presence in the Army would be most undesirable from the Internal Security point of view. He has been granted exemption until 31.12.41, and subject to your approval, I propose to ask the Ministry of Labour to take the necessary action to ensure that he is not then called up . . . Springhall is a dangerous type of Communist agitator . . . His presence in any branch of H.M. Forces would certainly constitute a serious menace to morale and discipline.[73]

In another lucky break for the security services, Springhall was caught red-handed inveigling secret documents from Olive Mary Sheehan, a clerk working in the telecommunications office of the Air Ministry, and cadres leader of the Secret Air Ministry group of the Communist Party.[74] The espionage was uncovered by Sheehan's flatmate, who overheard them discussing classified information and saw Sheehan give Springhall an envelope full of documents. She later obtained a package intended for Springhall, and passed it on to the RAF, who forwarded it to MI5.[75] Following his arrest and interrogation, on 28 July 1943 Springhall was found guilty under the Official Secrets Act of obtaining 'for a purpose prejudicial to the safety or interests of the State information which might be useful to the enemy' and was sentenced to seven years' imprisonment.[76]

Evidence suggested that Springhall had been spying since the beginning of the war and certainly since June 1941.[77] At least two other Spanish veterans were believed to have been involved. Former IRA man Danny Gibbons, an inmate of San Pedro[78] and the brother of John Gibbons, the *Daily Worker* correspondent in Moscow during the Second World War, was suspected to be assisting Springhall's armed forces work. Richard Kisch, wounded fighting in Mallorca in September 1936 and editor of *Volunteer for Liberty* in 1941–2, allegedly told Springhall in August 1942 'that he was bringing him some stuff'.[79]

Springhall's conviction provided ample evidence to elements in the British establishment that, as Sir James Grigg, the Secretary for War, later stated, 'members and adherents of the Communist Party could not be trusted not to communicate secret information to that party.'[80]

It has been known to the Security Service for some time that the Communist Party has been receiving secret information, some of it of vital importance to the success of the war effort . . . There is no reason to believe that the information obtained by the Party is being passed to the enemy, but the mere fact of an accumulation of secret information in the Party's hands, where its custody and dissemination is beyond the control of the authorities, is a grave menace to security. The Party makes use of this information for its own purpose, without regard to the national interest.[81]

The HDSE were quick to appreciate that Springhall's activities and his conviction could be used to undermine the Party and determined to make details of his Communist membership and activities public.[82] However, the potential for damage did not escape the attention of the CPGB either, and Springhall was swiftly and prudently excommunicated.

Despite Springhall's expulsion, suspicions remained that other veterans were involved in espionage. Both Wilf Macartney and Peter Kerrigan were suspected at some stage, though no conclusive evidence was ever discovered.[83] Rather more evidence existed, if only circumstantial, to doubt Alex Tudor-Hart, former head of the British Medical Unit in Spain, who, until 1940, had been married to long-time NKVD agent Edith Suschitsky.[84]

Tudor-Hart had joined the Communist Party in 1929 and though he was half-French and had been born in Italy was, nevertheless, a British subject. Therefore, as a report drawn up by MI5 in July 1939 recognised, he was 'eligible for a commission as regards nationality'. However, the report continued, 'from a security point of view, and his character generally, he is considered an undesirable person to be in close contact with service personnel.'[85] A short attachment to the report stated that:

> He was not popular with his medical colleagues [at the North West London Hospital in Hampstead], and ridiculed to a great extent on account of his effeminate manner, and was generally looked upon as a crank . . . It is understood the Spanish Government was looking upon the members of the British Medical Services in Spain with disapproval owing to their loose morals. Tudor-Hart was one of those in disfavour, but whether for incompetency or immorality it is not known.[86]

His application for a commission was therefore refused.

The following year, in a somewhat hysterical letter, the Assistant Chief Constable of Birmingham reported to Major General Sir Vernon Kell, Director-General of MI5, that Tudor-Hart was holding Party meetings in his mother-in-law's flat. The 'Red Flag' was sung at the conclusion of proceedings, and 'another song which refers to the fall of Buckingham Palace and the conversion of it into a public lavatory'[87] was also performed. The letter alleged, correctly, that between 1932 and 1934 Tudor-Hart had studied at the Lenin School in Moscow.[88] In a remarkably sanguine response, Kell replied that he believed Tudor-Hart 'is not a person who carries a great deal of weight [in the Communist Party]' but perhaps a post in a hospital where there were no security concerns might not be such a bad idea.[89] However, when it was appreciated that Tudor-Hart's job involved the monitoring of blood supplies and required access to information on the location of casualties (and therefore troop movements), his services were summarily dispensed with.[90]

Discreet surveillance was maintained on Tudor-Hart, partly in case he attempted to join up, but also because MI5 had a professional interest in his wife's activities. Nevertheless, despite his marriage and his contacts with members of Soviet intelligence such as the head of the NKVD in Spain, Alexander Orlov, MI5 did not seem to feel that the doctor presented a serious security risk and did not oppose his admission into the Royal Army Medical Corps (RAMC). Surveillance continued throughout 1942 and 1943, but as Tudor-Hart appeared not to be engaging in any questionable behaviour, in March 1943 he was 'cleared of suspicion of engaging in subversive activities or propaganda' and his file was ordered to be destroyed.[91] By 1944, Tudor-Hart was working in the Yugoslav Medical

Mission to the British Army and he ended the war with the rank of captain.[92]

Although he was not involved in espionage, the efforts of the former battalion secretary, Ted Edwards, nevertheless managed to cause the British security services a huge amount of hard work and embarrassment.[93] Edwards apparently possessed a remarkable determination to rejoin the war against fascism, whether His Majesty's Government wanted him or not, and his story demonstrates the strong sense of continuity many of the veterans felt between their experiences fighting Franco and the violence now erupting across Europe.

After Edwards was released from Wakefield at the end of his sentence for leaking the War Office memo, he was kept under surveillance, yet, despite an absolute ban on his admission into uniform, in October 1942 it was discovered, to the dismay and irritation of MI5, that he had managed to enlist in the Home Guard.[94] He was dismissed on 7 January 1943, and returned once again to civilian life.[95] To ensure that he did not slip through the net again, his post was monitored.[96]

It was soon realised, from what was referred to as 'a delicate source' (the opening of a letter from Edwards to his friend Sam Wild), that, despite MI5's best efforts, Edwards had managed to enlist in the army at the British Army Transportation Centre at Longmoor in Hampshire. A recommendation that 'in the interests of both Military and Internal Security' Edwards should be discharged once more was not long in coming and he was ejected again on 4 May 1943.[97] A mischievous article in the *Daily Worker* which referred to Edwards' 'exemplary character', entitled 'A Trained Fighter, but the Army Sacks Him', did not go down well with the security services.[98]

To make absolutely sure that Edwards could cause no further embarrassment, a memo was sent out from the Director of Recruiting and Demobilisation in July 1943 to all chief recruiting officers. Entitled 'Undesirable Recruit', it stated categorically that Edwards should not under any circumstances be admitted into the armed forces. Despite this, on 11 September 1943, it was discovered that Edwards had managed once again to sneak into the Home Guard. Following 'extensive and exhaustive' enquiries by the Manchester police into how he had managed to outwit the best efforts of the British security services, it was revealed that he had simply lied on a form completed for the Ministry of Labour and National Service. This time, the response from MI5 was almost admiring, admitting that he was 'a fairly tricky individual', and that they would 'not be at all surprised to hear that he has once more succeeded in pulling our legs'.[99] Nevertheless,

Edwards was thrown out for the third time and the security services continued to monitor his post until the end of the war. He worked for a brief period on the docks, causing a momentary panic, but by April 1945 he had, at last, elected to take employment in a sector not likely to cause the security services too many sleepless nights: he became a bus conductor.

23

We Shall Pass!

July 18, 1936, the day the Fascist Dictators launched open war in Europe, and the day when the people of Spain stood up to defend liberty with their lives.

Today, after eight years, the battle which began in the towns and villages of Spain is nearing its climax . . .

The pledge of the Spanish fighters and the International Brigades, the famous battle cry of Spanish democracy – 'No Pasaran' – has been fulfilled. The Fascists have not passed. Hitler's dream of a Nazi Europe has faded, the walls of his European Fortress have been breached, and his armies everywhere are facing destruction.

Volunteer for Liberty, July 1944

Despite the relaxation of the government's ban on International Brigaders following the Communist Party's conversion to the war, veterans still continued to find themselves rejected for service in the British armed forces and even the Home Guard and the ARP (Air Raid Precautions) services. Others struggled to find work connected with war industries, despite government claims that only 'a very short list of men with a long record of Communist activity' had been rejected.[1] In November 1941, Harry Pollitt claimed that he could provide the names of a number of Party members who had been dismissed, in military parlance, 'service no longer required', and he later wrote to War Secretary Sir James Grigg demanding an end to the discrimination:

During the course of the war, a number of men called to the armed forces have been discharged, despite the exemplary characters they have gained during their period of training, apparently for no other reason than their membership of the Communist Party . . . We believe that this . . . is absolutely unjustified . . . [and] not in the best interests of the nation in the struggle against fascism. The record of Communists in the International Brigades in Spain, in China, in the Red Army, in the fight against Hitler in Germany must be well known to you as being of a splendid and exemplary character.[2]

Gradually, though, increasing numbers of former Brigaders did manage to enlist. Some were even called up, despite appearing to be exactly the sort of veterans the War Office had sought to exclude: long-standing, active Communists, who had been among those 'undergoing training in revolutionary propaganda' while awaiting repatriation from Spain at the end of 1938. Yet, even after veterans had been accepted, many continued to experience harassment or prejudice. When Roderick MacFarquhar joined the British Army in 1941, he found it to be 'very, very strongly biased against people like myself who had been in the Spanish war'.[3] In line with the secret memorandum, veterans were discreetly put 'under quiet observation' and found themselves watched secretly for any signs that they might be attempting to politicise their fellow soldiers. Dossiers (often inaccurate) on the pre-war political activities of the individuals concerned were sent to their commanding officers[4] – although instructions were given that 'no man reported should become aware that he is viewed with suspicion, as it is not desired to prejudice any recruit who may have merely gone to Spain out of adventure and not become imbued with revolutionary doctrines.'[5] John Longstaff was in no doubt that he was kept under observation:

> George Tumbler was going on leave and I asked him to send me some copies of the *Daily Worker*. Returning from leave he asked me if I had received any. 'Not one,' I replied. A few weeks later I went on leave and sent him copies but, like me, he did not get them. Pauline, my girlfriend, had sent me some tins of cream biscuits. When I received them not only were they broken but each biscuit had been removed from its cellophane or silver paper wrapping. It was, of course, obvious that some watch was being kept on me as a possible enemy.[6]

Like numerous others, some of whom were hardly revolutionaries, Longstaff found himself denied overseas service. When he attempted to volunteer for a commando operation, he was turned down. 'I think you understand why you have not been picked,' his commanding officer told him. Other former Brigaders found themselves actually ejected from the armed forces or discharged from their war work. Anti-tanks veteran Fred Thomas, whose assessment in Spain had praised his military record while simultaneously expressing disappointment at his lack of interest in joining the Communist Party, was working as a carpenter building air-raid shelters until the War Office discovered his background. His work was stopped forthwith.[7] Those dismissed were not usually informed why, though the reasons were not hard to guess.

> I was ordered to appear before the colonel or adjutant. I stood to attention outside his office and was marched in.
>
> And the adjutant said, 'You are being discharged from the Army.'
>
> And I said, 'May I know the reason?'
>
> He said, 'I'm not allowed to give it to you. But you are being discharged under sub paragraph – I can't quote the exact number – of King's Rules and Regulations.'
>
> So I said, 'Well, may I know what the sub paragraph says?'
>
> And he reached for a copy and turned it up and said, 'I don't think you'll learn very much from it, but this is what it says: "This sub paragraph only applies to a soldier who cannot be discharged under any other sub paragraph."'[8]

Having himself been sacked from his Home Guard training centre at Osterley, Tom Wintringham wrote scathingly of what he saw as the traditional and reactionary manner of the British Army towards Spanish veterans:

> Clearly it is absurd that the military experience of those who fought in Spain with the International Brigade and other sections of the Republican Army, should be disregarded by those responsible for the training and organisation of the British Army. When I hear of some of my friends, who I know to be excellent officers, acting as despatch-riders or lance-corporals, and given no chance to show their capacity in fighting, I sometimes wonder if the powers who run this country are determined to lose this war in their own way without interference.[9]

However, in fairness to the security services and the War Office, there was evidence to suggest that when Party members did get into the armed services, many went on behaving much as they had done at their former workplaces. They contacted one another, met unofficially in groups, recruited new members, and sent regular reports to the *Daily Worker* about life in the services.[10]

Others were more discreet; some, aware that they might be discriminated against, even attempted to disguise the military proficiency they had gained in Spain. When Jack Edwards volunteered for the RAF, his skill with a rifle was noted by an NCO, who was extremely sceptical of Edwards' denials that he had ever served in the British Army. His explanation was unlikely to have been convincing: 'I used to have an air gun,' he claimed innocently.[11] Having already been rejected by the armed forces, Roderick MacFarquhar deliberately tried to keep his military experience secret when he began training with an artillery regiment. He was soon interrogated by an extremely suspicious corporal:

'How long have you been a soldier, MacFarquhar?'
  I looked at him with mock astonishment and said, 'Six weeks, Corporal.'
  'Six weeks,' he said. 'You fucking liar,' he said.[12]

Among those who had been accepted, many felt that the treatment they received was extremely arbitrary, citing the manifestly different war experiences of long-standing Communist, political commissar and battalion commander Bill Alexander and 15th Brigade Chief of Staff Malcolm Dunbar, both of whom had exemplary records in Spain. Despite the security services' suspicions that Alexander, in his role as organising secretary of the Russia Today Society, was contacting a representative of the Russian Embassy, responsible for channelling funds from the Soviets to the CPGB, he was drafted into the Royal Artillery on 11 August 1941.[13] Initially rejected for officer training, Alexander's ability to prove himself 'a keen and intelligent soldier', backed up with a supportive letter from the Independent MP Eleanor Rathbone to the Parliamentary Under-Secretary of the War Office, made the case for him to become an officer.[14] Shortly afterwards, in May 1942, he and another former commander of the British Battalion, Paddy O'Daire, were both recommended for officer training at Sandhurst.[15] The top cadet of his intake, Alexander passed out with the 'belt of honour' and continued to impress: in 1943 his commanding officer declared him to be 'the best subaltern he had had in his unit for some time'.[16] Commissioned into the Reconnaissance Corps in May 1943, he was posted overseas, serving in North Africa, Italy and Germany, and was promoted to captain in August 1944.[17]

Dunbar's experiences could not have been more different. In the summer of 1940, he was drafted into the army as a private. By May 1941 his military experience had earned him a promotion, marked by a sarcastic piece in the *Volunteer for Liberty*:

Malcolm Dunbar was up on leave last week. He has now reached the dizzy heights of becoming a corporal. Malcolm, as we all know was the very capable Chief of Staff, Fifteenth Brigade, ranking as Major. He served through most of the big battles, and was in Spain for a couple of years. In addition to the military qualifications he has all the other necessary 'qualifications' for an officer in the British Army. He was actually put forward for a commission, but they then learnt that he had been in Spain and nothing further has been heard of it. Of course there is nothing political about that – much. Politics don't enter into the British Army, my dear fellow. Says you. But didn't Sir Edward Grigg [*sic*] [the joint parliamentary Under-Secretary of State for War] say that it was the policy of the War Office to use to the full the experiences of those who served in Spain. And we can tell Sir Edward that we learnt more than how to blanco gaiters and slope arms in Spain. How about it Sir Edward? Must we, too, put questions in the House before a man's merits can be recognised?[18]

Dunbar's case was sufficiently glaring for Aneurin Bevan to raise it in the House of Commons:

The Prime Minister must realise that in this country there is a taunt on everyone's lips that if Rommel had been in the British Army he would still have been a sergeant. Is that not so? It is a taunt right through the army. There is a man in the British Army – and this shows how we are using our trained men – who flung 150,000 men across the Ebro in Spain: Michael [*sic*] Dunbar. He is at present a sergeant in an armoured brigade in this country. He was Chief of Staff in Spain; he won the battle of the Ebro, and he is a sergeant in the British Army.[19]

Eventually Dunbar was promoted to sergeant, but this was as high as he ever reached. Many of Dunbar's former comrades from Spain – including Bill Alexander himself – remarked pointedly at the injustice.[20]

However, Dunbar's case might not have been the clear evidence of government prejudice that it appeared. In fact, he had actually been recommended for a commission, but turned it down so that he could remain with his unit when they were posted overseas.[21] And while Dunbar never gained officer rank, his indisputable military prowess did receive official recognition when he was awarded the Military Medal for a display of 'cool calculating courage in the face of the enemy' during an action east of the River Orne in Normandy, on 18 July 1944.[22]

Other senior figures from the British Battalion also met with mixed fortunes during the Second World War. Senior political commissar and Politburo member Peter Kerrigan was, unsurprisingly, never called up and continued to play a central role in both the CPGB and the IBA.[23] Will Paynter also continued his political and trade union work as a miners' agent in the Rhondda.[24] And while Bob Cooney did manage to join what the *Volunteer for Liberty* referred to as 'The British Liberation Army', he was removed from the draft to go overseas, following instructions by the War Office.[25] However, John Angus, despite being refused a commission in the navy and discharged for poor eyesight, managed to join the army, where he rose to the rank of captain and served with the 14th Army in India.[26]

Of the former battalion commanders, Fred Copeman perhaps had the best war, giving lectures on the dangers of aerial bombardment to, among others, the royal family, though they came to a sudden end once the Blitz was under way: 'People did not want to hear what had happened somewhere else when they had already begun to experience bombing on their own homes,' Copeman discovered.[27] Instead, he took on responsibility for managing the public shelters for the London Borough of Westminster before being transferred to the Ministry of Home Security in 1941, 'to take over management of the new deep tunnels that were being laid throughout the London region.'[28] In November 1945 Copeman was awarded an OBE for his work with London's civil defence.[29]

While Paddy O'Daire and Bill Alexander managed to get commissions, Joe Hinks never rose above the rank of lance-corporal. He was captured at Singapore and died of malnutrition in a Japanese POW camp in Sumatra, in December 1943.[30] 'Military man' George Fletcher became a commanding officer once more, though only within the Home Guard rather than the army. Jock Cunningham was discharged from the army without explanation in 1942,[31] while neither Tom Wintringham nor Wilf Macartney entered the armed forces.[32]

Sam Wild, widely accepted to have been one of the most able of the British commanders in Spain, was rejected for anything and everything he applied for, having been deemed 'undesirable' by the Chief Constable of Manchester:[33]

> The powers that be decided that I was a bad element. Couldn't get in the army, couldn't get in the navy. Made applications for civil defence, demolition, air-raid warden. But the Chief Constable that was in charge of all these bodies of anti-Nazi auxiliaries just refused to have me. And when I challenged him, he threatened to take it to higher bodies. He just told me by letter that he was the authority and that he would decide the personnel of any one of the wartime auxiliaries. Well, that was it. They wouldn't let me in.[34]

This may have been a consequence of Wild's time in Spain and his continuing political activism, but it is more likely that the cause was his dishonourable discharge from the Royal Navy in the 1930s after deserting from his ship, HMS *Resolution*.[35]

Despite being a trusted member of the Communist Party who had worked for the SIM in Spain, gifted linguist David Crook was another veteran to serve without apparent discrimination. Having been an MP's private secretary before going to Spain, he possessed powerful friends and connections, and his time in the International Brigades seemed to present him with few obstacles.[36] When he returned to Britain in June 1942, having spent three years in China, Crook applied to join an RAF unit formed to rescue aircrew shot down by the Japanese over occupied China. He was given an interview at the Air Ministry, where he was questioned in French, Spanish and German (though surprisingly not in Chinese): 'A few days later I was informed that I was earmarked for "Clerk S.D.", the S.D. for Special Duties meaning Intelligence.'[37] He was posted to Bimlipatam, on the east coast of India, halfway between Madras and Calcutta.[38] En route, his ship stopped off in South Africa, where he was introduced to the social and political mores of the white residents:

> The well-to-do local whites (except for the Afrikaners) offered hospitality to the troops, entertaining them with drives round local sights and to

sumptuous meals in their homes . . . One family issuing its invitation added a P.S. 'No Jews please'. At the appointed time five soldiers arrived at the house and the butler opened the door to five Blacks. The lady of the house said there seemed to be some mistake. 'Oh no,' said the men. 'Our colonel never makes mistakes. Not Colonel Cohen.'[39]

Crook was sufficiently trusted to become an intelligence officer, charged with observing the movements and operations of the Japanese air force. However, after the defeat of Japan in August 1945, Russia returned to its pre-1941 pariah status. Crook's star similarly waned and he was relieved of his intelligence duties. He was, instead, put in charge of incoming supplies of beer and spirits.[40]

Walter Gregory too found his Spanish experiences to be no disadvantage. Gregory served in the navy, despite having a disabled thumb from the battle at Jarama. His petty officer was fully aware of his time in the Brigades and sent him on a torpedo course, stating: 'Oh, you've been to Spain, you'll be useful.' Gregory didn't feel that he suffered any discrimination: 'I don't think it was ever a secret on any ship I was on, that I'd fought in Spain. Sometimes it was a bit of a joke, [and people would ask] "What the devil did you go there for?"'[41]

Others had similar experiences. At the same time that the War Office was rejecting veterans of the International Brigades from the British Army, British agents based in the USA were asking American veterans to fight in Europe behind Nazi lines.[42] Bernard Knox, who had left Britain for America following his repatriation, was approached in 1941 by Milton Wolff, the last commander of the American battalion in Spain, asking whether he would be prepared to take part in dangerous work in occupied Europe. Knox, and various American ex-brigaders, were chosen precisely because of their status as linguists politically acceptable to the partisans with whom they would be working. This meant, in practice, that they were often Party members; Knox himself was described by the British security services as 'on intimate terms with a number of important members of the B.C.P.'[43] He was parachuted into Europe to work with the resistance in helping to supply arms and organise sabotage against the German occupying army:[44]

I fought in Europe in a special force organized by the American OSS [the Office of Strategic Services, the precursor to the CIA], the British SOE and the Free French to coordinate the action of the French Resistance forces with the advance of the Allied armies. It was the OSS too that later sent me to North Italy to work with large partisan formations that were operating on our side of the lines but in mountainous areas where heavy American equipment could not be used. The OSS also gave many Americans who had fought in the Brigades a chance to use their skills. General Donovan didn't care what your politics were or might have been as long as you were willing to fight, and there were many ex-Brigaders who did dangerous and effective work between and behind the lines in Italy.

It was in Italy, too, that I had a sudden reminder of Spain. I was discussing operations with the staff of the Divisione Modena, a large partisan formation, and sometimes getting my newly acquired Italian mixed up with my half-forgotten Spanish, saying *fuego* instead of *fuoco*, for example, and *frente* instead of *fronte*. Suddenly, after another such fumble, the division commander stood up, smiling, walked over to me and patted me on the shoulder. 'Spagna, no?' he said. He had been in the Battaglione Garibaldi that had fought next to us in the Casa del Campo. From that point on, relations with the partisans were no problem.[45]

Former doctors from Spain seem to have been almost universally welcomed into the British Army. Len Crome, former chief medical officer of the 35th Division of the Spanish Republican Army, was drafted in 1941 as a captain in the RAMC and posted to north Africa.[46] While helping many survivors of the International Brigades who had escaped there, Crome wrote a critical article in *The Lancet* complaining that medical lessons learned in Spain were not being fully utilised by the RAMC. Despite this, he eventually rose to the rank of lieutenant-colonel. Another senior medic from Spain, New Zealander Douglas Jolly, was appointed a divisional surgeon in the North African campaign, even though his time in Spain had prevented him from taking his Fellow of the Royal College of Surgeons examinations before the Second World War broke out. Reg Saxton, who had worked with Canadian doctor Norman Bethune in Spain developing his revolutionary blood-transfusion techniques, enlisted in the British Army Blood Transfusion Service, where he remained for the duration of the war, serving in Burma and India.[47] Crome and other former medics – mainly middle-class, well-educated and highly trained – seem to have been valued, and experienced less discrimination than their more proletarian comrades from the British Battalion. Nevertheless, even the doctors were not above suspicion: Crome, Kenneth Sinclair-Loutit and Alex Tudor-Hart were all

the subject of a vindictive anonymous tip-off by 'A. Warden', who alerted
the authorities to their Communist backgrounds. The author claimed to
have served as a medical worker with them among 'that crowd of hooligans
and Communists' in Spain. Though admitting that 'excellent surgical work'
had been done, he argued that:

> No man could have been a stronger communist, with hatred against this
> Government and its KING, than Dr. Tudor Hart and his other communist
> friends Dr. Sinclair Lutit, now here at Finnsbury A.R.P. as assistant Medical
> Officer, and Dr. Croom.[48]

Service in the British Army, of course, could be a very different experience
to fighting with the International Brigades in Spain. David Crook was rather
taken aback by the gallows humour displayed by RAF pilots:

> It took me some time to adjust to the ironical anti-heroics of the airmen.
> They were of the same stock as the heroes of the Battle of Britain, but
> marched back from the sea-front parade-ground singing such songs as 'We'd
> be far better off in a home' . . . whereas I recalled the songs we sang in Spain:
> 'We are the youthful guardsmen of the proletariat' and, of course, the
> Internationale.[49]

Many others commented on the differences. Alec Marcowich found that
his superiors were determined that he shouldn't forget it:

> I'm walking, foolishly, across the parade ground, which you're not supposed
> to do under any circumstances. [According to] proper military etiquette,
> you do not cross a parade ground, you circle it. Well, I crossed the parade
> ground, I'd got my hands in my pockets, you know, and I'm sauntering
> across and all of a sudden a voice from high says, 'Marcowich, get your
> bloody hands out of your pockets, you're not in Spain![50]

In a letter to the Volunteer for Liberty, an anonymous draftee complained
about his poor experience of the British Army, which he believed was 'due
to the whims and ideas of stupid and bumptious staff colonels. Their
attitude is that the troops should accept what they are given and be
satisfied.'[51] One issue, devoted solely to an examination of the differences
between the Spanish and British armies, claimed that, in Spain, 'the soldiers

in the People's Army knew that there were no vested interests behind the war.'[52] Roddy MacFarquhar echoed this, declaring – just as Tom Wintringham had in 1940 in *New Ways of War* – that the Spanish Republican Army compared very well with the British Army because the soldiers in Spain knew what they were fighting for.[53] Max Colin agreed:

> The International Brigade largely rested on a lot of self-discipline . . . Whereas the British [Army] was . . . about drills and marching and polishing and cleaning and saluting . . . I don't think it compared – anywhere near it.[54]

But not everyone looked back on the International Brigades so positively. Penarth volunteer Bob Peters was in no doubt that life in the British Army was an improvement: 'The training was completely different from Spain. We had good food, we had good uniforms, and we had armaments which we didn't have in Spain.'[55] Food had, of course, been a constant bone of contention in Spain and Bill Alexander was one of many to consider the British Army food 'infinitely superior'.[56]

Rather more serious than the change in diet were the military differences. John Longstaff remarked significantly that his training in the London Rifle Brigade benefited immeasurably from the ready availability of equipment that non-intervention had denied the Spanish Republicans:

> Training went on each day. There was map reading, distance judging, small arms training, compass reading and a first aid course. I realized at the time, how useful this particular course was to prove to the soldier in combat. All the courses and training were, in my opinion, well thought out and well instructed. Soon the Riflemen became reasonably proficient. I appreciated those training courses as the difference between soldiering in the International Brigade and now in the Rifle Brigade was profound. This was due to the fact that in Spain we had to make maps in the front lines and there were hardly any compasses in Spain's Republican Army.[57]

Longstaff's first posting was to North Africa, where he knew other ex-International Brigaders were already fighting Rommel, as part of the French Foreign Legion. As he prepared to go into combat with his unit, vivid memories of his experiences in the Spanish Civil War came back to him:

> It was only when I saw lads in the Battalion busy making the necessary

preparations that my memories flew back to the battles I had fought in
Spain. I knew that some of my friends would die during the first day of our
battle. I knew that others would be wounded and possibly lose a limb. I
knew that I was fully prepared mentally and physically, and I knew that I
would have to set an example to all around me. I had not lost the scent of
battle, the smell of blood, the stench of the bloated dead, the cries of the
wounded, the smell created where our artillery, and that of the enemy, had
disturbed the earth. Once again I would be seeing fear in men's faces and
experiencing the long dark nights where every shadow represented an
enemy. I would experience again the quietness of the battlefield just before
the attack. I remembered the shooting up of flares which would mean us,
or the enemy, were alert. The sound of rifle fire, machine guns, the thud of
shells, ours and those of the enemy, as they blasted into the earth. Many of
my friends looked to me to give leadership and that is what I had worked
myself up to do. My mind, in anticipating the future, could not forget the
past. I recalled how bravely the Republican Army and International Brigades
had fought even though ill clad, ill armed and hungry and [with] little else
but high morale and a will to win. Our last main offensive was on 25th July
1938 when, having crossed the Ebro, we had fought and defeated Franco's
elite troops . . . Now, in a few days' time, I would once again be fighting
the same enemy as I had fought years before. My morale was great. I could
see the 7th Rifle Brigade was ready for battle and was not, in any sense,
daunted by the knowledge that we were to fight a well-armed and equipped
enemy.[58]

As Longstaff knew full well and as many of their fellow soldiers at arms
discovered, the lessons learned in Spain meant that former International
Brigaders were often highly skilled and motivated fighters. During the
Italian campaign of 1943–4, a sapper in the Royal Engineers described how
impressed he had been by his corporal, a veteran of the Spanish Civil War,
who was 'slightly mad and brave, and a little out of place in a section that
hoped to avoid being heroic at all cost'. According to the sapper, the former
International Brigader 'volunteered for everything and we had never seen
him show any fear'. The veteran's enthusiasm inspired courage in the
formerly cautious Engineer: 'the experience was terrifying but exhilarating
. . . Against all my instincts I had put my life at risk.'[59]

Of course, lessons had also been learned in Spain by those fighting on
the other side; following the Allied victory at El Alamein in November 1942,

the journalist William Forrest, who had reported on the Spanish war for the *Daily Express*, was accompanying the commander of the Allied 8th Army, Field Marshal Montgomery:

> We met him down in his tent by the sea. After telling us that, 'We've won the victory, beaten the Bosch,' he said, 'I've just captured [Major-General Wilhelm Ritter] von Thoma. He spent last night in my tent and we fought our battle out again over the oil cloths on our table. He told me, among other things, that he'd been in command of German airmen in Spain – the men who bombed Guernica – and he told me the Germans used the Spanish Civil War as a sort of preliminary rehearsal for the [Second World] war.' Montgomery said this as if he'd learned that for the first time, but it was something I and the other correspondents in Spain could have told him six years before.[60]

The veterans of the International Brigades had experienced six difficult years. Having been defeated in Spain by Franco and his German and Italian allies, the former volunteers had ended up continuing their fight in the very war they had been so desperate to prevent. Spanish veterans participated in all the major battles of the Second World War. Charlie Goodman, who had been arrested and roughed up at Cable Street, was wounded in the evacuation from Dunkirk. Frank Ellis, a former prisoner in San Pedro, took part in the over-ambitious glider and parachute drop at Arnhem in Holland, made famous by the movie *A Bridge Too Far*.[61] A number fought alongside Scot John Tunnah in North Africa, and 'revolutionary lobster' John Sommerfield, a veteran of the battle for Madrid of November 1936, was among several to serve in India.[62] Indeed, he was one of many dispatched to the other side of the world, fuelling veterans' suspicions that they were seen as too untrustworthy to be deployed in the European theatre. Another former San Pedro prisoner, amateur astronomer George Wheeler, was posted to Freetown in Sierra Leone to train troops, in 'the middle of nowhere' as he described it.[63] His fellow inmate, *San Pedro Jaily News* artist Jimmy Moon, ended up as a dispatch rider in Burma despite his request to be posted to a front-line unit, and remarked pointedly upon the large number of former brigaders he encountered in the Far East:

> Morrie Levitas, Charlie Matthews, Tony Gilbert . . . they thought we might desert to the Russians in Europe I think. It was funny, we were all prisoners

at San Pedro – too much of a coincidence . . . we all landed up at Burma, Mandalay![64]

Yet, in early 1944, when another former inmate of San Pedro de Cardeña, Bruce Allender, found himself sent to North Africa, he found reason to celebrate rather than curse his posting. Though he was, once again, among the prisoners held in a concentration camp, the situation was rather different, for he was now a guard. 'This time THEY'RE inside!' Allender wrote triumphantly. 'This is what is known as a full turn of the wheel!'[65]

That same year, many former brigaders – including Peter Elstob (who had narrowly escaped being shot as a spy in Spain), Eddie Brown, the anti-Mosley protester from Perth, and former Kinder trespasser Maurice Levine – were involved in the June D-Day landings.[66] Despite the inevitable heavy casualties, the success of the invasion was acclaimed by the International Brigade Association as a clear signal that, after eight years of war, the defeat of Hitler's Nazi Germany was finally imminent.[67] As Allied forces advanced eastwards through occupied Europe, the prospect moved ever closer. Famously, the first Allied tanks to enter Paris in August 1944 were driven by exiled Spanish Republicans in General Leclerc's Second French Armoured Division. The tanks bore the names of Brunete, Guadalajara and other battles from the civil war painted on their sides.[68] 'This time we shall do the job completely,' declared Charles West, a former member of the Machine-Gun Company, that October.[69] He did. Just over six months later, as Allied troops occupied the ruins of Berlin, with the leaders of fascist Italy and Germany's thousand-year Reich either dead, captured or in hiding, the determination of West and all his former comrades to, in Louis Hearst's words, 'defend democracy with deeds' was at long last rewarded.

EPILOGUE

'Two down – one to go'

Never again will men of every creed and tongue go to war with the ideals with which the volunteers went to Spain. It was indeed a time of hope, when a man with a rifle had some power to divert the tide of human affairs. Now, we drift at the mercy of events too vast and complex to be managed. Men will never go to war like that again, for war will never be as simple.

Interview with International Brigader John H. Bassett

For British veterans of the struggle against fascism, it had been a very long war. Since 1932, they had battled Mosley's Blackshirts on the streets of Britain and volunteered to fight for the Republican government against Franco and his German and Italian allies on the battlefields of Spain. Only six months after defeat there, they had been recalled to continue their struggle against Hitler and Mussolini in military campaigns around the globe during the Second World War. Consequently, of those fortunate enough to survive the Spanish war, several were killed between 1939 and 1945.[1]

Just over two years after returning from Spain, Winston Churchill's nephew, Esmond Romilly, had left for America with his wife, Jessica (née Mitford), following the tragic death of their baby daughter in a measles epidemic.[2] Despite his terrible experiences in Spain, where most of his comrades had been slaughtered, Romilly was unwilling to watch the war against Hitler from the sidelines and returned to Britain during 1941 as a bomber pilot with the Canadian Air Force. On Sunday 30 November 1941, at the age of twenty-three, Romilly was killed in action in a raid over Hamburg. Like countless other women during the war, his wife received the heart-breaking news by telegram:

REGRET TO INFORM YOU THAT ADVICE RECEIVED FROM ROYAL
CANADIAN AIR FORCE CASUALTIES OFFICE OVERSEAS YOUR
HUSBAND PILOT OFFICER ESMOND MARK DAVID ROMILLY CAN
J FIVE SIX SEVEN SEVEN MISSING ON ACTIVE SERVICE NOVEMBER
THIRTIETH STOP LETTER FOLLOWS.[3]

Others to die in the war included Tommy McGuire, described by one
Scottish volunteer as 'one of the toughest soldiers I ever saw' and commended
for his bravery in Spain. McGuire served in the Commandos and the
Parachute Regiment, making forty-two perfect jumps before he was killed in
action in North Africa on 5 February 1943.[4] Clive Branson, the popular and
brilliant artist who had been a prisoner at San Pedro, died in Burma on 25
February 1944.[5] Henry Johnson (who had fought under the name Lionel East
in Spain) took part in the D-Day offensive on 11 June 1944 with the Royal
Marine Commandos and was one of almost three thousand British soldiers
to lose their lives during the Normandy landings.[6]

Monty Rosenfield, killed fighting on the Italian front in 1944, was among
several former International Brigaders to be decorated – though, ironically, he
had only been accepted for foreign service after the Independent MP Eleanor
Rathbone had raised his case with the War Office.[7] Rosenfield received the
Military Medal, awarded to 'other ranks' for conspicuous bravery in battle, as
did Willie Aird, from Edinburgh, while serving with the Royal Commandos
in Burma, and Liverpool Communist George Magee, who like Rosenfield had
initially been refused admission into the armed forces.[8] Len Crome, the doctor,
was awarded the Military Cross (the officers' equivalent of the Military Medal)
for his professionalism and bravery under heavy enemy fire in the battles
around Monte Cassino in Italy in 1944 and Lieutenant-Colonel Douglas Jolly
was awarded a military OBE.[9] But for most veterans their greatest reward
was surely to live to see the toppling of the Axis. Now, these fighters against
fascism could finally return home to peace - at least for a short while.

With the final defeat of Hitler and Mussolini in 1945 and the demobilisation
of the armed forces, the thoughts of the former International Brigaders
returned to Spain. During the Second World War, the International Brigade
Association had continued to campaign, but the increasing number of
members in the armed forces had limited the scale of its activities. As Bill
Alexander reluctantly accepted, 'wartime conditions – black out, rationing
of paper supplies, bombing – made activity difficult.'[10]

However, there had been some progress. The IBA was foremost in a successful campaign to save the life of Italian communist Luigi Longo, one of the founders of the International Brigades, who had been handed over from a French internment camp to Mussolini's political police.[11] Moreover, the association had managed to raise a great deal of money for Spain and medical supplies and food parcels were sent to both Republican refugees and the families of political prisoners. Pressure on the British War Office regarding former International Brigaders held in French camps also continued; at an IBA conference in London on 3 April 1943, several motions were passed concerning the fate of veterans who remained incarcerated in liberated North Africa.[12] And in the summer of 1945, Sam Wild was instrumental in a campaign to secure the release of former Spanish Republican soldiers held in a converted mill in Chorley, near Preston.[13] Having been interned in French camps at the end of the civil war, when France was overrun by Germany the unfortunate Spaniards had been forced into Nazi labour battalions building railways in north Africa. After liberation they had been transferred to Allied concentration camps and eventually ended up in Chorley.[14] The strain had already led one Spanish inmate to commit suicide and Wild later claimed the successful campaign was 'the greatest achievement of his adult life'.[15]

During the war, the removal of Franco's dictatorship had been of minor concern to the Allied powers, whose priority was that Spain should not actively join the Axis. Even the former volunteers recognised that Franco could not be overthrown without first defeating Hitler and Mussolini. However, their hopes for future political change were boosted by the Allies' obvious distaste for General Franco's regime and his support of Hitler. Though Franco had declared Spain neutral at the outset of the Second World War, he had always hoped for an Axis victory, writing to Hitler in 1940 of his 'unchangeable and sincere adherence' to him and the German people's cause.[16] As a report by the United Nations disclosed, Franco's deeds showed clearly enough where his loyalties lay. During the war, Spain had provided Nazi Germany with intelligence, armaments and valuable mineral supplies; perhaps 100,000 workers were sent to work in German factories, U-boats refuelled in Spanish ports, air bases were provided for the Luftwaffe and 20,000 Spaniards fought in the Blue Division on the Russian front.[17]

Following Labour's landslide victory in the 1945 General Election, the Party's chairman, Harold Laski, further encouraged veterans' hopes when he declared that they 'were going to be in a position to do full justice to our Spanish comrades' and parts of the Labour movement also pledged support for the restoration of a free Spanish Republic.[18] But it quickly became apparent that the British left was still divided, with the Foreign Secretary, Ernest Bevin, making it transparently clear that government support for any kind of military intervention was out of the question. Bevin believed that 'further civil war and bloodshed were too high a price for the disappearance of General Franco', and that foreign intervention might actually strengthen Franco's position.[19] Among conservatives, there was even less appetite for the removal of Franco: with the destruction of Hitler's regime, there was no longer any bête noire to compete with Stalin. The West's preoccupation with the Soviet Union was enshrined in Churchill's famous 'iron curtain' speech in March 1946 and reiterated in the doctrine of US President Harry Truman, which stated that America was willing to grant economic and military aid to Greece and Turkey in order to prevent them falling into the Soviet sphere. This ensured a vital strategic role for Spain as a further bulwark against Russian expansionism and allowed Franco, the arch anti-Communist, to become indispensable as 'the sentinel of the west'. As world war was replaced by Cold War, the veterans were faced with the dismal realisation that the western powers were no more likely to support the Republican cause than they had been ten years earlier.

Moreover, Bill Alexander later admitted, campaigns on behalf of Republican Spain by the IBA were probably not helped by their 'tendency to follow Communist Party policy'.[20] The common perception, certainly in government circles, was that the IBA was controlled directly by the party, not least because 'most International Brigaders were members'.[21] Yet, while many veterans remained committed to the cause of Spanish democracy, loyalty to the Communist Party and the IBA did not prove so enduring. A number had already left over the Hitler–Stalin pact and the Soviet invasion of Finland and the descriptions of Stalin's purges had led many others, such as Bernard Knox, to follow suit:

> I was appalled . . . by the show-trials of the Old Bolsheviks, Bukharin and the rest; I read the verbatim accounts of their so-called confessions, published by Moscow in English and available at left-wing bookshops in London. I was . . . sickened too by reports, later confirmed, that our General Kleber, whose coolness under fire at University City had taught us all how to face danger, had been recalled to Russia and executed. Loyalty to the ideals for which my friends had died in Spain was undermined by the grim realities which I could no longer ignore.[22]

When Tito's Yugoslavia was expelled from the Cominform (the Comintern's successor) in 1948, the IBA slavishly defended Stalin's action, despite an appeal from the Yugoslav veterans to their British comrades.[23] In consequence, the Communist Party lost still more members, including the former censor in Spain, Tony Maclean, and Jud Colman, one of numerous Manchester volunteers:[24]

> Disillusionment set in . . . [with] . . . the attacks on Tito. Tito's government was composed mostly of Yugoslav brigaders. Stalin was accusing them of being anti-communist traitors . . . It didn't change my belief in Socialism and a better world, but I will no longer show blind loyalty to an ideology that will not allow another point of view.[25]

Two years later, the Scottish branch of the IBA resisted the Executive Committee's labelling of the Yugoslav veterans as 'liars and traitors', forcing Peter Kerrigan, who was on the National Executive Committees of both the IBA and the CPGB, to make an emergency visit to Glasgow. Having already been expelled from the Communist Party, George Murray –a former SIM agent in Spain – was consequently removed from his post as the IBA's Scottish Branch Secretary.[26]

Once the 1956 'Krushchev revelations' exposed the full extent of Stalin's murderous regime, any lingering gratitude the veterans felt for the Soviet Union's support of the Spanish Republic drained away. Many in Britain felt great sympathy with the Hungarians' stand against the Soviet Red Army, which created feelings of solidarity not seen since the civil war in Spain.[27] As George Leeson admitted, 'the final blow, of course, was Hungary . . . I just would not accept the version put forward on Hungary at all.'[28]

Nevertheless, the IBA continued campaigning against the brutal extremes of Franco's regime. In 1962, they took a major role in protesting against the arrest, imprisonment and torture of Julián Grimau, a member of the central committee of the Spanish Communist Party. Having been sadistically tortured and then thrown out of a window in a clumsy attempt to simulate suicide, Grimau somehow survived despite having, his wife recounted, 'both wrists broken, a dent in his skull, shattered face and jaw, a damaged back and spine'.[29] The IBA sent a barrister to Madrid to try and represent him, but despite appeals for clemency from around the world, he was put to death on 20 April 1963. The execution generated widespread revulsion; Sam Lesser's pamphlet *Murder in Madrid* (written under the pen

name given to him in Spain, Sam Russell) sold over five thousand copies.[30]
Yet with the passing of time, not to mention Spain's increasing popularity
as a holiday destination, many came to the depressing conclusion that little
could be done about Franco's regime. The ageing veterans – and their cause
– became increasingly sidelined.

It was only on 20 November 1975, with the death of Franco, that hopes
of a return of democracy to Spain were rekindled. The remarkably smooth
political transition which followed, the legalisation of the Communist Party
in 1977 and, five years later, the election of the Socialist government of
Felipe González and his consequent offer of Spanish nationality to the
surviving veterans, all heralded a new era. Gradually, interest returned in
the actions of the men and women who had been derided during the Cold
War as 'premature anti-fascists'.

A conference at Loughborough University held in 1976, for the fortieth
annual reunion of the International Brigade Association, brought together
many former volunteers to record their recollections and several took the
opportunity to publish memoirs.[31] The 1980 BBC documentary on the
veterans, *Return to the Battlefields*, and the unveiling of the IBA's national
monument in London on 5 October 1985 – attended by former Labour
Party leader Michael Foot, TUC General Secretary Norman Willis, and the
Labour MP for Newham, Tony Banks – helped restore the veterans to
public awareness. But it was the *homenaje*, the veterans' triumphant return
to Madrid – and to a newly democratic Spain – in October 1986 that seemed
to mark the major turning point in their lives.[32]

When the former volunteers were called upon to talk about their time
in the Spanish Civil War, most remained overwhelmingly positive about
their experiences. 'The war was the biggest event in my life,' declared Frank
McCusker. 'I'm gled I was there. I'm gled I came back, of course, but I'm
gled I was there.'[33] Spanish Civil War diarist Fred Thomas expressed his
feelings with characteristic eloquence:

> There were no medals to be won in Spain. But I believe that no man, not
> even that band of brothers who fought upon St. Crispin's Day, nor that later
> Few of 1940, justly honoured though they may be, was ever prouder of his
> part than we who were of the International Brigade.[34]

Many echoed the view of Phil Gillan, expressed more than fifty years
after the war, that 'there's no way I could fault myself for going there. I

think it was absolutely right and the longer I think about it the more convinced I am that I was right. And I think that events proved conclusively that we were right.'[35] His fellow Scot, Frank McCusker, agreed, arguing that the political changes experienced in Spain following Franco's death signified a kind of victory, albeit long overdue:

> Looking back now on the Spanish War I say it was well worth while because even though Franco won, he never won – in the sense that they've got a socialist government now in Spain. So I think the International Brigade did one little thing anyway in helping to get a real democratic government elected in Spain later on.[36]

Spain undoubtedly maintained a great significance in the lives of the majority of the veterans, though this always had to be balanced with more prosaic concerns. At the end of the war, like other demobilised soldiers, the veterans had to return to everyday life. For some this was not so easy; for those wounded in the nine years of fighting between 1936 and 1945 there was a constant physical reminder. IBA secretary Jack Brent was among many crippled by his injuries; Scottish volunteer Eddie Brown, blown up by a shell at Brunete and shot through the knee at the Ebro, was still experiencing painful sensations in his feet and knee and other problems with his health fifty years later.[37] However, many more were able to resume normal working life, some of them establishing highly successful careers.

As befitting their role as 'British volunteers for liberty', many senior figures in Spain later became influential players in left-wing politics and the Labour movement. Former ILP volunteer Bob Edwards was the successful Labour Party candidate for Bilston in the 1955 General Election. In 1983, as MP for Wolverhampton South East, he became the oldest sitting member of the House of Commons. Bill Alexander stood as the Communist Party candidate for Coventry East in the 1945 General Election and between 1959 and 1967 was assistant general secretary of the Party. Sam Wild also worked full-time for the Communist Party and stood unsuccessfully as a local councillor in Manchester before taking work as a scaffolder. A blue plaque commemorating his achievements is now mounted on the old family home on Birch Hall Lane in Manchester.[38]

Will Paynter became President of the South Wales Miners' Federation in 1951 and General Secretary of the National Union of Mineworkers from 1959 to 1969, while Paddy O'Daire became a Transport and General

Workers' Union shop steward. However, the most famous of the trade unionists was Jack Jones, leader of the TGWU in the 1970s and later president of the Pensioners' Convention. Rather less conventional was the political trajectory of former San Pedro inmate Alfred Sherman, one of a number of veterans to be expelled from the Party in 1948 for 'Titoist deviationism'. Following his expulsion, Sherman embarked on a remarkable political journey from Communist to zealous free-market economist. In 1974, he founded the Thatcherite think-tank, the Centre for Policy Studies, which he ran virtually single-handed during the 1970s. Sherman's work informed many of the most radical policies of Margaret Thatcher's governments and in 1983 he received his reward with a knighthood.[39]

A number of medics went on to become particularly successful after the Second World War. Len Crome, who trained under Alexander Fleming as a pathologist, became a distinguished neuropathologist. And Archie Cochrane, recently cited as 'one of the grandfathers of evidence-based medicine', became the director of the Medical Research Council's Epidemiology Research Unit in Cardiff.[40]

Bernard Knox left the US Army at the end of the Second World War with the rank of captain, two Bronze Stars and the *Croix de Guerre avec Palme*. Upon returning to America he resumed his studies at Yale, where he took a doctorate on Greek tragic narrative in 1948 and became a professor in 1959. In 1961 he was invited to be the director of Harvard's newly founded Center for Hellenic Studies in Washington.[41] *News Chronicle* reporter John Langdon-Davies founded the child-sponsoring organisation Foster Parents Plan for Children in Spain, now known as Plan International, a charity which works for children's rights and against poverty in developing countries around the globe. Richard Bennett, the Cambridge student who had arrived in Spain with John Cornford, served in the Army Bureau of Current Affairs during the war, wrote for the *Sunday Telegraph* and later edited *Lilliput* between 1946 and 1950. Nathan Clark, the great-grandson of the founder of Clark's shoes, invented the ubiquitous desert boot in 1947, drawing inspiration from *alpargatos*, the rope-soled shoes worn by Spanish peasants he had observed while an ambulance driver in Spain.[42] And despite his record in Spain, actor James Robertson Justice went on to become one of the most recognisable faces in British cinema in the 1960s and 1970s.

But many simply returned to their normal working lives. After a time working with the Squatters' movement after the war, Bob Cooney worked as an industrial crane operator in Birmingham, while simultaneously building up a successful reputation as a folk singer. George Fletcher found employment at the Rolls-Royce factory in Crewe and, apart from occasional contact with his friend Sam Wild, seems to have had little or nothing to do with other veterans or their association.[43] Similarly, former prisoner David Lomon returned to his work in a wholesale firm, where he remained until retirement. 'Wrapped up in work and family life', he made no attempt either to contact his former comrades or the International Brigade Association itself.[44] However, in 2009, seventy-one years after leaving Spain, he happened to see an article in *SAGA*, the magazine for the over-fifties, on the Spanish government's awarding of nationality to surviving British veterans, and he was spurred to make contact.[45] After decades of silence, he rapidly became actively involved in the activities of the International Brigade Memorial Trust and in 2011 he returned to Madrid for the seventy-fifth anniversary of the foundation of the Brigades. Aged ninety-three, he was still able to deliver a passionate speech: 'Today, more than ever, we say *"¡No pasarán!"*' he declared, to huge and sustained applause.[46]

Inevitably, not all the veterans' stories after Spain are so heart-warming. George Orwell, who died prematurely of tuberculosis in January 1950, still outlived the former 'English Captain' and instigator of the Home Guard, Tom Wintringham, who had died of a heart attack the previous August.[47] In July 1963, the taciturn and reserved Malcolm Dunbar walked into the ocean at Milford-on-Sea near Southampton, having deliberately removed all forms of identification from his pockets and clothing.[48] A heavy drinker, he was apparently virtually penniless and depressed at the time of his death.[49] And four years later, Esmond Romilly's brother Giles 'was found dead in a lonely hotel room in America', having taken an overdose of tranquillisers.[50] As long ago as 1952, Jock Cunningham had been reported as 'tramping the roads up and down the country';[51] he died in February 1969, having apparently 'never fully settled down' after returning from Spain.[52]

However, the later life of Anton Miles, a former laboratory assistant and Communist Branch organiser in Brighton, can only be described as bizarre.[53] Having served with the 15th International Brigade Medical Services in Spain,[54] Miles cut all links with the Communist Party after the war, travelled to India to train as a sadhu (holy man) and then trekked, penniless, around south-east Asia, before becoming initiated as a Buddhist monk in Bhutan.[55] Miles is undoubtedly unique among Britons involved in the Spanish Civil War for having been initiated into a coven of witches in Bricket Wood in 1959.[56]

★

As time passed and the ranks of surviving veterans began to dwindle, a remarkable number of their obituaries appeared in national newspapers. Most were overwhelmingly positive and saluted their decision to go to Spain. Not all, however: the deaths of two of the best-known British volunteers were to provoke bitter controversies. Following the passing of Laurie Lee in May 1997, an article in *The Spectator* revived a long-standing accusation that Lee had 'never joined the International Brigades'.[57] This led to a fierce row in the British press. A history of epilepsy disbarred him from front-line service, so his account of hand-to-hand combat with a 'frantically spitting Moor' must have been the work of a writer rather than a fighter, but there was plenty of documentary evidence to prove that Lee had joined the Brigades.[58] A second storm erupted following the death of Jack Jones in April 2009. Since his time in Spain, there had been persistent whispers that Jones had once been a member of the Communist Party, though he had always denied it. But an article in the *Daily Mail*, drawing on an account by former Soviet spy Oleg Gordievsky, claimed that not only had Jones been a Communist, but he had received payments from Soviet intelligence agents.[59] Unsurprisingly, Jones' friends and family were furious at what they saw as a deliberate slur on his character.

Certainly there is strong evidence that Jones, like the majority of International Brigaders, was a member of the Party in Spain; indeed, his name appears on a number of lists of Communist cadres.[60] More significantly, on an application to join the Spanish Communist Party completed just before his departure from Spain, Jones himself describes how Liverpool Communist Leo Magee recruited him in 1930.[61] However, while he may have been an 'open member' from 1932 to 1941, MI5 believed that Jones had probably left the Party by 1949.[62] Like Denis Healey and many others in the 1930s, Jones had in any case been inspired to join the Communist Party by 'the awful realisation that black fascism was on the march right across Europe', rather than by a slavish loyalty to Russia.[63] British volunteers such as Jones and Healey were not 'Stalin's henchmen'. As journalist Geoffrey Cox (who was certainly no Communist) put it, the British veterans of the Brigades were 'mostly strong, forthright individuals . . . very different from the wary, set-faced Party *apparatchiks* of post-war Communism'.[64]

The claim that Jones had worked as a Soviet agent is another matter entirely and appears to rest solely on Gordievsky's account.[65] In fact, covert surveillance by MI5 later confirmed that Jones was not under Soviet influence and, if anything, had increasingly distanced himself from the

CPGB.[66] But once again the story of the volunteers had become entangled with the politics of the Cold War

As long as seventy-five years ago, two young writers articulately explained why they went to Spain and why it was important that they had done so. The first, John Sommerfield, stated simply that 'there are things worth fighting for and things that must be fought against.'[67] The words of his comrade, eighteen-year-old Esmond Romilly, could just as well apply to many of the conflicts that have erupted across Europe since his premature death in November 1941:

> I am not a pacifist, though I wish it were possible to lead one's life without the ugly intrusion of this ugly monster of force and killing – war – and its preparation. And it is not with the happiness of the convinced communist, but reluctantly that I realize that there will never be peace or any of the things I like and want, until that mixture of profit-seeking, self-interest, cheap emotion and organized brutality which is called fascism has been fought and destroyed for ever.[68]

Decades later Tommy Bloomfield summarised the feelings of many former members of the British Battalion in the Spanish Civil War when he described how 'today, as a pensioner, I live on social security, but I'm the richest man in the world having known my comrades in the International Brigades.' Time had done little to dampen his ardour either for the cause of Republican Spain or for his choice to risk his life fighting for it. 'If I had my life to live over again,' he stated confidently, 'I would do the same.'[69]

Three-quarters of a century on, the Spanish Civil War remains a live issue. In Spain, the controversial disinterring of victims continues and an acrimonious battle rages over whether the future of that still young democracy depends on the memory or the deliberate forgetting of the conflict. Yet many in Spain still harbour intense gratitude for the sacrifices made by the 35,000 men and women who came from around the world to fight for the Spanish government in the legendary International Brigades. During the two-minute silence of remembrance at a football match between England and Spain at Wembley on 12 November 2011, a Spanish supporter held aloft a sign bearing the image of four bright red poppies. Beneath the flowers, it bore a simple, poignant message: 'We also remember. XVth International Brigade. British Battalion '36.'

Notes

Key

ALBA   Abraham Lincoln Brigade Archive, New York

BLPES   British Library of Political and Economic Science, London

IWM   Imperial War Museum, London

IWMSA   Imperial War Museum Sound Archive, London

IBA MML   International Brigade Archive, Marx Memorial Library, London

IBMT   International Brigade Memorial Trust (digital Moscow files)

IBC   International Brigade Collection, Moscow

LCP   Len Crome papers, private collection

LHASC   Labour History Archive and Study Centre, Manchester

MHA   Manchester History Archive, Ashton-under-Lyne

NA   National Archives, Kew

WCML   Working Class Movement Library, Salford

Introduction

1 'Spain remembers: war veterans honoured', *The Guardian*, 9 June 2009.

2 http://www.english.illinois.edu/maps/scw/farewell.htm

3 Dewar, p. 109.

4 Francis, *Miners Against Fascism*, pp. 80–1.

5 Alexander, *British Volunteers*, p. 30.

6 Interview with Sam Wild in Corkhill and Rawnsley, pp. 18–19.

7 Interview with Jack Jones in Corkhill and Rawnsley, p. 139.

8 Romero Salvadó, pp. 50–1; H. Graham, *Spanish Civil War*, pp. 16–17.

9 *News Chronicle*, 2 September 1936, p. 2.

10 Hearst, MS, pp. 6–7.

11 Interview with Sam Lesser, IWMSA 9484, reel 6.

12 For the naval volunteers see, for example, interview with Tommy Hadwin, Manchester 190, reel 1, side 1 and IBC 545/6/89, p. 1. For the pilots see Bridgeman.

13 For a full breakdown of the background of the volunteers, see Baxell, *British Volunteers*, pp. 8–24.

14 Albert Camus, preface to *Espagne Libre*. Paris: Calmann-Levy, 1945.

15 Orwell, 'Looking Back on the Spanish Civil War', p. 155.

16 Interview with John Londragan in MacDougall, *Voices from the Spanish Civil War*, p. 181.

17 Hopkins, p. 151.

18 Colman, p. 13.

19 See, for example, Baxell, 'Laurie Lee in the International Brigades: writer or fighter?', pp. 157–75. There are a number of manuscripts of questionable veracity.

20 Fred Thomas, p. 70.

21 Helen Graham, interview online at: http://www.youtube.com/watch?v=3UcoZzWWQIk

22 Orwell, 'Looking Back', p. 151.

23 Interview with Freddie Brandler, 16 May 2000.

24 Interview with Hugh Sloan in MacDougall, *Voices from the Spanish Civil War*, p. 203.

1 The politics of dissent

1 Stevenson and Cook, p. 12.

2 E.D. Simon and J. Inman, *The Rebuilding of Manchester*, 1935, pp. 60–1, cited in Stevenson and Cook, p. 59.

3 Gardiner, *The Thirties*, p. 69.

4 Fyvel, p. 8.

5 Interview with Eddie Brown in MacDougall, *Voices from the Spanish Civil War*, p. 107.

6 Greening, p. 66.

7 Interview with Tommy Bloomfield in MacDougall, *Voices from the Spanish Civil War*, p. 50.

8 Interview with Syd Booth, MHA 200, reel 1, side 1.

9 Interview with Jim Brown in Corkhill and Rawnsley, p. 47.

10 Jack Jones, *Unfinished Journey*, Oxford, 1937, pp. 256–7, cited in Gardiner, *The Thirties*, p. 134.

11 Interview with Jim Brewer, IWMSA 9963, reel 1.

12 N. Branson, *History of the Communist Party 1927–1941*, p. 214 and, for example, interview with

David Goodman in Corkhill and Rawnsley, p. 96.

13 One of its first popular reads was *Walls Have Mouths: A Record of Ten Years Penal Servitude*. Described as 'the most genuine and damningly revealing account of prison life in Britain', it was a memoir of his time in Parkhurst by Wilf Macartney, who had been convicted for spying for the Soviet Union. Cox, *Defence of Madrid*, p. 147.

14 Ellen Wilkinson, cited in A. Jackson, *British Women in the Spanish Civil War*, p. 22.

15 Interview with Jim Brewer, IWMSA 9963, reel 1.

16 Wintringham, *English Captain*, p. 98.

17 Interview with Lillian Urmston, MHA 203, cited in Jackson, p. 17.

18 Cited in Hopkins, p. 106.

19 Copeman, p. 49.

20 Interview with Sam Wild in Corkhill and Rawnsley, p. 17.

21 Interview with George Leeson in Corkhill and Rawnsley, p. 76.

22 Eddie Brown cited in Cook, p. 19.

23 Dowse, p. 189.

24 Green, pp. 51–3; Gardiner, *The Thirties*, pp. 378–9.

25 Stevenson and Cook, p. 151.

26 Stevenson and Cook, p. 155.

27 Haldane, p. 89.

28 As Tom Buchanan points out, 'On most political issues in the later 1930s, the Communist Party was undoubtedly the most energetic force on the British left.' Buchanan, *Britain and the Spanish Civil War*, p. 74.

29 N. Branson, *History of the Communist Party 1927–1941*, pp. 116–17.

30 'The most striking feature of the character of the British Labour movement in the thirties was its uncompromising stand against communist influence.' Stevenson and Cook, p. 160.

31 Interview with Leslie Preger in Corkhill and Rawnsley, pp. 28–9.

32 Churchill, *The Grand Alliance*, 1950, p. 331.

33 Interview with George Leeson, IWMSA 803, reel 1.

34 Levine, p. 21.

35 Mitford, 1989, p.165.

36 Interview with Syd Booth, MHA 200, reel 1, side 1.

37 Healey, p. 34.

38 Toynbee, 'Journal of a Naïve Revolutionary', *The Distant Drum*, p. 147.

39 'The one thing that, where Spain was concerned, that made a tremendous impression on us as miners, was Franco's putting down of the Asturian miners. That really went to the quick.' Interview with Jim Brewer, IWMSA 9963, reel 2; H. Sloan, p. 30.

40 Francis, *Miners Against Fascism*, p. 193.

41 Greening, p. 58.

42 Interview with David Goodman in Cook, p. 96.

43 Interview with David Goodman in Corkhill and Rawnsley, p. 96.

44 Interview with Stafford Cottman, IWMSA 9278, reel 2.

45 Interview with Leslie Preger in Corkhill and Rawnsley, pp. 27–8.

46 Interview with Maurice Levine in Corkhill and Rawnsley, p. 3.

47 Interview with Maurice Levine in Corkhill and Rawnsley, p. 4.

48 Levine, pp. 24–5.

49 Rothman, p.53; Joe Norman memoir, IBA MML Box 50, File Nr/1a.

50 Longstaff, MS, p. 29.

51 Hynes, p. 17. See also Francis, *Miners Against Fascism*, pp. 80–1, which outlines the connection between the NUWM and Spain.

52 Stevenson and Cook, p. 163.

53 Interview with Frank Graham in Corkhill and Rawnsley, pp. 35–6. Similarly, the Welsh miners' leader Will Paynter joined the Communist Party in 1929, but did not join the NUWM until 1931. Paynter, pp. 84–5.

54 Longstaff, MS, p. 8.

55 Longstaff, MS, p. 15 and interview, IWMSA 9299, reel 1.

56 'There was a logical, sequential development of issues in the lives of many British militants: first, looking for explanations for the unemployment and repression they experienced; second, seeing the rise of fascism on the continent as an issue that concerned them; and third, seizing the opportunity to strike back at oppression, if not in Great Britain, then in Spain.' Hopkins, p. 107.

57 These were Tim Harrington, D.R. Llewellyn, Will Paynter and J.S. Williams. Francis, *Miners Against Fascism*, pp. 80–1.

58 Interview with Lance Rogers, South Wales Miners' Library, cited in Francis, *Miners Against Fascism*, p. 161.

2 Fighting the Blackshirts

1 Copsey, p. 14.

2 Hope, pp. 46–8.

3 Thurlow, 'The Failure of British Fascism 1932–40' in A. Thorpe, *The Failure of Political Extremism in Inter-War Britain*, p. 75.

4 Stevenson and Cook, p. 225.

5 Both Italy and Germany provided funding for Mosley's British Union. See Dorril, pp. 376–7.

6 Morgan, *Against Fascism and War*, p. 19.

7 Copsey, p. 23.

8 Almost half of those arrested at anti-fascist demonstrations in 1933–4 had a Jewish background. Thurlow, 'The Straw that Broke the Camel's Back', p. 76.

9 Gregory, p. 171.

10 Interview with George Watters in MacDougall, *Voices from the Spanish Civil War*, pp. 33–4. William Joyce, better known as 'Lord Haw-Haw', was an American-born fascist who made radio broadcasts for Nazi Germany during the Second World War. In 1946, he was hanged for treason.

11 Interview with Eddie Brown in MacDougall, *Voices from the Spanish Civil War*, p. 108.

12 Levine, pp. 26–7.

13 Copsey, p. 46.

14 Interview with Sam Wild in Corkhill and Rawnsley, p. 19; Cook, p. 24.

15 Copsey, pp. 20–1.

16 Copsey, pp. 21–2.

17 After the violence at Olympia, the final rally planned at White City was cancelled by the venue.

18 Interview with Tony Gilbert, IWMSA 9157, reel 1.

19 L.W. Bailey, 'Olympia', The Times, 6 March 1996, cited in Eaden and Renton, p. 17.

20 In Philip Toynbee's account of the demonstration, the chant is the rather less obscene: 'Hitler and Mosley mean hunger and war!' See Toynbee, Friends Apart, p. 21.

21 Toynbee, Friends Apart, p. 21.

22 Interview with Frank Graham in Corkhill and Rawnsley, p. 36.

23 Copsey, p. 32.

24 Copsey, p. 39.

25 Newsinger, 'Blackshirts', p. 832.

26 Copsey, p. 42.

27 Copsey, p. 51; Benewick, p. 217.

28 Interview with Tony Gilbert, IWMSA 9157, reel 1.

29 British Library of Political and Economic Science (BLPES), NCCL report, ch. 3, p. 3.

30 BLPES, NCCL report, p. 6.

31 Interview with Max Colin, IWMSA 8639, reel 1.

32 Benewick, p. 209.

33 Benewick, p. 212.

34 The Oxford Mail, 26 May 1936, cited in Benewick, p. 211.

35 Ewing and Gearty, p. 329.

36 Dorril, p. 395.

37 Dorril, p. 307; Newsinger, 'Blackshirts', p. 835.

38 Dorril, p. 371.

39 Daily Worker, 13 July, 7 and 9 December 1936.

40 Cullen, pp. 257–60.

41 Haldane, p. 94.

42 Copsey, p. 44.

43 David Renton, 'Docker and Garment Worker, Railwayman and Cabinet Worker: The Class Memory of Cable Street', in Kusher and Valman, p. 102 [orig. appears in P. Cohen, Children of the Revolution: Communist Childhood in Cold War Britain, London: Lawrence and Wishart, 1977, p. 61].

44 Thurlow, 'The Straw that Broke the Camel's Back', p. 82; Eaden and Renton. p. 58.

45 NA HO 144/21060, pp. 335–6.

46 Daily Herald, 1 October 1936; Benewick, p. 225.

47 Jacobs, pp. 237–8.

48 Copsey, p. 55.

49 'It could have been a very, very bloody affair, for many of the dockers had First World War rifles. And they were on the roofs of Cable Street and the areas leading up to Cable Street, and if the Fascists had started the march . . .' Interview with Tony Gilbert, IWMSA 9157, reel 1.

50 Report on Cable Street demonstration, NA HO 144/21061, p. 113.

51 NA HO 144/21061, p. 153; interview with Joe Garber, IWMSA 12291, reel 3.

52 Kushner, pp. 117–18.

53 Interview with John Longstaff, IWMSA 9299, reel 3.

54 Longstaff, MS, p. 33.

55 IBA MML Box D7-A2.

56 Crook, ch. 3, p. 2.

57 A. Williams, pp. 144–5.

58 Interview with Charlie Goodman, Searchlight, October 1996.

59 Many other protestors acted in the same way. When Harry Dobson, one of the imprisoned Tonypandy miners, was released from prison in December 1936, having served six months' hard labour, he immediately asked, 'How do I get to Spain?' Francis, Miners Against Fascism, p. 94. Dobson served as a political commissar in Spain and was mortally wounded on 1 August 1938 at Gandesa.

60 Interview with Tony Gilbert, IWMSA 9157, reels 1–2.

61 Interview with Alf Salisbury, Searchlight, October 1996. This estimate also appears on the ILP leaflet 'They Did NOT Pass'. Police estimates put the crowd at nearer 100,000. Copsey, p. 58.

62 Interview with Tony Gilbert, IWMSA 9157, reel 1.

63 Anon, 'They Did NOT Pass', p. 3.

64 Dorril, p. 395.

65 Benewick, p. 272.

66 Benewick, pp. 264–5.

67 Thurlow, Fascism in Modern Britain, p. 78.

68 Gregory, p. 173. Many historians agree with him: 'British fascism was considered an irritant, rather than a mortal threat,' argues Richard Thurlow. Fascism in Modern Britain, p. 79.

69 Magee, p. 312.

70 Gurney, p. 30.

71 Eaden and Renton. p. 57.

72 Interview with Jack Shaw, Searchlight, October 1996.

73 Interview with Alf Salisbury, Searchlight, October 1996.

74 Interview with Josh Davidson, MHA 193, reel 1, side 1.

75 Interview with David Goodman in Corkhill and Rawnsley, p. 95.

76 Interview with Tony Gilbert, IWMSA 9157, reel 1.

77 NA HO 144/21043. Report on political violence at public meetings, 1934–1938. The file lists numerous people arrested demonstrating in London who would later go to Spain, including Hugh Slater, David Guest, Harold Horne, Hamish Fraser, Jeffries Mildwater, James Pugh, Winifred Bates, Donald Renton and many others.

78 Sid Quinn, cited in Cook, pp. 17–19.

79 Horne, p. 43.

80 Interview with Wally Togwell in Hynes, p. 27.

81 Interview with Maurice Levine in Corkhill and Rawnsley, pp. 6–7.

3 Aid Spain! or 'keep out of it'?

1 *The Times*, 18 July 1936, p. 12.

2 Moradiellos, 'The Origins of British Non-Intervention in the Spanish Civil War', pp. 347–8.

3 According to the official history of the newspaper, *The Times* was 'rigidly disinterested in the Spanish Civil War'. There were extremely close links between senior members of the government such as Eden's predecessor as Foreign Secretary, Sir Samuel Hoare, and the editor of *The Times*, Geoffrey Dawson, and relations between the Foreign Office and the paper were as close during the period of the civil war as they had ever been. *History of the Times*, Part 2, 1921–1948, published in London, 1952, pp. 914, 1142.

4 'The Spanish Tragedy', *The Times*, 29 July 1936, p. 13.

5 *Daily Mirror*, 5 August 1936, from Shelmerdine, *British Representations of the Spanish Civil War*, p. 174.

6 Edwards, p. 38.

7 The infamous Oxford Union debate of 1933, in which the motion that 'this House will in no circumstances fight for its King and Country' was carried by 275 votes to 153, is often cited as an example of the depth of pacifism resulting from the horrors of the First World War. See, for example, Gardiner, *The Thirties*, p.498.

8 Bereton, *Inside Spain*, cited in Shelmerdine, *British Representations of the Spanish Civil War*, p. 176.

9 Buchanan, *Impact*, p. 20.

10 Many Blackshirts did have sympathies with the Spanish Nationalists and rallies in support of the Spanish Republic were targeted, but this probably had as much to do with the perception that supporters of the Spanish Republic were 'Jews and Reds' than with any particular fondness for Franco's Nationalists. Buchanan, *Britain and the Spanish Civil War*, p. 90.

11 Florence Farmborough, *Life and People in National Spain*, p. 5, cited in A. Jackson, *British Women in the Spanish Civil War*, 2009, p. 229. The attitudes of some Catholics towards the Spanish Republic in general and volunteers for the International Brigades in particular can be gauged by the experience of a mother who received a telegram to say her son had been injured in Spain. As the postman handed it to her he said, 'A pity he wasn't killed'. Suart, p. 211.

12 *Morning Post*, 1 October 1936, p. 10.

13 Aldgate, p. 116.

14 Aldgate, p. 117.

15 See 'Lord Rothermere and the "Reds"', *News Chronicle*, 18 August 1936, p. 8, in which A.J. Cummings (the paper's political editor) argues that the 'Christian' forces of Franco could not win without the Moors. The article is a fierce attack on Rothermere's 'Red' versus 'Anti-Red' coverage. As Tom Buchanan argues, the pro-Rebel press rather 'overplayed their hand by exaggerating what had, in fact, been a shocking slaughter'. *Britain and the Spanish Civil War*, p. 26.

16 Bertrand Russell, 'The Spanish Conspiracy', letter to the editor, *New Statesman and Nation*, 15 August 1936, p. 218. Although ascribed to Russell, the letter was in fact written by famous Hispanist and author Gerald Brenan. Faber, p. 157.

17 Letter from Arthur F. Loveday, *Morning Post*, 29 July 1936, p. 9. The majority of the British press gradually came to adopt the terminology 'Republicans' and 'Nationalists' for the two sides. However, the *Daily Worker* referred to the Rebels as 'Fascists', whereas the *Daily Mail* called them 'Patriots'. Deacon, p. 129.

18 *The Times*, 24 July 1936, p. 13.

19 *Morning Post*, 21 July 1936, p. 11; 'Spain: The Truth', 12 January 1937, p. 10.

20 O'Duffy, p. 43.

21 O'Duffy, p. 71.

22 *Morning Post*, 5 August 1936, p. 8.

23 Arthur Bryant cited in O'Duffy, p. 189. According to the most recent estimates, Bryant exaggerated the number of those murdered in the Republican zone by as much as a factor of seven. Preston, *Spanish Holocaust*, p. xvi.

24 Buchanan, *Britain and the Spanish Civil War*, pp. 118–19; Day, p. 117.

25 H. Thomas, *Spanish Civil War*, p. 567.

26 Toynbee, *The Distant Drum*, p. 59. Charlotte Haldane later admitted that the *Daily Worker* 'was not meant to be a newspaper at all, but a propaganda sheet'.

27 *Morning Post*, 1 August 1936, p. 11.

28 Dorril, p. 379.

29 'How I Flew Franco to the Revolution', *News Chronicle*, 7 November 1936, p. 1.

30 FO minute, 13 August 1936, cited in Moradiellos, 'Appeasement and Non-Intervention', p. 95.

31 *The Times*, 1 October 1936, p. 13.

32 'Europe and Spain', *The Times*, 21 August 1936, p. 11.

33 Edwards, p. 18.

34 Edwards, p. 41.

35 E.H. Carr, p. 17.

36 'Leave Spain Alone', *Morning Post*, 5 August 1936, p. 8.

37 Fiercely anti-Communist and sceptical of the democratic credentials of the Spanish Republic, the Labour leadership were determined to avoid becoming embroiled in the Spanish war. A wariness of the potential loss of Catholic members probably also played a part. See Mates, *The Spanish Civil War and the British Left* and Buchanan, *The Spanish Civil War and the British Labour Movement*.

38 A. Lockwood, 'Reflections on Spain', *Reading Citizen*, 148, September 1936, from Cooper and Parkes, p. 101.

39 'Spain's Civil War', *News Chronicle*, 21 July 1936, p. 10; 'Spain's Hour', *News Chronicle*, 25 July 1936, p. 8.

40 *News Chronicle*, 24 July 1936, p. 2.

41 Stratton, p. 26.

42 Interview with Bob Cooney, IWMSA 804, reel 3; MHA 179, reel 1, side 1.

43 Interview with Walter Greenhalgh, IWMSA 11187, reel 2.

44 Interview with Bill Feeley, MHA 191, reel 1, side 1. The extent of support in 1936 and early 1937 is difficult to quantify. In January 1937 an opinion poll carried out by the British Institute of Public Opinion had asked whether the British government should recognise Franco's government. Of those who expressed an opinion, an overwhelming majority – over four in five – were opposed to the idea (14 per cent said yes, 86 per cent said no). BIPO survey, January 1937, Gallup Social Services. The notorious questionnaire of 1937, published as *Authors Take Sides*, which had been sent to prominent writers, contained an overwhelming majority in support of Republican Spain. However, it was rendered essentially meaningless as it was principally sent out to Republican sympathisers. Buchanan, *Britain and the Spanish Civil War*, p. 159.

45 Griffiths, MS, p. 1.

46 Interview with Alec Ferguson, MHA 239, reel 1, side 1.

47 Interview with Syd Booth, MHA 200, reel 1, side 1.

48 Squires, p. 11.

49 Haldane, p. 89.

50 Interview with Syd Booth, MHA 200, reel 1, side 1.

51 Atholl, p. 316. For the Duchess of Atholl see Ball, pp. 49–85.

52 Fyrth, p. 198.

53 Buchanan, *Impact*, p. 91.

54 Theodore Repard is a pseudonym of Theodore Draper, the American *Daily Worker* foreign correspondent. Repard is, of course, Draper written backwards. This was a familiar Communist ploy: when the English volunteer Sam Lesser returned to Spain to broadcast for the Republic and write for the *Daily Worker* he was advised to change his name from Lesser to Russell.

55 The British security services held a file on Langdon-Davies which noted his membership of the National Joint Committee for Spanish Relief. NA KV/5/126, pf. 47004.

56 García, 'Unofficial Missions', p. 227.

57 Little, p. 292. Little explains: 'What one critic has labelled Britain's "malevolent neutrality" in the Spanish Civil War, then, stemmed more from ideological than from strategic considerations.'

58 *News Chronicle*, 17 August 1936, p. 2.

59 Sir Maurice Hankey, 'The Future of the League of Nations', 20 July 1936, NA FO371/20475 W11340, cited in Moradiellos, 'Appeasement and Non-Intervention', p. 97.

60 No doubt many in the Admiralty were mindful of the Invergordon Mutiny in the British navy in 1931. A number of those involved in the mutiny later served in Spain.

61 There would have been no shortage of evidence, not least from Nationalist radio transmissions, which were sufficiently powerful to be overheard in Britain. While the radio traffic was encrypted by ENIGMA machines, they had been cracked by British code-breakers as early as April 1937. The results were not passed to the Republicans. Graham Keeley, 'Nazi Enigma machines helped General Franco in Spanish Civil War', *The Times*, 24 October 2008, p 47.

62 Edwards, p. 396.

63 'Restricted Intervention', *The Times* 28 July 1937, p. 15; 'Call The Bluff', *News Chronicle*, 25 October 1936, p. 8.

64 Admiral Sir Hugh Sinclair to Sir Warren Fisher, 19 October 1937, cited in Jeffery, p. 286.

65 NA FO 371/2415-W973/5/41, Vansittart to Halifax, 16 January 1939, cited in Edwards, p. 212.

66 NA FO800/323, cited in Day, p. 125.

67 H. Thomas, 'The Spanish Civil War', p. 1601.

68 'No Intervention', *The Times*, 9 October 1936, p. 15. In fact the non-intervention agreement, as 'a series of unilateral statements', had no powers to limit the scale of imports at all. Foreign Office considerations also included adopting a policy to 'endeavour to be on good terms with the victor at the end of the Spanish War', NA FCO 73/265 SP/38/1-4, from Day, p. 125.

69 Interview with Chris Thornycroft, IWMSA 12932, reel 3.

70 Atholl, p. 336.

71 *Daily Worker*, 19 February 1936, p. 5.

72 Buchanan, *Britain and the Spanish Civil War*, p. 81.

73 H. Sloan, p. 31.

74 Introduction by Jack Jones in Cook, pp.vii–ix.

75 Fred Thomas, p. 5.

76 Cited in Mates, p. 209.

77 Interview with Jack Jones in Corkhill and Rawnsley, pp. 139–40.

78 Alexander, *British Volunteers*, p. 44.

79 Interview with John Dunlop in MacDougall, *Voices from the Spanish Civil War*, p. 117.

80 Interview with John Londragan in MacDougall, *Voices from the Spanish Civil War*, p. 171.

81 Gregory, p. 20. Most volunteers from Britain and Ireland have always seen the war as an anti-fascist war, rather than a civil war.

82 Interview with Garry McCartney in MacDougall, *Voices from the Spanish Civil War*, p. 241.

83 Gurney, p. 36.

84 As David Corkhill and Stuart Rawnsley discovered when interviewing veterans for their study of the motivations of the British volunteers, the ratio of Party men is skewed by the large number that joined in 1936 in order to go to Spain.

85 Interview with David (So)Lomon, 16 February 2011.

86 Interview with George Leeson, IWMSA 803, reel 1.

87 Interview with Sam Wild, IWMSA 10358, reel 2.

88 Interview with Bill Cranston in MacDougall, *Voices from the Spanish Civil War*, p. 185.

89 Angus, p. 3.

90 Hyde, p. 60.

91 Interview with Alec Marcowich, MHA 182, reel 2, side 1. Marcowich is presumably referring to Jimmy Queen from Airdrie and Allan Kemp (a pseudonym) from Port Glasgow. The precise identity of the other volunteer is uncertain. Queen was imprisoned by the Republicans as an undesirable: 'Criminal record in England. Absolutely lumpen. Drunkard. Sentenced to 4 months labour battalion.' IBC 545/3/99, p. 6.

92 'Britons Lured to Red Front', *Daily Mail*, 18 February 1937, p. 13. Graham Greene's brother, Herbert, who was involved in espionage in Spain, argued strongly that the British International Brigaders were 'all keen volunteers and the stories in the English papers that they are inveigled into going by false pretences are untrue'. Greene, p. 284.

93 There was perhaps a tension between London and Spain over recruits. For Robson and the British Communist Party it was a matter of prestige to recruit a large number of volunteers, and quantity over quality may sometimes have taken precedence. However, within Spain, particularly for political commissars such as Peter Kerrigan and Will Paynter who had to look after the volunteers, quality – and political commitment – was vital.

94 Interview with Will Paynter, IWMSA 10359, reel 2.

95 Interview with George Aitken, IWMSA 10357, reel 2.

96 'Records in London – Observations' enclosed in Marty to Pollitt, 22 December 1937. IBC 545/6/87/39–40.

97 Toynbee, 'Journal of a Naive Revolutionary', *The Distant Drum*, p. 163.

98 Interview with Maurice Levitas, MHA 955, reel 1, side 1.

99 Gregory, pp. 19–20.

100 Interview with Steve Fullarton in MacDougall, *Voices from the Spanish Civil War*, p. 303.

101 Watkins, p. 172.

102 Interview with David Stirrat in MacDougall, *Voices from the Spanish Civil War*, p. 263.

103 Interview with Maurice Levitas, MHA 955, reel 1, side 1.

104 Deacon, p. 146.

105 Churchill, 'The Spanish Ulcer', *Step by Step*, pp. 304–5.

106 Seven per cent in March 1938, 9 per cent in October and 9 per cent in January 1939.

107 'An appeaser is one who feeds a crocodile, hoping it will eat him last,' said Winston Churchill in the House of Commons in January 1940.

108 *Britain* by Mass Observation, p. 32. Surveys also demonstrated that by the end of the civil war public opinion very much opposed the 'better Hitler than Stalin' view that prevailed in certain circles of British society. A BIPO survey in January 1939 asked, 'In a war between Germany and Russia who would you rather see win?' Fifty-nine per cent said Russia, 10 per cent Germany and 31 per cent expressed no opinion. *News Chronicle*, 9 January 1939, p. 7.

109 Sáinz Rodríguez cited in Moradiellos, 'The Origins of British Non-Intervention in the Spanish Civil War', p. 340.

4 To Spain!

1 'Stalin's decision [to support the creation of brigades of international volunteers] was eventually reached apparently as a result of a visit to Moscow on September 21 by Thorez, the French Communist leader.' H. Thomas, *Spanish Civil War*, pp. 295–6.

2 'The idea of the International Brigade arose spontaneously in the minds of men who, up to July 1936, were engaged in peaceful pursuits, and were probably taking but little interest in the affairs of Spain.' Rust, p. 4.

3 Gurney, p. 62.

4 Interview with George Aitken, IWMSA 10357, reel 1.

5 Review of Antonio Elorza and Marta Bizcarrondo, *Queridos camaradas. La Internacional Comunista y España 1919–1939*, Barcelona: Planeta, 1999 by Helen Graham, in *The Volunteer*, 23:5, Winter 2001, pp. 17–19.

6 Viñas, *Looking Back*, p. 131.

7 See Volodarsky, 'Soviet Intelligence Services in the Spanish Civil War, 1936–1939'.

8 Viñas, *Looking Back*, p. 134.

9 H. Thomas, *Spanish Civil War*, 2nd edn, p. 453.

10 Suart, pp. 202–8. See also Francis, '"Say Nothing and Leave in the Middle of the Night"', pp. 69–76.

11 Interview with Albert Charlesworth, IWMSA 798, reel 4, cited in Suart p. 203.

12 Gregory, p. 21.

13 Fred Thomas, p. 4.

14 Alexander, *British Volunteers*, p. 34; Dolan, p. 60.

15 Green, p. 69.

16 Alexander, *British Volunteers*, pp. 34–5; Gregory, p. 19 and interview IWMSA 8851, reel 1.

17 Haldane, p.100. Initially Peter Kerrigan interviewed potential volunteers, but was replaced by Robson. Special Branch report on Robert Robson, 'Robbie'. NA KV2 1177.

18 Gurney, pp. 37–8; interview with John Londragan in MacDougall, *Voices from the Spanish Civil War*, pp. 171–2.

19 Interview with Bert Ramelson, IWMSA 6657, reel 1.

20 Interview with John Longstaff, IWMSA 9299, reel 4.

21 Interview with Syd Booth, MHA 200, reel 1, side 2.

22 Crook, ch. 3, p. 3.

23 Interview with Harry Fraser, MHA 241, reel 1, side 1.

24 Following the deaths of influential figures such as Ralph Fox and John Cornford in December 1936 and the bloodbath at Jarama in February 1937, the Communist Party became increasingly nervous about allowing senior cadres to go to Spain. As Anne Murray remembered, her brother Tom 'volunteered to come to Spain, but the people in the

Communist Party – he was in the Communist Party in Scotland – they didn't want him to come, because it was thought that he was too valuable in Scotland'. Interview with Anne Murray in MacDougall, *Voices from the Spanish Civil War*, p. 72. However, Murray was eventually allowed to go and served as an 'outstanding' political commissar. Assessment by battalion commander Sam Wild, 5 October 1938. IBMT: IBC 545/6/176, p. 112.

25 Interview with George Drever in MacDougall, *Voices from the Spanish Civil War*, p. 270.

26 Interview with Tom Murray in MacDougall, *Voices from the Spanish Civil War*, p. 308.

27 Interview with Bob Cooney in Corkhill and Rawnsley, p. 118.

28 Interview with Charles Bloom, IWMSA 992, reel 1.

29 Greening, p. 67.

30 Gregory, p. 22.

31 Interviews with Edwin Greening, IWMSA 9855, reel 2 and Charles Morgan, IWMSA 10362, reel 1.

32 NA KV2 1611/50a.

33 NA KV5/112. The list is a huge over-exaggeration and included 'a number of writers, journalists and other visitors to Spain, plus a number who never fought.' See Baxell, 'Have We Underestimated the Number of Volunteers?' *IBMT Newsletter*, 30, Autumn 2011, p. 9 and Buchanan, 'The secret history of Britain's Spanish civil war volunteers', *Guardian on-line*, 28 June 2011.

34 Interviews with Edwin Greening, IWMSA 9855, reel 2 and Charles Morgan, IWMSA 10362, reel 1. As S.P. Mackenzie has shown, the authorities recognised that there were major legal problems in applying the nineteenth-century legislation to volunteering for the Spanish war. Mackenzie, p. 63.

35 Interview with Hugh Sloan in MacDougall, *Voices from the Spanish Civil War*, p. 196.

36 John Lochore, unpublished memoir, from MacDougall, *Voices from War*, p. 113.

37 Interview with James Jump, IWMSA 9524, reel 1.

38 Greening, p. 63.

39 Stratton, p. 41.

40 Wintringham, *English Captain*, p. 54.

41 LHASC, CP/IND/POLL/2.

42 Interview with Steve Fullarton in MacDougall, *Voices from the Spanish Civil War*, p. 291.

43 Interview with Martin Bobker, MHA 185, reel 1, side 1.

44 Interview with Benny Goodman, MHA 174, reel 1, side 1.

45 IBA MML Box D-7, File A/1.

46 Letter from Peter Kerrigan to Harry Pollitt, 6 February 1937, IBA MML Box C, File 10/3.

47 B. Clark, p. 13.

48 Interview with Bill Feeley, MHA 191, reel 1, side 1.

49 Haldane, pp. 112–13.

50 Interview with Bill Cranston in MacDougall, *Voices from the Spanish Civil War*, p. 187.

51 Haldane, p. 114.

52 Arnold Reid, originally Reisky, known as 'Jack' in Spain. Haldane's memoir *Truth Will Out* is dedicated

to 'Jack' from 'Rita' (Rita was her pseudonym in Paris).

53 Haldane, pp. 103–4.

54 Interview with Frank McCusker in MacDougall, *Voices from the Spanish Civil War*, p. 42.

55 Interview with Sam Lesser, *The Guardian*, 10 November 2000.

56 Interview with Tommy Bloomfield in MacDougall, *Voices from the Spanish Civil War*, p. 47.

57 Interview with John Dunlop in MacDougall, *Voices from the Spanish Civil War*, p. 123.

58 Interview with Frank McCusker in MacDougall, *Voices from the Spanish Civil War*, p. 42.

59 Interview with Syd Booth, MHA 200, reel 1, side 2.

60 Interview with Harry Fraser, MHA 241, reel 1, side 1.

61 Interview with Arthur Nicoll, IWMSA 817, reel 2.

62 Interview with Syd Booth, MHA 200, reel 1, side 2.

63 Copeman cited in Cook, p. 32.

64 Gregory, p. 57.

65 Interview with Les Gibson in Arthur, *The Real Band of Brothers*, p. 258.

66 Guest, p. 189.

67 Interview with Hugh Sloan in MacDougall, *Voices from the Spanish Civil War*, p. 199.

68 Interview with Frank McCusker in MacDougall, *Voices from the Spanish Civil War*, p. 42.

69 Interview with Garry McCartney in MacDougall, *Voices from the Spanish Civil War*, p. 243. Not everyone greeted the Internationals with enthusiasm: Anarchist supporters were rather less happy to see the arrival of thousands of International Communists.

70 Interview with Jim Brewer, IWMSA 9963, reel 3.

71 See, for example, Percy Ludwick: 'The first bright rays of the sun now hit the snowy mountain tops, imparting them a pinkish tint which quickly turned into white. From these snowy heights, which seemed to us to be the top of the world, we looked far, far down into tiny valleys in which blue ribbons of water sparkled – beautiful Spain stretched out before us like on a wonderful landscape canvas. "Viva Republica!" we shouted enthusiastically.' Ludwick, *Notes*, p. 64.

72 Interview with Hugh Sloan, IWMSA 11354, reel 3.

73 Interview with John Dunlop in MacDougall, *Voices from the Spanish Civil War*, p. 125.

5 The army in overalls

1 A. Williams, pp. 163–4.

2 Ludwick, *Notes*, p. 58.

3 A. Jackson, *For Us It Was Heaven*, p. 22; Purcell, p. 140.

4 John Lochore, unpublished memoir, from MacDougall, *Voices from War*, p. 114.

5 B. Clark, p. 16.

6 Gregory, p. 25.

7 Longstaff, MS, p. 57.

8 Interview with Donald Renton in MacDougall, *Voices from the Spanish Civil War*, p. 22.

9 Hearst, MS, p. 27.

10 Interview with Tom Murray in MacDougall, *Voices from the Spanish Civil War*, p. 310.

11 Interview with Garry McCartney in MacDougall, *Voices from the Spanish Civil War*, p. 245.

12 This number is an estimate based upon lists of British men leaving for and repatriated from Spain held in the National Archives: KV5/112, FO369/2514-K14742/12563/241 and FO371/22654-W13505.

13 B. Clark, p. 18.

14 Interviews with William Feeley, IWMSA 848, reel 1 and MHA 191, reel 1, side 1.

15 Interview with Jim Jump, IWMSA 9524, reel 2.

16 Interview with Sam Wild, IWMSA 10358, reel 1.

17 Report by Comrade T. Wintringham, 20 November 1936. IBA MML Box C, File 7/2.

18 Gregory, p. 26.

19 Hearst, MS, p. 63.

20 Gregory, p. 27.

21 IBA MML Box A15; Buchanan, *Impact*, p. 79.

22 IBA MML Box 21, File A; Box D-7, File A/1.

23 These were Richard Kisch, Tony Willis and Paul Boyle. IBA MML Box C, File 5/2.

24 IBA MML Box C, File 5/2.

25 Stansky and Abrahams, p. 316.

26 Alexander, *British Volunteers*, p. 51.

27 Borkenau, p. 108.

28 Letter from John Cornford to Margot Heinemann, 16–30 August 1936, from Cornford, *Collected Writings*, p. 171.

29 Rust, p. 4.

30 Letter from John Cornford to Margot Heinemann, 16–30 August 1936, from Cornford, *Collected Writings*, p. 172.

31 Letter from John Cornford to Margot Heinemann, 16–30 August 1936, from Cornford, *Collected Writings*, p. 174.

32 Letter from John Cornford to Margot Heinemann, 16–30 August 1936, from Cornford, *Collected Writings*, pp. 175–6.

33 Hearst, MS, pp. 6–7.

34 Hearst, MS, p. 5.

35 Ironically, Orwell's 'great friend' Georgio Tioli was himself involved in secretive work on behalf of members of the British ILP group in Spain and the POUM. Tioli later disappeared in mysterious circumstances and is assumed to have been murdered by the Russian GRU or their agents. See Orwell, *Homage*, p. 170; Newsinger, 'Death of Bob Smillie', p. 575; Volodarsky, pp. 221–2.

36 Interview with David Marshall, IWMSA 9330, reel 2.

37 Purcell, pp. 11, 106–7.

38 Wintringham, *English Captain*, p. 23.

39 Letter from Tom Wintringham to Harry Pollitt, 10 September 1936. IBA MML Box C, File 5/3.

40 Interview with Phil Gillan in MacDougall, *Voices from the Spanish Civil War*, p. 13.

41 Watson, p. 30.

42 Interview with John Tunnah, IWMSA 840, reel 3.

43 As London volunteer Jason Gurney recognised, 'the myth of an army of middle-class writers and poets has arisen from the obvious fact that these were the most vocal section of the organization and that their work forms the easiest form of source material for writers of a later generation.' Gurney, p. 69.

44 Interview with John Anthony Myers, *West London Observer*, 24 February 1939, p. 5.

45 Interview with Sam Lesser, IWMSA 9484, reel 2.

46 Watson, pp. 71–2.

47 Watson, p. 79.

48 Watson, p. 82.

49 Interview with David Marshall, IWMSA 9330, reel 2.

50 Delmer, p. 311.

51 Stansky and Abrahams, p. 365.

52 Sommerfield, p. 12.

53 Sommerfield, p. 25. Orwell was rather dismissive of Sommerfield's memoir, describing it as 'sentimental tripe'. Orwell, review of *Volunteer in Spain*, in *Time and Tide*, 31 July 1937. Orwell has a point, for there is more than a whiff of the 'revolutionary heroic' in Sommerfield's account.

54 Kurzke, MS, p. 5.

55 Kurzke, MS, p. 7.

56 Crook, ch. 3, p. 4.

57 Ralph Fox, 'Letters from Spain', 10 December 1936, in Cunningham, *Spanish Front*, p. 277; Kurzke, MS, p. 10.

58 Kurzke, MS, p. 10; P. O'Connor, p. 14.

59 Watson, p. 109.

60 Gurney, p. 56.

61 Watson, p. 113.

62 Knox, *Essays*, p. 268.

63 Thomas, *Spanish Civil War*, 3rd edn, p. 459.

64 Gurney, p. 54.

65 Hearst, MS, pp. 54–5.

66 Kurzke, MS, p. 18.

67 On arrival one British volunteer, S.H. Charvet, 'demanded' to be transferred to a stretcher-bearer as he had 'personal objections to the taking of human life'. The demand was refused and Charvet deserted from Madrigueras in January 1937. Wintringham, *English Captain*, pp. 112–13 and letter to Harry Pollitt from Peter Kerrigan and Dave Springhall, 10 January 1937. IBA MML Box C, File 9/6.

68 Interview with Peter Kerrigan in Corkhill and Rawnsley, pp. 56–7.

69 Gurney, p. 63.

70 Letter from Peter Kerrigan to Harry Pollitt, 6 January 1937. IBA MML Box C, File 9/3.

71 Kurzke, MS, p. 15.

72 Knox, 'John Cornford in Spain', in P. Sloan, p. 187.

73 Gregory, p. 28.

74 Sommerfield, p. 31.

75 Knox, *Essays*, p. 267.

76 Hearst, MS, p. 51.

77 Kurzke, MS, p. 11.

78 Hearst, MS, pp. 51–3.

79 Sommerfield, p. 31.

80 Sexton, p. 3.

81 Knox, 'John Cornford in Spain', in P. Sloan, p. 188.

82 Sommerfield, pp. 49–50.
83 John Lochore, unpublished memoir, from MacDougall, *Voices from War*, p. 116.
84 B. Clark, p. 25.
85 Gurney, p. 55.
86 Kurzke, MS, p. 21.
87 Sommerfield, p. 48.
88 Kurzke, MS, p. 32.
89 Sommerfield, p. 49.
90 Kurzke, MS, p. 33.
91 Letter from John Cornford to Margot Heinemann, 21 November 1936, from Cornford, *Collected Writings*, p. 184.

6 The battle for Madrid

1 Several observers, such as *New York Times* journalist Herbert L. Matthews and Soviet journalist Mikhail Koltzov, have suggested that Miaja was anything but the courageous and determined figure of his reputation and that, on the contrary, he was 'weak, unintelligent [and] unprincipled'. Certainly Franco considered him an 'incompetent coward'. In reality, Miaja's Chief of Staff, General Vincente Rojo, was the true director of operations. Preston, *Concise History*, pp. 118, 130.
2 Colodny, p. 9.
3 Interview with Maurice Levitas, MHA 955, reel 1, side 1.
4 'Kleber' was a pseudonym for Lazar or Manfred Stern, a Hungarian with a colourful history. See H. Thomas, *Spanish Civil War*, p. 459.
5 Haldane, p. 87.
6 Kurzke, MS, p. 8.
7 Cox, *Defence of Madrid*, p. 67.
8 Barea, p. 595.
9 Kurzke, MS, p. 40.
10 Letter from John Cornford to Margot Heinemann, 21 November 1936, from Cornford, *Selected Writings*, p. 187; Cox, *Defence of Madrid*, p. 96.
11 Alexander, *British Volunteers*, p. 56.
12 Sommerfield, p. 57.
13 Letter from John Cornford to Margot Heinemann, 8 December 1936, from Cornford, *Selected Writings*, p. 188.
14 Interview with Sam Lesser, IWMSA 9484, reel 2.
15 Interview with Sam Lesser, IWMSA 9484, reel 6.
16 Sommerfield, pp. 91–2.
17 IBA MML Box 21a, File A.
18 Hearst, pp. 160–1; Kurzke, MS, p. 44; IBA MML Box 21a, File A.
19 Letter from John Cornford to Margot Heinemann, 8 December 1936, from Cornford, *Selected Writings*, p. 187.
20 Sommerfield, pp. 119–20.
21 Knox, 'John Cornford in Spain', in P. Sloan, pp. 189–90.
22 Kurzke, MS, p. 57.
23 Letter from John Cornford to Margot Heinemann, 21 November 1936, from Cornford, *Selected Writings*, p. 184.
24 Sommerfield, p. 138.
25 Kurzke, MS, p. 30.

26 Sommerfield, p. 92.
27 Sommerfield, p. 139; Borkenau, p. 95.
28 Interview with Sam Lesser, IWMSA 9484, reel 3.
29 Sommerfield, p. 146.
30 Letter from John Cornford to Margot Heinemann, 8 December 1936, from Cornford, *Selected Writings*, p. 188; Knox, *Premature Anti-Fascist*, online at http://www.english.illinois.edu/maps/scw/knox.htm, p. 7.
31 Sommerfield, p. 150.
32 Knox, 'John Cornford in Spain', in P. Sloan, p. 190. In Stansky and Abrahams, pp. 380–1, the quote is attributed to a pseudonymous Andrew Knight, to protect Knox, who was by the time Stansky and Abrahams' book was published a distinguished university professor. Conversation with Peter Stansky, April 2011.
33 Sommerfield, p. 151.
34 Knox, 'John Cornford in Spain', in P. Sloan, p. 191.
35 Sommerfield, p. 151; interview with Sam Lesser, IWMSA 9484, reel 3.
36 Kurzke, MS, p. 52.
37 Sommerfield, p. 155.
38 Delmer, p. 311.
39 Interview with Chris Thornycroft, IWMSA 19232, reel 2.
40 Interview with Phil Gillan, IWMSA 12150, reel 2.
41 Romilly, p. 130.
42 Romilly, p. 130.
43 Interview with Phil Gillan in MacDougall, *Voices from the Spanish Civil War*, p. 14.
44 Romilly, p. 36.
45 Interview with David Marshall, IWMSA 9330, reel 2.
46 Interview with Chris Thornycroft, IWMSA 12932, reel 1.
47 Delmer, p. 304; Watson, p. 122.
48 Phil Gillan quoted in Rust, p. 24.
49 Interview with Phil Gillan in MacDougall, *Voices from the Spanish Civil War*, p. 15.
50 Watson, p. 129.
51 Watson, p. 133.
52 Watson, p. 141.
53 Romilly, pp. 42–3.
54 Interview with David Marshall, IWMSA 9330, reel 1.
55 Romilly, p.43.
56 Interview with Phil Gillan in MacDougall, *Voices from the Spanish Civil War*, p. 15.
57 Romilly, p. 122.
58 Romilly, p. 121.
59 Romilly, p. 121.
60 Romilly, p. 134.
61 Knox, 'John Cornford in Spain', in P. Sloan, p. 192.
62 Knox, 'John Cornford in Spain', in P. Sloan, p. 193.
63 Rust, p. 22.
64 Kurzke, MS, p. 103.
65 Knox, 'John Cornford in Spain', in P. Sloan, p. 194.
66 Knox, *Premature Anti-Fascist*, p. 9.
67 Romilly, p. 181.
68 Romilly, p. 191; letter dated 4 January 1937 from Peter Kerrigan to Harry Pollitt, LHASC, CP/IND/POLL/2/5–6.

69 Watson, pp. 245–6. According to Esmond Romilly, Keith Scott Watson is mistaken here, and Bill Scott was not killed at Boadilla. He left Spain in 1937, having fought with a Spanish battalion. See Romilly, p. 102.

70 Interview with Phil Gillan, IWMSA 12150, reel 4; 'On Leave from Spain', *Irish Times*, 4 January 1937, p. 3. IBA MML Box A2, File A/3.

71 'Nazi Troops Kill Six Britons In Madrid', *Daily Worker*, 28 December 1936, p. 1.

72 Interview with Phil Gillan, IWMSA 12150, reel 2.

73 Interview with Joe Monks, IWMSA 11303, reel 2.

74 Figure cited in a report from Peter Kerrigan to Harry Pollitt, undated, LHASC, CP/IND/POLL/2/5-6.

75 Spender, p. 223.

76 Gurney, pp. 94–5.

77 Monks, p. 12.

78 Peter Kerrigan, 'The First British Company', *Volunteer for Liberty*, Vol. 2 No. 29, 13 August 1938, p. 4; Stansky and Abrahams, p. 387.

79 Interview with Mike Economides, IWMSA 10428, reel 2.

80 Hallett, p. 128.

81 Monks, p. 4.

82 H. Thomas, *Spanish Civil War*, 1961, p. 347.

83 Interview with James Brown, IWMSA 824, reel 2.

84 ALBA Moscow 545/3/479, p. 56; interviews with Walter Greenhalgh, IWMSA 10356, reel 1 and Joe Monks, IWMSA 11303, reel 2. Both the quantity and quality of the level of *matériel* supplied to the Republic have been grossly exaggerated. Howson, p. 250.

85 Interview with James Brown, IWMSA 124, reel 3.

86 Kerrigan, 'The First British Company', p. 4.

87 Copeman, pp. 82, 98; ALBA Moscow 545/3/479, p. 56.

88 Colman, p. 4.

89 Kerrigan, 'The First British Company', p. 4.

90 Hugh Slater, 'How Ralph Fox was Killed', cited in Cunningham, *Spanish Front*, p. 332. Originally from *Ralph Fox: A Writer in Arms*, 1937.

91 *Cambridge Review*, 5 February 1937, cited in P. Sloan, p. 252.

92 ALBA Moscow 545/3/478, p. 162; report from Peter Kerrigan to Harry Pollitt, undated, LHASC, CP/IND/POLL/2/5-6.

93 Interview with Walter Greenhalgh, IWMSA 11187, reels 3–4.

94 ALBA Moscow 545/3/479, pp. 54–5.

95 Monks, p. 18.

96 Herbert Greene also accused Delasalle of being a traitor, claiming that he was responsible for 'the betrayal of the volunteers' by leading them (presumably, deliberately) into an ambush. Greene, p. 141.

97 Gurney, p. 82.

98 Interview with Walter Greenhalgh, IWMSA 11187, reel 4.

99 Ralph Cantor diary, WCML. Cantor's real name was Ralph Cantorovitch. Like a number of Jewish volunteers, including David [So]Lomon and Charles Gautzman (Charles Boyd), he anglicised his name in Spain.

100 Interview with James Brown, IWMSA 824, reel 3.

101 Alexander, *British Volunteers*, p. 88.

102 Rust, p. 26; Alexander, *British Volunteers*, p. 89.

103 ALBA Moscow 545/3/479, p. 57.

7 The British Battalion

1 Copeman, p. 82; ALBA Moscow 545/3/479, p. 57.

2 Interview with Donald Renton in MacDougall, *Voices from the Spanish Civil War*, p. 23.

3 Crook, ch. 3, p. 6.

4 Gurney, p. 58.

5 Gregory, p. 28.

6 Gurney, p. 59.

7 Crook, ch. 3, p. 6.

8 Gurney, p. 60.

9 Interview with Tony Hyndman in Toynbee, *The Distant Drum*, p. 124.

10 Interview with John Dunlop, IWMSA 11355, reel 4.

11 Interview with John Dunlop, IWMSA 11355, reel 4.

12 John Lochore, unpublished memoir, from MacDougall, *Voices from War*, p. 116.

13 Interview with Mary Whitehead (née Beckett), MHA 211, reel 1, side 1.

14 IBA MML Box A/2, File A/130; Lochore, p. 118.

15 Maro's real name was William Rowney. Stratton, p. 33.

16 Interview with David Anderson in MacDougall, *Voices from the Spanish Civil War*, p. 95.

17 Gurney, p. 65.

18 Gregory, p. 31.

19 Interview with Bruce Allender, IWMSA 11300, reel 3.

20 Interview with John Dunlop in MacDougall, *Voices from the Spanish Civil War*, p. 132.

21 Wintringham, *English Captain*, p. 42.

22 Interview with Tommy Bloomfield in MacDougall, *Voices from the Spanish Civil War*, p. 51.

23 IWM, Fred Copeman collection.

24 Fred Thomas, p. 21.

25 Anon., 'Memories of a veteran', ALBA Moscow 545/2/266, p. 162.

26 Interview with George Watters in MacDougall, *Voices from the Spanish Civil War*, p. 35.

27 Interview with Bill Feeley, MHA 191, reel 1, side 1.

28 Fred Thomas, p. 18.

29 Rust, p. 30.

30 Interview with Donald Renton in MacDougall, *Voices from the Spanish Civil War*, p. 24.

31 Interview with Frank McCusker in MacDougall, *Voices from the Spanish Civil War*, p. 45.

32 Interview with Donald Renton in MacDougall, *Voices from the Spanish Civil War*, p. 24.

33 Alexander, *British Volunteers*, p. 73.

34 Baxell, *British Volunteers*, p. 14.

35 Alexander, *British Volunteers*, p. 65.

36 Copeman, p. 80.

37 Letter from Peter Kerrigan to Harry Pollitt, 6 January 1937. IBA MML Box C, File 9/3.

38 Gurney, p. 61.

39 Gregory, p. 29.

40 John Halstead and Barry McLoughlin, 'British and Irish Students at the International Lenin School, Moscow, 1926–37', Conference Paper, MHA, April 2001, p. 3.

41 Gurney, p. 61.

42 Interview with George Watters in MacDougall, *Voices from the Spanish Civil War*, pp. 35–6.

43 Monks, p. 12. Campeau's nationality is unclear: he is believed to have been French, though he is listed in the British Security Services' files as 'Raol Auguste Campero'. NA KV/5 112.

44 Purcell, p. 39.

45 Watson and Corcoran, pp. 28–9.

46 IBMT 545/6/182, p. 34.

47 John Lochore, unpublished memoir, from MacDougall, *Voices from War*, p. 117.

48 Interview with T.A.R. Hyndman in Toynbee, *The Distant Drum*, pp. 123–4.

49 'To Our Comrades: The Epic of Arganda Bridge'. IBA MML Box B-4, File L/8.

50 Wintringham, *English Captain*, p. 55.

51 Interview with John Tunnah, IWMSA 840, reel 3.

52 Interview with George Murray in MacDougall, *Voices from the Spanish Civil War*, p. 101.

53 Wintringham, *English Captain*, p. 41.

54 Interview with Hyndman in Toynbee, *The Distant Drum*, p. 124.

55 Spender, p. 213.

56 Rust, p. 29.

57 Wintringham, *English Captain*, p. 51.

58 Wintringham, *English Captain*, p. 52.

59 Interview with Maurice Levitas, MHA 955, reel 1, side 1.

60 Interview with John Tunnah, IWMSA 840, reel 3.

61 Interview with George Leeson, IWMSA 803, reel 2.

62 Interview with Sam Wild, IWMSA 10358, reel 1.

63 Wintringham, *English Captain*, pp. 51, 52.

64 Brome, p. 106. The standard period of basic training for the British Army is six months.

65 Interview with Cypriot volunteer Nicholas Vassilious, IWM Film Archive. Thanks to Toby Haggith at the IWM for access to this video footage.

66 For a meticulous analysis of the shenanigans surrounding arms procurement for the Republic, which ensured they were equipped with sub-standard armaments, see Howson.

67 John Lochore, unpublished memoir, from MacDougall, *Voices from War*, p. 119.

68 Interview with Eddie Brown in MacDougall, *Voices from the Spanish Civil War*, p. 110; Wintringham, *English Captain*, p. 54.

69 Wintringham, *English Captain*, p. 76.

70 Copeman, p. 81.

71 Gurney, p. 78.

72 Fred Thomas, p. 18.

73 Interview with John Dunlop in MacDougall, *Voices from the Spanish Civil War*, p. 136.

74 Interview with Jimmy Jump, IWMSA 9524, reel 3.

75 Gurney, p. 78.

76 Letter from Tom Wintringham to Harry Pollitt, 19 January 1937, IBA MML Box C, File 9/7.

77 Interview with Jack Edwards, MHA 171, reel 1, side 1.

78 Interview with John Tunnah, IWMSA 840, reel 3.

79 Monks, p. 21.

80 Angus, p. 1.

81 Interview with Tom Clarke in MacDougall, *Voices from the Spanish Civil War*, p. 60.

82 Interview with Eddie Brown in MacDougall, *Voices from the Spanish Civil War*, pp. 109–10.

83 Interview with John 'Bosco' Jones, IWMSA 9392, reel 3.

84 Gregory, p. 33.

85 Ivor Hickman cited in Wainwright, p. 81.

86 Gurney, p. 84.

87 IBA MML Box C, File 8/5. Report 20 January 1937; Box C, File 9/9.

88 Cox, *Defence of Madrid*, p. 171.

89 Gurney, p. 97.

90 Interview with Sam Wild, IWMSA 10358, reel 1.

91 Ruskin, from a White Russian family and whose real name was Doumont Zubchaninov, actually spoke eight languages. He had previously worked as a communications technician in Spain, France and Argentina and was later seconded to take command of the 15th Brigade Transmissions. IBC 545/6/89, pp. 12–13; Alexander, *British Volunteers*, p. 118.

92 Letter from Tom Wintringham to Harry Pollitt, 19 January 1937, IBA MML Box C, File 9/7.

93 Richard Bennett, 'Portrait of a Killer', pp. 471–2; *The Black and Tans*, p. 147; F.P. Crozier, *Impressions and Recollections*, London: T.W. Laurie, 1930, pp. 264–5. I am grateful to Melody Buckley, who uncovered the latter reference to Macartney.

94 Levine, p. 39.

95 Alexander, *British Volunteers*, p. 69.

96 Emmet O'Connor, 'Mutiny or sabotage? The Irish defection to the Abraham Lincoln Battalion in the Spanish Civil War.' On-line at http://irelandscw.com/docs-Division.htm

97 Cronin, p. 90, cited in P. O'Connor.

98 Interview with Charles Bloom, IWMSA 992, reel 2.

99 IBC 545/3/467, p. 21.

100 'A Documentary History of the XV International Brigade', IBC 545/3/467, p. 20. Irish volunteer Peter O'Connor believed that 'the reason for the Irish joining the Americans is because they cannot bunk with the Englishmen.' Letter from Peter O'Connor to Bill Alexander, 7 November 1976, IBA MML Box 50, File C/1.

101 Letter from D.S. Springhall to Harry Pollitt, 19 January 1937, IBA MML Box C, File 9/8.

102 Letter from George Aitken to Political Bureau, IBA MML Box C, File 17/7.

103 See Macartney, *Walls Have Mouths*.

104 Interview with Peter Kerrigan in Corkhill and Rawnsley, p. 59.

105 See, for example, Hopkins, p. 170.
106 LHASC, CP/IND/POLL/2/5-6.
107 Letter from Peter Kerrigan to Harry Pollitt, 19 January 1937, IBA MML Box C, File 9.
108 There is a strange footnote to this story. In August 2010 the author had a conversation with a former member of the Communist Party who claimed to have been present at a Party meeting, when Kerrigan confessed with no further explanation that he had in fact deliberately shot Macartney.
109 Letter from Peter Kerrigan to Harry Pollitt, 10 February 1937, IBA MML Box C, File 10/6.
110 Rust, p. 62.
111 Gurney, p. 63.
112 Interview with Hyndman in Toynbee, *The Distant Drum*, p. 124.
113 Copeman, p. 80; interview with Donald Renton in MacDougall, *Voices from the Spanish Civil War*, p. 22.
114 Cook, p. 28; Gurney, p. 88.
115 Anon., 'Memories of a veteran', ALBA Moscow 545/2/266, p. 163.
116 Interview with George Leeson, IWMSA 803, reel 2.
117 Lochore, p. 121.
118 Crook, ch. 3, p. 11.

8 Their finest hour?

1 Beevor, *The Battle for Spain*, p. 209.
2 H. Thomas, *Spanish Civil War*, p. 589.
3 Originally a Hungarian, Gal's real name was Janos Galicz. Wintringham, *English Captain*, p. 65.
4 Interview with George Aitken, IWMSA 10357, reel 2.
5 Figure quoted in a letter of 4 January 1937 from Peter Kerrigan to Harry Pollitt. LHASC, CP/IND/POLL/2/5-6.
6 According to Jud Colman, who had fought with No. 1 Company at Lopera, the veterans of No. 1 Company were mainly kept back as the brigade guard, and thus didn't fight much at Jarama. As he later recognised, he had been very fortunate: 'I was very relieved. I'm not that sort of a hero. I'd be a fool if I was.' Interview with Jud Colman, IWMSA 14575, reel 2.
7 Gurney, p. 64.
8 Wintringham, *English Captain*, p. 77.
9 Colman, p. 7.
10 Tom Wintringham, 'We held Them', ALBA Moscow 545/3/479, p. 158.
11 Interview with Bob Doyle in Arthur, *The Real Band of Brothers*, p. 174.
12 Wintringham, *English Captain*, p. 70.
13 Gurney, p. 85.
14 Interview with Tony Gilbert, from *Yesterday's Witness*, 'A Cause Worth Fighting For', BBC, 1972.
15 Interview with Albert Charlesworth, IWMSA 9427, reel 2.
16 John Lochore, unpublished memoir, from MacDougall, *Voices from War*, p. 122.
17 Interview with Patrick Curry, IWMSA 799, reel 1.
18 Gurney, p. 105.
19 Gurney, p. 86.
20 Gregory, p. 45.
21 Interview with Fred Copeman, IWMSA 794, reel 2.
22 Gurney, pp. 112–13.
23 Interview with Albert Charlesworth, IWMSA 798, reel 1.
24 Gurney, p. 102.
25 Wintringham, *English Captain*, p. 63.
26 Gurney, pp. 103–4.
27 'A Documentary History of the XV International Brigade', pp. 7–8. IBC 545/3/467.
28 Interview with Albert Charlesworth, IWMSA 798, reel 1.
29 Wintringham, *English Captain*, p. 65.
30 Wintringham, *English Captain*, p. 67.
31 Tom Wintringham's description of the engagement contains a useful sketch map of the positions during the morning of 12 February 1937. See Wintringham, *English Captain*, p. 62.
32 Tom Wintringham later acknowledged this, recounting that the battalion had held 'an untenable position for some six hours'. 'We Held Them', ALBA Moscow 545/3/479, p. 161.
33 Interview with George Leeson, IWMSA 803, reel 2.
34 John Lochore's unpublished memoir, from MacDougall, *Voices from War*, p. 123.
35 Interview with Tony Gilbert, from 'A Cause Worth Fighting For'.
36 Gurney, p. 109.
37 Interview with Sam Wild, IWMSA 10358, reel 1.
38 Jim Prendergast, ALBA Moscow 545/3/478, p. 121.
39 Account by Frank Ryan from Ryan et al, p. 62.
40 Interview with Tom Clarke in MacDougall, *Voices from the Spanish Civil War*, p. 61.
41 Interview with John 'Bosco' Jones, IWMSA 9392, reel 3.
42 Gurney, p. 71.
43 W.E. Johns, 'What a waste', *Popular Flying*, May 1937 in Cunningham, *Spanish Front*, p. 333. See also Shelmerdine, *British Representations*, p. 161.
44 Interview with Frank Graham, IWMSA 11877, reel 2.
45 Wintringham, *English Captain*, pp. 79–80.
46 Interview with Albert Charlesworth, IWMSA 798, reel 1.
47 Interview with James Brown, IWMSA 124, reel 3.
48 Gurney, pp. 104, 108.
49 Interview with George Leeson, IWMSA 803, reel 2.
50 Gurney, p. 103.
51 Wintringham, *English Captain*, pp. 76–7.
52 Account by Tom Wintringham, ALBA Moscow 545/3/480, p. 168.
53 Wintringham, *English Captain*, p. 69.
54 Bill Rust (in *Britons in Spain*, p. 44) erroneously claimed that the battalion had been equipped with obsolete ammunition. In fact, there was a mix-up between the ammunition for the German 7.92mm and the Soviet 7.62mm Maxims. I am grateful to Jim Carmody for this information.

55 LHASC, CP/IND/POLL/2/5-6.
56 Account by 'Bill' [Meredith] (whose real name was actually Bob Dennison), Harold Fry's observer and courier, in F. Graham, *The Battle of Jarama*, p. 17.
57 Rust, p. 45.
58 As Charlesworth retreated he also joined the long list of casualties when he was blown into the air by an artillery shell. After a spell in hospital he rejoined the battalion and became its postman. Interview with Albert Charlesworth, IWMSA 798, reel 1.
59 Copeman, p. 92.
60 Wintringham, *English Captain*, p. 91.
61 Account by Tom Wintringham, ALBA Moscow 545/3/480, p. 173.
62 IBC 545/3/467, p. 2.
63 Anonymous account by a 'member of the battalion staff', from Ryan et al, p. 52.
64 Gurney, p. 110.
65 Wintringham, *English Captain*, p. 93. Rust estimates that, including officers and members of the Machine-Gun Company, a total of 275 British were still in action by the end of the first day. Rust, p. 46.
66 Gurney, pp. 113–14. Maurice Davidovitch, from Bethnal Green in London, was a stretcher-bearer at Jarama. Copeman, p. 89.
67 Wintringham, *English Captain*, pp. 94–5; interview with George Aitken, IWMSA 10357, reel 1.
68 Copeman, p. 94.
69 Interview with John Tunnah, IWMSA 840, reel 7.
70 Rust, p. 46; 'A Documentary History of the XV International Brigade', p. 11. IBC 545/3/467.
71 Gurney, pp. 117–18.
72 Gurney, p. 118.
73 'A Documentary History of the XV International Brigade', p. 11. IBC 545/3/467.
74 Wintringham, *English Captain*, p. 99.
75 Account by Tom Wintringham, ALBA Moscow 545/3/480, p. 180.
76 Rust, p. 47.
77 Interview with George Aitken, IWMSA 10357, reel 1.
78 See written reports from members of the Machine-Gun Company captured that day: Harold Fry, Bert Levy, Donald Renton, Charles West and Basil Abrahams undated, LHASC, CP/IND/POLL/2/5-6.
79 Interview with Donald Renton in MacDougall, *Voices from the Spanish Civil War*, p. 25.
80 Copeman, p. 96. Copeman always insisted that this version was correct: 'Well, I know bloody well they were because I was there . . . They got our uniforms from blokes who were killed.' Interview with Fred Copeman, IWMSA 794, reel 1.
81 Jimmy Rutherford, 'I was a fascist prisoner for three months', ALBA Moscow 545/3/478, pp. 68–9.
82 See Interview with George Leeson, IWMSA 803, reel 3.
83 Account by Bill Meredith, from Ryan et al, p. 56.
84 Report by George Aitken, ALBA Moscow 545/3/497, p. 87.
85 Account by 'O.R.' from Ryan et al, p. 56.
86 Account by 'O.R.' from Ryan et al, p. 57.
87 Account by Frank Ryan from Ryan et al, p. 58.
88 Account by Frank Ryan from Ryan et al, p. 60.
89 Interview with John 'Bosco' Jones, IWMSA 9392, reel 3.
90 Wintringham, *English Captain*, p. 117. As Wintringham notes, more significant than good fortune were the vigorous attacks of the Dimitrov Battalion to the north of the British, who eventually pushed the Rebels back to the river valley gorge.
91 Interview with Sid Quinn, cited in Cook, p. 74.
92 H. Thomas, *Spanish Civil War*, p. 378.
93 In the first edition of Hugh Thomas's *The Spanish Civil War* (p. 380) he cites 25,000 Republicans killed and wounded and 20,000 Nationalists (first edition published by Eyre & Spottiswoode, 1961. Third, revised and enlarged edition published simultaneously by Hamish Hamilton and Pelican, 1977). These figures reappear throughout the literature: see, for example, Preston, *Concise History*, p. 141. However, in Thomas's third edition (p. 596) the figures have been revised down to 10,000 and 6000. These revised estimates appear in the most recent work on Jarama: Jesús González de Miguel's *La Batalla de Jarama*, 2009 (p. 707) and are probably nearer the truth. Precise figures of the casualty numbers at Jarama are obviously hard to pin down, so some historians are now understandably circumspect. See, for example, Beevor, *The Battle for Spain*, p. 214, in which he states, 'estimates varied from 6000 to 20,000.'
94 *Daily Worker*, 6 March 1937, p. 1.
95 H. Thomas, *Spanish Civil War*, 3rd edn, p. 592.
96 Stradling, *Irish and the Spanish Civil War*, p. 166.
97 Wintringham, *English Captain*, p. 65.
98 Interview with Frank McCusker in MacDougall, *Voices from the Spanish Civil War*, p. 43.

9 'The old men waiting patiently'

1 Copeman, p. 98.
2 Letter from Harry Pollitt to Mrs Craig, Springburn, Glasgow, 5 March 1937.
3 In fact, as Keith Scott Watson, who left the International Column to work as a reporter with Sefton Delmer of the *Daily Express*, described, 'while relations mourned the misguided, but gallant lad, he was leading an attack on the wireless station in the Casa de Campo.' Mackenzie bumped into Esmond Romilly and three of his companions in a café in Madrid: 'I'm here to deny the report that I've been killed,' he informed them. Romilly, p. 157; Hearst, p. 33; Watson, p. 170.
4 Ivor Hickman cited in Wainwright, p. 112. On occasion, relatives could wait for months, if not years, for confirmation of their relative's death. 'Fred White was killed in July 1937, but his wife did not receive the death certificate until March 1939. George Fretwell's family had to wait over a year to be informed that he was "missing, believed killed".' Suart, p. 225.
5 Stratton, p. 35. 'Jock McCrae' was probably William Macrae from Glasgow, who was repatriated in September 1937 after being wounded in the left leg. IBMT 545/6/166, p. 101.

6 Wintringham, *English Captain*, p. 117.
7 Gurney, p. 126.
8 P. Carroll, p. 99.
9 Interview with Charles Morgan, IWMSA 10362, reel 1.
10 For the American involvement in the 27 February disaster, see P. Carroll, pp. 101–2.
11 Springhall was invalided home to Britain the following month. Hopkins, p. 274; Alexander, *British Volunteers*, pp. 101–2.
12 IBC 545/3/467, p. 32.
13 Interview with Jud Colman, IWMSA 14575, reel 3.
14 Letter from Walter Tapsell to Harry Pollitt, undated [May–June?] 1937, IBA MML Box C, File 13/1. In March, a number of new arrivals, formed into No. 2 Section of an Anglo-American company in the 20th Battalion of the 86th (Mixed) Brigade, were also involved in fighting at Pozoblanco and Chimorra in southern Spain. In a disastrous error they were attacked by an Anarchist battalion and several were killed. Not surprisingly, many of the new volunteers were badly disheartened and there were a number of desertions, before Will Paynter managed to get them transferred to the British Battalion. 'Chimorra – Torrehermosa, Pozoblanco and Estremadura Fronts, March–July 1937,' ALBA Moscow 545/3/478, pp. 101–2: IBA MML Box 50, File Mk.
15 Interview with James Brown, IWMSA 124, reel 3.
16 IBC 545/6/93, p. 1.
17 On 5 March, three senior British volunteers received notice of their promotion to captain: battalion commander Jock Cunningham, commissar George Aitken and the doctor Colin Bradworth. IBC 545/3/498, pp. 2–6.
18 IBC 545/6/93, p. 1; letter from George Aitken to Harry Pollitt, LHASC CP/IND/POLL/2/6.
19 Gurney, p. 71.
20 Interview with Tom Clarke in MacDougall, *Voices from the Spanish Civil War*, p. 61.
21 Interview with John Tunnah, IWMSA 840, reel 7.
22 Interview with John Tunnah, IWMSA 840, reel 7.
23 George Aitken, 'Remarks on The Morale of the Troops', undated, ALBA Moscow 545/3/497, p. 96.
24 Interview with George Aitken, cited in Cook, p. 82.
25 Interview with John 'Bosco' Jones, IWMSA 9392, reel 3.
26 Interview with Joe Norman, IWMSA 818, reel 2.
27 Ryan et al, p. 84.
28 Copeman, p. 107.
29 Gurney, p. 141.
30 Copeman, p. 107.
31 Paynter, p. 65; letter from Will Paynter to Harry Pollitt, 30 May 1937, Box C, File 13/8.
32 Interview with Joe Norman, IWMSA 818, reel 2.
33 'Battalion has bad name (unmerited) probably started by base clique.' Ralph Cantor diary, 1 April 1937, WCML.

34 Interview with George Aitken, IWMSA 10357, reel 2.
35 Interview with George Aitken, IWMSA 10357, reel 2.
36 Interview with John Tunnah, IWMSA 840, reel 6. However, despite his opposition at Jarama, Wild was later involved in the execution of a volunteer accused of opening fire on his own comrades. See Chapter 13.
37 Interview with Joe Norman, IWMSA 818, reel 2.
38 Interview with John 'Bosco' Jones, IWMSA 9392, reel 3.
39 Interview with Sid Quinn, cited in Cook, p. 74.
40 Interview with Walter Greenhalgh, IWMSA 11187, reel 5.
41 Lee, *A Moment of War*, p. 94.
42 Alexander, *British Volunteers*, pp. 79–80.
43 Gurney, p. 141.
44 Interview with John Tunnah, IWMSA 840, reel 1.
45 Knox, *Essays*, p. 248.
46 F. Graham, *The Battle of Jarama*, p. 71; Gregory, p. 59.
47 Ryan et al, p. 84. Spanish members of the battalion were just as disheartened, arguing that 'it was a disadvantage to belong to the International Brigade, because if they had been in a Spanish brigade they would never have been kept in the line for so long.' 'Minutes of the meetings of Political Commissars of the Battalions held June 8, 1937', ALBA Moscow 545/3/435, p. 11.
48 Interview with John 'Bosco' Jones, IWMSA 9392, reel 3.
49 Gregory, p. 59.
50 Copeman, p. 105.
51 Interview with James Brown, IWMSA 824, reel 4.
52 Interview with Claud Cockburn, from 'A Cause Worth Fighting For'.
53 Battalion orders of 11 April 1937. IBC 545/3/495, p. 4.
54 IBC 545/3/467, p. 40.
55 Stratton, p. 38.
56 John Lochore, unpublished memoir, from MacDougall, *Voices from War*, p. 133.
57 Letter from Alec Cummings to Frank Crabbe, 19 March 1937. IBA MML Box A-15/11.
58 Interview with Robert Walker, MHA 240, reel 1, side 1.
59 Gurney, pp. 134–5.
60 IBC 545/3/496, pp. 91–3.
61 Battalion orders for 15 May 1937, signed by Charlie Goodfellow. IBC 545/3/495, p. 8.
62 'A Documentary History of the XV International Brigade,' p. 47. IBC 545/3/467; Battalion orders 11 April 1937. IBC 545/3/495, p. 6.
63 Copeman, p. 105.
64 Copeman, p. 110; diary of Sid Hamm, in Stradling, *Brother Against Brother*, p. 164.
65 Stratton, p. 41.
66 Gurney, p. 140.
67 IBC 545/3/451, p. 49.

68 Hearst, MS, p. 84.

69 Stratton, p. 38.

70 Gurney, p. 147.

71 Ćopić diary, 29 April 1937, from IBC 545/3/467.

72 Ralph Cantor diary, 28 April 1937, WCML.

73 ALBA Moscow, 545/3/478, pp. 145–6.

74 Gurney, p. 148. See also Stradling, 'English-speaking Units', p. 754.

75 Letter from Will Paynter to Harry Pollitt, 9 June 1937. IBA MML Box C, File 14/5.

76 Alexander, British Volunteers, p. 107.

77 Interview with George Aitken, IWMSA 10357, reel 1.

78 Wintringham, English Captain, p. 113.

79 Interview with John 'Bosco' Jones, IWMSA 9392, reel 6.

80 Alexander, British Volunteers, p. 107.

81 Interview with Fred Copeman, IWMSA 794, reel 3; Hopkins, p. 268.

82 Ralph Cantor diary, 4 May 1937, WCML.

83 Interview with Walter Greenhalgh, IWMSA 11187, reel 5. The writer of the lyrics of the song, Alec Macdade from Glasgow, who was killed at Brunete in July 1937, is sometimes confused with Willie MacDade from Dundee, Tom Wintringham's adjutant, who was repatriated later in the year.

84 Alexander, British Volunteers, p. 109.

85 Gregory, p. 60.

86 Letter from George Aitken to Harry Pollitt, 8 May 1937, IBA MML Box C, File 13/2.

87 Interview with John 'Bosco' Jones, IWMSA 9392, reel 3.

88 Interview with Tommy Bloomfield in MacDougall, Voices from the Spanish Civil War, p. 48.

89 Report by Thomas Bloomfield, 5 February 1938, IBC 545/6/107, pp. 58–64. With thanks to Rachel Seiffert for the translation from German.

90 Interview with James Maley, IWMSA 11947, reel 2.

91 Jimmy Rutherford, 'I was a fascist prisoner for three months', ALBA Moscow 545/3/478, p. 68.

92 Interview with Donald Renton in MacDougall, Voices from the Spanish Civil War, p. 26.

93 IBC 545/6/107.

94 IBA MML Box 28.

95 The executed volunteers were Phil Elias, a tailor from Leeds, and John Stevens, an engineer from Islington in London. IBA MML Box 28.

96 Interview with Tommy Bloomfield in MacDougall, Voices from the Spanish Civil War, pp. 48–9.

97 Interview with Tommy Bloomfield in MacDougall, Voices from the Spanish Civil War, p. 49.

98 'Britons Captured in Spain', Daily Mail, 31 March 1937, p. 20.

99 Interview with Donald Renton in MacDougall, Voices from the Spanish Civil War, p. 26; Geiser, pp. 15–16.

100 Rutherford, 'I was a fascist prisoner for three months', ALBA Moscow 545/3/478, p. 71; IBC 545/6/107.

101 'Voice of Madrid' radio broadcast by Jimmy Rutherford, 28 April 1938, cited in Geiser, pp. 15–16.

102 Rutherford, 'I was a fascist prisoner for three months', ALBA Moscow 545/3/478, p. 71.

103 Interview with Donald Renton in MacDougall, Voices from the Spanish Civil War, p. 28.

104 Kemp, Mine Were of Trouble, p. 67.

105 García, The Truth About Spain, p. 35.

106 IBMT Moscow 545/6/107.

107 IBA MML Box 28, File A/4.

108 Alexander, British Volunteers, p. 184.

109 Rutherford, 'I was a fascist prisoner for three months', ALBA Moscow 545/3/478, p. 72.

110 Notebook of A.C. Williams, from the family papers. I am very grateful to Lisa Croft for allowing me access to the papers.

111 Interview with Donald Renton in MacDougall, Voices from the Spanish Civil War, p. 27.

112 Interview with Tommy Bloomfield in MacDougall, Voices from the Spanish Civil War, p. 50.

113 NA FO371/21287 W6098; IBA MML Box 28, File A/18.

114 IBA MML Box 33, File 16/6.

115 IBC 545/6/107.

116 The Times, Saturday 29 May 1937.

117 IBMT 545/6/107.

118 Of the twenty-three released prisoners, five were back in Spain fighting with the British Battalion within six weeks, including Harold Fry, Basil Minsk (a Jewish volunteer from London fighting under the name of Basil Abrahams), Tom Bloomfield, a Scot from Kirkcaldy in Fife, and Jimmy Rutherford, the Edinburgh delegate to the YCL annual conference in 1934. 'Jimmy Rutherford Died for Freedom', Challenge, 20 February 1939, p. 7.

119 'Prisoners Released by Franco: a generous parting gesture', The Times, 29 May 1937, p. 13.

120 IBA MML Box 28, Files A2, A/56.

121 Alexander, British Volunteers, p. 185.

122 Geiser, p. 17.

10 'The May Days'

1 G. Jackson, Juan Negrín, p. 77.

2 Orwell, Homage, pp. 201–2.

3 Thwaites, p. 52.

4 Report by Harry P. Thomas, IBA MML Box C, File 13/12. In fairness to Edwards, this report was clearly written to conform to Communist Party sensibilities.

5 Interview with Frank Frankford, IWMSA 9308, reel 2.

6 Interview with Stafford Cottman, IWMSA 9278, reel 2.

7 Interview with Stafford Cottman, IWMSA 9278, reel 4.

8 Hall, *Not Just Orwell*, pp. 106–7.

9 Shelden, p. 274.

10 Orwell, *Homage*, pp. 3–4.

11 *The Spanish Revolution*, 3 February 1937, cited in Shelden, p. 278.

12 Orwell, *Homage*, p. 10.

13 Born of Russian parents, Kopp had grown up and been educated in Belgium, training as an engineer. Bowker, p. 206.

14 Orwell cited in Thwaites, p. 55.

15 John Cornford, 'A letter from Aragon', in Cornford, *Collected Writings*, p. 41.

16 Interview with Frank Frankford, IWMSA 9308, reel 3; Thwaites, p. 55.

17 Orwell, *Homage*, p. 48; interview with Stafford Cottman, IWMSA 9278, reel 3.

18 Orwell, *Homage*, pp. 43–4.

19 Interview with Frank Frankford, IWMSA 9308, reel 2.

20 Orwell, *Homage*, pp. 99–100.

21 Orwell, *Homage*, p. 27.

22 Orwell, *Homage*, p. 37.

23 Orwell, *Homage*, p. 75; interview with Stafford Cottman, IWMSA 9278, reel 4.

24 Interview with Frank Frankford, IWMSA 9308, reels 2–3.

25 Interview with Frank Frankford, IWMSA 9308, reel 3.

26 Shelden, p. 290.

27 Interview with Stafford Cottman, IWMSA 9278, reel 5.

28 Orwell, *Homage*, pp. 138, 141.

29 'Report on the English Section of the P.O.U.M.' IBA MML Box C, File 13/7a.

30 Orwell, *Homage*, p. 146.

31 Viñas, *Looking Back*, pp. 133, 149. Suspicion of the POUM actually existed in Spain before Russian involvement in the civil war. As the Communist dissident Franz Borkenau pointed out, 'It is difficult to say whether it [the POUM] was more hateful to the PSUC on account of its anti-Stalinism in Russian affairs or its extreme Leftist tendencies in Spanish questions.' Borkenau, p. 182.

32 Interview with J.R. Jump in Toynbee, *The Distant Drum*, p. 118.

33 Hall, *Not Just Orwell*, pp. 53–4.

34 D.J. Taylor, p. 223.

35 Harrisson, MS, pp. 103–5.

36 Harrisson, MS, p. 105.

37 Interview with Stafford Cottman, IWMSA 9278, reel 5; Copeman, p. 119.

38 Report on the position with regard to the ILP Group, 28 May 1937. IBA MML Box C, File 13/10.

39 IBA MML Box C, File 13/13.

40 IBC 545/3/99.

41 IBC 545/9/96, 545/6/215.

42 Orwell, *Homage*, pp. 250, 252.

43 For the most detailed and informed account of Nin's assassination, see Volodarsky, pp. 249–50.

44 Although many suspected that Smillie was murdered by Russian agents, the illness – albeit the result of official neglect – was almost certainly the cause of his death. See Buchanan, *Impact*, pp. 98–121.

45 Thwaites, p. 57.

46 Alexander, *British Volunteers*, p. 108.

47 Copeman, p. 119.

48 Interview with J.R. Jump in Toynbee, *The Distant Drum*, p. 118.

49 Fred Thomas, p. 110.

50 Fred Thomas, pp. 24–5.

51 Interview with Len Crome, IWMSA 9298, reel 3.

52 Gurney, p. 143.

53 Angus, p. 4.

54 Copeman, p. 122.

55 Interview with Sam Wild in Cook, p. 73.

56 Crook, ch. 3, p. 18; Bowker, p. 213.

57 Crook, ch. 4, p. 6. For Kurt Landau's disappearance see Pierre Broué, 'Kurt Landau', *Revolutionary History* 9:4, 2008, pp. 229–36.

58 Volodarsky, p. 267. O'Donnell alluded to his activities in a letter to Harry Pollitt in the spring of 1937: 'The work given to me was that of representing the English section of the Foreigners Department of the P.S.U.C. . . . I should explain that the nature of my work cannot be fully explained in a letter, and that much of it is of a character which can only be undertaken by a party comrade who has had previous experience in this work.' Letter from Hugh O'Donnell to Harry Pollitt, 18 March 1937, IBA MML Box C, File 11/2.

59 Crook, ch. 4, p. 2.

60 Interview with Hugh Sloan in MacDougall, *Voices from the Spanish Civil War*, p. 199.

61 *Daily Worker*, 17 May 1937.

62 Ralph Cantor diary, 14 May 1937, WCML.

63 *News Chronicle*, 10 May 1937, p. 5.

64 *Daily Worker*, 11 May 1937, p. 1; Pettifer, pp. 182–8.

65 *Daily Worker*, 14 September 1937.

66 R. Armstrong, 'Against the Slanders', *Workers Fight*, 2:3, July 1939.

67 Orwell, 'Eye-witness', p. 87.

68 Interview with Stafford Cottman, IWMSA 9278, reel 7.

69 Orwell, 'Eye-witness', p. 86.

70 Interview with Frank Frankford, IWMSA 9308, reel 4.

71 Orwell, *Homage*, pp. 87–8.

72 Alexander, *British Volunteers*, p. 27.

73 See interview with Albert Cole, MHA 212, reel 2, side 2. Cooney makes a number of interjections during Cole's interview.

74 Interview with Frank Frankford, IWMSA 9308, reel 2.

75 F. Graham, *The Battle of Jarama*, p. 71.

76 'During the rest of 1937 and well into 1938, many thousands of POUM members, and indeed other Leftists of all descriptions, were executed or tortured to death in Communist prisons.' Paul Johnson, *Modern Times: The World from the Twenties to the Eighties*. New York, NY: HarperCollins, 1983, pp. 334–5, taken from Volodarsky, p. 237.

77 Orwell, *Homage*, pp. 237–8.
78 A.J.P. Taylor, *Origins of the Second World War*, p. 159. As Angel Viñas argues, 'no significant aspect of communist or Soviet policies during that period can be understood without reference to the action against Trotskyism.' Viñas, *Looking Back*, pp. 133, 149.
79 Borkenau, p. 235.

11 ¡Sanidad!

1 Palfreeman, p. 3.
2 Hall, *Not Just Orwell*, p. 61.
3 Gray, p. 85.
4 Interview with Roderick MacFarquhar in MacDougall, *Voices from the Spanish Civil War*, p. 84.
5 Gray, p. 85 and Delmer, p. 344.
6 Delmer, p. 344.
7 Kurzke, MS, p. 40.
8 Interview with Roderick MacFarquhar, IWMSA 9234, reel 3, cited in Darman, p. 188.
9 Interview with Len Crome, IWMSA 9298, reel 1.
10 According to Slater, he was shown a solid gold crucifix between nine inches and a foot long, some gold ornaments, three gold and amber ashtrays and a set of silver fish knives. Hugh Slater, 'Report on the Spanish Ambulance Unit', 21 October 1936, IBA MML Box C, File 6/1; Gray, p.88.
11 The unit returned to Spain in September 1937, again led by Jacobsen, and remained in Spain, helping both sides in the war, until finally repatriated in July 1938. MacDougall, *Voices from the Spanish Civil War*, p. 342; Gray, pp. 85–92.
12 García, *The Truth About Spain*, p. 77.
13 Interview with Annie Murray in MacDougall, *Voices from the Spanish Civil War*, p. 69; Fyrth, p. 47.
14 Fyrth, pp. 49–50.
15 Total taken from Len Crome memorial lecture by Linda Palfreeman, London, 5 March 2011.
16 Kenneth Sinclair-Loutit and Aileen Palmer, 'Survey of a year's work with the British Medical Unit in Spain', p. 1. IBMT 545/6/88.
17 Cochrane, 'One Man's Medicine', p. 26, from Buchanan, *Impact*, p. 48.
18 Buchanan, *Impact*, p. 54.
19 Interview with Len Crome, IWMSA 9298, reel 2.
20 Interview with Annie Murray in MacDougall, *Voices from the Spanish Civil War*, p. 71.
21 Kenneth Sinclair-Loutit, cited in Toynbee *The Distant Drum*, p. 105.
22 Fyrth, p. 51.
23 Annie Murray, cited in Fyrth, p. 56.
24 Report by Sylvia Townsend Warner and Valentine Ackland, IBA MML Box C, File 7/1.
25 Report by Winifred Bates, IBC 545/6/88, p. 16.
26 Buchanan, *Impact*, p. 61.
27 Report by Winifred Bates, IBC 545/6/88, p. 17.
28 Loutit and Palmer, 'Survey of a year's work with the British Medical Unit in Spain', pp. 6–8.
29 Buchanan, *Impact*, p. 47. Not surprisingly, given the stresses of their life in Spain, Sinclair-Loutit was not the only medical worker to have a relationship. For example, Nan Green had a brief affair with a patient and Patience Darton met and married a German brigader. Green, p. 87; A. Jackson, *For Us It Was Heaven*, esp. pp. 58–9.
30 Palmer cited in Palfreeman, p. 45.
31 Interview with Reg Saxton, IWMSA 8735, reel 3.
32 Gregory, p. 50.
33 Wogan Philipps, 'An Ambulance Man in Spain', in Cunningham, *Spanish Front*, p. 45.
34 Interview with Reg Saxton, IWMSA 8735, reels 4 and 5.
35 Coni, p. 156.
36 Gregory, pp. 50–1.
37 'Position in the BMU', report by Walter Tapsell. IBA MML Box C, File 12/3.
38 Letter 4 May 1937, London to Albacete, IBA MML Box 21B, File 2i.
39 IBA MML Box 21B, File 2i.
40 IBA MML Box 21B, File 2i.
41 Interview with Annie Murray in MacDougall, *Voices from the Spanish Civil War*, p. 69.
42 B. Goldman, 'Report of work of British Medical Aid Unit in Spain'. IBMT Moscow 545/6/88, p. 49.
43 Philipps, 'An Ambulance Man in Spain', in Cunningham, *Spanish Front*, p. 45.
44 Coni, p. 160.
45 Interview with Alun Williams, IWMSA 10181, reel 3.
46 Fyvel, p. 28.
47 Interview with William Henry 'Harry' Stratton, IWMSA 9393, reel 4.
48 See Leonard Crome, 'The Death of Julian Bell', *New Statesman & Nation*, 28 August 1937; Stansky and Abrahams, p. 405.
49 Interview with Reg Saxton, IWMSA 8735, reel 9.
50 Stansky and Abrahams, p. 412.
51 Harrisson, MS, p. 118.
52 Interview with John Kiszely, IWMSA 12934, reel 1.
53 Interview with John Kiszely, IWMSA 12934, reel 1.
54 Fyrth, p. 94.
55 Letter from John Mahon to Harry Pollitt, 29 October 1937, IBA MML Box C, File 18/3.
56 Nan Green cited in Fyrth, p. 120. A slightly different version appears in Green, p. 85.
57 Report for Harry Pollitt from John Mahon, 2 November 1937, IBA MML Box C, File 19/1.
58 Interview with Margaret Powell, from 'A Cause Worth Fighting For'.
59 Interview with Tom Clarke in MacDougall, *Voices from the Spanish Civil War*, pp. 63–4.
60 B. Clark, p. 112.
61 Interview with Len Crome, IWMSA 9298, reel 2.
62 Patience Darton cited in A. Jackson, *Beyond the Battlefield*, p. 38.
63 Aurora Fernández cited in Fyrth, p. 142.
64 Leah Manning cited in A. Jackson, *Beyond the Battlefield*, p. 36. Jackson identifies the dying brigader as Harry Dobson, the Welsh political commissar of the Major Attlee Company, who was mortally wounded on Gandesa's Hill 481 on 28 July 1938.
65 A. Williams, p. 166.

66 A. Williams, p. 178.
67 Gregory, p. 128.
68 Bury, pp. 40–1. After being wounded at Jarama, Noel Carritt became a driver in an ambulance convoy. His younger brother, Anthony, was killed at Brunete. IBMT Moscow 545/6/113, p.89; IBA MML Box 21a, File A.
69 Interview with John Tunnah, IWMSA 840, reel 4.
70 For the medical advances in Spain see Coni, esp. pp. 47–81, and Palfreeman, pp. 219–30.
71 Douglas Jolly cited in Fyrth, p. 140.
72 Fyrth, p. 144.
73 Coni, p. 160; interview with Harold King, IWMSA 839, reel 2.
74 Coni, p. 126.
75 Interview with Tommy Bloomfield in MacDougall, Voices from the Spanish Civil War, p. 54.
76 Interview with Tom Clarke in MacDougall, Voices from the Spanish Civil War, p. 60.
77 A. Williams, p. 166.
78 Gregory, pp. 50–1.
79 Watson, pp. 173–4. It would appear that Watson was correct. Nationalist orders noted how the destruction of hospitals 'has a highly demoralising effect on troops'. Palfreeman, p. 54.
80 Interview with Margaret Powell, from 'A Cause Worth Fighting For'.
81 Coni, p. 107.
82 A. Williams, p. 166.
83 Palfreeman, pp. 226–7.
84 Fyrth, p. 147.
85 Bury, pp. 38–9. See also Josep Trueta, Trueta: Surgeon in War and Peace, London: Victor Gollancz, 1980.
86 Interview with Len Crome, IWMSA 9298, reel 2.
87 Interview with Reg Saxton, IWMSA 8735, reel 4.
88 Fyvel, p. 22.
89 Green, p. 94.
90 Interview with Reg Saxton, IWMSA 8735, reel 4.
91 Interview with Reg Saxton, IWMSA 8735, reel 6.
92 Douglas Jolly cited in Fyrth, p. 146.
93 Interview with Sam Lesser, London, April 2001.

12 'The good-looking students'
1   Alexander, British Volunteers, p. 109.
2   Azaña cited in Beevor, The Battle for Spain, p. 278.
3   Copeman, p. 122; Copeman interview IWMSA 794, reel 6.
4   Ryan et al, p. 131.
5   Rust, pp. 57–8.
6   Anon. 'Memories of a veteran'. ALBA Moscow 545/2/266, p. 163.
7   Interview with David Anderson in MacDougall, Voices from the Spanish Civil War, p. 93.
8   Interview with Fred Copeman, IWMSA 794, reel 8.
9   Interview with Fred Copeman, IWMSA 794, reel 8.
10 Letter from Bill Alexander to the author, 26 August 1999.
11 Letter from Fred Thomas to James Hopkins, 8 June 1999 (courtesy of Fred Thomas).
12 Report on the formation of the British Anti-Tank

Battery by Malcolm Dunbar. ALBA Moscow 545/3/479, pp. 62–3.
13 IBC 545/6/126, p. 26.
14 Dunbar has been listed as having studied at Trinity College with Julian Bell and the Cambridge spies Anthony Blunt and Guy Burgess and, like them, named as a member of the Apostles, the secret left-wing debating society. However, Dunbar graduated from Christ's, rather than Trinity, and the evidence strongly suggests he was not an Apostle either.
15 Interview with Hugh Sloan, IWMSA 11354, reel 4.
16 Interview with Hugh Sloan in MacDougall, Voices from the Spanish Civil War, pp. 202–3.
17 IBC 545/6/126, p. 37.
18 IBC 545/6/126, p. 36.
19 IBC 545/6/126, p. 31.
20 Though George Murray claims his responsibilities were 'guarding against insertion of enemy agents etc.' Interview with George Murray in MacDougall, Voices from the Spanish Civil War, p. 103.
21 H. Thomas, Spanish Civil War, pp. 22–3; interview with John Dunlop in MacDougall, Voices from the Spanish Civil War, p. 136.
22 Alexander, British Volunteers, p. 219.
23 ALBA Moscow 545/2/262, p. 60.
24 Interview with Jim Brewer, IWMSA 9963, reel 3.
25 Interview with Jim Brewer, IWMSA 9963, reel 7, cited in Darman, p. 160.
26 Alexander, British Volunteers, p. 219.
27 ALBA Moscow 545/2/262, p. 60.
28 Fred Thomas, p. 23.
29 Letter from Jim Brewer to Bill Alexander, 3 December 1979, IBA MML Box A/12, File Br.
30 Interview with Fred Copeman, IWMSA 794, reel 8.
31 Fred Thomas, p. 30.
32 Interview with John Dunlop, IWMSA 11355, reel 4.
33 IBC 545/3/451, p. 66.
34 Alexander, British Volunteers, p. 109.
35 F. Graham, Battles of Brunete and the Aragon, pp. 1–2.
36 Fred Thomas, p. 108.
37 Interview with John Dunlop, IWMSA 11355, reel 5.
38 Interview with Joe Garber, IWMSA 12291, reel 7.
39 Gregory, p. 69.
40 Gregory, p. 67; interview with Albert Charlesworth, IWMSA 798, reel 1.
41 Alexander, British Volunteers, p. 121.
42 Interview with Robert Walker, MHA 240, reel 1, side 2.
43 Interview with Albert Charlesworth, IWMSA 798, reel 1.
44 Gregory, pp. 70–1.
45 Frank Ryan, 'Franco Forces use Women and Children as Cover', Irish Democrat, 28 August 1937.
46 See, for example, interviews with Sid Quinn, IWMSA 801, reel 2 and John 'Bosco' Jones, IWMSA 9392, reel 4; Jack Roberts, 'How Fascists Fight: An Incident at the Front', ALBA Moscow 545/2/266, p. 61.
47 Copeman, pp. 130–1; interview with Fred

Copeman, IWMSA 794, reel 7.

48　Interview with John 'Bosco' Jones, IWMSA 9392, reel 4.

49　Interview with Joe Garber, IWMSA 12291, reel 9.

50　Copeman, p. 131.

51　Harrisson, MS, p. 117.

52　Alexander, British Volunteers, p. 122.

53　Interview with Albert Charlesworth, IWMSA 798, reel 1.

54　Colman, p. 9.

55　Interview with Eddie Brown in MacDougall, Voices from the Spanish Civil War, p. 112.

56　Fred Thomas, p. 37.

57　Interview with Sid Quinn, IWMSA 801, reel 2.

58　Interview with Hugh Sloan in MacDougall, Voices from the Spanish Civil War, p. 205.

59　Čopić diary, 7 July 1937, IBC 545/3/467.

60　Interview with Frank Graham, IWMSA 11877, reels 3–4.

61　Harrisson, MS, p. 117.

62　Copeman, p. 134.

63　Fred Thomas, p. 43.

64　Sexton, p. 31.

65　Interview with Alec Ferguson, MHA 239, reel 1, side 1.

66　Copeman, p. 135.

67　Interview with David Anderson in MacDougall, Voices from the Spanish Civil War, p. 92.

68　Letter from Harry Pollitt to Will Paynter, 13 July 1937. IBC 545/6/87, p. 4.

69　P. Carroll, p. 142; Petrou, p. 68.

70　Letter from Will Paynter to Harry Pollitt, 14 July 1937. IBA MML Box 21b, File 3/G.

71　Diary of Vladimir Čopić, 18 July 1937, IBC 545/3/467.

72　IBMT Moscow 545/5/148, p. 35.

73　Letter from Walter Tapsell to Unknown [Harry Pollitt?], 9 June 1937. IBA MML Box C, File 14/4.

74　Letter from Walter Tapsell to Unknown [Harry Pollitt?], 4 June 1937. IBA MML Box C, File 14/2.

75　Alexander, British Volunteers, p. 128.

76　Beevor, The Battle for Spain, p. 284.

77　Interview with Chris Smith, IWMSA 12290, reel 5.

78　Interview with Hugh Sloan, IWMSA 11354, reel 5.

79　Interview with Jim Brewer, IWMSA 9963, reel 5.

80　Fyvel, p. 29.

81　Interview with George Aitken, IWMSA 10357, reel 3.

82　Interview with George Aitken, IWMSA 10358, reel 2.

83　Angus, p. 7. See also IBA MML Box C, Files 16/1, 17/1.

84　Interview with Jim Brewer, IWMSA 9963, reel 5; Čopić diary, 27 July 1937, IBC 545/3/467.

85　Fred Thomas, p. 26.

86　Gregory, p. 77.

87　If Aitken really does mean his Corps commander, this would have been the Communist General Juan Modesto.

88　Interview with George Aitken, IWMSA 10357, reel 2.

89　Reynolds News, 23 July 1961, cited in Brome, p. 205.

90　Gallo estimated that of the 2144 troops of the 15th International Brigade taking part in the Brunete offensive, 293 had been killed, 735 wounded and 167 were missing. IBC 35082/1/42, cited in Radosh, p. 238.

91　IBA MML Box C, File 16/1.

92　Interview with Jim Brewer, IWMSA 9963, reel 5.

93　Malcolm Dunbar, then commander of the Anti-Tank Battery, later promoted to the 15th Brigade staff, admitted as much to Fred Thomas. Fred Thomas, p. 36.

94　Alexander, British Volunteers, p. 131.

95　IBA MML Box C, File 14/5.

96　Letter from George Aitken to Political Bureau, IBA MML Box C, File 17/7.

97　Letter from George Aitken to Political Bureau, IBA MML Box C, File 17/7.

98　IBA MML Box C, File 16/1.

99　IBA MML Box C, File 16/1.

100　An official report published previously in April 1937 had also not been very complimentary about Aitken. Describing him as 'a good comrade who works hard', it continued, 'I believe that comrade Aitken could work better in the brigade than in the battalion'. IBC, 545/6/93, p. 1.

101　IBA MML Box C, File 16/2.

102　Alexander, British Volunteers, p. 131.

103　Letter from George Aitken to the Political Bureau, undated, IBA MML Box C, File 17/7.

104　Letter from Bill Rowe to Harry Pollitt, 28 July 1937, IBA MML Box 39/A/26; IBC 545/6/451, p. 65.

105　Report from Albacete, [end of] July 1937. IBC 35082/1/90, cited in Radosh, p. 246.

106　Letter from Will Paynter to Harry Pollitt, 14 July 1937. IBA MML Box 21b, File 3/G.

107　Letter from Will Paynter to Harry Pollitt, 20 July 1937, IBA MML Box C, File 15/3.

13　¡Disciplina Camaradas!

1　Gurney, p. 148.

2　The popular and widespread use of the term 'volunteers' to describe the men of the battalion has not helped for, of course, they were only volunteers up to the moment they joined.

3　Interview with Jim Brewer, IWMSA 9963, reel 5.

4　IBA MML Box C, File 14/5.

5　ALBA Moscow 545/2/262, pp. 107, 109.

6　Senior British commissars who had attended the Lenin School included George Aitken, Bob Cooney, George Coyle, Thomas Degnan, Harry Dobson, Peter Kerrigan, Will Paynter and Walter Tapsell. See John Halstead and Barry McLoughlin, 'British and Irish Students at the International Lenin School, Moscow, 1926–37', Conference paper given at University of Manchester, April 2001.

7 Letter from Peter Kerrigan to Harry Pollitt, 6 January 1937. IBA MML Box C, File 9/3.

8 Report on British Political Commissars Conference, IBA MML Box C, File 19/8.

9 Report on British Political Commissars Conference, IBA MML Box C, File 19/8.

10 Gurney, pp. 64–5.

11 Copeman, p. 137.

12 ALBA Moscow 545/3/479, p. 21.

13 ALBA Moscow 545/3/479, p. 21; interview with Tom Murray in MacDougall, *Voices from the Spanish Civil War*, p. 317.

14 Wogan Philipps in Cunningham, *Spanish Front*, p. 47.

15 Hearst, MS, p. 56.

16 Interview with Syd Booth, MHA 200, reel 2, side 2.

17 ALBA Moscow 545/3/438, p. 52.

18 Jason Gurney argued that 'The nearest thing to a good Political Commissar that I saw was George Aitken, who took over that function in the British Battalion at Jarama. He was a Scots Communist about forty years of age, strong in his Communist convictions but by no means uncritical. If he thought that the leadership was wrong he didn't hesitate to say so, with the result that he was eventually sent home and resigned from the Party.' Gurney, p. 62.

19 ALBA Moscow 545/3/479, p. 22.

20 Gurney, p. 144.

21 Volodarsky, p. 297.

22 IBMT Moscow 545/6/138, pp. 28–33, 545/6/218, pp. 69–70; conversation with Freddie Shaw, July 2011.

23 Anon. *In Spain with the International Brigade*, p. 8.

24 Ralph Cantor diary, 16 April 1937, WCML.

25 Interview with George Gowans, IWMSA 12095, reel 2.

26 Interview with Jim Brewer, IWMSA 9963, reel 5.

27 Fred Thomas, p. 70.

28 Interview with Tom Murray in MacDougall, *Voices from the Spanish Civil War*, pp. 314–15.

29 Interview with John Dunlop in MacDougall, *Voices from the Spanish Civil War*, pp. 143–4.

30 A friend of the Anarchist Ethel McDonald, the Scottish volunteer Robert Martin was predictably suspected of being politically unreliable and arrested on his arrival in Spain. He was sent home without taking part in any action. Robert Martin, 'With the International Brigade', *Workers' Liberty*, November 1995, pp. 28–30. Originally published in *Controversy*, September 1937, p. 28.

31 Ralph Cantor diary, 2 May 1937, WCML.

32 B. Clark, p. 26; ALBA Moscow 545/2/262, p. 110.

33 The note was signed 'Salud, S——'. ALBA Moscow 545/3/438, p. 72.

34 IBC 545/3/435, p. 7.

35 According to the list of undesirables held in Moscow there were over 250 deserters from the British Battalion, while Bill Alexander estimated

298. There may well have been more. IBC 545/6/99, pp. 14–19; Alexander, *British Volunteers*, p. 81.

36 Will Paynter to Harry Pollitt, 9 June 1937. IBA MML Box C, File 14/5.

37 Angus, p. 7.

38 Letter from Walter Tapsell to Harry Pollitt, 25 April 1937. IBA MML Box C, File 12/4.

39 IBA MML Box C, File 15/3.

40 'Records in London. Observations', 22 December 1937, IBMT Moscow 545/6/88, p. 40.

41 Letter from George Aitken, undated, IBA MML Box C, File 17/7.

42 Diary of Vladimir Čopić, 15 September 1937, IBC 545/3/467.

43 Sexton, p. 38.

44 Ralph Cantor diary, 10 April 1937, WCML.

45 Angus, p. 7.

46 John Lochore, unpublished memoir, from MacDougall, *Voices from War*, p. 129.

47 Letter from George Aitken to Political Bureau, IBA MML Box C, File 17/7.

48 IBMT 545/6/119, p. 75. He was also suspended from the Party for two months. IBA MML Box C, File 17/7.

49 Letter from Walter Tapsell to Alexander Anderson, IBA MML Box 39, File A/10.

50 The senior Italian member of the Comintern, Palmiro Togliatti, admitted in a report at the end of August 1937 that many of the American, English and Italian volunteers had been promised they would be in Spain for no more than six months. Report by Togliatti, 29 August 1937. IBC 33987/3/961, cited in Radosh, p. 253.

51 Interview with John Peet in Corkhill and Rawnsley, p. 111.

52 Interview with Frank Frankford, IWMSA 9308, reel 2.

53 Interview with Jack Edwards, MHA 171, reel 1, side 2.

54 B. Clark, p. 72.

55 Letter from Laurence Collier to Bill Alexander, 23 December 1982, p. 4. IBA MML Box C, File C4/7c.

56 Interview with John Peet, IWMSA 800, reel 7.

57 While one might not expect him to say otherwise, there is no reason to disbelieve him. Hickman frankly admits that some men 'had whores' while on leave in Barcelona, but that those who indulged were a small minority. Ivor Hickman cited in Wainwright, p. 195.

58 B. Clark, pp. 112–13.

59 Interview with Walter Greenhalgh, IWMSA 10356, reel 1.

60 The 'honest neutral' George Ogilvie-Forbes, the British chargé d'affaires, who seems to have been more fair-minded than many of his colleagues, apparently raised the issue of deserters with Largo Caballero. See Buchanan, 'Edge of Darkness: British "Front-line" Diplomacy in the Spanish Civil War, 1936–1937', pp. 289–90. Some deserters

were certainly helped out of Spain on board British ships such as HMS *Devonshire*.

61 John Lochore, unpublished memoir, from MacDougall, *Voices from War*, p. 129.

62 Jones, p. 69.

63 IBA MML Box C, File 14/5.

64 Boon was docked three days' pay and Cranfield and Steventon two days. IBC 545/3/495, p. 22.

65 ALBA Moscow 545/2/262, p. 107.

66 Copeman, p. 109.

67 Interview with Bob Cooney in Corkhill and Rawnsley, p. 121.

68 Ruiz, p. 440.

69 IBA MML Box C, File 14/5.

70 IBA MML Box C, File 14/5.

71 Interview with Tony Hyndman in Toynbee, *The Distant Drum*, p. 127.

72 Letter from Walter Tapsell to Harry Pollitt, undated [May–June?] 1937, IBA MML Box C, File 13/1.

73 Gurney, pp. 69, 67.

74 Spender, p. 228.

75 Letter from Stephen Spender to Harry Pollitt, 18 June 1937, IBA MML Box C, File 15/1.

76 IBC 545/6/151, p. 4.

77 IBC 545/6/89, p. 25.

78 IBC 545/6/93; 545/3/451, p. 156.

79 Hopkins, pp. 258–64.

80 Interview with Alec Marcowich, MHA 182, reel 1, side 1.

81 Interview with Alec Marcowich, MHA 182, reel 1, side 1.

82 IBC 545/6/99, p. 11.

83 Interview with Bob Cooney, IWMSA 804, reel 5, cited in Darman, p. 178.

84 Sexton, p. 43.

85 Paynter, p. 71.

86 Angus, p. 7.

87 Copeman, p. 108.

88 Interview with Bob Cooney in Corkhill and Rawnsley, p. 121.

89 *Our Fight*, 10 January 1938.

90 Interview with John Dunlop, IWMSA 11355, reels 7–8.

91 Interview with John Dunlop, IWMSA 11355, reel 10.

92 IBC 545/6/99.

93 Interview with Jim Brewer, IWMSA 9963, reel 5.

94 Letter from Tony de Maio to Leppo, 6 November 1937. IBMT Moscow, 545/6/195, p. 58.

95 Interview with John Dunlop in MacDougall, *Voices from the Spanish Civil War*, p. 145.

96 Interview with Tom Murray in MacDougall, *Voices from the Spanish Civil War*, p. 324.

97 IBC 545/6/99 and 545/6/195, p. 62.

98 Interview with Eugene Downing from http://irelandscw.com/docs-3Deaths.htm.

99 Interview with John Dunlop, IWMSA 11355, reel 10.

100 Griffiths, MS, p. 37.

101 IBMT 545/6/111, p. 72.

102 Interview with Tony Gilbert, IWMSA 9157, reel 10.

103 IBMT 545/6/111, p. 71.

104 IBMT 545/6/111, p. 75.

105 IBMT 545/6/121, p. 12, pp. 27, 29.

106 Griffiths, MS, p. 21.

107 Stradling, *Wales and the Spanish Civil War*, pp. 145–50.

108 IBA MML Box 39/A, File 49, p. 3.

109 '*Proponemos que sería mas conveniente de dar la noticia en Inglaterra que el camarada Broadbent cayo en el combate.*' Note signed by Lon Elliott, 16 September 1938, IBMT 545/6/111, p. 3.

110 Many critics, somewhat anachronistically, situate the Brigades within Soviet history, post-Spain, comparing the commissars in Spain to those at Stalingrad and referring to the role of Spanish veterans in Eastern bloc regimes. Madrid in 1937 is not Stalingrad in 1942, just as Spain is not Hungary, or Czechoslovakia.

111 The Brigades, 'standard-bearers of the USSR's international prestige . . . were agents of the Kremlin first and soldiers of the Spanish Republic only second', argues Robert Stradling in 'English-speaking Units,' pp. 752–3.

112 However, as a recent ground-breaking work on Soviet intelligence in the civil war argues, 'Though archival materials show Marty's moral responsibility for many violent acts against the volunteers, his personal participation in executions seems only to be in Hemingway's intoxicated imagination . . . André Marty was *not* [emphasis added] "Le Boucher d'Albacete" who in concord with the SIM let dozens of members of the International Brigades (who could be somehow categorized as opposition) be sentenced to death and executed, as asserted by the French rightists since 1939 and as the Communist party renegades and in part Ernest Hemingway made it seem.' Volodarsky, p. 180.

113 Delmer, pp. 307–8.

114 IBC 545/6/156 p. 19; IBA MML Box 21, File B/2i.

115 Copeman was 'not developed politically', Sam Wild and Malcolm Dunbar were both 'weak politically', Jock Cuningham was 'theoretically absolutely crude'. IBMT Moscow 545/6/118, p. 63; 545/6/215, p. 33; 545/6/126, p. 29; 545/6/121, p. 46.

116 'Criminal in England. OK here.' IBMT 545/6/171, p. 108.

117 Letter from Commissar of the British Battalion [Bob Cooney] to John Gates [the American 15th Brigade Commissar], 8 May 1938. IBC 545/3/497, p. 63.

118 I am grateful to Dr Freddie Shaw for this information.

14 The 'turn of the tide'

1 Walter was a contradictory figure. According to Len Crome, who knew him well in Spain, Walter was universally popular with his troops and 'unfailingly generous and kind'. However, the hard-

drinking and hot-tempered Pole was also capable of acts of utter callousness and brutality, to friend as much as foe. See Crome, *General Walter, 1897–1947*, esp. pp. 8–9.

2 Petrou, p. 73.

3 Interview with Jim Brewer, IWMSA 9963, reel 4. Slater was 'very brave, but extremely arrogant', according to the British research clerk and military censor in Spain, Tony McLean. Interview with Tony McLean, IWMSA 838, cited in Darman, p. 65.

4 By the end of 1937, Internationals made up approximately half of the 15th International Brigade. Report by General Walter, IBC 35082/1/95, cited in Radosh, p. 452.

5 Alec Donaldson in Ryan et al, p. 287.

6 Alexander, *British Volunteers*, p.111.

7 IBA MML Box 21b, File 4a.

8 Gregory, p. 77.

9 Gregory, p. 77.

10 Rust, p. 90.

11 Alexander, *British Volunteers*, p. 148.

12 Letter from Tom Wintringham to his son O.J., cited in Purcell, p. 152.

13 H. Thomas, *Spanish Civil War*, pp. 725–6.

14 Sexton, p. 39.

15 Sexton, p. 39.

16 Sexton, p. 40.

17 Alexander, *British Volunteers*, p. 149.

18 Gregory, p. 79.

19 Gregory, p. 80.

20 Interview with Harry Fraser, MHA 241, reel 1, side 2.

21 Ćopić diary, IBC 545/3/467; interview with Marvin Penn, cited in Petrou, p. 72.

22 Len Crome, chief of the 35th Division medical services, later confessed to personally witnessing 'the execution of two groups of prisoners, most of whom were officers. Once on the order of Modesto, who explained to me personally that he did so as punishment or revenge, for the killing of my friend Dubois. He saw me having tears in my eyes. That was when we took Quinto. The second group was executed on the order of Walter, after we took Belcite.' LCP: Letter from Len Crome to Santiago Alvarez, 28 November 1988.

23 Geiser, pp. 30–1.

24 Interview with Hugh Sloan in MacDougall, *Voices from the Spanish Civil War*, p. 218.

25 Alexander, *British Volunteers*, p. 150.

26 Gregory, p. 81.

27 Alexander, *British Volunteers*, p. 151.

28 Interview with Roderick MacFarquhar, IWMSA 9234, reel 4.

29 Gregory, p. 82.

30 Gregory, p. 82.

31 Letter from Will Paynter to Harry Pollitt, 4 September 1937, IBA MML Box C, File 17/1.

32 Interview with David Stirrat in MacDougall, *Voices from the Spanish Civil War*, p. 266.

33 Interview with Tony McLean, IWMSA 838, reel 2, cited in Darman, p. 186.

34 ALBA Moscow 545/2/262, p. 109.

35 Interview with Walter Greenhalgh, IWMSA 11187, reel 6.

36 Rust, p. 98.

37 Copeman, p. 143.

38 Interview with Charles Bloom, IWMSA 992, reel 2.

39 Alexander, *British Volunteers*, p. 158.

40 Interview with Harry Fraser, MHA 241, reel 1, side 2.

41 Gregory, p. 83.

42 Interview with Hugh Sloan in MacDougall, *Voices from the Spanish Civil War*, p. 215.

43 Interview with Bill Alexander, IWMSA 802, reel 3.

44 Interview with Hugh Sloan in MacDougall, *Voices from the Spanish Civil War*, p. 217.

45 Interview with Bill Williamson, IWMSA 12385, reel 17.

46 Alexander, *British Volunteers*, p. 154.

47 These were Eric Whalley from Mansfield, C. Larlham from Chelsea, Frederick McCulloch from Glasgow, Arthur Robinson from Hartlepool and George Westfield from Liverpool. IBA MML Box C, File 2/1.

48 Interview with Robert Walker, MHA 240, reel 1, side 2.

49 Interview with Harry Fraser, MHA 241, reel 1, side 2.

50 Alexander, *British Volunteers*, p. 159.

51 O'Daire did not rejoin the battalion until July 1938. Alexander, *British Volunteers*, p. 152.

52 Interview with Jack Jones in Corkhill and Rawnsley, p. 143.

53 Alexander, *British Volunteers*, p. 154.

54 Report on British Political Commissars Conference, IBA MML Box C, File 19/8; Ivor Hickman cited in Wainwright, p. 193.

55 Alexander, *British Volunteers*, p. 160.

56 Steve Fullarton cited in Gray, p. 70.

57 ALBA Moscow 545/2/266, p. 109.

58 Hopkins, p. 247.

59 Interview with Hugh Sloan, IWMSA 11354, reel 4.

60 Interview with Jim Brewer, IWMSA 9963, reel 6.

61 George Murray cited in Gray, p. 71.

62 Letter from John Mahon to Harry Pollitt, 15 November 1937, IBA MML Box C, File 19/3.

63 Handwritten report by Bill Rust, dated 17 December 1936, Politico-Social-Arágon P5 AR 6, AHN Salamanca.

64 Bill Rust report, p. 3.

65 Bill Rust report, p. 5.

66 Bill Rust report, p. 7.

67 Bill Rust report, p. 6.

68 Interview with Joe Norman, IWMSA 818, reel 3.

69 Rust, p. 101.

70 B. Clark, p. 33.

71 B. Clark, p. 36.

72 Beevor, *The Battle for Spain*, p. 315.

73 *News Chronicle*, 23 December 1937, p. 8.

74 B. Clark, p. 39.

75 Ivor Hickman cited in Wainwright, p. 117.

76 Interview with Frank West, IWMSA9315, reel 5.

77 Interview with Charles Morgan, IWMSA 10362, reel 1.

78 IBMT 545/6/89, p. 38.

79 Report by General Walter, commander of the 35th Division, 14 January 1938, IBC 35082/1/95, cited in Radosh, pp. 440–4.

80 Anon., *In Spain*, p. 6.

81 Letter from Will Paynter to Harry Pollitt, 19 January 1938, IBA MML Box C, File 21/3.

82 Copeman, p. 143.

83 The chief instructor, known as Captain Ramon, was actually an officer in the Russian army. Interview with John Dunlop in MacDougall, *Voices from the Spanish Civil War*, p. 141; letter from George Aitken to Political Bureau, IBA MML Box C, File 17/7.

84 Petrou, p. 110.

85 Louis Tellier cited in Petrou, p. 17.

86 Interview with John Tunnah, IWMSA 840, reel 6.

87 Interview with David Anderson in MacDougall, *Voices from the Spanish Civil War*, p. 95.

88 Letter from Will Paynter to Harry Pollitt, 19 January 1938, IBA MML Box C, File 21/3.

89 B. Clark, p. 46.

90 Fred Thomas, p. 65.

91 Alexander, *British Volunteers*, p. 163.

92 Interview with Harry Fraser, MHA 241, reel 1, side 2.

93 Interview with Jack Edwards in Arthur, *The Real Band of Brothers*, p. 161.

94 Interview with Fred Thomas, IWMSA 9396, reel 7.

95 Alexander, *British Volunteers*, pp. 164–5.

96 Steve Hurst is probably correct to describe the order for the British to descend from the safety and magnificent position in the mountains onto the plain beneath as 'insane'. Hurst, p. 184.

97 Interview with Garry McCartney in MacDougall, *Voices from the Spanish Civil War*, p. 247.

98 B. Clark, p. 51.

99 Interview with Hugh Sloan, IWMSA interview 11354, reel 8.

100 Interview with Hugh Sloan, IWMSA interview 11354, reel 8.

101 Interview with Garry McCartney, IWMSA 809, reel 3.

102 Alexander, *British Volunteers*, p. 166.

103 Cooney, p. 71.

104 Alexander, *British Volunteers*, p. 167.

105 Interview with Sam Wild, IWMSA 10358, reel 2.

106 B. Clark, p. 53.

107 Alexander, *British Volunteers*, p. 168.

108 Greening, p. 71.

109 Interview with Robert Walker, MHA 240, reel 1, side 2.

110 Report by General Walter, commander of the 35th Division, 14 January 1938, IBC 35082/1/95, cited in Radosh, pp. 440–4.

111 B. Clark, p. 97.

112 Cooney, p. 78.

15 Bearing witness

1 NA KV5/112.

2 NA KV2/1012; Preston, *We Saw Spain Die*, pp. 163–5.

3 Scammell, p. 126.

4 Koestler, *Spanish Testament*, p. 211.

5 Sperber, p. 78.

6 Peter Kemp, in A.J.P. Taylor, *History of the Twentieth Century*, p. 1606.

7 Steer cited in Kemp, *Mine Were of Trouble*, pp. 52–3.

8 Delmer, p. 277.

9 Barea, p. 684; Preston, *We Saw Spain Die*, pp. 94–6.

10 García, 'Unofficial Missions', p. 220.

11 Cox, *Defence of Madrid*, p. 195.

12 Preston, *We Saw Spain Die*, p. 20

13 Deacon, p. 46.

14 Langdon-Davies, p. 205.

15 Koestler, *Invisible Writing*, pp. 333–5; Knightley, pp. 195–6. 'Writers such as Ernest Hemingway, John Dos Passos, W.H. Auden and others travelled there and wrote about the civil war, and Orwell and André Malraux actually fought (and still others like Julian Bell and Christopher Caudwell perished), but only Koestler sat in a cell expecting execution and survived to transmute that experience into fiction.' Review of Scammel's *Koestler*, by John G. Rodwan, Jr, *Logos*, 11:1, 2012.

16 Interview with Peter Kemp in Toynbee, *The Distant Drum*, p. 74. Claud Cockburn later admitted to inventing a completely fictitious battle 'to illustrate the gallant but unequal struggle the Republicans were waging'. Knightley, pp. 195–7.

17 Spender. p. 244. Herbert Greene came to a similar conclusion: 'Untrue propaganda is not an attribute of one side only, and there are few people, let alone those who go to Spain on safely conducted tours, seeing what they are shown, their bedrooms masses of flowers, who know or can discriminate between the truth and lies poured out equally by both sides.' Greene, p. 286.

18 George Orwell, 'Looking back on The Spanish War', in *New Road*, 1943, p. 478.

19 Orwell, *Homage*, p. 86.

20 Preston, *We Saw Spain Die*, p. 165.

21 Watson, pp. 171–2.

22 Cox, *Defence of Madrid*, p. 95.

23 Cox, *Defence of Madrid*, p. 95.

24 Cox, *Defence of Madrid*, p. 60.

25 Cox, *Defence of Madrid*, pp. 66–7.

26 Matthews, p. 92, taken from Deacon, p. 56.

27 Delmer, p. 299.

28 Steer, p. 258.

29 *The Times*, 28 April 1937, p. 17.

30 Watkins, p. 52. For a masterly account of the Guernica bombing and the ensuing Nationalist attempts to cover it up, see Southworth, *Guernica! Guernica!*

31 Kemp, *Mine Were of Trouble*, p. 89; Southworth, *Guernica! Guernica!*, p. 392.

32 Interview with Peter Kemp in Toynbee, *The Distant Drum*, p. 71.

33 Bell, p. 9.

34 Steer, pp. 263–4.

35 Bell, p. 9; Buchanan, *Britain and the Spanish Civil War*, pp. 57, 115.
36 Preston, *We Saw Spain Die*, pp. 282–5.
37 García, 'Unofficial Missions', p. 221.
38 Barea, pp. 656–7.
39 García, 'Unofficial Missions', p. 227.
40 García, *The Truth About Spain*, p. 85.
41 Spender, p. 244.
42 The story is almost certainly apocryphal, as is A.L. Rowse's insinuation that Ralph Fox's death was deliberately sought: 'He was ordered to Spain by the Party, which wanted martyrs for the cause.' See Cunningham, *Penguin Book of Spanish Civil War Verse*, pp. 41–2; Morgan, *Harry Pollitt*, p. 99.
43 Gascoyne, pp. 43–4; Spender, p. 218.
44 Other Britons making radio broadcasts in Republican Spain included John Cornford's companion Richard Bennett, who worked for Barcelona radio, and Sam Lesser, who fought alongside Cornford in Madrid.
45 Spender, pp. 214–16.
46 I am very grateful to Alan Lloyd and Jim Carmody, who identified Livesay.
47 Spender, pp. 223–4. Michael E.J. Livesay was killed at Segovia on 2 June 1937.
48 Watson, pp. 198–9.
49 Romilly, p. 133.
50 Toynbee, *Friends Apart*, pp. 95–6.
51 Toynbee, 'Journal of a Naïve Revolutionary', *The Distant Drum*, p. 150.
52 Delmer, p. 304.
53 Toynbee, 'Journal of a Naïve Revolutionary', *The Distant Drum*, p. 157.
54 W.H. Auden, 'Impressions of Valencia', *New Statesman & Nation*, 30 January 1937, in Cunningham, *Spanish Front*, pp. 115–17.
55 Langdon-Davies, p. 95.
56 Delmer, pp. 316–19.
57 Morgan, *Pollitt*, p. 96.
58 Interview with Jimmy Jump, IWMSA 9524, reel 4.
59 LHASC, CP/IND/POLL/2/5.
60 Cooney, p. 156.
61 Interview with Walter Greenhalgh, 1187, reel 5; Alexander, *British Volunteers*, p. 75. According to Herbert Greene, Haldane's expertise in poison gases very nearly scuppered an international arms dealer's devious attempts to flog sub-standard gas masks to the Republic. Greene, p. 112.
62 J.B.S. Haldane, 'A Tourist in Loyal Spain', ALBA Moscow 545/3/478, p. 127.
63 Interview with Fred Copeman, IWMSA 794, reel 3.
64 Interview with John Dunlop in MacDougall, *Voices from the Spanish Civil War*, p. 149.
65 Joe Norman memoir, p. 2. IBA MML Box 50, File Nr/1.
66 J.B.S. Haldane, 'A Tourist in Loyal Spain', ALBA Moscow 545/3/478, p. 127.
67 Ludwick, *Notes*, p. 74.
68 Letter from Clement Attlee to his brother, cited in Beckett, *Clem Attlee*, p. 135.
69 Attlee, p. 94.

70 Interview with John Dunlop in MacDougall, *Voices from the Spanish Civil War*, p. 149.
71 B. Clark, p. 33.
72 *Volunteer for Liberty*, 13 December 1937, p. 1, cited in Hopkins, p. 196.
73 Interview with John Dunlop in MacDougall, *Voices from the Spanish Civil War*, p. 149.
74 Harry Pollitt's account of his visits to the British Battalion, LHASC, CP/IND/POLL/2/5.
75 Longstaff, MS, p. 87; Cooney, p. 128.
76 Guest, p. 187.
77 Heath's companions were also Oxford undergraduates: 'Richard Symonds, a socialist from Corpus Christi . . . Derek Tasker, a Liberal from Exeter College . . . and George Stent, a South African from Magdalene, who was probably furthest to the left of us.' Heath, p. 52.
78 Edward Heath cited in Jones, pp. 69–70.
79 Interview with David Anderson in MacDougall, *Voices from the Spanish Civil War*, p. 96.
80 Sexton, p. 44.
81 Gray, pp. 73–4.
82 Gurney, p. 146. George Orwell was similarly scathing of those who attended Madrid's International Congress of anti-fascist writers in the summer of 1937: 'To the Spaniards the war was not a game, as it was to the "Anti-Fascist Writers" who held their congress in Madrid and ate banquets against a background of starvation.' See Orwell's review of Arturo Barea's *The Clash* in *The Observer*, 24 March 1946, from *Orwell in Spain*, p. 372.
83 Spender, p. 229.
84 Interview with Fred Copeman, IWMSA 794, reel 3.
85 Interview with Hugh Sloan in MacDougall, *Voices from the Spanish Civil War*, p. 201.

16 The great retreat

1 Rust, p. 104.
2 Griffiths, MS, p. 1.
3 Rust, p. 104.
4 Interview with Bob Doyle in Arthur, *The Real Band of Brothers*, p. 184.
5 Alexander, *British Volunteers*, pp. 169–70.
6 Brome, p. 245.
7 Kemp, *Mine Were of Trouble*, pp. 156–7.
8 Gregory, p. 102.
9 Sam Wild, 'Report by Battalion Commander on the last action', 23 May 1938. IBC 545/3/497, p. 22.
10 Interview with Hugh Sloan in MacDougall, *Voices from the Spanish Civil War*, pp. 222–3.
11 Fred Thomas, p. 96; Alexander, *British Volunteers*, p. 172.
12 Cooney, p. 84. Many volunteers disappeared during the retreats never to be seen or heard from again. Unusually, the fate of one, Percy Williams, an engineering officer on the Blue Star Shipping Line, was revealed by a Nationalist chaplain when Belchite was overrun. The chaplain, who spoke English, told a newspaper reporter that the dying man was found near the Goya Gate in Belchite. The identity of the volunteer – given by the chaplain as

Percival Ernest – remained a puzzle for years, until he was identified by Jim Carmody, the IBMT's researcher, as Swindon volunteer Percival Ernest Williams, originally believed to have been killed at Caspe. See *Liverpool Echo*, 11 March 1938.

13 H. Thomas, *Spanish Civil War*, p. 798.

14 Sam Wild, 'Report by Battalion Commander on the last action', 23 May 1938. IBC 545/3/497, p. 22.

15 Interview with Robert Walker, MHA 240, reel 2, side 1.

16 B. Clark, p. 73. Sproston was killed at the end of March 1938.

17 Cooney, p. 85.

18 Bob Cooney, 'The retreat from Belchite', IBA MML Box C, File 22/1.

19 Cooney, pp. 89–90.

20 Sam Wild, 'Report by Battalion Commander on the last action,' 23 May 1938. IBC 545/3/497, p. 22.

21 Interview with Robert Walker, MHA 240, reel 2, side 1.

22 B. Clark, pp. 74–5.

23 Sam Wild, 'Report by Battalion Commander on the last action', 23 May 1938. IBC 545/3/497, p. 23.

24 Interview with Frank Graham, IWMSA 11877, reel 4.

25 Sam Wild, 'Report by Battalion Commander on the last action,', 23 May 1938. IBC 545/3/497, p. 23.

26 Gregory, p. 106.

27 Alexander, *British Volunteers*, p. 176; Sam Wild, 'Report by Battalion Commander on the last action,' 23 May 1938. IBC 545/3/497, p. 23.

28 Interview with Robert Walker, MHA 240, reel 2, side 2.

29 However, the majority of this number were Spaniards. Only a third were British. Alexander, *British Volunteers*, pp. 159–60.

30 Ludwick, *Notes*, p. 94.

31 Rust, p. 148.

32 Fred Thomas, p. 102.

33 Ludwick, *Notes*, p. 99.

34 Greening, pp. 105–6.

35 Report by Sam Wild, IBC 545/6/495, p. 27.

36 Doyle, p. 63.

37 Alexander, *British Volunteers*, p. 178.

38 Gregory, p. 107.

39 Bob Cooney, 'Report by Battalion Commissar on the action commencing at Calaceite, 31.3.38', IBC 545/3/497, p. 17.

40 Report by George Fletcher, 5 May 1938, IBC 545/3/497, p. 30.

41 Cooney, p. 97.

42 Report by George Fletcher, 5 May 1938, IBC 545/3/497, p. 30.

43 Cooney, 'Report by Battalion Commissar', p. 17.

44 Cooney, p. 97.

45 Interview with Robert Walker, MHA 240, reel 2, side 2.

46 IBA MML Box C, File 3/1a.

47 Report by George Fletcher, 5 May 1938, IBC 545/3/497, p. 33.

48 Gregory, p. 108; interview with Robert Walker, MHA 240, reel 2, side 2.

49 Interview with Robert Walker, MHA 240, reel 2, side 2.

50 Interview with Garry McCartney, IWMSA 809, reel 1.

51 Doyle, p. 64.

52 Interview with Syd Booth, MHA 200, reel 2, side 1.

53 Interview with Harold Collins, IWMSA 9481, reel 3; Doyle, pp. 63–4.

54 Angus, pp. 10–11.

55 Interview with Syd Booth, MHA 200, reel 2, side 1.

56 Interview with George Drever in MacDougall, *Voices from the Spanish Civil War*, p. 281.

57 IBA MML Box C, File 3/1a; interview with Joseph Leo Byrne, IWMSA 12930, reel 2.

58 Gregory, p. 110.

59 Sam Wild, 'Report by Battalion Commander on the last action', 23 May 1938. IBC 545/3/497, p. 23.

60 Cooney, p. 108; Gregory, p. 112.

61 Ludwick, *Notes*, pp. 107–8.

62 Letter from Will Paynter to Harry Pollitt, 8 April 1938, IBA MML Box C, File 22/1.

63 Letter from Bob Edwards to 15th Brigade Estado Mayor, 22 April 1938, ALBA Moscow 545/3/497, p. 21.

64 Letter from Will Paynter to Harry Pollitt, 8 April 1938, IBA MML Box C, File 22/1.

65 Ludwick, *Notes*, p. 108.

66 Letter from Will Paynter to Harry Pollitt, 8 April 1938, IBA MML Box C, File 22/1.

67 Griffiths, MS, p. 14.

68 H. Thomas, *Spanish Civil War*, p. 803.

69 *News Chronicle*, 7 April 1938, p. 10.

70 Britten Austin, p. 1.

71 Gregory, p. 116.

72 Gregory, p. 113.

73 Cooney, p. 126.

74 Cooney, p. 126.

75 Alexander, *British Volunteers*, p. 203.

76 Interview with Steve Fullarton in MacDougall, *Voices from the Spanish Civil War*, p. 294.

77 Interview with John Dunlop in MacDougall, *Voices from the Spanish Civil War*, p. 158.

78 Fred Thomas, p. 108; Alexander, *British Volunteers*, p. 201.

79 Gregory, p. 115.

80 B. Clark, p. 95.

81 Interview with Steve Fullarton in MacDougall, *Voices from the Spanish Civil War*, p. 297.

82 Green, MS, p. 69.

83 Interview with James Jump, IWMSA 9524, reel 5.

84 Sexton, 'Memories', p. 51.

85 Interview with John H. Bassett in Toynbee, *The Distant Drum*, p. 140.

86 Griffiths, MS, p. 26.

87 Fred Thomas, p. 112.

88 Cooney, p. 138; IBA MML Box C, File 24/2.

89 Gregory, p. 121.

17 The last throw of the dice
1 Fred Thomas, p. 115.
2 Interview with Robert Walker, MHA 240, reel 2, side 2.
3 Interview with Hugh Sloan in MacDougall, *Voices from the Spanish Civil War*, p. 228.
4 B. Clark, p. 99.
5 Interviews with Tom Murray in MacDougall, *Voices from the Spanish Civil War*, p. 317 and with Hugh Sloan, p. 227.
6 Longstaff, MS, p. 94.
7 'Republicans Sweep On', *Daily Worker*, 26 July 1938, p. 1.
8 Interview with Hugh Sloan in MacDougall, *Voices from the Spanish Civil War*, p. 227.
9 B. Clark, p. 102.
10 Henry, p. 37.
11 Edmund Updale, a former training instructor at Tarazona, was seriously wounded by a bomb while rowing across the river and later had to have a leg amputated. IBC 545/6/209, p. 4.
12 Ludwick, *Notes*, pp. 114–18.
13 B. Clark, p. 100; Griffiths, MS, p. 28.
14 Interview with John Dunlop in MacDougall, *Voices from the Spanish Civil War*, p. 161.
15 Cooney, p. 145.
16 Interview with Tom Murray in MacDougall, *Voices from the Spanish Civil War*, p. 317.
17 Longstaff, MS, p. 98.
18 Interview with David Anderson in MacDougall, *Voices from the Spanish Civil War*, pp. 94–5.
19 Interview with David Anderson in MacDougall, *Voices from the Spanish Civil War*, p. 95.
20 'Key Franco Town Surrounded on Three Sides', *Daily Worker*, 29 July 1938, p. 1.
21 Preston, *Franco*, pp. 310–11; Hughes and Garrido, pp. 109–10.
22 Interview with Hugh Sloan in MacDougall, *Voices from the Spanish Civil War*, pp. 228–9.
23 Interview with Steve Fullarton in MacDougall, *Voices from the Spanish Civil War*, p. 298.
24 Griffiths, MS, p. 32.
25 Longstaff, MS, p. 99.
26 B. Clark, p. 107.
27 Gregory, pp. 124–5.
28 Jones, pp. 75–6.
29 Gregory, pp. 125–6.
30 Cooney, pp. 146–7.
31 Peter Kerrigan report to Harry Pollitt on the Battle for Hill 481, 2 August 1938. IBA MML Box C, File 24/2.
32 Cooney, p. 151.
33 'Rowing Blue Dies for Democracy in Spain', *Daily Worker*, 8 August 1938, p. 1.
34 Longstaff, MS, p. 102. Guest was actually shot through the heart and the pocket-book that he carried, complete with bullet hole, was passed on to his sister, Angela Haden-Guest, who was working in Spain as a nurse. Longstaff may be confusing David Guest with Lewis Clive, who was hit in the head a few days after Guest was killed. See letter from

Peter Kerrigan to Harry Pollitt, 15 August 1938, IBA MML Box C, File 24/7.
35 *Illustrated London News*, 13 August 1938, p. 272.
36 Anon., 'In Memoriam', *The Eton College Chronicle*, 6 October 1938, pp. 620–1.
37 Interview with George Wheeler, IWMSA 11442, reel 2.
38 Wheeler, p. 70.
39 Interview with John Dunlop in MacDougall, *Voices from the Spanish Civil War*, p. 162.
40 IBA MML Box C, File 24/2, p. 2.
41 Jones, pp. 73–4.
42 Ivor Hickman cited in Wainwright, p. 147.
43 Interview with John Peet, IWMSA 800, reel 3.
44 Griffiths, MS, p. 33.
45 Ludwick, 'Fortification Work', p. 10. For the story of the rediscovery of the monument, see the documentary, 'Voices from a Mountain'. Andrew Lee/David Leach, Narrative Productions, 2001.
46 Fred Thomas, pp. 128, 130.
47 Greening, p. 83.
48 P. Carroll, p. 199.
49 Interview with Syd Booth, MHA 200, reel 2, side 1.
50 Longstaff, MS, pp. 113–14.
51 Interview with John Dunlop in MacDougall, *Voices from the Spanish Civil War*, pp. 163–4.
52 Alexander, *British Volunteers*, p. 210.
53 Greening, p. 83.
54 Greening, p. 83.
55 Interview with Alun Menai Williams in 'Voices from a Mountain'.
56 Alexander, *British Volunteers*, p. 211.
57 Jones, p. 75.
58 IBC 545/6/89, p. 21.
59 IBA MML Box 39/A, File 49, p. 3.
60 Fred Thomas, p. 141.
61 H. Thomas, *Spanish Civil War*, p. 843.
62 Known as 'Sandesco' since the civil war by the British veterans, the town was recently identified in John Wainwright's biography of Ivor Hickman as Ascó, which lies on the River Ebro to the south of Flix.
63 Gregory, pp. 130–1.
64 Interview with Robert Walker, MHA 240, reel 2, side 2.
65 Gregory, p. 131.
66 Interview with John Dunlop in MacDougall, *Voices from the Spanish Civil War*, p. 165.
67 Alexander, *British Volunteers*, p. 212.
68 Interview with John H. Bassett in Toynbee, *The Distant Drum*, p. 138.

18 Defeat and withdrawal
1 See IBC 33987/3/1149, cited in Radosh, p. 469. A copy of the Spanish resolution for withdrawal of non-Spanish combatants from Spain put to the League of Nations in September 1938 is held in the National Archives in Kew. See NA FO371/22696 W12789.
2 Interview with Syd Booth, MHA 200, reel 2, side 1.
3 Cooney, p. 161.

4 Gregory, p. 132.

5 Cooney, p. 161.

6 Interview with Robert Walker, MHA 240, reel 2, side 2.

7 Interview with John Peet, IWMSA 800, reel 6.

8 Interview with John Dunlop in MacDougall, *Voices from the Spanish Civil War*, pp. 166–7.

9 Alexander, *British Volunteers*, p. 214.

10 Longstaff, MS, p. 125; interview with Robert Walker, MHA 240, reel 2, side 2.

11 Letter from Peter Kerrigan to Harry Pollitt, 27 September 1938, IBA MML Box C, File 25/5.

12 Interview with John Dunlop in MacDougall, *Voices from the Spanish Civil War*, pp. 166–7.

13 Cooney, p. 162.

14 Interview with Syd Booth, MHA 200, reel 2, side 1.

15 Cooney, p. 162.

16 Interview with Tommy Bloomfield in MacDougall, *Voices from the Spanish Civil War*, p. 54.

17 Interview with Robert Walker, MHA 240, reel 2, side 2. Walker is here probably referring to Johnny Lobban, who despite having a reputation for drunkenness and desertion, was a very good and brave soldier at the front. The 'tough character' Lobban was killed on 23 September 1938. IBC 545/6/164, pp. 1–5.

18 Longstaff, MS, p. 125.

19 Cooney, p. 163; Wainwright, p. 215.

20 Green, pp. 96–7.

21 Letter from George Green to his mother, Jessie Green, 21 August 1938, cited in Preston, *Doves of War*, p. 170.

22 Longstaff, MS, p. 125.

23 Letter from Peter Kerrigan to Harry Pollitt, 27 September 1938, IBA MML Box C, File 25/5.

24 Copeman, p. 150.

25 P. Carroll, p. 162.

26 Fred Thomas, p. 158.

27 Cooney, p. 165.

28 Interview with Edwin Greening, IWMSA 9855, reel 6.

29 Greening, p. 97.

30 Peet, p. 95.

31 Interview with Hugh Sloan in MacDougall, *Voices from the Spanish Civil War*, p. 232.

32 Greening, p. 98.

33 Ludwick, *Notes*, p. 128.

34 Greening, p. 99.

35 Alexander, *British Volunteers*, p. 239.

36 Alexander, *British Volunteers*, p. 240; Greening, p. 100.

37 Griffiths, MS, p. 46.

38 Greening, p. 101.

39 Interview with Jim Brewer, IWMSA 9963, reel 8.

40 The three flag bearers, Jim Brewer, John Peet and Alun Menai Williams, marched near the front of the parade, with the battalion following further behind. Interview with Jim Brewer, IWMSA 9963, reel 8.

41 Peet, pp. 96–7.

42 Longstaff, MS, p. 126.

43 Interview with Chris Smith, IWMSA, reel 9. 'It was

so emotional it hurt,' interview with Joe Fuhr, IWMSA 11305, reel 11.

44 Fred Thomas, p. 164.

45 A. Jackson, *For Us It was Heaven*, p. 120.

46 http://www.english.illinois.edu/maps/scw/farewell.htm.

47 Interview with Jim Brewer, IWMSA 9963, reel 8.

48 Letter from John Peet, 1 November 1938, from Peet, p. 96.

49 IBMT 545/6/87, p. 28.

50 IBMT 545/6/89, p. 30.

51 Griffiths, MS, p. 46.

52 IBMT 545/6/87, pp. 34–5.

53 Assessment by Brigade Party Committee, 21 October 1938. IBMT 545/6/215, p. 30.

54 Letter from André Marty to the British Secretariat in London, 12 December 1938. IBMT 545/6/87, pp. 34–5.

55 Interview with John Peet, IWMSA 800, reel 9.

56 Fred Thomas, p. 168.

57 This number includes British volunteers with 15th Brigade staff and other units. Alexander, *British Volunteers*, p. 241.

58 Alexander, *British Volunteers*, p. 240.

59 Greening, p. 108.

60 Fred Thomas, p. 169.

61 Interview with John Peet, IWMSA 800, reel 9.

62 Cooney, p. 171.

63 Fred Thomas, p. 169.

64 Ludwick, 'Notes', p. 136. Unlikely as this account of the final image of Republican Spain may seem, it is supported by Bob Cooney's recollection: 'My last memory of Spain is the sight of a wrinkled old lady standing with her clenched fist raised in silent salute as our train steamed over the frontier.' Cooney, p. 171.

65 Conversation with Sam Lesser, 14 May 2001.

66 Interview with Lillian Urmston, MHA 215, reel 1, side 1.

67 Interview with Annie Murray in MacDougall, *Voices from the Spanish Civil War*, p. 73.

19 'You'll all be shot!'

1 Many thanks to David Lomon for both informing me of the existence of this version and providing the words.

2 NA FO371/21287 W6098.

3 Report on International Brigades by M.V. Miller, Barcelona, 5 April 1939. NA FO371/24124-7458.

4 David Goodman, 'Franco Will Never Conquer the Spanish', *Challenge*, 25 February 1939, p. 6.

5 Report of Franco Prisoners, March 1938–February 1939, p. 4.

6 Interviews with Joseph Leo Byrne, IWMSA 12930, reel 2 and Morien Morgan, IWMSA 9856, reel 2.

7 Joe Norman memoir, IBA MML Box 50, File Nr/1a.

8 Report of Franco Prisoners, pp. 4–5.

9 Cyril Kent, 'I Was in a Franco Prison', *Challenge*, 5 January 1939, pp. 10–11.

10 Interview with Garry McCartney in MacDougall, *Voices from the Spanish Civil War*, p. 250.

11 Geiser, p. 96.

12 *New York Times*, 3 April 1938, cited in Geiser, p. 96. The reporting by Carney – a Catholic – was clearly influenced by his horror of the atrocities inflicted on the Spanish clergy. Knightley, p. 199.

13 The cartoon appears in Alexander, *British Volunteers*, p. 190.

14 Doyle, p. 79.

15 Joe Norman memoir, IBA MML Box 50, File Nr/1a.

16 Interview with Garry McCartney in MacDougall, *Voices from the Spanish Civil War*, p. 251.

17 Interview with James Maley, IWMSA 11947, reel 2.

18 Report of Franco Prisoners, p. 7. IBA MML Box C, File 3/1a.

19 Report of Franco Prisoners, pp. 10–11.

20 Doyle, p. 71; Gregory, p. 143.

21 Report of Franco Prisoners, p. 8; Wheeler, p. 134.

22 Joe Norman memoir, IBA MML Box 50, File Nr/1a. In addition to the Internationals, about 3000 Spaniards were packed into the camp, kept separate while they awaited transfer to labour battalions. *They Fought in Franco's Jails*, p. 7.

23 Interview with Dougal Eggar, IWMSA 9426, reel 4.

24 Alexander, *British Volunteers*, p. 188; Report of Franco Prisoners, pp. 8–9.

25 Gregory, p. 144.

26 Kent, 'I Was in a Franco Prison', pp. 10–11.

27 Report of Franco Prisoners, p. 9.

28 Report of Franco Prisoners, pp. 8–9.

29 Interview with George Wheeler, IWMSA 11442, reel 6.

30 Interview with George Wheeler, IWMSA 11442, reel 6.

31 Interview with Garry McCartney in MacDougall, *Voices from the Spanish Civil War*, p. 254.

32 Interview with David 'Tony' Gilbert, IWMSA 9157, reel 9.

33 Kearney 'Castles' (whose real surname was Cassells). See Hall, *Disciplina Camaradas*, p. 103.

34 Interview with Bob Doyle, IWMSA 806, reel 4.

35 Interview with Bruce Allender, IWMSA 11300, reel 3.

36 Kent, 'I Was in a Franco Prison', pp. 10–11.

37 Geiser, pp. 102–3.

38 Doyle, pp. 73–4.

39 'From irresponsible and uncontrollable elements, came much criticism and condemnation of the Party leaders,' admitted the official report. Report of Franco Prisoners, p. 16.

40 Interview with Jimmy Moon, IWMSA 15729, reel 2.

41 Report of Franco Prisoners, p. 17.

42 Interview with Garry McCartney in MacDougall, *Voices from the Spanish Civil War*, pp. 252–3.

43 Interview with Garry McCartney in MacDougall, *Voices from the Spanish Civil War*, p. 251.

44 John Anthony Myers, 'Franco's Prisoner', *West London Observer*, 24 February 1939, p. 5.

45 IBA MML Box C, File 3/1a; interview with William Kelly, IWMSA 819, reel 1.

46 Interviews with Bob Doyle, IWMSA 806, reel 4 and in Cook, p. 121.

47 Interview with George Wheeler, IWMSA 11442, reel 6.

48 Interview with George Wheeler, IWMSA 11442, reel 6.

49 Report of Franco Prisoners, p. 10.

50 Doyle, pp. 74–5.

51 *They Fought in Franco's Jails*, p. 8.

52 Report of Franco Prisoners, p. 25.

53 Bandrés and Llavona, p. 4.

54 A. Vallejo, 'Biopsiquismo del Fanatismo Marxista', 1938, p. 189, cited in Bandrés and Llavona, p. 5.

55 Doyle, p. 81.

56 Interview with Garry McCartney, IWMSA 809, reel 5.

57 Doyle, p. 81.

58 Interview with George Wheeler, IWMSA 11442, reel 7.

59 Bandrés and Llavona, p. 7.

60 Interview with Garry McCartney in MacDougall, *Voices from the Spanish Civil War*, p. 258.

61 Wheeler, p. 145.

62 Interview with Jimmy Moon, IWMSA 15729, reel 3.

63 Interviews with Morien Morgan, IWMSA 9856, reel 4 and Joe Norman, IWMSA 818, reel 4.

64 Myers, 'Franco's Prisoner', p. 5.

65 Report of Franco Prisoners, pp. 10, 25.

66 Report of Franco Prisoners, p. 26.

67 Interview with Garry McCartney in MacDougall, *Voices from the Spanish Civil War*, p. 257.

68 Wheeler, p. 155.

69 Report of Franco Prisoners, p. 15.

70 IBA MML Box C, File 3/1a.

71 *They Fought in Franco's Jails*, pp. 12–13.

72 Morgan Havard, 'Concentration Camp', *Our Time*, 1943, p. 10.

73 Gregory, p. 149; Kent, pp. 10–11.

74 Havard, p. 10.

75 Wheeler, p. 147.

76 IBA MML Box C, File 3/1a.

77 Doyle, p. 80.

78 NA MH 55/703.

79 *They Fought in Franco's Jails*, p. 13; Alexander, *British Volunteers*, p. 191.

80 Geiser, p. 174.

81 IBA MML Box D-7, File A/1. A collection of Branson's drawings still exists in the Marx Memorial Library in London.

82 Geiser, p. 159; Alexander, *British Volunteers*, p. 191.

83 Report of Franco Prisoners, p. 27.

84 Shaer-West, MS, p. 22.

85 Wheeler, p. 151.

86 Report of Franco Prisoners, pp. 28–9. The 'English' prisoner, Kennedy, was probably David Fleming Kennedy, who lived in Greenock in Scotland.

87 Wheeler, p. 153.

88 Report of Franco Prisoners, p. 30.

89 Doyle, p. 84.

90 Myers, 'Franco's Prisoner', p. 5.

91 Doyle, p. 85.

92 Geiser, pp. 188–9; *They Fought in Franco's Jails*, p. 11.

93 Geiser, p. 191.

94 Wheeler, p. 166.
95 David Goodman, 'Franco Will Never Conquer the Spanish', *Challenge*, 20 February 1939, p. 6; 'General Franco Frees 67 Britons', *Daily Telegraph*, 6 February 1939, p. 7.
96 Interview with Garry McCartney in MacDougall, *Voices from the Spanish Civil War*, pp. 255–6.
97 While most British prisoners were kept together, a handful were kept in other jails. John Firman Danson from Chatham (actually a Canadian), and Archibald Bartlett from Pontypridd (whose real name was Archibald Yemm), were both kept as prisoners in Duesto prison in Bilbao. IBA MML Box 28a, File A/6.
98 Interview with Garry McCartney in MacDougall, *Voices from the Spanish Civil War*, p. 255.
99 NA MH 55/703.
100 Doyle, p. 81.
101 Seven Americans wrote a letter to *The Times* denying the charges against Ryan. *The Times*, 1 June 1938, cited in Geiser, p. 133.
102 For the debate surrounding Ryan's time in Nazi Germany see Sean Cronin, *Frank Ryan*; Enda Staunton, 'Frank Ryan and Collaboration: a reassessment', *History Ireland*, autumn 1997, pp. 49–51; Fearghal McGarry, *Frank Ryan*, 2003; and Manus O'Riordan's review of McGarry's biography of Ryan in *Irish Literary Supplement*, fall 2003.

20 The English Rebels and the Irish Bandera

1 H. Thomas, *Spanish Civil War*, 1990, p. 980 fn 2, suggests that perhaps a dozen British fought for Franco, though 'half of these seem to have been at least partially Irish,' presumably Catholics. Judith Keene only discusses four (including an Italo-American and an Australian), though Christopher Othen has shown that there were certainly more than that.
2 Skidelsky, p. 435.
3 Buchanan, *Britain and the Spanish Civil War*, p. 90.
4 Bridgeman, p. 43; Othen, p. 57.
5 Othen, p. 57–60; Kemp, *Mine Were of Trouble*, p. 15.
6 Kemp, *Mine Were of Trouble*, p. 15.
7 Kemp, *Mine Were of Trouble*, p. 16.
8 Other British pilots of whom little or no information remains also served with the Nationalists, such as Peter Humbertum, an aeronautical engineer from 'a titled English family'. Bridgeman, pp. 45–9.
9 Othen, pp. 84, 88.
10 Keene, p. 122.
11 Kemp, *The Thorns of Memory*, p. 56.
12 O'Duffy, p. 148; Kemp, *The Thorns of Memory*, p. 53.
13 Kemp, *Mine Were of Trouble*, p. 113; *The Thorns of Memory*, p. 74.
14 Othen, p. 208.
15 Othen, p. 93.
16 H. Thomas, *Spanish Civil War*, 1990, p. 980 fn 2.
17 Kemp, *The Thorns of Memory*, p. 9.
18 Othen, p. 160.
19 Kemp, *Mine Were of Trouble*, p. 152.
20 Othen, p. 92.
21 Interview with Frank Thomas's father in the *Western Mail*, November 1936, cited in Othen, p. 92.
22 Frank Thomas, 'Spanish *Legionario*', in Stradling, ed., *Brother against Brother*, p. 53.
23 Keene, p. 100.
24 Frank Thomas, p. 41.
25 As one recent study observed, one of the most striking features to emerge from Kemp's account is not his candid admission of the atrocities committed by the side on which he fought, but his snobbery: 'Unknowingly, Kemp divides the world into two unequal halves: fellows that one might have met at Cambridge or at an embassy reception with their sisters and wives on one hand; and on the other the vast majority of humankind who are not out of the top drawer.' Hurst, pp. 67–8.
26 Interview with Peter Kemp in Toynbee, *The Distant Drum*, p. 67.
27 Interview with Peter Kemp in Toynbee, *The Distant Drum*, p. 68.
28 Frank Thomas, pp. 50–1.
29 Kemp, *Mine Were of Trouble*, p. 46.
30 Frank Thomas, p. 55.
31 Frank Thomas, p. 78.
32 Kemp, *Mine Were of Trouble*, p. 48.
33 Kemp, 'I Fought for Franco', p. 1606.
34 Kemp, *Mine Were of Trouble*, p. 60.
35 Kemp, *Mine Were of Trouble*, p. 59.
36 Frank Thomas, p. 95.
37 Frank Thomas, p. 97.
38 Kemp, 'I Fought for Franco', p. 1608.
39 Kemp, *Mine Were of Trouble*, p. 77.
40 Kemp, *Mine Were of Trouble*, pp. 78–9; *The Thorns of Memory*, p. 46.
41 Letter from Bishop of Dromore, 20 September 1936, read out at mass. Cited in O'Riordan, p. 212.
42 O'Duffy, pp. 13, 52.
43 O'Duffy, pp. 31–2.
44 O'Duffy, p. 32.
45 See, for example, interview with Patrick Smith, IWMSA 14891, reel 1.
46 Interview with William Geraghty, IWMSA 14893, reel 2; *Irish Independent*, 26 October 1936, cited in Stradling, *Crusades in Conflict*, p. 29.
47 O'Duffy, p. 14; Stradling, *Crusades in Conflict*, p. 25.
48 Shelmerdine, *British Representations*, p. 122.
49 Kemp, *Mine Were of Trouble*, p. 86.
50 Kemp, *Mine Were of Trouble*, p. 87.
51 Stradling, *Crusades in Conflict*, p. 51.
52 Interview with James Kavanagh, IWMSA 14894, reel 2.
53 O'Duffy, p. 110.
54 Interview with William Geraghty, IWMSA 14893, reel 2; Stradling, *Crusades in Conflict*, p. 55.
55 Interview with William Geraghty, IWMSA 14893, reel 2.
56 O'Duffy, p. 138.
57 Othen, p. 117.
58 O'Duffy, p. 143.

59 Interview with Tom Murphy, IWMSA 805, reel 2.
60 Stradling, *Crusades in Conflict*, p. 70.
61 Othen, pp. 159–60.
62 Cardozo, p. 177.
63 Frank Thomas, pp. 116–17.
64 Frank Thomas, p. 118.
65 Frank Thomas, pp. 119–20.
66 O'Duffy, pp. 248–9.
67 George Orwell's review of Eoin O'Duffy's *Crusade in Spain*, *New English Weekly*, 24 November 1938, cited in *Orwell in Spain*, p. 316.
68 Interview with Peter Kemp in Toynbee, *The Distant Drum*, p. 72.
69 Kemp, *Mine Were of Trouble*, pp. 110, 112.
70 Kemp, *Mine Were of Trouble*, p. 120.
71 Interview with Peter Kemp, IWMSA 9769, reel 3.
72 Kemp, 'I Fought for Franco', p. 1608.
73 Kemp, *Mine Were of Trouble*, p. 164.
74 Kemp, *Mine Were of Trouble*, p. 166.
75 Kemp, *Mine Were of Trouble*, p. 169. Some Nationalist prisoners were certainly shot on sight. During the course of the war, a number of Nazi pilots were captured when their aircraft were shot down; some were apparently shot immediately, though others were used in exchanges for Republican prisoners, as were Italian soldiers captured at Guadalajara and elsewhere. Many British volunteers were categorical that prisoners, including Legionaries, were not ill-treated, though as we have seen, the testimony from brigaders at Brunete and Quinto demonstrates that there were lapses. On the treatment of prisoners by the Republicans see, for example Proctor, p. 254; interview with John Longstaff, IWMSA 9299, reel 11.
76 Regular officers of the armed forces were often executed as traitors, for the Rebels argued – using utterly convoluted logic – that the Republican soldiers had participated in a rising against the legitimate government of Spain: that is, the military junta who had themselves risen against the government in July 1936.
77 Kemp, *Mine Were of Trouble*, pp. 170–3. The date suggests that the executed brigader could have been Ben Murray, a Communist Party branch secretary born in County Tyrone. However, reports suggest that Murray was actually killed by a bomb during the retreat in March 1938. I am grateful to Jim Carmody for this information.
78 Kemp, *Mine Were of Trouble*, p. 184.
79 Scott-Ellis, pp. 232–3.
80 Preston, *Doves of War*, p. 13; Kemp, *The Thorns of Memory*, p. 129.
81 Preston, *Doves of War*, pp. 2, 34–5.
82 Scott-Ellis, p. 98.
83 Kemp, *Mine Were of Trouble*, p. 191.

21 From Spanish war to world war

1 When the train stopped briefly at Versailles, Malcolm Dunbar took the opportunity to disappear. Most assumed that the 'intensely private' Dunbar wished to avoid participating in any public ceremony upon their arrival in Britain; however, he later told a former comrade from the anti-tanks that, in fact, he returned to Spain as a correspondent for the *Daily Worker*. Interview with Hugh Sloan in MacDougall, *Voices from the Spanish Civil War*, pp. 234, 349 fn 155; Alexander, *British Volunteers*, p. 241.
2 Interview with John Londragan in MacDougall, *Voices from the Spanish Civil War*, p. 177.
3 Fred Thomas, pp. 169–70.
4 Greening, p. 110.
5 Greening, p. 110.
6 Interview with George Aitken, IWMSA 10357, reel 3. Heath's 'sympathies were firmly with the elected government of the Spanish Republic', so he 'joined colleagues from across the political spectrum to welcome them home'. Heath, p. 53.
7 Cooney, p. 175.
8 Tommy Bloomfield cited in Gray, p. 202.
9 Longstaff, MS, p. 133.
10 Tommy Bloomfield cited in Gray, p. 202.
11 Gray, p. 203.
12 Quinn, p. 5.
13 N. Branson, *History of the Communist Party 1927–1941*, pp. 259–60.
14 Interview with Jim Brewer, IWMSA 9963, reel 9.
15 *Daily Herald*, 9 January 1939.
16 Peet, p. 98.
17 Interview with Hugh Sloan in MacDougall, *Voices from the Spanish Civil War*, p. 236.
18 Interview with Chris Thornycroft, IWMSA 12932, reel 3.
19 Knox, *Premature Anti-Fascist*.
20 Interview with Sam Wild, IWMSA 10358, reel 1.
21 Alexander, *No to Franco*, p. 18.
22 Alexander, *No to Franco*, p. 18.
23 Interview with George Leeson, IWMSA 803, reel 3.
24 Alexander, *British Volunteers*, p. 248.
25 Bury, p. 50.
26 Interview with Rose Kerrigan, IWMSA 796, reel 1.
27 Interview with Walter Gregory, IWMSA 8851, reel 8.
28 Buchanan, *Impact*, p. 127.
29 H. Francis, 'Say Nothing and Leave in the Middle of the Night', pp. 69–76.
30 Stratton, p. 51.
31 Interview with Roderick MacFarquhar in MacDougall, *Voices from the Spanish Civil War*, p. 87.
32 Interview with George Leeson, IWMSA 803, reel 1.
33 Sexton, p. 60.
34 Alexander, *No to Franco*, p. 18.
35 Alexander, *British Volunteers*, p. 243. Perhaps half of the families of brigaders received some level of financial assistance. Suart, p. 173.
36 Deegan, p. 57.
37 Longstaff, MS, p. 130.
38 Unsigned letter to Peter Kerrigan, 10 October 1938, IBA MML Box C, File 26/2.

39 Interview with Walter Greenhalgh, IWMSA 11187, reel 7.

40 Letter from Charlotte Haldane, 29 December 1937, cited in Buchanan, *Impact of the Spanish Civil War*, p. 138.

41 Alexander, *No to Franco*, p. 19; Buchanan, 'Holding the Line', p. 296.

42 Wintringham foolishly used 'the great talker' Kitty Bowler as an unofficial courier between himself and Harry Pollitt in London. Senior Party figures in Britain were appalled. More damaging by far was Wintringham's request to Kitty to consult experts in Valencia on a solution to the jamming Colt machine-guns. When she arrived at Madrigueras on 20 January with the technical information, she was arrested as a spy and interrogated by André Marty. Purcell, pp. 114, 122, 161–2.

43 Buchanan, 'Holding the Line', pp. 294–5. The issue of conscription divided many; some elements in the Party welcomed conscription as a necessary response to fascist militarism and felt that the need to strengthen their country's defences overrode their antipathy to Chamberlain. Morgan, *Against Fascism and War*, p. 79.

44 'The International Brigade Association . . . was under Communist control and described itself as the association in the United Kingdom of the men who fought in the International Brigades in the Spanish Civil war. A watch was kept upon its activities.' Report by Security Intelligence Centre Liaison Officers' Conference, 18 March 1941. NA CAB 93/4; HO 45/25575/865000/147, 17 July 1943.

45 N. Branson, *History of the Communist Party 1927–1941*, p. 260.

46 The IBA's membership numbered less than 500, about 25 per cent of the veterans. As the Party possessed detailed records of veterans' addresses and next of kin, it seems reasonable to conclude that a large number of the remaining 1500 veterans elected not to join the association. Buchanan, 'Holding the Line', p. 296.

47 *Volunteer for Liberty*, Vol. 1, No. 9, 1940, p. 5. Copeman was later described as 'a renegade' in his Moscow file. IBMT Moscow 545/6/118, p. 62.

48 Copeman states that he was also incensed by a demand from R.W. Robson that the IBD&WAC should repay to the Communist Party a sum of £1600 which Copeman claimed had been a loan, rather than a gift. Copeman, p. 153.

49 Greening, pp. 103–6, 110–11.

50 R. Armstrong, 'Against the Slanders', *Workers Fight*, Vol. 2, No. 3, July 1939.

51 R. Armstrong, 'Against the Slanders', *Workers Fight*, Vol. 2, No. 3, July 1939.

52 'Spain Fighters Say: "Duped by Reds",' *Sunday Dispatch*, 19 February 1939, p. 3.

53 Wattis named a 'Major Stefanovitch' as the senior NKVD figure in the Brigades and James Hopkins guessed that this might be a reference to a Bulgarian Communist called S. Mineff. In fact, there was no 'Major Stefanovitch' in the NKVD in Spain. Wattis may be referring here to Major David Oskarovich Lvovich of the GRU. Whatever else Stefanovich/Lvovich was, he certainly wasn't a senior NKVD figure in the Brigades. The widespread use of different pseudonyms, code names and the dissembling nature of the material makes drawing straightforward conclusions about Russian operations a difficult and hazardous business. My thanks to Boris Volodarsky for this information.

54 How reliable a witness Wattis was is not clear; he had been discharged with ignominy from the Royal Warwickshire Regiment in 1926, from the Birmingham Special Constabulary for fraud in 1932 and was sentenced for fraud 'and other offences' in 1938. In an interview in a local paper in 1946, Wattis claimed that he had commanded the 15th International Brigade as a lieutenant-colonel and ended up with fifty-three wounds. His membership of the 'Friends of Franco' reveals the extent of Wattis's political journey. *The Codonian*, 8 February 1946, p. 3; NA KV/5/31 pf 46530.

55 *Spain*, No. 78, 30 March 1939, p. 254.

56 Alexander, *British Volunteers*, p. 249. It is certainly true that the organisation never became more than a minor irritant. Buchanan, 'Holding the Line', p. 295.

57 García, *The Truth About Spain*, p. 190.

58 'Recognition', *News Chronicle*, 28 February 1939, p. 8.

59 As Paul Kennedy has argued, 'the real flaw in Chamberlain's strategy, understood by some in Europe but not the majority, was that Hitler was fundamentally *unappeasable*.' Kennedy, p. 437.

60 Interview with Sam Lesser in Arthur, *The Real Band of Brothers*, p. 241.

61 H. Graham, *Spanish Civil War*, pp. 111–13.

62 Interview with Max Colin, IWMSA 8639, reel 6.

63 Interview with Annie Murray in MacDougall, *Voices from the Spanish Civil War*, p. 74.

64 Interview with Lou Kenton in Arthur, *The Real Band of Brothers*, p. 43.

65 Deegan, p. 57.

66 Longstaff, MS, p. 140.

67 Bury, pp. 47–8.

68 Fyrth, pp. 147–8; Coni, p. 7.

69 Copeman, pp. 182–3.

70 Copeman, p. 183.

71 As Richard Thurlow has argued, divisions ran deeper than many at the time were able to grasp: 'The authorities failed to realize that the divisions in the CPGB represented the clash between those who saw international communism purely as the interest of the Soviet Union, and those who saw British communism as the leader of an anti-fascist crusade . . . The authorities failed to distinguish, let alone take advantage of, the significant difference between the "revolutionary pragmatism" of the Popular Frontists in the CPGB and the "revolutionary defeatism" of Stalin's British henchmen.' Thurlow, *The Secret State*, p. 232.

72 Interview with Tony McLean, IWMSA 838, reel 4.

73 Peet, p. 101.
74 George Aitken cited in Cook, p. 143
75 Interview with David Lomon, 16 February 2011.
76 Interview with Albert Cole, MHA 212, reel 1, side 1.
77 Coward, p. 22; Longstaff, MS, p. 135.
78 Interview with Josh Davidson, MHA 193, reel 1, side 2.
79 Video interview with Joe Garber, Toby Haggith material, 1987, IWM.
80 N. Branson, *History of the Communist Party 1927–1941*, p. 266.
81 Haldane, p. 180.
82 Morgan, *Against Fascism*, p. 96.
83 Moore and Barnsby, p. 1.
84 N. Branson, *History of the Communist Party 1927–1941*, p. 268.
85 Andrew Flinn, 'William Rust: the Comintern's Blue-Eyed Boy?' in McIlroy, Morgan and Campbell, *Party People, Communist Lives*, p. 94.
86 Beckett, p. 95.
87 Thurlow, *Clever Capitalist Class*, p. 6.
88 Buchanan, *Impact*, p. 179.
89 Calder, p. 244.
90 The Soviet-Finnish war left the Communist Party 'in the unenviable position of demanding peace at a time when the only bloodshed in Europe flowed from an act of aggression which every Communist was obliged to condone if not celebrate'. Morgan, *Against Fascism*, p. 124. A number of Swedish veterans of the Spanish Civil War fought actually against Russia in Finland. Roberts, *Freedom, Faction, Fame and Blood*, p. 170.
91 Alexander, *No to Franco*, p. 34.
92 Buchanan, *Impact*, pp. 179–80.
93 Copeman, p. 181.
94 See interview with Bob Cooney in Cook, p. 148. YCL and NUWM member John Henderson argued of the war in Spain that 'Franco was being used by Hitler to form part of an international fascist conquest and unless this was stopped there'd eventually be another world war. This was quite apart from the domestic issue of here was an army general who'd attacked a duly and properly elected government.' Henderson cited in Watson and Corcoran, p. 29.
95 Interview with Patrick Curry, IWMSA 799, reel 3.
96 Deegan, p. 58.
97 Buchanan, *Impact*, p. 179. Pollitt found under-standing from a rather unlikely quarter, as a secret report composed for the Prime Minister on the Communist Party's policies and tactics noted: 'The Communist Party had represented itself for so long as the only consistent opponent of fascism that it was not surprising that Harry Pollitt and the Party generally should have been carried away into support of the war against Germany when it broke out in September 1939.' Memo from Lord Swinton, 2 October 1941, NA PREM 4/64/5B.
98 Healey, p. 44.
99 Fernbach, p. 73.
100 Interview with Jack Edwards, IWMSA 808, reel 3 and in Arthur, *The Real Band of Brothers*, p. 165.

101 Hyde, p. 69. His fellow *Daily Worker* correspondent, Sam Lesser, registered for the armed forces when he returned to Britain from Belgium in late 1940, having managed to secure an interview with the leader of the French Communist Party, Maurice Thoreau, who was then in hiding. He received no response, though he did receive a letter confirming that he had been removed from the list of Royal Scots Guards reserve officers. Harry Pollitt suggested to him that he had done enough fighting (he was still recovering from his wound from Spain) and found him a reserved job in an arms factory in Acton, where he remained until the end of the war. Interview with Sam Lesser, 28 January 2006.
102 Sexton, p. 62. Another British veteran and ex-POW from San Pedro, Robert Watts, survived the sinking of the *Lancastria*, but died in 1943 from malaria in 'a Middle East hospital'. *Volunteer for Liberty*, Nov–Dec 1943, p. 18; Stratton, p. 55.
103 *The Western Sun*, 186, 5 May 2005, p. 5.
104 Interview with Albert Charlesworth, IWMSA 798, reel 4.
105 One veteran of the British Battalion – the 'Anglicised Egyptian' and gifted linguist André Diamant, who lost a leg in Spain – was unfortunate enough to be trapped in France when the Germans invaded. IBMT 545/6/93, p. 2; Colman, p. 6.
106 *Daily Worker*, 9 July 1940.
107 Morgan, *Against Fascism*, p. 175.
108 Statement of the International Brigade Association in the *Daily Worker*, 12 June 1940, cited in Morgan, *Against Fascism*, p. 175.

22 Return of the anti-fascist war

1 NA PREM 4/64/5B.
2 Churchill, *The Second World War, Volume III, The Grand Alliance*, p. 402; Buchanan, 'Holding the Line', p. 299.
3 Interview with Max Colin, IWMSA 8639, reel 6.
4 Crook, ch. 4, p. 27.
5 Orwell, *Homage to Catalonia*, p. 73.
6 Tom Wintringham, *The Politics of Victory*, London, 1941, pp. xvii, xix, cited in Fernbach, p. 82.
7 Report on CPGB for War Cabinet by The Security Executive, 19 October 1941. NA CAB 66/19/17 (41) 244.
8 Letter from Viscount Swinton, 2 October 1941, NA PREM 4/64/5B.
9 Thurlow, 'Clever Capitalist Class', p. 15.
10 Longstaff, MS, p. 143.
11 Interview with James Maley, IWMSA 11947, reel 3. George Leeson, who had been a member of the British Machine-Gun Company captured at the Battle of Jarama, was also rejected: 'I was called up, I was taken for my medical exam, examined Grade 1. I remember the officer interviewing me, he said, "Oh, with your experience Mr Leeson, you'd be a marvellous candidate for the commandos." I said, "Oh yes, that would suit me marvellously", you see,

I said, "Or the Navy," I said, "I've served in the
Navy." But from that time I was never called up.
Never a word . . . I volunteered. I wrote a letter to
the Admiralty saying that I had had service in the
Royal Navy, I'd been a seaman-gunner, and I would
like to volunteer for service. And they said, "Well,
I'm afraid we can't do this . . . We call people up as
and when we need them." And then I wrote to the
Merchant Marine . . . Well, the same thing.'
Interview with George Leeson, IWMSA 803,
reel 3.

12 Peet, p. 100.
13 The restrictions also appeared to extend to veterans
from the Independent Labour Party group. Bob
Edwards discovered that as a former 'officer in a
foreign army' he would not be accepted for service.
Interview with Bob Edwards, IWMSA 4669, reel 3.
14 NA CAB 93/5.
15 NA KV 2/609 37d.
16 NA KV 2/609 37d.
17 NA KV 2/609 37d.
18 The US army also firmly denied that such
discrimination existed. However, requests made
under the Freedom of Information Act revealed that
the systematic discrimination against Lincoln
veterans in the armed services reflected a deliberate
military policy formulated in the war department
against 'potentially subversive personnel'. P.
Carroll, pp. 262–3.
19 Though it is also perfectly possible that recruiters
were unwilling to become involved in a time-
consuming and bureaucratic correspondence with
the security services.
20 Interview with John Longstaff, IWMSA 9299, reel
12.
21 Interview with David Marshall, IWMSA 9330,
reel 3.
22 IBC 545/6/127, p. 61.
23 NA KV 2/609/18a.
24 Interview with Chris Smith, IWMSA 12290, reel 9.
25 Edwards had, somewhat naively, left his real
address when taking the clerk's job. Report for
Chief Constable Major James, NA KV2/609/16a &
18a.
26 Interview with Chris Smith, IWMSA 12290, reel 9.
27 NA KV2/609/18a.
28 NA KV 2/609/ PF47319 VOL 1; 610/ PF47319
VOL 2.
29 R. Clark, p. 123.
30 R. Clark, pp. 146–7; Jackson, *Juan Negrín*, p. 309; NA
HW17/20. Kahle's presence on the project was
raised in a report by the Security Intelligence Centre
Liaison Officers' Conference. NA CAB 93/4. Kahle
disappeared in June 1940, having been interned and
transported to Canada.
31 A brief assessment by the security services in a list of
all individuals suspected of having gone to fight in
Spain read: 'In Spain – political comissar [sic] anti-
tank batt. In England – Communist.' NA KV/5/112.
For Alexander's personal file see KV2/2036.
32 Further experiments carried out the following year

involved Duff and three other veterans, all from
Ireland: John Larmour, who had been repatriated
from Spain in 1937 having been wounded at
Lopera; Dublin company commissar Jim
Prendergast; and former battalion commander
Paddy O'Daire. See letter to *Saothar*, journal of the
Irish Labour History Society, 18, 1993, and replies.
Available online at http://irelandscw.com/ibvol-
EDThetis.htm.
33 Duff, a member of the TGWU from Ireland, was
wounded four times in Spain, including being badly
wounded in both arms in the Republican Ebro
offensive which caused him to miss the Barcelona
farewell parade.
34 R. Clark, p. 138.
35 J.B.S. Haldane, 'Life at High Pressures', *Science
News*, 4, London: Penguin 1947, pp. 9–29, cited in
Calder, p. 465.
36 R. Clark, p. 135. Haldane later published a research
paper on the experiments and sent a copy of it to all
the volunteers involved. See J.B.S. Haldane, 'After
Effects of Exposure of Men to Carbon Dioxide', *The
Lancet*, 19 August 1939, pp. 419–22.
37 On 21 January 1943 a letter to MI5 from Lt.
Anderson at the Admiralty asked for several of
Haldane's assistants to be vetted. NA KV2/1832.
38 NA ADM 178/313.
39 Fernbach, p. 70.
40 S.P. Mackenzie, 'The Real Dad's Army: the British
Home Guard 1940–1944', from Addison and Calder,
pp. 50–9.
41 John Newsinger, 'My Country, Right or Left:
Patriotism, Socialism and George Orwell, 1939–
1941', in Kirkham and Thomas, pp. 29–31.
42 Wintringham, *New Ways of War*, p. 118.
43 Orwell, *The Lion and the Unicorn*. pp. 100–1.
Wintringham was seen by many in the government
as a dangerous figure who, despite his expulsion
from the Communist Party, remained communist
in all but name: 'Like Orwell, Wintringham
believed that war provided the best opportunity for
revolution and that a revolution was necessary for
fascism to be defeated.' Purcell, p. 170.
44 Tom Wintringham, 'Train the Home Guard for a
Modern War', *Picture Post*, 12 May 1941, p. 28, cited
in Fernbach, p. 76.
45 Wintringham, *New Ways of War*, p. 73.
46 Like British military strategist Basil Liddell Hart,
Wintringham argued that the Allies' policy of
bombing German cities was a mistake, both
militarily and politically, for as he had seen in Spain,
it merely strengthened resolve and at the same time
was 'bombing the revolution', thus preventing any
chance of a popular uprising against Hitler in
Germany. See Fernbach, p. 90.
47 The *News Chronicle* reporter in Spain, John Langdon-
Davies, also had a significant involvement in the
Home Guard and wrote extensively on the danger
of a fifth column. He established a field craft school
at his farm in Burwash, Sussex, which he presided
over as a Captain. Buchanan, *Impact*, p. 154.

48 Slater, pp. 69–73.

49 In 1941, *Guerilla Warfare*, a Penguin special, was written by Yank Levy, with assistance from both Kitty Bowler and Wintringham.

50 Fernbach, p. 73.

51 Fernbach, p. 77.

52 Wogan Philipps, later Lord Milford, the only Communist in the House of Lords, was convinced that he was rejected for the Home Guard because he had driven an ambulance in Spain. *Reynolds News*, 18 August 1940. According to the file held on Philipps by MI5, he applied to join the Home Guard in 1940. He joined the Communist Party – and was expelled from the Labour Party – the following year. NA KV/5/129, pf. 52255.

53 Purcell, p. 193.

54 Purcell and Smith, p. 202.

55 *Daily Mirror*, 21 June 1941; NA KV2/1612.

56 Gardiner, *Wartime Britain 1939–1945*, p. 244. The National Service Bill of December 1941 included the Home Guard as a force to be conscripted into, and from 1942 onwards, a significant proportion were conscripts.

57 Interview with Sam Russell (Lesser), IWMSA 9484, reel 6. Some were also recruited before Spain: at least three of the British volunteers, William Ivy Morrison, Sydney Fink and George Ives, had previously been trained as radio operators in the Soviet Union. NA HW17/20; KV 2/606/PF44912; Andrew, p. 176.

58 Petrou, p. 41.

59 Foote, pp. 8–9. Foote's assessment by his superiors in Spain credited him with 'a long and excellent record' and stated that he 'always impressed as having good political understanding'. IBC 545/6/135, p. 9.

60 Report 3 July 1947, NA KV2/1611.

61 Foote also recommended another Spanish veteran, Leon Beurton, who had previously worked with him in the 15th International Brigade auto-park. 'Sonia' divorced her German husband to marry Beurton, thereby gaining British citizenship, and after training up an operative, Beurton followed his wife to England using a false passport.

62 Volodarsky, p. 317.

63 Report 23 February 1945, NA KV2/1611.

64 Report 3 July 1947, NA KV2/1611.

65 Report 8 July 1947, NA KV2/1611.

66 NA KV 2/1615.

67 NA KV 2/1616 307a.

68 IBC 545/6/142, p. 103.

69 Volodarsky, p. 351. Alonzo Elliot, a senior and trusted member of the Party, had worked under the senior Italian Communist Luigi Longo, at the Political Commissars' headquarters in Madrid. Joe Garber served initially as a machine-gunner before becoming a censor with the Special Military Investigations Unit, which involved being sent to Russia for training. Interview with Joe Garber, IWMSA 122291, reel 9; conversation with Dr Freddy Shaw.

70 MI5 also discovered that John William Reid, known as Jack Reid in Spain, was involved in espionage work, though he was only suspected of low-level work as a courier. Andrew, p. 277; NA KV/2/2073, p. 35a.

71 Andrew, p. 278.

72 NA KV 2/1596.

73 Letter from MI5, 19 November 1941, NA KV2/1596/255b, 355a. In 1920, Springhall had been discharged from the navy for distributing seditious material during the First World War. NA KV/2/1594.

74 NA KV 2/1597/300z.

75 Andrew, p. 278.

76 In the same court case a Captain Uren, with whom Springhall had also been working, was dismissed from the army, and also given seven years' imprisonment for passing on secret details of SOE headquarters. NA KV2/1597/304a1.

77 NA KV2/1596.

78 IBMT 545/6/91; IBA MML Box D-7, File A/1.

79 NA KV2/1596.

80 N. Branson, *History of the Communist Party 1941–1951*, p. 75.

81 NA KV/2/1598/10a.

82 Minutes of the Home Defence (Security) Executive committee meeting, 7 July 1943. NA CAB 93/5.

83 Macartney's file also includes the accusation that Harry Pollitt, Raj Palme-Dutt and Bill Rust had all provided information to the Russians at some stage. NA KV2/1596 and 2073.

84 See NA KV 2 1603–4 and Volodarsky, p. 187.

85 NA KV2/1603/105a.

86 NA KV2/1603/106.

87 NA KV2/1603/109a.

88 Most senior Communist Party figures and many of the British political commissars in Spain had studied at the Lenin School. See Halstead and McLoughlin, 'British and Irish Students at the International Lenin School, Moscow, 1926–37', unpublished conference paper, 2001.

89 Letter from Major General Sir Vernon Kell to the Assistant Chief Constable of Birmingham, 9 May 1940. NA KV2/1603/110.

90 NA KV2/1603/111a.

91 Captain I.R. Deacon to Major J.P. McGeagh, Northern Command HQ, NA KV2/1603.

92 *Volunteer for Liberty*, July 1944, p. 19.

93 The case of the 'serial fantasist' Eric Camp, who Robson believed had 'wanted to go to Spain, principally so that his wife would get an allowance', also caused the security services a great deal of time and trouble. Camp claimed to be both a 'professional crook' and to be involved in espionage work for the Soviet Union. Both claims were established to be as false as his marriage vows, when the Metropolitan Police brought charges of bigamy against him. A rather sardonic assessment by the security services concluded that 'We have little evidence to show that he has been any more faithful to the Party than he has been to his wife.' IBC 545/6/113, p. 37; NA KV2/2030.

94 NA KV 2/610/66a.
95 NA KV 2/610/78a.
96 NA KV 2/610/87a.
97 *Volunteer for Liberty*, Vol. 4, No. 4, June 1943, p. 3. Edwards' MI5 file states 3 May. NA KV/2/610, 93a, 99b.
98 NA KV/2/610 99b.
99 NA KV 2/610, 142a.

23 We shall pass!
1 Meeting of HDSE, 17 November 1941, NA CAB 93/5.
2 NA HO 45/25574/865000/94.
3 Interview with Roderick MacFarquhar in MacDougall, *Voices from the Spanish Civil War*, p. 87.
4 N. Branson, *History of the Communist Party 1941–1951*, p. 55.
5 NA KV 2/609 37d.
6 Longstaff, MS, p. 154.
7 Fred Thomas's assessment in Spain read: 'Was Party member in Britain. Made no effort to join here. Good record. Cynical.' IBC 545/9/96. For his dismissal from building air-raid shelters, see *Volunteer for Liberty*, No. 4, April 1940.
8 Interview with Ernest Troy, IWMSA 4693, cited in Gardiner, *Wartime Britain*, pp. 124–5.
9 Tom Wintringham, *Volunteer for Liberty*, February 1942, p. 15.
10 N. Branson, *History of the Communist Party 1927–41*, p. 307.
11 Interview with Jack Edwards, MHA 171, reel 1, side 2. Edwards' political history and his time in Spain were, in fact, well known to the British security services. See NA KV/5/121, pf 119479.
12 Interview with Roderick MacFarquhar, IWMSA 9234, reel 5.
13 NA KV2/2036, 29 May 1940 and 21 February 1941.
14 NA KV2/2036, Reports 28 November 1941 and 27 July 1942; letter from Eleanor Rathbone to Parliamentary Under-Secretary of the War Office, 6 July 1942. NA 2/2036.
15 O'Daire was admitted into the army as a private in the Royal Army Service Corps, but after being recommended for a commission in 1942 was made a second lieutenant the following year. *Volunteer for Liberty*, Vol. 3, No. 7, 1942, p. 8; Vol. 4, No. 5, 1943, p. 11.
16 *Daily Worker*, 3 March 1943; *Volunteer for Liberty*, Vol. 4, No. 4, June 1943, p. 4; NA KV2/2036, HQ West Command, ISWC 204/NISC, 5 August 1943.
17 Interview with Bill Alexander, IWMSA 16216, reel 1.
18 *Volunteer for Liberty*, No. 12, 12 May 1941, p. 5.
19 House of Commons debate on motion of 'No Confidence', 7 July 1942, cited in Churchill, *The Second World War, Volume IV: The Hinge of Fate*, p. 359.
20 Alexander, *British Volunteers*, p. 246.
21 *Hansard*, 1 October 1942.

22 Citation of 11 August 1944, announced in the *London Gazette* on 21 December 1944. NA WO 373/50.
23 *Volunteer for Liberty*, No. 14, Aug–Sept 1941, p. 16.
24 Paynter, p. 121.
25 *Volunteer for Liberty*, Vol. 4, No. 4, June 1943, p. 5, July 1944, p. 17, Vol. 4, No. 6, 1943, p. 4 and October 1944, p. 9; Alexander, *British Volunteers*, p. 246.
26 Angus, p. vi.
27 Copeman, p. 187.
28 Copeman, p. 192.
29 Copeman, p. 192.
30 Henderson, p. 43.
31 *Volunteer for Liberty*, Vol. 3, No. 6, 1942, p. 5.
32 Macartney's conviction for spying for the Soviet Union in the 1920s was probably more than enough to keep him out of the armed forces. Moreover, the security services also suspected Macartney of financial impropriety. NA KV2/648.
33 IBC 545/6/215, p. 33.
34 Interview with Sam Wild, IWMSA 10358, reel 2.
35 Conversation with Mike Wild, 16 October 2010.
36 Interview with Sam Wild in Cook, p. 73.
37 Crook, ch. 5, p. 13.
38 Crook, ch. 6, p. 7.
39 Crook, ch. 6, pp. 1–2.
40 Crook, ch. 6, p. 16.
41 Interview with Walter Gregory, IWMSA 8851, reel 8.
42 P. Carroll, p. 245.
43 NA KV/5/125, pf.220483.
44 Knox, *Essays Ancient and Modern*, p. 269.
45 Knox, *Premature Anti-Fascist*.
46 Crome was informed that regulations stipulated that every candidate for a commission in the Territorial Army must be 'a British subject and a son of British subjects' and as the child of Latvian immigrants he was therefore ineligible. LCP. Letter from D.A.D.M.S. 44th (H.C.) Division to Len Crome, 23 June 1939.
47 Interview with Reg Saxton, IWMSA 8735, reel 9.
48 Letter to the Inspector of Police, Birmingham, undated, NA KV2/1603/119a.
49 Crook, ch. 5, p. 15.
50 Interview with Alec Marcowich, MHA 182, reel 2, side 1.
51 'From the I.B. to the British Army', by Militiaman, *Volunteer for Liberty*, No. 5, May 1940, p. 7.
52 *Volunteer for Liberty*, Vol. 1, No. 10, 1941, p. 3.
53 Interview with Roderick MacFarquhar, IWMSA 9234, reel 4.
54 Interview with Max Colin, IWMSA 8639, reel 6.
55 Lewis, p. 57.
56 *Volunteer for Liberty*, Nov–Dec 1943, p. 18.
57 Longstaff, MS, p. 147.
58 Longstaff, MS, pp. 195–6.
59 Richard Holmes, 'The Italian Job: Five Armies in Italy, 1943–45', from Addison and Calder, p. 209.
60 Interview with William Forrest, IWMSA 12416, reel 4.

61 Interview with Walter Gregory, IWMSA 8551, reel 8.
62 *Volunteer for Liberty*, July 1944, p. 19.
63 Interview with George Wheeler, June 2000.
64 Interview with Jimmy Moon, IWMSA 15729, reel 4.
65 *Volunteer for Liberty*, Jan 1944, p. 18
66 Interview with Maurice Levine in Cook, p. 148; interview with Eddie Brown in MacDougall, *Voices from the Spanish Civil War*, p. 115.
67 *Volunteer for Liberty*, July 1944, p. 2.
68 Stein, pp. 148–9.
69 *Volunteer for Liberty*, October 1944, p. 20.

Epilogue: 'Two down – one to go'
1 The *Volunteer for Liberty* carried the obituaries of more than twenty killed during the Second World War, though there were undoubtedly others. Some were not reported, such as Cypriot George Demitriou, who survived the sinking of the SS *Ciudad de Barcelona*, only to be killed serving in the Merchant Navy in the Atlantic in 1940, when his ship was torpedoed by a U-boat. Philipou Strongos, pp. 265–6.
2 Mitford, 2007, pp. 148, 183.
3 Ingram, p. 222.
4 Interview with Tommy Bloomfield in MacDougall, *Voices from the Spanish Civil War*, p. 53; *Volunteer for Liberty*, Vol. 4, No. 3, April–May 1943, p. 8; Cooney, MS, p. 164.
5 Branson, *History of the Communist Party 1941–51*, p. 55.
6 *Volunteer for Liberty*, Vol. 4, No. 6, 1943, p. 10.
7 LCP, Letter from Tony Miles to Len Crome, 21 September 1944, *Volunteer for Liberty*, Vol. 4, No. 4, June 1943, p. 5, July 1944, p. 17, October 1944, p. 9; Alexander, *British Volunteers*, p. 246.
8 *Volunteer for Liberty*, Vol. 6, No. 3, July 1945, p. 7.
9 NA Citation for the Military Cross for Captain Leonard Crome, 23 May 1944. The record of Herbert George Rowlands (known as Roland Miller in Spain) was rather less glorious. During the evacuation of Norway in June 1940, he was taken prisoner by the Germans. Exactly four years later Rowlands was released when, despite his International Brigade past, he agreed to join the British Free Corps, a Waffen SS unit made up of pro-Nazi Britons. After the war, he was brought to trial and, on 19 February 1946, sentenced to two years' imprisonment for conspiracy and assisting the enemy. *Evening News*, 19 December 1945; NA KV 2/625/ PF90889.
10 Alexander, *No to Franco*, p. 34.
11 *Volunteer for Liberty*, Vol. 4, No. 5, 1943, p. 19.
12 *Volunteer for Liberty*, Vol. 4, no. 4, 1943, p. 4; Harrison, p. 30.
13 Alexander, *No to Franco*, p. 44.
14 Cleminson, pp. 167–8.
15 B.H. Philips, 'No Other Way', p. 21.
16 Watkins, p. 196.
17 Report of the [United Nations] Sub-Committee on the Spanish Question, cited in Watkins, pp. 197–201.
18 Watkins, p. 205.
19 Watkins, p. 212.
20 Alexander, *No to Franco*, p. 58.
21 Alexander, *No to Franco*, p. 34.
22 Knox, *Premature Anti-Fascist*.
23 Buchanan, 'Holding the Line', p. 304.
24 Interview with Tony Maclean, IWMSA 838, reel 4.
25 Colman, p. 17.
26 Report on Scottish District of the IBA, NA KV 5/54.
27 Buchanan, *Impact*, p. 190.
28 Interview with George Leeson, IWMSA 803, reel 3.
29 Alexander, *No to Franco*, pp. 69–70.
30 Alexander, *No to Franco*, p. 71.
31 These interviews form the basis of the sound archives held at the Imperial War Museum, London and at the Tameside Local Studies and Archives Centre, Ashton-under-Lyne.
32 Williams et al, p. 5. The monument's site on London's South Bank was consequently used for the annual commemorations of the IBA and, later, its successor, the International Brigade Memorial Trust.
33 Interview with Frank McCusker in MacDougall, *Voices from the Spanish Civil War*, p. 45.
34 Fred Thomas, p. 170.
35 Interview with Phil Gillan in MacDougall, *Voices from the Spanish Civil War*, p. 19.
36 Interview with Frank McCusker in MacDougall, *Voices from the Spanish Civil War*, p. 45.
37 Interview with Eddie Brown in MacDougall, *Voices from the Spanish Civil War*, p. 115.
38 Thanks to Dolores Long for the information on her father, Sam Wild.
39 Obituary of Sir Alfred Sherman, *Daily Telegraph*, 28 August 2006.
40 Goldacre, p. 44.
41 Obituary of Professor Bernard Knox, *Daily Telegraph*, 16 September 2010.
42 IBMT 545/6/115, p. 30; obituary of Nathan Clark, *The Guardian*, 3 July 2011.
43 I am grateful to the family of George Fletcher for this information.
44 Interview with David Lomon, 16 February 2011.
45 *SAGA* Magazine, April 2009, pp. 67–8, 70; June 2009, p. 46.
46 'Return to Madrid', *IBMT Newsletter*, 31, New Year 2012, p. 1.
47 Purcell, pp. 209, 246.
48 IBA MML Box D-4, File Db.
49 Morris Riley and Stephen Dorril, 'Rothschild, the right, the far-right and the Fifth Man', *The Lobster*, 16; Brome, p. 280.
50 Toynbee, *The Distant Drum*, p. 130.
51 IBA MML Box 45 B/44.
52 My thanks to Wendy-Anne Cunningham for this information. More dreadful than tragic is the case of George Alexander Robertson from Edinburgh. On 23 June 1954, Robertson became the last man to be hanged for murder in Edinburgh. Six months earlier, the 'violent, abusive and intensely jealous' Robertson had been let back into the family home

by his estranged wife, Elizabeth. He had responded to this act of kindness by seriously wounding his daughter and brutally murdering his wife and son. 'Lothian Murder Files: Brutal man was city's last to hang', news.Scotsman.com, 14 January 2011.

53 IBMT 545/6/173, p. 30.

54 IBC 545/6/96; IBMT 545/6/173, p. 32.

55 http://www.shivashakti.com/dadaji.htm.

56 http://www.thewica.co.uk/Others.htm.

57 Simon Courtauld, 'A Not Very Franco Account', The Spectator, 3 January 1998, p. 17.

58 See, for example, IBC 545/6/91, p. 142. Much of Lee's memoir, A Moment of War, is probably not reliable. See Baxell, 'Laurie Lee in the International Brigades', pp. 165–8; Grove, pp. 515–16.

59 'Jack Jones, Soviet spy', Daily Mail, 8 October 2009.

60 See, for example, IBMT 545/6/94, p. 3.

61 IBMT 545/6/155, pp. 49–51.

62 Andrew, p. 535.

63 Jack Jones cited in Cook, p. vii.

64 Cox, Eyewitness, p. 218.

65 When the Sunday Times printed Gordievsky's allegation that Michael Foot was a KGB agent, the former Labour leader successfully sued for libel, winning substantial damages. 'Oleg Gordievsky has spent much of his adult life as a spy,' said a leading article in the Independent. 'His stock-in-trade is lying and deceit.' 'Michael Foot's tainted accuser', Independent, 20 February 1995.

66 Andrew, p. 589.

67 Sommerfield, p. 157.

68 Romilly, p. 196.

69 Tommy Bloomfield cited in Gray, p. 209.

Bibliography

If I were to list all the sources I referred to in researching and writing this book the finished tome would be far longer and considerably less wieldy. Consequently, I have chosen to include only works quoted in the text, as well as a short list of recommended reading for those who wish to explore the Spanish Civil War and the lives of the volunteers more deeply, or more widely. For a complete bibliography, please visit www.richardbaxell.info.

Suggested further reading

For British politics in the 1930s, see John Stephenson and Chris Cook's *Britain in the Depression* and Juliet Gardiner's *The Thirties*. Joe Jacobs' memoir *Out of the Ghetto* is good for a view from the street.

There are many published accounts by British volunteers in the International Brigades; of those still in print, Walter Gregory's *The Shallow Grave* and Fred Thomas's *To Tilt at Windmills* are justifiably popular. George Orwell's *Homage to Catalonia* and the Spanish-born Arturo Barea's *The Forging of a Rebel* are both important and highly readable. Many works focus on the national and ethnic groups within the 'British' volunteers, of which Hywell Francis' reissued *Miners Against Fascism* and Daniel Gray's *Homage to Caledonia* are two notable recent additions. Paul Preston's *We Saw Spain Die* is a fascinating account of the foreign correspondents who witnessed the conflict.

For the war itself, Hugh Thomas's *The Spanish Civil War* in its fully revised third edition is always useful, though Helen Graham's *The Spanish Civil War* and Paul Preston's *Concise History* offer more accessible introductions to the subject. Ronald Fraser's *Blood of Spain* remains a shining example of the merits of oral history.

For the role of the former volunteers after the civil war and the continuing relevance of the conflict, see Tom Buchanan's *Impact of the Spanish Civil War on Britain*.

Archives

Abraham Lincoln Brigade Archives, Tamiment Library, New York University.
Archivo General Militar de Avila, Avila.
British Library of Political and Economic Science, London.
British Newspaper Library, London.
International Brigade Archive, Marx Memorial Library, London.
International Brigade Collection, Russian Centre for the Preservation and Study of Recent Historical Documents, Moscow.

International Brigade Memorial Trust, London.
Labour History Archive and Study Centre, People's History Museum, Manchester.
Len Crome Papers (courtesy of the family).
Manchester History Archive, Tameside Local Studies and Archives Unit, Ashton-under-Lyne.
National Archives, Public Record Office, Kew.
Spanish Civil War Collection, Imperial War Museum Sound Archive, London.
Spanish Civil War Collection, Working Class Movement Library, Salford.
Swansea Miners' Library, Swansea.
Trades Union Congress Archive, University of Warwick.

Unpublished memoirs
Anon. *The Epic of Arganda Bridge*. International Brigade Archive, London.
Cantor, Ralph. Unpublished diary. Working Class Movement Library, Salford.
Cooney, Robert. *Proud Journey*. International Brigade Archive, London.
Crook, David. Autobiography. Online at www.davidcrook.net
Green, Oliver; Piper, Alec; Aitken, George; Meredith, Bill; Diamant, André; McElroy, James; McAnaw, T. *The British Brigade*. Fred Copeman Collection, Imperial War Museum, London.
Griffiths, W.J. *Spain. Memoirs of the Spanish Civil War*. Swansea Miners' Library.
Harrisson, P.D. *Interesting Times*. Author's copy, courtesy of David Leach.
Hearst, Louis. *The First Twelve*. Author's copy, courtesy of David Marshall.
Jump, James. Unpublished memoir. Imperial War Museum, London.
Kurzke, Jan. *The Good Comrade*. Author's copy.
Longstaff, John. Unpublished memoirs. Author's copy, courtesy of the family.
Ludwick, Percy. *Notes of a Muscovite*. International Brigade Archive, London.
Norman, Joe. Untitled, International Brigade Archive, London.
Sexton, Cyril. *Memories of the Spanish Civil War*. International Brigade Archive, London.

Published primary sources
Anon. NCCL report on Albert Hall meeting, London: NCCL, 22 March 1936.
Anon. *They Did NOT Pass: 300,000 Workers say NO to Mosley*. London: ILP, 1936.
Anon. *In Spain with the International Brigade: A personal narrative*. London: Burns, Oates and Washbourne, 1938.
Anon. *They Fought in Franco's Jails*. London: CPGB, 1939.
Alexander, Bill. *British Volunteers for Liberty*. London: Lawrence and Wishart, 1982.
Angus, John. *With the International Brigade in Spain*. Loughborough: Loughborough University, 1983.
Atholl, Katherine. *Searchlight on Spain*. London: Penguin, 1938.
Attlee, C.R. *As It Happened*. London: Heinemann, 1954.
Barea, Arturo. *The Forging of a Rebel*. London: Granta, 2001.
Borkenau, Franz. *The Spanish Cockpit*. London: Ann Arbor, 1963.
Britten Austin, F. *On the Aragon Battlefront*. London: Spanish Press, 1938.
Bury, Henry Saunders. *Medicine, Politics and War*. New York: Cenda, 1993.
Cardozo, Harold. *The March of a Nation: My Year in Spain's Civil War*. London: Eyre and Spottiswoode, 1937.

Churchill, Winston. *Step by Step 1936–1939*. London: Macmillan, 1943.

——. *The Second World War*. London: Cassell and Co., 1949–1950.

Clark, Bob. *No Boots to my Feet: Experiences of a Britisher in Spain 1937–38*. Student Bookshops, 1984.

Colman, Jud. *Memories of Spain, 1936–1938*. Manchester: Privately printed, date unknown.

Colodny, Robert. *The Struggle for Madrid*. New York: 1958.

Copeman, Fred. *Reason in Revolt*. London: Blandford Press, 1948.

Cornford, John. *Collected Writings*. Manchester: Carcanet, 1986.

Coward, Jack. *Back from the Dead*. Liverpool: Merseyside Writers, date unknown.

Cox, Geoffrey. *The Defence of Madrid*. London: Gollancz, 1937.

——. *Eyewitness: A Memoir of Europe in the 1930s*. Dunedin, NZ: University of Otago Press, 1999.

Deegan, Frank. *There's No Other Way*. Liverpool: Toulouse Press, 1980.

Delmer, Sefton. *Trail Sinister*. London: Secker and Warburg, 1961.

Doyle, Bob. *Brigadista*. Currach Press, 2006.

Foote, Alex. *Handbook for Spies*. New York: Doubleday, 1949.

Fyvel, Penelope. *English Penny*. Ilfracombe: Arthur Stockwell, 1992.

Gascoyne, David. *Journal 1936–1937*. London: Enitharmon Press, 1990.

Geiser, Carl. *Prisoners of the Good Fight*. Connecticut: Lawrence Hill, 1986.

Graham, Frank, ed. *The Battle of Jarama*. Newcastle: Frank Graham, 1987.

——. *Battles of Brunete and the Aragon*. Newcastle: Frank Graham, 1999.

Green, Nan. *A Chronicle of Small Beer*. Nottingham: Trent Editions, 2004.

Greene, Herbert. *Secret Agent in Spain*. London: Robert Hale, 1938.

Greening, Edwin. *From Aberdare to Albacete*. Pontypool: Warren and Pell, 2006.

Gregory, Walter. *The Shallow Grave: A Memoir of the Spanish Civil War*. London: Victor Gollancz, 1986.

Guest, Carmel Haden. *David Guest: A Scientist Fights for Freedom 1911–1938*. London: Lawrence and Wishart, 1939.

Gurney, Jason. *Crusade in Spain*. London: Faber and Faber, 1974.

Haldane, Charlotte. *Truth Will Out*. London: Weidenfeld and Nicolson, 1949.

Healey, Denis. *The Time of My Life*. London: Michael Joseph, 1989.

Heath, Edward. *The Course of My Life*. London: Hodder and Stoughton, 1998.

Henderson, Stan. *Comrades on the Kwai*. Ceredigion: Socialist History Society, 1998.

Horne, Harold. *All the Trees Were Bread and Cheese*. Luton: Owen Hardisty, 1998.

Hyde, Douglas. *I Believed*. New York: G.P. Putnam's, 1950.

Jacobs, Joe. *Out of the Ghetto*. London: Phoenix Press, 1978.

Jones, Jack. *Union Man*. London: Collins, 1986.

Kemp, Peter. *Mine Were of Trouble*. London: Cassell, 1957.

——. 'I Fought for Franco', in A.J.P. Taylor, ed., *History of the Twentieth Century*. London: Purnell, 1968, pp. 1604–9.

——. *The Thorns of Memory*. London: Sinclair-Stevenson, 1990.

Kisch, Richard.——. *The Days of the Good Soldiers*. London: Journeyman, 1985.

Knox, Bernard. *Essays Ancient and Modern*. Baltimore: John Hopkins University Press, 1989.

——. *Premature Anti-Fascist*. New York University, 1998. Online at http://www.english.illinois.edu/maps/scw/knox.htm.

Koestler, Arthur. *Spanish Testament*. London: Victor Gollancz, 1937.

——. *Invisible Writing*. London: Collins, 1954.

Langdon-Davies, John. *Behind The Spanish Barricades*. London: Secker and Warburg, 1936.

Lee, Laurie. *A Moment of War*. London: Viking, 1991.

——. *To War In Spain*. London: Penguin, 1996.

Lehmann, John, ed. *Ralph Fox: A Writer in Arms*. London: Lawrence and Wishart, 1937.

Levine, Maurice. *Cheetham to Cordova: Maurice Levine – A Manchester Man of the Thirties*. Manchester: privately published, 1984.

Macartney, W.F.R. *Walls Have Mouths*. London: Victor Gollancz, 1936.

Madge, Charles and Harrison, Tom. *Britain by Mass Observation*. London: Penguin, 1939.

Magee, Bryan. *Clouds of Glory*. London: Pimlico, 2004.

Mitford, Jessica. *Hons and Rebels*. London: Victor Gollancz, 1960.

Monks, J. *With the Reds in Andalusia*. London: privately printed, 1985.

O'Connor, Peter. *Recollections of a Socialist and Anti-Fascist Fighter*. Dublin: MSF, 1996.

O'Duffy, Eoin. *Crusade in Spain*. Dublin: Brown and Nolan, 1938.

O'Riordan, Michael. *Connolly Column*. Dublin: New Books, 1979.

Orwell, George. 'Eye-witness in Barcelona', *Controversy*, August 1937, pp. 85–8.

——. 'Spilling the Spanish Beans', *New English Weekly*, 29 July and 2 September 1937.

——. *Homage to Catalonia*. London: Secker and Warburg, 1938.

——. *The Lion and the Unicorn: Socialism and the English Genius*. London: Secker and Warburg, 1941.

——. 'Looking back on the Spanish Civil War', *England Your England and Other Essays*. London: Secker and Warburg, 1953, pp. 151–76.

Paynter, Will. *My Generation*. London: George Allen and Unwin, 1972.

Peet, John. *The Long Engagement: Memoirs of a Cold War Legend*. London: Fourth Estate, 1989.

Romilly, Esmond. *Boadilla*. London: Hamish Hamilton, 1937.

Rothman, Benny. *The Battle for Kinder Scout*. Altrringham: Willow, 2012.

Rust, William. *Britons in Spain*. London: Lawrence and Wishart, 1939.

Ryan, Frank, ed. *The Book of the XVth Brigade: Records of British, American, Canadian and Irish Volunteers in the XV International Brigade in Spain 1936–1938*. Madrid: War Commissariat, 1938.

Scott-Ellis, Priscilla. *The Chances of Death: A Diary of the Spanish Civil War*. Norwich: Michael Russell, 1995.

Slater, Hugh. *Home Guard for Victory*. London: Victor Gollancz, 1941.

Sloan, Hugh. 'Why I Volunteered', *Scottish Trade Union Review*, 51, July–September 1991, pp. 30–1.

Sommerfield, John. *Volunteer in Spain*. London: Lawrence and Wishart, 1937.

Spender, Stephen. *World Within World*. London: Readers Union, 1951.

Steer, G.L. *The Tree of Gernika*. London: Hodder and Stoughton, 1938.

Stratton, H. *To Anti-Fascism by Taxi*. West Glamorgan: Alun Books, 1984.

Thomas, Frank. *Brother Against Brother*, ed. Robert Stradling. Stroud: Sutton, 1998.

Thomas, Fred. *To Tilt at Windmills: A Memoir of the Spanish Civil War*. East Lansing: State University of Michigan Press, 1996.

Watson, Keith Scott. *Single to Spain*. London: Arthur Barker, 1937.

Wheeler, George. *To Make the People Smile Again*, ed. David Leach. Newcastle: Zymurgy, 2003.

Williams, Alun Menai. *From the Rhondda to the Ebro*. Pontypool: Warren and Pell, 2004.

Wintringham, Tom. *English Captain*. London: Faber and Faber, 1939.

——. *New Ways of War*. London: Penguin, 1940.

Secondary sources

Addison, Paul and Calder, Angus, eds. *Time To Kill: The Soldier's Experience of War in the West, 1939–1945*. London: Pimlico, 1997.

Aldgate, Anthony. *Cinema and History: British Newsreels and the Spanish Civil War*. London: Scolar Press, 1979.

Alexander, Bill. *No to Franco: The Struggle Never Stopped, 1939–1975!* London: Bill Alexander, 1992.

Andrew, Christopher. *The Defence of the Realm*. London: Allen Lane, 2009.

Arthur, Max. *The Real Band of Brothers*. London: Collins, 2009.

Ball, S. 'The Politics of Appeasement: The Fall of the Duchess of Atholl and the Kinross and West-Perth By-election, December 1938', *Scottish Historical Review*, 187, April 1990, pp. 49–85.

Bandrés, Javier and Llavona, Rafael. 'Psychology in Franco's Concentration Camps', *Psychology in Spain*, 1:1, 1997, pp. 3–9.

Baxell, Richard. *British Volunteers in the Spanish Civil War: The British Battalion in the International Brigades, 1936–1939*. London: Routledge / Cañada Blanch Studies on Contemporary Spain, 2004; Pontypool: Warren and Pell, 2007.

——. 'Laurie Lee in the International Brigades: Writer or Fighter?', in Jim Jump, ed., *Looking Back at the Spanish Civil War*. London: Lawrence and Wishart, 2010, pp. 157-175.

Beckett, Francis. *Enemy Within: The Rise and Fall of the British Communist Party*. London: John Murray, 1995.

——. *Clem Attlee*. London: Richard Cohen, 1997.

Beevor, Anthony. *The Spanish Civil War*. London: Orbis, 1982.

——. *The Battle for Spain*. London: Weidenfeld and Nicolson, 2006.

Bell, Adrian. *Only for Three Months*. Norwich: Mousehold Press, 1996.

Benewick, R. *The Fascist Movement in Britain*. London: Penguin, 1972.

Bennett, Richard. *The Black and Tans*. London: Edward Hulton, 1959.

Bowker, Gordon. *George Orwell*. London: Little, Brown, 2003.

Branson, Noreen. *History of the Communist Party of Great Britain 1927–1941*. London: Lawrence and Wishart, 1985.

——. *History of the Communist Party of Great Britain 1941–1951*. London: Lawrence and Wishart, 1997.

Bridgeman, Brian. *The Flyers: The Untold Story of British and Commonwealth Airmen in the Spanish Civil War and other Air Wars from 1919 to 1940*. Swindon: B. Bridgman, 1989.

Brome, Vincent. *The International Brigades: Spain, 1936–1939*. London: Heinemann, 1965.

Buchanan, Tom. *The British Labour Movement and the Spanish Civil War*. Cambridge: Cambridge University Press, 1991.

——. *Britain and the Spanish Civil War*. Cambridge: Cambridge University Press, 1997.

—— 'Holding the Line: The Political Strategy of the International Brigade Association, 1939–1977', *Labour History Review*. 66:3, Winter 2001, pp. 294–312.

—— 'Edge of Darkness: British "Front-line" Diplomacy in the Spanish Civil War, 1936-1937', *Contemporary European History*, 12, 2003, pp. 279-303.

——. *The Impact of the Spanish Civil War on Britain*. Brighton: Sussex University Press, 2007.

Calder, Angus. *The People's War*. London: Jonathan Cape, 1969.

Carlton, David. 'Eden, Blum, and the Origins of Non-Intervention', *Journal of Contemporary History*, 6:3, 1971, pp. 40–55.

Carr, E.H. *The Comintern and the Spanish Civil War*. London: Macmillan, 1984.

Carroll, Peter N. *The Odyssey of the Abraham Lincoln Brigade*. California: Stanford Press, 1994.

Clark, Ronald. *J.B.S.: The Life and Work of J.B.S. Haldane*. Oxford: Oxford University Press, 1984.

Cleminson, Richard. 'Spanish Anti-Fascist "Prisoners of War" in Lancashire, 1944–46', *International Journal of Iberian Studies*, 22:3, 2009, pp. 163–83.

Coni, Nicholas. *Medicine and Warfare: Spain, 1936–1939*. London: Routledge, 2008.

Cook, Judith. *Apprentices of Freedom*. London: Quartet Press, 1979.

Cooper, Mike and Parkes, Ray. *We Cannot Park on Both Sides: Reading Volunteers in the Spanish Civil War 1936–39*. Reading: Reading International Brigades Memorial Committee, 2000.

Copsey, Nigel. *Anti-Fascism in Britain*. London: Macmillan, 2000.

Corkhill, D. and Rawnsley, S., eds. *The Road to Spain: Anti Fascists at War 1936–1939*. Fife: Borderline, 1981.

Crome, Len. 'Walter, 1897–1947: A Soldier in Spain', *History Workshop Journal*, 9, Spring 1980, pp. 116–28.

Cronin, Seán. *Frank Ryan: The Search for the Republic*. Dublin: Repsol, 1979.

Cullen, Stephen. 'Political Violence: The Case of the British Union of Fascists', *Journal of Contemporary History*, 28, 1993, pp. 245–67.

Cunningham, Valentine, ed. *The Penguin Book of Spanish Civil War Verse*. London: Penguin, 1980.

——. *Spanish Front: Writers on the Civil War*. Oxford University Press, 1986.

Darman, Peter. *Heroic Voices of the Spanish Civil War*. London: New , 2009.

Davison, Peter, ed. *Orwell in Spain*. London: Penguin, 2001.

Day, Peter. *Franco's Friends*. London: Biteback, 2011.

Deacon, David. *British News Media and the Spanish Civil War*. Edinburgh University Press, 2008.

Dewar, Hugo. *Communist Politics in Britain: The CPGB from its Origins to the Second World War*. London: Pluto, 1976.

Dolan, Chris. *An Anarchist's Story: The Life of Ethel Macdonald*. Edinburgh: Berlinn, 2009.

Dorril, Stephen. *Blackshirt: Sir Oswald Mosley and British Fascism*. London: Viking, 2006.

Dowse, R.E. *Left in the Centre: The Independent Labour Party, 1893–1940*. London: Longmans, 1966.

Eaden, James and Renton, David. *The Communist Party of Great Britain since 1920*. Basingstoke: Palgrave, 2002.

Edwards, Jill. *The British Government and the Spanish Civil War*. London: Macmillan, 1979.

Ewing, K.D. and Gearty, C.A. *The Struggle for Civil Liberties: Political Freedom and the Rule of Law in Britain, 1914–1945*. Oxford: Clarendon Press, 2000.

Faber, Sebastiaan. *Anglo-American Hispanists and the Spanish Civil War*. New York: Palgrave Macmillan, 2008.

Fernbach, David. 'Tom Wintringham and Socialist Defence Strategy', *History Workshop Journal*, 14, Autumn 1982, pp. 63–91.

Francis, Hywel. *Miners Against Fascism: Wales and the Spanish Civil War*. London: Lawrence and Wishart, 1984.

——. '"Say Nothing and Leave in the Middle of the Night": The Spanish Civil War Revisited', *History Workshop Journal*, 32, Autumn 1991, pp. 69–76.

Fyrth, Jim. *The Signal Was Spain*. London: Lawrence and Wishart, 1986.

García, Hugo. *The Truth About Spain! Mobilising British Public Opinion, 1936–1939*. Eastbourne: Sussex Academic Press, 2010.

——. 'Potemkin in Spain? British Unofficial Missions of Investigation to Spain during the Civil War', *European History Quarterly*, 42:2, 2010, pp. 217–39.

Gardiner, Juliet. *Wartime Britain 1939–1945*. London: Headline, 2004.

——. *The Thirties: An Intimate History*. London: Harper Press, 2010.

Goldacre, Ben. *Bad Science*. London: Harper Perennial, 2009.

Graham, Helen. *The Spanish Civil War*. Oxford: Oxford University Press, 2005.

Gray, Daniel. *Homage to Caledonia*. Edinburgh: Luath Press, 2008.

Grove, Valerie. *Laurie Lee: The Well-Loved Stranger*. London: Viking, 1999.

Hall, Christopher. *Disciplina Camaradas: Four English Volunteers in Spain 1936–39*. Pontefract: Gosling Press, 1994.

——. *Not Just Orwell: The Independent Labour Party Volunteers and the Spanish Civil War*. Barcelona: Warren and Pell, 2009.

Hallett, Don. '"The Hand that History Dealt", Ralph Fox 1900–1936', *Transactions of the Halifax Antiquarian Society*, 17, 2009, pp. 110–40.

Harrison, Stanley. *Good to be Alive: The Story of Jack Brent*. London: Lawrence and Wishart, 1954.

Henry, Chris. *The Ebro 1938: The Death Knell of the Republic*. Oxford: Osprey, 1999.

Hope, John. 'Blackshirts, Knuckle-Dusters and Lawyers: Documentary Essay on the Mosley versus Marchbanks Papers', *Labour History Review*, 65, 2000, pp. 41–58.

Hopkins, James K. *Into the Heart of the Fire: The British in the Spanish Civil War*. California: Stanford, 1998.

Howson, Gerald. *Arms for Spain: The Untold Story of the Spanish Civil War*. London: John Murray, 1998.

Hughes, Matthew and Garrido, Enriqueta. 'Planning and Command: the Spanish Republican Army and the battle of the Ebro, 1938', *International Journal of Iberian Studies*, 12:2, 1999, pp. 107–15.

Hurst, Steve. *Famous Faces of the Spanish Civil War*. Barnsley: Pen and Sword, 2009.

Ingram, Kevin. *Rebel: The Short Life of Esmond Romilly*. London: Weidenfeld and Nicolson, 1985.

Jackson, Angela. *British Women and the Spanish Civil War, 1936–39*. London: Routledge, 2002; Barcelona: Warren and Pell, 2009.

———. *Beyond the Battlefield: Testimony, Memory and Remembrance of a Cave Hospital in the Spanish Civil War*. Pontypool: Warren and Pell, 2005.

———. *For Us It Was Heaven: The Passion, Grief and Fortitude of Patience Darton*. Brighton: Sussex Academic Press/Cañada Blanch Centre for Contemporary Spanish Studies, 2012.

Jackson, Gabriel. *Juan Negrín*. Brighton: Sussex Academic Press/Cañada Blanch Centre for Contemporary Spanish Studies, 2010.

Jeffery, Keith. *MI6: The History of the Secret Intelligence Service, 1909–1949*. London: Bloomsbury, 2010.

Jump, Jim, ed. *Looking Back at the Spanish Civil War*. London: Lawrence and Wishart, 2010.

Keene, Judith. *Fighting for Franco: International Volunteers in Nationalist Spain during the Civil War, 1936–39*. Leicester: Leicester University Press, 2001.

Kennedy, Paul. *The Rise and Fall of the Great Powers*. London: Fontana, 1989.

Kirkham, Pat and Thomas, David, eds. *War Culture: Social Change and Changing Experience in World War Two*. London: Lawrence and Wishart, 1985.

Knightley, Phillip. *The First Casualty*. London: Andre Deutsch, 1976.

Kushner, Tony and Valman, Nadia. *Remembering Cable Street: Fascism and Anti-Fascism in British Society*. London: Valentine Mitchell, 2000.

Lewis, Greg. *A Bullet Saved My Life*. Pontypool: Warren and Pell, 2006.

Little, Douglas. *Malevolent Neutrality: The United States, Great Britain and the Origins of the Spanish Civil War*. New York: Ithaca, 1985.

MacDougall, Ian, ed. *Voices from the Spanish Civil War: Personal Recollections of Scottish Volunteers in Republican Spain, 1936–1939*. Edinburgh: Polygon, 1986.

———. *Voices from War: Personal Recollections of War in our Century by Scottish Men and Women*. Edinburgh: Mercat Press, 1995.

Mackenzie, S.P. 'The Foreign Enlistment Act and the Spanish Civil War, 1936–1939', *Twentieth Century History*, 10:1, 1999, pp. 52–66.

Mates, Lewis. *The Spanish Civil War and the British Left*. London: Taurus, 2007.

McIlroy, John; Morgan, Kevin and Campbell, Alan, eds. *Party People, Communist Lives*. London: Lawrence and Wishart, 2001.

Moore, Bill and Barnsby, George, eds. *The Anti-Fascist People's Front in the Armed Forces: The Communist Contribution 1939–1946*. London: Communist Party History Group, 1990.

Moradiellos, Enrique. 'The Origins of British Non-Intervention in the Spanish Civil War: Anglo-Spanish Relations in Early 1936', *European History Quarterly*, 21:3, July 1991, pp. 339–64.

———. 'Appeasement and Non-Intervention: British Policy During the Spanish Civil War', in Peter Catterall and C.J. Morris, eds, *Britain and the Threat to Stability in Europe, 1918-47*. London: Leicester University Press, 1993, pp. 94–104.

Morgan, Kevin. *Against Fascism and War: Ruptures and Continuities in British Communist Politics 1935–1941*. Manchester: Manchester University Press, 1989.

———. *Harry Pollitt*. Manchester: Manchester University Press, 1993.

Newsinger, John. 'The Death of Bob Smillie', *The Historical Journal*, 41:2, June 1998, pp. 575–8.

———. 'Blackshirts, Blueshirts and the Spanish Civil War', *The Historical Journal*, 44:3, September 2001, pp. 825–44.

Othen, Christopher. *Franco's International Brigades: Foreign Volunteers and Fascist Dictators in the Spanish Civil War*. London: Reportage Press, 2008.

Palfreeman, Linda. *SALUD! British Volunteers in the Republican Medical Service during the Spanish Civil War, 1936–1939*. Eastbourne: Sussex Academic Press/Cañada Blanch Centre for Contemporary Spanish Studies, 2012.

Petrou, Michael. *Renegades: Canadians in the Spanish Civil War*. Vancouver: UBC Press, 2008.

Philippou Strongos, Paul. *Spanish Thermopylae: Cypriot Volunteers in the Spanish Civil War, 1936–39*. Barcelona: Warren and Pell, 2009.

Preston, Paul. *Franco: A Biography*. London: HarperCollins, 1993.

——. *A Concise History of the Spanish Civil War*. London: Fontana, 1996.

——. *Doves of War*. London: HarperCollins, 2002.

——. *We Saw Spain Die: Foreign Correspondents in the Spanish Civil War*. London: Constable and Robinson, 2008.

——. *The Spanish Holocaust*. London: Harper Press, 2012.

Purcell, Hugh. *The Last English Revolutionary: Tom Wintringham, 1898–1949*. Stroud: Sutton, 2004.

Purcell, Hugh with Smith, Phyll. *The Last English Revolutionary: Tom Wintringham, 1898–1949*, 2nd Edition. Brighton: Sussex Academic Press/Cañada Blanch Centre for Contemporary Spanish Studies, 2012.

Quinn, Michael. *The Life and Times of Michael O'Riordan*. Dublin: Connolly Books, 2011.

Radosh, Ronald; Habeck, Mary M. and Sevostianov, Grigory, eds. *Spain Betrayed: The Soviet Union in the Spanish Civil War*. London: Yale University Press, 2001.

Roberts, Elizabeth. *'Freedom, Faction, Fame and Blood': British Soldiers of Conscience in Greece, Spain and Finland*. Eastbourne: Sussex Academic Press, 2010.

Romero Salvadó, Francisco. *The Spanish Civil War*. Basingstoke: Palgrave Macmillan, 2005.

Ruiz, Julius. '"Work and Don't Lose Hope": Republican Forced Labour Camps during the Spanish Civil War', *Contemporary History*, 18:4, 2009, pp. 419–41.

Scammell, Michael. *Koestler*. New York: Random House, 2009.

Shelden, Michael. *Orwell: The Authorised Biography*. London: Heinemann, 1991.

Shelmerdine, Brian. *British Representations of the Spanish Civil War*. Manchester: Manchester University Press, 2006.

Skidelsky, Robert. *Oswald Mosley 1896-1980*. London and Basingstoke: Macmillan, 1975

Sloan, Pat, ed. *John Cornford: A Memoir*. Jonathan Cape: London, 1938.

Southworth, Herbert R. *Guernica! Guernica!* London: University of California Press, 1977.

Sperber, Murray. *And I Remember Spain*. London: Hart Davis MacGibbon, 1974.

Squires, M. *The Aid to Spain Movement in Battersea 1936–1939*. London: Elmfield Publications, 1994.

Stansky, Peter and Abrahams, William. *Journey to the Frontier: Two Roads to the Spanish Civil War*. London: Constable. 1966.

Stein, Louis. *Beyond Death and Exile*. Cambridge, Massachusetts: Harvard, 1979.

Stevenson, John and Cook, Chris. *Britain in the Depression: Society and Politics 1929–1939*. New York: Longman, 1994.

Stradling, Robert. *The Irish and the Spanish Civil War 1936–1939: Crusades in Conflict*. Manchester: Manchester University Press, 1999.

——. *History and Legend: Writing the International Brigades*. Cardiff: University of Wales Press, 2003.

——. *Wales and The Spanish Civil War: The Dragon's Dearest Cause?* Cardiff: University of Wales Press, 2004.

——. 'English-speaking Units of the International Brigades: War, Politics and Discipline', *Journal of Contemporary History*, 45:4, 2010, pp. 744–67.

——. ed. *Brother Against Brother*. Stroud: Sutton, 1998.

Taylor, A.J.P. *The Origins of the Second World War*. Harmondsworth: Penguin, 1964.

——. *English History 1914–1945*. Oxford: Oxford University Press, 1992.

Taylor D.J. *Orwell: The Life*. London: Chatto and Windus, 2003.

Thomas, Hugh. *The Spanish Civil War*. London: Eyre and Spottiswoode, 1961.

——. 'The Spanish Civil War', in A.J.P. Taylor, ed., *History of the Twentieth Century*. London: Purnell, 1968, pp. 1598–1603.

Thorpe, Andrew, ed. *The Failure of Political Extremism in Inter-War Britain*. Exeter: Department of History and Archaeology, University of Exeter, 1989.

Thurlow, Richard C. *The Secret State*. Oxford: Oxford University Press, 1994.

——. 'A Very Clever Capitalist Class: British Communism and State Surveillance, 1939–45', *Intelligence and National Security*, 12:2, April 1997, pp. 1–21.

——. 'The Straw that Broke the Camel's Back: Public Order, Civil Liberties and the Battle of Cable Street', in Tony Kushner and Nadia Valman, eds., *Remembering Cable Street: Fascism and Anti-Fascism in British Society*. London: Vallentine Mitchell, 1999.

——. *Fascism in Modern Britain*, Stroud: Sutton, 2000.

Thwaites, Peter. 'The ILP Contingent in the Spanish Civil War', *Imperial War Museum Review*, 1987, pp. 50–61.

Toynbee, Philip, ed. *The Distant Drum: Reflections on the Spanish Civil War*. London: Sidgwick and Jackson, 1976.

——. *Friends Apart*. London: Sidgwick and Jackson, 1980.

Viñas, Angel. 'September 1936: Stalin's Decision to Support the Spanish Republic', in Jim Jump, ed., *Looking Back at the Spanish Civil War*. London: Lawrence and Wishart, 2010, pp. 129–55.

Wainwright, John L. *The Last to Fall*. Southampton: Hatchet Green, 2012.

Watkins, K.W. *Britain Divided: The Effect of the Spanish Civil War on British Political Opinion*. London: Nelson, 1963.

Watson, Don and Corcoran, John. *An Inspiring Example: The North East of England and the Spanish Civil War 1936–1939*. Newcastle: McGuffin, 1996.

Williams, Colin; Alexander, Bill and Gorman, John. *Memorials of the Spanish Civil War*. Stroud: Sutton, 1996.

Yesterday's Witness, 'A Cause Worth Fighting For', BBC, 1972.

Unpublished secondary sources

Halstead, John and McLoughlin, Barry. 'British and Irish Students at the International Lenin School, Moscow, 1926–37'. Conference paper given at University of Manchester, April 2001.

Hynes, M.J. 'The British Battalion of the XVth International Brigade'. BA dissertation, University of Manchester, 1985.

O'Connor, Emmet. 'Mutiny or sabotage? The Irish defection to the Abraham Lincoln

Battalion in the Spanish Civil War'. Online at http://irelandscw.com/docs-Division.htm.

Phillips, B.H. 'No Other Way. Major Sam Wild, 1908-1983.' Courtesy of the family.

Shaer-West, Dolly. 'Frank West: A Biography'. Courtesy of the author.

Suart, Natalie. 'The Memory of the Spanish Civil War and the Families of British International Brigaders'. PhD thesis, De Montfort University, 2001.

Volodarsky, Boris. 'Soviet Intelligence Services in the Spanish Civil War, 1936–1939'. PhD thesis, London School of Economic and Political Science, 2010.

Index